FRONTIERS
in
SEMIOTICS

ADVANCES IN SEMIOTICS

Thomas A. Sebeok, General Editor

Edited by John Deely,
Brooke Williams, and Felicia E. Kruse

FRONTIERS
in
SEMIOTICS

INDIANA UNIVERSITY PRESS

Bloomington

Library of Congress Cataloging-in-Publication Data

Main entry under title:

FRONTIERS IN SEMIOTICS

    Bibliography: p.
    Includes index.
    1. Semiotics—Addresses, essays, lectures.
I. Deely, John N.   II. Williams, Brooke.   III. Kruse, Felicia E.
P99.F76   1986   001.51   85-45982
ISBN 0-253-34605-3
ISBN 0-253-20371-6 (pbk.)

1   2   3   4   5   90   89   88   87   86

This collection is dedicated to

the editors of

Speech Surrogates: Drum and Whistle Systems

(= Approaches to Semiotics 23; Den Haag: Mouton 1976)

William Blake marvelled
at those able to see the world in a grain of sand;
we marvel as well
at those able to see a grain of sand in the world.

The philosophers speak of universal reason;
the linguists, anthropologists, folklorists, and their kin
speak rather of infinite detail,
while the physicists confirm both.

In medias stat virtus:
ab ambos et ad invicem dedicatur sequelus scriptus.

CONTENTS:

III. Developing Themes

IV. Reshaping Traditional Spheres:
Some Regional Applications

V. The Name and Its Direction

"Pars pro Toto"

"Pars pro toto"—a part taken to represent a whole—is familiar as an expression used to name the literary device of synecdoche, as when the proud youth pulls up to a friend's house in a new car, and asks the friend what he thinks of her "wheels".

Here, however, we are using this ancient expression to name rather a fallacy, one that is in many respects distinctively modern (a byproduct, as it were, of overspecialization), namely, the fallacy of mistaking the part for the whole, or of treating some part as if ("practically speaking") it were the whole.

A. *Fad* versus *Revolution*

Wray Herbert, writing in a recent issue of *Humanities Report* III.1 (January 1981), 4-9, rightly pondered whether semiotics is a fad or a revolution. Our answer is that it is indeed both, but the fad should not be taken for the revolution.

The "fad" aspect of semiotics is well-represented in the recent collection of essays edited by Marshall Blonsky, *On Signs* (Baltimore, MD: The Johns Hopkins University Press, 1985). In his "Preface", Blonsky, with wistful nostalgia, refers two of the three parts of his collection to "the heady days" of "the seventies" (VII), days of which "probably it will be difficult for the reader to form a concept" (VIII). Even the third—and final—part (VIII-IX) looks forward only to carrying the "clean theory" of the "heady days" into "turbulent application", to realizing "a desire for a new life for semiotics" in the wake of the deaths of Foucault, Lacan, and Jakobson. In short, Blonsky sees semiotics as a retrospective development ("Introduction", L), applying to it Hegel's metaphor of the Owl of Wisdom who only flies toward evening.

The perspective of the present collection of essays is just the opposite. We see semiotics as a radically prospective development. It is a phenomenon of dawn rather than twilight. We agree with Blonsky that we have reached the point "when a period is ending". We agree that the fad for semiotics is part of that ending. Where we disagree is in our assessment of the fad's fading. The problem is not to revive it somehow. The fad is passing. It is time to get on with the revolution.

Semiotics in popular consciousness is misleadingly identified with structuralism and literary criticism, with exclusively cultural concerns. Such a view both distorts the actual state of semiotics today* and conceals the breadth of possibilities that the development of a doctrine of signs provides. Arthur Berger, for example (1982:

---

* Sebeok describes it as follows (1977: 182): "The chronology of semiotic inquiry so far, viewed panoramically, exhibits an oscillation between two seemingly antithetical tenden-

14, 17), writes that "semiology" is "also sometimes called semiotics", and that "the essential breakthrough of semiology is to take linguistics as a model and apply linguistic concepts to other phenomena—texts—and not just to language itself." In representations such as this, the part is not only mistaken for the whole, but actually conceals it. Thomas Sebeok, writing for the *International Semiotic Spectrum* (No. 2, June 1984), puts the matter bluntly:

> Terence Hawkes recently informed his readers [1977: 124] that the boundaries of semiotics "are coterminous with those of structuralism" and that "the interests of the two spheres are not fundamentally separate . . .". Nothing could be a more deluded misconstrual of the facts of the matter, but the speciousness of this and associated historical deformations are due to our own inertia in having hitherto neglected the serious exploration of our true lineage.

This assessment is harsh as well as blunt, but, in this regard, the actual development of semiotics in our time provides a number of clues which should not be neglected in our attempts to interpret what sort of phenomenon we are dealing with.[1] "While every contributor" to semiotic matters, Sebeok remarks below (p. 256), "may indulge his personal taste when attaching a label to the theory of signs", the terminology within the same piece of discourse will not oscillate ad libitum, for the "initial selection will have signaled" to the sophisticated readership with what tradition the author in question has chosen to align himself or herself.

It is well known that semiotics as we find it around us today is a highly diversified and vigorous intellectual phenomenon whose dynamics and nature are far from well understood, but which traces itself back to two contemporaneous pioneers, one in the field of linguistics, and one in the field of philosophy. The first of these, Ferdinand de Saussure, envisioned the possible developments under the label of semiology, a term he adapted from existing usage, fashioned of course from the Greek *sēmeîon*. The second, C. S. Peirce, chose rather the name semiotic, also fashioned from the Greek, but not of Peirce's own coining. Peirce derived his vision of the possible development we now see being actualized, as he himself tells us, from the text with which Locke concludes his *Essay Concerning Human Understanding*. Though often regarded and treated (e.g., Parret 1984) as opposed and competing factions, these two sociologically distinct traditions are better understood under a "part-whole" analogy, inasmuch as the Poinsot-Locke-Peirce[2] tradition is inclusive of, rather than in opposition to, the more limited glottocentric perspective developed out of Saussure.

For Saussure, the "science" of signs was to be a branch of social psychology, and linguistics a subspecies within that branch, albeit the most important one. Of this "possible science", of course, Saussure himself did not say a great deal.

---

cies: in the major tradition (which I am tempted to christen a Catholic heritage), semiosis takes its place as a normal occurrence of nature, of which, to be sure, language—that paramount known mode of terrestrial communication which is Lamarckian in style (that is, embodies a learning process that becomes part of the evolutionary legacy of the ensuing generations)—forms an important if relatively recent component. . . .

"The minor trend, which is parochially glottocentric, asserts, sometimes with sophistication but at other times with embarrassing naivete, that linguistics serves as the model for the rest of semiotics—Saussure's *le patron général*—because of the allegedly arbitrary and conventional character of the verbal sign."

But he did wisely caution that, "since it does not yet exist, one cannot say what form it will take" (i.1906-1911: 33)—a wise caution largely ignored, it must be said, by even the most brilliant of those in our own day who took their inspiration from Saussure and proceeded to develop a "science" of signs centered exclusively on literary texts and the other artifacts of culture which were always treated on the patterns of language and almost as of a piece with it. Within this tradition, it must be said, the possibilities of semiotic understanding, though very rich and diversified, have always been restricted in highly artificial ways in terms of what has been called—for present purposes indifferently—by some *glottocentrism* and by others *logocentrism*.

To this extent, semiotic development has undoubtedly been unable to free itself from the coils of modern philosophy, and the work of the Kantian critiques in particular, according to which precisely there is no world known or knowable beyond the phenomena constructed by the understanding itself according to its own hidden mechanisms and ineluctable laws. Writing within this tradition, Terence Hawkes reminds us (1977: 18) that:

> It follows that the ultimate quarry of structuralist thinking will be the permanent structures into which individual human acts, perceptions, stances fit, and from which they derive their final nature. This will finally involve what Fredric Jameson has described as [1972: 209] "an explicit search for the permanent structures of the mind itself, the organizational categories and forms through which the mind is able to experience the world, or to organize a meaning in what is essentially in itself meaningless".

This tradition, as noted above, originally flourished under the banner of semiology, a term which today remains far from desuetude. It has, however, been greatly and increasingly influenced in recent years by the other semiotic tradition, which develops not from Saussure but from Peirce and Morris and a number of scientific workers. It does not seem too much to say that it has been under the pressures of this influence that we have witnessed the coming into being, alongside the term "sémiologie", the newer term "sémiotique", a term which, without displacing "sémiologie" entirely, has come to dominate over it and, to a certain extent, replace it, without, however, so far removing the intractable bias toward glottocentrism and philosophical idealism that has so far characterized semiotic development, particularly in the Romance areas. We are dealing here with something more than "the simultaneous multilingual interplay of polysemy" described below by Sebeok (p. 254). We are dealing with that, but as indexical in the circumstances of something more fundamental.

Martin Heidegger, for example, himself a German, is among modern philosophers the one who struggled most against the coils of modern idealism, and in the direction of a semiotic. His failure to free himself from the modern logocentrism is a testimony to its pervasiveness in modern culture, to be sure, and to the scale of the task semiotic in its fullest possibilities has to face (see Reading 23 below); yet in the debate between realism and idealism, he is the one (1927: 207) who perhaps most clearly brought to the fore the fact (highlighted in Section II of Reading 3 below) that, whatever its drawbacks and "no matter how contrary and untenable it may be in its results," idealism "has an advantage in principle" over realism, by the simple fact that whenever we observe anything, that observation already presupposes a semiosis whereby the object observed came to exist *as* object—that is to say, as perceived or known—in the first place.

No one, including Heidegger, realizes this fact better than the semiotician. Indeed, it is the realization that the whole of human experience, without exception, is an interpretive structure mediated and sustained by signs, that is at the heart of semiotics. So it is perhaps not surprising that much of the original semiotic development in our times took place along the tracks and lines of a classical idealism in the modern sense.

The structuralist analysis of texts and narratives is particularly comfortable within such an environment and climate of thought. Yet we are entitled to wonder if such a perspective is enough to allow for the full development of the possibilities inherent in the notion of a doctrine of signs—to wonder if the "way of signs" Locke concludes his *Essay* by suggesting does not lead outside of and well beyond the classical "way of ideas" with which rather he began the *Essay* and which almost exclusively influenced the classical formation of modern thought.

Such a development seems to be what is taking place in the larger tradition of semiotics today, if we keep in mind that what we are faced with under this label is not a purely contemporary development but, as Sebeok remarks (1976a: 272), "an ancient discipline" or stream of thought that winds backward from Peirce to the remotest times, as recent work has begun to exhibit.

This development does not take its principal or almost exclusive inspiration from human language and speech. It sees in semiosis a much more fundamental and broader process, involving the physical universe itself in the process of human semiosis, and making of semiosis among humans a part of semiosis in nature. Abduction, the process whereby alone *new* ideas are seized upon, later to be developed deductively and tested inductively, beginning again the cycle—or, rather, *spiral* (see p. 29 below)—is first of all, as Peirce remarked (1898b: 30-31), a phenomenon of nature. It works with constructed signs, but not only with constructed signs, and not with constructed signs first of all.

Consider the "two fundamental insights" on which the semiological side of semiotics today rests (Culler 1976: 4): social and cultural phenomena "are objects or events with meaning, and hence signs", and they "do not have essences but are defined by a network of relations". If it is a question of phenomena which have a meaning, the discovery of evolution at every level of nature has long since shown that nothing in the universe can rightly be excluded, if we but look long enough and wait to see where things lead; and as to the matter of "essences", Culler's negative assessment can just as well (if not better) be put positively: the essence of a semiotic phenomenon as such consists in the network of relations whereby one thing stands for and leads to another.

No matter how we approach the matter, in short, the study of signs cannot be confined to the boundaries of the artifactual nor measured by the paradigm of linguistic exchanges. To study the sign is to uncover a web as vast as nature itself, a whole of which, to borrow Sebeok's recent formulary (1984b: 2), "that miniscule segment of nature some anthropologists grandly compartmentalize as culture" remains but a part, even if, from our point of view, the most privileged part—the part from which our interpretations always arise and to which, inevitably, they recur, in our asymptotic efforts to encompass by understanding the web of nature in its totality and in all its implications for anthroposemiosis.

Even as a provisional sketch, many of whose terms are far from fixed, the following diagram, deploying from Sebeok's metaphor of the web, is useful as a measure of the actual scope and potential development of the current semiotics movement:

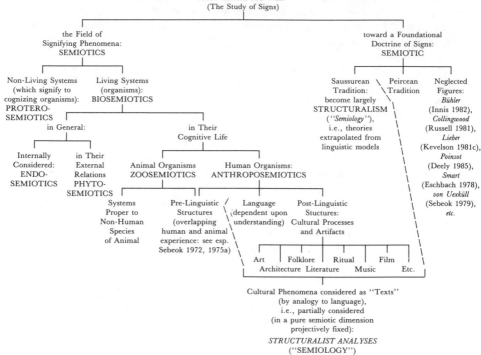

THE "SEMIOTIC WEB"
(The Study of Signs)

B. Attaining the Being Proper to Experience

The semiotic revolution concerns, first of all, our understanding of human experience itself, and therewith all of human knowledge and belief. What semiotics at this point has shown is that the whole of human experience—the whole of it— is mediated by signs. Root and branches, to borrow Descartes' metaphor (1648: 14), knowledge and experience in their development and structure throughout are a local product of semiosis.

For Locke, the first task of semiotic was to bring ideas along with words into the perspective of the sign. In fact, unbeknownst to Locke, this task had already been completed in a work published in the year of his birth by his older Iberian contemporary, John Poinsot. Manifestly, with the idea or concept (the intraorganismic means of cognizing, let us say) established as a sign in its proper being, interpretation generally, the whole of understanding and perception, including its "transmission" in communication, had been identified as a semiotic phenomenon. Sensation itself* might still arguably lie outside the prospectus of

---

*particularly the "simple sensations" of the Empiricists or "proper sensibles" of the Aristotelians—the bedrock of experience and ultimate referent of understanding for all but the partisans of innate ideas (but innate ideas, being ideas, are already within the orbit of semiotic).

the new Division of the Sciences as concerns the means of achieving speculative
and practical grasps of things: but this redoubt too had already fallen to Latin
and Iberian analyses summarized and extended by Poinsot, in his demonstration
that even the most irreducible and proper of the ''sensibles'', the most limited
and subjective of the purviews whereby an organism takes account of its surroundings, let us say, are irretrievably semiotic in their deliverances to the deliberating
organism seeking its needs beyond itself.

With this comes the realization that nothing of the conscious mind extends
beyond the nourishing surround of the signifying, neither the sensory roots of
thought nor its perceptual and intellectual branches: whatever leaves and variety
of fruit this mind might later achieve, it achieves on the basis of its semiosis, be
the achievement gnoseological or ideological. *Nil est in intellectum nec in sensum quod
non prius habeatur in signo*—''There is nothing in the understanding nor in sense
which was not first contained in a sign''.

Implied is *an integral model of human experience* in which language has its place
and decisive place within anthroposemiosis, but without being absorbtive of all
that precedes and follows upon it in experience—a model, as it were, responsive,
in the larger perspective of semiosis as a phenomenon of nature, to Benveniste's
penetrating question (1969: 1): ''What is the place of language among the systems
of signs?'' A first answer to the query might be represented in the following schema
(which we abstract from the fuller narrative context accompanying the presentation of the model in Part II of *Introducing Semiotic*):

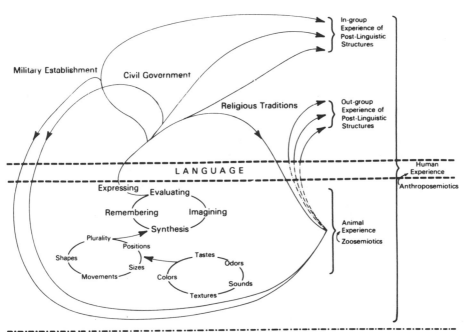

Based on such a model, if we adopt in imagination the point of view of an alien—either a cultural outsider or a visitor from another planetary system— observing afresh life in a given region of anthroposemiosis, what would appear at the outset would be a series of regularities or "natural systems". These, upon examination, would reveal themselves as objects or patterns at once of perception and of understanding—that is, as perceivable patterns (such as the bowing toward Mecca at specific times among devout Moslems) ultimately dependent upon shared customs sustained by linguistic contents directly inaccessible to pre-linguistic and nonlinguistic channels of interpretation. Sustaining these patterns, in the sense of being presupposed to their possibility in the first place, would be a further set of regularities or "natural systems" comprised of cognition-independent relations of the human organisms to one another and to their surroundings.

The dependent and derivative patterns, in short—those whose proper content requires language to access directly, for all that they have of outward perceptibility—reveal themselves eventually as carried by and conflated with the independent networks. (Whether these networks are antecedently or subsequently independent would have to be further determined, but, at a given moment, they are independent nonetheless.) The whole network, at first apparent simply as a web of perceptible patterns, finally appears as dependent for its interpretation on an *imperceptible* content lending structure to the perceptible insofar as it signifies and conveys precisely the historical experience of the individual and group.

It is *this* content that properly constitutes anthroposemiosis in its distinction from zoosemiosis and the further forms of physiosemiosis. This content transpires through the "feeding into" the diaphanous interface of language of so-called primary networks—i.e., those comprised of perceptually accessible elements as such—carried by social interaction. What emerges "across the interface" and "on its other side", so to speak, is not language, but enculturated social interactions— an animal society no longer just zoosemiotic but now a potentialy cultural system as well, which will become actualized in this new and further dimension without losing something of its foundational character as zoosemiotic, with all the physiosemiological elements that zoosemiosis further involves.

It is a question of transformation, but transformation from within, and using all the former means according to a new formality and content no longer irrecusably tied to the physical organism as such in its here and now interaction with other organisms or other physical elements as such of the environment. It is a question now of a *content cognitively separable* and *linguistically conveyed* in vehicles which *depend upon perception* (and therefore zoosemiosis) at every point but are *not reducible to what perception as such attains*. Now the cumulative transmission of learning— cultural tradition as distinct from social tradition and life, and separable from it* —for the first time becomes possible, at the anthroposemiotic summit of biosemiosis. This cumulative transmission presupposes all that goes before it in semiosis, but constitutes a new and distinct dimension or level, different in kind, and not reducible, as appears in the following table:

---

*not as *here and now realized*, but *as transmissible*, or, rather, *recoverable even by outsiders later in time*, as the Middle Ages "recovered" Aristotle, or the Renaissance, Plato.

But the clarification along such lines is predicated on an accurate understanding of the structure of human experience—that is to say, an integrally semiotic one—and of the central, but not all-consuming, role of language therein.

Much, of course, remains to be clarified. It is a work of many hands and many generations; but to begin it well is for that reason all the more important, according to the saying of Aristotle (c.335-334BC: 1098a20-25) that time is a good partner in the work of advancing what has once been well outlined.

C. The Structure of the Volume

The individual readings are treated in the descriptive list following. Here we need explain only the structure of the volume as a whole, and in its specific articulation. We have already indicated the general perspective which animates the book. In terms of this perspective, which thinks in terms of the whole of semiosis and not just that part of the whole, as Paul Perron put it (1983: 1), where the sign is "first of all a construct", a number of clarifications become possible which are of the first importance for semiotics itself as a movement defining its own future and seizing upon the unique opportunities opened up by the developing doctrine of signs in our day. For the first time in perhaps three hundred years, we have a perspective which is inherently transdisciplinary. As a consequence, this perspective makes it possible to lay new foundations for the human sciences, foundations projecting in turn the possibility of a new superstructure for the humanities and the so-called hard or natural sciences alike. Such a framework has been often dreamed of, but semiotics for the first time puts it within our reach, provided only that, escaping the *pars pro toto fallacy*, we entertain an understanding of the sign and its essential functionings sufficiently rich to preclude the closing off of semiotic research within the sphere of language and the constructed signs of which Perron speaks.

It is its interdisciplinary, or, rather, *trans*disciplinary, character, in fact, which is the key to semiotics' appeal and its future success; and it is this character of the current movement that we have tried to emphasize in our collection. Inasmuch as every activity of the interpreting animal moves in the environment of the signifying, it is reflection on this dimension as pervading all experience that constitutes

semiotics in the broadest sense. The semiotic dimension of specific kinds of interpretive activity (concerned, for example, with film arts rather than with cyclotrons
or neurosurgery, or, conversely, with chemistry rather than with architecture and
linguistics) gives rise similarly to specific semiotic reflections; yet these varieties
of interpretive activity, for all their specificity, depend on semiosis as their ground
of prior possibility and share its properties in both overlapping and sometimes
fully common ways.

This breadth of the semiotic perspective—all-encompassing, as we have said,
and enhancive of rather than competitive with or alternative to the traditional
concerns of academic lines of specialization—has best been shown, perhaps, in
the writing of the group of researchers, too loose to be called a school, too diversified to be called American, associated with the Research Center for Language
and Semiotic Studies at Indiana University in Bloomington under the Chairman-
ship of Thomas A. Sebeok.

In fact, all of the authors brought together in this volume, excepting of course
John Locke, have been associated directly with Professor Sebeok in his work. The
concern of this collection is to show that the perspective in semiotics which Sebeok
has long promoted through his own work and that of others is in fact the purview
which derives most directly from and expresses the integrity of the original notion of semiotic limned by Locke, in naming it, in 1690.

The readings, therefore, again with the exception of Locke, are all of them
contemporary readings: they reflect in this sense less where semiotics comes from
than where it is right now; and, in their collectivity, they suggest where we think
it is going—where the frontiers are. Being entirely contemporary (all the authors
save Locke and Maritain are still living), the collection provides both a corrective
and an enhancement of popular conceptions of "semiotics" today, in a format
designed to encourage curiosity from an illustratively broad range of "specialties". We hope the book will be useful in the classroom, both for those already
convinced of the possibilities of semiotics as an interdisciplinary forum, and for
those in search of some such forum.

To enhance its utility in the undergraduate classroom particularly, we have
provided, in square brackets, often supplemented by italics, an English translation for most "foreign" language phrases, sentences, or passages that occur in
any of the readings. The frequency with which such "foreign" passages occur
should be regarded as indexical of the the transnational, as well as transdisciplinary,
character of the perspective that the "doctrine of signs" realizes.

The collection is complementary to the sister collection of Robert Innis,
Semiotics: An Introductory Anthology (Bloomington: Indiana University Press, 1985),
which is a superb assemblage of neoclassic authors, contemporary more or less,
but most now dead, and mirroring the embryonic stage through which semiotics
first established itself on the contemporary scene. The two collections represent,
respectively, points of departure, on the one hand, and trajectories of travel since.

There remains to explain the articulation of the parts of the present collection
in their specific character.

Part I explains the origin of the term "semiotic" as it comes to us from Locke,
and conveys specifically a perspective, as Winance put it (1983: 515), "able to
assimilate the whole of epistemology and natural philosophy as well", where
"nature" is understood, as Aquinas explained in such a context (c.1269: I.1.2),

"ita quod sub naturali philosophia comprehendamus et metaphysicam"—"in such a way as to include whatever there is of being".

Part II does not treat of all the main semiotic systems known to exist, but only of those three concerning which programmatic research statements are as such extant. This part treats therefore of the three main semiotic systems so far explored as such by teams of researchers cognizant of their orientation and concerned to establish it as such. Further frontiers remain, and some of them (by no means all, or even always accurately) have already been indicated in the position paper of Anderson *et al.* (1984), "A Semiotic Perspective on the Sciences: Steps Toward a New Paradigm".

Part III concerns themes common to the breaking down and breaking through of the confines imposed by the various linguistic paradigms, as semiotics has moved into its broader perspective of development.

Part IV illustrates the penetration of semiotics into some areas already well established in traditional terms. This section is the most incomplete, inasmuch as the influence of semiotics extends to many "traditional spheres" besides those specified here; but we have chosen the readings for this section with an eye to their exploratory merit. The point of the section is to illustrate lines of possible over already achieved development.

Part V, finally, returns to the name, for the purpose of exploring now not its origins, but its future. It might equally well have been titled "Prospective Semiotics".

In short, the volume begins with the text of Locke's original proposal, followed by a philosophical-historical exegesis of that proposal, and develops through a series of essays establishing the connection of the original semiotic perspective to traditional lines of specialized thought (including philosophy itself) and exhibiting the possibilities of that original perspective in more or less detailed applications to major problem areas. The readings globally taken provide, as we have said, a corrective and an enhancement of popular conceptions of semiotic today.

We aim at nothing less than a full-scale "paradigm shift", in the popular consciousness, from the exclusively literary, structuralist, and Saussurean *pars* to the inclusive biological, philosophical, and Peircean *totum*.

DESCRIPTION OF CONTRIBUTIONS
AND LIST OF PERMISSIONS

Complete identification of the original sources of the readings assembled in this volume follows, with glosses as seems useful to the particular case. The readings are identified by number according to the sequence of their appearance in the volume, as specified in the Contents. A full statement of permissions for reprinting, along with the requisite disclaimers and acknowledgments, is provided at the end of the descriptions.

Reading 1: John Locke, "Coining the Name". This selection, the title of which has been added editorially, is the concluding chapter of John Locke's 1690 *Essay concerning Human Understanding*, "On the Division of the Sciences". It is from this source that the name "semiotic", with its long train of congeners (see Reading 22 below), first enters the English language and the mainstream of philosophical tradition.

Reading 2: John Deely, "The Coalescence of Semiotic Consciousness", is a revision of Deely 1982: 47-62 (Part I, Sections 5 and 6), rewritten to stand as an independent whole and especially to incorporate the several historical discoveries of theoretical import (notably in the work of Kaczmarek and Doyle) that have come to light since that earlier attempt to map the semiotic matrix of, on the one hand, early modern thought in the Latin tongue (against the background of which Locke's seminal naming occurred) and, on the other hand, the development between Locke's day and our own in what concerns the proper florescence of semiotic consciousness, which, in the argument of the last of our readings, is a strictly contemporary (or 'post-modern') as distinct from a modern development.

Reading 3: Thomas A. Sebeok, "The Doctrine of Signs", is an essay written by Sebeok for the *Journal of Social and Biological Structures* 10.1, where it is scheduled to appear in January of 1987 along with some commentaries. This essay has a twofold merit: in its first part (35-39), it provides one of the best descriptive statements available to students who wish to gain access in a single sweep to the kinds of considerations which give rise to the perspective of semiotic as encompassing both the foundations of experience and the very idea of nature which arises therein; in its second part (39-42), it provides just as splendid an example of the difficulty of conceptualizing this new paradigm in formularies which transcend the snares of the modern epoch ("realism vs. idealism") and achieve semiotic's proper footing "prout includit tam signum naturale quam ad placitum", as Poinsot early put it (1632a: 118/3-4), or, in Sebeok's pungent phrase (1975a: 85), "at the intersection of nature and culture".

Reading 4: Donald Preziosi, "The Multimodality of Communicative Events", originally appeared as Appendix A of a pioneering book, *The Semiotics of the Built Environment* (Bloomington: Indiana University Press, 1979), 96-102. The essay introduces the complexity of anthroposemiosis under the central theme of this anthology, namely, the irreducibility of semiosis to a glottocentric model.

Reading 5: Jacques Maritain, "Language and the Theory of Sign", originally appeared in English as Ch. V of *Language: An Enquiry into Its Meaning and Function*, ed. Ruth Nanda Anshen (New York: Harper & Brothers, 1957), 86-101. In his earlier semiotic sketches of 1937-1938, Maritain was the first thinker to introduce leading ideas from the 1632 semiotic of John Poinsot into the national language traditions. This essay, which extends and specifies that earlier work, develops a properly semiotic way of grounding the distinction between understanding and perception, between language as a phenomenon of anthroposemiosis and the zoosemiotic components of anthroposemiosis.

Reading 6: Umberto Eco, Roberto Lambertini, Costantino Marmo, and Andrea Tabarroni, "Latratus Canis or: The Dog's Barking", sketches, in effect, the "interface in retrospect" between anthropo- and zoösemiosis. The essay has the following background. The original version of the paper was presented to the Convention on Animals in the Middle Ages held at Spoleto by the Centro Italiano di Studi sull'Alto Medioevo (1983); an Italian text is being published in the Proceedings of that convention. A further-developed English version of the paper has been published in *Versus* 38/39, 1-38, under the title "On Animal Language in the Medieval Classification of Signs". A third version was presented as a conference of Umberto Eco at the University of Leuven, May 1984, and is now published as "Latratus Canis" in *Tijdschrift voor Filosofie* 47.1 (March, 1985), 3-14. The English text presented in this anthology is a synthesis of these previous papers made by the editors in consultation with U. Eco, and adding notably the historical layering of the references as explained on page 290 below.

Reading 7: Thomas A. Sebeok, "The Notion of Zoösemiotics", reprints from *Language* 39.3 (1963), 448-466, under an editorially assigned title, the paragraph opening on p. 465 with "The term *zoosemiotics*. . ." and continuing to the end of the "Review of Communication among Social Bees; Porpoises and Sonar; Man and Dolphin". Like Locke's chapter with which our volume opens and which named the entire field, this brief text of Sebeok (brief in itself, but effective only by the support of the preceding review which it concludes, and to which we refer our readers) succeeded in naming the broad area within semiotics concerned with specifically animal communication modalities beyond, as well as within, the human species. Something of the subsequent history of this neologism is traced by Sebeok himself (1968, substantially reprinted in Sebeok 1970).

Reading 8: Thomas A. Sebeok, "Talking with Animals: Zoosemiotics Explained", originally appeared in the journal *Animals*, 111.6 (December), 20ff. It explains in layman's terms the scope and interest of one of the most important research areas in semiotics for the forseeable future. The literature of this area has become so vast as to require the development of a bibliography in its own right (not that earlier bibliographies have not been attempted, just that they are, as such, already obsolete); suffice to mention here that Sebeok has done pioneering work within zoösemiotics proper himself (e.g., 1979a), and, with Donna Jean-Umiker Sebeok, particularly decisive work in clarifying the relation between zoösemiosis and anthroposemiosis (notably Sebeok and Umiker-Sebeok 1981, 1982, and the landmark 1980 collection edited by the two, q.v.; and their current Animal Communication Series with Indiana University Press).

Reading 9: Martin Krampen, "Phytosemiotics", is reprinted from *Semiotica* 36.3/4 (1981), 187-209, but omitting the quantitative discussion between pp. 197-203, as explained in the note on p. 277 below. We have not been able to determine with certainty the origin of the term "phytosemiotics". It occurs already in Golopentia-Eretescu 1977 (a significant review of Sebeok 1976); but Krampen's is the first programmatic statement of research within this further semiotic domain explicitly identified as such, and was a decisive stimulus to the general paradigm considerations later proposed in Anderson et al. 1984.

Reading 10: John Deely, "On the Notion of Phytosemiotics", defends and clarifies grounds within philosophical tradition for a statement of the type proposed by Krampen. It was originally presented at a session of the Seventh Annual Meeting of the Semiotic Society of America held in Buffalo, New York, in October of 1982.

Reading 11: Thomas L. Short, "Life among the Legisigns", is reprinted from *Transactions of the Charles S. Peirce Society* XVIII.4 (Fall 1982), 285-310. This essay develops Peirce's trichotomic sign classification, and in particular establishes philosophically how the production and interpretation of legisigns (i.e., whatever law insofar as interpreted) takes place across the biosemiotic spectrum. It is a companion piece to Short 1981, which we recommend to the reader for its distinctive clarification of the fundamental Peircean and semiotic notion of the *Interpretant*.

Reading 12: Floyd Merrell, "Structuralism and Beyond: A Critique of Presuppositions", is reprinted from *Diogenes* 92 (1975), 67-103. This essay clarifies the relation of 'structuralism' to the larger possibilities of semiotics, anticipating views developed in the author's subsequent books of 1982, 1985, and 1985a.

Reading 13: Eugen Baer, "The Medical Symptom", is reprinted from *The American Journal of Semiotics* 1.3 (1982), 17-34. This reading clarifies in contemporary terms what Sebeok (1975: 181) described as "the third, admittedly uneven leg upon which semiotics rests, very likely the most deeply rooted", namely, medicine, "the revered ancestral figure surely being Hippocrates (c.460-377BC)". See the gloss on Baer's 'curious and all-encompassing' work listed in this volume as Baer 1983.

Reading 14: Umberto Eco, "On Symbols", originally appeared in *Recherches Sémiotiques/Semiotic Inquiry* 2.1 (March 1982), 15-44, and subsequently as Ch. 4 of Eco 1984. The topic forms one of the three main categories (alongside icons and indices) identified by Peirce for semiotic analysis. In preparing the text for this volume on the plan of the SSA Proceedings Style Sheet (see p. 290 below), we found that both the 1982 and 1984 texts had proofreading and referential deficiencies, although in general the 1984 text was to be preferred. The English text presented here, while doubtless not without flaws, has the merit (e.g., p. 169 below) of no textual passages left untranslated for the beginning student, in addition to the clarification of sources (notably, e.g., as regards the identity of "Gilbert of Stanford") resulting from historical layering.

Reading 15: Irene Portis Winner, "Semiotics of Culture", appeared originally as the "Concluding Remarks" to *Semiotics of Culture: The State of the Art* (Victoria University: Toronto Semiotic Circle Publication Series, 1982 No. 1), 60-64, and is reprinted here as modestly revised by the author for independent presentation. It limns an overview of the topic of culture conceived semiotically, one which includes the East European traditions of semiotic development, which deserve a reader in their own right.

Reading 16: Michael Herzfeld, "Disemia", is reprinted from *Semiotics 1980*, the Proceedings of the Fifth Annual Meeting of the Semiotic Society of America, held October 16-19, 1980, in Lubbock, Texas, compiled by Michael Herzfeld and Margot D. Lenhart (New York: Plenum Press, 1982), 205-215. In this essay, Herzfeld provides, as it were, "from within" an anthropological perspective, a vignette illustrative of this anthology's central theme, to wit, the inadequacy of linguistic paradigms to provide a basis for the whole of semiotics, even within the realm of culture.

Reading 17: Roberta Kevelson, "Prolegomena to a Comparative Legal Semiotic", is a revision prepared with the author specifically for this volume on the basis of "Comparative Legal Cultures and Semiotics: An Introduction", *The American Journal of Semiotics* 1.4 (1982), 17-34. This reading points to a specific universal dimension of cultural organization exceptionally important in practical affairs, but heretofore little understood in its intrinsically semiotic character.

Reading 18: Richard Lanigan, "Semiotics, Communicology, and Plato's Sophist", originally appeared under the title "Semiotic Phenomenology in Plato's *Sophist*", in *Semiotica* 41.1/4, 221-245. The essay, in consultation with the author, was retitled for publication here, better to reflect its contemporary bearing and interest. This reading provides a sustained comparison of information theory and communication theory, taking for its vehicle models of discourse analysis initially drawn from Roland Barthes on the one hand and Plato on the other. The upshot of the comparison—with references throughout to a broad range of semiotic literature—is the exposure of key structuralist problems, which find their solution in phenomenological developments of the Platonic model (exhibited particularly through the work of Merleau-Ponty) connecting the ontology of the speaking subject and the epistemology of the discourse system through the sign relation.

Reading 19: Brooke Williams, "History in Relation to Semiotic", was presented originally at the Eighth Annual Meeting of the Semiotic Society of America in October of

1983 at Snowbird, Utah. Subsequently expanded into a major article (Williams 1985), this reading demonstrates how the perspective of semiotic provides a way of reconceptualizing the foundations of the discipline of history that clarifies the logic actually used by historians— something that has resisted long-standing attempts of analytic philosophers, as well as recent attempts of semioticians (e.g., Haidu 1982) working from literary models.

Reading 20: Luigi Romeo, "Heraclitus and the Foundations of Semiotics", is reprinted from *Versus* 15.5 (dicembre 1976), 73-90, but omitting pp. 75-79, as explained in the note on p. 279 below, and incorporating narrative footnotes into the body of the text where this seemed appropriate. This reading places the philosophical leg of Sebeok's "Semiotic Tripod" (medicine, philosophy, linguistics) at the very interface of history with prehistory, deeper in time even than the explicit semiotic texts of medical tradition favored by Sebeok. In any event, Romeo's semiotic reading of the inscrutable Oracle at Delphi cogently suggests how fruitful the semiotic re-reading of previous tradition is bound to be.

Reading 21: Joseph Ransdell, "Semiotic Objectivity", is reprinted from *Semiotica* 26.3/4, 261-288, with very modest editing by the author of concluding Section V. Ransdell argues at the level of philosophical principles and from the nature of experience itself against the 'scientific' and for the 'doctrinal' development of contemporary semiotics, a debate resumed recently in Williams 1985a. From the standpoint of intertextuality, Ransdell's arguments anticipate suggestions on objectivity made elsewhere in the volume.

Reading 22: Thomas A. Sebeok, " 'Semiotics' and Its Congeners", originally written in 1971, is here reprinted from Sebeok 1976: 47-58. This essay outlines, as it were, a kind of 'sociology of language' wherein the direction and development of semiotics are construed from the polynymic and polysemic interplay of the main competing theoretical terminologies derived respectively from the seminal work of de Saussure on the one hand and Peirce (after Locke) and Charles Morris on the other, out of which interplay the current "semiotics" emerges as from "irreversible inroads".

Reading 23: John Deely, "Semiotic as Framework and Direction", was originally presented as a paper in the October 10 Morning Session of the "Semiotics: Field or Discipline" State-of-the-Art Conference organized by Professor Michael Herzfeld at the Bloomington campus of Indiana University, 8-10 October 1984. This reading provides a summary statement of the perspective of the volume as a whole and a programmatic statement anticipating further development.

Each of the readings assembled in this volume are reprinted with the permission of the author. Where the copyright was held by someone else than the author, further permission to reprint was obtained, as follows: Permission was granted for the inclusion of Reading 3 by the Academic Press, London; for Reading 4, by Indiana University Press, Bloomington; for Reading 5, by Harper & Row Publisher, Inc., New York; for Reading 6, by Umberto Eco, on behalf of the co-authors; for Reading 7, by the Editor of the journal *Language*, Los Angeles; for Readings 9, 18, and 21, by Mouton Publishers, Berlin; for Reading 11, by the Editor of the *Transactions of the Charles S. Peirce Society*, Buffalo; for Reading 12, by the editorial office of *Diogenes*, Paris; for Readings 13 and 17, by the Editors of *The American Journal of Semiotics*, Davis; for Reading 14, by the Editor of *Recherche Sémiotique/Semiotic Inquiry*, Toronto, and by Indiana University Press, Bloomington; for Reading 16, by Plenum Publishing Corporation, New York; for Reading 22, by the Indiana University Board of Trustees.

The State-of-the-Art Conference at which Reading 23 was first presented was jointly funded by the National Endowment for the Humanities, the Indiana University Office of Research and Graduate Development, the Institute for Advanced Study, the Patten Foundation Lecture Fund, the Indiana University Department of Anthropology, the Folklore Institute, and Qantas Airways (without, of course, any of the papers presented officially representing the views of any sponsoring organization).

The seminal chapter from John Locke's *Essay concerning Humane Understanding* presented here as Reading 1, along with the title page of the *Essay*, is reproduced from the original 1690 first edition by the courtesy of the Lilly Library of rare books on the Bloomington Campus of Indiana University.

Grateful acknowledgment is made to Mr. Czeslaw Jan Grycz for his assistance in all aspects of the design for this volume.

I

The Name and Its Context

A N
E S S A Y
CONCERNING
𝕳umane 𝕌nderstanding.

In Four BOOKS.

Quam bellum est velle confiteri potius nescire quod nes-
cias, quam ista effutientem nauseare, atque ipsum sibi
displicere ! Cic. de Natur. Deor. *l.* 1.

L O N D O N:

Printed by *Eliz. Holt*, for 𝕿homas 𝕭asset, at the
George in *Fleetstreet*, near St. *Dunstan's*
Church. MDCXC.

1

JOHN LOCKE

Coining the Name

C H A P. XX.

Of the Division of the Sciences.

§. 1. ALL that can fall within the compass of humane Understanding, being either, *First*, The Nature of Things, as they are in themselves, their Relations, and their manner of Operation: Or, *Secondly*, that which Man himself ought to do, as a rational and voluntary Agent, for the Attainment of any Ends, especially Happiness: Or, *Thirdly*, The ways and means, whereby the Knowledge of both the one and the other of these, are attained and communicated; I think, *Science* may be divided properly into these *Three sorts*.

§. 2. *First*, The Knowledge of Things, as they are in their own proper Beings, their Constitutions, Properties, and Operations, whereby I mean not only Matter, and Body, but Spirits also, which have their proper Natures, Constitutions, and Operations as well as Bodies. This in a little more enlarged Sense of the Word, I call φυσικὴ, *or natural Philosophy*. The end of this, is bare speculative Truth, and whatsoever can afford the Mind of Man any such, falls under this branch, whether it be God himself, Angels, Spirits, Bodies, or any other of their Affections, as Number, and Figure, &c.

§. 3. *Secondly,*πρακτικὴ, The Skill of Right applying our own Powers and Actions, for the Attainment of Things good and useful. The most considerable under this Head, is *Ethicks*, which is the seeking out those Rules, and Measures of humane Actions, which lead to Happiness, and the Means to practise them. The end of this is not bare Speculation, and the Knowledge of Truth; but Right, and a Conduct suitable to it.

§. 4. *Thirdly,*The third Branch may be called σημιωτικὴ,or *the Doctrine of Signs*, the most usual whereof being Words, it is aptly enough termed also λογικὴ, Logick; the business whereof,is to consider the Nature of Signs,the Mind makes use of for the understanding of Things, or conveying its Knowledge to others. For since the Things, the Mind contemplates, are none of them, befides it felf, prefent to the Underftanding , 'tis neceffary that fomething elfe, as a Sign or Reprefentation of the thing it confiders, fhould be prefent to it: And thefe are *Ideas*. And becaufe the *Ideas* of one Man's Mind cannot immediately be laid open to the view of another ; nor be themfelves laid up any where, but in the Memory, which is apt to let them go and lofe them: Therefore to communicate our *Ideas* one to another, as well as record them for our own ufe, Signs of our *Ideas* are alfo neceffary. Thofe which Men have found moft convenient, and therefore generally make ufe of, are articulate Sounds. The Confidera-tion then of *Ideas* and Words , as the great Inftruments of Knowledge, makes no defpicable part of their Contemplation, who would take a view of humane Knowledge in the whole Extent of it. And, perhaps, if they were diftinctly weighed, and duly confidered, they would afford us ano-ther fort of Logick and Critick, than what we have been hitherto ac-quainted with.

§. 5. *This* feems to me *the firft and moft general, as well as natural divi-fion* of the Objects of our Underftanding. For fince a Man can employ his Thoughts about nothing, but either the Contemplation of Things themfelves for the difcovery of Truth ; Or about the Things in his own Power, which are his own Actions, for the Attainment of his own Ends; Or the Signs the Mind makes ufe of, both in the one and the other, and the right ordering of them for its clearer Information. All which three, *viz.* Things as they are in themfelves knowable ; Actions as they depend on us, in order to Happinefs ; and the right ufe of Signs in order to Know-ledge, being *toto cælo* different, they feemed to me to be the three great Provinces of the intellectual World , wholly feparate and diftinct one from another.

F I N I S.

2

JOHN DEELY

The Coalescence of Semiotic Consciousness

No discipline is more fundamental than semiotic, compassing, as it does, the very foundations and origin of experience and knowledge; so it is not surprising that it has been in its integral possibilities one of the slowest of the philosophical disciplines to mature toward anything like an explicit and thematic self-consciousness, as it finally seems to be doing in our day, spurred by the need for a framework to overcome the excessive compartmentalization of research that has been brought about by modern science. Consequently, since writing a history of anything presupposes an understanding of what it is that the history is about, neither should we be surprised that the history of semiotic is "yet to be written" (Sebeok 1974: 213 n. 9; Romeo 1976: 74), and that the writing of this history must eventually take the form also of a *rewriting* of the entire history of ideas and of philosophy such as to bring to the fore and make explicit the semiotic components latent by the nature of the case (all thought being through signs) in each of the previous thinkers who have wrestled since ancient times with foundational questions of knowledge, experience, and interpretation generally. This is already plain even in the preliminary sketches that have been made toward such a history-to-be-written (e.g., Rey 1973, Eschbach and Trabant 1983, etc.).

Meanwhile, no more valuable preparatory work can be done than the task of conceptualizing in hindsight the achievements of our predecessors as they appear from the semiotic point of view, so as to establish for future workers landmarks and beacons showing over the ages where and how principal contributions toward the doctrine of signs were first adumbrated or secured.

In executing such a task, we often find that figures long well known and dominant in traditionally established perspectives sometimes are *also* pioneers in the development of semiotic—the case of St. Augustine is an outstanding example of this. But we also find that figures known secondarily or not at all (quite forgotten) in the currently established histories must be reckoned as primary sources and pioneers of the first importance for the history of semiotic. Indeed, the neglect of such figures in traditional perspectives sometimes stems directly, it would seem, from their importance for semiotic—that is to say, from the fact that their semiotic contribution as such precisely *had no place* in the traditional interests and perspectives of their own age. In short, their neglect has been almost *because of* their importance for a discipline and doctrinal point of view whose time had not yet come, and whose possibilities, even when articulated or indirectly implied in forays of pioneering genius, remained virtually invisible to

5

contemporary eyes accustomed only to the light of concerns prevailing in the public life of the period.

I. Modern Times: The Initial Latin Phase

In treating of a "coalescence" of "semiotic consciousness", we are concerned not with an implicit or virtual awareness, so to say, but with the explicit suspicion and attempt to thematically realize the fact and implications of the ideas whereby consciousness is structured being themselves already signs of objects, with the immediate and unrestricted consequence that the whole of "objectivity" depends upon and is a creation throughout of semiosis, the singular triadic action of signs standing in its own right outside the order of efficient causality.

The historical unit of focus for further research into the original coalescence of a thematically semiotic consciousness turns out to be a period about which, unfortunately, "there is little accurate writing or knowledge" (Randall 1961: 71), the period roughly between 1350 and 1650. These dates conveniently represent the death of the last seriously studied figure of mainstream Latin development, practically speaking, namely, William of Ockham, on the one side (about whom Gilson writes [1955: 491], with what appears from our standpoint as exquisite irony, that "the only difficulty there is in understanding Ockham is related to his fundamental notion of 'natural sign' ", which "is in fact a concept" or idea); and, on the other side, the death of the first seriously studied post-Latin mainstream thinker, namely, Descartes (who first firmly established the radically antisemiotic standpoint of modern philosophy whereby ideas are construed as objects before being signs, exactly as sensible things). Such is the sorry state of research into the history of philosophy in the contemporary period that this interlude is *terra incognita*, the "least known period in the history of Western philosophy" (Randall 1962: vii-viii)—a situation quite detrimental for the development of semiotics, as very recent studies (e.g., Herculano de Carvalho 1969, 1970; Romeo 1979) have begun to make clear. The common prejudice, established in the century after Descartes and prevailing down to the present day, has been stated with perfect clarity by Charles Sanders Peirce (1871: 14):

> With Ockham, who died in 1347, scholasticism may be said to have culminated. After him the scholastic philosophy showed a tendency to separate itself from the religious element which alone could dignify it, and sunk first into extreme formalism and fancifulness, and then into the merited contempt of all men.

Professor Savan has observed in discussing this remark that Peirce made it at a very young age, and that a man so young, breathing the air of the age, should perhaps not be held too strictly to account for so gross and fallacious a generalization. With this I am inclined to agree, particularly when one considers how extraordinarily at variance Peirce's thought stands in its totality with the complacent contemporaneity with which philosophers today, as in Peirce's time, continuing the Cartesian heritage as though the intervening centuries had revealed nothing of its limitations, shamelessly indulge what Lévy-Bruhl once described (1899: ix) as "a taste for abstract and too simple solutions, a conviction that it is sufficient to argue soundly upon evident principles in order to discover the truth, even in the most complex problems of social life—in short, a lack of historical

spirit'', an almost total naiveté regarding the historicity of man and ''the fact
that'', as Apel observed of Peirce against the moderns (1967: 19), ''all thought
is mediated through tradition'', that is to say, semiotically (Williams 1985).

Nonetheless, in that early statement, Peirce truly represents the prevailing
prejudice at the turn of the century which endures, although it has most recently
begun to be qualified, and the period which it has consigned to oblivion may soon
(let us hope) be invaded by intellectual explorers who will bring its true character
and riches into the light of day. In this regard, Gilson (1952: 657), speaking of
course of Latin philosophy after Ockham, well remarked: ''We enter here upon a
doctrinal territory ill understood, extremely complex and of which we know at least
this much going in, namely, that the term 'nominalism','' a term long used to characterize the totality of post-Ockhamite scholasticism, ''does not in any wise suffice
to define it.'' Kristeller, whose work has gone further in this area than that of any
other toward undermining the ignorant prejudices that have shrouded the early
Latin phase of modern thought in myths and caricatures, suggests summarily how
the present situation came about. ''Historians of thought'', he remarks (1961: 34),
''have been sympathetic to the opponents of Aristotelianism in the Renaissance,
whereas most of the defenders of medieval philosophy have limited their efforts
to its earlier phases before the end of the thirteenth century, and have sacrificed
the late scholastics to the critique of their contemporary and modern adversaries.''

The situation that confronts us here may be described as follows (Kristeller
1961a: 114-116 *passim*):

> . . . Renaissance Aristotelianism continued the medieval scholastic tradi-
> tion without any visible break. It preserved a firm hold on the university
> chairs of logic, natural philosophy, and metaphysics, whereas even the
> humanist professors of moral philosophy continued to base their lectures
> on Aristotle. The literary activity of these Aristotelian philosophers . . .
> is difficult of access and arduous to read, but rich in philosophical prob-
> lems and doctrine. It represents the bulk and kernel of the philosophical
> thought of the period, but it has been badly neglected by modern histo-
> rians. . . . Consequently, most modern scholars have condemned the
> Aristotelian philosophers of the Renaissance without a hearing. . . . If we
> want to judge the merits and limitations of Renaissance Aristotelianism
> we will have to proceed to a new direct investigation of the source materials,
> instead of repeating antiquated judgments

—such as the one enunciated by Mr. Peirce in 1871. We should note here, as
the above passage from Kristeller already suggests, how little useful for our purposes is the division which standard historiography makes into ''early''
(''Frühscholastik''—1050-1200), ''high'' (''Hochscholastik'' —1200-1300), and
''late'' (''Spätscholastik''—after 1300) scholasticism. This division, especially as
between ''high'' and ''late'' Latin philosophy, and particularly if we look to the
lines of development linking the Paris of Thomas Aquinas with the Iberian schools
at Coimbra, Salamanca, Alcalá, and elsewhere, is arbitrary to a fault, chronological
in the thinnest sense. The truth is that there is no name or place in the currently
conventionalized ''history of philosophy'' for the epoch of *philosophia naturalis* that
begins with the 12th century translations of Aristotle and culminates in the cur-
ricula of the 17th century Spanish schools.

The translation of the works of Aristotle in the 12th century coincided within about seventy years with the founding of the European universities, as they continue to this day. A look at the contents of the entire works of Aristotle reveals that they comprise in their own way practically the whole range of academic studies down to this day. What the contents of the works of Aristotle became in those early times, therefore, was, not surprisingly, the basis for the university curriculum of the West throughout the later Latin age. By comparison, the developments of humanism (literary humanism, not the secular and philosophical humanism meant by the term today) and of Platonism in the renaissance were something beside or sustained within this mainstream. After Descartes, where today a graduate student's continuous historical knowledge of philosophy typically ends (when it even goes back that far), "everyone knows" that those earlier Latin Aristotelians were victims of idle speculation, having nothing worthwhile to say to later ages. So why study them? Almost any professor of philosophy in the mainstream departments of universities in the English-speaking world can tell you that, without even having to look at the books of the period.

On the other side, even when the great revival of medieval studies took place, largely, in the "English-speaking world", owing to the great and recently deceased Gilson, the new interest in Latin philosophy only carried its workers up to the time of Ockham, usually to limn in him the clear beginnings of a "decadence" that would only advance in the remaining Latin ages (a view indeed not wholly wrong as far as education in the English universities was concerned!), but sometimes to champion him rather as the last outpost of Latin greatness in philosophy, as in the work of Boehner (cf. Deely 1982: 165 n. 3). Thus, from both sides—whether one deals with the historians of the middle ages moving toward the present, or with the contemporary philosophers so far as they see themselves as heir to an historical tradition—a point is reached, Ockham in the former case, Descartes in the latter, where there is simply a gap, populated it is true by a few odd figures like Nicolas of Cusa, Marsilio Ficino, Pomponazzi; but basically the period in question resembles what astronomers might call a "black hole". Yet precisely in that "black hole", there is good reason to suspect, lies the richest and most fertile ground for understanding the epigenic unfolding in our own times of semiotics. I would suggest that this is precisely the principal gestation period for the development historically of the semiotic point of view.

First of all, not only from the point of view of philosophy proper, as we have seen, but particularly from the point of view of semiotic, this period (1350-1650) does not at all develop along those lines of vision that are familiar in the standard histories, which tend to concentrate on the renaissance in Europe and the Italian peninsula, and on figures that are identified either with the humanist movement, or with Platonic movements that were indigenous to the renaissance with its newly awakened sensitivity to and interest in linguistic diversity which, as much as anything, sets the renaissance apart from the earlier "middle ages".

The recovery of Greek and awakening awareness of the feedback effect of language on underlying structures of thought and experience are events of first importance to the gestation of semiotics. Initially, apart from ecclesiastical concerns with "orthodoxy", scholars were delighted at the great find made available by the early translations of Aristotle. But as time went on, particularly as scholars fleeing Constantinople made Greek more and more accessible to the Latin West, further translations of the same works were made, with the semantic fields distributed often in troublingly alternative ways on key points "settled" in earlier commentaries. Two or three hundred years of such endeavor, needless to say, created a situation of some considerable complexity.

We have already noted Gilson's ironic observation (1955: 491) that "the only difficulty there is in understanding Ockham" relates to his attempt to bring the ideas or concepts of the mind into the perspective of a semiotic. It is possible to find anticipations of such a move also in Aquinas (though Gilson did not find them interesting), Albert the Great (c.1250-1252: 4. tract. 3. cap. 2), Aegidius Romanus (1247-1316), and many others of the medievals (see Eco et al., in this volume). But preliminary studies of Kaczmarek (1980, 1981, 1983) and Spade (1980) suggest that it may well have been under the principal influence initially of followers of Ockham—I am thinking particularly of Pierre d'Ailly c.1372, a.1396—that an inclination among the Latin philosophers came about to develop a special terminology for the basic problems of semiotic, one adding to the traditional ontological-epistemological analysis of knowledge not just another set of terms for dealing with the already complex notion of *conceptus* or "ideas" (see Deely 1982: Part I, Section 4), but a development specifically striving to assimilate the entire prejacent analysis developed from the point of view of ontology to the quite different standpoint of signification, or, as we would now say, *semiosis*.

From the point of view of the main semiotic development, the crucial lines of reflection and controversy over the period in question seem to lie in the university traditions of Iberia, Spain and Portugal, with commentators on Aristotle and Aquinas soon taking over the initial impetus of the Occamites. These university traditions, above all others, maintained substantial continuity with the doctrinal achievements of the high middle ages, particularly in the three great centers already mentioned, namely, Coimbra (the principal university of Portugal), Salamanca (the principal center in Spain), and Alcalá (rival to Salamanca in the late 16th and early 17th centuries, thereafter to fade and eventually be absorbed through relocation elsewhere in our own century). In these and related schools, dispute over signs and signification became rampant—"a matter of daily dispute in the schools", as one author of the period put it (Poinsot 1632a: 194/39-40—"quotidianis disputationibus agitare solent").

Within the summulist logical tradition, therefore—that is (as explained in Deely 1982), within the mainstream interpretation and teaching of logic within the Latin world everywhere from the 1200s to the Latin twilight at the dawn of modern times—at least within the Iberian university world, there is a considerable development of controversies over signification during the period we have circumscribed. The possibility of a unified science or doctrine or "theory", of abstracting, as it were, a *common object* in the experience of signification, was, by the end of the 16th century, a matter on which sides were being taken, often against, as in the case of the celebrated Suarez (1605: disp. 1, par. 6).

How central semiotic notions were becoming in the thought of this period can be indicated best, perhaps, by the case of Petrus Fonsecus ("Pedro da Fonseca", 1528-1599), a Portuguese philosopher who became the principal professor ("Professor Primarius") at Coimbra and the organizing force of the group of thinkers there whose work came to be known collectively as the *Cursus Conimbricensis*, and whose treatise *De Signis* (1607), Professor Doyle has recently brought to light (1984), proves to have been a most influential work within the immediate context of the 17th century, possibly known even to Locke. Of particular interest for present concerns was the publication in 1564 of Fonseca's *Institutionum dialecticarum libri octo*, essentially a summulist logic text, which was read far and wide in the Latin world, having gone through some fifty-three editions by the year 1624 (Romeo 1979: 190).

In Pedro's work, we find the special terminology first proposed (the Conimbricenses indicate, 1607: q. 2. art. 1. p. 15) by Aegidius Romanus and deployed by d'Ailly in a manner if not primitive, at least certainly filled with paralogisms, now refined to a high degree. Signs themselves we find divided, according to this way of speaking and thinking, into "formal" and "instrumental", the former being the "forms" (*species expressae*) or ideas within the mind whereby experience is structured, the latter being words and, more generally, any sense-perceptible item or object of experience which functions as a sign, i.e., to bring something other than itself into awareness. In Pedro's own words (1564: lib. I, cap. VIII):

> Formal signs are similitudes or a certain type of forms of things signified [*species*, as Albertus Magnus had already intimated c.1250-1252] inscribed within the cognitive powers, by means of which the things signified are perceived. Of this sort is the similitude which the spectacle of a mountain impresses upon the eyes, or the image which an absent friend leaves in another's memory, or again the picture one forms of something which he has never seen. These signs are called "formal", because they form and as it were structure the knowing power.
>
> Instrumental signs are those which, having become objects for knowing powers, lead to the cognition of something else. Of this sort is the track of an animal left in the ground, smoke, a statue, and the like. For a track is a sign of the animal which made it: smoke the sign of an unseen fire: a statue finally is a sign of Caesar or someone else. These signs are called "instrumental", either because through them as instruments we signify to others our ideas; or because just as an artist must move his instrument in order to shape his material with it, so must powers able to know first perceive these signs in order to know anything through them.
>
> Hence may be gathered the most striking difference between instrumental and formal signs: since indeed formal signs do not have to be perceived by us in order for us to come to an awareness of the thing signified by the perception they structure; but unless instrumental signs are perceived, they lead no one to an awareness of anything.

It seems probable that this division, developed indigenously throughout our neglected period, was developed specifically in light of a growing uneasiness with the long-accepted definition from Augustine's *De doctrina christiana* (c. 397-426: Book II, c. 1), which had been taken over (as remarked in Deely 1982: Part I, Section 3) first in the *Sentences* of Peter Lombard (c. 1150), and thereafter by all of the Latin writers on sacramental theology (cf. Conimbricenses 1607: cap. 1. q. 2. art. 1. pp. 14-15., art. 3., esp. "sectio artic. prima", p. 21ff., and "sectio articuli II", p. 24ff., "sectio artic. tertia", p. 27ff.). According to the terms of this definition, being sense-perceptible is essential to the proper being of a sign.

By Fonseca's time—as already with Albertus Magnus' and later Ockham's forth-right designation of ideas in the mind as *signa naturalia*—it was becoming evident that the concepts of the mind, being the very structures which form our experience of nature, indeed function as sense-perceptible signs function *insofar as* these latter function *as* signs—yet without being for all that in anywise accessible to sense perception as such.

Moreover, not only concepts were designated by the Latins as *signa naturalia*, but all those phenomena of human experience which seem to have a connection with what they signify antecedent to and independent of social interaction. For these and other reasons, the need had been felt for a new way of thinking about signs, and the division of signs into formal and instrumental, probably proposed first by Aegidius (a.1316), as the Conimbricenses tell us (1607: q. 2. art. 1. p. 15), appears to have been the most seminal coinage within the period to accom-modate this need, as evidenced in the lecture course given by Professor Bosserel at the University of Graz, Austria, in 1615 (MS 133 of the University) on the logical doctrines of Fonseca (*Synopses in quibus doctrina dialectica R.i P.i Petri Fonseca ad ordinem Aristotelicam revocatur*), particularly at the point where Bosserel synthesizes Fonseca's 1564 discussion of signs (translation of Bosserel basically from Romeo 1979: 201 n. 1, retouched by comparison with the Latin):

> To signify means to represent something to a being able to know, as, for example, to the sense, the imagination, the understanding. Signs are divided into two groups. The first comprises formal and instrumental signs. The formal ones are similitudes, like images of things signified that exist in cognitive powers, through which the things signified are apprehended, as, for example, the resemblance of a friend. In order that these signs may be known, it is not necessary to see the eyes through which one sees the signs. Instrumental signs are those which are represented to cognitive powers as soon as they are recognized by them, and also when they lead to the recognition of other things, as the footprint of an animal, smoke, or wrinkles in the forehead.
>
> The second group contains natural and conventional signs. Natural signs are those which signify the same thing to everybody, such as moans and laughs. Conventional signs are those which signify through as it were a socially structured human intention, such as words and letters, as well as those which have entered the usage of all people, such as ivy and cypress. [In Greek and Latin cultures, Bacchus, crowned with ivy during his debauches, made of ivy a universal symbol of drunkenness and revelry. Similarly, the common use of cypress boughs in ancient funeral rites and of cypress trees to mark burial sites made cypress a signifier of death.]
>
> Note that natural signs can also be formal, but not all of them. For a concept and a moan are both natural signs, yet a moan is not formal, but instrumental.

We now know with certainty (thanks to the singular work of Doyle 1984, along with the already mentioned studies of Kaczmarek and Spade) that this division of signs based on their function in experience relative to the cognizing organism, with the revision of the classical Augustinian definition that the new division implies (by restricting it to the one class of instrumental signs only), was far from original with Fonseca. (Cf. Deely 1982: 55-56.)

Of greater importance than the question of authorship (*doctrinaliter si non personaliter*) is the fact of a new, specialized terminology, attesting to a new, unmistakable direction—the direction of semiotic—in which the late Latin renaissance mainstream in its most vigorous current was unmistakably moving.

In line with this development, we find in Fonseca also an explicit attempt to identify the precise role of representation in signification (1564: lib. I, cap. VIII):

> To signify is nothing else than to represent something to a cognizing power. But since everything that represents something is a sign of the thing which it represents, it happens that whatever signifies something is its sign.

As this text shows, for Fonseca, the relation of representation to signification is one of identity, one wherein the two are equated.

But thirdly, as a consequence of his reservations concerning the notion of formal "signs" (noted in Deely 1982: 55-56 in connection with the since richly confirmed hypothesis of Fonseca's derivative authorship in respect of this notion)—namely, that "they are not called signs in full accordance with the customary usage" ("nec admodum usitate nominantur signa"), that is, the usage established by Augustine; "nor are they said to represent with sufficient propriety" ("nec satis proprie dicuntur repraesentare")—we find in Fonseca (and this goes *against* the line of development otherwise indicated thus far), a specific denial that there is really a common notion that unites these two kinds of signs. This in effect is a denial of a unified object at the base of semiotic analysis, and hence of the possibility of a general account, theory, or doctrine of signs.

In other words, we find in Fonseca a man pressured by the development of thought and terminology in the summulist tradition to envisage the specific possibility of a semiotic, who resists the prospect and in the end denies it. The possibility, he says in effect, is not a real one, in this regard anticipating the view of the major Latin professor to influence the specifically modern thinkers of the 17th century such as Descartes and Leibniz, thinkers who in turn would set the direction of mainstream philosophical development in the national language traditions. I refer to the magistral Francis Suarez, already mentioned above (1605: disp. 1, par. 6; cf. Poinsot 1632a: 141/12-142/13), who has found in our own time an unknowing disciple and unwitting echo in Roger Scruton's denial (1980: 14) that clouds signify rain in any sense univocal with the way that words signify.

Fourthly therefore we find in Fonseca, contrary to the obvious sense of his own words, and again *contrary* to the semiotic development he otherwise furthers, an effort to promote continued acceptance of St. Augustine's definition of the sign as a correct general definition, that is, one valid for all cases—the definition, it will be remembered, from the *De doctrina christiana*: "A sign is something which, on being perceived, brings something other than itself into awareness". This definition plainly applies to instrumental signs—sense-perceptible realities which function subsequently as signs; so, if it is truly a general definition of signs, then indeed the possibility of treating ideas in semiotic perspective is precluded.

But, finally, to return to a positive point, we also find at this period, clearly illustrated in Fonseca's work, proof of a developing sophistication in the understanding of the distinction between natural and conventional signs, as involving in fact more than two terms. This is a point of considerable theoretical importance, as I have tried to show elsewhere (1978a; cf. Rollin 1976). Here, I want only to note its active presence in the summulist currents of the Latin renaissance (Fonseca 1564: lib. I, cap. IX):

> Conventional signs are those which signify by deliberate intention and as if by a kind of compact. Such signs are of two types. For some signify as the result of stipulations, such as the words by which men converse, or the letters by which absent parties communicate; others, however, signify as the result of customs and traditions of use, in the way that items displayed in a shop signify what is for sale. And of those signs which signify by stipulation, there is again a twofold signification, proper and improper . . . . Indeed, practically all words have an improper signification as a result of adaptation and change in use, through metaphor, catachresis, metalepsis, or metonymy.

What is clear at this point—roughly two-thirds of the way through our "lost period" in the history of philosophy and semiotic—is that there is a growing complexity of considerable interest and not without its antinomies in the understanding of signs. The definition of sign is becoming unsettled, the division of signs is ramifying and intersecting in unexpected ways that demand further analysis and, in particular, have consequences for the very attempt at definition.

This situation is well reflected in the complex of analyses put forward under the title "De Signis" (1607), as the first chapter in their commentary on Aristotle's *De Interpretatione*, by the group of thinkers inspired by Fonseca, the Conimbricenses. The authors of this important work, it would appear, were among the professors instructing John Poinsot in his undergraduate years at the University of Coimbra. Certainly the discussions of the Conimbricenses provided the decisive counterpoint against which Poinsot developed his own thinking in this area, and much of the clarity Poinsot eventually achieves is owing directly to his wrestling with the difficulties the Conimbricenses bring into focus without being able to fully resolve.

Poinsot, an Iberian philosopher of mixed Burgundian and Portuguese descent (Deely 1985: 421-424, esp. n. 32), is the first thinker that we encounter who both debates the possibility of a unified doctrine or "general theory" of signs and affirms it unequivocally, setting himself to work out precisely such a doctrine in a unified treatise. He published an introductory logic text under the rubric of *Summulae* in 1631, the year before Locke's birth. He preceded his *textus summularum* with a very interesting announcement of his own forthcoming *Treatise on Signs*, to be published in the following year as part of the course in material logic; and with an equally interesting complaint. The introductory logic texts that have been written in recent generations have become excessively complicated, he asserts, through the intrusion into the introduction of the problems attendant upon the notion of sign, which involves many matters from metaphysics and psychology which are customarily treated at length only toward the end of the curriculum (see Deely 1982: 36-40, sequence of tables redone as a foldout chart in Poinsot 1632a: 372-375)—the whole problem of knowledge and ideas. As a result, beginners have experienced needless and excessive difficulty in getting clear about the more simple business (being exclusively glottocentric) of formal logic as traditionally conceived (in contrast with signs as such, which are coextensive with the whole of cognitive life, perceptual as well as conceptual, pre- and post-linguistic).

Therefore, he says, what he has done (in this following the example of the Conimbricenses), in order to simplify the *summulae* texts and at the same time clarify the larger logical and philosophical tradition in this area, is to reduce to their proper unity all the basic issues which have been raised concerning signs, and insert the discussion of these issues into its proper place in the tradition of logic and philosophy, by substituting a general treatise on signs (*tractatus de signis*) for the heretofore customary commentary on the *De Interpretatione (Peri Hermenias)* of Aristotle. The reason for this substitution, he explains (1632a: "Super libros perihermenias", 38/1-39/18), is that in the logical tradition up till now, e.g., in the commentary of St. Thomas (c.1269-1274) on the *Peri Hermenias* or in its completion by Cajetan (1496), or in the writings of the other Latins on the subject all the way down to the 17th century, *interpretation*, following Aristotle, has been treated solely in terms of intellectual or *logical* interpretation. But logical interpretation itself is only one mode or form of interpretation; interpretation as such is rather co-extensive with the cognitive life of organisms; and logic achieves its specific forms of interpretation (not only in dependence upon enculturated perceptual and sensory habits—such as the ability to recognize the words and syntax of a given language, but) entirely through the use of signs. And therefore, lest the foundations of the exposition of logical form go unexamined, it is necessary to substitute for the narrow logical discussion of interpretation customary in the second part of logic (i.e., in the problematic of "material" logic) rather a general treatise on signs, which is what the name "perihermenias" properly would mean.

In 1632, the year of Locke's birth, Poinsot's *Treatise* proper is published. Needless to say, an examination in all the subtle abstract detail (matched in my opinion only by Heidegger's *Sein und Zeit* in our own time, which produces a similar exhaustion in the reader) and far-reaching exposition of this early and perhaps first systematic semiotic treatise is out of the question here. Since, however, Poinsot, being himself a graduate of Coimbra (1605), was thoroughly familiar with the work of da Fonseca and the Conimbricenses, it will perhaps suffice for present purposes to single out against the background of Fonseca's work in particular, as already presented above, three points of basic theoretical importance, which may serve to indicate the thrust of Poinsot's comprehensive doctrine.

First of all, the critique of the definition of the sign handed down by all the Latin generations from Augustine, implicit in the introduction of the division of signs into formal and instrumental, as we have seen, but hedged by Fonseca, is on the contrary made explicit and championed by Poinsot (1632a: 27/14-18, 116/1-13; resumed in Deely 1978a: 5-7). The ground of this critique, as of the existence of a unified subject matter for semiotic, is the insight that what is essential in our experience to the being and functioning of a sign is not that it be something perceived but that it bring something other than itself into the awareness of an organism, which is exactly how ideas function within the mind—to bring something other than themselves into awareness. When one thinks of a horse, for example, it is the horse one is thinking of, a determinate object among many alternative determinations of thinking, not the subjective mental state, the idea in your mind, that objective presence presupposes. The consequence of this is that formal and instrumental signs, precisely as signs, are indeed univocal in their way of being, and are therefore equally truly signs: the crucial point of doctrine that Poinsot establishes from a number of angles (e.g., 1632a: Book I, Questions 1 and 2; Question 5 at 202/19-45) before tackling it *ex professo* in the opening Question of Book II, "Whether the Division of Signs into Formal and Instrumental Is Univocal and Exhaustive"; discussion in Deely 1978, Williams 1985a).

What is crucial in this connection is to see that the distinction between formal and instrumental signs as it comes to Poinsot from previous tradition, however important, is assimilated by him in a way that makes it derivative from, rather than constitutive of, the foundation of semiotic. Given the novelty of the perspectives opened up by the notion of formal signs once it has been introduced, it is perhaps not surprising that this has been the one element of Poinsot's semiotic that was fastened upon (even in the absence of any understanding of his unique way of grounding that distinction in the relative) in the polemical climate of the last quarter century of logic and philosophy in the English-speaking world, by philosophers interested primarily in a "realist" epistemology and logic—thus Maritain (1924, 1943, 1957, 1959, etc.), Oesterle (1944), Adler (1967), Simon (1961), Veatch (1952), Parker and Veatch (1959), Wild (1947). The strictly limited success met with by these attempts to appropriate this conception from Poinsot's context traces directly to the fact that each of these authors attempts to employ the distinction of formal signs directly, as if it were independent of Poinsot's prior account of relative being (but then, it is no longer *Poinsot's* distinction); yet it is precisely that prior account which gives to the distinction its proper force (see Deely 1974: 875 n. 26, 1985: 479-481) and sets its use apart in Poinsot's context from the earlier discussions—as from the contemporary ones. Indeed, in the case of Wild (1956: 558) and Adler (1968: 582), so "independent" is the use made of the notion taken from Poinsot, in terms of its semiotic origin, that they deploy it in the context of a view of relation that is the contrary opposite of the one Poinsot regards as indispensably propaedeutic to the possibility of *any* finally coherent unified account of signifying. For Poinsot, when the notion of formal sign is advanced in detachment from an account of the relative being constitutive of *all* signs and is treated rather, not as a particular instance of *this* being (the intraorganismicly founded instance), but as something posited independently, cut, as it were, out of whole cloth, it appears inevitably as an extremely interesting but essentially arbitrary or *ad hoc* construct (as Ransdell 1966: 143 expressly pointed out), lacking proper philosophical justification and hence finally unconvincing in its own right. This is a point to which Poinsot, in taking over the terminology of earlier discussion, gave a great deal of thought, as Herculano de Carvalho well notes (1969: 139).

Secondly, Poinsot expressly denies the equation (explicit in Fonseca and implicit in most writers on signs down to the present day) between *representation* and *signification* (1632a: 26/39-27/6, 116/14-117/17, 122/17-123/32). Representation and signification differ in this: an object can represent another than itself, and thus be a sign, but an object can also represent itself; whereas it is a contradiction for a sign to be a sign of itself: a sign is a sign only if it is a sign of something at least modally other. Representation and signification differ as the foundation of a relation differs from the relation it founds.

Poinsot, thus, explains this distinction too by taking over the terms of the account of relation traditional in Latin thought from the time of Boethius. According to this tradition, relation involves three basic elements: what they called the foundation, or *ground*, in our terms—some characteristic of an individual; the relation itself, which is over and above the individual—supra- and inter-subjective, we would say; and that *to which* the thing is related through its foundation, which they called the term or *terminus* of the relation. In terms of signs, what Poinsot is saying is that the sign—signification—consists in the relation, the second of the three elements. Representation at best is the *foundation* for the relations of signification. So, apparently for the first time, Poinsot establishes a systematic distinction between signification and representation, where the role of representation is isolated and identified within signification. All signs, thus, involve representation, but not all representations are signs (*pace* Fonseca).

As an aside, in order to glimpse in passing the theoretical importance of this point, recall how Locke begins his *Essay Concerning Human Understanding* with the notion of ideas as directly apprehended representations of objects. At the conclusion of his *Essay*, when calling for a semiotic analysis of ideas, he suggests that such an analysis will perhaps result in a different sort of logic and critic than we have been acquainted with hitherto. What Poinsot shows in the course of his treatise is that when indeed ideas are analyzed as signs, it is impossible for them to be the direct objects of our awareness in the sense that Locke lays down at the beginning of his *Essay* (Introduction, par. 8), and again at the opening of Book IV (par. 1). Viewed in this light, Poinsot's semiotic appears historically as an alternative epistemology to the solipsistic course that modern thought actually takes in the national language traditions (see Deely 1978b, 1982: 168-179, 1983, 1985b). For given the distinction between representation and signifying as Poinsot construes and applies it first to the distinction between representation and signification and then to the further distinction of formal from instrumental signs, there is some irony in the discovery that the closing chapter of Locke's famous *Essay*, where he marks out the domain of semiotic and identifies ideas as signs (Book IV, Chapter XXI, esp. par. 4), is at variance in principle—contradictory variance—with the doctrine of ideas as objects with which he introduced the *Essay* and on which he grounded the body of its expositions. It was this earlier doctrine, basically consistent with Descartes' *cogito* (a fact more fundamental than the rejection of innate ideas) that became through the unfolding of its implications the common doctrine of the modern mainstream, rationalist and empiricist alike.

How precisely is the doctrine of ideas as signs contradictory to the modern doctrine of ideas as objects directly cognized? Even here in passing this contradiction bears a closer look.

Consider how signs function in our experience of what is essential to them as signs: they bring into awareness something other than themselves, what they themselves are not. (By construing ideas as that which the mind is directly aware of, Descartes, Locke, and those after them must posit *something else* on the basis of which the "idea-objects" are presented. What this "something else" would be—the mind itself precisely as acting, perhaps, as opposed to any results of such acting—they do not discuss in express detail. It is this, however, that constitutes the idea as we are defining it and as Locke proposed that it should be considered in the perspective of semiotic, namely, as a sign.) Immediately we are struck by how much closer to unreflected usage in the natural languages such a formula brings us when applied to ideas than does the standard modern formula which makes of ideas objects in their own right. When we apprehend of some natural or cultural entity—a tree, say, or a flag—we are not aware directly of any mental state as such. Rather, we are aware of a tree or a flag, something an idea most definitely is not. At the same time, it is clear that a tree we are looking at, in order to be present not merely in the physical environment but in our awareness as well, requires for this relative-to-an-observer existence some factor within the observer on the basis of which the tree presumably existing in nature *also* exists as terminus of awareness (as item in an Umwelt and intersection in a web of sign relations, as we explain later in this volume). This intraorganismic factor on the basis of which a given object, concrete or abstract, perceptual, real or unreal, exists for an individual as something of which that individual is aware, i.e., as terminus of his or her cognition, is what an "idea" is seen to be in semiotic perspective. Of course, any object, once cognized, may further become a sign in its own right for the one cognizing it, as a certain tree may lead the biologist on to consider an entire evolutionary history, or the lover to recall a former tryst.

Note the procedure here. The basis for positing the existence of ideas is our awareness of objects—any objects, including perceived objects with a physical dimension—not, as in modern philosophy (cf. Hume 1748: 680) or the introspective psychology that preceded behaviorism, the other way around. Conformably with our spontaneous interpretation of experience and in line with the "opinion" noted by Berkeley (1710: 524) as "strangely prevailing amongst men", we affirm *first* the indubitable experience of apparently cognition-independent aspects of things both natural and artificial of which we become aware, and *from the fact of that awareness* we infer the existence of ideas—an "Abstraction" in the Peircean sense (c.1902a: 1.227).

In other words, in approaching cognition from a semiotic point of view (Deely 1981), the first requirement is to distinguish between signs which make possible the existence of objects cognized—ideas in the generic sense—and signs which must be perceived as objects even in order to function as signs. Both types of signs, those which are such precisely because they are not what we directly apprehend and those which are such precisely as part of what we are aware of, function *as* signs in exactly the same way, to wit, to bring to awareness another than itself. This precisely is the relativity constitutive of the sign in its proper being. But signs of the former sort, ideas ("concepts or ideas"), are not known or knowable through direct perception. On the contrary, they are cognized, if at all, only on reflection, and as the foundation or ground in the knower of what is apprehended directly. As private, i.e., inasmuch as each organism forms its *own* ideas, they are not objects at all, but the foundation or basis for relations of cognition to objects, which, owing to the indifference of relation to its subjective ground, may be "real" or "unreal".

Thus, solipsism, the persistent proclivity of classical modern thought, is overcome at a stroke, and the semiotic approach to cognition explains the possibility of communication in the same way that any two things can be related to a common third. Ideas as belonging to an individual are private, but as signs they relate that individual to objects that are other than private states, objects that still other individuals may also form "ideas of", and so enter into communication about through the use of extraorganismic elements—such as sounds, marks, or gestures—as signs (see Deely 1982: Appendix II). Signs of this latter sort, being fundamentally objects first of all, may or may not be successfully used to signify in any given case, as the first-time visitor to a foreign culture learns all too well. Their being as signs depends on their ontological difference from the being as signs of ideas, the intraorganismic factor identified above.

In sum, the definition of ideas as objects of awareness, which Descartes made the center of his *Meditations* (1641) and with which Locke began his *Essay* (1690), the definition which unremittingly influenced the classical modern formulation of theories of knowledge and psychology, especially in the work of Hume with impact on Kant (awakening him from one dogmatic slumber only to induce another far deeper), is incompatible with common experience and incompossible with the definition of ideas as signs which Locke proposed on concluding the *Essay*. If the concluding proposal is more sound than the opening one, it is not too much to say that the introduction of the semiotic point of view into the account of cognition portends a revolution for philosophy and psychology alike, and an end to the modern era of solipsism and reductionism.[1]

Thirdly, our author in some sense sees that an essential feature of semiotic analysis (*"doctrina signorum"*, in his terms) is that it is a new beginning for the whole enterprise of philosophy. For one thing it entails a new analysis of experience that subsumes what were previously the last conclusions of the system within its experiential starting point (Poinsot 1632a: Second Preamble, esp. 86 n. 16; Deely 1982: 168-173, 1985: 404-411; Winance 1983). For another, the analysis of sign—semiotic—provides a point of view that is superior to, that literally transcends, the traditional division of being into what is independent of the mind (*ens reale*) and what is dependent upon it (*ens rationis*), because in the sign, as in experience, both orders of being are found (Poinsot 1632a: 117/28-118/6). The foundational importance of this point in Poinsot's thought cannot be overstated (Deely 1977). When clouds, through our experience, come to function as signs of rain, we have a natural sign; but of course, in some culture, clouds might also function as signs of a particular relationship to the gods, which is to us obviously not a question of something natural. Social and natural being come together in the sign.

It is in the identification of this standpoint as the one proper to semiotic that Poinsot finds his originality as the first systemizer of the foundations of the doctrine of signs, beyond realism and idealism. It is from this vantage that Poinsot unfolds his semiotic systematically, not in counterpoint to other views but as determined directly by the matter-at-issue, the "proper object" of semiotic, namely, semiosis. And it is to this vantage that he assimilates all counterpoint—what the contemporary "realists" missed. The first task of the semiotician (Poinsot 1632a: 117/25-118/18) is to secure a standpoint superior to the division of being into what exists independently of our cognition (*ens reale*, "mind-independent being") and what exists dependently upon cognition (*ens rationis*, "mind-dependent being"). For Poinsot, semiotic must take its stand, in the felicitous description of Sebeok (1975a), squarely "at the intersection of nature and culture".

This new, wholly experiential point of departure selected for Poinsot's philosophical account of signs (Ransdell speaks similarly—1980: 181—of the "basic phenomenological stance" endemic to semiotic) is what sets his semiotic on a path toward reconciling in the sign the seemingly opposed orders of nature and culture—"seemingly", that is to say, in modern thought at least since the famous *Critique of Pure Reason* of Immanuel Kant (1781, 1787). Kant's conclusions in this regard merely systematized and made unmistakable inclinations that had been at work from the beginnings of modern thought in its manner of treating knowledge. But Poinsot's simple recognition of semiotic's basic task also amounts to a revolution within the perspective of natural philosophy or "physics" traditional in Poinsot's day. For the sole concern of that tradition was to uncover and explicate the structure of *ens reale*, which they thought to have achieved, after Aristotle, with the division of mind-independent being into *substances* or natural units of independent existence (see Ashley 1973) with their *accidents* or various properties and characteristics. Thus, the division of being into the Aristotelian categories of substance and the various types of accident was generally thought to be the permanent achievement of ontology in the Latin age.

Poinsot's approach to semiotic, his point of departure, that is, simply undercuts this categorial scheme, not in the sense of invalidating it or showing it to be false, but in the sense of *going below* it and beginning at a more fundamental point, with an analysis of experience prior to the possibility of the working out of *any* such scheme, Aristotelian ("realist") or Kantian ("phenomenalist") equally (Deely 1977). Comparatively to the traditions of ancient Greek and mediaeval Latin philosophy alike, Poinsot establishes a *fundamental ontology* in just that sense which Heidegger calls for in our own time namely, an "ontology" which accounts for the categorial interconnections (1927: 3) and lays bare the ground of the prior possibility of truth as a "coming together" or "correspondence" (*convenientia*) between thought and being (1929). Poinsot finds this fundamental ontology in our experience of *the way in which things appear to be relative*. The simplicity of his analysis on this point is nothing short of ingenious, although his terminology and style of expression are so history-laden with the concerns of previous traditions of discussion in this area, going back continuously some eleven hundred years in the Latin (to the work of Boethius—discussions in Krempel 1952, Deely 1982, Eco et al. in this volume), that it makes for difficult access on the part of contemporary readers separated by linguistic tradition as well as centuries from contact with that then-living community of discourse. I will try to recapture the central insights of concern here by the use of some simple examples to illuminate the introduction of the minimum technical terms.

Consider the twofold case of a room in which all the furniture has just been moved in but not yet arranged, and that same room after each item of furniture has been "placed". *No thing*, literally, has been altered in the two cases—each thing in itself, each item of furniture, remains just as it was, assuming no damage in the rearrangements; and yet the simple "fact" of arrangement makes all the difference in the world between the two cases. It is not *in the things* that a difference has been made, but *in between* them. Moreover, this "in between" difference is there in both cases, whether or not anyone happens to be contemplating it. We have here the matter of what Poinsot calls, among other things, "categorial", "predicamental", or "real" (physical) relations.

Now consider further the case of the "unarranged" room while its inhabitant-to-be is deciding how to arrange it. Suppose, for simplicity's sake, that the person in question completely thinks out in advance the exact position for each item, and only then proceeds to place the furnishings exactly according to plan. At the moment when everything has been thought out but nothing yet placed, there exists in thought a network of objective and communicable but cognition- or mind-dependent ("mental") relations (*relationes rationis*); yet once the furnishings have been moved "according to plan", this very same network has been made to exist in the physical order of what stands independently of cognition. Thus Poinsot observed (1632a: Second Preamble, esp. 93/16-96/36, in this following Aquinas c.1266: q. 28. and Cajetan 1507 before him) that as a mode of "reality" relation is unique in that its essence (*esse ad aliud*, "being between") is separate from its cause or ground of existence (*esse in alio*, "the character or feature upon which a relation is as such founded and dependent here and now"), which is not the case for any other mode of reality, any other feature of cognition-independent being as such. Poinsot sees in this the ultimate reason for the possibility of semiosis: relation in what is proper to it, namely, suprasubjectivity (*esse ad*), is indifferent to realization now in nature, now in thought, now in both at once (Deely 1971a, 1972, 1972a, 1974, 1985: 472ff.). Relation in this sense, precisely as indifferent to the opposition of what depends upon and what is independent of cognition, Poinsot calls *relatio secundum esse*, "relation according to the way it has being" or *ontological relation*. (It is in this relation that any sign as such will consist.)

Consider now the case of some "individual" being, whether "natural"— say, a dinosaur—or "artificial"—say, a lamp in the newly arranged room. Such individuals are emphatically not relations in the being proper to them (*secundum esse*): they exist subjectively as something in their own right, not just (merely and solely) between other things sustaining them in a derivative way, but as sources of resistance and interaction. And yet, if we seek to *explain* why they are or how they might be altered from their present state, we find it necessary to refer to what the individuals in question themselves are not. Thus, even the individual entities and "natural units" of experience existing in their own right—even substances in Aristotle's scheme, the most absolute of the subjective entities—are seen to be in some sense *relative* when it comes to the question of how they come to be or of how they are to be accounted for. Relativity in *this* sense, precisely as infecting the whole scheme of categories of cognition-independent existents (as also of phenomenal entities physically sustained, as a *liber clausus*), Poinsot termed *relatio secundum dici*, "relation according to the way being must be brought to expression in discourse", or (synonymously) *relatio transcendentalis*, "transcendental relation". (It was here that the Conimbricenses thought to locate signs.)

With this division of being, then, into transcendental and ontological relation, Poinsot has in hand two simple "categories" which are exhaustive and exclusive, but whose terms are entirely matters of *direct experience* (unlike Aristotle's division of being into substance and accident, which was also exhaustive and exclusive, but directly experienced only on the side of certain accidents: discussion in Powell 1983), and whose relevance to the doctrine of signs is immediate: for all authors agree (cf. Williams 1985a: xxxii-xxxv), and indeed experience makes quite unmistakable, that every sign as such is a *relative* being (something making known another than itself); and since, by the prior terms of the analysis of relative being, we know that there are only two irreducible types of relativity, it remains only to apply that analysis to our experience of semiosis in order to determine in what precisely a sign consists (the *formalis ratio signi*, as Poinsot puts it), that is to say, what is it that constitutes a sign in its proper being?

The answer to this question is ontological relation, an answer which enables Poinsot to resolve a number of aporia which have plagued accounts of signifying from ancient times down to the present, and which turn out to be decisive for epistemology and philosophical thought generally.

To mention only some of the most salient points, this resolution enables Poinsot to explain the indifference of discourse to physical reality (the possibility of lying, scientific posits like Eudoxus' spheres that prove to be mythical, talk about past or future, fiction, etc.) and, at the same time, the power of discourse to express a factual situation. In sharp contrast to the direction his contemporary Descartes was even then giving to what was to become the modern mainstream of philosophy on the other side of the transition from Latin to the national languages, Poinsot was able to provide an analysis of ideas as signs which short-circuited the potential problem of how we can come to know any reality other than our own minds. He did so by showing that ideas in their existence as "private" (*esse in*) are mere transcendental relations serving to ground in their proper being (*esse ad*) relations to objects which by definition are in every case suprasubjective and accessible to many—in the same way, as we have noted, that any two or more things can be related to something in common. Communication and public life, immediate components of common experience, are thus verified theoretically by the terms of Poinsot's semiotic, as is also the possibility of a science of nature which attains its object by the critical control of objectivity through the isolation of variables.

Notice that these remarks, confined to the central point of the doctrine (the foundation of semiosis in the nature of relative being), have made no mention at all of the distinction between formal and instrumental signs, or of any other division of the sign, for that matter. Considerations of specific types and contexts of signs, for Poinsot, refer back to and are best treated only in light of the foundational semiotic doctrine, securing the nature of signification in ontological relativity and showing its contrast to representation: while every sign involves representation fundamentally, yet formally the sign in its proper being goes beyond the representative on which it is as such founded, exactly by leading awareness to something other. In Poinsot's *termini technici*, the representative element in signification is a transcendental relation, whereas the signification proper is in every case an ontological relation, and a categorial or "real" one—cognition-independent in this sense, *even though*, as actually semiotic, occurring precisely within and *constituting* the cognition in its suprasubjective reach—when the conditions for relation to obtain in the physical order (Poinsot 1632a: 91/31ff., 137/9ff.)—principally the cognition-independent or "subjective" existence of its term—are fulfilled. Thus, while the concept as a similitude or "representation" is but a remote connection with existing entities, as Descartes and Hume brought out so forcefully, it is not in this capacity that ideas, understood semiotically, provide the objects of apprehension, being (in this capacity) but transcendental relatives founding ontological relations, which latter alone are the proximate means for apprehending objects, whether "real" or not. As Powell summarized (1977, published in Deely 1985: 470):

> Thanks to these innovations, Poinsot can be seen as a bridge for a philosophy of realism between medieval philosophy of real individual substance and modern philosophers of empiricism and of social world. Empiricism is satisfied in terms of realism by making transcendental relations and categorial relations the empirical origin of realism in philosophy. Social

world is made intelligible in terms of realism by the univocity *as known* of real and unreal relations in language as customary signs.

Or again (ibid. 471):

> Poinsot wrote many purely traditional treatises as well as this one, but this *Treatise on Signs* contains in the concept of *formalis ratio signi* a moment when medieval realism of individual substance was passing into modern philosophies of empiricism and social world. We do not claim that Poinsot's concept of the *formalis ratio signi* is the only such moment. But the "formalis ratio signi" *defined* as *relatio secundum esse* expressed both the "realist reason" of medieval substance philosophy and the "subjective empiricist reason" of modern philosophies.

Compare this last point to Locke's notion of semiotic, as put forward in 1690. In concluding his *Essay*, Locke proposes his new division of knowledge, which we may schematize thus:

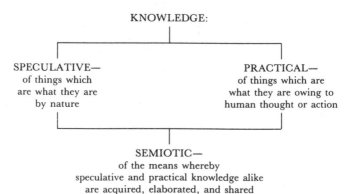

This proposed division is reminiscent in different ways both of Aristotle's division of the sciences,

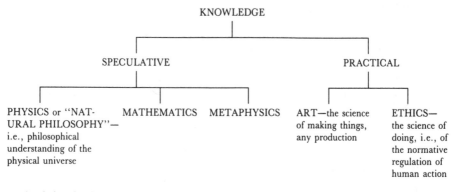

and of the Stoic Division,

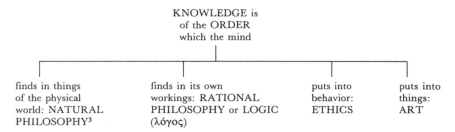

KNOWLEDGE is
of the ORDER
which the mind

finds in things of the physical world: NATURAL PHILOSOPHY[3]	finds in its own workings: RATIONAL PHILOSOPHY or LOGIC (λόγος)	puts into behavior: ETHICS	puts into things: ART

but with a very important difference which I failed to notice before in another treatment of this matter (Deely 1978: 152-154).

Notice that in the Stoic division, as also in that of Aristotle, the various types of objects specifying the various types of knowledge are distinguished, and they are kept distinct. Locke divides knowledge at first exactly the way Aristotle does—essentially he divides it into *speculative* (the knowledge of things which are what they are, independently of us, which Locke calls *physics*, betraying not only a Greek influence but, much more proximately, the influence of the Latin renaissance) and *practical* (that is, the knowledge of things which depend for their coming into existence upon human thought and action). So far he is merely repeating Aristotle. But now, when he brings in his semiotic, what we are confronted with is a proposal for studying in a systematic and unified fashion the ways and means whereby speculative and practical knowledge alike are acquired, developed, and communicated. This establishes a threefold division of the sciences, all right, but it is more unlike than it is like the division either of the Stoics or of Aristotle; because with Locke's third branch we are given a *distinction which unites*: it distinguishes the different orders only in order to show how they are brought together in the sign—and this is exactly the point of view superior to the division of being into *ens reale* (the principal object of speculative thought in the Aristotelian tradition) and *ens rationis* (certain forms of which are the object of practical thought) that we already encountered as the entrance to Poinsot's *doctrina signorum*. The object of semiotic is neither *ens reale* nor *ens rationis* preclusively, but both in the ways they get mixed up with and compenetrate one another in experience.

What is being drawn here, by Poinsot, by Locke, by—more fundamentally—semiotic, is a new line: in the old tradition (cf. Russman 1981), the basic concern is with what is what it is independently of man, and secondarily with the things that are brought about by and depend upon man. With semiotic, the basic concern is with both equally. For the first time, the standpoint is achieved which of itself opens—to borrow an apt formulary from a contemporary philosopher (Maritain 1966: 32)—"onto the avenues of non-being windows as large as those open onto the avenues of being"; and the basic realization behind this achievement is that "what is" is circumscribed not by a fixed but by a shifting line whose shifts are determined precisely by the interaction between the two orders of being through the function of signs, through semiosis. The study of that shifting reality, that shifting line, is semiotic. Clouds as signs of rain is the classical case of the natural sign as something which is what it is independent of man. Now of course there are people trying to seed the clouds to produce rain, bringing what was formerly wholly outside human control partially within that control—hardly a possibility the medievals envisaged. More centrally, "heroes" for a given culture shape the development of that culture through myth and folklore in ways that cannot be reduced to causal lines stemming from actual achievements in the order of physical events, just as stories false in their origin can become true shapers of a course of social events, thus acquiring a reality which must be dealt with in its own right and even in the "institutionalized forms" and customs of cultural life, so that "the paths of non-being" become "as difficult as those of being".

The older divisions separated the various orders of knowledge, the "sciences". This division shows how they are united in human experience. We may schematize the relation of knowledge to experience on this basis thus:

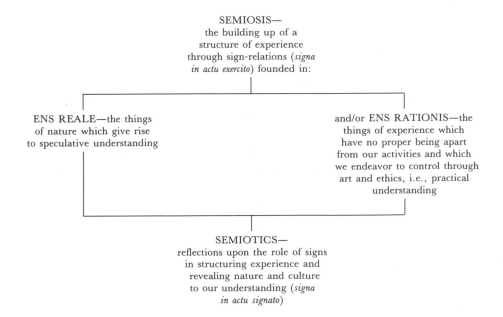

SEMIOSIS—
the building up of a
structure of experience
through sign-relations (*signa
in actu exercito*) founded in:

ENS REALE—the things
of nature which give rise
to speculative understanding

and/or ENS RATIONIS—the
things of experience which
have no proper being apart
from our activities and which
we endeavor to control through
art and ethics, i.e., practical
understanding

SEMIOTICS—
reflections upon the role of signs
in structuring experience and
revealing nature and culture
to our understanding (*signa
in actu signato*)

It is with Poinsot, we may say, that the long tradition of Logic and *Philosophia*, winding back over the centuries to ancient Greece and beyond, finally achieves semiotic *in actu exercito*, while with Locke it is achieved *in actu signato*, that is, the *doctrina signorum* first systematized by Poinsot receives from Locke what was destined to become its "logically proper name". From the 17th century onwards, the relation of logic to semiotics is something achieved both in fact and in name, though the achievement will not be recognized for another three hundred years.

II. Modern Times: The Intermediate National Language Phase

Keeping within our chosen perspective of logical development, what happens between Locke and our own day?

From the point of view of semiotic, just as Poinsot's *Tractatus de signis*, so also Locke's proposal for a new approach to the sciences, falls still-born from the press. If one looks at the posthumous editions of Poinsot's *Ars Logica*, one finds that the editors unmistakably and systematically misunderstand or make nothing of the standpoint of his semiotic, concerning themselves only with reducing it so far as possible to the prejacent perspectives of logical and ontological philosophical analyses, as witnessed in Gredt in our own time (discussion in Deely 1985: 461 n. 97). Except for some honorific references on the matter of signs (e.g., Makowski 1679: 248), the limited example of Comas del Brugar 1661 is the only trace of further development along the lines indicated by Poinsot's semiotic that I have found in the Latin. If one looks in the national language traditions for traces of Locke's influence, indeed one finds it everywhere, but nowhere on the point of semiotic as "another sort of logic and critic than we have been hitherto acquainted with." Indeed, the chapter proposing semiotic is commonly omitted from the many abridged editions of Locke's celebrated work that appear in succeeding centuries. The silence is broken, it would seem, only by Leibniz's superficial criticisms in his *Nouveaux Essais sur l'entendement humain* (composed 1704; published 1765), which Fraser appends in the notes to his classical 1894 edition of Locke's text (p. 463), and for the evaluation of which the best preparation might well be a careful reading of the Aristotelian tract so influential in the 13th and 14th centuries, *De Sophisticis Elenchis*, on the unmasking of spurious arguments. Until of course Peirce's reading of Locke's proposal (cf. Sebeok 1974a: 5-10), soon after which the silence is thoroughly shattered!

From the point of view of logic too, whether "formal" or "material", as from the point of view of semiotic itself, we encounter from the 17th century an extended period of barrenness, curiously styled "classical" logic (cf. Bochenski 1970: 14), and which is characterized by a diffuse interest centered "much more on rhetorical, psychological, and epistemological problems than on logical ones" (Bochenski 1970: 254)—and, in general, by a drift away from awareness of foundations. As a consequence, if we omit, as (we have seen) has long been the custom of researches in these areas, consideration of the contributions of the Latin Iberian mainstream, it can be said that "from the 400 years between the middle of the fifteenth and the middle of the nineteenth century we have", as the Kneales (1962: 298) put it, "scores of textbooks but very few works that contain anything at once new and good." Bochenski (1970: 9) speaks just as harshly of "the utterly barren period" stretching from Descartes to the mid-nineteenth century, when the new development of formal logic begins. Typical of and early in this decadent phase was the famous *La Logique ou l'Art de Penser*, the so-called *Port Royal Logic*, of Arnauld and Nicole (1662).

Barren as this period seems to have been respecting the problematic of formal logic, if we recall the more integral problematic adumbrated by the entire organon, it should be noted that this period at least stands out in the work of thinkers who sought to flesh out in the context of experimental science our understanding of *induction*. This general process, whereby the mind forms its commerce with sensible nature *ideas* about how that nature works, had of course been recognized and set in contrast to the syllogism (deductive reasoning) from the earliest times, and indeed by Aristotle (e.g., *Topics* 1.12). That there is such a process is evident from the fact that we are not born with a predetermined set of notions about the world, but develop our concepts first from experience. As a late modern author summarized (Maritain 1923: 272), "there must indeed be two distinct kinds of inference, one of which will lead or introduce us to the knowledge of universal things starting from singular facts of experience, and the other which will lead us from previously formed universal propositions to other propositions on the same universal plane'', that is to say, one process by which we first reach our ideas, and another by which we are able to elaborate those ideas once acquired.

It is also true that the Greek and Latin periods of logic developed primarily in terms of the understanding of deductive reasoning, so that inductive reasoning, though known, was underdeveloped in these traditions, and indeed, with a few exceptions (notably Albertus Magnus, e.g., c.1250-1264: II, tract. 7, ch. 4; c.1264-1270: I, tract. 3, ch. 4), neglected. Thus the way was prepared in early modern times for an emphasis on inductive reasoning to appear as something almost entirely new, "ignorantly or perversely rejected by our forefathers in favour of the deductive reasoning, which they associated with the name of Aristotle, and now held to be in comparison an idle thing'', as Joseph described the situation (1916: 394).

This was precisely the situation Bacon sought to cultivate and exploit with his *New Organon* (1620) and *De Dignitate et Augmentis Scientiarum* (1623), not altogether fairly from the standpoint of an integral familiarity with the "old" *Organon* of Aristotle, it is certain (Joseph 1916: 391-392; Maritain 1923: 282-283), but with a virtually complete success from the standpoint of sociology of knowledge. In the process, as we will shortly see, the interrelation of certain essential structures of the mind's working were lost from view, structures which had nonetheless been clearly labelled and recognized, even if not thoroughly utilized or analyzed, in the older Latin traditions. In the modern period, following in the line of Bacon (and not helped in this particular by the influential "lack of subtlety on Hume's part'' concerning the nature of necessities outside of thought, as Wallace remarks [1980: 127]), induction, conceived simply as the ascent from particular facts to general conceptions, laws, or principles, came to be the subject of studies going far beyond anything to be found in the earlier periods, but with the curious result that, instead of bringing about a progressive clarification of our understanding of the matter, induction became "one of the most confusing terms in Logic'' (Joseph 1916: 395). The mid-19th century brought in many respects the climax of this modern development, in the works particularly of Herschel (1831), Whewell (1837, 1840), Lotze (1843, translated into English 1884), and Mill (1843). Of Mill's *System of Logic* Joseph writes (1916: 395):

> To that more than to any other work is to be traced the prevalence of the opinion, that inductive reasoning, or Inductive Logic as the theory of it, is a discovery of the moderns—an opinion which certainly contains less truth than falsehood. The name induction may be said with him to have stood for more than a particular form of inference; it was the battle-cry of a philosophical school, the school, as it is called, of experience. But as a result of this, and of its previous history, it has become one of the most confusing terms in Logic.

Knowing apparently nothing of Peirce, Joseph summarized the results of the post-Baconian studies of induction thus (p. 397):

> We incline to think of Deduction and Induction as processes moving between the same points, but in opposite directions; Deduction, we think, argues from general principles to particular facts, Induction from particular facts to general principles. Even if this were true, such a statement tells

us nothing of the difference in the nature of the reasoning between the two cases; and in point of fact, though there are arguments of those two kinds, the distinction is by no means the most important that can be drawn, does not coincide with the distinction between the arguments traditionally assigned to Deductive and Inductive Logic respectively, and leaves out some of the operations of reasoning that best deserve to be called scientific.

In terms of the clarifications in principle that such a situation cries out for, it would seem that the most fertile development for semiotics in this area of logic comes with the re-discovery by C. S. Peirce around 1866 that the notion of induction is heterogeneous, comprising not one but two distinct species of movement: the movement of the mind whereby we form an hypothesis on the basis of sensory experience, which Peirce called *abduction* (sometimes "hypothesis", also "retroduction"), and the movement back whereby we confirm or infirm our hypothesis with reference to the sensory, for which movement Peirce retained the name *induction*. Fisch (1980: 11) writes as follows:

> The extreme diversification of Peirce's work had a focus and a purpose. The focus was in logic, conceived at first as a branch of semiotics, but eventually as nearly coextensive with it, though with a distribution of emphasis different from those of semioticians who are not logicians. The purpose was to distinguish the possible kinds of semioses or sign-functions, and, among them, to make the most thorough study he could of arguments in particular, and above all of their functions in mathematics and in the sciences. His major single discovery was that what he at first called *hypothesis* and later *abduction* or *retroduction* is a distinct kind of argument, different both from deduction and from induction, and indispensable both in mathematics and in the sciences. This discovery came at least as early as 1866. . . .

I call this a re-discovery, because it seems to be a fruitful elaboration of the distinction commonly taught in the summulist tradition under the heading of induction, between *ascensus* ("abduction") and *descensus* ("induction"). For example, Poinsot 1631:

> *Liber Tertius Summularum*, cap. 2: . . . St. Thomas [c. 1269-1272a: Book I, lect. 30] posits but two ways of acquiring scientific knowledge, to wit, demonstration [deduction] and induction. Demonstration indeed is a syllogism, which proceeds through universals: whereas induction proceeds in terms of singulars, by the fact that all of our knowledge originates from the particulars perceived by sense. Induction accordingly is defined as "a movement from sufficiently enumerated particulars to a universal"; as if you were to say: "This fire heats, and that one, and that one, etc. Therefore all fire heats." And since opposites have a common rationale, under this definition of induction, which is in terms of ascent, its opposite is understood, namely, descent, that is to say, the movement from universals to singulars. And induction, as regards *ascent*, is ordered to the discovery and proof of universal truths as they are universals, that is, insofar as they correspond with the particulars contained under them. For it cannot be

shown that anything is the case universally except from the fact that its particular instances are such. *Descent* from a universal to particulars, on the other hand, is principally ordered to showing the falsity of a universal as such. For the falsity of a universal is best established by showing that something that falls under it is not the case. At the same time, supposing the truth of a universal established and discovered through ascent [abduction], descent [induction] also serves to show the correspondence of the universal to those singulars contained under it.

   Liber Tertius Summularum, cap. 3: "On the Manner and Means of Resolving Terms by Ascent and Descent."

   In this way of understanding the matter, a simplistic "contrast of opposite directions in the reasoning process between the same two points" (cf. Eco 1976: 131-133) is replaced rather by the phenomenological contrast between thought in its interaction with the realm of material things outside itself, on the one hand, which interaction moreover is of a twofold character, and thought considered in its internal development according to the relations which are proper to its own realm.[2] Thus we have the three irreducibly distinct movements recognized in common by Peirce and some among the older Latin authors grounded in the integral treatment of the *Organon:*

   This diagram brings out clearly that there are three irreducibily distinct movements of the mind, not just two, as modern tradition customarily implies; but it should be well understood that we are dealing with anything but a static situation. It is a structural matter precisely and only as (semiosically) developmental, as I have tried to bring out in a supplemental diagram (1985a, 1985b: 19-20) showing that we are confronted here with a kind of spiral, beginning at conception in the acquiring of ideas through experience (even intrauterine, as Margaret Mead considered in some later studies), which ideas, as tested in interaction, seldom prove to be adequate (i.e., "quite as we thought"), thereby giving rise to a second and third ascent and so on in a kind of spiral, interrupted, mayhap rudely, by death:

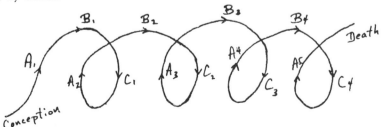

So we have a kind of integral notion of "logic" (far from a purely "formal" logic, be it syllogistic or calculistic), developing temporally—and hopelessly developmental, short of psychosis—along the pattern of the proposed model.

The reversal of terminology here—reserving the traditional term "induction" for the phase of the process least commonly but properly associated with it in tradition, while substituting the new term "abduction" in place of the erroneously univocal common use of the term "induction" for the ascent wherein the mind unifies experiences through the formation of representative notions—has considerable pedagogical merit. In conceptualizing the matter thus, Peirce characteristically transcends his modern contemporaries in the direction of a different and more profound understanding of the foundations and origin of thought in experience, that is to say, in the direction of semiotic. But, equally characteristically, coming late in the modern development, it is not with him a question of any simple *return* to a prior understanding. With Peirce what is always at stake is a creative development of the basic problems. From this point of view, he considers (c.1902b: 2.98), "the division of all inference into Abduction, Deduction, and Induction may almost be said to be the Key of Logic", explaining (ibid.: 2.96):

> An Abduction is Originary in respect to being the only kind of argument which starts a new idea. A Transuasive Argument, or *Induction*, is an argument which sets out from a hypothesis, resulting from a previous Abduction, and from virtual predictions, drawn by Deduction, of the results of possible experiments, and having performed the experiments, concludes that the hypothesis is true in the measure in which those predictions are verified, this conclusion, however, being held subject to probable modification to suit future experiments.

The creative development of basic problems in philosophy, however, always has the result in principle of making possible a better integration of the *whole* history of thought. Thus, we are far removed here from the superficial contemporary contrast (e.g., Copi 1982: 389; Halverson 1976: 31) between arguments whose conclusions are necessarily true (deductive arguments) and arguments whose conclusions are only probably true (inductive arguments). The old notion of material logic may have gone out of fashion for good reasons, but that hardly justifies us in making light of or glossing over the fact that an argument can be deductive in form and hence necessary in its conclusion while being at the same time only probable in its truth by reason of uncertainties bearing on the matter or content of the premises. It is glib superficiality to contrast deductive to inductive arguments as arguments with necessary conclusions to arguments with probable conclusions, since conclusions can be necessary in point of form and still remain only probable in point of matter. What is required rather is an answer to Joseph's question of the difference in the *nature of the reason* in the two cases, and when this is given (e.g., Maritain 1923: 206-213, 258-287, one of the few modern authors, and perhaps the only one of genius, to be steeped—if anything, overly so—in a philosophical awareness of the Latin past), it becomes clear that the *reason for probability* in the conclusion of *any* argument is always *the same*, namely, a material deficiency (cf. Maritain 1923: 276-278). It is not probability and necessity that fundamentally contrast induction and deduction, therefore (*pace* Cohen and Nagel 1934: 278-279), but rather the very nature of the mind's movement as proceeding in terms of the connection between propositions or concepts as such (deduction) or in terms of the connection between propositions or concepts as representing sensible data under a determinate form of unity (induction, whether ascending or descending).

In the line of formal logic itself, the middle of the 19th century also brought a more or less sudden awakening with the pioneer work of George Boole, *The Mathematical Analysis of Logic*, published in 1847, the same year as De Morgan's *Formal Logic*. From that time to the present, in several different directions (Jevons 1864; Schröder 1877, 1890-1905; Frege 1879; Peano 1889; Hilbert 1905; Whitehead and Russell 1910-1913; Carnap 1934; and many others), we might say of "formal logic" that if the Aristotelians of the Latin period developed a formal logic, then the development over this recent period (in which Frege plays a privileged role—some, e.g., Quine 1952, Dummett 1967, Sluga 1980, etc., would say rather the *founding* role—through the introduction of the quantifier-variable notation for expressing generality) must be called formal with a vengeance!

Leibniz (1646-1716) envisioned the possibility of a logical language so perfect that merely by mechanical manipulation it would be capable of traversing all the possibilities of human knowledge (see entry for Leibniz in Deely 1982: 220-221). In the spirit of Lull before him (1274; discussion in Deely 1982: 184-185), Leibniz dreamed indeed of a kind of religious order that, by this logistic method, would resolve the theological disputes which had plunged Europe of his day into unending sectarian warfare!

Russell's theory of descriptions in our own day (1905, 1910, 1919), or Carnap's work on a logical language (1934), is not so different. What happens in logic to inspire such dreams in periods otherwise so diverse?

I think basically two things, one fundamentally erroneous, the other ingenious and of considerable technical merit, but both of which have the effect of divorcing logic from concerns of common life or substantive use in philosophy, and reducing it to a sub-species of semiotics far removed from the foundations of a doctrine of signs.

The first and chimerical notion is that mathematics is essentially continuous with logic, such that the one is a part of the other. In the most extreme form owing especially to Frege, the contention was that all mathematical terms can be defined by logical terms, and all mathematical theorems can be deduced from logical axioms. Russell and Whitehead set themselves to demonstrate this thesis in their *Principia Mathematica* and failed. Indeed, that the thesis in question is not only difficult to establish, but false and therefore impossible to establish, came to be the accepted view.

The other notion, which has merit on its own terms if pursued for what it is, is that the understanding of purely logical relations might in some respects be advanced if the semiotic web of natural language were abandoned, and in its place were substituted an artificial symbolic system totally controlled by stipulations. The pure forms of inner consistency within such a system of axioms and stipulated markers can then be explored with a thoroughness and rigor that proves impossible in the complex historical system of actual language. Moreover, within such a construct, the use of methods of calculation becomes possible to such a degree that this latest phase of formal logic is commonly called "mathematical", a designation which has not advanced clarity in the understanding of what is fundamentally involved in the study of inner consistency when an artificial symbolic system is substituted for one that is capable of performing the actual task of sustaining a socio-cultural system in its manifold relations to the extra-linguistic realities which surround and penetrate human life. Nonetheless, what is revolutionary about contemporary logic is not the aspect of calculus. On the contrary, the aspect of calculus is itself entirely dependent upon, becomes possible only in function of, the fundamental innovation that, in contrast to all the previous forms of logical development, as Bochenski puts it (1970: 412), the so-called "symbolic" or "mathematical" logic

> proceeds *constructively*, i.e., by investigating logical laws in an artificial language that it has devised. Such artificial languages exhibit very simple syntactical and semantic relations, as compared with natural languages, with the result that formal logic has undergone a change very like that effected by Galileo in the domain of physics. Instead of the immediate, but complex facts, the simpler underlying connections can now be investigated.

All the earlier varieties of logic, notably the Latin summulist traditions in Iberia and elsewhere between 1350 and 1650, this same author notes (p. 266):

> make use of an *abstractive* method; the logical theorems are gained by abstraction from ordinary language. Mathematical logicians proceed in just the opposite way, *first constructing* purely formal systems, and later looking for an interpretation in every-day speech.

The constant and deliberate increase in formalism, i.e., use of a calculus as the general principle of logical method in the late modern period, especially after Frege, becomes possible precisely and only because, as in mathematics, "the *shape* and not the *sense* of the symbols" (Bochenski 1970: 266) is the matter of the rules of operation. Where a natural language is concerned, resort to formalism is possible only within the limits imposed by the *sense* of what is being formalized: hence the importance of the discussion of *suppositio* among the scholastic logicians (Deely 1985a: esp. chs. 6-7), which cannot be directly compared with the use of quantifiers in symbolic logic, let alone be dispensed with in favor of them, as some contemporary logicians think (e.g., Kneale and Kneale 1962: 511; Geach 1968: esp. chs. 3-5). The reason for this is straightforward, as can be gleaned from the following remark of Copi 1982: 380, substituting the expression "natural language" where he uses the expression "English":

> One cannot translate from a natural language into our logical notation by following any formal or mechanical rules. In every case one must understand the meaning of the sentence in the natural language, and then symbolize that meaning in terms of propositional functions and quantifiers.

But it is precisely the understanding of sentences in a natural language that the doctrine of *suppositio* is designed to express. Hence it deals with a concern that is presupposed as settled whenever quantification is employed.[3] Since they do different jobs, the one cannot be replaced by the other. Hence also the fact that while formalism has already been employed and highly developed "in scho-

lasticism especially'', it could never there receive ''such thorough-going application'' as to become the general principle of method it becomes in 'mathematical'
logic (cf. Bochenski 1970: 266-412).

In the early stages of this development, as by a remnant today (e.g., Geach
1968, 1972), it was commonly held that there was an opposition and competition
between the ''old'', ''Aristotelian'' logic and the ''new'', ''true'' logic. Of course,
the mere fact that no scientific history of formal logic existed at the time, and
that a few centuries had intervened between the ''new'' logic and any tradition
that could seriously and substantively be called Aristotelian, did not at first in-
terfere with anyone's enthusiasm, least of all Bertrand Russell's. ''No wonder
then'', comments Bochenski (1970: 9, cf. Dumitriu 1977), ''that with the rise
of mathematical logic theorems belonging to the elementary wealth of past epochs
were saddled with the names of De Morgan, Peirce, and others.''

As sanity and sobriety began to prevail, thanks to the more profound inquirers
in the new area such as Peirce, Lukasiewicz, and most recently Bochenski, it
became possible to see that the logic of Frege's *Begriffsschrift* (Bochenski 1970: 268),
no less that that of the *Principia*, can more profitably be viewed as an outgrowth
and a development and, in one very precise sense, the perfection of the formal
problematic of the *Analytica Prior*, because now the entire philosophical-epistemolog-
ical baggage of ''material logic'' has been, through the simple expedient of purely artificial language, effectively jettisoned in favor of a study of the inner consistency of symbolic forms purely and entirely for its own sake, divorced from
any check of further concerns. In this sense there is a continuity, it is possible
to argue, between mathematical logic and the problematic of the prior analytics,
if that problematic is first isolated within the *Organon* and then pursued entirely
for its own sake—no longer for the purpose of an *ars seu logica utens*, but solely
for the purpose of developing a ''science'' in its own right, the science of necessary
relations so far as they can be traced to the control and stipulations of men. Viewed
in this light, ''mathematical'' logic does indeed appear as an outgrowth, development, and perfection of the constant tradition of formal logic, so that, as Bochenski says (1970: 413), ''there can be no doubt that in this period formal logic once
more attained one of its peaks of development'', or that ''by using the formalized
languages of symbolic logic as a means of representation'', as Menne remarks
(1962: VIII), ''classical and traditional theory can be made more precise logistically
and its consequences more easily examined''—although, Bochenski warns (1970:
22) at ''appreciable risk of misunderstanding,'' not only because such is present
''in every case of translation'', but particularly because it is a question of translation into ''a terminology with so narrowly defined a sense as that of mathematical
logic.''

From the point of view of semiotic, however, ''perihermenias'' (Deely 1982:
188ff. n. 16) in that full sense of the interpretive activity coextensive with cognitive
life, mathematical logic appears only as a most restricted form of interpretation,
far more restricted even than the too narrow tradition of Aristotelian commentary on the *De Interpretatione* criticized so effectively by Poinsot and others for leaving
the *foundations* of logical form unexamined.

To appreciate this, recall the division of instrumental signs into ''ex instituto''
(stipulated) and ''ex consuetudine'' (customary). Applied specifically to the signs
of language, linguistic forms, it is possible to show that both these aspects are

constantly at play in ordinary language and in fact that it is precisely this interplay that defines the term "natural" as it functions in the expression "natural language" (cf. Deely 1978a; 1982: Part II Section 87-92). The habit structures of a population, the experiences of a people; the fact that when I communicate with you using words of a common language, those words yet have resonances in your mind that they don't have in mine, and conversely; the fact that there are riches of connections in the linguistic traditions of the English language or of the Nahuatl tongue or of the Eskimo tongues—sign relationships that are carried there embodying a collective history of the peoples and specific populations: when you substitute the element of *ex instituto* so far as possible for all elements of custom, when you cut off what is arbitrary from all that has become naturalized in a language, such exactly are the factors that drop out—history, experience, the past of a people. These are the very elements that, by their presence and incremental growth, gradually pressured thinkers of the renaissance in the summulist tradition who strove constantly to take account of them—instead of devising ways to anesthetize and amputate them—in the direction of an ever richer understanding of signification culminating eventually, in a privileged instance, with a grasp of the foundations of logical interpretation in semiosis, with all that that implies for the theories of knowledge and truth.

With the dominant contemporary logic, the pressures on the movement of thought tend in precisely the opposite direction. In the context of natural language, the understanding of logical interpretation tends to broaden beyond the confines of what can be stipulatively controlled. Ultimately, following out this tendency leads from within logic itself to a foundational doctrine of signs, both philosophically and historically. In the context of an artificially stipulated symbolic system, the understanding of logical interpretation tends rather to narrow itself precisely to the elements of control, and become a pure technique, a calculus of consequences more and more empty of natural substance. In the extreme, this tendency leads logic itself into a hollow or empty formalism, more and more technically perfect, as relations of reason build upon one another constructs ever more intricate and subtle, but by the same token further and further removed from foundations in reality—what the older logicians used to call "distinctions of reason reasoning" (cf. Poinsot 1632: 294a1-300b48).

The philosophers of our universities today who have attached themselves to such a method and see in its exercise the very progress of philosophy, therefore, not surprisingly find themselves without a great deal to say of general interest for semioticians. Theirs is a technique which belongs to the field of semiotics, not to the area of semiotic foundations (Deely 1976: 171-173; 1977; 1978a; and esp. 1985: 411-417); a technique which is not even by itself properly logic (Bochenski 1970: 17), and which has an *ad hoc* rather than properly systematic value (which can nevertheless be considerable) for the exposition of any given problem or set of problems in philosophy or anywhere else (Deely 1975, 1975a: 254-271). Thus (Bochenski 1970: 22):

> For particular logicians, or a particular form [of logic], the use of an artificial symbolism is not only possible, but to be desired. But then every case requires a *special* symbolism. What we cannot do is to create a unique symbolism suitable for all the ideas that have been developed in the different varieties of logic

—particularly when it is a question of investigating the very foundations and prior possibility of logical form!

You can see then that the maturation of semiotic imposes the conditions of a revolution on contemporary philosophers. It will, for the first time, exhibit unmistakably the proper and central place of historical experience in philosophical reflection; secondarily, as a consequence of this if nothing else, it will force an overall re-evaluation and redistribution of the materials of intellectual history; and it will end the diverting of students away from questions that properly form the substance of philosophical education.

Of course, it may be, as Heidegger believed (1947: 119), that the logistic and "scientific" philosophers are so far gone down their by-way that future thought in these areas will no longer be called philosophy.

Be that as it may, semiotic and semiotics are here to stay.

3

THOMAS A. SEBEOK

The Doctrine of Signs

*I am inclined to think the doctrine of signs a point of great
importance and general extent, which, if duly considered, would
cast no small light upon things, and afford a just and
genuine solution of many difficulties.*

—George Berkeley 1732: 307—

Consider what these ten little dramas have in common:

—A radiologist spots a silhouette on a chest x-ray photograph of a patient and diagnoses lung cancer;

—A meteorologist notes a rise in barometric pressure and delivers next day's forecast taking that change into account;

—An anthropologist observes a complex of ceremonial exchanges practiced among members of a tribe; she draws analytical insights about the polity, economy, and social organization of the people she is studying;

—A French language teacher holds up a picture of a horse. His American pupil says "horse". The teacher shakes his head and pronounces "cheval";

—A historian takes a look at the handwriting of a former President and gains insight therefrom of her subject's personality;

—A Kremlin-watcher observes the proximity of a member of the Politburo to the Party Secretary on Mayday and surmises his current status;

—A compromising fingerprint is introduced at a trial and the defendant is convicted on that evidence;

—A hunter notices in the snow sets of rectangular tracks of pointed hoofs with an impression of dew claws; the fore-foot track is 15 cm. long and 13 cm. broad, and the corresponding measurements for the hind-foot track are 15 cm. and 11 cm. There are spherical droppings on the trail 20-30 mm. long and 15-20 mm. broad. The hunter surmises, with a high degree of probability, that a fully grown bull elk is trotting ahead of him.

—A man finds himself being stared at by a dog whose head is held high and neck is arched, growling, barking, lips contracted vertically and teeth bared, ears erect and turned forward; he concludes he is in danger of imminent attack and takes evasive action.

—A peacock displays to a susceptible peahen; she circles rapidly, squats, and coition ensues.

Those of us who practice semiotics tend to treat these happenings the same way despite their manifest substantive differences of setting, cast of human or speechless characters, and many other variables. What entitles us to do so is an abstractive operation which resolves each episode to an instance of *semiosis*, or sign action. In this view, semiotics is not about the "real" world at all, but about complementary or alternative actual models of it and—as Leibniz thought—about an infinite number of anthropologically conceivable possible worlds. Thus semiotics never reveals what the world is, but circumscribes what we can know about it; in other words, what a semiotic model depicts is not "reality" as such, but nature as unveiled by man's method of questioning. It is the interplay between "the book of nature" and man its decipherer that is at issue. The distinction may be pictured by the simile of a fisherman casting his net; the size of the fish he can catch is limited by the morphology of the net but this fact does not provide tutorage in ichthyology. A concept of "modeling systems" has been central to Soviet semiotics of the so-called Moscow-Tartu school since the 1960s, but, having been derived from a representation of language in structural linguistics, it has focused on culture to the exclusion of the rest of nature. In the age-old philosophical quest for reality, two alternative points of departure have been suggested: that the structure of being is reflected in semiotic structures, which thus constitutes models, or maps, of reality; or that the reverse is the case, viz., that semiotic structures are independent variables so that reality becomes the dependent variable. Although both views are beset by many difficulties, a version of the second view, proposed by the remarkably seminal German biologist, Jacob von Uexküll, under the watchword *Umwelt-Forschung*—approximately translated as "research in subjective universes"—has proved to be in best conformity with modern semiotics (as well as ethology). The same attitude was expressed by Niels Bohr when he answered an objection that reality is more fundamental than the language which it underlies; Bohr replied: "We are suspended in language in such a way that we cannot say what is up and what is down". Signs have acquired their effectiveness through evolutionary adaptation to the vagaries of the sign-wielder's *Umwelt*. When the *Umwelt* changes, these signs can become obstacles and the signer extinct.

According to the incomparable polymath, C. S. Peirce (1839-1914), who has justly been called "the most original and the most versatile intellect that the Americas have so far produced", and who uniquely reinvigorated semiotics, the antique doctrine of signs, semiosis involves an irreducibly triadic relation between a sign, its object, and its interpretant. This trio of terms and their next of kin have far resounding philosophical overtones. Before rehearsing some of these, let me dwell on a common definition of semiotics, and pause to consider its components and a few of its consequences.

I. *A Common Definition of Semiotics*

The subject matter of semiotics, it is often credited, is the exchange of any messages whatsoever, in a word, *communication*. To this must at once be added that semiotics is also focally concerned with the study of *signification*. Semiotics is therefore classifiable as that pivotal branch of an integrated science of communication to which its character as a methodical inquiry into the nature and constitution of codes provides an indispensable counterpoint.

A message is a sign, or a string of signs, transmitted from a sign-producer, or source, to a sign-receiver, or destination. Any source and any destination is a living entity or the product of a living entity, such as a computer, a robot, automata in general, or a postulated supernatural being, as when a boy (source), on bent knees (nonverbal message), beseeches his deity (destination), "I pray the Lord my soul to take" (verbal message). It is important to realize that only living things and their inanimate extensions undergo semiosis, which thereby becomes uplifted as a necessary, if not sufficient, criterial attribute of life. By "living things" are meant not just the organisms belonging to one of the five kingdoms, consisting of the Monera, Protocista, Animalia, Plantae, and Fungi, but also their hierarchically developed choate component parts, beginning with a cell, the minimal semiosic unit, estimated to correspond to about 50 genes, or about a thousand billion (10^{12}) intricately organized atoms. (Viruses are omitted because they are neither cells nor aggregations of cells.) Our bodies are assemblages of cells, about a hundred thousand billion (10^{14}) of them, harmoniously attuned to one another by an incessant flux of vital messages. The origin of nucleated cells is a dimly apprehended story of the symbiotic and semiosic collaboration among single cells— populations of blue algae and bacteria without apparent internal components; they evolved less than a billion years after the formation of the Earth (and ample traces of them were harvested in Greenland). Simple cells, it is thought, fused to form the complex confederations of cells composing each living being. They, in turn, are integrated into organs, organs into organisms, forming social systems of ever increasing complexity. Thus physics, biology, psychology, and sociology each embodies its own peculiar level of semiosis. The genetic code governs the exchange of messages on the cellular level; hormones and neurotransmitters mediate among organs and between one another (the immune defense system and the central nervous system are intimately interwreathed by a dense flow of two-way message traffic); and a variety of nonverbal and verbal messages conjoin organisms into a network of relations with each other as well as with the rest of their environment. As François Jacob picturesquely described the progression: "From family organization to modern state, from ethnic group to coalition of nations, a whole series of integrations is based on a variety of cultural, moral, social, political, economic, military and religious codes. The history of mankind is more or less the history of these integrons and the way they form and change". Semiosis on a superior level in the hierarchy of integrons is irreducible to that on a lower level, viz., ultimately to physics.[1]

The semiosic comportment of even the major organismic groupings, with differing lifestyles, has been unevenly studied. In the web of nature, plants are, above all, producers; an examination of their communicative behavior, under the banner of "phytosemiotics", began only in 1981, when the German semiotician, Martin Krampen, published an insightful programmatic article under that title. The polar opposite of plants are the fungi, nature's decomposers; our knowledge of their peculiar brand of semiosis is even more rudimentary. Primary interest has hitherto focused on animals (zoosemiotics), the ingesters, which mediate between the other two, and, according to what they consume, may be categorized either as herbivores or as predators; their nutritional mode may also mark the character of their respective reliance on sign-use.

Note that message traffic in four out of the five kingdoms is exclusively nonverbal; verbal messages have been found only in animals and there surge solely in one extant subspecies, *Homo sapiens sapiens*. Man's most distinctive trait is that he, alone throughout terrestrial life, has two separate, although, of course, thoroughly commingled repertoires of signs at his disposal: the nonverbal— demonstrably derived from his mammalian (especially primate) ancestry—and a uniquely human verbal overlay. The latter constitutes the subject matter of the most advanced and highly formalized branch of semiotics, general linguistics, the study of verbal commerce and its subjacent grammatical foundation. This essay, however, by and large concentrates on the nonverbal—as in most examples which opened this essay—or on issues concerning both, because the former are overwhelmingly more copious, not only in nature but even in human-to-human interchanges.

The definition advanced here presupposes a message-producer, or source, and a message-receiver, or destination. In the samples above, extant or formerly alive sources and destinations figure in roles like a patient and his physician; an ethnographic fieldworker and her informants; a teacher and his pupil; a historian and a late public figure; a remote foreign official and a political scientist; an elk and a hunter; a dog and his potential casualty; a peacock and a peahen. The barometer read by the weather forecaster is a man-made instrument of observation, one of a class of sense-enhancing devices like a bubble chamber, constructed to render ineffable messages effable; thus no physicist can really "see" subatomic particles, not even aided by the most powerful electron microscope (or accelerator-detector complex), but only (in the simple case) the tiny bubbles of hydrogen produced by them—the vaporous beads in the tank "stand for", i.e., model, their interactions. As for the dermatoglyph presented to the court, this functions here as a probatively synecdochic message-by-contiguity about the guilt of a presumed criminal.

In any given transaction, a source is necessarily coupled by means of a channel to a destination; the variety of such passage-ways is constrained by the specific sensorium of both. This state of affairs was neatly summed up by George Dalgarno (the Scottish author of *Ars signorum*, a fascinating semiotic treatise from the mid-seventeenth century): "It is true", he wrote in 1661, "that all the Senses are Intelligencers to the Soul less or more; for tho they have their distinct limits, and proper Objects assigned them by nature; yet she is able to use their service even in the most abstracted Notions, and Arbitrary institution". Dalgarno adds "that Nature seems to have fitted two, Hearing and Seeing, more particularly for her service", but this is a superficial view. By far the most hoary messages are molecular, and the chemical channel is the most prevalent. Three of the hierarchical levels of basic endosemiotic control are regulated, respectively, by the genetic code, by humoral as well as cell-mediated immune reactions, and (since the appearance of the sponges) by the large number of peptides present in the central nervous system, functioning as neurotransmitters. The olfactory and gustatory senses are likewise semiochemical. Even in vision, the impact of photons on the retina differentially affects the capacity of the pigment rhodopsin (which fills the rods) to absorb light of different wave lengths, the condition for the univariance principle. Acoustic and tactile vibrations, and impulses delivered via the thermal senses are, as well, finally transformed into electrochemical messages. Humans and many other animals are routinely linked by several channels simultaneously or in succession. Parallel processing of messages introduces a degree of redundancy, by virtue of which it becomes more likely that errors in reception will be minimized; however, it is also possible for collimated messages to contradict one another—this is how a rhetorical figure such as irony performs in spoken or written discourse, as does the back-arch display of a house cat in zoosemiotics.

It is unknown how most sources generate—or, to use a less overburdened term, formulate—a message. Human beings are capable of launching an enormous number of novel messages appropriate to an indefinite variety of contexts, but the electrochemical intricacies of their initial entrainment by that cramped globe of tissue known as the brain remain an enigma. Plainly, however, the message-as-formulated must undergo a transductive operation to be externalized into serial strings appropriate to the channel, or channels, selected to link up with the destination. This neurobiological transmutation from one form of energy to another is called *encoding*. When the destination detects and extracts the encoded messages from the channel, another transduction, followed by a series of still further transformations, must be effected before interpretation can occur; this pivotal reconversion is called *decoding*. Encoding and decoding imply a code, a set of unambiguous rules whereby messages are convertible from one representation to another; the code is what the two parties in the message exchange are supposed to have, in fact or by assumption, totally or in part, in common. Using Joseph Weizenbaum's famous computer program, aptly named Eliza, human interlocutors tend to project sympathy, interest, and intelligence upon Eliza, as they would upon a psychotherapist. In fact, Eliza "knows" nothing (Weizenbaum 1977). A similar fallacy about shared codes is the theme of Jerzy Kosinski's brilliant novelette, *Being There* (and the faithful movie based on it—Ashby 1979), in which an illiterate, retarded gardener is ascribed supreme gnostic attributes because he—essentially a blank page—mimics, echoes, and reflects back the interactive codes of every one of his conversational partners, whatever their native speech community may be.

Receivers interpret messages as an amalgam of two separate but inextricably blended inputs: the physical triggering sign, or signal, itself, but as unavoidably shaped by the context. The latter plays a cardinal role, yet the concept has eluded definition; too, it is generally unknown how destinations "take account of" context. In semiotics, the term is used both broadly and loosely to encompass preceding messages (anaphoric presuppositions), and probably succeeding messages (cataphoric implicatures), environmental and semantic noise, all filtered by short- and long-term memory, genetic and cultural.

These six key factors—message and code, source and destination, channel and context—separately and together make up the rich domain of semiotic researches. However, the pivotal notion remains the *sign*.

II. *Components, Consequences, and Philosophical Overtones*

This term has been defined in many different ways since its introduction in Ancient Greece. In medical semiotics, for example, sign is used in conjuction with, or, rather, in opposition to symptom, since at least Alcmaeon (6th-5th cent. BC), Hippocrates (c.460-377BC), and especially Galen (c.130-200AD). Clinical practitioners usually distinguish between "soft data", or subjective signs, dubbed symptoms, meaning by this whatever the patient relates verbally about his feelings ("I have a pain in my chest") or exhibits nonverbally (groans while pointing to the chest); and "hard data", or objective signs, which clinicians actually call "signs", meaning whatever the physician observes with his eyes and ears (bloody sputum, wheezing) or with his instruments (shadow on an x-ray photograph). Many philosophers also use the term "sign"; however, not a few contrast it with symbol rather than with symptom. Ernst Cassirer (1923-1929), for instance, claimed that these two notions belonged to different universes of discourse, and that "a sign is a part of the physical world, a symbol is a part of the human world of meaning". Minimalist approaches such as these are far too imprecise and superficial to be serviceable, as Peirce painstakingly demonstrated throughout his voluminous writings. For Peirce, "sign" was a generic concept, of which there are a very large number of species, multiplying from a trichotomous base of icon, index, and symbol, each defined according to that sign category's relation to its object in a particular context.

To clarify what a sign is it is useful to begin with the medieval formula, *aliquid stat pro aliquo*, broadened by Peirce, (c.1897: 2.228) to "something which stands to somebody for something in some respect or capacity". To the classic notion of *substitution* featured in this famous phrase—the late Roman Jakobson (1896-1982) called it *renvoi*, translatable as "referral"—Peirce here added the criterion of *interpretation*. At this point, let us take a closer look at the Object-Sign-Interpretant trichotomous cycle alluded to earlier, and also pause to consider Peirce's "somebody": the destination or other receiver of the message.

The initial distinction between object (O) and sign (S) raises profound questions about the anatomy of reality, indeed about its very existence even, but there is nothing approaching a consensus about these riddles among physicists, let alone philosophers. One obvious implication of this postulated duality is that semiosis requires at least two actants: the observer and the observed. Our intuition of reality is a consequence of a mutual interaction between the two, von Uexküll's private world of elementary sensations (*Merkzeichen*, or perceptual signs) coupled to their meaningful transforms into action impulses (*Wirkzeichen*, or operation signs), and the phenomenal world (*Umwelt*), that is, the subjective world each animal models out of its "true" environment (*Natur*, or reality) which reveals itself solely through signs. The rules and laws to which those sign-processes—viz., semiosis—are subject, are the only actual laws of Nature. "As the activity of our mind is the only piece of nature known to us", he argued, in 1920, in his great work on *Theoretical Biology*, "its laws are the only ones that have the right to be called laws of Nature." Any observer's version of his *Umwelt* will be one unique model of the world which is a system of signs made up of genetic factors plus a cocktail of experiences, including future expectations. A complicating fact of life is that the bare act of observation entails a residual juncture that disturbs the system being observed. The essential ingredient, or nutriment, of mind may well be information, but to acquire information about anything requires, via a long and complex chain of steps, the transmission of signs from the object of interest to the observer's central nervous system. Its attainment, moreover, takes place in such a manner that this influential action reacts back upon the object being observed so as to perturb its condition. In brief, the brain, or mind, which is itself a system of signs, is linked to the putative world of objects not simply by perceptual selection, but by such a far-off remove from physical inputs—sensible stimuli—that we can safely assert that the only cognizance any animal can possess, "through a glass darkly", as it were, is of signs. Whether there is a reality behind signs—perhaps what Heraclitus called *logos*, the repeatable structure that secures for any object its ideal unity and stability, and which the topologist René Thom and I have independently rendered as "form"—mankind can never be sure of. As Heraclitus so eloquently put it, "You could not discover the limits of soul, even if you traveled every road to do so; such is the depth of its form." In sum, this reasoning entitles us to rewrite O as S_{I_n}, so the initial twofold distinction is resolved to one between two sorts of signs.

What about the third correlate, Peirce's interpretant (I)? What did he mean by this much-discussed (and even more often misunderstood) concept? True, no single, canonical definition of it is to be found in his voluminous writings, but he does make it clear that every sign determines an interpretant "which is itself a sign, [so] we have a sign overlying sign." He also points out that an interpretant can be either an equivalent sign or "perhaps a more developed sign", which is where novelty enters the system, enabling us to increase our understanding of the immediate object. To illustrate all this, ponder some interpretants of the English noun *horse*. They could be (partial) synonyms like *colt, gee-gee, gelding, hinny, mare, pony, stallion, stud,* or *thoroughbred*—to say nothing of *heroin*—and the like, or the interpretant could be a monolingual rewording, including standard dictionary definitions, as the OED's beginning: "A solid-hoofed perissodactyl quadruped . . . having a flowing mane and tail, whose voice is a neigh". Another of its interpretants is the scientific name *Equus Przewalski caballus*, as are all (roughly equivalent translations into verbal signs in other languages, like *cheval, Pferd, losad, hevonen,* etc. Historical tokens, such as Bucephalus, Morocco, Clever Hans, and all the Lippizaners of the Spanish Riding School of Vienna belong here, along with literary representations like Dean Swift's Houyhnhnms (1726), Peter Shaffer's play "Equus" (1974), Conan Doyle's saga of "Silver Blaze" (1892), Eco's creature Brunellus (1980: 23), and entire scientific treatises as different as Xenophon's disquisition *Treatise on Horsemanship* (c.365BC), Stefan von Maday's *Psychologie der Pferde und der Dressur* (1912), and E. H. Gombrich's penetrating essay, "Meditations on a Hobby Horse" (1951). Intersemiotic transmutations into nonverbal signs include innumerable and world-wide engravings and paintings of horses (notably from the Magdalenian caves), sculptures (from the Neolothic onward, including the Chinese tradition since Lung-shan), Scythian friezes, Greek centaurs as well as modern filmic portrayals, as "National Velvet" (Brown 1944), or "The Black Stallion" (Ballard 1979). Finally, of course, any "actual" horse I point to may become, by virtue of that gesture, which is an indexical sign (an "object of direct experience so far as it directs attention to an object by which its presence is caused"), an interpretant. There is no doubt that an intralingual synonym or paraphrase of, or extended discourse on, any sign will enrich comprehension of the object it represents, as will also its interlingual translations and intersemiotic transmutations. Each further interpretant tends to amplify intelligence and afford opportunity for a cascade of semantic innovation and therefore change. (Another, more technical way of putting this is that any metalanguage explicating an object language is always richer than the latter.)

In brief, it follows from Peirce's way of looking at the sign that the second distinction, as much as the first, resolves itself into two sorts of signs, to wit, S and S_{I_n}. Once more, here are his words: a sign is anything "which determines something else (its *interpretant*) to refer to an object to which itself refers (its *object*) in the same way, the sign becoming in turn a sign, and so on *ad infinitum*."

If objects are signs, in indefinite regression to a supposititious *logos*, and if interpretants are signs marching in progression toward the ultimate disintegration of mind, what is there left that is not a sign? What of the "somebody" mentioned by Peirce—the observer or the interpreter of the train after train of sign-actions? In a celebrated article he published in 1868, Peirce anticipated and answered this question, contending "that the word or sign which man uses *is* the man himself", which is to claim that "the man and the external sign are identical, in the same sense in which the words *homo* and *man* are identical. Thus my language is the sum total of myself, for the man is the thought."[2] In short, the "somebody" is also a sign or a text. What of man's faculty of procreation, shared with all other life forms? Peirce showed that even this capacity is inherent in signs, a parallel that has been elaborated by the French topologist Thom, in his path-breaking "From Icon to Symbol" (1973). *Omne symbolum de symbolo*—signs come into being only by development out of other signs.

The position adverted to in the foregoing paragraphs, according to which, at a certain point in the semiosic cycle, there are objects, included among them conscious observers or interpreters (which Charles Morris defined as organisms for which something is a sign)—such as people, porpoises, and perhaps Phobians— and there are, at another point in the cycle, interpretants, both being kinds of signs, is a familiar one in philosophical tradition. This position—one that surely follows from Peirce's wistful throw-away remark (1906a: 5.448 n.1) about something he took to be a fact, "that the universe . . . is perfused with signs, if it is not composed exclusively of signs"—is known as idealism, and that of a particular hue, sometimes called "conceptual idealism", which maintains that our view of reality, viz., our *Umwelt*, entails an essential reference to mind (*Gemut*) in its constitution. As Kant insisted—and, of course, both Peirce and von Uexküll had thoroughly assimilated Kantian principles—"raw experience" is unattainable; experience, to be apprehended, must first be steeped in, strained through, and seasoned by a soup of signs. For this reason, this brand of idealism can be called "semiotic idealism", in the apt designation recently put forward (1983) by the Toronto philosopher David Savan. Furthermore, to paraphrase Savan, semiotic idealism comes in two flavors, strong or radical, and mild or tolerant, as between which he leans toward the latter, namely, "the thesis that any properties, attributes, or characteristics of whatever exists depend upon the system of signs, representations, or interpretations through which they are signified'. Without necessarily committing oneself to this or that brand of idealism—only the realist positions are, I think, altogether devoid of interest—it is clear that what semiotics is finally all about is the role of mind in the creation of the world or of physical constructs out of a vast and diverse crush of sense impressions.

A few months ago, I was an auditor at an international state-of-the-art conference, co-sponsored with my university by the National Endowment for the Humanities. The topic debated was whether semiotics is a field or a discipline—a question Umberto Eco had suggested in a speech delivered ten years earlier on the same campus. Most speakers were specialists in one or more of the complex historical sciences the French call *les sciences humaines*. The designated formal discussant was the illustrious and skeptical English social anthropologist, Sir Edmund Leach, who had detected undue hubris in the presentations, pointing out to the speakers that "others were there before you". As to this, he was undoubtedly correct. Mankind's obsessive concern with signs dates from the appearance of the most dramatic of all steps in hominoid evolution, the emergence of verbal signs and the changes in information storage and transmission that accompanied this transition. The same preoccupation with signs is evident throughout infant and child development. When my five-year-old daughter asked me, a few weeks ago, "Daddy, just what does the Salivation Army do?", and, some time ago, when my seven-year-old wondered just how Dracula was killed by a "steak" driven into his heart, I knew I was not being led into the tangled thickets of philanthropy or Transylvania, but that *locus classicus* of signs in action, paranomasia.

A few lines above, I used the expression "historical sciences", but this, too, may well perpetuate an illusion. According to at least one version of quantum theory, John Archibald Wheeler's highly imaginative rendition (1981) of the so-called "Copenhagen interpretation", the past is theory, or yet another system of signs; it "has no existence except in the records of the present". At a semiotic level we make the past as well as the present and the future.

II

Semiotic Systems:

Anthroposemiotics
Zoosemiotics
Phytosemiotics

4

DONALD PREZIOSI

The Multimodality of Communicative Events

In the semiotic task of revealing more precisely the *place* of the built environment—or any other system of signs—in communication, the analysis of *communicative events* in their multimodal totality has acquired today a fundamental urgency and importance. In the present section I would like to discuss the complexities inherent in such events as well as our current abilities to adequately model such complexities.

Communication, in the broadest sense, involves the transmission of information regarding the perception of similarities and differences. Any semiotic system is a complexly-ordered device for the cuing of such perceptions in given sensory channels and in conventionally-delimited media.

A communicative act such as a verbal utterance does not normally exist *in vacuo* (except perhaps in the fictitious atmosphere of certain recently fashionable linguistic models); rather, speech acts are invariably co-occurent with communicative acts in distinct signalling media. This state of affairs is neither accidental nor circumstantial, for on the basis of internal evidence alone, it is increasingly evident that each of the isolable sign systems evolved by humans has been designed from the outset to function both semi-autonomously and in deictic concert with other sign systems.

But beyond an understanding of certain formative entities in the linguistic code—whose meaningfulness, as in the case of "shifters", can only be disambiguated through cross-modal indexing—we remain at a serious loss to account for the extraordinarily complex systematicities of normal (i.e., multimodal) communication in daily life.

It has been clear for a long time that an adequate account of communicative events demands of us more than a mechanical summation of the organizational properties of particular codes as analytically isolable, and more than is currently offered by the hybrid heuristics of sociolinguistics and "pragmatics", which, while admirable for their remarkable rediscovery of the wider world in which verbal language is embedded, nevertheless rarely escape an implicit verbocentrism. One can only stretch paralinguistics so far.

In the ongoing semiotic bricolage of daily life, we orchestrate and intercalate anything and everything at our disposal to create and maintain a significant world, or simply to get a message across. It is clear that the attempt to understand such complexities through the scientistic superimposition of design features, analytic methods and even data language drawn from the study of one of its embedded components—for example verbal language—upon other significative modalities has, by and large, been a failure. While it is true that much has been learned by such activity, it must be decisively admitted that the ultimate expected illumination has tended to be rather dim and fleeting in comparison to the energies expended—or, as more often has happened, the mute stones and gestures have remained mute.

Of course this is not to deny the importance and relevance of a semiotics of the code—whether architectonic, gustatory, linguistic, or somatotopic; rather it becomes increasingly urgent to reaffirm the status of such models as selective, partial and synecdochal fictions.

If we are to augment the ongoing multiplication of semiotic models of specific codes in given cultural contexts beyond the trivial reductionisms of currently available ''semiotics of culture'', our focus must be held tenaciously upon the actualities of semiosis in daily life which implicate and combine varieties of significative formations drawn from distinct signalling media. Moreover, general sign theory itself must push beyond the ultimate propositional logics which, perhaps not so curiously, seem to privilege the perspective (verbal or visual) of the given analyst.

None of this criticism is particularly new or original. It is raised again, and must be continued, until our picture of the extraordinarily complex nature of normal human semiosis begins to be clarified in a non-trivial fashion. Clearly, this is not intended as an indictment of the semiotic enterprise itself, rather only its dominant priorities. If semiotics is to realize its potential as a principled, insightful and radical contribution to the problem of meaning in human life, it must remain absolutely clear about the relative urgencies of its priorities.

Additionally, if semiotics is to be more than merely a new formalism, I think that we must be prepared to admit that it may be at least theoretically possible for semiotics to learn from the experience of other perspectives which in the past or at present have attempted to wrestle with equivalent problems. There is nothing more vacuous than a semiotics of art (for example) which is less well-informed or insightful than the received art history.

Again, I think these issues are self-evident, and rather than continue to pursue them in the abstract, I would like to begin to address the question of the implications of a holistic and multimodal approach to semiosis.

It is clear that communicative acts in a given medium are normally co-occurrent with acts in other modalities which may or may not implicate or address distinct sensory channels, and I think it is also clear that communicative events resemble complex, dynamically equilibrated spatiotemporal arrays of such acts, of which the basic primate display is a simple, but (in the human line) radically apotheosized analogue.

Furthermore, it is evident that the analysis of transmissions in any one of a series of copresent modalities in a communicative event may not necessarily result in an entirely complete, coherent, or homogeneous semantic domain. Much of the information simultaneously broadcast is often redundant and perceptually augmentative, and some of it may be contradictory. Some of it may be supplementary in providing collocational semantic markings with respect to information in another modality.

I think it is a reasonable assumption that each of the various sign systems employed by humans in social communication has been designed or evolved to operate in concert with all others. Crossmodal indexing, redundancy, complementarity, and supplementarity are properties of any code, perhaps to a greater degree than we may have been willing to admit in the past. Any human sign system is *de facto* not merely an open system, but it is an asymmetrical and dynamic system: it possesses both dynamism in its synchronicity and stability in its diachrony.

This is an extremely complex state of affairs, since it situates human sign systems somewhere between mechanistic well-formedness and idiosyncratic bricolage; but I will also take it as a reasonable assumption that this state of affairs has not only been highly adaptive in the evolution of the human line, but that it has, in a variety of imaginable ways, been responsible for what it is we have become as a species.

The peculiar internal nature of human sign systems is both a concomitant of and a contributor to our characteristically crossmodal behavior. Moreover, the human grade of intelligence is such that when faced with a choice, we invent a third possibility, or we answer a question with a question. We contrast with our nearest primate relatives not merely by the possession of any one code (whether verbal or visual), but rather by the globality of our intelligence in all modalities.

The chief task of semiotics—its highest priority—is the clarification of the multidimensional geometries of relationship underlying this multimodal behavior, which is manifest in even the most simple communicative events in daily life. The question is, what is minimally implicated in any such event?

If we situate ourselves at the locus of verbal language, it will be evident that any speech act is co-occurent, minimally, with the following:

> (1) some state of gestural, somatotopic or spatiokinetic signing, involving the significative use of the body and its culturally and conventionally-delimited components; (2) some state of costuming or dermal patterning, involving the significative use of artifactual markings or materials which figure a body's topologically-defined ground; and (3) some state of architectonic or environmental structuration, involving the significative use of a built environment or an appropriated topography.

Each of these modalities—which, depending upon the conventions of a given culture, may themselves incorporate more than one "code" as such—may be said to broadcast simultaneously with a particular speech act. In concert, these intercalated transmissions define and delimit a communicative event.

As important as it may be to identify and define the modal components of a given communicative event, it is no less important to stress and explicate their salient contrastive structural properties, for it is not the case that we are dealing with topologically identical cells in a matrix, or merely different shapes in a jigsaw puzzle. Nor for that matter will the relative contributions of copresent signings in different modalities necessarily be equivalent; nor will it be necessarily the case that they will always be hierarchicalized in any one linear direction, wherein any one set of signings invariably stands as a "figure" to the "ground" of other signings in other modalities.

There are significant structural differences among the copresent signings in a communicative event, which in large part are concomitants of the particular sensory channels implicated in a transmission. Vision is directional; audition is omnidirectional. Moreover, there are important differences with respect to relative permanence of broadcast: speech signals decay instantaneously; buildings and their infrastructures remain perceptually available for use across a multitude of different speech acts. Clearly, there is an ascending scale of relative "object-permanence" in the list of modalities given above.

Thus, any nontrivial understanding of the inherent multimodality of communicative events must reject a simple summation or communicative relationship of its components, for we are dealing with different kinds of components which have been evolved to do partially different things.

The cases where a speech act occurs outside this multimodal context are relatively minimal. But the situation is not necessarily symmetrical with other modalities, and speech acts may be absent in communicative events, whether or not they are replaced by surrogate or complementary signings in other modalities. Various kinds of gestural signings may serve in such a capacity, whether derived metaphorically or synecdochally from verbal structure, or arising independently of a linguistic code. Some such systems may be truly "deponent", in the sense of being ancillary or paralinguistic, operating in rhythmic synchrony with speech, while others will be capable of semantic disambiguation without the copresence of verbal transmission.

There is an enormous amount of redundancy in even the simplest communicative event, and a great deal of redundancy is built into the operant behavior of any code. But this phenomenon is not only infra-modal, it is cross-modal, and information supplied by one modality may be augmented by distinct formations in other codes. It may well be that the particular effability of any one code is to a certain degree a concomitant of its embeddedness in arrays of copresent codes, both actually and potentially. In visual communication, the symbolic and significative potential of a given gestalt is a necessary coefficient of its ground, in mutual reciprocity. From the perspective of communicative events, this codeterminate "ground" involves both inframodal and crossmodal contextualization.

The real question here is the extent to which we are capable of modelling such complexities. Taking merely the four modal activities noted above—namely, verbal utterances, dermal patterning, somatotopic signing, and architectonic appropriation—then our task will be to clarify the relationships defined by the operant behaviors of copresent signings in these domains. It seems evident that these relationships will not only be linearly syntagmatic, metonymical or commutative— since however useful it may be to model such phenomena as if they were "texts" or complicated "rebuses", they are more than these. Nor are they merely paradigmatically associated, or metaphorically related: a communicative event is necessarily more complex than a linguistic unit such as a phoneme, defined by the intersective copresence of a simultaneous bundle of distinctive features.

The relationships in question will be both metonymical or synecdochal, and metaphorical—that is to say, both syntagmatic and paradigmatic. Furthermore, whether a given relationship between signings in any two modalities is paradigmatic or syntagmatic may well be a function of the stance of the analysis. In other words, the relationship may be non-transitive or irreversible: a metaphorical relationship from one direction may be synecdochal when modelled from the other direction. All of this may be over and above the patent syntagmatic-paradigmatic oscillation among units in a particular code at different levels in its hierarchy of sign formations. It may very well be the case that not only will such relationships be asymmetrical, they may be differently asymmetrical from the standpoint of different modalities.

But there are two further complications. The first concerns the phenomenon of markedness which pervades any code: to what extent do we really understand markedness relations as applied cross-modality? I am not aware of any study which addresses this problem either directly or indirectly, although the work on palaeolithic symbol systems by the Soviet writer Toporov (1972) and the American anthropologist Marshack (1976) may lead to insights into this problem. It is most clearly understood in work in linguistic semiotics, notably in the work of Jakobson and others (see especially Jakobson and Waugh 1979), where its relationship to metaphor and metonymy is distinctly specified.

The second complication regarding the nature of crossmodal relationships in communicative events has to do with the problem of the relative dominance of various functions in a transmission in a given signing, and its copresent associations in other modalities. In other words, will it necessarily be the case that a focus upon conative, or phatic, or aesthetic functions in a given signing will be equilibrated with an equivalent focus in another modality? I suspect that here also the situational possibilities are quite complex, for it is evident that from the perspective of a communicative event in its totality, distinct modalities may contribute different weightings in functional dominance: otherwise equivalent verbal utterances with a dominance on one function may acquire different transmissive foci in different settings. Once again, this fact suggests that a semiotics of the code *per se* is a selective fiction in isolation from its multimodal communicative context. And taken together, the various complexities just outlined suggest that the relationship between a semiotics of the code and general sign theory is necessarily not metaphorical, but inevitably synecdochal.

The calibration of these possible geometries of relationship is precisely what is the most urgent task facing semiotics. As it is, it is exceedingly complex in merely dealing with the four modal domains abstractly and generically discussed here, let alone in the actual pluralistic conditions of semiosis in daily life, which involves the intercalation of signings drawn from many distinct codes—both those inherited from our palaeolithic past, such as verbal language and the architectonic code (the latter of which is now evidenced as early as 300,000 B.C. in its present form), as well as those assembled yesterday.

The situation is precisely this: if it is the case that each of the various semiotic codes evolved by humans are irreducible with respect to each other—in other words, that the contents expressed by complex nonverbal units cannot be translated into one or more verbal units, and vice-versa, except by weak approximation—then the hope to find some uniformitarian common denominator, some "meta" language, some non-trivial and non-reductionist general theory of semiosis, is an illusion except as a selective and synecdochal fiction. There are no metalanguages; rather (and much more interestingly) only selective infralanguages which are part and parcel of given codes. And since any infralanguage by its very nature adds to the body of a given code itself, and thereby alters its topology, so in any attempt to see itself as an object it must undoubtedly act so as to make itself distinct from, and thereby false to, itself. In this condition it will always partially elude itself. The kitten will always chase its own tail.

I suspect it is in the very nature of any human sign system to partially elude itself, and herein lies the very effability of the semiotic codes which we have evolved. But if there is no truly synoptic picture of semiosis in a value-neutral sense, no one perspective which subsumes all others, we are left with something which in the long run is inherently much more useful—namely a mutable focus on communicative events which affords a temporal and syntagmatic cascade of perspectives which selectively illuminate a situation in a stereoscopic and overlapping fashion.

It is precisely the operant nature of our multimodal understanding which privileges each perspective selectively and successively. Since any analysis is a function of the purposes to which it is put, it is in the nature of any analysis to be provisional, for there are many different functions and purposes, some of which are contradictory and irreducible, even if they may be copresent in the same analysis to varying degrees of dominance.

Consequently, it will be necessary to be explicit regarding the inevitable teleological determinants in any semiotic analysis, even if this implies not only an abandonment of a semiotics of the code except as a provisional fiction, but also an abandonment of a uniformitarian theory of semiosis itself in favor of a holographically-overlapped matrix of generic and irreducible semiotic theories.

Of course this is not to deny the necessary operational paradox that any code can be employed, in communication, as a *provisional* metalanguage. Nor is it to deny the evident fact that even though many codes are mutually irreducible in a strict sense, they may reveal correlative processes of formation and transmission, as we have argued in the present study. But whatever they share is shared by virtue of their status as human sign systems with partly-overlapping and mutually-implicative functions. Codes are necessarily correlative rather than isomorphic. The role of semiotics is to provide a clearer understanding of how and why each copresent system provides its own particularly powerful perspective on the totalities of human experience, and the ways in which each such perspective necessarily implicates all others. The most urgent task awaiting semiotics is precisely a principled attention to the directional geometries of this implication.

And in addressing these implicational relationships our analyses will be most productive when the essential and fundamental difference between meaning and reference are clearly borne in mind. Meaning is the specification of an ordered trace of relationships which a given sign or matrix of signs prescribes with respect to other signs within the same code, whereas reference is not an indexical relationship which a given sign bears to formations outside of semiotic systems, toward some fictive "real" world, but rather involves cross-modal implications. In verbal language, for example, "shifters" are cross-modally indexical with respect to significative formations in a somatotopic modality (i.e., the relative placements and perspectival positionings of addressers and addressees in communicative events). In an identical fashion, the "meaning" of a given painting or environmental construct is internal to its own code, whereas the "reference" of a mediaeval religious composition (or any other) may implicate a culturally copresent set of texts, doctrines or beliefs, which themselves comprise significative formations in their own right in adjacent codes. And the relationships among all these may be metonymic or indexical, or metaphoric.

I believe strongly that a clarification of these issues can only lead to a salient enhancement of the semiotic enterprise, shunting our focus more tenaciously upon the nature of *relationship* itself, which after all is what semiotics is all about, from its conceptual foundations to the fine grain of its ongoing analysis. I have tried to suggest here that the most productive direction such analysis can take today is in the direction of the disambiguation of the cross-modal relationships manifest in their totality primarily in the complexities of communicative events. In addition, it is only in this way that our understanding of the internal structural nature of individual codes can be made less fictive.

5

JACQUES MARITAIN

Language and the Theory of Sign

A treatise on the sign and symbol, such as I hope may one day be written, would on the one hand endeavor to winnow out what is essential in the extensive intellectual elaboration to which mediaeval thinkers subjected this matter, above all in logic (theory of concepts and judgment) and in theology (theory of the sacraments). On the other hand, it would endeavor to link up with this, making use of the conceptual procedure thereby established, the scientific investigations of our own day and that vast assemblage of problems of whose importance various contemporary schools of thought . . . have been so well aware, and which relate to the symbolic, its role in primitive civilizations, in magic, in the arts and sciences, in the social life of our more developed civilizations, etc. The project for such a treatise, it seems to me, should include: 1. a philosophical theory of the sign (general theory of the sign—the speculative sign; the practical sign); 2. reflections and hypotheses with regard to the magical sign; 3. reflections on art and the sign, science and the sign, social life and the sign, religion, ethics, mysticism and the sign. The present study will attempt only to clear the ground for the subject by suggesting certain very incomplete notions on a few of the themes which arise from the first two parts of the project outlined above [and as restricted, moreover, to the specific subject of language as it forms but a part of the larger consideration of the sign].

—Jacques Maritain 1943: 191—

I should like here to take up again some parts of an outline on a general theory of the sign I wrote a number of years ago (1937-1938, 1938; also, with additions, 1943, 1956 [comment in Williams 1981: 318 n. 17]), and to make use of them to propose some considerations on language. These considerations may be grouped under three headings: language and awareness of the relation of signification; language and the magic sign; language and reverse or inverted signification. [This threefold grouping is preceded by a brief precis or synopsis of the general theoretical considerations as first advanced in 1937-1938, with the corresponding references to the Latin text of Poinsot 1632a, from which Maritain principally derived the general considerations, restored here in square brackets exactly according to the footnotes appended by the author to the texts of 1938 and 1943.]

1. Recapitulations of the General Theory of the Sign

No problems are more complex or more fundamental to the concerns of man and civilization than those pertaining to the sign. The sign is relevant to the whole extent of knowledge and of human life; it is a universal instrument in the world of human beings, like motion in the world of physical nature. [Gloss in Deely 1985: 490 n. 2 par. 2.]

Signum est quod repraesentat aliud a se potentiae cognoscenti: A sign is something that makes something other than itself present to knowledge. A sign manifests and makes known something for which it stands vicariously and to which it is related as the measured is to the measure. [Poinsot 1632a: 25/11-13, 116/3-5, 116/14-117/17.]

The ancients drew a distinction between the natural sign (*signum naturale*) and the conventional sign (*signum ad placitum*). In their view, a sign is what it is by virtue of its specific and characteristic function of making known some other thing. [Poinsot 1632a: 119/10-15, 119/30-39, 119/50-120/6, 121/21-30, 123/13-25, 125/35-39, 128/14-18, 137 n. 4.] The relation of the sign to what it manifests is a real relation, i.e., is founded in reality in the case of a natural sign, since a natural sign is better known than that which it manifests, and since the property of being more knowable, and this in relation to something else that is thereby made knowable, is a real property, not a purely ideal relation (*relatio rationis*) existing as such in thought only. [Poinsot 1632a: 137/9-14, 138/16-41, 140/7-15, 141/4-11, 141/12-18, 154/21-30, 161/32-34, 164/13-165/8.] The fact that smoke gives us knowledge of fire rather than of water, and that tracks of oxen give us knowledge of the ox rather than of man, and the concept of a horse of the horse rather than of stone—all this is based on a real intrinsic proportion between these signs and the things they signify. This realistic notion of the natural sign rests, in short, on a metaphysics for which intelligibility and being are consubstantial (*verum et ens convertuntur*).

This real relation is not one of efficient causality. Sign strictly keeps to the order of "objective causality" or of the formal causality of knowledge, not of efficient or productive causality. When a sign produces an effect it is never by virtue of being a sign. The sign is not even the efficient cause of the knowledge of the thing signified; it makes it known only by standing in lieu of the object within the cognitive faculty to which it brings the presence of the object, thus functioning in the same line of causality as the object itself (formal causality). [Poinsot 1632a: 194/31-37, 195/3-9, 195/18-29, 202/46-203/14.]

Not every image is a sign, and not every sign is an image. For the image (which "proceeds from another as from its principle and in the likeness of that other") may be of the same nature and have the same ontological status as that of which it is an image (the son is the image, not the sign, of his father). And many signs are not images (smoke is not the image of fire, nor is a cry the image of pain). [Poinsot 1632a: 218/29-48, 219/29-48.] We might define a symbol as a *sign-image* (both *Bild* and *Bedeutung*), a sensible thing *signifying* an object by reason of a presupposed relation of *analogy*.

Signs have to do with all types of knowledge. They are of considerable importance in the psychic life of nonrational animals [Poinsot 1632a: 204/9-205/3], and here I think we should interpret the data concerning conditioned reflexes from the point of view of psychology, not merely of physiology [Poinsot 1632a: 278/11-29].

The external senses make use of signs (I see Socrates when I see his statue; my eye sees him in it), for the use of signs does not necessarily imply discourse. Thus the thing signified has a kind of presence—the presence of knowability—in the sign; it is there *in alio esse* ["in another mode of existence". The summarized text of 1943 continues at this point—p. 193—after a comma: "in another mode of existence. Here is a point of capital importance from which flow many great truths, and which must be noted in passing as absolutely characteristic: *'Quid est illud in signato conjunctum signo, et praesens in signo praeter ipsum signum et entitatem ejus? Respondetur esse ipsummet signatum in alio esse'*—'What may be that element of the signified which is joined to the sign and present in it as distinct from the sign itself and its own entity? I answer: No other element than the very signified itself in another mode of existence' (Maritain's citation and translation of Poinsot 1632a: 209/1-5, with further cross-references noted to 205/35-37, 206/6-31, 207/26-28, 208/34-47). Hence the content of significance with which overflowed the statues of the gods. The god did not exist; but all the cosmic and psychic forces, the attractions, the passions which took shape in him, the idea which the artist and his contemporaries conceived of him—all that was *present* in the statue, not in a physical sense but *in alio esse*, in another mode of existence, and after the manner of the presence of knowability. For the statue had been made precisely to make all that known, to communicate it. In our museums, this pagan content is asleep, but it is always there. Let some accident take place, an encounter with a soul itself sensitized by some unconscious content: contact is established; the pagan content will be awakened and will unforgettably wound that soul"].

The birth of ideas and thus of intellectual life in us seems bound up with the discovery of the signifying value of signs. Animals make use of signs without perceiving the relation of signification. To perceive the relation of signification is to have an *idea*, i.e., a spiritual sign. Nothing throws more light on this subject than the miracle of the first dawning of intelligence in people who are deaf and dumb and blind (like Marie Heurtin, Helen Keller, Lydwine Lachance). It depends essentially on the discovery of the relation of signification between a gesture and the object of a desire. The keystone of the life of the mind is the sign.

In the realm of social life, the part played by signs is no less important: they give rise to social as well as to individual consciousness. It is through its symbols that a city, a class, or a nation becomes conscious of what it is.

Only in God does the life of the intellect make no use of signs. He knows Himself and all things by His essence. That is the privilege of the pure Act.

2. Language and the Intellectual Awareness of the Relation of Signification

At this point I should like to submit my first remarks about language. I just alluded to the first awakening of intelligence in blind deaf-mutes. Let us look a little more closely into the case.

For the first stirring of the idea as distinct from images, the intervention of a sensible sign is necessary. Normally in the development of a child it is necessary that the idea be "enacted" by the senses and lived through before it is born as an idea; it is necessary that the relationship of signification should first be actively *exercised* in a gesture, a cry, in a sensory sign bound up with the desire that is to be expressed. *Knowing* this relationship of signification will come later, and this will be to have the *idea*, even if it is merely implicit, of that which is signified. Animals and children make use of this signification; they do not perceive it. When the child begins to perceive it (then he exploits it, he toys with it, even in the absence of the real need to which it corresponds)—at that moment the idea has emerged.

But in "imprisoned souls", among blind deaf-mutes, the first stirring of an idea cannot spontaneously arise for lack of natural sensory signs. These require the convergence of all the senses; a cry which is not heard, a gesture which is not seen—how can these poor walled-in souls actively make use of such to express a desire? With them there can be no natural and spontaneous exercise of a relationship of signification, preceding the knowledge thereof, and hence preceding the birth of the idea.

In order to *exert* the first relationship of signification of which they are to make use, they must *know* this relationship; the idea, the very knowledge of signification must needs come to life at the same time as its first practical use! That is why some external help is indispensable. The miracle of awakening to the life of thought will come to pass precisely when—owing to the patiently repeated attempts of the teacher, who denies a desire and then suggests a sign, an *artificial, conventional* sign, intended to procure the satisfaction of the desire he has denied— the child suddenly *discovers* by some sort of sudden eruption of the idea the signification of this conventional sign (for example, of some gesture or other, in the language of the deaf), and from that moment on progresses with astonishing rapidity. A Marie Heurtin, a Helen Keller achieved the higher levels of intellectual life.

Now it seems to me that the way in which ideas are born to blind deaf-mutes can help us to picture how the discovery of language may have taken place.

The discovery of language, then, coincides with the discovery of the relation of signification, and this would explain why, as a matter of fact, the invention of language and the birth of ideas, the first release of the intellect's power, probably took place at the same time.

It is conceivable, I think, that a genuine language of *natural* sensory signs may have preceded language strictly so called (made up of conventional sensory signs), and that the latter may have developed out of the former. The "miracle" would have happened at the moment when man, beyond the fact of using natural gestures to express hunger, anger, or fear, would also have grasped the notion that this gesture was possessed of the virtue of signifying. By the same stroke a field of infinite possibilities would have opened. Then, once the relation of signification was discovered, the process of arbitrarily selecting or inventing other gestures and of using them as *conventional* signs no doubt developed quite rapidly.

Did a language made up of simple natural signs ever actually exist? Did, on the other hand, a language made up of conventional signs which were only gestures ever actually exist? It is not within my province to discuss such hypotheses. Moreover, my private opinion is rather that things took place in a dramatically different way. But as a philosopher I wish to point out that such hypotheses are logically conceivable. I do so in order to emphasize that what defines language is not precisely the use of words, or even of conventional signs; it is the use of any sign whatsoever *as involving the knowledge or awareness of the relation of signification*, and therefore a potential infinity; it is the use of signs *in so far as it manifests that the mind has grasped and brought out the relation of signification*.

Granted the imaginary possibility that a language of gestures ever existed, we might also imagine that later some kinds of vocal gestures or wordless singsongs led to articulate language. In any case, the invention of those particular conventional signs which are words, the creation of a system of signs made up of "phonemes" and "morphemes" was in itself a second "miracle", a further discovery of human intelligence, no less characteristic of man, but less essential than, and by nature not prior to, the discovery of the relation of signification.

So far we have spoken of genuine language. Let us point out that the word "language", when referring to animals, is equivocal. Animals possess a variety of means of communication but no genuine language. I have observed that animals use signs. But, as I also pointed out, no animal knows the relation of signification or uses signs as involving and manifesting an awareness of this relation.

The full import of this is best realized in connection with the use of conventional signs by animals. Karl von Frisch's admirable studies have shown (1950) that bees use conventional signs: he has observed that a scouting bee performs two types of dance (a round dance and a wagging dance) to indicate to the other members of the hive in what direction and at what distance the source of food it has visited is to be found. Yet, as Professor Benveniste rightly points out (1952: 5,6,7), such conventional signs do not truly constitute a language in the genuine sense of this word.

> The bee's message does not call for any reply from those to whom it is addressed, except that it evokes a particular behaviour which is not strictly an answer. This means that the language of the bees lacks the dialogue which is distinctive of human speech. . . . Moveover, the bee's message cannot be reproduced by another bee which has not seen for itself what the first bee has announced. . . . The bee does not construe a message from another message. Each bee, once advised by the scouting bee's dance, flies out and feeds at the spot indicated, reproducing the same information on its return, not with reference to the first message but with reference to the fact it has just verified itself. Now the characteristic of language is to produce a substitute for experience which can be passed on *ad infinitum* in time and space. This is the nature of our symbolism and the basis of linguistic tradition. If we now consider the content of the message it is easy to see that it always concerns only one fact, viz., food, and that the only variations of this theme concern the question of space. The contrast with the boundless possibilities of human language is obvious. Furthermore, the behaviour which expresses the bee's message is a special form of symbolism. It consists in tracing off an objective situation of fact, the only situation which can be translated into a message, without any possibility of variation or transposition. In human language, on the contrary, the symbol as such does not trace out the facts of experience in the sense that there is no necessary relationship between the objective reference and the linguistic form. . . . The essential difference between the method of communication discovered among bees and our human language . . . can be stated summarily in one phrase which seems to give the most appropriate definition of the manner of communication used by the bees: it is not a language but a signal code. All the characteristics of a code are present: the fixity of the subject matter, the invariability of the message, the relation to a single set of circumstances, the impossibility of separating the components of the message, and its unilateral transmission.

All this means, in the last analysis, that the relation of signification remains unknown to the bees. They use signs—and they do not know that there are signs.

By what process the dance of the bees developed as a conventional sign is a great mystery of biology and animal psychology. But in itself it no more implies language, in the genuine sense of the word, than the fact of a dog's barking when he sees a stranger, or of his crouching down or sitting up when his master utters certain words. The whole thing belongs to the realm of conditioned reflexes, whereas language pertains to the realm of the intellect, with its concepts and universal notions.

3. Language and the Magical Sign

A particularly important place in a general theory of sign should be given, I think, to the distinction between *logic* and *magic* signs.

By a *logic* sign, I mean a sign operating under certain functional conditions through which it is a sign *for the intellect* (whether speculative or practical), that is, when the predominance of the intellect defines a particular psychological or cultural regime. Under such conditions the sign, be it in itself sensible or intellectual, speaks ultimately to the intellect and refers ultimately to a psychic regime ruled by the intellect.

I call *magic* a sign operating under a different functional regime, where it speaks primarily to the imagination, regarded as the supreme and ruling standard of the psychic or cultural life as a whole. The sign, be it in itself sensible or intellectual, ultimately speaks to the imaginative faculties and refers ultimately to a psychic regime immersed in the vitalizing depths of the imagination.

My working hypothesis is here the new notion of "functional conditions" or "states" (using the word "state" here in a sense similar to that intended by chemists when they speak of the solid, liquid, and gaseous "states" of matter, or by theologians when they speak of the "state of pure nature", the "state of innocence", etc.), and I am pointing to a fundamental distinction between the state of our developed cultures and another state, in which for the psychic and cultural life as a whole the last word rests with the imagination as the supreme and final law. No doubt the intellect is present, but, in a way, it is not free. That is the kind of "state" I am calling the "magic" regime of psychic and cultural life.

May I add that this working hypothesis was lucky enough to reconcile opposed points of view in a particularly controversial field. Some time before his death, Professor Lucien Lévy-Bruhl was so kind as to write me of his agreement on this point. "As you put it quite rightly", he said, "'primitive' mentality is a *state* of human mentality, and I can accept the characteristics through which you define it" (1938).

As we have seen above, animals make use of signs. They live in a kind of magical world; biologically united to nature, they use signs belonging to a psychic regime which is entirely imaginative.

Intellect in primitive man is of the same kind as ours: it may even be more alive in him than in some more civilized people. But the question here is that of its "state" and of the existential conditions under which it operates. The whole mental regime of primitive man is under the authority of the imagination. In him the intellect is in every way involved with and dependent on the imagination and its savage world. This kind of mental regime is one where acquaintance with nature is experienced and lived through with an intensity and to an extent we cannot easily picture.

This is a state of inferiority, but it is by no means despicable. It is a human state, the state of mankind in its infancy, a fertile state through which we have had to pass. Under this regime humanity enriched itself with many vital truths, a number of which were perhaps lost when it passed on to an adult state. These truths were known by way of dream or instinct and by actual participation in the thing known—just as if we imagined that in the knowledge a bee has of the world of flowers a light which the bee does not possess, the light of reason or of the intellect, were present in a diffused, undifferentiated state, before becoming condensed into stars and solar systems separating daylight from darkness.

Here we meet with a difficulty analogous to that which we find when we try to penetrate the mental life of animals. Whatever *we* picture to ourselves is bathed in intelligence, and in intelligence which is free. We have great trouble in depicting to ourselves what another mental regime can be like. (And if we are Cartesians, it is impossible for us to do so.)

Let me say in brief that in our logical state, sensations, images, and ideas are *solar*, bound up with the luminous and regular life of the intellect and its laws of gravitation.

In the magic state they were *nocturnal*, bound up with the fluid and twilight mental life of the imagination and of an experience which was astonishingly powerful but entirely lived through and dreamed.

The same is true of the sign, and of the relation of sign to thing signified.

3.1. Since truth is a relation of the cognitive faculty to the thing and belongs only to the judgment of the intellect which grasps it as such, it should be said that in primitive man this relation is experienced but is not winnowed out for its own sake. It is known, of course, because the intellect is present, but it is known in a nocturnal manner, since intelligence is in this case immersed in the powers of the imagination.

When we consider primitive man we may say that in him the relation of the mind to the thing is ambivalent: the same relation is "false" (in the eyes of our evolved consciousness) to the extent that it asserts, for instance, the existence of composite tribal ancestors (like duck-men or kangaroo-men). It is "true" to the same extent that it affirms the vital union of man and nature of which this myth is the symbol. But for primitive man a distinction of this kind has no meaning. This is because his very adhesion to truth is not ours, since for him the idea of truth has not been winnowed out for itself.

He adheres *en bloc*, at the same time and indistinctly, to the symbol and the symbolized: here is for him, in indivisible fashion, an image or a likeness of truth, an equivalent, an *als ob* of truth, without his having winnowed out the idea of truth for its own sake. In similar fashion a child believes in a story, in the adventures of Alice in Wonderland; awaken the child, withdraw him from the world of the imagination and he knows very well that a little girl cannot enter a rabbit hole. But primitive man does not wake up; he is not yet withdrawn from the motherly bosom of the imagination, which makes him familiar with the whole of nature and without which he could not face the relentless severity of his existence as a cave dweller at war with the beasts. He lives in the world of *make-believe*.

3.2. Bergson has admirably shown that what is to be found at the source and basis of magic as a primordial element is the relationship of causality (1932: 175-177, = 1935: 155-157):

. . . [Man] realized at once that the limits of his normal influence over the outside world were soon reached, and he could not resign himself to going no further. So he carried on the movement, and since the movement could not by itself secure the desired result, nature must needs take the task in hand. . . . [Things] will then be more or less charged with submissiveness and potency: they will hold at our disposal a power which yields to the desires of man, and of which man may avail himself. . . . [The workings of Magic] begin the act which men cannot finish. They go through the motions which alone could not produce the desired effect, but which will achieve it if the man concerned knows how to prevail upon the goodwill of things. Magic is then innate in man, being but the outward projection of a desire which fills the heart.

That which I believe to be lacking in Bergson's theory is that it does not take into account the indispensable instrument of magical activity—the *practical sign*. [In his texts of 1937-1938, 1943, Maritain takes this notion from Poinsot a.1644e— i.e., the sixth and last posthumous volume of Poinsot's *Cursus Theologicus* which reached publication in 1667—disp. 22. art. 1. dub. 4. par. 83, dub. 5. pars. 99-102, 108, 110-111, 114-115.] It is surely true that magic implies an appeal to some cosmic power which brings the desire of man to a happy outcome, an appeal which itself presupposes some sympathy, some compliance in things. But it must be added that magic makes use of signs. Here the relationship proper to the sign, and to the practical sign, necessarily intervenes. Man does not merely outline some causal action; he *makes a sign* (to semi-personal cosmic elements). It is needful that we insist upon the mental characteristics of these practical signs, subject as they are to the nocturnal regime of the imagination.

3.3. First of all, in my opinion, we here find ourselves confronted with a refraction in the world of imagination, or with a nocturnal deformation, of the practical sign in its quality as sign, or considered in the order of the *relationship itself of signification*, that is to say, in the order of *formal* causality, wherein the sign is, by its essence, the vicar of the object. Let us not forget that this relationship of sign to signified is, in its own order, singularly close. The motion toward the sign or the image, says St. Thomas [1272-1273: III.25.3.], following Aristotle [c.330BCb: ch. 1, 450b27-31], is identical with the motion toward the object itself: *"Sic enim est unus et idem motus in imaginem cum illo qui est in rem"* ["So the movement toward an image is one and the same as a movement toward that which is imaged": discussion in Poinsot 1632a: 211/29-212/18]. In the formal-objective order the sign is thus something most astonishing, whereat the routine of culture alone prevents our wonder. And this marvelous function of containing the object— with respect to the mind—of having present in itself the thing itself *in alio esse*, is fully exercised in primitive man. Words are not anemic or colorless, they are overflowing with life—with their life as signs—for primitive man. But that in itself sets a snare for his imagination. Thanks to the condition of experienced and lived participation wherein is established his whole mental life, the presence as to knowledge of the signified in the sign becomes for him a presence as to reality, a physical interchangeability, a physical fusion, and a physical equivalence of the sign and the signified (invocation of mythical names; magic objects, spells, idolatry). Primitive man is intoxicated with the excellence of the sign; yet the sign never altogether loses its genuine relationship of signification (to some *other* thing). The idol is god and yet is never altogether god.

3.4. Then again a slurring takes place from formal-objective causality to *efficient causality*. The creation of signs is a mark of the preeminence of the mind, and the instinct of the intelligence quickly informed man that symbols make him enter into the heart of things—in order to know them: at once, in a psychic regime wherein the imagination is dominant, this slurring will take place, man will think that symbols make us enter into the heart of things in order to act physically upon them and in order to make them physically subject to us and in order to effect for us a real and physical union with them. Moreover, are not the signs in question first and foremost practical signs? At once the imagination will take a sign directive toward an operation as an operating sign. And why should we be astonished that the imagination of primitive man cannot distinguish between formal causality and efficient causality, when the intelligence of philosophers so often confuses them?

The sign, then, not only makes men know, it makes things be; it is an efficient cause in itself. Hence all the procedures of sympathetic magic. In order to make rain, the sorcerer waters the ground. In order to obtain abundant tubers, he buries in the ground at seed time magical stones of the same shape as the desired tubers, which shall "teach" the yams and the taro to grow big, to reach the same size as the stones. The stones make them a sign, they are pattern symbols. The theory of *mana* among the Melanesians (*avenda* among the Iroquois, *wakonda* among the Sioux), the theory of a force spread throughout nature wherein all things participate in various degrees, seems to be the fruit of a later reflection upon this use of the sign. To the extent that reflection will be intensified, the idea of this semi-physical, semi-moral environment will become more materialized.

3.5. But the sign, in spite of everything, remains a sign. Inevitably there will take place a return of the order of causality to which it belongs, that is, of formal causality and of the relationship of signification—which with primitive man becomes a relationship of fusion and of physical equivalence—upon the relationship of efficient causality and of operation. And the imagination will oscillate from one way of thinking the sign to the other. In the perspective of efficient causality (as well as in the perspective of the relationship of signification understood in accordance with its true nature) there is a *distinction*, a difference, between the cause and the effect (as well as between the sign and the signified). In the perspective of formal causality denatured by the imagination, and of that intoxication with the sign induced in primitive man by the relationship of signification, there is a physical *interpenetration* and fusion of the sign and the signified.

Since we are by hypothesis dealing with the nocturnal regime of the imagination, and since for the imagination as such (as dreams bear witness) the principle of identity does not exist; and then again, since the intelligence is still present, bound up with and clothed in the imagination, it is easy to understand that for primitive man the identity of things is constantly unmade and made again. It is altogether too hasty for us to say that with him there is simply an identity between the sign and the signified. No, there is an oscillation, there is a going and coming from distinction to identification. When children play by building sand castles, these castles are truly castles for them. If you trample them, the children will cry with rage and indignation. But once their play is at an end, what were castles are only sand. Primitive man believes to be identical (through the living power of the imagination) that which he obscurely knows to be different (through his intelligence, bound up in the imagination). It is impossible to understand anything about his thought if it be conceived from the point of view of the logical or daylight state of the intelligence, taken as the rule and measure of all thought. It is the thought of an awakened dreamer, wherein the role of *play* (and the allowance of *play*) is tremendously great.

   3.6. If the above remarks are true, we may conclude that language began in mankind in the form of "magical" language. To the mind of the primitive man the word does not signify a concept, and, through the concept, a thing; it directly signifies a thing; and the word and the thing it signifies are both distinct and one, for the word, in so far as it remains a sign (formal causality), is not physically the thing, and in so far as it is a magical sign (confusion between formal and efficient causality), is physically the thing or causes it to exist. Nothing is more natural for primitive mentality than to make the name into a real equivalent of the thing named, suchwise that a sick person will swallow the paper on which the name of a remedy is written with the same confidence as the medicine itself. Under the cover of the mirage and illusion proper to magical thought, at least the dignity and sacred mystery of the words were felt and recognized (even though overrated). [Compare Heidegger 1927:81ff.]

   Once the mind and the society have passed under the solar regime of intelligence, the sense of this dignity and sacred mystery—now purified of its magical connotations—remains essential to human civilization. When civilization decays, the sense in question dissipates itself and is finally lost. Then, in order to recover it, poetry may possibly be tempted to return to magic and to crave for *the power of words* (cf. Tate 1952), as can be seen in Mallarmé and many other modern poets. There is a curious—and tragic—phenomenon, where something great and invaluable is looked for, and missed (namely, the genuine dignity of words, which refers to truth, not to power), and where by dint of refinement the civilized mind retrogresses to that magical notion of the sign which was normal in the childlike state of mankind, yet is for mankind in its adult state but a pathological symptom.

4. Language and the Reverse Sign

   As appears with particular clarity in the consideration of works of art, a final distinction must be made, namely, between the *direct* sign (which denotes an object) and what might be called the *reverse* or *inverted* sign (which manifests the subject). All the signs which we have been considering in this study are direct signs. The letter *A* signifies the sound *A*, mourning weeds signify death. But the sign can also act in the inverse way. While manifesting an object it can by a kind of inverted or retroverted signification also denote the subject itself which is using the sign and its states, its dispositions, and its secrets which it does not admit to itself, the subject being in that case taken as object by some observer. This is the sense in which Freud and his disciples understand the word "*symbol*"; they no longer think of its direct but only of its reverse or inverted signification. The Freudian symbol is a conscious content caused by the unconscious states of which it is the symptom. The birth of Minerva from the forehead of Jupiter is no longer the symbol of the divine origin of wisdom; it is the "symbol" of the idea of physiological birth *ex utero* which has been thrust back into the unconscious, and the idea of the divine origin of wisdom becomes itself the "symbol" of this unconscious representation. As has been pointed out by Roland Dalbiez (1936), it would be better in this case to say "psychic expression", a notion that is valid especially for the products of "dereistic" thought (dreams, hallucinations, neurotic symptoms).

But even in normal thought the signs which man uses to signify things (direct signs) signify man himself (reverse signs). Every work of art is a confession, but it is by discovering the secrets of being (guessed at by dint of suffering the things of this world) that it makes confession of the poet's secret.

4.1. As far as language is concerned, the part played by the *reverse* or *inverted* sign appears in an arresting way in those kinds of slang which are not simply spontaneous appropriations of speech to a special (and especially trying) human task or a closed (though possibly large) environment, divided from the society, manners, and speech of "cultivated" people, but which are, in actual fact, discriminating languages, typical for groups which segregate themselves from the community, either because they are composed of derelict, potentially delinquent, or criminal people at war with society or because they are composed of highbrow people who consider themselves privileged, as happens with young persons who have been selected to be trained in certain prominent institutions especially devoted to the formation of a vocational or intellectual elite.

The phenomenon is particularly interesting in this latter case, and it seems to be linked, as a rule, with those rites of initiation which are called *brimades* in French, and which correspond roughly to "hazing". As an instance among thousands, I would refer to the book in which Romain Rolland tells us of his recollections as a student in the École Normale Supérieure of Paris, a highbrow school for future intellectuals; he gives us a curious lexicon of the slang that was used there at that time. For example, with reference to the Director of the School (Georges Perrot), to some professors (La Coulouche, Chantavoine, and Fortunat Strowski), and to a general in charge of military instruction (General Jeanningros), *faire un Perrot* meant to make a blunder; *faire un Coulouche*, to play the phrasemonger; *faire un Chantavoine*, to play the euphuist; *faire un Tunat*, to make a bad pun; *faire un Jeanningros*, to utter a stupidity (Rolland 1952: 18-19).

Slang, as a rule, not only signifies concepts and things but also, and first of all, the subjective behavior, the feelings, habits, oddities, jokes, tricks, collusions, experiences, and resentments which are peculiar to the group and differentiate it from any other; it alludes to the secret life of the group and strengthens this collective life. It affords a particular delight because only the man who belongs to the group can understand it, and because in using it he immerses himself in this incommunicable hermetic life. Each time he uses the slang of the group, he affirms and reinforces his communion with the group and, in one sense, the giving up of his own personality to the group. The word becomes a kind of magic and operative sign of the unity of the group, and of its difference from ordinary mankind. Then, indivisibly from its function as direct sign, the word is essentially a reverse or inverted sign of the subjectivity, self-love, and pride of the group.

That is why slang cannot really be translated into ordinary language without losing its meaning and flavor. More than an object of thought, it means the overtones that accompany this object in terms of human and social subjectivity. The human despair and abjection with which certain abject writers have to saturate the world of things could not be expressed except in their slang.

Now, if it is true that the essence of language is to manifest thought and objects of thought, it is difficult not to conclude that the various slangs of which I spoke involve a kind of perversion of the function of language.

Finally, the question I would like to raise in this connection no longer deals with slang. It is whether, since the event of Babel, all tongues of the earth—though they are in no way slang but genuine types of language—do not run the risk of being tinged with some admixture of a similar impurity. For peoples divided from each other by their languages, and walled up in their own particular means of intelligible communication, there is an inherent temptation to yield to an inner spiritual trend toward cherishing over and above all the closed subjectivity of the group, its difference from the rest of mankind.

No doubt an element of reverse or inverted signification is inseparable from the direct signification of the words. But genuine language, while expressive of the group's subjectivity, gives unquestionable prevalence to objectivity, and direct sign, and to the universality of direct, intellectual meaning; and then the secondary function of language, i.e., the intention of expressing subjectivity, remains itself *open*, it is oriented toward a *communication* of the collective self, which tends to make itself sincerely known to others. The risk of impurity of which I am speaking materializes when this intention of expressing subjectivity becomes oriented toward the *self-assertion* of the group in a *closed*, aristocratic, or resentful manner, and as against all other groups.

The primary and the secondary functions of language are both human. Language attains complete freedom, and the excellence of its own nature, when these two functions are perfectly fused. The subjective function, however, is, as I have said, secondary. Furthermore it remains, as a rule, in an inchoate and unsatisfactory condition, because our words are primarily destined to designate material and external things. As a result, in their secondary function itself they signify the subjectivity of the social group rather than that of the individual person, and they do so in a more or less awkward and rough manner, which depends on the particular history and accidental experiences of the group. Let me say, therefore, that if Angels used words, it is only in the language of Angels that the two functions of which I am speaking would be really and perfectly fused. It is only in the tongue of Angels that language could attain complete freedom and the excellence of its own nature.

But Angels use no words.

Poets, in mankind, desperately endeavor to achieve a certain similarity of the language of Angels, or of perfect language, capable of expressing things and the self together in one and the same breath. Thus, what birds realize by music only, man can somewhat realize by poetry, and his music has also an intelligible significance, a spiritual meaning.

6

UMBERTO ECO, ROBERTO LAMBERTINI,
COSTANTINO MARMO, AND ANDREA TABARRONI

"Latratus Canis" or: The Dog's Barking

In the Middle Ages, how did dogs bark?

The question is not so whimsical as it seems. It opens for exploration the whole area of medieval zoosemiotics.

I. The Center and the Margins

Aquinas and the medieval thinkers knew well that the strength of a philosophical system is measured best not in the academic lessons wherein the philosopher expounds his own doctrine *ex cathedra*, but in the course of the *quaestiones quodlibetales* wherein the master is requested to establish, for example, whether it is the king, woman, wine, or truth which acts most potently on the human will. The marginality of the problem does not represent an intellectual diversion, but a critical mode in which the system ought to show its flexibility and explanatory power. From its center a system always seems well defined and all but beyond challenge; it is at its periphery that it gets put to the test.

In discussing language, logicians and grammarians of the middle ages commonly cited, among their examples of pseudo-language—that is, at the margins of true language—the *latratus canis*. Indeed, not only the dog's bark, but also the horse's whinney, the pigeon's coo, the cow's moo, the pig's oink, and—it goes without saying—the speech of parrots and magpies. What is curious about this particular example, always or nearly always present in the medieval classifications of signs, is that, without explanation and so, as it were, unnoticed, it appears in a different position in each classification. The question is, why? What lies behind and motivates the unremarked shifts?

This problem of how to classify the bark of the dog, or, for that matter, the wail of the infirm (*gemitus infirmorum*), nests in a problematic doubtless marginal with respect to the problems which modern logic and contemporary philosophy of language recognize as central for a theory of signification and reference.

Nonetheless, for and in the "middle ages", animals used "to say" many things, even entirely without knowing it. In the Bestiaries, for example, they show up as living signs of something other than themselves, characters of a book *scriptus digitus Dei*, 'words' of a symbolic lexicon, regardless of any "language" they might produce themselves.

But philosophers and grammarians—in ways different and of different import, as we shall see—were interested throughout this period in the *latratus* and the other *voces animalium* as a kind of linguistic phenomenon, mentioned frequently enough, as we have said, in relation to the wailing of sick persons (the *gemitus infirmorum*), and to other kinds of interjections. But when one extrapolates from these various discourses a taxonomic tree, it results that in certain trees the *latratus* is a sprig on the same branch as the *gemitus infirmorum,* while in other trees it is on another branch entirely.

This discovery is enough to pique anyone's curiosity. For medieval materials at first glance normally appear to be stubborn repetitions of a common archetype or model, differing not at all or at least not perceptibly. But here, accessed from the margin and viewed, as it were, in a slanted light, this appearance disappears to some extent, as concealed differences stand out against the background of seeming repetitions—differences of the sort promising to reveal the heart of systems in reality very different.

Viewed from the center, animals other than man—'brute' or 'irrational' animals—find only a generic place in the Latin writings, and only to play an oppositional role against the *animalia rationalia* in the framework of essential definitions on the Tree of Porphyry. Beyond this, the central philosophical theories of the middle ages leave the brutes to their collective destiny, furnishing no instructions whatever for distinguishing the dog from the wolf, or for that matter from the horse or any other species of the genus animal beyond the human. Refinements along this line have to wait for naturalists and artificial language theorists of the 17th century, particularly in England.

It is not that medieval scholars were lacking texts on animal behavior. It is rather that, unfortunately, even though as early as the 12th century attention was beginning to be paid directly to the observation of natural phenomena, as in the works of Aquinas' teacher, Albert the Great (a trend which would find a kind of maturation in the *scientia experimentalis* of Bacon), observations which are not second-hand are not what we find in the many medieval texts. Even the *Historia Animalium* of Aristotle becomes available only much later in the Latin age. The dog and the other animals appear rather as a *topos*, framed by the inertia of *auctoritas* and the migration of examples drawn from tradition rather than from the direct observation of nature. The Schoolmen knew various discussions about the natural characteristics of dogs, not to mention the problem of the noises of fish and the voices of birds (including parrots and magpies), through the mediation of Pliny and of Ammonius.

Likewise, something must have filtered down from the discussions which took place between the Stoics, Academicians, and Epicureans about the possibility of an "animal logos". Sextus Empiricus says (c.200: 1.1, 65-77) that the dogs manifest, through their behavior, various capacities of reflection and apprehension. Sextus quotes an observation of Chrysippus, according to which, when a dog follows his prey to a point where three roads meet, having sniffed the two ways not taken by the hoped-for victim, forms a flawless dialectical syllogism: "the beast must have passed by here, or by there, or by there. By here, no; by there, no; therefore by there". It is debatable whether Sextus was known to the middle ages, but it is certain that this same argument is repeated in the *Bestiary of Cambridge*. Since it appears neither in Isidore nor in the *Physiologus*, a great part of the Greek discussion must have migrated somehow through other secondary sources.

The mass of ancient "naturalistic" observation carried in the Stoic legacy survived in the work of the Latin philosophers, notably through the mediation of Augustine. Nonetheless, generally speaking, every appearance of the dog among the Latins shows a dependency on that passage of Aristotle's *De Interpretatione* (c.330BC: 16a ff.) which controlled the entire medieval discussion on human and animal language. Thus the dog circulates in the philosophical and linguistic literature of the Latins mainly as a barking animal, making noise along with parrots, cocks, and horses—sometimes along with the *gemitus infirmorum*, sometimes under another heading. The barking of the dog, born as a *topos*, a *topos* remains.

Nevertheless, as we will see, the authorities have a nose of wax, and beneath literal appearances, every time the *topos* is cited, one has grounds for suspecting that a slight or more than slight shift of perspective has taken place; and that medieval semiotics knows on this point not one but two lines of thought, within which the *latratus canis* comes to occupy positions which are different in substance in differing classifications according to whether the classifications are mainly of signs in general (a concern Stoic in origin) or of *voces* (a concern Aristotelian and Hippocratic in origin, according to the ancient tradition clearly distinguishing between the theory of verbal language conventionally related to its objects and the theory of signs as rather natural givens entertaining with what they signify a relation of inferentiability).

II. Signs and Words

To accomodate the ambiguous position of the latratus canis in the medieval theories of language, therefore, one must realize that Greek semiotics, from the corpus Hippocratum up to the Stoics, made a clearcut distinction between a theory of verbal language (*onomata*) and a theory of signs (*sēmeîa*). Signs are natural events acting as symptoms or indices, and they entertain with that which they point to a relation based upon the mechanism of inference ("if such a symptom, then such a sickness"; "if smoke then burning"). Words stand in a quite different relation with what they designate or point to, as with the "passions of the soul" which they signify. This relation is based upon the mere equivalence or biconditionality which appears also in the influential Aristotelian theory of definition and tree of Porphyry which springs from it.

It was Augustine who first proposed a "general semiotics"—that is, a general 'science' or 'doctrine' of signs, where sign becomes the genus of which words (*onomata*) and natural symptoms (*sēmeîa*) are alike equally species.

With Augustine, there begins to take shape this '*doctrina*' or 'science' of *signum*, wherein both symptoms and the words of language, mimetic gestures of actors along with the sounds of military trumpets and the chirrups of cicadas, all become species. In essaying such a doctrine, Augustine foresees lines of development of enormous theoretical interest; but he suggests the possibility of resolving, rather than effects a definitive resolution of, the ancient dichotomy between the inferential relations linking natural signs to the things of which they are signs and the relations of equivalence linking linguistic terms to the concept(s) on the basis of which some thing 'is'—singly or plurally—designated.

Medieval semiotics knows at this point two lines of thinking as possibly unified, but without having achieved their actual unification. This is a crucial observation, inasmuch as a main reason why the latratus canis occupies different positions in different classifications of signs stems from whether the given classification is one in the Stoic and Augustinian mode or of *voces* in the Aristotelian mode of a theory of spoken language. Out of the tension of this opposition—under the provocation, as it were, of Augustine—is born much of the distinctively Latin development of semiotic consciousness. It is this increasing of semiotic awareness that we want to explore, by way of examining a series of figures strategic for the medieval Latin development.

III. Aristotle

The Latin controversy *latratus canis* has as its detonator the passage of the *De Interpretatione* where Aristotle, intending to define nouns and verbs (c.330BC: 16-20a), makes to this end some marginal statements about signs in general.

To summarize the results of an unending discussion among the interpreters of the passage in question, Aristotle basically says that nouns and verbs are cases of *phonē semantikē kata synthekēn*, which is what the post-Boethian Latins call *vox significativa ad placitum*. Aristotle remarks that words are symbols of the affections of the soul (''passiones animae''), and that written words are symbols of the spoken ones. He takes symbol here for a conventional device; and he assigns this 'conventionality' as the reason why symbols are not the same in every culture. The passions of the soul, by contrast, are alleged to be the same for all, since they are images (we could also say ''icons'') of the things they manifest. It is in speaking of the passions of the soul that Aristotle adds, somewhat parenthetically, that words are of these passions ''before all else'' signs.

Have we here an instance of mere redundancy, in which the word ''sign'' is used synonymously with the word ''symbol''? Indeed not, for when Aristotle speaks expressly of signs (*sēmeîa*) in his *Rhetoric* (c.335-334BC), he makes it plain that symptoms, natural events from which one can infer something else, are what is at issue.

In context, Aristotle is simply saying that, even though words are conventional symbols, they can, insofar as they are uttered, also or in the first instance be taken as symptoms of the fact they make evident, to wit, that the one who speaks has something in mind.

This becomes clearer a few lines further on, where Aristotle remarks that, since even vocal sounds can be taken as signs (that is, as symptoms), so also can non-articulated noises emitted by animals function as symptoms. He says ''noises'' (*agrammatoi psophoi*) rather than ''sounds'' because, as Ammonius and all subsequent commentators will explain, he is also thinking of certain animals, such as fishes, which do not emit sounds vocally but make noises nonetheless (''quidam enim pisces non voce, sed branchiis sonant'', Boethius will say, ''et cicada per pectum sonum mittit''). Aristotle says that these noises manifest (*dēlousi*) something.

Now, what happens with the first influential translation of *De Interpretatione* made by Boethius? Both 'symbol' (*symbolon*) and 'sign' (*sēmeîon*) are translated with the term *nota*, with the result of suppressing, in effect, the Aristotelian nuance. Moreover, *dēlousi* is translated not as *manifestant* (''they show'') but as *significant* (''they signify''). Where Aristotle spoke of the noises of animals, and lexically distinguished noise from sound, the medieval commentators from Boethius onward translate *phonē* (sound) with *vox* (voice) and *psophos* (noise) with *sonus* (sound).

Thus, for the medieval commentators, animals without lungs emit sounds, but animals with lungs utter voices, and *voces* can be *significativae*.

The road is open for a significant bark of the dog.

IV. Boethius latrans

The bark of the dog appears for the first time in Greek in the commentary of Ammonius on the *De Interpretatione* (c.400); but this work does not appear in Latin until the translation of Moerbeke in 1268. It is Boethius who brings it into the Latin world as an example of *vox significativa* not *ad placitum* (by convention) but rather *naturaliter*, as set forth in Table 1:

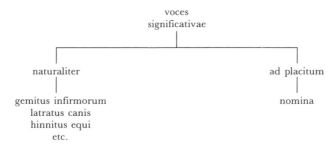

A sound that for Aristotle was a sign in contrast to symbols falls here rather under the heading of the *vox significativa* which also includes words or symbols. Under this same heading or category Boethius also places the *gemitus infirmorum*, the whinney of horses, and even the sounds of animals without lungs that "tantu sonitu quodam concrepant". Why do these sounds signify *naturaliter*? Evidently because through them one is able to know their cause by a symptomatic inference.

In grouping things thus, Boethius leaves out of account two important differences. First, the difference emphasized by the Stoics between natural events which 'happen' but are not emitted by living beings, like the smoke from which fire can be inferred or the medical symptom from which a disease can be inferred. Second, the difference between sounds emitted intentionally and those emitted unintentionally. Infirms wail often unintentionally. Do dogs bark without intentions? Or do dogs have an intention to communicate? Boethius says of the horse that "hinnitus quoque eorum saepe alterius equi consuetudinem quaerit", that is, the horse whinnies to call another horse, intentionally and with a precise sexual purpose. He also says (Boethius, that is, not the horse) that animals frequently utter voices "aliqua significatione praeditas", that is, sounds endowed with some meaning. But endowed by whom? By the animal uttering or by the man listening? Boethius disregards this question, just as he has disregarded the difference between animate and inanimate nature in the giving of signs.

Thus the dog is put in an awkward situation. It emits *voces*, but it does so naturally. Its voice stands ambiguously poised between natural event and intentional utterance. If it barks intentionally, it is not clear whether in doing so it intentionally talks to another dog or to men—not a minor question from the viewpoint of zoosemiotics. Moreover, does man understand the dog (or horse) because man has a natural disposition to interpret symptoms, or because man has a natural disposition to understand the canine (or equine) language?

Boethius, in transferring the dog from Greek to Latin, has launched a tradition of classifying *voces* that merges the Stoic classification of signs with the Aristotelian classification of symbols but leaves unresolved the problem of intentionality in the emission of these "voces".

V. Aquinas

Thomas Aquinas takes over the Boethian classification, and develops from it only a more complex taxonomy. He deals with the problem in more than one page of his commentary on the *De Interpretatione* (c.1269-1274), but his remarks are shaded by a number of ambiguities, ambiguities which echo various influences. In some passages, Aquinas, along Augustinian lines, calls *signum* every *vox significativa*. In other passages the sound of a military trumpet, evidently not a case of *vox vocalis*, is also spoken of as a *signum*. It seems that, for Aquinas, *signum* is every utterance endowed with meaning, whether it be vocal or not. But he does not here take into account the *signa naturalia* (the *semeia*), even though natural signs will play an important role in the theory of the sacraments and in the theory of analogy. Interpreting Aquinas in terms of the sources probably echoed in his text, his elaboration of the Boethian classification beginning with *sonus* as the genus of *vox* can be synthesized in the following Table[1]:

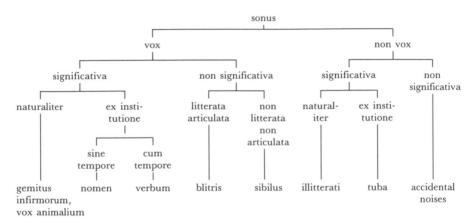

In this scheme, the bark stands together with meaningful vocal sounds, even though it is natural and non-conventional; while the unarticulated whistle emitted without the intention of communicating anything stands together with articulated vocal utterances, such as *blitris*, since all together they belong to the species of meaningless sounds.

But it is not at all in the opposition between intentional and unintentional that Aquinas locates the main difference between human and animal sounds, between a man's utterance and a dog's bark. The situation is much more complicated than that—and much more interesting. To see where Aquinas steps beyond Boethius (perhaps inspired by the Boethian question about the whinney of the horse), we must turn from his commentary on the *De Interpretatione* to his commentary on the *Politics* (c.1269-1272: Bk. I. lect. 1. nn. 36-37), where he turns again to the difference between human and animal sounds, with some supplementary observations. Just as men have ways of deliberately signifying to one another pain and pleasure, so too have the animals, ways which are comparable to what are called interjections among men.

Here Aquinas touches a problem treated more broadly by Roger Bacon (1267: I.9), who distinguishes between a wail of an infirm emitted involuntarily, which is a pure symptom of illness, and an interjectory wail emitted in order to signify the same pain but now intentionally and according to a definite linguistic convention. In such a way, inside the same Aquinian framework, the *latratus canis* changes position: it is as if in between the *voces significativae naturaliter*, where the *gemitus* stands, and the *voces ad placitum*, where spoken language stands, an intermediate zone were posed, where man produces—paralinguistically, we would say now—interjections and the dog barks. The key difference between human language and the pseudo-language of the dog does not consist in the opposition intentional/non-intentional, nor in the opposition natural/ad placitum (vaguely hinted but substantially eluded, as the later discussions of Poinsot in particular demonstrate), but in the opposition between mere interjections and those devices (namely, words) by which human language is able to express, over and above feelings of joy and sorrow, abstractions concerning good and evil, just and unjust. Only through such abstractions does human language establish cultural institutions within human society —*domum et civitatem*—as distinct from the society of animals without such capacity.

VI. The Stoic Legacy among the Latins: Augustine

The confusions we have witnessed in the Latin interpreters of *De Interpretatione* is absent from those thinkers, such as Augustine, who were not exposed to the Aristotelian influence, but were more directly subject to the Stoic tradition.

In *De doctrina christiana* (c.397-426) Augustine, having given his famous (and later much criticized) definition of the sign as "that which, beyond the impression it conveys to sense, makes something besides itself come into awareness", develops the distinction between what he terms *signa naturalia* and *signa data*. Natural signs are ones that "apart from any intention or desire to signify make something besides themselves known", such as the smoke which reveals burning and the face of the enraged which of itself reveals anger without any intention to do so. *Signa data* are those exchanged by living beings in order to convey "motus animi", i.e., inward states, which are not necessarily concepts but can be sensations or psychological states—any subjective condition or state of which the one seeking to communicate has awareness. And what these signs produce or evoke in the soul of the addressee similarly need not be a concept.

With this stroke of genius, and without a tremor of doubt, Augustine places among the *signa data* both the words of Holy Scripture (*verba divina*) and the utterances of animals ("Habent enim bestiae inter se signa, quibus produnt appetitus animi sui"), abandoning the wail of the infirm among the natural signs together with the smoke of fires and the tracks of animals:

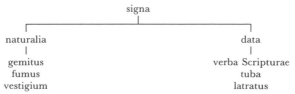

signa

naturalia   data
gemitus   verba Scripturae
fumus   tuba
vestigium   latratus

However, having located the dog's bark surely among the *signa data*, Augustine becomes not so sure about the exact nature of the intention expressed and whereby the animals give signs; but this doubt he waves aside as "not pertaining to the point at hand" ("Quae utrum, sicut vultus aut dolentis clamor sine voluntate significandi sequantur motum animi, an vere ad significandum dentur, alia quaestio est, et ad rem, quae agitur, non pertinet"—*loc. cit.*, II, 1-3).

VII. Abelard

Does the dog mean what he says, or not?

The problem finds an original solution in Abelard. In his *Dialectica* (i.1118-1137), his classification of signs can be traced back to the Boethian one, dividing *voces significativae* into those signifying *naturaliter* and those signifying *ex impositione* (by convention). But in his *Logica seu Summa Ingredientibus* (a.1120), Abelard adds a new opposition, that between *voces significativae* and *voces significantes*, which arises from speaking either *ex* or *sine institutione*.

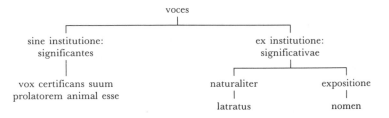

The *impositio* in this scheme is a convention, but the *institutio* is not a convention: it is rather a decision which precedes both the conventional meaningfulness of human words and the natural meaningfulness of animal sounds. One can see this "institution" as very close to an intention. Words are meaningful by virtue of the institution of the human will, which orders them *ad intellectum constituendum*—to the production of 'something' in the mind of the hearer, perhaps, as Augustine maintained, something less than a concept. The bark of the dog has equally some meaning, even though a natural one, and the institution (the intentionality) of his expression is provided by nature, or by God. In this sense the bark is as *significativus* as the human word, and in this sense it must be distinguished from those phenomena which are only *significantia* or merely symptomatic: "ita non omnia in actu significantia sunt significativa, sed ea sola quae ad significandum sunt instituta" ("not all things actually signifying are significative, but only those which are instituted for the purpose of signifying"). One and the same bark can be considered as emitted *ex institutione* and therefore *significativus*, or as heard from afar allowing one to simply infer that "down there is a dog".

It is clear that Abelard, in an Augustinian vein, is following the Stoic line of thought by distinguishing between signs which function on the basis of an inference (*significantia*) and words or pseudo-natural words which function on the basis of an intention of some sort (*significativa*). The same bark can act as a symptom in the case where the intentionality belongs to the interpreter and the event has not been instituted for the purpose of that interpretation, or as a naturally signifying utterance by which the dog expresses himself in order to *constituere intellectum*—to ''get a point across''. This does not mean that the dog ''wants'' to do what he is doing: his intention (*institutio*) is not his own, but rather a ''natural'' intention impressed by nature, so to speak, in the neural circuits of the whole canine species. We are seeing here the curious proposal of a sort of Agent Will, modelled upon the Agent Intellect of Avicenna. (An analogous suggestion appears later in the *De Anima* of Albert the Great [i.1254-1257].) Thus the agent of the dog's bark is not individual, but it is yet intentional.

VIII. Roger Bacon

The provocation of Augustine shows up in yet another classification of signs in the medieval period, that which can be extrapolated from the *De Signis* of Roger Bacon (1267). But the classification which can be extrapolated from *De Signis* is highly syncretic and far from homogeneous in its principles:

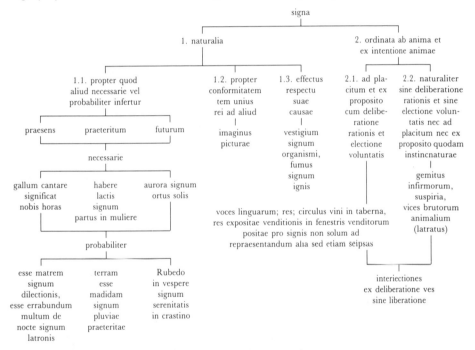

In this table, the natural signs seem to be those of Augustine emitted without intention, but we could spend a lot of time trying to figure out the criteria followed on this left side of the classification.[2] For present purposes, our main interest is in the signs of type 2., which are produced by an intention of the soul. Here we find, as in Abelard, the distinction between a voluntary intention and a natural one.[3]

It is definitely interesting to note that, once again, there is a difference between the crowing of the cock taken as symptom of the presence of a cock in an area and that same crowing taken as a somewhat intentional sound emitted in order to communicate. When it appears among the signs *ordinata ab anima* Bacon calls it the *cantus Galli*, while when it appears among the *signa naturalia* he characterizes it by an infinitive construction, gallum cantare—the fact that a cock crows as proof of its presence in an area. This is, as the Stoics would have said, an "incorporeal", a symptomatic sequence of events. As such, it can be interpreted by human beings without any knowledge whatever of the intentionality filling the cock's soul and overflowing in its crow: "the crow of a cock signifies nothing to us in its own right as a significative voice, but the fact of the cock's crowing signifies to us a definite time of the day" (Bacon c.1250).

Bacon does not go as far as Augustine dared to—that is, he is not putting the barking of dogs and the words of God within the same subheading. But neither does he incline, as Abelard did, to reduce the voice uttered by the animal when communicating by a natural impulse to the status of a mere symptom. His description of animal language is as sensitive in its own way as was that of Augustine. Dogs, hens, and pigeons, in his examples, are not mere *topoi* but 'real' animals observed with naturalistic—and not merely grammatical—interest in their usual behavior. In *De Signis* of 1267, Bacon implies with his twofold classification but does not expressly ask for whom—its conspecifics or men—the cock crows; but he had taken this up earlier in his *Sumule Dialectices* (c.1250), and made explicit what his later classification implies: "A significative voice is that through which every animal conveys something to every other or rather to each member of its own species." Thus a cock speaks to its hens differently in different circumstances, and by careful observation and analysis we can come to understand this language of poultry and of any species ("... ex industria et assuetudine possit aliquod animal uti voce alterius"). In addition to these *voces significativae naturaliter* which signify properly within a species and improperly to members of other species, there are other *voces*—those *significativae ad placitum*—which are understood only by subgroups of the same species ("Gallicus Gallico, Graecus Graeco, Latinus Latino").

The Baconian classification in a sense mirrors a new attitude toward nature and direct experience—new at least to us who are more used to prejudices when it comes to the matter of understanding the Latins, for even in Albert the Great and others both earlier and later there can be seen a preference for observation over authority. Bacon has a sharp feeling for the relativity of human languages (Gallicus Gallico, Anglicus Anglico) and also for the necessity of learning languages. He has no doubt that cocks crow and dogs bark in order to communicate with their conspecifics and sometimes with aliens. We may not understand their language in the very sense in which a Greek does not understand a Latin and vice versa, but the ass is understand by the ass, the lion by the lion, and the bee by the bee. For man, it is enough to have a little training—or perhaps a good deal of training—and, as Latins can come to understand Englishmen, and Frenchmen Greeks, so will it be possible to understand the languages of the beasts. Such a conclusion, at least, is reached within almost less than a century by the pseudo-Marsilius [4] of Inghen (1495):

> It is clear that the bark of the dog is also the sound of a voice. And when it is argued that "yet a dog's barking does not occur with an intention of signifying something", response is made by denying what has been assumed. Nor is it necessary that all should understand that barking, but it is enough that those familiar with the breed and habits understand the bark. For the bark of dogs signifies delight to one, anger to another.

IX. Finale

The night of the Latin Ages seems to be haunted by a crowd of barking dogs and wailing sick people: the landscape designed by so many theoretical and theological pages cannot but suggest a more real landscape of stray dogs and vagabonds roaming the streets of the medieval cities, while Christians, not yet comforted by aspirin, celebrated in an unending cycle of ritual the approach of the Last Day.

In this landscape, hens and parrots scratch about but, as far as I have found, no cats show up. They were probably reserved for more intimate sorcery parties and could not be recognized as usual inhabitants of the official and orthodox city.

The Middle Ages did not develop in a rigorous sense what we call today a "zoosemiotics", but they were sensitive to the problem of animal language— even though they used it as a term of comparison in order to understand the nature of the human one.

7

THOMAS A. SEBEOK

The Notion of Zoosemiotics

The term *zoosemiotics*—constructed in an exchange between Rulon Wells and me—is proposed for the discipline, within which the science of signs intersects with ethology, devoted to the scientific study of signalling behavior in and across animal species. A survey of the vast and widely ramified literature of ethology, supplemented by repeated spot checks of ongoing research projects, reveals that the study of signaling behavior in animals has, by and large, been taxonomically parochial: even Darwin's great pioneer work, on *The expression of the emotions in man and animals* (1872), dealt, in the main, with the domestic cat and dog. A great variety of animals has since been more or less minutely scrutinized, both in the natural environment (after J. S. Huxley and K. Lorenz) and in captivity (after H. Lissman and N. Tinbergen), but usually in one particular species (or, sometimes, in closely related forms, say, of the genus *Apis*) rather than guided by overarching theoretical considerations relevant to problems of communication in general, including especially speech. The task for the immediate future will be to treat, comprehensively and exhaustively, the achievements of zoosemiotics from Darwin through J. von Uexküll to the present day; to arrange and display the data in a format relevant to the study of language, that is, by matching logical concepts derived from sociobiology with those developed in linguistics; and, using each species, so to say, as a miniature paradigm which throws light upon language observed as a peculiar combination of distinctive features, of which all or almost all components, considered alone, have their separate evolutionary roots (cf. Koehler 1956), to consolidate and build upon what has been established about the protocultural foundations of human adaptation.

Whitney's conception of language as a social institution, unfolded in necessary antithesis to Schleicher's simple-minded Darwinism, is now itself in need of revision as we recollect L. Bloomfield's aphorism (1939): "Language creates and exemplifies a twofold value of some human actions." Language has, as he put it, both a biophysical and a biosocial aspect. Speech is, of course, a biological phenomenon in several related senses. Since all systems in science have a biological component, the linguistic system observed includes the linguist-observer (cf. Simpson 1963). Speech, furthermore, is carried on by human beings, a species of animal; it is not only a part of animal behavior but undoubtedly the principal means of biological adaptation for man, an evolutionary specialization that arose from prehuman behavioral adaptation of which we seek to trace the paths as one objective of zoosemiotics.

In 1936 (1.254) Jakobson asked, in Copenhagen: "Est-il besoin aujourd'hui de rappeler que la linguistique appartient aux sciences sociales et non à l'histoire naturelle? N'est-ce pas un truisme évident?'' [*"Is it necessary today to recall that the study of language pertains to the social sciences, and not to natural history? Is this not an evident truism?"*] Twenty-five years later, he himself gave the answer as, in Helsinki (1962), he called attention to the "direct homology between the logic of molecular and phonemic codes", implying a vision of new and startling dimensions: the convergence of the science of genetics with the science of linguistics. A fundamental unity of viewpoint has been provided by the discovery that the problem of heredity lies, in effect, in the decipherment of a script, that genes are sections of the molecular chains of DNA which contain messages coded in particular sequences of nucleotide bases (Dobzhansky 1962: 39), in a manner persuasively reminiscent of the way in which bundles of binary features are linked into sequences of phonemes. Genetics and linguistics thus emerge as autonomous yet sister disciplines in the larger field of communication sciences, to which, on the molar level, zoosemiotics also contributes.

8

THOMAS A. SEBEOK

"Talking" with Animals: Zoosemiotics Explained

Semiotics is, quite simply, the exchange of messages. A message consists of a sign or a string of signs. "Zoosemiotics" is a term coined in 1963 to delimit that segment of the field which focuses on messages given off and received by animals, including important components of human nonverbal communication, but excluding man's language and his secondary, language-derived semiotic systems, such as sign language or Morse code.

Biologists define life as a system capable of evolution by natural selection. This genetic definition, which places great emphasis on the importance of replication, is entirely compatible with the modern semiotic point of view, which asserts that all communication is a manifestation of life, and that it is the capacity to communicate that distinguishes living beings from inanimate substances. Reproduction is itself a matter of communication, the molecular code being one of the two master sign-systems on earth. The other one is the verbal code—our language. The molecular code is apparently the same in all terrestrial organisms; the verbal code is fundamentally the same—with superficial variations—in all the peoples of the globe.

Scholars distinguish two varieties of animal communication: intraspecific and interspecific. Intraspecific communication refers to all of those devices at the disposal of an animal that link it to every other member of its own species, and all others to it. Territory delineation, and the location of kin, competitors, and prospective mates, are among these devices. Examples of intraspecific messages are the bright flashes of light used in the dialogue among fireflies, an exchange of coded information about species identity, sex and location. The flash code used varies from species to species within the family of beetles to which fireflies belong. Certain fishes communicate with their own kind by broadcasting different patterns of electric pulses to threaten, indicate submission, carry on courtship, or even, by discharging a particular set of signs, to insure individual recognition from a mate, a companion or rival, and thus to help promote cohesiveness within its social group.

Although "flehmen", or lip-curl, which involves the closure of nasal openings when the head is jerked back, is a widely distributed behavioral trait in mammals, this facial expression has evolved into a particular sign in horses which elicits particular responses on the part of other horses. A fearful rhesus monkey carries its tail stuck stiffly out behind, while a baboon will convey the same emotion to its fellows by holding its tail vertically.

In brief, each kind of animal has at its command a repertoire of signs that forms a system unique to it or is, in biological parlance, species-specific. Language is a species-specific trait of man; it is therefore counterproductive and misleading to ascribe language to any other animal, except, perhaps, metaphorically. Some features of tail signaling, as of any other kind of communicative device, may vary geographically; linguistic diversity in space may produce dialects, a term which is also used in zoosemiotics to characterize behavioral differences in populations of the same species occupying different areas. Thus langur monkeys in northern India carry their tails up and arched over the back, while the same species in the south carry them up and then looping backward to signify an individual's degree of "confidence".

No species, however, can survive in isolation from other sorts of animals. Each species must live in a vast ecosystem which requires its members to coexist with a variety of neighbors on certain terms. In order to avoid predators, capture prey or in other ways further the mutual advantage of two or more species, animals must have additional code-switching capabilities, an *interspecific* communication system. In parts of India, for example in Kanha Park, some half a dozen hoofed animals occupy a range which they must share with the tiger and lesser carnivores, like the leopard and jungle cat, sloth bear, striped hyena, jackal and an occasional python—to say nothing of man. Each prey and each predator species must communicate with every other within range to enhance the survival of its own kind.

A number of marine fishes specialize in eliminating parasites that plague another species of fish. The "cleaner" fish entices its hosts by means of a sign— the "cleaner dance" or nod swim—which the hosts acknowledge by permitting themselves to be cleansed. The hosts, in turn, know how to invite the cleaners to perform their lustral chores.

The saber-toothed blenny is, by contrast, a fake and a natural opportunist: it mimics the communicative behavior of the harmless cleaner fish in order to deceive the hosts, enabling the impostor to bite chunks off their fins and gills and get away with it. Such deception by mimicry is a common perversion of interspecific communicative processes throughout the animal kingdom.

A famous example of interspecific communication to mutual advantage is found in the savannahs of Africa south of the Sahara, where a bird, called the honey guide, indicates to man the location of beehives that the bird cannot open but on whose honeycombs it likes to feed. This bird produces conspicuous beckoning calls, followed by certain optical signs, until a willing human being finds the hive, feeds the wax to the bird and consumes the honey himself.

How man and animals communicate with one another poses all sorts of interesting problems which require a great deal more study. Man may encounter animals under a wide variety of circumstances that make it necessary for each party to learn—even if never entirely master—the essential elements of the other's code.

Here are some possibilities for contact:
1. Man is an animal's despoiler (e.g., potential exterminator, such as of the starling); or
2. Man is an animal's victim (e.g., of our most devastating killer, the mosquito).
3. Man is an animal's (unequal) partner or symbiont (say, a human host and his household pet guest, like his goldfish or canary).

4. Man is a parasite on an animal (e.g., the reindeer) or the other way around (e.g., the flea and the louse); or the two exist in a state of commensalism (like seagulls following the plough or robins perched on a spade).
5. The animal accepts a human as its conspecific, even to the extent of attempting to mate (as a panda tried with her keeper in London, or a male dolphin with his female trainer in St. Thomas).
6. The animal defines humans as inanimate objects (e.g., when men are in a vehicle driving through a wildlife park).
7. Man subjects an animal to scientific testing and experimentation (*apprentissage*) in the laboratory or to performing in exhibitons (*dressage*), as in the circus.
8. Man tames animals and continues to breed them selectively (domestication).

Each of these situations—and others—involves a crucial understanding on our part of the animals' biologically-given communicative capacity. The success of processes like taming and training depends on our having mastered relevant elements of animals' codes. In order to flourish in our company, each animal must be able to discern man's verbal and/or nonverbal behavior.

All communication systems, especially those of animals, are studied under six major rubrics. I have already mentioned that messages, or strings of signs, are a chief focus of attention, but all messages have to be generated by an emitting organism (source or addresser) and interpreted by one or more receiving organisms (destination or addressee). The kind of messages emitted is dictated by the biological makeup of the source, particularly its sensory apparatus, and the environmental conditions, or context, to which the species has adapted. A message can but rarely be transmitted directly in the shape in which it was generated (quite probably, electrochemically). Messages have to be encoded in a form that the channel connecting the communicants can accommodate. For the message to have an impact the receiving animal must have the key for decoding it back into such a shape (also electrochemical) that its biological makeup enables it to interpret. This is the reason why messages appear in coded form, and why the source and the destintion must (at least partially) share either an inherited or a learned code, or, commonly, some mixture of both.

Picture, then, an organism which formulates a message—say, "I want you!"—directed at another individual, a very special one, of the opposite sex within its own species, as a gannet calling out to its mate after prolonged separation at sea during the winter, so that each member of the pair can recognize the other again as they both return to their nesting cliffs. This message is encoded in acoustic form, and the sound waves travel through the medium of air from the vocal organs of one gannet across to the auditory apparatus of the other. Contrast this with the promiscuous scented advertisement of a flightless female silk moth to any male flying by within a radius of a few miles: her glands emit a sex-attraction pheromone (or message-bearing chemical released to the exterior) called bombykol, which is then transported through the air surrounding her, eventually to be picked up by certain receptor organs on the male antennae. Bombykol molecules are absorbed by the hair surface, diffuse to and through the pores and tubules into a fluid, where they hit the membrane, eliciting a cell response which sets the male off traveling to and, perhaps, mating with the stationary female. A single odor molecule (or very few) can apparently trigger an explosive series of events. Among other things, this chain of happenings illustrates an important principle of animal communication: signing behavior often releases far more energy than is used for the act of launching a message.

All messages are encoded to suit the medium and can, accordingly, be conveniently classified in terms of the channel, or combination of channels, employed by the animal in question. Understandably, human beings, in whose daily lives speech plays such a prominent part, tend to think of the vocal-auditory link as the paramount channel. Actually, however, the use of sound in the wider scheme of biological existence is rather uncommon: the overwhelming majority of animals are both deaf and dumb. Of the dozen or so phyla of animals, only two contain creatures that can hear and produce functional sound: the arthropods and the chordates. Of the latter, the upper three and a half classes of vertebrates are unique in having all their members capable of sound production as well as—excepting only snakes—of hearing. The methods of sound production vary, of course, enormously from group to group. Not only does our own method seem to be unusual, but, to all appearances, evolved only once in the stream of life. The vocal mechanism that works by means of a current of air passing over the cords and setting them into vibrations is confined to ourselves and, with distinctions, to our nearest relatives, the other mammals—the birds, reptiles and amphibians. (Although some fish use wind instruments as well, they do so without the reed constituted by our vocal cords.) So far as we know, no true vocal performances are found outside the land vertebrates or their marine descendants, the whales. Acoustic communication may take place in air or in water and it varies in range. The human ear can register only a narrow portion of that range. In that respect, we are overshadowed by the smallest bat, by every dog, as well as by many rodents and, no doubt, countless other animals hitherto not investigated.

Optical communication is, similarly, much more extensive than the limits of the human eye might indicate. Our eyes can register only visible light, whereas bees and some other insects are able to communicate in the ultraviolet range. Nocturnal mammals, possessing a "tapetum lucidum" (an iridescent pigment choroid coat causing reflected night eye-shine), are able to "see in the dark", a feat man can accomplish only with the aid of specially-constructed infrared equipment. The sensitivity of our sense organs tends to vary from that of other species: the auditory reaction time of the avian ear has been estimated, for instance, to be ten times that of a human ear. African vultures were shown to be capable of distinguishing, from a height of about 13,000 feet, whether a gazelle lying on the ground is dead or only sleeping; we, even using field binoculars, are unable even to identify the bird soaring at such a height.

Beside the acoustic and the optical channels, animals may rely on chemical signs through their sense of smell, for example, as do many carnivores and ungulates. The dog's superior sense of smell is legendary. I have mentioned pheromones previously; more and more of them are being isolated and analyzed. The "flehmen" of horses, as well as that of bats and a variety of their predators and prey, is also a specialized device for closing the nostrils to rechannel such olfactory substances as female urine to the so-called vomeronasal organ, located on the roof of the palate of the male, where the chemical message is decoded for ultimate interpretation in the hypothalamus. In snakes and lizards, the vomeronasal organ simply registers olfactory substances, but in such animals as antelopes it enables bucks to know the state of a doe—whether, for example, she is in heat.

Advances are rapidly being made in our understanding of communication by means of electrically coded messages in both marine and fresh water environments. In certain animals, notably such reptiles as rattlesnakes and pit vipers, slight changes in temperature can have significance. Tactile communication—by direct contact or through physical conduits as different as the spider's web and tracks of silk or the slime trails of snails and slugs—is practiced in various corners of the animal world.

The integration of a species may be achieved via a hierarchical combination of channels: the social dynamics of a wolf pack depend, for example, on (a) visual signs, especially the subtle repertoire of tail and body displays and facial expressions; (b) vocal signs, including collective "singing"; (c) tactile signs, such as grooming, nibbling, licking, or just lying together in rest and sleep; and (d) olfactory signs, involving scent marking and rolling. These four channels are used either in alternation, according to certain rules (for instance, when a member has lost visual contact with the pack, he may continue to track, at high speed, following a scent) or to reinforce one another. Such supplementation, called redundancy, becomes necessary under certain unfavorable environmental conditions that introduce noise—unwanted signs—into the stream of communication.

People who want to understand how animals communicate must abandon the layman's traditional notion of the "five senses." Many more than five are already known to science, and many others undoubtedly remain to be discovered. Equally important, humans tend to underestimate many animals' sensorial efficiency. Such misestimates, based on ignorance, sometimes lead to ludicrous pronouncements claiming "extrasensory perception" on the part of certain animals, for example, horses. It has been known, however, since 1926, that horses are capable of detecting movements in the human face of less than one-fifth of a millimeter (one millimeter equals 0.0394 inch). A sign consisting of a movement so minute simply escapes the ken of human onlookers. There are assuredly many such phenomena that should be checked and checked repeatedly in every species of animal.

Specialists in zoosemiotics concentrate on one topic, or a combination of topics, among the following:

1. How does the source animal successively formulate and encode its messages? Squids and octopuses, which are mollusks with a truly extraordinary control of color and pattern, have, for instance, arranged their comportment so as to respect the demands of gravity; to be able to achieve this, they have evolved parts which by their physical structure symbolize gravity and movement. The English anatomist, J. Z. Young, has shown in detail how these internal structures are, as it were, miniature models of the universe, and how these features, among others, guide these cephalopods—whose social existence is confined largely to combat and copulation—in their communicative behaviors, or in other words, how the signs they use signify some change in their inner or outer world or embody some instructions for action.

2. Once encoded, how is the message transmitted—through what channel(s), operating under what conditions? If a multichannel system is involved, as with wolves, what rules determine how channels are to be combined or when an animal is to switch from one to another?

3. How does the receiving animal successively decode and interpret the incoming message? What is its sensory capacity like, what are its limitations? Cicadas are interesting in this respect. While calling to the female, the male abruptly turns deaf to its own raucous song; the female, however, perceives pulses (which, to us, sound like a mere rattle) from the time patterns of which she is able to sort out her species and fly to the correct type of male.

4. What is the total message repertoire in a given species? (Some investigators maintain that each species of birds and mammals has only from about fifteen to forty-five display messages, classifiable into a dozen or so categories.) What form does each sign take? How are signs arranged into strings and what does each concatenation signify—what information is embodied by each complex sign, and how can this be decomposed into smaller meaningful units?

5. What are the properties of the code used by each species? (A code is a transformation, or a set of rules, whereby messages are converted from one representation to another; an animal either inherits or learns its code, or both.) Thus, insects, which do not have a constant temperature, face a problem created by fluctuations in the environment: male grasshoppers are known to double their rates of singing for every 10°C rise in outside temperature, which means that, if the female recognizes the species solely on the basis of the number of pulses per unit of time, which she does, the code, inherent in her nervous system, must allow for temperature differences to enable her to locate the male. Such must indeed be the case, for females at 25 degrees Centigrade, for example, fail to respond to calls of males at 15 degrees Centigrade.

6. An animal always interprets messages it receives in the light of two different variables: the incoming signal itself; and the specific qualities of the context in which the message was delivered—such as whether the water was quiet or turbulent, whether the display was performed in the emitter's territory or the receiver's, near a cover or in the open, or whether, during the act of communicating, the animals were approaching one another, withdrawing or still. Every previous message, moreover, provides contextual information for the interpretation of every succeeding message. Very little is known about how animals or indeed, people, utilize contextual information, but there is no doubt as to its critical importance in every communicative transaction.

There are two fields of complex research that space will not permit me to more than touch upon in this brief survey. One focuses on the question: how have sign systems evolved—that is, changed into communicatory devices from some segment of behavior that previously fulfilled a different function—in one species or another (the study of what ethologists refer to as "ritualization")? For instance, the evolution of human laughter, which also occurs in monkeys and the chimpanzee as the "relaxed open-mouth display", interpreted as a friendly sign of play, has been traced back to a movement that was originally associated, as far back as primitive insectivores, with grooming and respiration.

The other field attempts to deal with the development (or ontogeny) of sign systems in the life of a given individual, from its birth or hatching to maturity. Much fascinating and useful information has come to light, for example, from longitudinal studies of the vocal development of a variety of songbirds, and the crystallization—the reaching of the final adult pattern—of this manner of territorial assertion.

There are many reasons for encouraging the serious study of zoosemiotics. Let me conclude by mentioning only two. We are as yet far from understanding the pathways along which our own nonverbal and verbal communicative abilities have evolved. Zoosemiotics searchingly illuminates both the commonalities and distinctions between human and animal communication.

Second, we share our globe with a great many fellow-creatures but are totally ignorant of—or worse, entertain childlike ideas about—most of them. Sentimental or outright mistaken notions must be replaced by sound knowledge. Therein lies our only hope for establishing realistic, workable communication links with the host of the speechless creatures that form a vital part of our environment.

9

MARTIN KRAMPEN

Phytosemiotics

The problem of this essay is to establish phytosemiotics, i.e., the semiotics of plants, as an area of inquiry into sign processes, parallel and on an equal footing with anthroposemiotics, the study of human communication, and zoosemiotics (Sebeok 1963, 1972), the study of sign processes occurring within and between species of animals, the three areas forming together the discipline of "biosemiotics".

The problem and its background

Subjective interest. For three years, I have been working, in my capacity as a psychologist and semiotician, in an interdisciplinary team together with a designer, a gardener, and a physician in an experiment in living and working among plants. The designer from this team moved, four years ago, into a normal commerical greenhouse that was empty at the time. After a preliminary failure with "laissez-faire" gardening and tropical vegetation, he planted, with the help of the gardener, a selection of subtropical plants around small platforms used for office work, sleeping, cooking, and sitting. These plants remain green all year round—regardless of the presence of snow and frost outside—if the greenhouse is moderately heated. The designer had his office there and lived there, the doctor monitored his health, and I observed the behavior of the designer, his employees, and his visitors (including myself). In addition, oxygen and carbon dioxide measurements were taken longitudinally under different weather conditions. A report on this experiment has appeared (Logid 1981). On the basis of the result, the team is suggesting a combination glass-and-stone house with a 50% surface for plants as an alternative architectural solution in the face of fading oil resources (the sunheat caught in the glasshouse can be stored), in the face of air pollution (the oxygen content in the glasshouse is, due to the plants, above the normal level of any room with open windows), and in the face of decreasing environmental quality in our cities. In contrast, the quality of life in this environment is rated very highly by the participants in this experiment (because of the colors of blossoms and leaves, the smells, and the constant change of space resulting from plant growth and seasonal cycles). This advantage must be paid for by way of an average of one hour per day spent on plant care.

I had, however, one problem with the experiment that I could not resolve at the beginning—the problem of its semiotic interpretation. For quite some time I thought that the semiotic content of this enterprise was negative only. This island of green represented, in my estimation, an escape from daily routine with its signs of human communication in bureaucracy and mass media. Plants, unlike letters, punched cards, and tapes, are not malleable. One cannot do with them as one pleases. They require care and grow according to their own plan.

Problem relevance and the semiotic approach. There is little doubt that the problem of new alternative forms of working and living is highly relevant if one considers the crisis of energy, environmental pollution, and the general loss of quality in daily life. This is at least true in western industrialized countries, where we witness mass tourism, suburban sprawl, and growing so-called "green" political movements. A project like the one described above seems to give a direct and practical answer to the problems mentioned. There seems to be little room for theoretical questions of semiotics. But the lack of a theory to back up a practice has always made me suspicious. I also find the escapist tendencies in mass tourism, urban sprawl, and "green" politics unsatisfactory. I therefore began to amplify my semiotic interests by searching for a solution to my "cognitive dissonance".

Jakob von Uexküll's biosemiotics. I had read Jakob von Uexküll's "Bedeutungslehre" ("theory of meaning", 1940) a long time ago. I had discussed the semiotic importance of the work of this unorthodox German biologist, forerunner of ethology, many times with his son, Thure von Uexküll, who is attempting to develop further the semiotic aspects of his father's work with "biology as a science of meaning in nature". These discussions were often very heated and controversial because I could not cope with what I thought to be a hermeneutic approach to natural science. It took the publication of Jakob von Uexküll's selected writings (1899-1940) by his son Thure von Uexküll (1980), and a careful rereading of the "Bedeutungslehre", to convince me that a basis for a semiotics of plants could be found in Jakob von Uexküll's work. The basic premises of Jakob von Uexküll's theory of meaning in nature may be summarized as follows:
(1) Living beings, from the cell to the most complex organism, are "autonomous". They do not react in a causal and mechanical way to impingements of objects or other living beings as material objects do. Living beings react in a way that is meaningful in terms of their own needs, i.e., they process information according to their specific receptors, nervous systems, and effectors and according to their own code. Therefore, biology can utilize causal and mechanical explanations only to a very limited degree. The main task of the biologist is to reconstruct the meaning of a living being's behavior. This implies finding out exactly which sign processes underly behavior. In other words, biology is biosemiotics (a term not used by Jakob von Uexküll).
(2) There is a structural correspondence between each living being as an autonomous subject and its own "Umwelt". The term "Umwelt" is difficult to translate into English. It means the subjective world of what is meaningful impingement for the living being in terms of its own information processing equipment, sign systems, and codes. Since "Umwelt" is not to be confused with "environment", the original term will be maintained. The structure of connection between a living being and its "Umwelt" is mediated by sign processes.
(3) There is a meaningful structural correspondence between the Umwelts of different living beings within a species and those of living beings of different species, according to a "general plan of nature".
(4) The ultimate task of the biologist is to reconstruct piece by piece, in keeping

with, and on the basis of, experimental evidence, the hypothesized general plan
of nature.

Jakob von Uexküll's anthroposemiotics and zoosemiotics. In order to describe in somewhat
more detail the biosemiotic theory of Jakob von Uexküll, one must start with his
anthroposemiotics. While this term, again, is not used by him, the meaning of
the relationship between each human subject and his Umwelt, as well as the meaningful correlation between the Umwelts of different human beings, is of special
importance in Jakob von Uexküll's biosemiotics. He gives many examples as
evidence of different kinds of Umwelts.

One example is a walk through a town. The tailor's shop contains the concave counterforms of human bodies specialized for different activities in their lives.
The clocks in the watchmaker's shop have replaced—according to abstract human
time measures—the natural one of the sun, which used to regulate human lives
by the presence or absence of its light. The book shop contains messages between
cardboard covers that are of great importance for communication from human
Umwelt to human Umwelt. The butcher's shop contains the carcasses of animals,
each of which was, at one time, an organism with an Umwelt of its own, etc.
Everything witnessed during a walk through town is geared to human needs. The
height of the buildings and of doors and windows is related to the size of the human
body. Stairs accommodate ascending legs, bannisters the arms. Each object is
given its form and its meaning by some function of human life. In every case,
some human affordance is backed up by a counteraffordance of an object. In fact,
the meaning of an object to human lives literally consists of its counteraffordance
to human affordance.

But the key role of anthroposemiotics in Jakob von Uexküll's conception arises
from the fact that the scientist himself, the biologist, is a human subject surrounded
by his Umwelt as if by a transparent bubble, on the surface of which appear his
scientific observations in keeping with his own sign systems and codes. Jakob von
Uexküll likes to quote, in this respect, the British astronomer and physicist Sir
Arthur Stanley Eddington, who said he had two desks, the one he used for writing
on, and the other a physical desk consisting of an immeasureably large number
of particles (Jakob von Uexküll 1940). For that matter, a biologist would investigate
a different desk from a physicist (Jakob von Uexküll 1935). Therefore, the scientific and especially the biosemiotic investigator must use a special method in order
to arrive at a careful reconstruction of the Umwelt of the observed living being
in his own Umwelt and on his own terms—a method that would now be called
participant observation.

The structural correspondence between each living human organism and its
Umwelt is described by Jakob von Uexküll as a "function cycle". The subject
literally "grasps" an object, in a doublepronged attack, either directly with his
receptors (e.g., eyes) and effectors (e.g., hands), or indirectly with amplifications
of his receptors (e.g., microscope) and his effectors (e.g., a tool or a machine).
There is a constant feedback of signals from the effectors to the receptors, which
is modified by the encounter with the object. The nervous system within the
organism mediates between receptors and effectors according to the needs of that
organism (e.g., hunger, defense, sexual drive, and the medium in which it lives).

According to Jakob von Uexküll, the receptors receive afferent signals from the object and the effectors are steered by efferent signals to carry out an action upon the object. Both kinds of signals are charged with meaning by the code constituted by the subject's needs. An object may thus be sensed differently and acted upon differently, depending on the actual need. The two faces of the object as a sign are the afferent signals as the signifier, and the induced efferent signals as the signified. The semiosis proceeds on the basis that the afferent signals are constantly cancelled by the efferent signals, either in terms of the consumption of the object, or in terms of a different "perspective", or in terms of a code-switching to another need. The sum of the object signals received and their corresponding action signals constitutes the Umwelt of the organism, which is mirrored by signs as an "inner" counterworld.

The task of the biologist is to study the code according to which a living being, be it human or animal, imparts meaning to its Umwelt, by studying the physical structure of receptors and effectors and by observing, through experimental variation, which signals are processed on each side, i.e., which signs are in the code of the living subject. The study of the Umwelt of human beings is thus, clearly, anthroposemiotic.

The role played by those particular objects in the Umwelt of human beings that are called signs has been studied by Thure von Uexküll (1980). The specific characteristic of the human Umwelt is that it is structured according to the species' framework of space and time; that, by reafferent feedback processes, the phenomenon of "consciousness" (or self-awareness) exists; and that by transmission of sign-objects, particularly of linguistic signs, a common social reality is established.

Following the suggestion of Marx (1857: 636) that it is scientifically more correct to explain apes by using knowledge about men than to explain men in terms of apes, the zoosemiotics of Jakob von Uexküll can now be sketched "by subtraction".

Returning to the example of Eddington's desk, this object becomes, in the Umwelt of a fly, a mere horizontal walking surface and is, in that respect, no different from the seat of the chair or the top of a cupboard. In fact, all objects in a human room are reduced, in the Umwelt of a fly, to objects to walk on, objects to feed on, and objects, a lamp for instance, to fly around in a kind of play activity. As Jakob von Uexküll cogently observes, the number of objects pertaining to the Umwelt of an animal corresponds exactly to the number of actions executed by it. But each animal, be it an amoeba, a fly, or a lion, behaves meaningfully on the basis of sign processes with a functional cycle forming signs from afferent signals as signifiers and corresponding efferent signals as signifieds.

The phytosemiotic hypothesis

It is the hypothesis of this study that, while plants are automomous living beings (in the sense of Jakob von Uexküll), their semiosis is different from that of human and animal subjects in such a way that it merits its own semiotic analysis. This semiotic analysis may well form the positive scientific basis lacking so far in the conservationist activities that have, until now, largely been based on negation and ideology. The method by which the specificity of plant semiosis can be shown is that of opposition, well known in semiotic inquiry. It would thus be necessary to show by which distinctive features phytosemiotic processes differ from anthropo- and zoosemiotic processes, and at the same time, what their common biosemiotic basis is.

Distinctive features of phytosemiotics

Fixation versus mobility. Jakob von Uexküll (1922) characterizes the most obvious difference between animals and plants as that of movement and quietness:

> The confusing aspect offered by the thousands of animal worlds is due to the impossibility of finding a moment of rest anywhere. Everything is constantly in the process of breathtaking movement. . . . Again and again the animal must exercise its organs to respond to the requirements of the Umwelt. Sometimes the animal is the persecutor and sometimes the persecuted. But it is always active and thus burns the materials which its digestive cells have extracted in painstaking labor from the nourishment which it has acquired in such a hard way.
>
> The aspect of the reign of plants is quite different. Hectic haste is replaced by comfortable calm. Not that work ceases for a moment, as long as the plant is alive. An uninterrupted stream of liquids enters by the roots, rises along the stem and branches out in all directions to the leaves where it evaporates again in a well-controlled fashion. This stream transports the nourishing salts gained from the earth into all those tissues of the plant which transform them into material of the plant's body. In the laboratory of the leafgreen, the important building block of carbon is produced with the help of the sun. Everything is handled by the fine detail work of living cells which remain autonomous subjects as do those in the bodies of animals. They work in union, according to a plan, by transmitting stimuli and material.

This quotation certainly should not be misunderstood in the sense that plants do not move. There is, for one thing, the phenomenon of phototropism (e.g., Presti et al. 1977), implying relatively slow movement of plants toward light sources. And there is, of course, very visible adaptive movement of plants in response to the pressure of air (wind) or water (stream).

Absence of effectors and receptors. The "comfortable calm" of the reign of plants is due to the fact that plants have no specific effector organs—no feet to run with, no arms to gesticulate with, etc.—and, correspondingly, no specific receptor organs—no eyes to look around with, no ears to hear with, etc. Consequently, there is no nervous system mediating between effectors and receptors.

This assertion appears to be in contradiction to an increasing—and quite "fashionable"—body of literature concerned with "plant receptors". For instance, so-called photoreceptors have been studied in different strains of Phycomyces, a species of fungus (Delbrück et al. 1977; Delbrück et al. 1976; Presti et al. 1977). It was found, in one study, that "the Phycomyces sporangiophore is a single cell and responds phototropically, adapting to various light levels. . . . The authors have analyzed the kinetics of this adaptation, using a tracking machine for greater precision. Dark adaptation is exponential . . . i.e., the threshold falls exponentially in the dark, in contrast to scotopic vision where the logarithm of threshold falls exponentially in the dark". In the other studies, the chemical functioning of these photoreceptors was analyzed, with the result that "the bluelight receptor" of Phycomyces is not carotene (as in animals), but riboflavin.

A similar topic in the literature is the search for a functional "plant hormone receptor" (e.g., Dodds and Hall 1980, a review on the problem with a bibliography of 65 titles). Animal hormone receptors are defined as follows:

> Animal hormones are synthesized in clearly defined organs and are then translocated to equally clearly defined "target" tissues organs . . . where they control specific biochemical processes . . . the sites with which they interact must have a very high affinity for the hormone. Equally, the sites must show very high specificity for the hormone. These sites, or rather the whole molecule of which they are part, are termed "hormone receptors". All such receptors which have been isolated so far have proved to be proteins.

In contrast to a large number of hormones found in animals (more than 40 have by now been identified), only five groups of plant hormones are known so far. These plant hormones have a much simpler structure than animal hormones. According to Dodds and Hall (1980), "The very term hormone is called into question in plants since the site of synthesis is not usually restricted to a specialized organ or tissue . . . most if not all plant cells have had the capacity for hormone synthesis at some time in their development and many retain this capacity, even if to a limited extent". In addition, "there is usually no one distinct target for a given hormone since at any one time many different tissues and organs in the plant are capable of responding to it—often in a different way". Obviously, it is this "totipotency of plant cells", a principle formulated already by Haberland (1902), that differentiates so-called photo- and hormone-receptors of plants from those in animals. This does not mean that there is no "differentiation", e.g., "division of labor", between plant cells during the development of plants.

It is typical for the modern conception of "plant receptors" in botany to refer to chemical "binding" processes that are treated, according to information theory, as processes between chemical "messengers" and "target substances", rather than referring to specialized cell compounds or receptor organs as these are present in animals. Moreover, the useful distinction between "exteroceptors" (e.g., photoreceptors) and "interoceptors" (e.g., hormone receptors) is neglected by botanical terminology. I would, therefore, like to maintain Jakob von Uexküll's conception denying plants the capacity of specialized receptor organs, and rather apply to what are called receptors in the above cited literature the term "sensors", according to the parlance of cybernetics with respect to feedback cycles.

Absence of the functional cycle. For the same terminological reason, I would agree with Jakob von Uexküll in maintaining that plants do not have a "functional cycle" connecting receptor organs via a nervous system to effector organs. What plants have is a feedback cycle between sensors and regulators. In the absence of a functional cycle in plants, there is no way by which afferent signals can be fitted together with efferent signals to form the signifiers and signifieds of "objects".

Casing versus Umwelt. Given the absence of a functional cycle, plants cannot have an Umwelt. As Jakob von Uexküll (1940) points out: "The plant does not possess Umwelt-organs, it is directly immersed into its habitat. The relationships of the plant to its habitat are quite different from those of the animal to its Umwelt". While humans and animals each have their own Umwelt, plants are confined to their casing.

Meaning factor versus meaning carrier. Due to the absence of effectors, nervous system, and receptors and the consequent lack of the functional cycle and the resulting Umwelt, plants have no objects that may become the sources or "carriers" of meaning for them. Meaning is mediated for plants by what Jakob von Uexküll calls "meaning factors". Meaning factors are those stimuli among the stream of impingements pressing upon the plants from all sides that are relevant to their life. The plant does not counter external impingements with the double-pronged operation of receptors and effectors, but uses the living sheet of cells of its casing to filter out relevant impingements. These relevant impingements are the meaning factors, i.e., the semiotic factors, for the living plant.

Using the example of the leaves of an oak tree, Jakob von Uexküll shows how phytosemiosis functions. One of the meaning factors, as far as oak leaves are concerned, is the rain. Falling raindrops follow precise physical laws governing the behavior of liquids upon striking a leaf. In this case, according to Jakob von Uexküll, the leaf is the "receiver of meaning", coupled with the meaning factor "rain" by a "meaning rule". The form of the leaves is such that it accommodates the physical laws governing the behavior of liquids. The leaves work together by forming cascades in all directions in order to distribute the rain water on the ground for optimal use by the roots. To put it in more common semiotic terminology, the leaf's form is the signifier and the physical behavior of a raindrop is the signified. The code coupling leaf and raindrop is the oak tree's need of liquid for the transport of nourishing salts into its cells.

Utilization of meaning by form versus utilization of meaning by function cycle. The difference between plant and animal is that the plant utilizes meaning by means of its form built up according to a "plan of nature", enabling the leaf to fit into the physical behavior of liquids, while humans and animals utilize meaning through their function cycle. The code of a plant's need is a superordinate rule coupling two subordinate rules, the physical laws governing the forming and flowing of drops and the biological formation rules according to which the leaves of a particular species of plants grow in its typical habitat. The code of an animal's need couples relevant objects or animals to the receptors and effectors of the receiving animal. The superordinate rule of the living being's needs may be considered a code to which subordinate rules relate as subcodes.

Predominance of indexicality versus iconicity and symbolicity. The classical trichotomy of possible relationships between the material aspect of the sign and the object it stands for is, in Peirce, reflected by degrees of iconicity, indexicality, and symbolicity (and in the Saussurean tradition by degrees of motivation, indexicality, and arbitrariness). If one wants to extend this trichotomy to plants on the one hand, versus animals and humans on the other, the absence of the function cycle would suggest that, in plants, indexicality certainly predominates over iconicity. In animals, however, iconicity seems to predominate over symbolicity, since the double-pronged action of receptors and effectors models the object almost as a concave negative image of the two actions. Finally, symbolicity predominates over iconicity in humans because of their widespread social use of language and other arbitrary sign systems.

There are three levels of meaningful cycles corresponding to predominance of indexicality, iconicity, and symbolicity, each higher process including also the lower. Indexicality, on the vegetative level, corresponds to the sensing and regulating, in a feedback cycle, of meaningful stimulation directly contiguous to the form of the plant. Iconicity, on the animal level, is produced by the function cycle, with receptor and effector activity representing, in a nervous system, the "image" of objects. Symbolicity, on the human level, is produced by perception and action in human society.

Communalities between phytosemiosis and zoosemiosis

Selection of impingements. While there are distinct differences between the sign processes in plants and animals or humans, there are also important communalities among them. One is that they all filter out a specific selection of all those impingements surrounding them. As living beings, they are all capable of drawing a borderline between "self" and "nonself", utilizing only those impingements that are meaningful to their needs.

Suffering the imposition of meaning. Plants, animals, and humans not only utilize impingements meaningfully, but also suffer the imposition of meaning. Jakob von Uexküll (1940) shows this with the example of the different roles a wild flower in a meadow may play as a meaningful object in different function cycles: It may be picked by a human for a bouquet of flowers, it is utilized as a walkway and plant-louse farm by ants, the larva of the cicada may bore its nest into its stem, and the cow may eat it together with a bunch of grass. Suffering the imposition of meaning is analogously applicable to animals and humans, as is proved by the roles of prey and predator between animals and between animals and humans, and by the suppression of humans by humans. In the "plan of nature", the meaning of suffering the imposition of meaning may range from the reduction of excess individuals in the interest of their own species to reduction in the interest of a whole ecological system, whereas social oppression among humans seems to be dictated by historical and dialectical laws.

Rules of correspondence between the Umwelts of humans, animals, and plants—the method of "counterpoint". With the example of oak leaf and raindrop, it was shown that meaning in nature is based on rules of correspondence bracketing subordinate formation rules and physical rules. The favorite example of Jakob von Uexküll for explaining the lawfulness of these meaningful correspondences or—as one would say in semiotics—codes is that of a musical composition of which "nature" is the composer. This whole composition, of which the biologist tries to write the score, i.e., to study the syntagmatic rules, is based on the technique of counterpoint. The method is to find the counterpoint to each note of the composition by following the motto: Wherever there is a point, its corresponding counterpoint can be found. The physical behavior of raindrops is the counterpoint corresponding to the point of the leaf's form, the soft skin of mammals corresponds to the tick's bite, the path corresponds to man's feet, nourishment to his mouth, an enemy to his weapon, as Jakob von Uexküll has pointed out.

There is one fundamental rule of correspondence between humans and animals on the one hand and plants on the other, this being of critical importance for life: Plants produce the oxygen all humans and animals breathe. In other words, the life of plants corresponds as a counterpoint to the breathing lungs of humans and other animals as a point. As Jakob von Uexküll (1940) paraphrased Goethe's verse

> Wär' nicht das Auge sonnenhaft
> *If the eye were not sun-like,*
> die Sonne könnt' es nie erblicken.
> *it could ne'er behold the sun.*

by postulating

> Wär' nicht die Sonne augenhaft
> *If the sun were not eye-like,*
> an keinem Himmel könnte sie erstrahlen.
> *It could not shine in any sky.*

we might say

> Wär nicht die Lunge pflanzenhaft.
> *If the lung were not plant-like,*
> das Atmen könnte nicht gelingen.
> *breathing could not comply.*

and

> Wär nicht die Pflanze lungenhaft
> *If the plant were not lung-like,*
> gäb's keinen Atemzug auf Erden.
> *respiration would pass earth by.*

Three forms of life and their common semiotic aspect.[1] The vegetative world, for all of its differences from the world of animals and humans, is nevertheless structured according to a base semiotics which cuts across all living beings, plants, animals, and humans alike.

As Thomas A. Sebeok and Thure von Uexküll have pointed out, many life processes within the animal and human organisms function according to the principle of the vegetative world, i.e., according to the principle of phytosemiotics. This field of semiotic inquiry had been labeled endosemiotics by them (Sebeok 1976, Thure von Uexküll 1980). As soon as a functional cycle is constituted by the presence of effectors and receptors, through the mediation of a "vegetative" nervous system, the phenomenon of Umwelt arises in animals and humans alike. The semiotic aspects of the Umwelt have been called "exosemiotics" (Thure von Uexküll 1980). Whereas endosemiotics is pertinent to all three forms of life, plants, animals, and humans, and thus pertinent to phytosemiotics, zoosemiotics, and anthroposemiotics, exosemiotics is pertinent to zoosemiotics and anthroposemiotics only. As Thure von Uexküll (1980) suggests, the age-old problem of the dualism of body and soul might thus find a biosemiotic answer. Plants would therefore exhibit predominantly indexical sign systems; in animals, both indexical and iconic signs would appear; whereas human sign processes would display the whole range of the trichotomy, from indexicality via iconicity to symbolicity.

Meaningful interactions between plants and animals. Thus far, only differences and communalities between the sign processes in plants, animals, and humans have been accounted for. Some examples of semiotic interactions between these living beings will now be presented.

It is well known that plants have chemical defenses against the attacks of herbivore animals such as insects. There are two classes of such defenses. Either chemical deterrents are already present before the attack occurs or such a deterrent is mobilized in response to such an attack. The latter defense is known as "induced resistance". It is practiced frequently in higher plants against infections by microorganisms. Induced resistance sometimes occurs, however, as a counterattack by the plant against the attack of an herbivore insect enemy. As far as this insect-induced resistance in plants is concerned, it is interesting to study the time plants need for mobilization. Most of the observed cases of this type of resistance have long response times, ranging from 12 hours to as much as several years. But there are examples of relatively rapidly induced resistance. I am grateful to Thomas A. Sebeok for drawing my attention to such an example published recently (Carroll and Hoffman 1980). It shows a complex sequence of animal attack on the plant, rapid counterattack by the plant, and adaptive countermeasures against this defense of the plant on the part of the animal. The crookneck squash is attacked by a beetle species labeled *Epilachna tredicimnotata* (Coleoptera: Coccinelidae). This bug first uses its specially formed apical teeth to cut a circular trench in the crookneck squash leaf and then feeds only on the cut-out disk. The trenching takes about ten minutes, obviously time enough to isolate a part of the leaf from the chemical deterrent that the plant mobilizes against the attack. The response time of the plant and some further circumstances connected with this interaction between "prey" and "predator" have been investigated experimentally by Carroll and Hoffman.

They used the circumstance that the deterrent mobilized by the crookneck squash against *Epilachna* is a feeding stimulant for another beetle (*Acalymma*). The latter refuses, for instance, to feed on crookneck squash leaves that have been recently removed from the plant and, therefore, cannot yet have been reached by the deterrent (unless it has been locally synthesized). The response time of *Epilachna* attacks on the crookneck squash can now be experimentally "chronometrized" by damaging crookneck squash leaves and varying the time between damaging and cutting a part of the leaf as food for the two kinds of beetles. The first kind should refuse, the second kind start feeding from the moment at which the deterrent has arrived at the damaged area of the leaf. Carroll and Hoffman found that it takes the crookneck squash about 40 minutes to mobilize the deterrent and to send it to the attacked area. *Epilachna* is faster, however, and takes only ten minutes to cut out an area from the leaf before the deterrent can reach it! (Or is it content to eat only what it can cut in ten minutes, the plant, in turn, tolerating this minor damage?) After reviewing some similiar cases of plant-animal interaction reported in the literature, Carroll and Hoffman suggest that the fact that herbivores often move from one plant to another before having finished feeding might be an adaptive response geared to avoiding the arrival of defensive deterrents at the feeding point.

Meaningful interactions between plants and men: (1) The "green thumb" theory. As far as the interaction between humans and plants is concerned, there is a widespread conviction that some people have "green thumbs": Whatever seed they put into the earth will grow and mature nicely. Others, not gifted with this magic capacity, can do whatever they like—the plants will die for them. I have heard people explain this phenomenon by the alleged radiation of an aura that is particularly "congenial" to plants. But even admitting that living beings possess their own "aura" of radiation (for instance, warm-blooded animals radiate heat), I would suggest that "green thumbs" is a phenomenon analogous to that of "Clever Hans" of which Sebeok (1977, 1978) has repeatedly warned us. The "magic", in this case, lies in the fact that some people have a different attitude toward plants, know more about them and, consequently, take better care of them. It is no wonder if plants react positively to this treatment.

(2) Caring for plants. Another concept of meaningful interaction between plants and humans could be based on the differentiation of "meaning" into two classes: There are objects that are "indirectly" meaningful to us, such as words or other communicative signs. But there are also objects that may acquire "direct" meaning. This is, for instance, the case with "cherished" possessions, which may become receptacles of personal memories, e.g., a gift from a friend, or tokens of attitudinal justification, e.g., a "status symbol" or a trophy. Plants, for instance, are generally present in the "object ecology" of a typical middle class home and tend to carry a special meaning for one or more members of the family. Csikszentmihalyi and Rochberg-Halton (1978) and Rochberg-Halton (1979) have shown in their studies on the meaning of "cherished household possessions" that, for children, parents, and grandparents, quite different objects acquire meaning for quite different purposes. The younger generation names, as its preferred possessions, objects that require active manipulation—e.g., stereo units, musical instruments, pets, etc. The grandparents, on the contrary, prefer objects of passive contemplation, such as family photographs, books, paintings, crockery, etc. The middle generation, the parents, take an intermediate position between their children and their own parents as far as the "motivation" of cherished objects is concerned. Their preference ranges from paintings and books to musical instruments, plants, and stereos (in that order). The middle rank of objects for the three generations shows a decrease in life characteristics: children prefer pets, parents plants, grandparents crockery. Also, the same objects may obtain different ranks, depending on whether they are ranked according to one or another of three different meaning dimensions: first, reference to self versus reference to other; second, current experience versus memory of the past, and third, personal values. The latter dimension of meaning reflects objects as models of the self or templates of self-development. It is in this dimension that plants, together with books, rank first, i.e., above all other objects. By analyzing the rank order of parents separately, i.e., women versus men, one finds plants only in the rank order of the former, whereas the latter have tools and trophies in their preference list as objects meaningful only to men. Obviously, in these choices, differences in the conception of self are involved that are due to stereotypes of sexual roles. As Csikszentmihalyi and Rochberg-Halton (1978: 12) put it: "The meaning system built by men is different from that of women partly because they learn to use different things to objectify experience. The feelings and thoughts one has in caring for a plant are bound to be different from the ones a person has when using a camera . . . We

are assuming that a plant produces, in its (characteristic) caretaker, feelings of nurturance while a trophy is more likely to invoke a feeling of pride in one's past accomplishment.''

This phenomenon of plants evoking the nurturance instinct in humans is nicely demonstrated in a report by Newman (1979) on a particular type of interaction with plants, exhibited by a woman who served as a subject in a study on a person's relation to objects. By eliciting accounts of this woman's most highly valued activities, Newman found that she focused her main interests on collecting, repairing, and nurturing. Her main collector items were valuable Indian prints, as well as stones she picked up. She repaired her own car and other objects around the house, being directly prompted to do so by her feminist orientation, prescribing that one has to learn to take care of oneself. The nurturing aspect of her activities was clearly visible by the mass of plants in her house. But this aspect was brought out even more by the fact that she used to go to supermarkets and plant stores every so often to buy plants that were dying. "Then she would nurse them back to health, propagate them and give them to friends who would be good to them. Thus, she said, she "worries a lot' about them" (Newman 1979: 4a). Apparently, her interaction with plants excluded aesthetic contemplation. Caring for plants was a very active form of "rescuing" in the women's life.

This example shows, in a psychological way, how important plants may become for humans. The study of the psychological relationships between men and plants is still in its very early stages. One of the tasks ahead lies in the development of an attitude-toward-plants-test, which could complement other "environmental inventories", e.g., the Environmental Response Inventory (ERI) of McKechnie (1977), already used in environmental decision making, planning, and aptitude testing.

(3) Learning from plants. Plants not only evoke nurturance behavior but often become something like "teachers" when we interact with them. The "comfortable calm" they radiate has already been mentioned (Jakob von Uexküll 1922). But they may also become "living examples" of "passive resistance". As Jakob von Uexküll (1940) says: "A plant solves its main task by passive surrender to the effects of the Umwelt into which it is slotted. Since the plant is not mobile, it has to face all those external effects which are present in its surroundings. The most efficient means of an animal's self-preservation—escape—is not available to the plant." In addition, the example of the plant's life rhythm can be very instructive to humans. Some plants certainly possess, in their genotype, the capacity to predict, independently from weather conditions, the change of seasons. And Jakob von Uexküll (1940) observes, in this respect:

Since plants are not dead cases, but are constantly forced to defend their lives, we recognize in them a life rhythm paralleling the change of the seasons. Our deciduous trees lose their leaves in autumn and change into plants, independent of water, in order to survive the effects of dehydration imposed on them by frost and frozen ground. The inner rhythm of plants, however, is adapted even more intimately to the changes of the year because it has been shown that our fruits grow best in hot houses, if one exposes the trees to the drop in temperature normal during their blossoming period.

Finally, plants impress us not only with the biotechnical solutions they find to their problems but also with their "wisdom" in architecture: "The houses of men are immobile and immediately betray their locality in their external habitus: Roofs and windows must be built differently, depending on whether snow, rain, storm or heat from the sun menaces the house. Plants, likewise, demonstrate through their form whether they must defend themselves against drought or water, against an excess or a lack of light." (Jakob von Uexküll 1940).

Generally, human aesthetic experience is heightened in symbiosis with plants, since the plant's foremost "receiver of meaning" is its form, linked with physical "meaning factors" that generally follow physical laws. Thus, plants not only adapt indexically to their environment but also iconically portray the forces of their environment through their meaningful form. A study of literature and poetry, of painting, religion, and other human endeavors should convince us that plants have served as meaningful signs, indexical, iconic, and symbolic, in many cultures because they are living beings possessing features that evoke the attribution of meaning to a very considerable degree.

Discussion and some conclusions

Jakob von Uexküll's approach to biology as a science of life is a holistic one: The whole is not explained by the functioning of its parts, but the meaning of the parts is explained according to the plan of the whole, a principle that is not unlike the fundamental proposition of Gestalt theory. Admittedly, with his postulate of a "general plan of nature", one reaches the borderline of the operational. But if the "general plan of nature" is taken as a hypothesis, guiding, step by step, the experimental verification of "rules of correspondence", it loses its pseudo-explanatory character.

It may also become a guideline for ecological research and, indirectly, for the political conclusions based upon it. The ideological veneration of greenery and its attendant blind search for alternatives can be replaced by the detailed study of the symbiosis between humans, animals, and plants, and ecologically sound solutions to contemporary problems can be deduced from it. Despite the impression of progress raised by the constant introduction of new and sophisticated tools between human effectors or receptors and the human Umwelt, the human organism cannot escape the basic vegetative rules of endosemiotics and remains locked together with plants by a mutual rule of correspondence: If men cease to care for plants, i.e., cease to understand their meaning factors and the meaning rules at the basis of their formation rules, they will asphyxiate themselves. As Thure von Uexküll (1980) has put it: "Man is led, from his extravagant position as the observer positioned outside nature and as its unscrupulous exploiter, back into nature, in which he must arrange himself for better or worse." Phytosemiotics can help to improve this arrangement.

10

JOHN DEELY

On the Notion of Phytosemiotics

> The action of a sign generally takes place between two parties, the
> utterer and the interpreter. They need not be persons; for a
> chameleon and many kinds of insects and even plants make their
> livings by uttering signs, and lying signs, at that. Who is the
> utterer of signs of the weather . . . ? However, every sign certainly
> conveys something of the general nature of thought, if not from
> a mind, yet from some repository of ideas, or significant forms, and
> if not to a person, yet to something capable of somehow
> "catching on", . . . that is, of receiving not merely a physical,
> nor even merely a psychical dose of energy, but a significant
> meaning. In that modified, and as yet very misty, sense, then, we
> may continue to use the italicized words . . . .
>
> —Peirce c.1907: MS 318, 205-206—

> . . . physical science . . . no less than biological science appears to
> manifest teleology . . . .
>
> —Henderson 1913: 305—

Writing in 1978, I criticized sharply the following view of Thomas A. Sebeok,
considering it excessive and pregnant with the kind of imperialism likely to discredit
the semiotics movement in the eyes not just of detractors, but even of traditional
academicians neutral but open-minded about whatever possibilities semiotics might
prove to offer:

> In the early 1960s, I called attention to a vision of new and startling dimen-
> sions: the convergence of the science of genetics with the science of linguis-
> tics, remarking that both are emerging "as autonomous yet sister disciplines
> in the larger field of communication sciences. . . ." It is amply clear . . .
> that the genetic code must be regarded as the most fundamental of all
> semiotic networks and therefore as the prototype for all other signaling
> systems used by animals, including man. From this point of view, molecules
> that are quantum systems, acting as stable physical information carriers,
> zoosemiotic systems, and, finally, cultural systems, comprehending
> language, constitute a natural sequel of stages of ever more complex energy
> levels in a single universal evolution. It is possible, therefore, to describe
> language as well as living systems from a unified cybernetic standpoint
> . . . A mutual appreciation of genetics, animal communication studies,
> and linguistics may lead to a full understanding of the dynamics of semiosis,
> and this may, in the last analysis, turn out to be no less than the definition
> of life (Sebeok 1968a: 627, as reprinted in Sebeok 1976: 69).

Today, almost five years later, I find myself again turning to the contemplation of Dr. Sebeok's singularly large view of semiotics, without repudiating my
earlier reservations about his stand from the strict perspective in which they were
conceived (the origins of full semiosis in cognition), but at the same time feeling

compelled to make some broad-gauge adjustments in that earlier perspective which have the effect, in effect, of subjecting Dr. Sebeok to yet another round of criticism for being—in this same grand vision—perhaps not grand enough! In discussing with my friend and colleague Dr. Russell the subject of today's discussion—phytosemiosis, whatever it may be—he repeatedly embarrassed me by noting that it sounded like "a clear case of Deely vs. Deely".

Be that as it may, I was led to reassess at once Dr. Sebeok's and my own views of semiotics by the appearance of a remarkable article by Martin Krampen in *Semiotica* 36-3/4 (1981) titled, simply enough, "Phytosemiotics", i.e., the semiotics of plants. Familiar with the opinion all too prevalent beyond semiotic circles proper that semiotics is a forum where nonsense abounds, I anticipated Krampen's article with much less than a positive frame of mind. Careful reading of his actual text nonetheless astounded me, and I believe it to Krampen's credit that his text achieved the rare effect of converting a hostile reader into a favorable admirer of his views, and perhaps of his daring even more.

For, as I was soon to learn, phytosemiotics is not a subject one who values social admiration broaches lightly. Privileged again to attend the Toronto version of ISISSS in 1982, and a confirmed admirer of the work of Donald Preziosi and others in the area of architectural semiotics, I particularly looked forward to the June 18-20 ISISSS Colloquium on "Urban Semiotics", and to the opportunity to follow in person the further development of Professor Krampen's novel perspective in his talk, " 'Green Arks'—Living in an Environment with More than 50% Plants", scheduled for the evening of June 19. Apprised of Krampen's contention (1981: 192) that "this semiotic analysis may well form the positive scientific basis lacking so far in the conservationist activities that have, until now, largely been based on negation and ideology", I looked forward to his presentation as a probable development of this particular feature of his phytosemiotics. I was not disappointed. He presented a fascinating and experimentally grounded discussion of the role and use of plants in helping to control the oxygen content and general purity of atmosphere in the human habitat. Plants, heretofore taken for granted in the physical environment and introduced into our dwellings largely for decorative and aesthetic purposes, Krampen proposed considering as being made integral parts of the interior of buildings, not for mere secondary purposes, but as *primary components* of the interior of dwellings helping to control and maintain the quality of air, in addition to their psychological benefits and so far largely subliminal and unexamined effects on the human psyche. In line with this, and in view of the substantially deteriorating atmosphere and physical environment of "post-industrial man" (a particularly fitting consideration in the country first experiencing on a large scale in its lakes and rivers the deadly impact of the singularly American-engendered "acid rains" which are sadly destined to become, in all probability, a planet-wide phenomenon), Krampen concluded his presentation with some proposals and considerations toward a city expressly conceived and designed to include plants not as mere outdoor growths to beautify the landscape, but as indoor growths contributing to the quality and regulation of the air we breathe as well as the sights we see.

From an architectural point of view, clearly, such a proposal is both novel and rich with possibilities. Krampen proceeded to describe an experimental community whose southward exposure enclosed large quantities of plant life. I thought too of the energy utilization possibilities of such structures. Imagine then my astonishment when the commentator, a professional architect, after making the usual comments about his pleasure and honor at being on this program, etc., announced that, that being said, he had nothing further to say, nor could he imagine any possible relevance of anything Professor Krampen had to say to any possible conception of semiotics.

With that inauspicious beginning, the matter was turned over to the floor for questions. Matters were not helped by the opening "questioner", a well-known but here unnamed Polish semiotician, who further disgraced a thoughtful and careful presentation by a purely *ad hominem* and thoroughly unworthy attack on Jakob von Uexküll, Krampen's avowed mentor on the subject of plants and bio-semiosis generally:

> Using the example of the leaves of an oak tree, Jakob von Uexküll shows how phytosemiosis functions. One of the meaning factors, as far as oak leaves are concerned, is the rain. Falling raindrops follow precise physical laws governing the behavior of liquids upon striking a leaf. In this case, according to Jakob von Uexküll, the leaf is the "receiver of m", coupled with the m factor "rain" by a "meaning rule". The form of the leaves is such that it accommodates the physical laws governing the behavior of liquids. The leaves work together by forming cascades in all directions in order to distribute the rain water on the ground for optimal use by the roots. To put it in more common semiotic terminology, the leaf's form is the signifier and the physical behavior of the raindrop is the signified. The code coupling leaf and raindrop is the oak tree's need of liquid for the transport of nourishing salts into its cells (Krampen 1981: 195).

So amazed was I by the contrast between Dr. Krampen's thoughtful presentation and the consternation—not to say hostility—with which it was met, that I left the session troubled for many hours—then and since—by trying to understand what had "really" gone on in the semiosis of the occasion. In what follows, I want to sketch out the general considerations that gradually clarified in these reflections.

First of all, in thinking about plants and in trying to engage others in discussions about them, I found them to be perhaps the factor most taken for granted in the human world. They simply are not considered seriously in their own right, despite their absolutely crucial evolutionary role first in bringing about an oxidizing atmosphere (about a billion years ago) and then in sustaining ever afterward the basic matrix required for the development and continuance of all animal life, as Krampen noted (1981: 197):

> There is one fundamental rule of correspondence between humans and animals on the one hand and plants on the other, this being of critical importance for life: Plants produce the oxygen all humans and animals breathe. In other words, the life of plants corresponds as a counterpoint to the breathing lungs of humans and animals as a point.

There is more to be considered here than a merely external correspondence and exploitive dependency, and I do not mean to suggest that Dr. Krampen is unaware of this. Consider the following text, singularly uncharacteristic of the

mainstream of modern philosophy, as it waxes increasingly glottocentric in contemporary times—a text I choose in part for its fortuitous extension of the
phytosemiotic image of the oak tree cited above from Krampen on the basis of
von Uexküll's work. The text is from the 19th century idealist philosopher, Jules
Lachelier (1933: XVIII-XIX):

> It seems to me, when I am at Fontainebleau, that I sympathize in all my
> energies with the powerful vitality of the trees which surround me. I am
> too encrusted in my own form to be able to reproduce their form; yet,
> on well considering the matter, it does not seem unreasonable to hold that
> all forms of being sleep more or less deeply buried in the ground of every
> being. Under the sharp contours of my human form any careful observer
> could see the vaguer contours of "animality", which veils in turn the even
> more fluid and incomplete form of simple organic life. Now one of the
> possible determinations of organic life is *tree*, which engenders in turn the
> oak tree. So the "being of an oak tree" is somewhere hidden in the foun-
> dations of my being, and may even strive sometimes to emerge and appear
> in its turn *dias in luminis oras* [on the beautiful shores of light]—but humanity,
> which has gotten ahead of it, prevents it from doing so and blocks its
> way.[1]

This text strikes one in our cultural milieu as something idiosyncratic, or even
bizarre. Yet in truth it is no more than a faithful echo of the older traditions of
the Western philosophical mainstream, if we recall the reflections in this area common to Greek and Latin thought, before the unique development of modern
philosophy entirely shifted concern away from natural being to the universe of
human discourse in such ways as effectively to close the range of philosophy within
the conventionalized realms of human culture. According to this older, broader
mainstream, the life of the plant exists *within* the animal itself precisely as base
and part of its proper life. That is to say, the life principle is the first principle
of *all* planetary life as such. I quote from a typical medieval commentary (Aquinas
c.1266-1272) on Aristotle's original conception (c.330BCa) of "psychology" as
the science of living things:

> Aristotle defines the primary principle of life, which is called the vegetative
> psyche or soul; in plants this is the entire soul, while in animals it is only
> a part of the soul . . . To understand his definition, it must be seen that
> there is a definite order among the three operations of the plant soul. For
> its first activity is taking food, through which the living thing preserves
> its existence. The second and more perfect activity is growth, by which
> the living thing develops both in size and vital energy. But the third, most
> perfect, and fulfilling activity is reproduction, through which something
> already as it were existing perfected in its own right, transmits being and
> perfection to another. For anything achieves its greatest perfection, as
> Aristotle observes in Book IV of his *Meteorology* (c.335-334BCa: ch. 1, 4-18),
> when it is able to make another such as it itself is. Since therefore things
> are appropriately defined and named by their outcome, whereas the fulfill-
> ment of the activity of plant life is the generation of another living being,
> it follows that it will be a proper definition of the first principle of life,

that is to say, of the plant soul, if we define it as *what is generative of another like itself on the plan of being alive.*[2]

This ancient way of conceptualizing the nature and essence of life in general—and of plant life in particular—coincides squarely, in contemporary terms, with our understanding of the genetic code. It places a wholly unexpected weight of tradition on the side of Sebeok's contention that, if indeed the genetic code is a semiotic system, such that genetics and linguistics, as codes, subtend the upper and lower reaches of semiosis, then indeed in the full perspective of Western philosophical tradition, "a full understanding of the dynamics of semiosis" would, in the last analysis, "turn out to be no less than the definition of life".

It is also clear in this perspective how the proposal of Krampen (1981: 187) "to establish phytosemiotics, i.e., the semiotics of plants, as an area of inquiry into sign processes, parallel and on an equal footing with anthroposemiotics, the study of human communication, and zoosemiotics, the study of sign processes occurring within and between species of animals, the three areas forming together the discipline of biosemiotics"—however much consternation this proposal may cause to those who remain under the sway of modern glottocentrism even in their conception of semiotics—is nonetheless an inevitable consequence of the "vision of new and startling dimensions" to which Sebeok pointed in the early 1960s (specifically, in 1963). From the point of view of the analogy between linguistics and genetics, and within the dialectic of concepts set up thereby, the establishment of phytosemiotics alongside anthroposemiotics and zoosemiotics completes a tryptich. Within this analogy, phytosemiotics has already a right to existence, its place marked out in advance. What is surprising, really, is not therefore Krampen's proposal, but rather the fact that almost twenty years elapsed between the time of Sebeok's original proposal and Krampen's concrete taking up, advancement, and elaboration of it under the rubric of phytosemiotics. Far from being the bizarre and aberrant proposal it seems to be when viewed from a standpoint of more or less explicit glottocentrism, from an integrally semiotic viewpoint, Krampen's work appears rather as an important and daring step in the dialectical maturation of the doctrine of signs.

This is not to say that the notion is without difficulties, or that its final status vis-à-vis anthroposemiosis and zoosemiosis is assured. In fact, even in Krampen's original proposal, two quite distinct possibilities for the definition of phytosemiotics are outlined. The first and explicit scheme is for a relatively autonomous area of inquiry, "on an equal footing with anthroposemiotics and zoosemiotics", as Krampen puts it, using *opposition* as "the method by which the specificity of plant semiosis can be shown" (p. 192). By the use of this method, Krampen is able to show, as the ancient philosophers also argued, that (p. 203) "many life processes within the animal and human organisms function according to the principle of the vegetative world, i.e., according to the principle of phytosemiotics".

Rich as are the results of this method in Krampen's hands, nonetheless, I am not wholly convinced that they succeed in establishing phytosemiotics on an *autonomous* footing. Or, to put it another way, I am not convinced that the communication between plants and the physical environment, and the communication between plants and animals, is, on *the side of the plants themselves*, truly a process of *semiosis*, such as it certainly is on the side of the animals.

My hesitations here can be exhibited in the form of a distinction between *communication* and *signification*. The two are often confused or treated as identical, owing to their common nature as *thoroughly relational* states of affairs, in addition to which all conscious communication, within or between organisms, is by means of signification. But, while it is true that all relational phenomena are communicative, it is not conversely true that all communicative events involve signification. All relation involves signification potentially, but this becomes actual only through the intervention of cognition.

With these distinctions in mind, the situation of semiosis in the context of communication phenomena (relations) can be outlined thus:

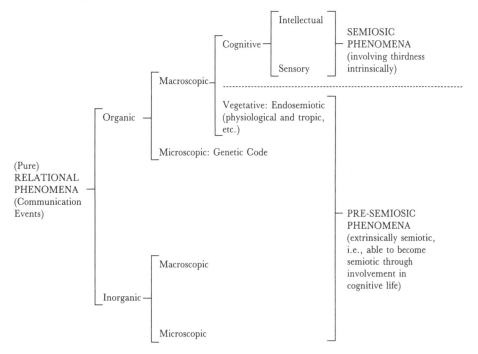

In this scheme, the dynamics of semiosis in the strict, intrinsic sense are co-extensive with the dynamics of cognitive life rather than with the dynamics of life itself. This was my original objection to Sebeok's proposal that the genetic code is already a semiotic network. And yet, it is unquestionable that the genetic code is a communicative network, and a communicative network whereby the present shapes the future which is not yet. Through the genetic code the limitless possibilities of organic life, including semiosis, are opened up, just as through the linguistic code the infinity of cognitive life is rendered possible in anthroposemiosis—which is, after all, "le coeur de l'analogie", as Sebeok pointed out.[3]

What should be stressed, therefore, is not the presemiosic character of plant life, or still more that of the process of formation of star and planetary systems in the first place, but rather the remarkable ordering whereby, thanks to the inorganic processes of planetary formation and the organic processes of vegetable life, semiosis first becomes sustained in its proper possibilities, then grows both in size and vitality, and finally transforms into itself (at least by tendency and right of domination) all that preceded and once lay outside its sphere. As Henderson remarked (1913: 312):

> The properties of matter and the course of cosmic evolution are now seen to be intimately related to the structure of the living being and its activities; they become, therefore, far more important in biology than has been previously suspected. For the whole evolutionary process, both cosmic and organic, is one, and the biologist may now rightly regard the universe in its very essence as biocentric.

If it is true that "things are appropriately defined and named by their outcome", the semioticist may with even greater right regard the universe in its very essence as "semiocentric". The "new and startling vision" of the sixties, which at first seemed too grand, proves rather not grand enough. Even the restriction of semiosis to the cognitive order (because of the type of thirdness it involves, which is not "dynamical" in the Peircean sense) ends by bringing everything under the rubric of semiotics, specifically, inasmuch as all things are in principle knowable. Anything can become an object of awareness, and any object of awareness can come to function as a sign. *Anything* can be a source of signification; all things are potentially signs. The point of the restriction is simply that only cognition can render something actually signifying this way or that way here and now.

In the post-modern era that semiotics introduces, no longer ontocentric as were classical and Latin times, neither anthropocentric as the Renaissance nor glottocentric as the moderns, but semiocentric, we can complete and complement the once-famous maxim of Aristotle, "anima est quoddammodo omnia" ("the soul in a certain way is all things"), by adding: "in a certain way, all things are semiotic" ("omnia sunt quodammodo semiotica")—*in a certain way* (quoddammodo), that is, inasmuch as they enter into knowledge. Anything can signify through cognition, but only through cognition can anything signify. Phenomena not in themselves semiosic, thus, nonetheless become semiotic once an awareness of them is acquired. Indeed, few if any are the things that can form part of conscious awareness without, willy-nilly, yielding signification. Semiosis is above all an organic process, assimilative, for it is a form of life, and dominative, for it is life's highest form. It is the process whereby phenomena originating anywhere in the universe become significant through the intervention of cognition.

This brings me to the second of the two possibilities for the definition of phytosemiotics I see outlined in Krampen's work, namely, the study of plants from the point of view of their symbiosis with animals. From this point of view, phytosemiotics would be defined as the study of the peculiar dependencies of animal upon plant life, and of the benefits to human life in particular that could be derived from such a study. The method of opposition used so skillfully by Krampen would necessarily form a substantial part and lay the foundations for this study. And yet, viewed in this way, phytosemiotics would be, to borrow an older terminology, a study subalternate to rather than on an equal footing with zoosemiotics and anthroposemiotics.

Since this definition in my opinion is unquestionably valid as an important and new semiotic perspective or field of inquiry, since further it includes the methods and results of the alternative definition, I might summarize by saying that from Krampen's work I am convinced of phytosemiotics, but not of phytosemiosis. In either event, from the point of view of an anthroposemiosis that has become transparent to itself and grounded in principle, forever free of the characteristically modern glottocentric bias so evident in the reaction of the Toronto audience to Krampen's ideas, it remains that "the vegetative world is nevertheless structured according to a base semiotics which cuts across all living beings, plants, animals, and humans alike" (Krampen 1981: 203). I would conclude then by giving the last words to this pioneer worker who has opened a new area important even to those who cannot yet recognize it (Krampen 1981: 208):

> Despite the impression of progress raised by the constant introduction of new and sophisticated tools between human effectors or receptors and the human Umwelt, the human organism cannot escape the basic vegetative rules of endosemiotics and remains locked together with plants by a mutual rule of correspondence: If men cease to care for plants, i.e., cease to understand their meaning factors and the meaning rules at the basis of their formation rules, they will asphyxiate themselves. As Thure von Uexküll has put it: "Man is led, from his extravagant position as the observer positioned outside nature and as its unscrupulous exploiter, back into nature, in which he must arrange himself for better or worse." Phytosemiotics can help to improve this arrangement.

III

Developing Themes

11

T. L. SHORT

Life Among the Legisigns

Let us journey into darkest semeiotica. I refer, of course, to Peirce's system for the classification of signs: immense, obscure, crabbed with dense tangles, and never before traversed. Previous explorers have touched upon its fringes or have mapped it from the air, at an altitude from which its general outline could be discerned. Of the multitude of tribes which dwell in this region, the legisigns are the most sophisticated yet treacherous and their folkways deserve particularly careful study. This expedition has been suggested, or rather required, by an earlier essay (Short 1981), in which I argued that Peirce's theory of signs can be fairly judged only by examining its detailed development and divers applications. His system of classification is the place where that development and those applications are to be found, so far as Peirce himself developed and applied his semeiotic.

I.

To prepare for our later adventures it will be best to review what we already know about the basic principles of Peirce's theory. A sign is one element of an indivisible triad: *object, sign,* and *interpretant.* Nothing is an object which is not signifiable; nothing is a sign that is not interpretable as signifying some object; and nothing is an interpretant that does not interpret something as signifying an object. An object need not be signified and a sign need not be interpreted; but they are what they are in virtue of potential signs and potential interpretants, respectively. These potentialities are more than mere possibilities. Something is a sign in virtue of a *ground*—or relation of sign to object—that would justify a particular interpretation of it. Significance, then, is grounded interpretability. But an interpretant can only be grounded or justified in relation to some goal of interpretation. Therefore, corresponding to each ground and to each sign there is an actual or possible goal of interpretation. It follows that the basic concept of semeiotic is not that of sign but is that of semeiosis, the process of sign-interpretation; and it follows, further, that semeiosis is essentially teleological. However, it does not follow that semeiosis involves consciousness; for the goal of a teleological process need not be a purpose consciously held. Indeed, since the human mind, according to Peirce, is constituted by semeiotic processes of a special type, it should be possible to use the concept of semeiosis to analyze consciousness, and that precludes using the concept of consciousness to analyze semeiosis.

In ways that I cannot repeat here [the reference is to Short 1981a, 1983, q.v.], the teleological structure of semeiosis accounts not only for the significance of signs and the intentionality of consciousness but also for the fact that we can distinguish two objects and three types of interpretant for each sign. The *immediate interpretant* is the potential interpretant that constitutes the grounded interpretability or significance of the sign. The *final interpretant* is also potential and is the best interpretant of the sign relative to the goal of interpretation. The *dynamic interpretant* is an actual interpretant of the sign, if any. The dynamic interpretant must in some manner actualize the immediate interpretant, but it may add to, refine, correct, or negate this interpretant. All that is required to form the immediate interpretant is acquaintance with the sign and its ground. Additional observation, "collateral" to the given sign, is required to form a dynamic interpretant that corrects, refines, or supplements the immediate interpretant. In some cases, sufficient collateral experience will result in a dynamic interpretant in which the final interpretant is achieved; in other cases the final interpretant can be approached but not attained. In some cases there may be many dynamic interpretants of the same sign; in other cases at most one. In the immediate interpretant the *immediate object* of a sign is grasped: this is the world, or some part of it, *as* the sign represents it to be. The world, or this portion of the world, as it really is—that is, as it is independently of what it is represented to be—is the *dynamic object* of the sign. The dynamic object is what would be fully and accurately apprehended in the final interpretant.

Each thing is as many signs as there are grounds for distinct interpretations. It follows that there are many more signs than are currently recognized. Progress in science, in scholarship, and perhaps in the other liberal arts, and in the fine arts as well, is the discovery of new signs. Since goals can often be obtained only by taking risks, there will be some fallible grounds of interpretation. This makes it possible for there to be false or misleading signs. These have significance or grounded interpretability, yet what they signify is not. That is, their immediate objects form no part of their dynamic objects. A sign is inaccurate when its immediate does not fit its dynamic object precisely enough, relative to the goal of interpretation. A sign will be true and accurate but incomplete or inadequate when, relative to the goal of interpretation, it does not convey enough about its dynamic object; in this case the immediate is an aspect of the dynamic object. We can thus discriminate several different types of mistaken interpretation. One is where there is no ground that justifies the interpretation: something is taken to be a sign which it is not. Another is where a false or inaccurate sign is taken at face value. In that case the significance of the sign is properly apprehended, but the sign itself ought to be corrected. A third is where an inadequacy goes unrecognized.

Object, sign, and interpretant are essentially triadic, since each is what it is only in relation to each of the others. But it is possible for any one of these to be less than triadic as it is in itself, that is, apart from its being an object or a sign or an interpretant. Employing Peirce's three categories (with which I assume the reader is familiar), an object may be either monadic, such as a quality or feeling or mere possibility, dyadic, such as an effort or resistance or any event or existent *qua* occurring or existing, or triadic, such as a process of inference by which a conclusion is made to follow from premises or such as any instance of continuity, combination of parts to form a whole, lawfulness, or anything *qua* lawful, continuous, or compound in nature. Anything of any of these categories may be signified, though not all in the same way. And, as we will see in more detail below, anything of any category may be a sign or, often, many different signs at once, though *qua* signs they are all triadic. Similarly, an interpretant, whether immediate, dynamic, or final, may be a mere feeling—that is, an actual feeling or a potential feeling—and that is what Peirce called an *emotional interpretant*. Or an interpretant may be an action—whether an action which remains potential or one that is actually performed—and that is what Peirce called an *energetic interpretant*. Or an interpretant may be a habit of action (including such rarefied actions as that of expectation)—whether it is a habit that would be formed or one that had been or is being formed—and that is a *logical interpretant*.

The interpretant of a sign may also be another sign and, in his early semeiotic writings, Peirce held that each interpretant is another sign of the object signified by the sign it interprets. But later he argued that for each interpretant that is such in virtue of being a sign, there must be another interpretant, potentially, that is *not* such in virtue of being a sign. These are what he called *ultimate interpretants*—ultimate, because they do not require interpretation in turn. I have described emotional, energetic, and logical interpretants in their ultimate forms. Non-ultimate logical interpretants are verbal signs, including thoughts (which Peirce conceived of as internalized verbalization). Peirce's pragmatism, in its later or semeiotic formulation, consists in identifying habit as the ultimate logical interpretant. Notice that ultimate interpretants need not be final. Ultimateness pertains to meaning and finality to truth.

Peirce's conception of the interpretant underwent continued revision until the end of his career; everything I have said about interpretants in the preceding paragraphs is contradicted at one place or another in his writings (critics can save themselves much labor by writing the author for a list of passages which contradict his interpretation). However, I believe that the preceding is the best reconstruction of Peirce's theory that can be made and I believe that it is very close to, if not identical with, Peirce's latest views, of 1908 and thereafter.[1]

II.

Partly in consequence of the changes he made in his conception of the interpretant, Peirce's classification of signs was also in constant flux. It is convenient to pick out two attempts at classification, one from c. 1903 (2.233-2.268) and the other from 1908 (8.343-8.376), though an examination of Peirce's "Logic Notebooks" (1865-1909: MS 339) and some of his other manuscripts reveals intermediate versions. The first version based ten classes of signs on three trichtomous divisions of signs and the second, sixty-six classes on ten trichotomies. The set of ten trichotomies, unlike the set of three, depends upon Peirce's divisions of objects into immediate and dynamic and of interpretants into immediate, dynamic, and final. The earlier is more fully described than is the later system and, therefore, I will make it the focus of my discussion and will refer to the later only to clarify, correct, or add to the earlier system. In the present section we will consider only the first two of the original three trichotomies. These are based, first, on what a sign is in itself and, second, on the relation of a sign to its object. In the next, and last, section we will look at the third trichotomy, which is based on the relation of a sign to its interpretant.

According to what it is in itself, a sign is either a *qualisign*, a *sinsign*, or a *legisign* (Peirce 1903: 2.243-246). A qualisign is a quality that is a sign; a sinsign is an existing individual thing or an occurrence that is a sign; and a legisign is a general type that is a sign. Of course, a quality in itself is a mere possibility. Therefore, no qualisign can actually signify except as it is embodied in some individual object or event. Still, an embodied quality remains a quality and, as significant, it is a qualisign.[2] Similarly, a legisign, being general, can signify only through its individual instances, called *replicas*. The legisign defines the characteristics (shape, sound) essential to any of its replicas, and determines *how* these replicas are to be interpreted (which is not always the same thing as determining *what* their interpretation is: *vide infra*). A replica is a sinsign, but it is one of a special type, since its significance (as a replica) depends not only on the unique features of its occurence but also on its being the replica of a legisign. The distinction between a legisign and its replicas is more usually known as the type/token distinction. Examples of these kinds of signs will be found anon, as we wend our way deeper into this thicket.

A sign in relation to its dynamic object—that is, with respect to its ground—is either an icon, an index, or a symbol (Peirce 1903: 2.247-249; 1906: 4.536). An icon exhibits its object in its own character: its object is the quality or other possibility that it exemplifies. An index is existentially related to its object, either as its effect or its cause, or at least by some spatio-temporal relation. Thus, smoke is a sign of fire, as its probable cause, while an outstretched finger, by its orientation in space, signifies a direction. A symbol is related to its object by a rule that specifies what its interpretant is to be. One might object that signs of every type are interpretable by rule. For example, to regard smoke as a sign of fire one must know the rule relating fire to smoke. But such a rule either formulates or is based on a causal relation, and it is that causal relation which is the real ground of significance. Such a rule only recognizes the ground, whereas the rule which makes something a symbol is itself the ground of that symbol's significance: it determines a potential interpretant that would not otherwise exist. The grounds of iconic and indexical significance are not intrinsically semeiotical, while that of symbolic significance is. The obvious examples of symbols are the parts of speech that signify by convention, but, as we will see later, on Peirce's view not all symbols are conventional.[3]

It is clear that a qualisign could never be anything more than an icon. For a quality, as such, can stand in no existential relation to anything and, thus, it cannot be an index; and since it is not a type, it cannot be a symbol. A sinsign can be an index, since singular things and events always stand in existential relations to other singular things and events. It will also be any number of iconic signs, both in virtue of embodied qualisigns and by exemplifying possibilities in other ways. In using a sinsign as an example of singularity—or as an example of sinsigns—we are using it as an icon for that of which no mere qualisign could be an icon. But sinsigns cannot be symbols. The significance of a symbol is established by a general rule. Such a rule cannot refer to an individual thing, but only to a type. Therefore, every symbol is a legisign. Legisigns, however, may be indexical or iconic instead of symbolic. We will encounter examples of iconic and indexical legisigns around the next twist in the trail.

These relations between the two trichotomies of signs, by which they yield not nine but only six classes of signs, follow rigorously from two principles which Peirce stated. The first of these is that the dynamic object of a sign determines the sign and the sign determines its interpretant (1908: 8.343). (By "determines"

Peirce means "delimits the possible" rather than "causes" (p.1903: 8.177). The nature of an object delimits what can be a sign of it, and a sign delimits the class of its possible interpretants.) The second principle is that nothing of a higher category can determine anything of a lower category. Hence, no object can be represented by a sign of lower category nor can any sign be interpreted by an interpretant of lower category (1903: 2.235-237). By extending the first principle to cover other factors of the sign situation, the second principle restricts the possible combinations of Peirce's various trichotomies of signs. Thus, his 1908 list of ten trichotomies yields only sixty-six instead of 3^{10} or 59,049 classes of signs.[4]

An example Peirce gives of a qualisign is "a feeling of 'red'" (1903: 2.254). Of course, this must be embodied and the result of that—say, a red patch of cloth—is an iconic sinsign (or, as Peirce sometimes called it, a hypoicon). Another example of an iconic sinsign is an individual instance of a geometrical diagram (ibid.: 2.255), which, *qua* diagram, represents the set of relationships which it exhibits among its own parts.

Indexical sinsigns do not exhibit their objects but, rather, point to them or in analogous ways "pick them out". Thus, a spontaneous cry (1903: 2.256) so affects our instinctual or conditioned reflexes as to draw our attention to its source. Similarly, a weathercock (ibid.: 2.257) indicates the direction of the wind to anyone who considers it in light of the fact that its direction is determined by the wind's direction, when there is a wind. Clearly, the weathercock must involve an icon of the wind's direction, viz. in the direction of its own longest horizontal dimension. But it is the *actual* direction of the wind that is signified, and not a merely possible direction. Therefore, the icon which it involves is part of a more complex sign. The whole is an index of the wind's actual direction, because it is the actual direction of the wind which determines the actual direction to which the weathercock turns. ". . . it is not the mere resemblance of its Object, even in these respects, which makes it a sign, but it is the actual modification of it by the Object" (ibid.: 2.248).

As we see in our two examples of indexical sinsigns, they will be properly interpreted only by individuals prepared, either by instinct or by training, to interpret them. And in the second, interest is also required; for one who knows how to read weathervanes but is not at the moment interested in determining the wind's direction might see a weathervane without any thought of what it indicates. The same applies more emphatically to hypoicons. Since every individual object and event exhibits any number of possibilities, each is many distinct icons at once. These icons will go unnoticed except when attention is drawn to them, either by one's interest or by a second sign that directs attention to a particular icon. Thus, one who is thinking about what color to paint a wall may be made to think of a particular shade by chancing to see it somewhere; another person might present a piece of cloth to a clerk, saying, "I want some material of that color." *Using* something as a sample of x is different from its *being* an icon of x, though nothing can be used to exemplify what it does not already exemplify.

In a well-known remark on ostensive definition, Wittgenstein shows that pointing does not suffice by itself to isolate an intended referent. But that is because the referent in question is one that is intended. Pointing alone does signify the actual direction defined by the finger (or stick or other pointer) in its actual spatial orientation. To signify some particular object lying in that direction, one must join other signs to the pointing. In that case, the pointing still signifies a direction only, but it occurs as part of a more complex sign which, as a whole, signifies something other than a direction. This is quite different from adding signs to pointing in order to direct attention to the pointing, as when someone says, "Look where I'm pointing."[5]

There is no similar problem of drawing attention to the replicas of legisigns. For legisigns only exist *in order* to be used[6]—that is, to signify through replication—and that presupposes the existence of creatures prone to interpret those replicas according to the rules associated with the legisigns replicated. Conversely, the interpretation of something as the replica of a legisign presupposes that it was produced *in order* to be interpreted *as* a replica of that legisign. Think of the difference between a pile of stones that just happen to be at one side of a forking path and that same pile placed there with the intention of marking a trail: the latter indicates which path to take, while the former has no such significance. In interpreting a pile of stones as a cairn marking a trail, we presume its having been placed there for the purpose of being so interpreted. In this respect, then, legisigns and their replicas differ essentially from signs of other kinds. Other signs may be used to signify, as a piece of cloth may be used as a sample of its color, but, normally, they do not exist in order to be so used, and their significance does not depend upon the fact that they are so used.

It follows that the creation and replication of legisigns is goal-directed. In no other case is sign-production necessarily teleological, even though sign-interpretation always is. But the great tribe of legisigns fall into two distinct groups, depending upon whether they are conventional and their replication intentional, or natural and their replication not intentional though still goal-directed. We will examine conventional legisigns first. The general principles of legisigns presented above, when applied to conventional legisigns specifically, can be expressed in this way: a person who wishes to convey a meaning intends to produce a particular sort of interpretant in the thought, the behavior, or the emotions of a person he is addressing,[7] and he intends to do this by replicating a legisign with which he assumes the person addressed is familiar. But in order to succeed in this the person addressed must recognize that such were the intentions of the speaker. Hence, the speaker must also intend that these intentions of his be recognized. Normally, there is no difficulty in this since legisigns are not usually replicated except with such intentions and since it is usually quite unlikely that the same sounds or shapes would be produced by sheer accident. If an auditor believes that the speaker is babbling insanely or is practicing elocution or is a parrot or otherwise "does not mean what he says", then he will not interpret the sounds heard as signifying what they would signify if meant. (Notice that a person can mean what he says and be lying.)

This is, in part, the same point which the contemporary philosopher, H. P. Grice, is best known for having made. Grice (1968: 1-18) distinguishes between hearer's meaning, word and sentence meaning, and utterer's meaning, and he holds that utterer's meaning is basic. In one place he writes (1957: 45), "'A meant something by x' is roughly equivalent to 'A uttered x with the intention of inducing a belief [or some other effect] by means of the [hearer's] recognition of this intention'." This analysis has been criticized by John Searle (1965: 45) for its having failed "to account for the extent to which meaning can be a matter of rules or conventions''. Searle also points out that Grice makes a related error of not distinguishing, among the effects which the utterer intends to produce in the hearer, between those which are a part of what is said and those that are not. This corresponds to J. L. Austin's distinction (1962: *passim*) between illocutionary force and perlocutionary force. The illocutionary force of a speech act is determined by the conventions governing the words used, while perlocutionary force is a further effect that may be intended or expected to be produced by that speech act in the given situation but which is not a function of linguistic convention.

Peirce's semeiotic not only embraces Grice's insight as a special case of more general principles, but it also anticipates Searle's corrections and forestalls his objections. On Peirce's view, the speaker can intend his intentions to be recognized by the auditor only because he is employing conventional legisigns with which he presumes the auditor is familiar. For the conventions which determine the meanings of these legisigns determine what the intended significance of their replicas may be. At the same time, any further purpose the speaker may have will not be delimited by these conventions and belongs, therefore, to the perlocutionary effect. The intended illocutionary effect is, in Peirce's terms, the immediate interpretant of the utterance. The intended perlocutionary effect may or might not be part of the dynamic interpretant, if any, and it may or might not be part of the final interpretant, depending upon whether the hearer's purposes agree, in that respect, with the speaker's.[8]

Legisigns can be iconic, indexical, or symbolic. Peirce's example (1903: 2.258) of an iconic legisign is "a diagram, apart from its factual individuality". The idea appears to be that a diagram (*qua* general) is a type of icon, replicas of which are readily recognized to be intended to be iconic, and not only iconic, but iconic in a specific way, viz., in respect to the spatial relations of their parts. The usefulness of such legisigns is that when they are used, attention is thereby directed to a specific iconic significance. Anyone educated in our society who sees certain types of lines, curves, etc. on a sheet of paper recognizes them to be diagrams of one sort or another.

There are several types of indexical legisigns, but each is a "general type or law, however established, which requires each instance of it to be really affected by its Object" (1903: 2.259, 2.260). "The demonstrative pronouns, 'this' and 'that' are indices. For they call upon the hearer to use his powers of observation, and so establish a real connection between his mind and the object; . . . The relative pronouns, *who* and *which*, demand observational activity in much the same way, only with them the observation has to be directed to the words that have gone on before" (Peirce 1893: 2.287). "Some indices are more or less detailed directions for what the hearer is to do in order to place himself in direct experiential or other connection with the thing meant" (ibid.: 2.288); the example Peirce gives involves a designation of latitude and longitude. Notice that such directions must make indexical reference, either by demonstrative pronouns or names (*vide infra*), to other individual objects, such as the Earth's equator and poles. Without the use of indices no set of directions would enable us to locate its referent in the actual world; for it would remain perfectly general. Again, indefinite pronouns or quantifying words, such as "any", "every", "some", "at least one", and "none", are indexical "because they inform the hearer how he is to pick out one of the objects intended" (ibid.: 2.289).

No indexical legisign of any of the preceding types signifies an individual; for different replicas of any of these will signify different things. But there are other indexical legisigns whose replicas always signify the same individual thing, class, or stuff, except when the legisign suffers from ambiguity. Ambiguity arises because a legisign is comprised of two sets of rules—one specifying how its replicas are to look or sound and the other specifying how they are to be interpreted. When there are two sets of rules of the latter type conjoined with one of the former type, we have an ambiguous legisign. Putting ambiguity aside, we can say that each replica of the same proper name, e.g., "Napoleon Bonaparte", signifies whatever earlier replicas signified, going back to its original replicas, assigned, by an act of naming—in this case, to a baby that had its hand stuck in its blouse. This account of how proper names signify is drawn from 1906: 4.544, where Peirce said that they "should probably be regarded as Indices, since the actual connection . . . of Instances of the same typical words with the same Objects, alone causes them to be interpreted as denoting those Objects." A similiar account of naming is presupposed in Saul Kripke's view of names as "rigid designators"—a view he extends to names for natural kinds, substances, etc. Kripke's rigid designators are a special type of indexical legisign, of which proper names are a paradigm.[9]

The difference between symbolic and other legisigns is that the rules for indexical or iconic legisigns refer interpreters to indexical or iconic grounds, whereas the rules for symbolic legisigns are themselves grounds of significance (see Peirce 1903: 2.261).[10] When we see a diagram we know that we are to attend to the spatial relations of its parts; when we hear someone say, "There!" we know that he means us to look where he is looking or pointing; but when we see or hear a replica of the word "red" we know, without further ado, what it is that the sign-utterer wishes to convey, namely, the thought of the color red (except in special circumstances, where a different, but equally immediate effect is intended, e.g., a clerk's grabbing a red one off the shelf). This thought, as it occurs in the mind of the sign utterer and again in the mind of the interpreter, is the symbol itself, each of its occurrences being distinct replicas of it. One replica is interpreted by another of the same symbol or by the ultimate interpretant of that symbol. Each replica is an index of the symbol replicated, since it causes interpreters to replicate that same symbol or to form its ultimate interpretant. In ordinary parlance, the word calls the thought to mind.

Examples of conventional symbols are some words—such as some common nouns, adjectives, verbs, and adverbs—statements, and arguments. Discussion of these examples is better postponed until the next section of this paper. Let us now leave the conventional legisigns and turn to their ruder brethren, the natural legisigns. Few explorers of semeiotica have noticed that Peirce explicitly admits the existence of natural legisigns of all kinds, including symbols. Yet in many places Peirce wrote much as he did in 1902, at 2.307, where he defined "symbol" as a sign "which is constituted a sign merely or mainly by the fact that it is used and understood as such, *whether the habit is natural or conventional* (my emphasis). It is easy to see why such passages have failed to register with readers of Peirce. For how can a legisign be *used* except intentionally, by one conscious of what he is doing? And how can the use or replication of a legisign be interpreted as such except by one who has a consciousness of legisigns and their use which answers to that of the user?

Yet we often speak of uses and of using without implying that there is any conscious purpose or intention involved. Infants and dumb brutes use their eyes to see with, a mother marsupial uses her pouch to carry her young, a clever chimpanzee uses a sharp twig to prick out succulent grubs, and so on. We speak of "use" where an artifact has been created or an object selected to do something or where a feature of an organism has been retained in the course of evolution because it has contributed in some way to the survival of the species. And we speak of "using" where that artifact or that organic feature performs its function through the action of some individual.[11] Similarly, we say that the use of the bright colors of male birds is to attract the attention of the females of the same species. But this is a semeiotic phenomenon. The function of these colors is fulfilled only through the response they elicit from the female of the species. The colors have a significance consisting in their potential interpretation by the behavior of female birds. They signify that their bearer is a young man of the right sort—that is the object signified—and this object is grasped in the interpretative response of the female when she acts towards the bearer of those colors as if he were indeed a young man of the right sort. Some male birds indulge also in mating displays. This is their way of saying, "O! What a lusty young fellow am I!"

These colors and antics replicate legisigns. For they would not have their sexual significance except for instincts in the female for so interpreting any such instance of the same pattern. As with the conventional legisigns of human speech, the legisigns of sexual display among male birds developed simultaneously with the disposition to use them (i.e., in actual displays) *and* with the disposition to interpret them. But, unlike the legisigns of human speech, there is with respect to these legisigns a dichotomy between users and interpreters. The male displays, the female reacts appropriately (sometimes).

These legisigns of sexual identity and display are indexical in part. For the attention of the female is directed to that individual bird which actually is so colored or which actually is prancing about, spreading its tail, and so on. However, such legisigns arc primarily symbolic. For the attention they elicit from the female is specifically sexual, answering to the sexual nature and readiness of the male bird. And this specifically sexual nature of the interpretant is determined directly by the female's instinctual rule for interpreting the color and behavior of the male. The individual instance of this color or display is an indexical sinsign of the symbolic legisign it replicates, since it acts directly on the observant female to react as she would react to any instance of that same legisign. But this symbolic legisign includes an indexical component, since the female is to react not only sexually but toward a specific object, viz., the lucky male who provoked that reaction.

Having informed the reader about birds, it is time for a lesson on bees. The dance of the honeybee is another good example of the use and interpretation of natural legisigns. Workers coming back to a hive move about and twiddle in various ways, in response to which departing workers buzz off in definite directions to where the returning workers had found but not exhausted supplies of nectar-laden blossoms. The steps of the dance mean what they do only because of the way in which other bees are programmed to interpret them. The steps are indexical legisigns so far as their replicas indicate definite directions in space, but they are symbolic insofar as they determine departing workers to go in those directions. The interpretant is energetic, not logical. It involves no thought of nectar, yet it is a goal-directed response grounded in the nature of bees.

Consciousness and intentionality are not essential to the existence, replication, or interpretation of legisigns. What is essential is a purpose or goal, whether consciously entertained or not, that is shared by sign-replicator and replica-interpreters.[12] For it is of the essence of legisigns that interpreters would not interpret replicas as they do if legisigns were not replicated in order to elicit those specific interpretations. Replicator and interpreter each presuppose the other and the legisign, and the existence of a legisign presupposes both replicators and interpreters. That is why the whole ensemble of legisign, its user, and its interpreter must come into existence simultaneously, even if gradually.

My purpose in these last paragraphs has not been to argue that animals and plants communicate in the way that humans do. Of course human speech is unique: it consists in the ability to replicate legisigns in ever new patterns, as well as in the ability to create new legisigns, not by the slow process of evolution, but within the lifetimes of individuals, and by their own volition. The point, rather, is that the distinctive power of human speech is not a supernatural gift but is a remarkable development of basic principles found elsewhere in nature. Peirce did not tell us something new and amazing about what animals and plants can do. Instead, he classified familiar phenomena in new and perhaps surprising ways, with the result that we now see connections hitherto obscure and understand much hitherto mysterious. There are signs throughout nature, but there are legisigns only where there is life, and legisigns always exist in order to serve the purposes of living things. Conventional legisigns, created and manipulated by individuals in ways that constantly produce new meanings, are distinctive—perhaps constitutive—of the form of consciousness found in human life.

The distinctive properties of human speech, and the bearing of these on the nature of human consciousness, have not yet been explored in light of Peirce's semeiotic. To do so may result in important contributions to the philosophy of mind. In many places Peirce made suggestions along such lines. I will quote just one of those passages (1906: 4.531):

> A Symbol incorporates a habit, and is indispensable to the application of any *intellectual* habit, *at least*. Moreover, Symbols afford the means of thinking about thoughts in ways in which we could not otherwise think of them. They enable us, for example, to create Abstractions, without which we should lack a great engine of discovery. These enable us to count; they teach us that collections are individuals (individual = individual object), and in many respects they are the very warp of reason.

III.

The third division of signs corresponds to the familiar triad, term/proposition/argument, but is of considerably broader scope (1904: 8.337). Peirce sometimes referred to the three types of sign that make up this trichotomy as *rhemes, dicisigns*, and *arguments*, and sometimes as *semes, phemes*, and *delomes*, respectively. His characterizations of these types of sign varied greatly. In 1908, when this third trichotomy had become the ninth of ten, Peirce presented it in this way (1908: 8.373): "IX. As to the Nature of the Influence of the Sign: Semes, like a simple sign: Phemes, with antecedent and consequent; Delome, with antecedent, consequent, and principle of sequence''. Yet, in 1906, Peirce argued that while terms, propositions, and arguments are traditionally distinguished by degrees of complexity, their distinction from one another ''is by no means a difference of complexity, and does not so much consist in structure as in the services they are severally intended to perform'' (1906: 4.572). These two passages can be reconciled only if we suppose that the structural differences referred to in 1908 pertain to the ''services they are severally intended to perform'' rather than to the signs themselves; that is, the structural differences are not syntactic. This interpretation is supported by the rubric under which Peirce presented the structural distinctions: ''As to the nature of the *Influence* of the Sign'' (my emphasis). Presumably, the reason why Peirce thought that signs of these types do not differ from one another by syntax, is that syntax is so wonderfully flexible and varied. In some contexts a single word can take the place of a proposition or even of an argument. Still, it is not obvious how these structural differences pertain to the services signs are intended to perform or the influence of signs.

In 1903 Peirce wrote that ''A Rheme is a sign which, for its Interpretant, is a sign of qualitative Possibility . . .'' (1903: 2.250); ''A *Dicent Sign* is a Sign which, for its Interpretant, is a Sign of actual existence'' (2.251); ''An *Argument* is a Sign which, for its interpretant, is a Sign of law'' (2.252). But a law could be asserted in a proposition or dicisign or named by a term or rheme. Similarly, a possibility can be asserted or argued for, and an existent can be either named or made the subject of argumentation. What, then, does Peirce mean to be getting at in this passage? The key, I believe, lies in the obscure qualification, ''for its interpretant'', which echoes the notions of influence and service. The emphasis is not on what is signified but is on how the sign ''appeals'' to its interpretant: Peirce makes this clear in the paper of 1906 (''An Apology for Pragmaticism'', 4.572) already referred to: ''. . . when an Argument is brought before us'', Peirce wrote, ''there is brought to our notice . . . a process whereby the Premises bring forth the Conclusion . . . this Process of Transformation is no more built out of Propositions than a Motion is built out of positions. The logical relation of the Conclusion to the Premises might be asserted; but that would not be an Argument. . .''. The assertion of the logical relation would be but one more proposition and not something by which several propositions are bound into one argument (as Lewis Carroll showed in his version of the Achilles and the Tortoise paradox). Whereas a proposition merely informs, an argument ''appeals'' to one (ibid.) ''in virtue of the logical habit which would bring any logical Interpreter to assent to it''. The differences in manner of influence are best stated by Peirce in this same year (1906: 4.538): ''By a *Seme* I shall mean anything which serves for any purpose as a substitute for an object . . .'' ''By a *Pheme* I mean a Sign . . . intended to have some sort of compulsive effect on the interpreter of it.'' ''[A *Delome*] is a Sign which has the Form of tending to act upon the Interpreter through his own self-control, representing a process of change in thoughts and signs, as if to induce this change in the Interpreter.''

A seme does not inform, since it does not compel belief. It serves merely to call something to one's attention. Even if this object is an actuality, that actuality is brought to mind only and, therefore, it is present to mind only as a possibility. If being present to mind does not serve to distinguish possibility from actuality, how is that distinction made? Peirce's answer is that actuality or other facts are represented *qua* facts in the forcefulness of their presentness to mind (see, e.g., c.1895: 2.337). A pheme signifies existence or fact through its own compulsiveness on the interpreter. Existence, for Peirce, consists in dyadic relations of action and reaction, and it is attested to or signified by a corresponding compulsiveness. And law, as that in accordance to which reactions occur, is known through our corresponding habits of self-control. These habits can be practical or purely intellectual; in the latter case they are the "principles of sequence" by which our inferences are governed. In an argument or delome, such laws are presupposed on the part of the interpreter, as that which the interpreter is asked to apply to the premises he is given, to see for himself whether the suggested conclusion follows. The peculiar syntax or other marks by which we know an argument to be one, signify only through the appeal they make to the interpreter to go through a process of inference himself.[13]

It seems to me that this conception of the differences among semes, phemes, and delomes is of great importance. In the first place, it shows that *what* is signified cannot be separated from the manner in which the sign addresses potential interpreters of it. In the second place, this notion of a correspondence of relation to object and relation to interpretant revives in a new and more acceptable form the old Greek idea that like is known by like. Possibility is known through the passive content of experience, actuality is known through the compulsiveness of experience, and laws are known by the habits of self-control in which they are mirrored. Our knowledge of actuality and of necessity cannot be passive, but is one with strenuous existence and deliberate conduct. Yet it does not follow that knowledge, however inseparable it is from practice, cannot be pursued for its own sake. In the third and last place, this fresh view of how signs relate us to the world presents us with many new questions and with new aspects of old questions. For example, in the broad category of delomes, other principles of self-control than the strictly intellectual might be appealed to. Thus, it is for good reason, we now see, that Aristotle discussed the "practical syllogism" in his ethics rather than in his logic; for the principle of sequence to which it appeals is a habit of action rather than a habit of thought.[14]

Despite the virtues of his way of formulating the third trichotomy, there are problems with it which Peirce seems not to have seen and did not resolve. These problems center around Peirce's conceptions of the proposition and of assertion. Before we can formulate these problems we need to see how the third trichotomy relates to the first two.

Any icon must, of course, be a rheme, and so, therefore, must every qualisign. Indices can be either rhemes or dicisigns. "A Rhematic Indexical Sinsign is any object of direct experience so far as it directs attention to an Object by which its presence is caused" (Peirce 1903: 2.256). "A Rhematic Indexical Legisign is any general type or law . . . which requires each instance of it to be really affected by its Object in such a manner as merely to draw attention to that Object" (ibid.: 2.259). In both cases we see the typical function of a rheme: that is, merely to bring something to one's attention. Peirce's example of the first is a spontaneous cry, and of the second, a demonstrative pronoun. "A dicent Sinsign", by contrast, not only draws attention to its object, but "affords information concerning [it]" (2.257).

Peirce's example of a dicent sinsign is a weathercock. The weathercock is by no means a proposition or assertion in the usual sense, and yet it does act compulsively on interpreters of it, causing them to form an opinion about the wind's direction. Not that interpreters are not free to deny what the weathercock indicates, if they have some reason to believe that it is not functioning properly. But in the absence of grounded doubt, a person who knows how to interpret weathercocks cannot help but be influenced by one if he sees it whilst pondering the wind's direction. The weathercock also shares the structural features of propositional significance: it is an index of the wind and it embodies an icon of direction, and the combination of these two signifies that that direction is the wind's direction. "Such a Sign must involve an Iconic Sinsign to indicate the Object to which the information refers. But the mode of combination, or *Syntax* of those two must also be significant" (1903: 2.257).

"A Dicent Indexical Legisign is any general type or law . . . which requires each instance of it to be really affected by its Object in such a manner as to furnish definite information concerning that Object" (1903: 2.260). Peirce's example is a street cry, that is, the typical cry of a vendor, replicas of which serve not only to call attention to their utterer but to inform one of what it is he is selling.

Symbolic legisigns may be either rhemes, dicisigns, or arguments. All arguments are symbolic legisigns. Terms, Peirce indicated, are rhematic symbols (hence, legisigns, since all symbols are legisigns), and propositions are dicent symbols (1903: 2.261-263). But here the trouble begins. The treacherous legisigns at first resist the suggestion that any of them are dicisigns, and then it turns out that even if some of them are dicisigns (of a peculiarly grudging sort), none of them can be propositions anyway.

A legisign in itself is not compulsive. It can act compulsively only through its replicas. But not all replicas, even of such a legisign as "The sky is falling! The sky is falling!" are compulsive. Only those which assert the proposition they express tend to compel belief. Other replicas of the same legisign might be produced non-assertively, e.g., as an hypothesis to ponder or as an exercise in chirography. Therefore, the compulsiveness of such replicas as are compulsive is due not to the legisign replicated but to the special characteristics of those replications. Hence, the legisign that is replicated in an assertion is not compulsive at all. Therefore, it seems that no legisign can be a dicisign. Peirce admitted the non-compulsiveness of any legisign when he wrote that the proposition or, as he maintained that it was, the symbolic dicisign only "*purports* to intend to compel . . . " (c.1902: 2.321, my emphasis). And an argument, he said (ibid.: emphasis added), only "*purports* to intend not compulsion but action by means of comprehensive generals . . . ."

But, then, in 1904 Peirce changed his definition of the dicisign. It became this: that a dicisign is either compulsive (dicent sinsigns) or it is what can be compulsively replicated (dicent legisigns). Thus, "A dicent is not an assertion, but is a sign *capable* of being asserted. But an assertion is a dicent." This requires modification, since not all dicent sinsigns are assertions. Only those which replicate dicent legisigns can be assertions. Other dicent sinsigns, like the weathercock, neither are nor make assertions but are compulsive in some other way.

In c.1902: 2.315, Peirce wrote that ". . . an act of assertion supposes that, a proposition being formulated, a person performs an act which renders him liable to the penalties of the social law (or, at any rate, of the moral law) in case it should not be true, unless he has a definite and sufficient excuse; . . . ." In 1903: 2.235, he made the complementary point that "The assertion consists in the furnishing of evidence by the speaker to the listener that the speaker believes something, that is, finds a certain idea to be definitely compulsory on a certain occasion". It is the speaker's making himself liable to censure if what he says should prove to be wrong which furnishes the evidence that he really believes it. And this, in turn, is reason (not indefeasible) for his auditors to believe it, too. *That* someone asserts something is, other things being equal, sufficient, indeed, compelling reason to believe it.[15]

But what is it that is asserted in an assertion? Peirce spoke, very naturally, of an assertion asserting the proposition which it expresses or formulates.[16] However, a proposition in this sense cannot also be the dicent symbol which the assertion replicates. It is declarative sentences, typically, which are replicated in assertions, but sentences are not what are asserted. Different sentences can sometimes be replicated to assert the same thing (e.g., when you say, "I ache", and when I say to you, "You ache", or, again, when the same thing is said in different languages). And some sentences are such that different assertive replications of them assert different things (e.g., when you and I both utter the words, "I ache"). Therefore, if a proposition is what is asserted, it cannot be the dicent symbol or sentence which the assertion replicates.

There is an interesting way out of these difficulties, but it requires placing propositions, and also concepts and arguments, into a class which Peirce, so far as I know, did not provide for in his classification of signs. A legisign, you will recall, consists of a rule determining the sound or shape of its replicas; but this rule must be associated with a second rule determining how those replicas are to be interpreted. Ambiguity consists in a plurality of rules of interpretation for the same legisign, and change of meaning consists in a change of these associated rules. It follows that the identity of a legisign is fixed only by the rule defining its replicas. Symbolic legisigns are words and sentences and combinations thereof. Now, how shall we describe what happens when the *same* rule of interpretation becomes associated with *different* symbolic legisigns? We could say, very naturally, that these different legisigns express the same concept, the same proposition, or the same argument (depending upon whether the legisigns are rhematic, dicent, or of the form of an argument). It does not follow that concepts, propositions, and arguments are separately existing entities—any more than legisigns exist separately from their replicas. Just as we say that two replicas are replicas of the *same word* when they both accord with the same rule defining replicas of that word, so also can we say that two words express the *same concept* when their replicas are to be interpreted by the same rule. Something similar holds for propositions, only here we must recognize that some dicent symbols do not express just one proposition, since various of their replicas are to be variously interpreted, albeit by the same rule. How all of this can be made to fit into a convincing revision of Peirce's classification of signs is a question that remains to be answered.

We turn, now, to further problems which the third trichotomy presents. If distinctions among rhemes, dicisigns, and arguments depend on a sign's influence on its interpretant, which interpretant is that—the immediate, the dynamic, or the final? In 1904: 8.337-338, Peirce held that rhemes, dicisigns, and arguments are distinguished by their relations to their "signified" (i.e., final) interpretants, while their being presented for contemplation, urged or submitted depends on their relations to their dynamic interpretants. (Arguments, only, can be submitted; but they can also be urged or contemplated; dicisigns can be either urged or contemplated; rhemes can only be contemplated.) (We see here, again, that Peirce changed his conception of this trichotomy, from how it tends to affect interpreters, to how it is *capable* of being used to affect interpreters. As we saw, this revision applies, strictly speaking, only to legisigns.) But, given that dynamic interpretants are formed through the influence of a sign and are steps on the way to the final interpretant, can we really distinguish between the influence of a sign on its final interpretant and its "appeal" (ibid.: 8.388) to its dynamic interpretant? In 1908b: 8.371, Peirce used the relation of a sign to its dynamic interpretant as a basis for a quite different trichotomy: "Suggestive, Imperative, Indicative". At that time semes, phemes, and delomes were still being distinguished by "The Nature of the Influence of the Sign" (ibid.: 8.344). Nevertheless, the same doubt arises: can we separate the appeal of a sign to its dynamic interpretant from its influence?

These and many similar questions must be raised about Peirce's later, expanded classification of signs. He himself made it clear in 1908b: 8.345 that the details of his division of signs according to ten trichotomies were tentative. However, the 1908 division of signs contains important new suggestions, even if they are not properly worked out. For example, imperatives had not earlier found a place in the classification of signs, even though Peirce did discuss imperative utterances in some earlier passages (especially the c.1906 passage, 5.473). Now an imperative seems to be a dicent symbol both in the structure of what it signifies, consisting as it does in a predicate describing what is to be done and a subject indicating who is to do it, and in the compulsiveness of its typical replications. We need to ask how these imperative dicisigns differ from indicative dicisigns. If it is not by their relations to their dynamic interpretants, is it by the nature of the immediate interpretant—energetic vs. logical—they are fit to elicit? In 1908: 8.369 we can see how Peirce first thought this himself but then "with great hesitation" changed his mind.

We are now at the heart of the wilderness. Our native bearers and guides have disappeared into the surrounding darkness. We are left on our own resources. We have followed Peirce's words to this point, but further progress must be made, if at all, on our own. I think we owe it to ourselves, if not to Charles Peirce, to raise the questions he did not live to raise and to see whether the system he originated can be developed to fruition.

12

FLOYD MERRELL

Structuralism and Beyond: A Critique of Presuppositions

The failure of past methods will force man to accept a new conviction lest the old Adam destroy him.

—Lancelot Law Whyte 1944: 245—

Structuralism, Robert Scholes tells us (1974: 3), embodies "a 'scientific' view of the world as both real in itself and intelligible to man". In order to achieve objectivity and descriptive adequacy in the human sciences, structuralists have generally adopted the linguistic model of Ferdinand de Saussure via Prague school structural linguistics.[1] The common assumption has it that structural linguistics, given its method of abstracting language into an autonomous object for empirical analysis, now constitutes itself as a true science, worthy of emulation by other disciplines in the social sciences and in the humanities (see, for example, Lévi-Strauss 1958: 66-79). However, there has been sparse inquiry into the validity of the general "scientific" foundations upon which the structuralist methodology rests.[2] In response to this critical deficiency the present commentary will aim: (1) to subject the underlying presuppositions of structuralism to close scrutiny in the light of past and present scientific paradigms, and (2) to suggest, as a consequence of the first objective, that structuralism is based on premises which are not consistent with current scientific and epistemological lines of reasoning.

All epistemologically sound analytical models must be constructed upon an intrinsically coherent set of presuppositions. On the surface it appears that structuralism complies with this exigency. The structuralists generally put forth the primary assumption that their field of study is analogous to a linguistic, or more precisely a phonological, system. For instance, Claude Lévi-Strauss (1958: 29-53) considers that kinship is governed by rules analogous to those governing phonology. Jacques Lacan (1966: 249-89), after postulating that the unconscious is structured like a language, reinterprets the Freudian topology of the human mind in linguistic terms. And Roland Barthes (1966; see also Kristeva 1967) proposes an analogy between the sentence (microcosm), which constitutes the limits of traditional linguistic study, and the literary text (macrocosm), which is the object of the critic's attention. It is further assumed, then, that the structuralist can study his *corpus* by use of a heuristic device analogous to that used by the structural linguist. Therefore, it follows that since the structuralist method is ultimately tied to a linguistic model, consideration of structuralism's underlying presuppositions entails simultaneously a general statement on the presuppositions of structural linguistics in so far as they overlap.

However, obvious pitfalls appear when attempting to generalize on the presuppositions of a heuristic model which is employed, now methodically, now indiscriminately, by a heterogeneous assemblage of analysts. An insect's eye view of all *ad hoc* analytical techniques formulated in the name of structuralism would be impossible, an interminable Cartesian division into smaller and smaller parts. Consequently, while certain facets of my statements on presuppositions may not apply to all varieties of structuralism, I have attempted to pinpoint in broad terms the general picture of the world which constitutes the epistemological foundations of the movement. These presuppositions are as follows:[3]

(1) The *corpus* chosen for study is an object of "empirical" analysis. However, since true reality "is never the most obvious of realities" (Lévi-Strauss 1955: 61), empirical observation of the entities making up this *corpus* is solely possible by the use of models which have been constructed *a priori*. Neither deductive principles nor empirical evidence can stand alone but they must complement and support one another.

(2) The *corpus* constitutes a closed, homogeneous system of signs which are related in terms of resemblances and differences (Barthes 1964: 97-98). In this system composed of interdependent terms, "the value of each term results solely from the simultaneous presence of the others" (Saussure i.1906-1911: 114). Such an "instantaneous arrangement" of terms must be analyzed as a static state of existence irrespective of time, for it is absolutely impossible to study simultaneously relations in time and relations within the system (ibid.: 81). For instance, in the case of language, the individual speaker is confronted with a system. As far as he is concerned at the moment he emits an utterance, time has no bearing; it is only a factor in the socio-historical context. His utterance exists instantaneously with all aspects of the linguistic system and past and future states are of no consequence. In other words, "language is for him a perpetual present, with the possibilities of meaning implicit in its every moment" (Jameson 1972: 6).

(3) The notion of a closed system implies an autonomous grouping of signs (linguistic or extralinguistic) which move laterally within the system from term to term rather than projecting outside the system from term to thing. This provides the system with an inner form where the concept of one sign becomes the denotate (object) of another sign. The relation between signifier and signified (the two elements making up the sign) is completely arbitrary since there are no physical cause and effect relations between them (Saussure i.1906-1911: 67-69).[4]

(4) The system must be methodically decomposed into a set of abstract parts which are analyzed in terms of their mutual relations. This is accomplished by constructing a taxonomic chart of all possible permutations between the elements making up the system. Such a chart represents the underlying reality of the *corpus* as opposed to its surface empirical phenomena, and its analysis involves a reconstruction of the *corpus* during which time meaning is disclosed. Meaning, therefore, is not derived directly from the content but by explicating the potential and actual relations between all elements making up that content (see Barthes 1964: 58-88).

(5) It follows from the preceding presupposition that the isolated terms, or elements, in the system are never absolute; they take on meaning only when integrated into the system. *Gestalt* psychology, an influence on both Lévi-Strauss and Jakobson, similarly focusses on patterns of mutual dependencies and indivisible

wholes rather than on isolated elements. Obviously in reaction against atomistic empiricism, both *Gestalt* psychology and structuralism attempt to move toward a "unified field" approach which is not without analogy to twentieth century theories in the physical sciences. Just as in the sciences doubt has recently arisen concerning the substantive quality of the atom, so the structuralist approach posits that content is in reality form, and analysis of this unobservable form calls for a model which reveals to the observer that which is unavailable to immediate perception (see Nutini 1970: 70-107).

(6) The *system* lies behind a general *process*. System is characterized as conservatism, stability, crystallization, process as a chaos of contingency, fortuitous links, and accidental encounters. Hence synchrony and diachrony (system and process) must be maintained in rigid opposition.[5] For instance, Saussure (i.1906-1911: 19) strictly distinguishes between *langue*, the social product which "exists in the form of a sum of impressions deposited in the brain of each member of a community", and *parole*, a conscious individual act. System, which can be analyzed objectively, must take precedence over process, which lends itself solely to subjective interpretation. By logical extrapolation of this postulate, it becomes possible to analyze the underlying reality of social phenomena and move from conscious phenomena to the study of unconscious infrastructure (Lévi-Strauss 1967: 31).

(7) Change, with respect to the system, is unintelligible. It is only understood as the passage from one state to another, as a series of discontinuous shifts (Lévi-Strauss 1966: 269-70). The system can never be modified directly. Certain elements replace others to throw the system out of equilibrium, but this disequilibrium will call for the establishment of new grounds of solidarity which bind all the elements to the whole. Although in this scheme linear cause and effect is of no consequence, a form of "structural causality" prevails wherein the system determines not only the nature of systematic equilibrium at a given moment, but immanently contains vestiges of all past equilibriums and the seeds of all future states of affairs. The underlying system is simultaneously mutable and immutable: mutable as a collective though intangible entity undergoing "structural changes" in time (Jakobson 1931: 334), and immutable since, in language for example, the utterances of the individual speaker represent mere "accidents" in time and are totally incapable of changing the linguistic system (Saussure i.1906-1911: 78).

(8) Man himself is excluded as an object of study. The subject and the situation cannot be considered since man (subject), his cultural products (object), and his socio-historical context (situation), are not susceptible to the same analytical model. Man is looked upon as the instrument through which cultural phenomena (i.e., language, myth, religion, art, etc.) manifest themselves, and he consequently "disappears", as a concrete being toward which inquiry is directed, to become an idealized abstraction. For instance, while existentialism and phenomenology attempt to know man through personal identity between analyst and analyzed, the structuralist, as a detached observer devoid of moral or metaphysical pretenses, considers not man nor his situation but the products of his mental activity. The first may be conceived as an attempt to understand Being "in relation to oneself", while the second is an attempt to understand "Being in relation to itself" (Lévi-Strauss 1955: 62).[6]

(9) The eighth presupposition implies a relatively uninvolved spectator who organizes his data in accordance with *a priori* assumptions as well as by means

of empirical observation. It follows, then, that if (a) the structures of the observed phenomena are organized by the preconceiving mind of the spectator, and (b) the *corpus* is studied in so far as it is the product of human mental processes, then (c) the true object of study is not substantive but mental; that is, a reciprocal exchange between the absent mind of the producer of cultural artifacts and the mind of the contemplator of those artifacts.[7] At the same time the structuralist, in contrast to the phenomenologist and the existentialist, purports to analyze the *corpus* from outside rather then relive the historical situation surrounding the phenomena. As a result, the structuralist perspective is doubly an abstraction. It abstracts by removing the observed data from its historical context (and hence the danger of falling into the "formalist fallacy"). And it abstracts in as much as man is removed from his cultural products (and the structuralists' "disappearance" of man threatens to become a reality). (See Krader 1974: 336-61.)

The epistemological roots of structuralism go deep. Embodied in the movement is a reaction against atomistic and mechanistic ways of thinking. Atomists conceive reality as an aggregate of individual elements while mechanists place their faith in a linear, materialistic cause and effect explanation of all phenomena. Structuralism, purportedly holistic, non-material, acausal, and non-linear, nonetheless discloses at the level of its root presuppositions, an incapacity to gain total emancipation from those very scientific conventions against which it is rebelling. It now becomes necessary to expound on those scientific conventions in order to determine the constraints preventing structuralism from constituting a truly novel approach to the study of man.

The scientific world view up to and including the nineteenth century was identified primarily with the names of Galileo, Descartes, and Newton. Classical physics conceived the cosmos as a "giant machine", a homogeneous universe of perfect symmetry and clockwork precision; and God was precisely the guardian of the key with which to wind that clock. The dream of this new science which could transform and perfect man by making him a manipulable working part in this "great machine" was brought to its most sublime expression by Laplace. At the end of the eighteenth century, he euphorically proclaimed that a superhuman Intelligence could know at any given instant the exact positions of all cosmic bodies and the forces between them, and could derive from this configuration a prediction of their positions at any future time. Nothing would be uncertain. The future, like the past, would be simultaneously present to the eyes of this omniscient observer (Matson 1966: 11).

Laplace's superintelligence became the paradigm to be emulated by science. Natural phenomena, it was assumed, consisted of an aggregate of objects entirely detached from, and independent of, the observer-scientist. This assumption logically led to the notion of a "common-sense" view of nature where there existed no discrepancy between appearance (the sense-data reaching the observer) and reality (the actual world of things). Such a belief constituted a philosophical creed in itself. No attempt was made to justify it by abstract argument; so long as it worked satisfactorily none seemed to be needed, the success of the science based upon it providing a sufficient justification (Jeans 1959: 1-2).

Moreover, according to classical physics, Euclidean space was regarded as a homogeneous, immutable medium whose existence was logically prior to the material objects contained within it. The binary opposition, "full: empty", became a fundamental scientific metaphor. Space, it was assumed, constituted a void (emptiness) in contrast to matter, which was defined as a *plenum*. Since space was a neutral container totally independent of its material content, changes could be perceived solely in the positions of the bodies in space but none in space itself since it was, *ipso facto*, unchangeable. Time, like space, was considered independent with respect to its content. Just as matter "filled" portions of space, so changes "filled" segments of time, and just as space was a receptacle for all matter, so time was a neutral container for all changes. The difference rested in that while spatial relations were defined as juxtaposition, temporal relations were conceived in terms of succession, or contiguity. Consequently, the uniformity of space became counterpart to temporal uniformity, or more expressively designated, to *uniform fluidity*. Material bodies in space changed in time, but time itself could not undergo a change for it was considered, like space, a homogeneous medium. Hence the homogeneity of space demanded temporal homogeneity (Capek 1961: 7-53).

The upshot of the above formulations was finally that both space and time must be *instantaneous* (de Broglie 1937: 14-15). Matter consisted of discrete, discontinuous corpuscles existing in empty, homogeneous space and time. The configuration described by the sum of these corpuscles was defined as a cross-section of simultaneous spatio-temporal entities. In this manner the universe was considered a succession of instantaneous configurations of matter, a static, closed, predetermined and forever determinable system. A moment of time became nothing but a "knife edge", as William James describes it, an instantaneous flash which photographs the simultaneous positions of matter partially filling up the void. At a given instant, the resultant configuration represented the predetermined effect of all past configurations and simultaneously implied all future configurations. Hence the universe was presented as a mathematical series of contiguous states, each constituting an instantaneous configuration of discrete corpuscles—quasi-infinite in number—with definite mass, position, and velocity. A transition from one state to another was no more than a variation in this configuration due to the physical interactions (mechanical cause and effect) between these corpuscles. As they were displaced in space a new configuration would ensue such that there could be no change in the inherent nature of the content (corpuscles) nor alteration in the attributes of the containers (space and time), but only in the positions of the elements composing that content. Matter thus became indifferent to the lapse of time, and time became a mere accident, a succession of instants totally independent of material attributes. Hence this quantitative and qualitative immutability of matter was counterpart to the homogeneous, but unrelated, flow of time (Whitehead 1948: 41-56).

In such a scheme of things, time became superficial, a dispensable entity delegated to secondary categories, while space, as the container in which material corpuscles must react, acquired paramount importance. This tendency to "spatialize time" may actually be traced to the dawn of Western thought, when Parmenides and the Eleatics attempted to reduce becoming to being, process to state, content to form (Capek 1961: 136).[8] According to the Eleatic conception of the universe the directional flow of time loses its objective meaning and the hoary image of Nietzsche's "eternal return" becomes not merely a romantic illusion but a mathematical possibility, for:

In infinity, at some moment or other, every possible combination must once have been realized; not only this, but it must have been realized an infinite number of times. And inasmuch as between every one of these combinations and its next recurrence every other possible combination would necessarily have been undergone, and since every one of these combinations would determine the whole series in the same order, a circular movement of absolutely identical series is thus demonstrated: the universe is thus shown to be a circular movement which has already repeated itself an infinite number of times, and which plays its game for all eternity (Nietzsche 1883-1888: 126).

The image of man suffers in this classical picture of the world for it ultimately implies: (1) the elimination of all notion of *purpose* from the universe, since changes and future states are described simply as the inevitable consequences of prior conditions (Bohr 1958: 95), and (2) the removal of man, as a subjective feeling being, from the center of a universe mathematically defined in terms of primary qualities (that which is not observable by the senses but which can be qualitatively measured). Hence, a "mathematical finality" was imposed on the physical as well as the human sciences (Bronowski 1955: 46).

It was mentioned above that structuralism generally adopts the linguistic model. For instance, Jakobson posits (1963: 157-62)[9] the existence of a hierarchy of ever-widening linguistic systems (i.e., phonemes ⟨ morphemes ⟨ sememes, et al.). These systems are "isomorphic"; that is to say, rules governing a lower system will also govern a higher system. By extrapolation, what is true of the hierarchy of linguistic systems must also be true of semiological systems in general. Therefore, the linguistic model, one semiological system in the hierarchy, becomes analogous to patterns of exchange and "primitive" myth (Lévi-Strauss' kinship and *Mythologiques*), foods (the "culinary triangle" of Lévi-Strauss), clothing styles (Barthes' *Système de la mode*), bourgeois "myths" (Barthes' *Mythologies*), literary structures (Barthes, Tzvetan Todorov, A. J. Greimas, et. al.), the topology of the mind (Lacan), economic intrastructures (Althusser), and even the myth of Superman (Umberto Eco).[10]

Structuralism, then, appears to be guided by a "law of relative magnitudes", the notion that as one proceeds from the infinitesimal to the infinite, he will encounter worlds within worlds, each "isomorphic" to the world enclosing it. What is true of the phoneme must obviously be true also for the morpheme, the sentence, discourse, myths, literature, kinship, culture, *ad infinitum*. This line of reasoning is analogous to the nature of Lilliput, that miniature world in *Gulliver's Travels* constructed as a scale model for our own world. Such "Chinese box" models have been posited time and time again as hypostats with which to interpret reality, but in general they have proved fallacious. For example, the "Lilliputian fallacy" was disclosed in the physical sciences when it was demonstrated that the assumed analogy between the atom and our solar system was false. Such fundamental errors in science may be construed as manifest proof that the tendency of the mind to move along pathways of least resistance does not necessarily lead to truth.[11] In reality, "macrosystems" do not always abide by the same rules nor do they inextricably manifest the same structures as the "microsystems" contained within them. On the contrary, while the phonemic system operates on a level of higher "logical typing" (i.e., greater simplicity and order) larger cultural systems manifest higher levels of organizational complexity whose "logical typing" is by nature highly differentiated, allowing for less order but more vagueness and ambiguity.[12]

The problematic involved in *ad hoc* models constructed on the basis of what is known to be "common sense" knowledge has become apparent. In addition to the potential falsity of the models, a greater danger rests in what Arthur Eddington (1958: 109, 112) terms the "Procrustean treatment", that is, the habit of forcing the data at hand into a preconceived mold. It will be recalled that Procrustes cut down or stretched his guests to fit the bed he had constructed, and then wrote a scholarly paper "On the Uniformity of Stature of Travellers". Unfortunately in a world which rewards him who is consistently "right"—even though many who have contributed most to the history of thought have in the long run been wrong—to expose the falsity of one's model is anathema. The more "respectable" alternative is to alter things a bit so as to assert the model's validity.

To reiterate conclusions derived from the second section of this article, the classical conception of an instantaneous universe presupposes space as a homogeneous "container" to be "filled" by material objects, and time as a chronically homogeneous "container" to be "filled" with a series of infinitesimal instants. Structuralism is founded upon presuppositions strikingly similar to those of Newtonian physics. An instantaneous configuration of structures is presumed to exist within an isolated system where the seeds of all future conditions of structure are contained within the present configuration which in turn is the logical culmination of all past states.

Furthermore, a form of "causality" is assumed possible in a system composed of a continuous series of instantaneous states, each being represented by a complex configuration of simultaneous, atomistic entities with sharply defined structures and boundaries. A given configuration is implied in all past configurations (since the structural changes consist of displacements of elements in the structures) and in turn implies all future ones. The root structural models (i.e., the "actantial" model of Greimas, the "triadic" model of Bremond, the "homological" model of Lévi-Strauss, the "generative-transformational" model of Todorov, the "Schemes" of Lacan, etc.) assume structures composed of homogeneously organized elements existing in space and time. The flow of time, however, has nothing to do with the nature of the structures. One structure is replaced by another in a reversible, atemporal scheme devoid of traditional considerations of physical cause and effect. It is nonetheless causal: a form of "structural causality". According to this conception of things, a given instant of time is independent of all other instants. The passage of time becomes mere illusion since structure and its laws of commutation, permutation, transformation, etc., are identical whether considered diachronically in time or "spatially" across cultures at a given instant of time.[13] Therefore, history, or the chronological flow of time, becomes a mere "myth" created by Western thought to perpetuate the bourgeois idea of progress (see "History and Dialectic", in Lévi-Strauss 1962a: 245-69).

"Structural causality", in the final analysis, implies that from one particular instantaneous state of the universe (past, present, or future) all other states can be derived, a mechanistic scheme whose terminology is remarkably compatible with the Newtonian corpuscular-kinetic picture of the world. Spatial configurations of immutable structures determine the distinctions to be found in all successive configurations while the content of those structures is of little consequence. In such a timeless scheme, the universe becomes a conglomerate of subsytems which set up constraints and limit man to certain predetermined paths. Ultimately the end product is a static state not unlike the second law of thermodynamics; that is, the entrophy principle, another convention of nineteenth century physics. This picture of the world is evoked by Saussure's monstrous chess game analogy to language. On the chessboard an aggregate of "objects" can be rearranged in a calculable but quasi-infinite number of possible combinations. Saussure's analogy automatically implies a closed universe, a Laplacean system *par excellence*, in which linguistic constraints are equally as immutable as the structures they determine. In such a universe the structuralist method of viewing man and his cultural products in terms of homogeneity, relations of similarity, opposition, reciprocity, etc., appears to be the line of least resistance.

The instantaneous arrangement structuralism posits is nowhere more explicit than in Lévi-Strauss' analogy (1964: 14-30) between music and myth. The "melody" (diachronic aspect) of the myth may be read as one reads any other story, but to derive meaning from the myth it must be read in terms of its "harmony" (synchronic aspect). This constitutes a timeless reading of "instantaneous chords" through space. Such a synchronic reading of the myth breaks it up into discontinuous (timeless) entities which are determined by their spatial relations rather than by their content. The subsequent system of relations must by nature be static, a hermetic chamber containing a finite number of elements continually displacing one another. Hence to base the study of myths, as does Lévi-Strauss, on a linguistic model implies automatic reduction of all myths to their discontinuous rudiments. The observation that the phonemic aspect of language consists primarily of discontinuous signs, oppositions, and static binaries is well taken and perhaps correct. However, explication of myths and other mental constructs in terms of these same discontinuous categories is undoubtedly tenuous. The problem hearkens back to Heraclitus. Oppositions such as night and day, this Greek philosopher says, are illusions, since there is always a continuum of gradations between each element of the binary. Man unconsciously confers upon a dynamic reality those static linguistic categories which distort rather than fully explicate. Hence although our awareness of reality may be, as Michael Polanyi tells us (1969 123-80), a form of "tacit knowledge", that reality must inexorably remain, due to our linguistic limitations, ineffable.[14]

As a result of the posited "instantaneous arrangement" of the *corpus*, structural analysis usually entails construction of static taxonomic systems. Taxonomy presumes a structured (dead) corpus as well as a closed system. It may appear at the outset that a rough analogy can be established between the present classificatory state of many structuralist studies and the state of botany under Linnaeus. Species and genera were, for Linnaeus, fixed forms, rather than stages in an ongoing theory of evolution.[15] This analogy, however, disintegrates upon realization that while the natural sciences progressed from static classificatory systems to the notion of evolution, for the human sciences the situation was reversed. The evolutionary concept derived from within the natural sciences was dumped on the human sciences when in their infant stage. This evolutionary vision of reality consequently abetted the idea that Western societies represent a superior, more highly evolved form of civilization. Structuralism, especially that of Lévi-Strauss, can be conceived as a reaction against such ethnocentrism, a reaction well taken. But the consequent reversion to a static science of taxonomy is fraught with difficulties, chief of which is the structuralist movement's discontinuous view of reality (see Culler 1973: 20-36). It is interesting to note that structuralism has been termed a "predialectics" (Seve 1969: 108-50). This label attests to the static quality of the structuralist method while placing it historically prior to the birth of modern sociology, anthropology, economics, and other human sciences. In the final analysis, rather than looking beyond, the structuralist movement gives in to a conservative tendency, propagating images of static equilibrium, enclosure, timelessness, and spatialization.[16] This conservative element becomes more evident when observing that structuralism has been influenced by mathematics only in so far as closure can be maintained. For instance, the cybernetic model adopted by Piaget and Lévi-Strauss is, strictly speaking, the earlier closed-system cybernetics entailing a static form of equilibration (homeostasis) developed by Wiener and others during the 1950's (Wilden 1972: 230-73, 302-50). Group theory, which has contributed much to structuralist methodology, implies a closed system of permutations wherein the "eternal return" is an ongoing reality, a system akin to the "cosmic cycle" of the Greeks (Keyser 1956: pp. 1538-1557). And information theory is adopted only in as much as it will not go beyond the hermetic enclosure established by structuralism (Wilden 1972: 351-94).

Therefore, the structuralist "rage" is in reality the stepchild of the classical model of the universe. Although Democritean atomism is presumably discarded, structuralism remains in essence "macroatomistic". That is to say, while the elements within a given system are not considered as "atoms" *qua* atoms, but "real" only in so far as they fit into a combinatorial system, that system is nevertheless effectively isolated from all other systems to become a "macroatom."[17] A few structuralists, such as Jakobson, voice vague speculations concerning an integrative "system of systems", but make little or no attempt to establish a rigorous intersystemic model. On the other hand, it has been proposed that "homologies" can be established between systems, but only a few, notably Lucien Goldmann, have attempted such a study.[18]

In short, the Newtonian model "spatializes" time whereas the structuralist model "synchronizes" process. Space, according to the classical notion of the universe, is the eternal and immutable medium providing for perpetuation of a clockwork universe. Similarly, structure gives order to an otherwise chaotic universe which consists of an incessant flow of meaningless sense perceptions. Whether the system behind randomness is conceived as space (the eternal void to be filled with neutral material) or structure (the neutral emptiness which provides for eternal orderliness), man in either case is displaced from the "center" to become a passive object, acted upon by opposing material objects or existing as a mere instrument by means of which the system discloses itself.[19]

Consider for a moment that in the classical view of the universe and in the structuralist system, the "spatialization" of time and the "synchronization" of process derive from a tacit avoidance of history, a non-conscious effort to halt the threat of continually generated novelty. The Newtonian model was founded upon a faith in indefinite and inevitable progress. This convention, fortified by nineteenth century utopian philosophy, was predicated upon a "doctrine" whose underlying structure revealed a fundamental antinomy: the inherently static, cyclical nature of the explanatory model which was finally revealed by Nietzsche and others. In contrast, the structuralist conceptual framework rejects faith in the inevitable progress of human culture. Does this indicate that no comparable anomaly exists at the roots of the structuralist world view? An answer must be voiced in the negative. For on further observation it is ascertained that, implicitly in structuralism and explicitly in existentialism (the philosophical movement it was to displace), there is a preoccupation with non-Being, or nothingness. This preoccupation goes back to the philosophy of Pascal, whose *angst* stems from the realization of man's finitude, in a Newtonian world, between the infinite vastness of an empty universe and the infinitesimal minuteness of atomic substance. In this classical view of the universe, space becomes paramount. Space is defined as non-Being (void) in opposition to Being, and it simultaneously takes on the attributes of the Deity, since by its very nature it must precede matter.[20] In a similiar manner, structuralism tacitly assumes that the "holes", or empty "slots" to be filled, precede the content. It is not as if Carroll's Cheshire Cat were erased to leave only the smile (structure). The smile is the "emptiness" which demands to be filled. It exists prior to the Cat and requires that the Cat be "structured" to fit.

The structuralist notion of "emptiness" is perhaps best illustrated by Lacan's "lack of being" (*manque d'être*) which is an attempt to conceptualize that persistent human yearning for the absent origin. The primordial "lack" is a sort of "hole" in the system, a basic fault whose fulfillment is prompted by the subject's desire.

It is the "movement" of language, an incessant play of signifiers taking place in a linguistic "space", which potentially fills the emptiness. Modern man, unlike the "primitive" described by Lévi-Strauss, enjoys no stable ontological "center". He has before him only the yawning void since the origin has been cut off from him. Consequently through language, desire attempts to symbolically fill up the "hole" and restore man's primordial "lack" to its full status as being (Lacan 1966).

A similiar notion is found in the analyses of Lévi-Strauss where the structures embody an intrinsic "free play" without any external fixed point of reference. Lévi-Strauss chooses a "reference myth" to function as a prototype, an autonomous point about which his study of other myths can revolve. But this reference myth itself holds no privileged position; it is simply employed as a handle by means of which reality can be grasped (see Derrida 1970). Hence Lévi-Strauss' reference myth temporarily occupies the elusive center, and the myths he studies are situated in a sort of complex mosaic where, as in Baroque style, the "empty spaces" are conveniently filled. However, this system is still "a sort of Newtonian universe without any God to wind it up" (Wilden 1968: 218). While Lacan's "emptiness" is potentially filled by the desiring subject, Lévi-Strauss' "empty slot" is temporarily filled—albeit at the expense of a stable point of reference—and the "center" becomes illusory, an "unmoved mover" which is neither God, nor man, but system. Through a series of myths which are not spoken by man but speak themselves through man, this system is revealed.

Although it is generally assumed that structuralism and existentialism are diametrically opposed, they remain on common grounds in so far as: (1) they reject conventional atomism, empiricism, and the Newtonian world, and (2) they have been unable to gain total emancipation from the earlier epistemological tradition. As was concluded above, according to the structuralist picture of the world, time is "accidental", structure (space) is paramount, and "emptiness" (nothingness in existentialist terminology) precedes substance. In contrast, the existentialist Martin Heidegger asks the fundamental question: Why is there something rather than nothing? Here the existence of "things" appears to be accidental, a situation brought about by the whims of contingency. Heidegger also contradicts structuralism's "synchronization" of process, contending that man is defined in and through time, and actively projects his temporality onto nothingness. However, contrary to Heidegger, who says that nothingness negates itself, Jean Paul Sartre claims that nothingness cannot negate itself but must be negated by an outside force: consciousness. In contrast to the structuralist view, then, man is defined by his consciousness rather than by motivations the nature of which he is unaware. This conscious being which brings nothingness into the world is its own nothingness; or in Sartre's words (1943: 21), "Nothingness lies coiled in the heart of being, like a worm". Therefore, according to the existentialist, nothingness comes into the world through being, which is its own nothingness. This conception is analogous to that of the classical thinker. Imbued with the Newtonian picture of the world, he postulates that space is the emptiness in which material objects exist, and those material objects contain their own emptiness: that is, the emptiness which remains when they are displaced. The Pascalian fear of "empty spaces", as they are conceived from within the Newtonian cosmological framework, becomes a variant of the existentialist dread of nothingness. Emptiness is necessary for the existence of materialness and material objects give rise to the need for emptiness, a complementary (dialectical in the terminology of Sartre) relationship where the annihilation of one brings forth the creation of the other.

Existentialist *praxis* constitutes an attempt to come to grips with the void and with the contingency of beingness and death, since the existence of nothingness is dependent on consciousness of being. Structuralism, on the other hand, aims at the unconscious in human culture. An invariant topology of the mind becomes the paradigm for all structures (predominantly binary) which provide the "slots" to be filled with content. However, structure, Lévi-Strauss tells us (cited in Caws 1970: 197-215), *is* content; it lies at the very heart of substantiality as the *conditio sine qua non* of the content's existence. Hence, the following schema of "structural permutations" between the classical, existentialist, and structuralist world views can be constructed.[21]

Structure "structurally" displaces space (the void) and nothingness in the first two cosmologies. This not only reveals the underlying import of the notion of non-Being but also further discloses the structural movement's incapacity totally to abolish past conventions. The structuralist paradigm represents in reality nothing more than a "permutation" of concepts rather than the replacement of one model by a new model. The above schema is analogous to the *Weltanschauung* approach to the philosophy of science which has become respectable in recent years. It behooves us to look into this approach in order to comprehend more adequately the structuralist movement.[22] According to Stephen Toulmin, a new scientific *Weltanschauung* is developed by a restatement of various laws, ideals, and

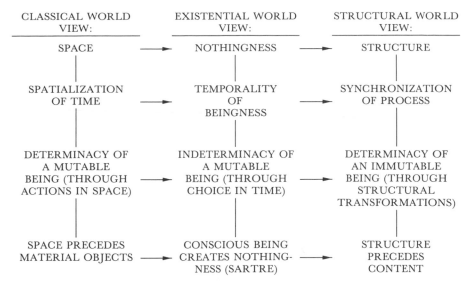

CLASSICAL WORLD VIEW:	EXISTENTIAL WORLD VIEW:	STRUCTURAL WORLD VIEW:
SPACE	NOTHINGNESS	STRUCTURE
SPATIALIZATION OF TIME	TEMPORALITY OF BEINGNESS	SYNCHRONIZATION OF PROCESS
DETERMINACY OF A MUTABLE BEING (THROUGH ACTIONS IN SPACE)	INDETERMINACY OF A MUTABLE BEING (THROUGH CHOICE IN TIME)	DETERMINACY OF AN IMMUTABLE BEING (THROUGH STRUCTURAL TRANSFORMATIONS)
SPACE PRECEDES MATERIAL OBJECTS	CONSCIOUS BEING CREATES NOTHING-NESS (SARTRE)	STRUCTURE PRECEDES CONTENT

hypotheses using terms borrowed from earlier scientific formulations. However, as the terms are transported from one *Weltanschauung* to another, their meanings are invariably altered. This incorporation of traditional terms into new explanatory models such that the meaning of the terms is changed constitutes what Toulmin calls a *language shift* (1953: 13-16, 159-170; 1961: 62-98). The meanings of semantically transmuted terms occurring in scientific theories are theory dependent, and, when taken out of the context of their scientific *Weltanschauung*, the semantic fullness of these terms is inevitably destroyed.

Thomas S. Kuhn (1962: 52-91), in contrast to Toulmin, is concerned with the "structural" analysis of scientific thought. Both epistemologists view science as operating from within particular world views which govern the perspectives by means of which phenomena are observed and regulate the criteria of theory formulation. However, while Toulmin maintains that science undergoes an evolutionary development by assimilating new concepts to the existing *Weltanschauung*, Kuhnian scientific thought is fundamentally discontinuous and revolutionary. All great scientific theories, Kuhn argues, have developed out of the general acceptance of a new pattern of thought, or a "paradigm", which leads to the construction of a particular view of reality. The acceptance of revolutionary paradigms such as the Copernican, Newtonian, and Einsteinian models of the universe, entails the construction of an entirely new map which is then used as a basis for further scientific theory making. However, "anomalies" gradually appear in a given scientific view of the world as it is subjected to successive refinement. The established paradigm is used to explain away the anomalies by auxiliary appendages. Gradual multiplication of these appendages leads to increased disenchantment within the scientific community until finally the model is rejected and another takes its place. Kuhn's "structural" interpretation contradicts the idea of progress inherent in Toulmin's conception of the history of science. Progress is only relative, for it is measured from within a given world of ideas that are conditioned by a choice of one from among a number of possible, but equally valid, models of the universe.

The general approaches of Toulmin and Kuhn are based on three assumptions: (1) perception is *Weltanschauung*-bound, since a given picture of the world determines to a large degree one's perception and consequent interpretation of reality, (2) meanings are perception-bound, since, if the *Weltanschauung* governs one's view of reality, the meaning conveyed to him by that reality will be incorporated into his mental scheme in a manner different from that of another person who possesses a distinct picture of the world, and (3) language does not imprison man's cognitive capacities, as the orthodox structuralists would have it, but it is used as an instrument by means of which man draws from the vast untapped pool of potential knowledge. Thus both epistemological hypotheses attempt to discover the underlying nature of scientific theories "through an examination of their linguistic formulatons, and on occasion even seem to assume that the theory is its linguistic formulation" (Suppe 1974: 221).[23]

The problem with Kuhn's revolutions and Toulmin's language shifts is that they do not readily go to completion. Rather than one paradigm "structurally" replacing another or one meaning being replaced by another, generations are required for a community to adjust to a new way of thinking (Bridgman 1950: 103). For instance, Capek asserts (1961: 264) that centuries of conditioning have integrated the Newtonian paradigm into our "intellectual subconscious". Consequently, "we fail to realize that the very terms 'motion' and 'displacement' are thoroughly inadequate because they are tinged with misleading classical associations. The continued use of these terms . . . indicates the reluctance of our Newtonian subconscious to depart from traditional habits of thought." This "semantic inertia" is responsible for numerous incidents in the history of science where obstinate terminology reflecting conservative underlying mental habits prevents novel ideas from emerging in their fullness. Similarly, Anthony Wilden demonstrates (1972: 230) how Piaget, Lacan, and Lévi-Strauss use "scientific terminology" in such a way as to depict a world view which is not compatible with contemporary scientific thought nor with what they are actually trying to say.[24]

In short, according to the *Weltanschauung* approach, cognition takes precedence over language. The latter does not rule over the former although it might appear that way given the conservative tendency to follow the line of least resistance and yield to "semantic inertia".

Let us consider further the structuralist movement in light of the twentieth century "Einsteinian paradigm". It is now commonplace in the physical sciences that the notion of a detached observer is illusory. The mind cannot be excluded from the world since it is an integral part of that world, and mental processes, both conscious and unconscious, must be included in that which is observed. The scientist cannot know anything about anything without getting involved, either directly or indirectly, with the object of observation. Thus "no knowledge of any physical property or even mere existence is possible without interaction" (Bridgman 1950: 95). In this context a scientific theory becomes a picture of man's relationship with nature, and as this relationship changes, the theory also must undergo alteration (Heisenberg 1967: 27-29). It is significant, then, that Eddington (1958: 16-27) calls contemporary scientific theory "a priori knowledge", an epistemological stance he justifies on the grounds that the universe described by the scientist is not wholly objective but partially subjective.

Leading structuralists often voice platitudes concerning the synthesis of the Cartesian subject-object dichotomy. Nevertheless, in actual practice the structuralist method generally presupposes an objective, uninvolved observer who discloses the structure of either the *corpus* or, especially in the case of Lévi-Strauss, the mind that created the *corpus* (Krader 1974: 352).[25] It is an ironical turn of events that while the physical sciences have been hard at work to liberate themselves from the "myth" of objectivity, predictability, and in general, the tyranny of method, in the human sciences the trend has been toward more rigidly defined methodologies. Models at times are taken at face value as *a priori* truths and relationships are usually considered to be invariant.

It is evident from the foregoing that structuralism's underlying presuppositions stubbornly reveal vestiges of archaic epistemological conventions. Just as the special and general theories of relativity were unable in the first decades to replace effectively the Newtonian primacy of space with a genuine relativistic space-time fusion (Capek 1961: 157-87), so structuralism has apparently been incapable of emancipation from an earlier dogmatic epistemology. For instance, the Newtonian timelessness of space is founded upon an assumed dichotomy and categorical separation between matter and space. Relativity theory dissolves this dichotomy, and space can no longer be considered merely a static, neutral container. Instead of matter partially filling the emptiness of space, "it would be more accurate to speak of space being fused with its changing and dynamic physical content" (ibid.). However, the classical distinction between "fullness" and "emptiness" was carried over into the early "unified field" theories of Einstein, Eddington, Schrödinger, and others, a notion that actually goes back to a Laplacean universe (Monod 1970: 43). Nevertheless, in spite of this inevitable tendency toward "linguistic conservatism", some of the great minds of the present century have brought forth a new image of the world which goes far beyond their original intent. The Newtonian image of empty space can now be looked upon as simply an artifact of our thinking (Bridgman 1959: 197-98). Recent theories more rightly postulate that space does not exist prior to matter nor is it a neutral homogeneous container. The very existence of space comes into being in simultaneity with the appearance of matter at a given stage in the space-time continuum.

Equally, we can postulate that the "full: empty" distinction is invalid with respect to structuralism. The universe, be it in the physical or the mental sense, does not consist of a system of invariant structures persisting through time and existing in space. Nor are structures simply empty containers, slots to be filled, prior to and independent of content. Structure comes into existence only as it is defined by content. It assumes a reality by virtue of the content's existence; and the content is a part of reality in so far as it is "structured". A qualitative change in the content leads to a warp, or distortion, in the structure which then, rather than reverting back to a static state of equilibrium according to Saussure's formulation, moves forward toward a higher, more complex system (the open world). Hence, content and structure are modifications of the notion of the diachronic-synchronic continuum, since the system is susceptible to changes in time and time is defined by those systemic changes. This suggests a priority of process rather than of structure, a transformation in human thinking not unlike that of twentieth century physics which ultimately abolished the classical notion of instantaneous states.

It may well be that the concept of *process* will dominate in the decades to come (Bertalanffy 1967: part II). This trend began in the sciences themselves during the present century. Heisenberg's principle of indeterminacy, to cite only one instance, stands in stark contrast to the mechanistic determinism of classical physics. His indeterminacy principle denies the exact prediction and simultaneous measurement of both the position and velocity of subatomic entities in space and time. Consequently, since neither position nor velocity can be defined together, the exact state of the system cannot be precisely known. Heisenberg himself suggests (1962: 180-81) that matter manifests to the physicist not a static state but a "potentia" in the sense of Aristotelian philosophy. In fact, he believes that "language actually used by physicists when they speak about atomic events produces in their minds similiar notions as the concept 'potentia'". However, "semantic inertia" often prevents this concept from effectively revealing itself.

The task now at hand is to "dynamize" the general structuralist interdisciplinary methodology, as Paul Ricoeur (1968: 114-29) believes Chomskyan linguistics is striving to dynamize structural linguistics in particular. How can the static categories of structuralism be transformed into historical, dynamic categories? In search for an answer let us refer back to the analogy of the physical sciences. It is now generally conceded that: (1) the Newtonian primacy of absolute space is invalid, (2) the notion of separateness of space and time is a mathematical abstraction, a fundamental axiom upon which the Newtonian system was deduced, and (3) homogeneous and instantaneous states in time and space are imaginative logical constructs by means of which Newtonian mechanics could operate.

The current view has it that space and time are fused together in nature to produce a four-dimensional continuum. In the words of James Jeans (1959: 104-05), our "human spectacles" have created that spurious differentiation between space and time. When these spectacles are removed, "we see that an event no longer occurs at a point of the continuum, this point identifying both the time and place of its occurrence; we discover that the primary ingredients of nature are not objects existing in space and time, but events in the continuum." Time, which must now be considered heterogeneous since events are not evenly spaced in the continuum, can no longer be separated from its own content. Moreover, content is merged into space while simultaneously space is fused with time. Time does not exist as an empty homogeneous flow prior to material content; its reason for existence is dependent upon that content. Hence, the "traditional distinction between time and concrete physical processes must be seen to be as artificial as that between *space* and its *material* content" (Capek 1961: 212). The physicist, then, observes not particles in time and space but spatio-temporal events in an ongoing transformational process. This is a radical departure from the notion of a discontinuous series of instantaneous states. Whereas it was once assumed that an individual particle could be observed in terms of its position during successive instants, now we realize that the same event can never be observed twice (Schrödinger 1945: 175). Cognizant of this new image, Capek proposes (1961: 328-29) a change in scientific terminology from "displacement" in space to "change" through time-space and from "particles" to "events". Therefore, the impossibility, in light of relativity physics, of an instantaneous configuration of independent, homogeneous, and empty time and space, of a universe of mechanistic determinism which, if logically extended, produces the image of a state of permanency, has been slowly eliminated. The static universe of classical physics has been superseded by an "open world" (Weyl 1932). This reassertion of a dynamic world of becoming supports the "philosophers of process" (James, Bergson, Whitehead, and more recently, Whyte), and in a different vein, the proponents of "general systems theory" (von Bertalanffy, Laszlo, et al.).

In this view of things, the mind is a creator, not a passive observer, a "great thought" rather than a "great machine" (Jeans 1958: 181). Mental creativity does not act on a static machinelike universe; it unfolds itself in conjunction with the universe to reveal higher, more complex cognitive constructs which are concomitant with what Whitehead terms the "creative advance of nature". Hence, the general epistemological transition I am proposing here is from configuration to process, static state to "potentia", surface relations to underlying reality, and certainty to indeterminism. The first term of each of these binaries terminates inevitably in a state of chaos (the entropy principle); the second implies evolution toward higher, more complex levels of organization. For the first the unreal is always an impossible world and vice versa, while for the second, potentia is, though for the moment unreal, not ultimately impossible. Norbert Wiener (1967: 19) remarks that indeterminacy, the idea of the possible, is a sort of parallel to Freud's irrationalism. In reality, indeterminacy is irrational only in a universe conceived of in static Newtonian terms founded upon the fundamental algorithm of determinism (Capek 1961: 337). Saussure himself alludes vaguely (i.1906-1911: 133) to a distinction between a destructive sort of "entropy principle" and an "ordering principle" which limits absolute arbitrariness:

> The whole system of language is based on the irrational principle of the arbitrariness of the sign, which would lead to the worst sort of complication if applied without restriction. But the mind contrives to introduce a principle of order and regulation into certain parts of the mass of signs, and this is the role of relative motivation. If the mechanism of language were entirely rational, it could be studied independently. Since the mechanism of language is but a partial correction of the system that is by nature chaotic, however, we adopt the viewpoint imposed by the very nature of language and study it as it limits arbitrariness.

Saussure pits the "unconscious" (irrational and arbitrary) against the "conscious" (ordering and motivated) aspects of language. One is more lexical (phonological) in nature while the other is more grammatical (syntactic). Saussure's formulation is understandably couched in mechanistic nineteenth century terminology much as is Freud's language. Nevertheless, the seeds of a philosophy of purpose, or "motivation" in Saussure's words, is present. If structuralism and the nineteenth century Newtonian world are generally devoid of the notion of purpose, the twentieth century scientific paradigm revives this aspect of Aristotelian physics. Purpose presupposes a universe where novelty rather than invariance is the rule. There is nothing mysterious in the affirmation that the universe is somehow incomplete. It is certainly less preposterous than to consider time a mere figment of the imagination as do some structuralists. The notion of novelty, unlike what Piaget designates (1968: 3-16) as "structureless genesis", does not indicate a chaotic, incoherent universe, nor does it, as the nineteenth century argument goes,

imply any sort of creation *ex nihilo*. On the contrary, novelty presupposes causal influence of the past due to principles of equifinality and multifinality (i.e., the same
result from different beginnings or different results from the same beginnings).
But there can be no casual factors between present and future. The future is potential, a probable state of affairs from among a quasi-infinite number of possibilities.

The structuralist might reject the concepts of potentiality and possibility as
absurd since, according to his heuristic model, the instantaneous state of a given
structure intrinsically possesses the character of all future constructions. Structures exist at present in the form of a sort of disguised reality which remains hidden from our present knowledge, but which can be discovered by the use of proper
models. Futurity is merely a label given to that part of the present state of things
which is unavailable to our immediate perception. Hence the temporal relationship between present and future is meaningless since future is not novelty but
exists in the present and effectively loses its futurity on becoming actual.

In contrast to this orthodox structuralist view, according to the notion of process, the present can only point toward a number of potential future states. Presentness contains within it the past, but, as Whitehead tells us, only "anticipation"
of the future. This is to say that it would not have been "scientifically" possible
for Goethe to predict a Joycean novel, for Marx to predict modern day "neo-
capitalism", or for Laplace to predict Heisenberg's principle of indeterminacy,
although in each case causal links leading up to the world views and works of
these three outstanding individuals might be established. Presentness stands on
the shoulders of pastness but is not bound by futurity.

To go beyond the limits of structuralism, therefore, we must consider "potentia" in terms of "space-time system", in terms of structure not as a static entity (in
space) but as an entity defined by its combinatorial properties in so far as they are
being transformed in (and through) time. The search focusses on *structuring process*. Whether or not a system is relatively static over a given period is not the only,
nor is it the chief concern. Analysis does not seek to disclose solely *what* a particular "configuration" is but, in addition, *how* it got that way and *why* it exists
as it does in its particular context. This does not imply that there is no room for
universals, for to state that all systems change is itself a universal. The objective
must be conscientiously to avoid a static classificatory schema of universals, and
to attempt in the future a formulation of universals of *becoming* rather than universals of *being*.

I believe that if structuralism is to survive the test of time, it must itself be an ongoing process, an evolution from the study of those intransigent antinomies of
human culture to an interpretation of the dynamic aspects of culture. This evolution demands the replacement of the notion of constraint by human choice and
selectivity, of the monolithic institutionalized system which uses and stultifies by innovation and human creativity, of closure by a system which opens out through the
use of a language continually referring to that which lies beyond itself. Ricoeur
(1968: 126) calls for a reappraisal of the *word*, the mediator between system and
event:

> The sentence . . . is an event: as such, its actuality is transitory, passing,
> vanishing. But the word survives the sentence. As a displaceable entity,

it survives the transitory instance of discourse and holds itself available for new uses. Thus, heavy with a new use-value—as minute as this may be—it returns to the system. And in returning to the system, it gives it a history.

Semiology involves analysis of the schema disclosing a system's combinatorial properties. It assumes a clear-cut dichotomy between *langue* and *parole*. Focussing on the taxonomic possibilities of *langue*, it denies *parole* the status of scientific *corpus* due to its transitory, incoherent qualities. Semantics, in contrast, is identified with *usage*: that which rests between and mediates *langue* and *parole*. Semantics focusses on the word, which, transitory by its very nature and emerging for use in ever-evolving contexts, projects synchrony into the diachronic axis. In an open system change cannot be described simply as a permutation of the elements in a system. Change implies a contextual transformation where the complex, more subtle relations between the elements in that system are radically altered. The system must be in dynamic equilibrium with respect to adjacent systems in the total hierarchy, which are themselves incessantly moving forward toward the undefined potentia. Hence, the structuralist technique must involve more than a gathering of observed structures to place them in a definite order, the nature of which is often decided upon *a priori*. It must ask how one structure comes forth from another, and seek an understanding of thought's processes in bringing about these transitions.

Consider the notion that structures emerge by means of cognitive rather than strictly defined linguistic processes. It has been generally concluded in the sciences that Einsteinian space-time is the product of "thought" and exists in basic conflict with sense-perception, or "common sense" knowledge. Thought, contrary to these structuralists who declare dogmatically that language "speaks itself" through man, is not a slave to language. The unfolding of thought is not uncompromisingly determined by language, nor is there a rigid correspondence between thought processes and discourse; their relation is organic. Thought without language lacks the framework by means of which knowledge's edifice is constructed. At the same time, language without thought is no more than a defunct repertoire of empty signs.[26]

Furthermore, language, as distinct from the contemporary positivist tradition, is not a direct reflection of, nor is it, nor should it necessarily be, a faithful reference to objective reality. The underlying, non-empirical reality postulated by modern physics is expressible solely by means of mathematical conventions, natural language being incapable of explicating these complex mental constructs (Eddington 1958: 85). This underlying reality is not the equivalent of the structuralist's so-called "deep structure", where the detached observer objectively, empirically, and consciously organizes, by the use of his model, the elements of a system which are to represent the product of unconscious human activity. Although the structuralist is correct in his assumption that true reality is never the most obvious of realities, he errs when positing that mental reality is nondevelopmental, or a closed system. Both thought and experience are ongoing dynamic processes. The problem is that when these processes are described in natural language they appear to be reduced to bits and pieces, binaries and static combinatory systems (the "Eleatic urge" again). In the long run, this linguistic system, or any other semiotic system, reveals a subject and object, matter and mind, motion and rest, reality demanding Parmenidean stasis. On another level, however, with its in-

cessantly evolving connotations, this same natural language reveals word meanings, indices, and referents: a world of becoming where analytical preciseness gives
way to synthesis although at the expense of inevitably introducing vagueness and
ambiguity.

At the outset it appears that vagueness and ambiguity are the inextricable result
of natural language's incapacity to depict faithfully the world as modern man conceives it, be he scientist, artist, or philosopher. Whereas natural language, it was
assumed, could quite effectively and precisely describe Newtonian principles, when
confronted with such products of the human mind as Bohr's "complementarity",
Heisenberg's "indeterminacy", Pauli's "exclusion principle", all of which can
be concisely described in mathematical terms, the inadequacies of traditional
Western languages becomes more apparent.[27] However, vague and ambiguous
language has nothing to do with human error or inadequacy; it is something at
the very heart of physical reality as reflected in recent theories of microphysics.
Vagueness, ambiguity, and even paradox, move hand in hand with the principles
of indeterminacy and complementarity. There is thus a degree of truth to Wittgenstein's principle of ineffability in all languages. It is possible that in recent
decades thought has drastically forged ahead of language, which is, Saussure tells
us, the most conservative of social institutions. Obviously it is beyond our capacity
to "purify" language; that was the abortive task of the logical positivists. We
must learn to live with ambiguity and vagueness, aware that Cartesian "clear
and distinct ideas" are impossible, at least given the present state of knowledge.
Ultimately the task will involve an arduous swim upstream, against the Eleatic
tradition, to abolish taxonomies, charts, and combinatory schemes, in favor of
emergent forms and structuring processes.

I do not wish to suggest in this paper that we submit the social sciences and
the humanities to methods created *sui generis* for the physical sciences. I do believe
that to tap more effectively the resources hidden at the underlying reality, the
structuralist method must undergo a "dynamization", shaking off those epistemological conventions of the past and abolishing the priority of structured events.
This involves simultaneously a re-emphasis on man as agent of his creations, rather
than the victim of demonic structures which take on a life of their own and reveal
themselves through man. The alternative in a vast, incomprehensible and apparently chaotic world is for the analyst to isolate himself, in the presumed autonomy
of those structures he intends to explicate, from which position he can do no more
than peer out either into the disorderly world of materialness or into the void of
nothingness, nostalgic for that long lost universe of total harmony.

IV

Reshaping Traditional Spheres: Some Regional Applications

13

EUGEN BAER

The Medical Symptom

*Denn darin gerade besteht das Leben, dass es nicht begriffen
werden kann. (For life consists precisely in this, that it
cannot be grasped in concepts.)*
—Novalis 1798: 222—

*Difficultés insurmontables que présentent les nombres premiers.
(The insurmountable difficulty that prime numbers present.)*
—Valéry 1894: I, 1172 (in the margin)—

*Et les dieux ont reçu de l'esprit humain le don de créer, parce que
cet esprit étant périodique et abstrait, peut agrandir ce qu'il
conçoit jusqu'à ce qu'il ne le conçoive plus. (And the gods have
received the gift of creation from the human mind, because
this mind, being limited in its span of attention and
abstract, can magnify what it conceives to a point beyond
its comprehension.)*
—Valéry 1894: I, 1182 lines 6-11—

This essay sketches first a phenomenological approach to Peirce's logic of events and then applies this logic to the phylogeny and ontogeny of the medical symptom. It appears from this application that the symptom figures in four universes of experience, only one of which is rational. The semiotic approach, as proposed here, can restore to the conception of symptoms its transrational, prerational, and irrational dimensions and put the various strands of its rational treatment (biomedical, sociological, psychological) on the common denominator of the sign.

Moreover, since the logic of events used here is at the same time the logic of evolution, the symptom can be shown to sit like a Russian doll within the isomorphic larger structure of life itself. This would restore to the medical vision, on semiotic grounds, its traditional relation of microcosm to macrocosm.

Semiotic Symptomatology

Novalis saw in disease an invitation for individuation. Illness, for him, had the purpose of initiating its bearer into the mysteries of the universe. The symptom was a hieroglyph, a mark of the sacred, a sign in which nature and spirit came together to celebrate an orphic wake. The symptom was the phenomenology of the spirit, the supreme metaphor, the self in action.

This is admittedly an allusion to a romantic symptomatology but one which probably was the original one. Sebeok's often repeated claim that symptomatology is the oldest branch on the semiotic tree, the oldest leg of the semiotic "tripod" (Sebeok 1976), consisting of medicine, philosophy, and linguistics, has to be taken beyond Hippocrates back to an era of mythical consciousness in which the symptom inscribed itself in narrative systems of ontological equivalences and proportions which crossed the now separated realms of biology, sociology, and psychology. The symptom "stood" for the whole order of world experience, it evoked the sum total of human relations, it individuated the universe and its religious depth in one concrete existential sign of the body: it was, in short, *the* concrete universal.

Today may be the time to restore to symptomatology its pluridimensional plenitude. To be true, this plenitude always coexisted as an undercurrent with official medical theory. One has only to think of the alchemists and Romantics to be reminded of the necessary complementarity of reduction and amplification, typical of the history of ideas. But it was not until Freud and his followers that the mythical archaic past (re)turned from diachrony to synchrony, from forgotten or repressed time to coexisting time, and restored to the symptom the semiotic fullness of the rebus (Baer 1983: see gloss in References).

What remains to be done is to articulate this fullness by means of a general theory of signs. This is all the more urgent as one of the protagonists of such a theory, Charles S. Peirce, had one of the most reductive notions of the symptom, one in which it is merely an indexical reaction to a stimulus, "without an utterer". The person who has or, rather, *is* the symptom is totally excluded from this conception. This leads straight to a "disease-oriented" instead of a "person-oriented" medical theory. A full or fuller theory, however, should assemble multiple orientations or universes of discourse in one enveloping universe of discourse. This is briefly attempted in this essay.

The Three Universes of Experience
While Peirce has a too narrow view of the symptom, his general theory of signs is most useful to adumbrate a full symptomatology. His ideas about three absolute universes of experience, firstness, secondness, and thirdness, disclose aspects of the symptom which integrate its diachronic and synchronic Sphinxian nature both on a phylogenetic and ontogenetic level. Since each of the three universes is an absolute, the experience or type of experience which is characteristic for each is absolute, too. We arrive thus at a conception of the symptom which— paradoxically—unites that which by definition cannot be united. This impossible unity is the sign which can be explained only *post factum* or *post hoc*, that is, only once an instance of firstness and an instance of secondness have happened. Thirdness, the only one of the three universes which is in any way rational, is a latecomer, an epi-genetic product. As such it is essentially *anamnestic*, that is, it remembers its nonintelligible precursive instances and is able to give form to those instances or, let us say, a semblance of form, since the "point" of such a form is its dissolution. An example: One can rationalize quality, one can talk about good and evil or attempt to explain it, but the *experience* of it eludes all forms given by the universe of "meaning" and is, in this sense, "formless". The experience of quality belongs to the universe of firstness. It is a monadic, absolutely self-referential relation and logically precedes all rationality as its nonrational foundation.

The Paradigm of Time
The three universes of experience which I shall use, in modified form, to sketch the outline of a holistic medical symptomatology, are best presented or introduced phenomenologically. The mathematician Brouwer (1913), taking a Kantian route,

does precisely that. His prose developing the three universal categories as a phenomenology of time-experience could not be clearer and more concise (Brouwer 1927: 1235):

> *Consciousness* in its deepest home seems to oscillate slowly, will-lessly, and reversibly between stillness and sensation. And it seems that only the status of sensation allows the initial phenomenon of the said transition. This initial phenomenon is a *move of time*. By a move of time a present sensation gives way to another present sensation in such a way that consciousness retains the former one as a past sensation, and moreover, through this distinction between present and past, recedes from both and from stillness, and becomes *mind*.

In this passage, the first category seems to be that of stillness. This logical moment of silence is an aural figuration of ontological absolute nothingness. Peirce, too (1898: 6.217), speaks of this nothingness as "the nothing of not having been born" and distinguishes this "state" from firstness. I shall therefore accept, instead of three, *four* universes of experience, modifying Peirce slightly, but, I think, along some traces of his thought, as the following passage suggests (Peirce c.1910: 6.490):

> whether in time or not, the three universes must actually be absolutely necessary results of a state of utter nothingness.

Brouwer's stillness, in the above quoted passage (from 1927), is, as I mentioned, the figuration (in Greimas's sense of temporalization) of this Peircean "state of utter nothingness", "a state of things in which the three universes were completely *nil*" (Peirce c.1910: 6.490). This "zero of bare possibility" (Peirce 1898: 6.220) is annulled through the absolute miracle disclosed in sensation, that, rather than absolutely nothing, *there may be some thing*. Sensation spreads as a mere first and fills consciousness, making it move from stillness to fullness: a move of time. But fullness as presence is annulled again, this time as giving way to another presence, another first which, in respect to the withdrawing former moment, is a second. We sense in this display, absolutely necessary as it is, the original play of nothingness at work. Past and present, otherness and self, are two and move as sheer togetherness in the permanence of the universe of secondness. In it, they are irreconcilable absolutes, in eternal strife, irrational abyss, irremediable fraction of being, brutal destruction, entropic dissolution. Now Brouwer introduces *mind* as that which from its aboriginal recess from both past and present can *hold* both together in a continuity (*con-tenere*: holding together) which is neither and, strictly speaking, not anything. It is *Entsprechung*, correspondence organization, a code. The play of time is thus enough to show us the universal logic of events. A symptom is an event. We can insert it or see it in this logic. It is the logic of the four absolutes of meaning.

The Four Absolutes of Meaning

The logic of meaning is conceptually generated. It belongs to the universe of third-ness, of symbolism, of language, but precisely as such it discloses that which make it work: (1) a dimension of play which Wittgenstein called "*Spiel*", (2) a dimension of monadic origin in which all iconicity is founded, and (3) a dimension of "blind" otherness which does not let it come to rest. Meaning, including the meaning of symptoms, is linguistically generated, but it involves and presupposes three other, nonrational universes of experience. Language, in this case, serves, as Peirce points out (c.1896: 1.493), as "scaffolding":

> To get at the idea of a monad, and especially to make it an accurate and clear conception, it is necessary to begin with the idea of a triad and find the monad-idea involved in it. But this is only a scaffolding necessary during the process of constructing the conception. When the conception has been constructed, the scaffolding may be removed, and the monad-idea will be there in all its abstract perfection.

In this sense of "scaffolding", I would like to offer first a brief exposition, suitably adapted to my own needs, of Peirce's universal categories of human experience. Then I am going to apply these categories to the symptom, mindful of my earlier remark that the symptom is a privileged place and mode of human experience. Finally, I shall portray the symptom as a micro-theater of a macrocosmic "logic".

The medical symptom is any sign which conveys to a perceiver that something is fine or wrong with the sender's existence. "Existence", in turn, is defined as a way of "being-in-the-world" (Heidegger), a way of having a world as an individual reality (Thure von Uexküll's *individuelle Wirklichkeit* [1979]). Because of its crisis-provoking character—I am using "crisis" here in the sense of Thom's "catastrophe" (1972)—the symptom is a privileged mode of human experience.

Elements of experience may be conveniently grouped into four structural moments which are irreducible to one another and in this sense are four absolutes.

First is the category of unbounded freedom. Peirce himself refused to call this element a category and therefore recognizes explicitly only the three which are to follow this one. However, he clearly acknowledged, as we have just seen, the logical need to distinguish, at the very beginning of everything, a state of "absolute nothingness". He explains (1898: 6.217):

> We start, then, with nothing, pure zero. But this is not the nothing of negation. For *not* means *other than*, and *other* is merely a synonym of the ordinal numeral *second*. As such it implies a first; while the present pure zero is prior to every first. The nothing of negation is the nothing of death, which comes *second* to, or after, everything. But this pure zero is the nothing of not having been born. There is no individual thing, no compulsion, outward nor inward, no law. It is the germinal nothing, in which the whole universe is involved and foreshadowed. As such, it is absolutely undefined and unlimited possibility—boundless possibility. There is no compulsion and no law. It is boundless freedom.

This category, then, designates a mode of "utter nothingness" (Peirce c.1910: 6.490), pure idling, pure play, without there being anything or anyone that plays. It is absolute nothingness, "not the nothing of negation", just pure nothing at all.

Second is the category of origin, Peirce's firstness. He claims that pure idling, if it is any good, spontaneously produces something, a *quale*, pure quality, something similiar to Thom's "attractor" (1972). He bases his claim on the phenomenology of play, for example, doodling, in which random processes usually result eventually in some compulsive morphology, some Rorschach-like configuration. In this universe of experience, compulsive forms are experienced as absolutely original, irreducible to anything else but itself. They are self-constituted and self-referring monads, pure *qualia*, genuine icons.

Third is the category of otherness, Peirce's secondness, something similiar to Heidegger's *Riss* (1957) or Derrida's *trace* (1972). In this category, everything is opposed, in conflict, clashing, irrupting. It is the moment of ek-sistence, of standing out through contrast like figure from ground, a unity constituted by sheer difference. This experience of everything bordering on or being part of something else constitutes indexicality.

Fourth is the category of meaning or of the sign. It is Peirce's thirdness, a triadic relation, in which incompatible or heterogeneous elements are brought into a relation of mutual containment. Circularity, reversibility, and chiasmus of the differentiated units are the main properties of this category. It is this fourth category, as universe of the symbol, which releases the preceding three. In this sense, the last category is the first and characteristically reverts the order of genesis adduced here. In other words—and this is typical of the symbol—it envelops that by which it is itself enveloped; it encloses that by which it is enclosed.

The Four Universes of the Medical Symptom

If we now apply Peirce's four universal categories of human experience to the symptom as privileged clearing (*Lichtung*) of the world, we can identify in it, as a matter of convention and convenience, four major universes—a Plotinian might be tempted to speak of four major hypostases—namely, the boundless Open, absolute origin, brute force, and law-likeness. These correspond, respectively, to the four absolute dimensions of the sign: absolute nothingness, the icon, the index, and the symbol.

The first category is perhaps the most difficult one to grasp. In it, the symptom is considered before its genesis, and this is an absolute sense, that is, without meaning, without causal connections, without content—no purpose, no cause, no quality—as an absolute nothing. It is a view of the symptom before it is born and without any frame or opposition to "place" it. In this universe, we experience the symptom as "the nothing that is" (Wallace Stevens), as pure nonrelatedness.

Difficult as it may be to consider a dimension of the symptom before it arises, there is another way of formulating it, and this is to say that the symptom, considered radically under the aspect of its *raison d'être*, its ultimate anchor in ontology, its basic support in some kind of foundation, *has no basis at all*. Philosophers who are mutually differing in other respects such as Schopenhauer, Wittgenstein, and Heidegger, agree with Peirce on this issue, that the foundation of all meaningfulness, all cause-effect relations, all forms of representation, is ultimately groundless (*grundlos*). Shocking as this thought may appear to some people at first, it can be quite liberating for many. It frees one not only from trying to find some ultimate meaning in symptoms of health and illness, but also from the search for an ultimate cause. It puts all symptom-formation into a frame of gratuitousness, of freedom, of play, of chance, much like biological morphogenesis and thought-formation which in Peirce's logic are seen as epigenetic phenomena (more about this below).

From a universe of absolute nothingness, we enter, by a switch of thought, the universe of firstness, of compulsive origins, an entry so startling and overwhelming in its mystery that it can best be represented by the Leibnizian question of which Heidegger was so fond:

"Why is there something and not rather nothing?"

Peirce answers this question by begging it:

"Where form is absent, there form can arise."

Phenomenologically, however, compulsive origins resulting from "differentiation" (Ehrenzweig 1967) can be experienced in experiments of thought or action: Where idling and play is perfect, it results in some spontaneous form which is accountable only to itself. Applied to the symptom, this means that in this universe of experience, the symptom is a first behind which one cannot ask, because *it is never really present as an object*. It is, in this mode of consciousness, an all-pervasive mood which is not graspable. Rather, we find ourselves *in* such moods. They are symptomatic in the sense that they color, "tone", qualify or modify the world we live in. In this dimension, symptoms are most deeply "ours" in the sense of an absolutely individual reality:

"Nobody can feel my pain."

Or,

"Nobody can share my insight."

The symptom, at this level, is identical with prerational selfhood. It releases prereflexive feeling-tones (Merleau-Ponty), for example, a sense of total fragility, of vulnerability, despair. Or a sense of excessive power, of titillating pleasure, of deep ecstasy, peace. It refers only to itself as a self and is thus consubstantial, of one substance, with the world it discloses. In this universe, I *am* the feeling, I do not *have* it (Gabriel Marcel). The symptom here is an *Urgefühl*, an absolute primary feeling, prerational, prereflexive, preobjective, prerepresentational.

Symptoms as instances of firstness are monadic relations, *states of nonduality*. Peirce puts it this way (1904b: 24):

Firstness is the mode of being of that which is such as it is, positively and without reference to anything else.

Instances of Zen-like illuminations, of feelings of an all-encompassing well-being, of an all-pervading pain, of flashes of insight, are examples of symptoms as firsts or, as Heidegger calls them, as *Stimmungen*, primary moods which imply a certain being attuned to the disclosed world (*gestimmtsein*) at a point at which it cannot become an object. Symptoms as firsts are prerational states, difficult to express symbolically but nevertheless that which all symbols are ultimately about.

Secondness is the dimension in which the symptom appears as irrational brute force, an outside or inside aggressor, an irresistible impulse or inexorable blind fate. Experiences of terminal illness or of obsessive ideas (*Zwangsideen*) are examples of this irrational dimension of the symptom. Here the relation is dyadic, a clash, brute conflict, struggle, resistance, a collision of ego and non-ego, sheer negation, without any sense, without meaning, without a third. Peirce puts it thus (1904b: 24):

Secondness is the mode of being of that which is such as it is, with respect to a second but regardless of any third.

This third absolute universe of the symptom is perhaps the most real one for most people in the sense of being the most brutal. It is, after all, the category of sheer otherness, of the symptom as totally and unspeakably other. Its limit case is the event of death as an occurence of an absolutely irrational physical break, completely overriding all our attempts at rationalizing it or coming to grips with it, and ridiculing all our attempts at explaining it.

And finally, there is the fourth dimension of the symptom: the symptom as symbol. All contemporary attempts at broadening and pluralizing the notion of symptom can be assigned to this dimension. I shall distinguish in this symbolic universe of experience three subdimensions. They address psychological, biomedical, and sociological aspects of the symptom.

The first symbolic dimension of the symptom is psychological. It is the dimension of the individual self, the person. After all, it is this person who is feeling fine or who is suffering and who is undergoing, in a heightened or symptomatic way, the drama of life and death. Individual life-events such as the loss of a loved person or falling in love play a crucial role in the way we produce and experience symptoms. Moreover, all persons perceive their symptoms through *individual* frames of meaning, although these frames, from another point of view, can be perceived as *social* constructs (provening from popular medicine, religion, art, literature, philosophy, the mass media).

The second symbolic dimension of the symptom is the natural-biological one. This is without a doubt the one in which our culture invests the most interests and which it considers the most "real". Indeed, for many physicians and patients, this is the only dimension of the symptom that "really counts"—the rest is talk, talk, and more talk. In this dimension, disease is construed as consisting of physical and molecular processes studied by the methods of the natural sciences. Taken in isolation, this model, in spite of its spectacular successes of treatment during the last hundred years or so (the treatments for diphtheria [Wood 1961] and tuberculosis [Sontag 1978] being prime examples), is deficient, mainly because, as Kleinman notes (1980:18), it does not "account for the meaning context of sickness" and, in addition, is not "self-reflexive", not aware of the basic cultural assumptions from which it proceeds (Kleinman 1980: 18).

The question of cultural assumption brings us to the third symbolic dimension: the cultural-social context, in which disease is given meaning. Arthur Kleinman points out (1980: 24), that "in the same sense in which we speak of religion or language or kinships as cultural systems, we can view medicine as a cultural system, a system of symbolic meanings, anchored in particular arrangements of social institutions and patterns of interpersonal relations" (Kleinman 1980: 24). Accordingly, and inversing the whole order of symptomatic genesis described so far, we can perceive the medical symptom first of all as a cultural product in the sense in which a language, a given form of life, a consciousness, are said to be constitutive of what can become meaningful by means of them. Heidegger (1927: 363) puts it this way:

> The articulation of the understanding of Being, the delimitation of an area of subject-matter (a delimitation guided by this understanding), and the sketching-out of the way of conceiving which is appropriate to such entities—all these belong to the totality of this projecting; and this totality

is what we call *"thematizing"*. Its aim is to free the entities we encounter within-the-world, and to free them in such a way that they can "throw themselves against" (*ob-icere: entgegenwerfen*) a pure discovering—that is, that they can become "objects". Thematizing objectifies.

Kleinman further calls attention to the "tremendous power of social reality" which fashions a world we accept as the only "real" one, to which we commit ourselves, often passionately, and react to so as to shape our own "life-trajectories" (Kleinman 1980: 36). The cultural institutions, by naming and ratifying *certain* diseases and not others, allow them to "exist" in a socially recognized space. Such "filters of disease", as we might call the consciousness and medical practice moulded by a given culture, are much more diversified than we customarily are ready to concede. (See Staiano 1979 for an excellent discussion of the ethnosemiotic dimension of the symptom.) Maybe the future will show whether semioticians, most likely of the Greimas school, will be attracted to the task of giving us detailed analyses of various types of symptomatic discourse.

The Meaning-Cycle of the Symptom

For now we can at least summarize the Peircean categories in Greimassian form. The symptom then appears as a transformational microsystem of prefixes to the word "rational". The system can be presented as a meaning-cycle in the form of the semiotic square (Figure 1):

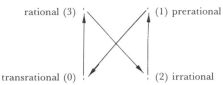

Figure 1. The meaning-cycle of the symptom.

Starting from the universe of thirdness (3), in which the symptom is treated rationally (e.g., biomedically, psychologically, sociologically), we jump through the logic of negation into its brute irrationality (2). This is the universe of blind fate, *ananke*, brute necessity, and coercion. Every attempt at explanation or rationalization fails. But this impossibility of explanation clears the way toward a form of consciousness which precedes duality (1) and in which the symptom is experienced as an absolute origin of consciousness. At the heart of that consciousness we find, like the emptiness in the seed of the huge nyagrodha tree of the Chandogya Upanishad, an absolute nothingness (0) as the free-play of any origin. At this point we can reenter the universe of rational meanings (3). The cycle is complete and without beginning and end. The syntagmatic itinerary (3, 2, 1, 0, 3 . . . .) discloses the paradigma of a timeless logic. This means, among other things, that the reentry into the rationality of the symptom is accompanied by an absolute freedom which releases and enhances the power of scientific explanation and treatment.

The Symptom as Life-Cycle

It would now be tempting to compare Peirce's categorial fourfold with that of Heidegger. This will be done in a later study (Baer 1983). We can, however, ex-

pand the present categorial model by showing how, in this view, the symptom
sits like a Russian doll in an encompassing icon of life itself. In other words, we
can show how the ontogeny of the meaning-cycle of the symptom recapitulates
the phylogeny of life itself. This might be a semiotic way of restoring to medical
theory the traditional relation of microcosm to macrocosm. The basis of this relation would be the sign. To be precise: the thought-sign. I have shown elsewhere
(Baer 1985) how thought-signs are the criterial attribute of life and would like
to reformulate here the symptom as a thought-sign or life-cycle. To do this, we
can represent the meaning-cycle of Figure 1 as a cycle of openness, iconicity, indexicality, and symbolicity (Figure 2):

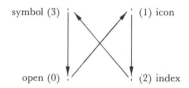

symbol (3)   (1) icon

open (0)   (2) index

Figure 2. The symptom as life cycle.

In this version of the four categories, we can read the symptom as a circle,
as a tropos of a topos: out of what Rilke called the Open (Eighth *Elegy*) arises
a topos (icon), say, a sharp backache, which incurs the twist of conflict (index),
for example in the form of paralyzing our habitual way of going about things.
The icon creates its correlative index: to the ache corresponds a new world to
which I have to adapt. The effort of adaptation invokes a holding together of icon
and index, a form of plan, in which the adaptation is worked out. This is done
by the symbol which transforms the mere reaction of the index into thoughtful
action.

With this reformulation of the symptom as thought-sign we are now in a position to establish its phylogenetic dimension with the help of Peirce's evolutionary
logic. To better appreciate this logic, I am going to frame it on one end of the
temporal scale with the logic of Pythagoras, on the other with that of modern
physics.

The Logic of Tautology

The number-logic of Pythagoras starts with a primary unity, much like the logic
of Peirce. And much like Peirce, Pythagoras apparently finds it difficult to maintain the primary unity as the number one. Rather, the primary unity is that which
allows the play of numbers, their harmony, their ratios, hence something like zero,
something like the empty slot ''between'' numbers which releases the numbers
one and two, odd and even, into their complementary contrast. The contrast is
one of topos and anti-topos, of ''limited'' (odd) and ''unlimited'' (even). The
unity lies in a nonsubstantial ratio, a law of correspondence, of complementarity, in short: a *code*.

It is easy to recognize in this logic not only the constitutive moments of an
open (living) system as described in modern systems theory consisting of a
homeostasis of closed (limited) and open (unlimited) states, but also an ingenious
theory of harmony (or unity) based not on substances but on signs, not on things
but on codes. Physics, at that early time, was already semiotics.

Linguistically, the "logic" of this harmony can be stated as being expressed by a tautology. Parmenides, in this sense, is entirely Pythagorean. His thought is tautologous. Consider, as a typical example, from fragment 8: "The same (*tauton*) is thinking (*noein*) and that about which (*houneken*, also: 'for whose sake' or 'because of which') there is thought." The unity of observer and observed (the problem of reference) is here presented in the form of participation: observer and observed participate in one another on the grounds (Peirce's icon) of sameness. The sameness becomes substantial only and precisely *in* the differentiation. Another way of putting this is to say that observer and observed produce one another and by doing so they make *mind* (code) come to light. Mind becomes a phenomenon in the participatory coupling of observer and observed.

Again, this production of sameness through differentiation can be aptly illustrated by tautologous predication. The differentiation which is necessary for predication executes the "return" of thought from differentiation to identity. Predication, in other words, "participates" both on the side of the subject as well as on that of the predicate in a purely relational (self-referential) unity.

Modern physics gets ready to catch a glimpse of this logic. At this point, though, it is "as yet not an idea, but an idea for an idea" (Misner et al. 1973: 1212), namely, that nature is a manifestation of a certain type of logic which was intuited by Aristotle and Hegel: a logic that can think about itself, a self-referential logic, a tauto-logic.

This is pregeometric logic, a logic which accounts for geometrical topologies by way of participation, and the question some physicists ask today is consequently the following (Misner et al. 1973: 1217):

> May the universe in some strange sense be "brought into being" by the participation of those who participate?

Although this question comes to physics in a belated way, it is never too late, because it addresses not linear time, but circular time, not the syntagma of the logic but its paradigma. This circular time is released by the sign (*Sein*). Heidegger's *Sein und Zeit* (1927) can show us just in what sense not only time, but all objectivity is circular by working on the basic insight of Fichte and Novalis, to wit, that "I" and "not-I" designate two participatory states of the same "system". Being (*Sein*) is "here" (*da*) only in the form of corresponding voices. Self and world, in this view, are mutual self-realizations governed by a single code. In other words: self and not-self together—and only together—are *one* sign, a thought-sign.

The Logic of Evolution

This brings us back to Peirce. The triadic structure of his evolutionary logic should be understood as a cycle which combines the paradigmatic and syntagmatic aspects of thought-signs. The cycle can be represented with the help of a Greimassian square (Figure 3, page following).

Life, according to this logic, arises from absolute nothingness by a kind of "jump" into a topos, an idea, an icon, a monadic form, which, for the human observer, takes on the form of a geometrical object. René Thom writes (1972: 151-152) that "we might look upon all living phenomena as manifestations of a geometric object, the *life field (champ vital)*, similar to the gravitational or electromagnetic field; living beings would then be particles or structurally stable

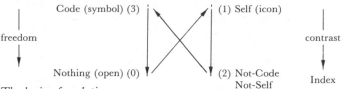

Figure 3. The logic of evolution.

singularities in this field, and the phenomena of symbiosis, of predation, of parasitism, of sexuality, and so forth would be the interactions and couplings between these particles''.

This view is very close to that of Whitehead, in whose cosmology eternal objects *ingress* concrete actual occasions. An eternal object consists of a monadic relation, much like Peirce's icon. Compare the two definitions—Whitehead in the Lowell Lectures of 1925 (published in Whitehead 1948: 159):

> Each eternal object is an individual which, in its own peculiar fashion, is what it is. This particular individuality is the individual essence of the object, and cannot be described otherwise than as being itself.

And Peirce in his lectures on pragmatism (1903a: 5.74):

> . . . a pure icon does not draw any distinctions between itself and its object. It represents whatever it may represent, and whatever it is like, it in so far is. It is an affair of suchness only.

Peirce is willing to call this self-referential suchness a Platonic form which, at some stage of evolution—and here the language is practically identical with that of Whitehead—''enters'' some theatre of reactions, such as the world we know (1898a: 6.195). But unlike Whitehead, for whom the icon was eternal, Peirce envisioned the icon itself as being subject to an evolutionary process. He writes in a Cambridge lecture (1898a: 6.194):

> The evolutionary process is, therefore, not a mere evolution of the *existing universe*, but rather a process by which the very Platonic forms themselves have become or are becoming developed.

Peirce then goes on to have the icon originate out of absolute nothingness, a state of boundless freedom, of utter arbitrary idling. It is this aspect of his ''logic of the universe'' which I would like to foreground here and to align it with contemporary views of biological morphogenesis. Form, for Peirce, originates out of an arbitrary play of differences. But once it has jumped into possibility, it tends toward spatiotemporal stabilization under the influence of a code. I suggest that one of the best models to make of this combination of arbitrariness and motivation is the combination of the two articulations (phonemic, morphemic) in linguistics.

One philosopher who has made this move, although only in passing, is Derrida. In his book *Of Grammatology* (1967), he develops in various ways the notion of difference (trace) as a constitutive element of meaning in a way which makes sheer difference (difference that does not make a difference) logically and temporally precede meaningful difference (difference that makes a difference). The basic idea is the *jump* of meaning out of meaninglessness. One can visualize the scene in the following way: one system of differences which in regard to a second system of differences is *meaningless*, is used by that second system to produce meaning. This is how phonemes are used by morphology to constitute morphemes. Derrida seems to think that all forms, including and especially biological ones, arise as *differences within differences*. Form is thus always necessarily *displaced*, and that means, conversely, that in order to account for it in principle at any level, one has to acknowledge *its absolute gratuity* or, as Peirce has it, its *freedom*. But an absolutely gratuitous form—because of its self-reference—is what I have chosen, following Peirce, to call an "icon".

Thom attempts to give expression to a similar idea when he uses the term "attractor" to denote an irreducible locally stable element of morphogenesis. "Irreducible", that is, to something else, but reducible, precisely for that reason, to itself alone. In other words, a first.

The startling way in which icons are absolute origins is indeed manifest in biological morphogenesis. There we notice, as everywhere in morphology, the combination of (a) lawlike factors (codes) involved in the conservation and development of forms, of which the genetic code is a prime example, and (b) jumplike factors, especially changes in structural genes and changes in gene regulation which are true firsts in Peirce's sense and assure the possibility of best designs to environmental changes, themselves a product of chance and lawlike factors.

One of the most interesting passages in Peirce's work relating to iconicity in biology is contained in one of his Cambridge lectures, entitled "The Logic of Continuity". There (1898a: 6.204) he writes, as he does many times elsewhere, that the clue to making our ideas clear is to make them iconic in the sense of "making our thought diagrammatic and mathematical". The diagram of thought is the thought itself: here we have a pure icon. By observing its genesis and "experimenting upon it", a process which Peirce calls "ideoscopy" or "phenomenology", Peirce assembles the logic of the universe with the logic of consciousness in the simple image of a blackboard (ibid.: 6.203), which stands for absolute nothingness, understood as boundless freedom of potential quality. On this imaginary blackboard he draws with a piece of chalk a line, a first, taken in its whiteness as pure icon, but in its contrast to the original blackness representing the "brute act" of secondness. The stage is set—at least in Peirce's consciousness—for the genesis of a possible universe. Peirce writes (1898a: 6.204):

> We see the original generality like the ovum of the universe segmented by this mark. However, the mark is a mere accident, and as such may be erased. It will not interfere with another mark drawn in quite another way. There need be no consistency between the two. But no further progress beyond this can be made, until a mark will *stay* for a little while; that is, until some beginning of a *habit* has been established by virtue of which the accident acquires some incipient staying quality, some tendency toward consistency.

This remarkable passage formulates in speculative thought—and with typical philosophic simplicity—the birth of an icon (or Platonic form) in very roughly the same terms as we encounter in empirical descriptions of biological morphogenesis, where it is said that "mutations occur at random . . . (i.e.,) the chance that a specific mutation will occur is not affected by how useful that mutation would be" (Futuyma 1979: 249). However, whether or not a spontaneous mutation is going to be "erased" or not seems to depend, much like the genetic variation of a given population, on selective pressures of the environment. We can say that a random—and in this sense arbitrary—genesis of a dialogue between gene variation or mutation and selective pressures yield morphological stability. The biological icon has both an arbitrary grounding (much like linguistic morphemes) *and* a "motivated" stability by way of repetition, reproduction, coping, etc.

The same is true of the symptom. It is both arbitrary and motivated. It repeats on the microscene of our bodies the macrocosmic drama of life (Eros) and death (Thanatos). Freud (1920) clearly saw this biological macrodimension of the symptom. Semiotics can refine his vision by means of Peirce's logic of events which lets biology and the human sciences meet in the common structure of thought-signs. The medical symptom, then, is that most concrete of all signs—a true event in Heidegger's (1957) sense (*Ereignis*)—where the meaning of life and death is most radically offered for individual appropriation, and where semiosis, much like psychoanalysis for the later Freud (1937), becomes most intensely interminable.

14

UMBERTO ECO

On Symbols

What is a symbol? Etymologically speaking, the Greek word σὐμβολον comes from συμβάλλω, "to throw-with, to make something coincide with something else". A symbol was originally an identification mark made up of two halves of a coin or of a medal: two halves of the same thing, either one standing for the other, both becoming, however, fully effective only when matched to make up, again, the original whole. In the semiotic dialectics between signifier and signified, expression and content, or name and thing, such a rejoining is always deferred, the first half of the couple being always *interpreted* by our substitution of another first half of another couple, and so on *ad infinitum*, so that the initial gap between *signans* and *signatum* grows more and more vast. On the contrary, in the original concept of symbol there is the suggestion of a final recomposition. Etymologies, however, do not necessarily tell the truth—or, at least, they tell the truth, in terms of historical, not structural, semantics. What is frequently appreciated in many so-called symbols is exactly their vagueness, their openness, their fruitful ineffectiveness in expressing a "final" meaning, so that with symbols and by symbols one indicates what is always *beyond* one's reach.

Are there in the specialized lexicons more technical definitions of this category and of the corresponding term? Alas! One of the most pathetic moments in the history of philosophical terminology occurs when the collaborators of the *Dictionnaire de philosophie* of Lalande (1902-1923) gather to discuss the definition of *symbol*. This page of a "technical" lexicon is pure Ionesco.

After a first definition according to which a symbol is something representing something else by virtue of an analogical correspondence (for example: the sceptre, symbol of royalty—where it is not clear where the analogy lies, because this is a paramount case of metonymical *contiguity*), a second definition is proposed, namely, that symbols concern a continued system of terms, each of which represents an element of another system. It is a good definition for the Morse code; unfortunately the illustrative citation [from Jules Lemaitre] following it speaks of a system of uninterrupted metaphors, and the Morse code seems hardly definable as a metaphorical system. At this point Lalande adds that a symbol is also a "formulary of orthodoxy", and he quotes the *Credo*. A discussion follows: Delacroix insists on the analogy; Lalande claims to have received from O. Karmin the proposal to define as a symbol every conventional representation; Brunschvicq speaks of an "internal" representational power and mentions the archetypical circular image of the serpent biting its own tail; van Biéma reminds the party that the fish was the symbol of Christ only for acronymic reasons; Lalande wonders how a piece of paper can become the symbol for a given amount of gold, while a

mathematician speaks of symbols for the signs of the square root; Delacroix is
caught by the suspicion that there is no relation between the sign for square root
and the fox as a symbol of cunning; someone else distinguishes between intellectual and emotional symbols; and the entry fortunately stops at this point. The
effort of Lalande has not been fruitless; it has suggested that a symbol can be
everything and nothing. What a shame!

There are undoubtedly among all the above definitions some family
resemblances. But family resemblances have a curious property (see, for instance,
Bambrough 1961). Let us consider three concepts A, B, and C analysable in terms
of component properties a . . . g:

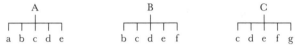

It is clear that every concept possesses some of the properties of the others, but
not all of them. But let us now broaden the series according to the same criterion:

In the end, no common property will unite A with F, save one: they belong to
the same network of family resemblance . . . .

When speaking of the concept of sign, it seems that it is possible to outline
a unique definition that can take into account the various senses attributed to
this expression, thus establishing a proper, abstract object for a general semiotics.
It seems, however, that when facing the various occurrences of a term such as
symbol, such a univocity is impossible.

Symbol is not an expression of everyday language. A word such as *sign* occurs
in many ready-made syntagms, and, when one is unable to give a univocal definition of the isolated term, one is still unable to give a certain interpretation of these
syntagms. It is, on the contrary, the pseudo-everyday language of the press or
of literary criticism that says that a certain merchandise is the symbol of the pro-
ductivity of a given country, that Marilyn Monroe was a sex symbol, that the
terrorists attempted to assassinate the American ambassador in Rome for symbolic reasons, that a certain word, description, or episode has to be read symbolically. A common speaker would have some difficulty in explaining the "right"
sense of these and other similar expressions.

In his exhaustive survey of all the possible uses of *symbol*, Raymond Firth (1973)
remarks that this term is used in place of *sign* when there is a certain *ineffectuality*:
a "symbolic" gesture does not attempt to get immediate concrete effects. He
notices that there is a web of contrasting relationships, from concrete to abstract
(fox for cunning), from abstract to concrete (logical symbols), of vague metaphors
(darkness for mystery). At its first level a symbol can also be conventional (the
keys of Saint Peter for the power of the church), but as soon as the symbol is
considered in transparence, one finds in it new and less conventional meanings
(since it is unclear what the gesture of Jesus, when he gives the keys to Peter,
means exactly—moreover, why does Jesus give the keys, not materially but
"symbolically"?)

At the end of his survey Firth shows a propensity for a provisional and "pragmatic" definition: "In the interpretation of a symbol the conditions of its presentation are such that the interpreter ordinarily has much scope for exercising his own judgment. . . . Hence one way of distinguishing broadly between signal and symbol may be to class as symbols those presentations where there is much greater lack of fit—even perhaps intentionally—in the attribution of the fabricator and interpreter" (1973: 66-67). This is a reasonable conclusion, stressing the vagueness of meaning and the gap between the intentions of the sender and the conclusions of the addressee. However, we cannot ignore that other theories provide different and far more contrasting definitions.

Thus, on the provisional basis of Firth's suggestion, we shall try three complementary critical moves:

(a) We must first isolate those cases in which *symbol* is plainly equivalent to *sign*. This first decision is certainly a terminologically biased one. It would not be forbidden to decide that it is better to call symbols what we have called signs, therefore [and thereby] considering signs a subclass of symbols. Why decide that signs will be a genus of which symbols (if any) are a species? There is, however, a reason for our choice: there are many people who call symbols what others call signs, but fewer people who call signs what other people call symbols. It seems, in other words, that in the couple sign/symbol, only the second term is the *marked* one; if there are theories where *symbol* is unmarked, there are no theories where *sign* is marked.

(b) Provided that *sign* expresses a genus, we shall then isolate many species of it that do not display the properties that, according to Firth, we have tentatively assigned to the symbolic experience.

(c) At this point we shall look for a "hard core" sense of *symbol*, that is, for a specific semantico-pragmatic phenomenon that we decide to label as *symbolic mode*.

The following diagram tries thus to outline the series of semiotic phenomena labelled as symbolic by many theories and that in the following sections (from 1 to 3) will be excluded from the rank of symbols. We shall see that many of them can provide polysemous interpretations, but that these interpretations are always controlled by certain rules (be they lexical, rhetorical, or whatever).

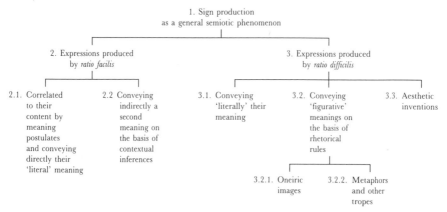

Once having eliminated all these improper senses, we shall be in the position to give a survey of many instances of a properly designated symbolic mode (see 4, p. 163ff.), as well as to provide a tentative description of the textual strategies implemented in order to produce interpretations in the symbolic mode (see 5, p. 174ff.).

1. *Genus and Species: the Symbolic as Genus*

There are, first of all, theories that identify the symbolic with semiotic activity in its entirety. In these perspectives symbolic activity is that by which man organizes his own experience into a system of contents conveyed by an expression system. The symbolic is the activity by which experience is not only coordinated but also communicated.

Goux (1973) has shown that such a notion of symbolic activity underlay Marx's theory, thus permitting the dialectic between structures and superstructures (see also Rossi-Landi 1974). Semiotic and symbolic activities are identical in Lévi-Strauss's structuralism (1950): culture is an ensemble of "symbolic systems" such as language, marriage rules, economic relationships, art, science, and religion. The possibility of the mutual transformation among structures is permitted by the existence of a more profound symbolic ability of the human mind, which organizes the whole of our experience according to the same modalities.

The symbolic and the semiotic also coincide in Lacan's thought. The registers of the psychoanalytic field are the *imaginary*, the *real*, and the *symbolic*. The imaginary is characterized by the relation between an image and a similar object, but the similarity of which Lacan speaks is not the one of so-called iconic signs: it is a phenomenon that takes place within the very perceptual mechanism. Men experience a mere relationship of similarity (an imaginary one) in the mirror stage, in the erotic dual relationship, and in many cases of isomorphism. In his "Seminar 1"(1953-1954), Lacan considers those images that in catoptrics are called "real" images, produced by curved mirrors (as opposed to the "virtual" images of plane mirrors), and that appear and disappear according to the position of the looking subject. This physical experience is used as an allegory of the constitution of the psychic subject, which is produced as subjective self-identity only by the phenomenon of the symbolic. The subject is an effect of the symbolic; the symbolic is the determining "order" of the subject. Wheras the imaginary is a simple relation between the ego and its images, the symbolic produces the subject through language (*la parole*) and realizes its closed order by the Law (*le Nom-du-père*). Only through the symbolic is the subject connected with the real, which is, so to speak, its umbilical cord. In Freud the symbolic is a store of oneiric symbols endowed with a constant signification (see 2.4.); that is, Freud attempts to set up a *code* of symbols. Lacan, on the contrary, flattens the relation between expression and content by considering only the internal logic of signifiers. Like Lévi-Strauss, Lacan is not concerned with the organization of sign-functions; he is, rather, concerned with the structural arrangements of signifiers. In "Seminar 1", he says that thinking means substituting an elephant with the word *elephant*, and the sun with a circle. But the sun, in so far as it is designated by a circle, is nothing if this circle is not inserted within a system of other formulations that, in their entirety, set up the symbolic order. A symbol becomes a signifying entity when it is inserted within a world of symbols (undoubtedly, for Lacan, the symbolic order is an *s-code* [Eco 1976: 38-40]). In this sense Lacan speaks of symbols both as words, as in the case of *elephant*, and as visual signs, as in the case of the sun-circle, even though the symbolic model in which he is more interested is undoubtedly the verbal one. Lacan is not as interested in a typology of signs as he is in the general category of the symbolic. It is, however, clear that for Lacan the symbolic order is what we can call the semiotic one. It is true that, in his interpretive practice, he introduces elements of what we shall call the symbolic mode, but this happens at the level of the interpretation of oneiric-verbal *texts*. From the point of view of a general definition, Lacan identifies the symbolic with the semiotic in general.

Symbolic and semiotic are also the same for Ernst Cassirer in *The Philosophy of Symbolic Forms* (1923-1929). Science does not mirror the structure of being (considered as the unattainable Kantian thing-in-itself): "The fundamental concepts of each science, the instruments with which it propounds its questions and formulates its solutions, are regarded no longer as passive images of something but as *symbols* created by the intellect itself" (1923-1929: 75). Cassirer mentions Hertz and Helmholtz's theory of scientific objects as "inner fictions" or symbols of outward objects: "These symbols are so constituted that the necessary logical consequences of the image are always images of the necessary natural consequences of the imagined objects" (ibid.). Cassirer does not identify symbols only with those *models* or *diagrams* ruled by *ratio difficilis* (see 2.3): his purpose is a wider one. He deals with the Kantian theory of knowledge as if it were a semiotic theory (even though Cassirer's *a priori* is more similar to a cultural product than to a transcendental structure of the human mind). The symbolic activity does not "name" an already known world, but establishes the very conditions for knowing it. Symbols are not translations of our thought; they are *its organs* (ibid.: 85-86):

> The logic of things, i.e., of the material concepts and relations on which the structure of a science rests, cannot be separated by the logic of signs. For the sign is no mere accidental cloak of the idea, but its necessary and essential organ. It serves not merely to communicate a complete and given thought content, but is an instrument, by means of which this content develops and fully defines itself . . . . Consequently, all truly strict and exact thought is sustained by the *symbolic* and *semiotics* on which it is based.

2. *Expressions Produced by Ratio Facilis*

2.1. *Symbols as Conventional Expressions.* C. S. Peirce defines an *icon* as "a sign which refers to the Object that it denotes merely by virtue of characters of its own", an *index* as "a sign which refers to the Object that it denotes by virtue of being really affected by that Object", and a *symbol* as "a sign which refers to the Object that it denotes by virtue of a Law, usually an association of general ideas. . . . It is thus itself a general type" (1903: 2.249).

As such, a symbol is correlated to its Object by an arbitrary and conventional decision. In this sense, words are symbols in so far as their lexical content depends on a cultural decision. Since Peirce had decided to use the term *sign* for the *genus generalissimum* of semiotics, he had to decide whether to reserve *symbol* for iconic signs (as Saussure and Hjelmslev did; see 3.1) or for the category of arbitrary signs. He made his choice following a rather frequent scientific usage, by which symbols are conventional signs standing for chemical, physical, or mathematical entities. It is true that Peirce knew very well that these scientific symbols display many "iconic" qualities (as we shall see when speaking in 3.1. of expression produced by *ratio difficilis* and conveying a "literal" meaning), but it is also true that Peirce never identified something as a mere symbol or as a mere icon. In any case, his decision contrasts with the most common terminological usage, and he certainly never thought that symbols convey a vague meaning. On the contrary, he speaks of symbols as those expressions that mean directly and univocally what they are designed to mean.

Curiously enough, many call symbols in the Peircean sense those *stylizations* (such as flags, emblems, astrological and chemical symbols) that Peirce would have recognized as abundantly endowed with iconic qualities. Probably at their very beginning, the alchemical symbol for the *Balneum Mariae* and the astrological symbol for Lion displayed some more or less evident "analogy" with their content, but nowadays they function as conventional devices. Emblems, coats of arms, and other heraldic devices do have a second sense: an image represents in first instance a tree, a hill, a city, while the heraldic meaning is a different one. But they are visual allegories whose meaning—even though multiple and difficult to guess—are already coded. Thus, either they are symbols in the Peircean sense, or they are "literal" expressions ruled by *ratio difficilis*; in both cases they must be excluded from the rank of the instances of a symbolic mode.

2.2. *Symbols as Expressions Conveying an Indirect Meaning.* The full content of a sign can be actualized only by progressive interpretations. But the notion of interpretation (rooted in that of inference) is not sufficient to characterize the symbolic mode. It characterizes every semiotic phenomenon at large.

There are, however, many expressions (usually sentences or texts) that suggest, beyond their *prima facie* interpretable "conventional" or "lexical" meaning, an additional "intended meaning" (see Grice 1957). If I tell a lady that I saw her husband in a cozy restaurant with a beautiful girl, I am undoubtedly trying to convey, along with the literal meaning, the intended meaning that the lady's husband is unfaithful to her. This second meaning is certainly "indirect", and, as such, it must be actualized by inferential labor on the part of the addressee; nevertheless, it is neither vague nor ambiguous.

Todorov (1978), aware of the difficulty of assigning a univocal sense to the term *symbol*, decides to provide a framework within which all its contrasting definitions can find a place, and wants to keep as "plural" what is in fact irreducible to a unique definition. In so doing, however, he accepts the line of thought criticized above: he identifies symbols with the whole gamut of indirect and even of direct meanings—connotations, presuppositions, implications, implicatures, figures of speech, intended meaning, and so on. Once again the symbolic is identified with the semiotic in general, since it is impossible to think of discourses that do not elicit some inferential response.

Many of the devices people call *symbols* have something to do with these phenomena of "indirect" meaning, but not every device conveying an indirect meaning can be called symbolic. Every semiotic device can be used, if not from the point of view of the sender, at least from the point of view of the interpreter, in order to actualize further meanings.

All these instances of indirect meaning say what they are intended to say on the basis of contextual inferences governed by semantic or pragmatic rules. What the sender intends to express—what he wishes to be understood—is so precise that the sender would be irritated if the addressee did not understand it. On the contrary, the genuine instances of a symbolic mode seem to be those where neither the sender nor the addressee really wants or is able to outline a definite interpretation.

3. *Expressions Produced by Ratio Difficilis*

3.1. *Symbols as Diagrams*. Saussure called symbols what Peirce called icons, and Hjelmslev ranked diagrams and games among the "symbolic systems", meaning by symbolic systems those which are *interpretable* but not *biplanar*. Thus Hjelmslev listed among symbols those signs that are *isomorphic* with their interpretation (1943: 113-114), as in:

> the case of pure games, in the interpretation of which there is an entity of content corresponding to each entity of expression (chess-piece or the like), so that if two planes are tentatively posited the functional net will be entirely the same in both . . . . *Symbol* should be used only for entities that are isomorphic with their interpretation, entities that are depictions or emblems, like Thorvaldsen's Christ as a symbol for compassion, the hammer and the sickle as a symbol for Communism . . . . There seems to be an essential affinity between the interpretable pieces of a game and isomorphic symbols, in that neither permits the further analysis into *figurae*. . . .

Saussure and Hjelmslev spoke in fact of signs ruled by *ratio difficilis* (Eco 1976: 183-184) where the expression maps, according to pre-established projection rules, some features of the corresponding content. In this sense one can call symbols those used by algebra and formal logic, at least insofar as their syntactic structure is concerned. They are such because every transformation performed upon the syntactical arrangement of the expression mirrors a possible rearrangement in the structure of their content. If, on a geographical map, one alters the borderline between France and Germany, one can forecast what would happen if, in a possible world (the new content corresponding to the manipulated expression), the geopolitical definitions of both countries were different. An algebraic formula and a map are *diagrams*. That is why in electrotechnics Seinmetz and Kennelly (following Helmholtz) called "symbolic" the method postulating biunivocal correspondence between the ensemble of sinusoidal functions of the same frequency (which incidentally are expressed by merely conventional and by no means "analogical" devices) and the ensemble of points upon an Arnauld-Gauss plane of rotating vectors. The rotation of a vector is a diagram that implies different sinusoidal functions.

It is, however, clear that there is a difference between diagrams and other phenomena labelled as symbols. Diagrams are based upon precisely coded transformational and projective rules, in the same way in which, in a musical score, the "symbolic" relation between rising points on the stave (spatial height) and frequency increments (phonic height) are ruled by a precise proportional criterion. On the contrary, many so-called symbols are characterized by the vagueness of their content and by the fact that the correlation is not pre-coded but invented

at the same moment in which the expression is produced. In Hjelmslev's definition the category of symbols encompasses both phenomena, without acknowledging
the radical difference between the way in which the Christ of Thorvaldsen is a
symbol for compassion and the way in which a move on the chessboard has a
symbolic nature. A different chess move would imply different interpretations of
the further course of the game, whereas we do not know how many manipula-
tions the Christ of Thorvaldsen should undertake in order to stand for something
other than compassion.

Moreover, a diagram such as the map of a subway is certainly ruled by *ratio
difficilis*, but it is neither vague nor indirect: its meaning is a "literal" one; one
can extrapolate from one's operations upon the map a precise possible state of
affairs. It could not be said that this possible state of affairs is a sort of "second"
sense that the map conveys. In the same way as one can interpret the word *father*
by inferring that if there is a father there should be either a son or a daughter,
thus if one detects on the map that, for reaching the node C from the node A,
one must pass through the node B, one can infer that if A and C were tied by
a direct connection, then B would be avoided. In both cases the word and the
map tell what they tell as soon as they are correctly interpreted according to given
cultural criteria.

Rather different, on the contrary, is the image of the serpent biting its own
tail. It is defined as a symbol because there is the strong feeling that it not only
represents a snake in an unusual position but that it also aims at communicating
something more.

3.2. *Symbols as Tropes.* **3.2.1.** *Oneiric Symbols.* Freud in *The Interpretation of Dreams*
(1900) speaks of oneiric symbols. Dreams convey images which stand for something
else, and Freud is interested in establishing how a "latent content" is organized
by the oneiric labor into the form of a "manifest content". The latent content
is transformed by the dream distortion (ibid.: ch. 4), and the dream is the disguised
fulfillment of repressed wishes. Freud does not interpret dreams (as ancient
oneiromancy used to do) as organic allegories. Allegories do have a logic, whereas
dreams do not. The psychoanalytic interpretation does not work upon organic
oneiric discourses but upon fragments and their idiosyncratic mechanisms of
substitution. Dreams work through condensation and displacement, and (even
though Freud does not say it explicitly), since they do not have a logic, they have
a rhetoric. Condensation and displacement are modalities of tropic substitution.

In the dream of the botanical monograph, the botanic symbol *condenses* Gärt-
ner, Flora, the forgotten flowers, the flowers loved by the author's wife, a university exam: "Each of the elements of the dream's contents turns out to have been
"overdetermined—to have been represented in the dream-thoughts many times
over" (1900: IV, 283).

Freud knows that the oneiric image is correlated to its content by a sort of *ratio
difficilis*, since it displays certain features that in some way map equivalent features
of the latent content. But, as happens in all cases of *ratio difficilis*, the mapping
relationship takes place between *selected features* of the expression and *selected features*
of the content. To decide which properties have to be selected, that is, which properties are co-textually pertinent, is exactly the typical labor performed by dreams,
according to certain requirements of plasticity, immediacy, representability.

Freud knows that oneiric symbols are not "stenographic" signs endowed with a pre-established meaning; however, he tries to anchor these expressions in an interpretable content. To find such an anchorage, Freud distinguishes between those oneiric symbols produced for idiosyncratic reasons which must be interpreted by using the patient's associations as their idiolectal encyclopedia, and those whose symbolism "is not peculiar to dreams, but is characteristic of unconscious ideation, in particular among the people, and it is to be found in folklore, and in popular myths, legends, linguistic idioms, proverbial wisdom, and current jokes" (1900: V, 351). It is true that every dreamer shows a remarkable plasticity in employing the most disparate images for symbolic purposes, but Freud tries repeatedly (see the various editions of the book: 1909, 1911, 1919) to find a *symbolic code* so as to explain the intersubjective (or cultural) meaning of umbrellas, sticks, railway travels, staircases and so on.

To look for an oneiric code means to touch on the hypothesis of a collective unconscious, as Jung would do; but Freud understands that in doing so one risks going backwards, to the very sources of human mental activity, where there will no longer be a *code*. On the other hand, a code is indispensable in order to speak intersubjectively of a semantics of dreams beyond the idiosyncratic attitudes of the dreaming subject. Thus Freud links the decoding of oneiric symbols to verbal puns, and in doing so he suggests that the knowledge of linguistic mechanisms can help one to understand the oneiric strategies of condensation and displacement. (The Lacanian decision to anchor the order of the imaginary in the order of the symbolic must be understood in this sense.) Freud suggests that the code can be reconstructed and that it is neither universal nor innate, but is historical, semiotic, and depends on the cultural encyclopedia of the dreamer.

This assumption is not, however, unambiguous. The dream must be interpreted according to a linguistic and cultural competence (that is, according to a competence which is external to the world of dreams); nevertheless, every oneiric image can be polysemous, as Freud explicitly says, and must be referred to the idiolect of the dreamer as well as to the whole dream as its co-text. Notwithstanding these perplexities and contradictions, Freud is undoubtedly looking for "correct" interpretations of dreams, and in this sense his oneiric symbols are not constitutively vague.

Freud has thus elaborated an oneiric rhetoric, with its own rules for generating and for interpreting images.

3.2.2. *Metaphors and Other Tropes.* Must we also exclude, from the rank of properly called symbols, metaphors, allegories, and other tropes? This is not to be taken for granted, because in many theories of literary criticism this distinction is not at all clear. However, even though they are "open" to various interpretations, metaphors are always governed by rhetorical rules and controlled by their co-texts.

In any case, there is a clear-cut test for distinguishing a metaphor from a symbol: a trope cannot be taken "literally" without violating a pragmatic maxim according to which a discourse is supposed to tell the truth; it must be interpreted as a figure of speech, since otherwise it would appear as senseless or blatantly false. On the contrary, the instances of the symbolic mode do suggest a second sense, but could also be taken literally without jeopardizing the communicational intercourse. (I shall further elaborate on this point in section 5).

More evident is the coded nature of allegories. They can be interpreted according to complementary senses (see, in 4.3, the medieval theory of the four levels of sense of the Scriptures), but these senses are never vague or indefinite.

A radical difference between symbol and allegory has been definitely established by Romantic theorists, who have, however, dangerously identified the symbolic with the aesthetic.

3.3. *The Romantic Symbol as Aesthetic Text.* Originally, a symbol was produced by the mutual relationship of two pieces of a coin destined to acquire their full purport through their actual or potential rejoining. In other sorts of signs the *signans* becomes irrelevant at the moment at which its *signatum* is caught (the *signans* is thrown away, so to speak); instead, in the signs that Romantic philosophers and poets called symbols, the *signatum* acquires its full purport only in so far as it is continually compared to the physical presence of its *signans*.

This idea suggests that there should be some resemblances between symbolic activity and the aesthetic function of language, where the message is self-focusing and speaks mainly of itself or of the relation between *signans* and *signatum*. The aesthetics of Romanticism has particularly insisted on this parenthood between symbolism and art. The work of art is conceived as an absolutely coherent organism in which expression and content are inseparable. A work of art is thus an untranslatable and unspeakable message (its ''meaning'' cannot be separated from what conveys it), and art is symbolic by definition because its discourse cannot but be undefinable or infinitely definable. Schelling identifies works of art with symbols because they are *hypotyposes*, self-presentations, and, instead of signifying an artistic idea, they are that idea *in themselves*. There is no ''semantic'' interpretation of a work of art.

Schelling distinguishes schemas, where the general provides us with an understanding of the particular, from allegories, where the particular provides us with knowledge of the general; in aesthetic symbols both procedures are at work simultaneously.

In the same line of thought, Goethe says that allegories designate directly, whereas symbols designate indirectly (1797: 94). Allegories are transitive, whereas symbols are intransitive. Allegories speak to the intelligence, whereas symbols speak to perception. Allegories are arbitrary and conventional, whereas symbols are immediate and motivated. A symbol is an image which is natural and universally understandable. Allegories employ the particular as an example of the general; symbols embody the general in the particular. Moreover, symbols are polysemous, indefinitely interpretable; they realize the coincidence of contraries; they express the unexpressible, since their content exceeds the capability of our reason (Goethe 1809-1832: nn. 1112-1113):

> Symbolisms transform the experience into an idea, and an idea into an image, so that the idea expressed by the image remains always active and unattainable and, even though expressed in all languages, remains unexpressible. Allegory transforms an experience into a concept and a concept into an image, but so that the concept remains always defined and expressible by the image.

In this sense the aesthetic and the symbolic come to coincide definitely, but they define themselves in terms of each other, in a circular way.

As a matter of fact, Romantic aesthetics does not explain the semiotic strategy by which, in the poetic use of languages, particular meanings are conveyed: it only describes the effect that a work of art can produce. By doing so, Romantic aesthetics flattens the concept of semiosic interpretation (which undoubtedly acquires a particular status in aesthetic texts) into the one of aesthetic enjoyment. On the other hand, semiotics can explain the phenomenon of symbolic mode, but it cannot fully explain aesthetic enjoyment, which depends on many extra-semiotic elements. In a work of art the expression is indefinitely interpretable, because the interpreter can continually compare it with its content and with the whole of his encyclopedic competence, but such a *semiosic* interpretation represents only one among the various aspects of aesthetic openness. A work of art can be aesthetically interpreted in many ways, because we compare its meanings (*interpreted* in the semiosic sense) with the individual structure of the token expression that conveys them. By displaying further and further new and uncoded possible relationships between these two planes, the work of art elicits also nonsemiosic reactions, such as synesthesiae, idiosyncratic associations, and more and more refined perceptions of the material texture of the conveying expression.

To interpret semiosically means to know better and better the possibilities of the encyclopedia; to interpret aesthetically also means to know more and more *intus et in cute* the details of an individual object. In Hjelmslev's terms, the semiosic interpretation has to do with *forms*; the aesthetic one has to do with *substances*. Thus if one uses the term *symbol* to describe the aesthetic experience, one has then to avoid the same term for other forms of "symbolic" understanding, such as, for instance, those that take place in mystical experience (where the mystic gets something beyond his own visionary experience).

The Romantic tradition is, instead, very ambiguous in this regard. Influential theorists of symbolism such as Creuzer (1810-12) speak of symbols as "epiphanies of the Sacred". The basic ideas of established religious doctrines spring from symbols that act as a light beam coming from the depths of the Being (I, 35). However, the same Creuzer says that a Greek sculpture is a plastic symbol, thus showing an oscillation between the idea of symbols as unattainable and transcendent revelations, and symbols as the self-evident presence of the artistic value embodied in a physical form. Is the Romantic symbol the instance of an *immanence* or of a *transcendence*?

4. The Symbolic Mode

4.1. *The Hegelian Symbol.* A radical attempt to distinguish the symbolic experience from the aesthetic one was performed by Hegel (1817-1829) in his philosophy of the fine arts.

The Hegelian symbol represents the first stage of artistic creativity (which dialectically progresses from symbolic to Classical and to Romantic art):

> Generally speaking, symbol is some form of external existence immediately present to the senses, which, however, is not accepted for its own worth, as it lies before us in its immediacy, but for the wider and more general significance which it offers to our reflection. We may consequently dis-

tinguish between two points of view equally applicable to the term: first, the *Significance*, and, second, the mode in which such a significance is *expressed*. The *first* is a conception of the mind, or an object which stands wholly indifferent to any particular content; the *latter* is a form of sensuous existence or a representation of some kind or other.

In symbols the correlation between signifier (expression) and signified (significance) is not a conventional one (the lion is a symbol for strength because it is strong); nevertheless, the motivation determining the correlation is in some way undetermined. The lion, for example, possesses qualities other than mere strength, and these qualities do not become relevant to the symbolic purpose. It is exactly this selection or reduction of the relevant qualities that provides for the ambiguity of symbols. Hegel refuses the idea of aesthetic symbolism as expressed by Creuzer: "In this sense the gods of Greece, insofar, that is to say, as the art of Greece was able to represent them as free, self-subsistent, and unique types of personality, are to be accepted from no symbolical point of view, but as self-sufficient in their own persons" (1817-1829: 21). The symbolic mode arises as a form of pre-art only when men look at natural objects as if they suggest something universal and essential, without a strict and absolute identity between expression and significance. In these first stages of artistic activity, when men try to spiritualize nature and to naturalize the universal, fantastic and confused results are produced: symbolic art experiences the inadequacy of its images and reacts to the sentiment of their limits by deforming them so as to realize an excessive and merely quantitative "sublimity".

Hegel outlines carefully these phases of symbolic activity (unconscious symbolism, symbolism of the sublime, conscious symbolism of the comparative type of art) through which mankind progresses from the symbols of Eastern art and religion to Western fables, parables, and apologues, to the allegory, the metaphor, the simile and the didactic poem. What is important, however, in Hegelian perspective, is the refusal to put together the symbolic and the artistic. The symbol always displays a certain disproportion, a tension, an ambiguity, an analogical precariousness. In "genuine symbolism" the forms do not signify themselves; rather they "allude to", hint at, a wider meaning. Any symbol is an enigma, and "the Sphinx stands as a symbol for symbolism itself" (ibid.: 83). In primeval symbolism a symbol has a meaning but it is unable to express it completely. The meaning of a symbol will be fully expressed only by the comparative mode of art, but at this point one is witnessing the dialectic "death" of the symbolic mode which transforms itself into higher and more mature forms of rhetorical expression. Hegel's whole argument is extraordinarily lucid, at least in distinguishing the symbolic from the aesthetic at large, as well as from the rhetorical. Hegel helps us in outlining a symbolic mode as a specific semiotic phenomenon in which a given expression is correlated to a *content nebula* (Eco 1976: 260).

4.2. *Archetypes and the Sacred.* Jung's theory of symbols as archetypes clearly outlines a notion of the symbolic mode as characterized by an analogy between expression and content and by a fundamental *vagueness* of the expressed content.

Jung (1954) opposes the personal unconscious to the collective one, which represents a deeper, innate layer of the human psyche and which has contents and modes of behavior that are more or less the same everywhere and in all individuals. The contents of the collective unconscious are the archetypes, archaic types, universal images, *représentations collectives*: lunar, solar, vegetal, meteorological representations—more comprehensible in myths, more evident in dreams and visions. Jung is explicit in saying that these symbols are neither mere signs (he uses the Greek technical word σημεῖα) nor allegories. They are genuine symbols precisely because they are ambiguous, full of half-glimpsed meanings, and in the last resort inexhaustible. They are paradoxical because they are contradictory, just as for the alchemists the spirit was conceived as *senex at iuvenis simul* ("an old man and a youth at once"). If the archetypes are indescribable and infinitely interpretable, their experience cannot but be amorphous, undetermined and unarticulated. Symbols are at the same time empty and full of meaning, and in this sense the experience of the mystics, which is strictly concerned with symbolic visions, is a paradoxical one. As Scholem (1960) also remarks about Jewish mysticism, mystical thought lives on a continual threshold between tradition and revolution: on one side the mystic is nourished by the tradition, but on the other side the visions he has can be interpreted so as to perturb the traditional truths. Usually the mystic uses old symbols, but fills them up with new senses and, in so doing, always challenges the authority, that is, the thought of the tradition he is supposed to follow and to reinforce. This kind of nihilistic experience is very well illustrated by the story of Brother Klaus von der Flue, mentioned by Jung. Brother Klaus has a vision of a mandala divided into six parts with in its center the "crowned countenance of God". His experience is defined as "terrifying", and the fifteenth-century humanist Woelflin describes it by saying that "all who came to him were filled with terror at the first glance". Jung remarks that visions such as the mandala are the usual and the traditional antidote for chaotic states of mind.

Brother Klaus has to choose between a free interpretation of the symbol and a traditional one. He relies on a devotional booklet by a German mystic, and assumes that what he has seen was the image of the Trinity. In this way the mystic, so to speak, "tamed" his unbearable experience (Jung 1954: 394):

> This vision, undoubtedly fearful and highly perturbing, which burst like a volcano upon his religious view of the world, without any dogmatic prelude, and without exegetical comment, naturally needed a long labor of assimilation in order to fit it into the total structure of the psyche and thus restore the disturbed psychic balance. Brother Klaus came to terms with his experience on the basis of dogma, then firm as a rock, and the dogma proved his powers of assimilation by turning something horribly alive into the beautiful abstraction of the Trinity idea. But the reconciliation might have taken place on a quite different basis provided by the vision itself and its unearthly actuality—much to the disadvantage of the Christian conception of God and no doubt to the still greater disadvantage of Brother Klaus himself, who would then have become not a saint but a heretic (if not a lunatic).

In the mystical experience symbols must be tamed exactly because they are exaggeratedly "open", and their force must be controlled. It obviously depends on one's religious and philosophical beliefs in deciding whether this force springs from a sacred source, or is nothing other than the way in which an interpreter, idiosyncratically, fills up the empty container of the symbolic expression. Firth (1973) observes that the mystical symbol is a private one: the mystic is the "detonator" of the symbol, but immediately afterwards a public "elaborator" is needed who establishes certain collective and understandable meanings for the original expression. In the story of Brother Klaus, both detonator and elaborator coincide. Firth mentions, on the contrary, the case of Saint Margaret Mary Alacoque who, as detonator, experienced the vision of the Sacred Heart of Jesus, while her Jesuit confessor interpreted and elaborated her symbolic material, providing the Catholic community with a new cult.

Incidentally, the case of this vision is interesting insofar as the pertinence of the so-called analogous properties is concerned: Saint Margaret Mary had her vision when both science and common opinion were definitely convinced that, physiologically speaking, the heart was not the seat of human feelings; nevertheless, in the first half of this century, Pope Pius XII still spoke of the Sacred Heart as a "natural symbol" of the Divine Love, a symbol that was "natural" only for those who, with an unconscious semiotic sensitivity, identified nature with encyclopedia. Pius XII certainly knew that the human heart was not the seat of emotions, but he also knew that, according to a nonspecialized competence (such as is expressed in and supported by many ready-made syntagms and by love songs), it was still considered so. What counts, in the symbolism of the Sacred Heart, is not the weakness of the analogical correlation but the vagueness of the correlated content. The content of the expression *Sacred Heart* (be it uttered in words or visually represented) is not a series of theological propositions but an uncontrollable ensemble of mental and affective associations that every believer can project onto the cardiac symbol. On the other hand, the symbol is the device by which a given authority controls these associations, as well as the profound drives that elicit them—in the same way in which the saint herself had probably projected into the mystical symbol a series of obsessions that, without the symbolic discipline, could have driven her to insanity.

But this is a positivist interpretation of a mystic experience. Usually, in the symbolic line of thought, symbols are considered as the vehicle of a transcendent Voice who speaks through them. Such is the perspective of Ricoeur's hermeneutics (1962). Symbols are opaque because they are analogic; they are bound to the diversity of languages and cultures, and their interpretation is always problematic: "There is no myth without exegesis, no exegesis without confrontation". But if there are recognizable symbols, there must be a Truth that symbols express, and symbols are the voices of Being: "The implicit philosophy of any phenomenology of religion is the renewal of a theory of reminiscence" (ibid.: 22). Ricoeur knows very well that, along Freudian lines of thought, religious symbols do not speak of the Sacred but of what has been removed. But in his hermeneutic perspective, these two possibilities remain as complementary, and symbols can be interpreted in either way. They tell us about the unconscious that *we were* and the Sacred that *we ought to become*. Freud and Heidegger are re-read in a Hegelian mood. The eschatology of human consciousness is a continual creative repetition of its archeology. In this way, naturally, nobody can assign to symbols a final truth or a coded meaning.

4.3. *The Symbolic Interpretation of the Holy Scriptures.* The symbolic mode is a recurrent tendency in many cultures and can coexist with other ways of producing or interpreting texts. Since this mode appears in many historical stages, it would be sufficient to isolate some of its instantiations: one of its characteristics is to reproduce itself in different epochs with the same features, so that an historical survey need not be exhaustive and can proceed through examples.

We can start from one of the most influential instances of the symbolic mode, the one developed by late Antiquity and the Middle Ages, not only because it has represented one of the most impressive and long-lasting cases of the symbolic mind, but also because our civilization is still dependent in many respects on that historical experience.

Pagan poets believed, more or less, in the gods of which they were speaking. But in the sixth century B.C., Theagenes of Regium tried to read these poets allegorically, and so did the Stoics many centuries afterwards. This allegorical reading had secular purposes: it aimed at discovering some "natural" truths beneath the mythical surface. However, once this way of reading was outlined, why not turn the method, and its purposes, the other way around? Thus, while, in the first century A.D., Philo of Alexandria was still attempting a secular interpretation of the Old Testament, Clement of Alexandria and Origenes attempted the opposite, that is, a nonsecular and, if possible, more mystical reading of religious texts.

At the moment in which the newborn Christian theology dared to speak of God, the Fathers of the Church realized that, in order to speak of Him, they could only rely on what He had told them: the Holy Scriptures. The Holy Scriptures were two, the Old Testament and the New Testament. At that time the Gnostics assumed that only the New Testament was true. Origenes wanted to keep the continuity between the two Testaments, but he had to decide in what way they were saying the same thing, since apparently they were speaking differently. Thus he made the decision to read them in a parallel way: the Old Testament was the signifier, or the "letter", of which the New Testament was the signified, or the spirit. At the same time, the New Testament was also speaking of something concerning the Incarnation, salvation, and moral duties. The semiosic process was thus rather complicated: a first book speaking allegorically of the second one, and the second one speaking—sometimes by parables, sometimes directly—of something else. Moreover, in this beautiful case of unlimited semiosis, there was a curious identification between, on the one hand, sender, message as signifier or expression, and signified or content, and on the other hand, referent, *interpretandum*, and interpretant—a puzzling web of identities and differences that can hardly be represented by a bidimensional diagram (see, for a splendid discussion on these points, Compagnon 1979):

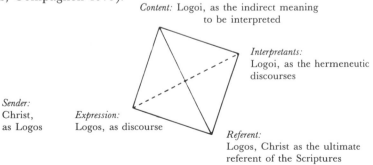

Content: Logoi, as the indirect meaning to be interpreted

Interpretants: Logoi, as the hermeneutic discourses

Sender: Christ, as Logos

Expression: Logos, as discourse

Referent: Logos, Christ as the ultimate referent of the Scriptures

This semiosic web was encouraged by the ambiguous status of the term *logos*, which is at the same time *verbum mentis* and *verbum vocis*, as well as the name and the nature of the second person of the Trinity. Moreover, the first interpreter of the ancient law was still Christ as *Logos*, and every commentary of the Holy Texts was an *imitatio Christi*, so that in the light of the *Logos* all faithful interpreters can become *Logikoi*. To make the web even more inextricable, Christ, in so far as He was the *Logos* (that is, the knowledge that the Father had of Himself), was the ensemble of all the divine archetypes; therefore, He was fundamentally polysemous.

Thus both Testaments speak of their sender and of their own polysemous nature, and their content is the nebula of all the possible archetypes.

What the first exegetes understood was that, at that point, the Scriptures were in the position of saying everything, and everything was too much, for any exegesis looks for a translatable Truth. The Church is the divine institution supposed to explain the truth, to make it understandable, even to the illiterate. The symbolic nature of the Books had thus to be tamed and reduced, in the same way in which the mystic vision of the detonator has to be tamed by its elaborator. The *symbolic* mode had to be transformed into the *allegorical* one. The Scriptures potentially had every possible meaning; but in fact their reading was susceptible to being governed by a code, and the meanings of the text had to be reduced to a manageable format. That is why the first Fathers proposed the theory of allegorical senses. In the beginning these were three: literal, moral or psychic, mystic or pneumatic. According to Origenes, the moral sense also held for the unfaithful and was thus immediately dependent on the literal one. Later the senses became four (literal, allegorical, moral and anagogical). As Dante explained in the *Epistula XIII* (i.1312-1317; but the theory was already fully elaborated by Bede in the seventh century), given a verse such as *in exitu Israel de Aegypto*, "if we look at the letter it means the exodus of the sons of Israel from Egypt at the time of Moses; if we look to the allegory it means our redemption through Christ; if we look at the moral sense it means the conversion of the soul from the misery of sin to the state of grace; if we look at the mystical sense it means the departure of the sanctified spirit from the servitude of this corruption to the freedom of eternal glory."

With this further elaboration, the moral sense can be understood only through the mediation of the allegorical one, and is attainable only by the faithful. The whole medieval tradition elaborated upon this theme, which can be summarized by the line of Nicholas of Lyra (c.1330): "*Littera gesta docet, quid credas allegoria, moralis quid agas, quo tendas anagogia*" [Literature teaches what people have done, allegory teaches what you should believe, morality what you should do, anagogy where you should direct yourself]. (But the same formulation appears in many other authors; for an impressive survey of all these theories, see De Lubac 1959).

The theory of the four senses provided a sort of guarantee for the correct decoding of the Books. But the Patristic and Scholastic mind could never avoid the feeling of the inexhaustible profundity of the Scriptures, frequently compared to a forest or to an ocean. According to Saint Jerome (c.397: *Ep.* 64.21) they are an "*infinita sensuum sylva*" [infinite forest of senses] and (c.411: col.448[1]) an "*oceanum et mysteriorum Dei, ut sic loquar labyrinthum*" ["ocean of the mysteries, or if I may so put it, of the labyrinth, of God"]. Origen speaks of a "*latissima sylva*" [broadest forest] (c.232-250: *In Ez.* 4, col. 696) or of a sea where, if we enter in a small boat, our mind is caught by fear and we are submerged by its whirls (c.232-250a: *In Gen.* 9.1, col.210).

Gilbert of Stanford (a.1153: *In Cant. 20.225*) tries to show how many senses can be found in the rapids of the divine discourse:

Scriptura Sacra, morem rapidissimi fluminis tenens, sic humanarum mentium profunda replet, ut semper exundet; sic haurientes satiat, ut inhexausta permaneat. Profluunt ex ea spiritualium sensuum gurgites abundantes, et transeuntibus aliis, alia surgunt: immo, non transeuntibus, quia sapientia immortalis est; sed, emergentibus et decorem suum ostendentibus aliis, alii non deficientibus succedunt sed manentes subsequuntur; ut unusquisque pro modo capacitatis suae in ea reperiat unde se copiose reficiat et aliis unde se fortiter exercent derelinquat. [*Sacred Scripture, like the rapids of a river, fills the depths of human minds, while it forever rushes onwards. Great whirlpools of spiritual meanings are formed within it, and while some whirlpools dissolve, others arise. Indeed, even when the former whirlpools do not dissolve, new ones appear, because wisdom is immortal. But, as the new ones arise and show their beauty to the previous ones, the newer ones follow the previous whirlpools. Thus each person finds in Scripture wherewith to be fully satisfied according to capacity, yet leaves to others wherewith they can also be absorbed.*]

Which is to say that, even though the senses of the Scriptures are infinite, none of them annuls the others; each increasingly enriches this immense store of meanings, where everyone can find what he is able to find according to his interpretive capabilities.

The metaphor of the ocean or of the forest alluded to the symbolic structure of the Books, and this symbolic structure was the continual challenge to their allegorical interpretability. Either the Books had infinite readings (therefore they were ambiguous expression correlated to the content nebula of all possible archetypes) or they had only the four canonical ones. But, if the four senses were coded, there was no further possibility of interpreting the Books, therefore of exploiting their admirable profundity. The problem was how to reconcile these two trends, so that it was possible to read the texts, continually discovering in their pages, if not new things, at least the same and everlasting truth rephrased in ever new ways: *non nova sed nove*, no new things but the same things retold in a new way.

The early Christian theology had then to find a way of controlling (by an allegorical code) the free interpretation of the (symbolic and uncoded) nature of the Books. A rather oxymoronic situation, indeed. At this point, the topological model capable of representing this situation should be even more complex (perhaps a Moebius Ring), since the only authority that could establish the right way of interpreting the Books was the Church, founded upon the Tradition; but the Tradition was represented exactly by the series of "good" interpretations of the Holy Scriptures. In other words, the Tradition draws its right to control the interpretation of the Books from the interpretation of the Books. *Quis custodiet custodes* [who will guard the guardians]? How can the authority legitimate the interpretation, since the authority itself is legitimated by the interpretation?

This question had no answer; no theory of types or of metalanguage was elaborated to legitimate the circle of hermeneutic legitimation (no theory of hermeneutic legitimation can indeed be legitimated, if not by the very process of hermeneutic reading). At the origins of the hermeneutic practice there is a circle; it does not matter how holy or how vicious.

The only possible answer to this question was a practical one: the rules for good interpretation were provided by the gatekeepers of the orthodoxy, and the gatekeepers of the orthodoxy were the winners (in terms of political and cultural power) of the struggle to impose their own interpretation. Such a rule also holds for a more secular hermeneutics: the text will tell the truth in so far as the reader has the rhetorical power to make it speak. And the reader will be sure to have seen right in so far as he has seen—in the text—his own image. The same, albeit less secular, procedure held for the interpretive practice in Jewish mysticism (Scholem 1960: 15):

> The literal meaning is preserved, but merely as the gate through which the mystic passes, a gate, however, which he opens up to himself over and over again. The Zohar expresses this attitude of the mystic very succinctly when, in a memorable exegesis of Genesis 12.12, God's words to Abraham, *Lekh lekha*, are taken not only in their literal meaning, "Get thee out", that is, they are not interpreted as referring only to God's command to Abraham to go out into the world, but are also read with mystical literalness as "'Go to thee', that is, to thine own self".

We feel here, pre-echoed, the Freudian maxim, as re-read by Lacan: *Wo Es war, soll Ich werden* [where the *id* was, the *ego* should be].

The whole history of medieval exegesis is the story of the establishing and, at the same time, of the fair challenging of exegetical *auctoritates*. First of all, from the time of Augustine, it was discovered that, if the Books always tell something Other, they do so not only by the *words* they use but also through the *facts* they tell about. The allegory is not only *in verbis* but also *in factis*. The problem was how to assign an allegorical value to facts, that is, to the furniture of the existing world, to animals, to plants, to stones, to actions, to gestures, and so on. In *De Doctrina Christiana*, Augustine decides that in order to understand the Scriptures the exegete must know physics, geography, botany, mineralogy. Thus the new Christian civilization accepts and introduces (by further and further re-elaborations) into the interpretive circle (that is, into its own growing encyclopedia) all the knowledge of classical civilization, as it was inherited by the late Roman culture, under the form of a syncretistic encyclopedia. This is the origin of the acceptance of the Hellenistic *Physiologus* and of the successive production of herbaries, bestiaries, lapidaries, *Imagines* and *Specula Mundi*.

The main characteristics of these texts are: (a) Since every visible entity has an allegorical meaning, the world's creatures are not described according to their empirical properties, but according to those properties that display some analogy with the content they are supposed to represent. So the lion is described as an animal which cancels with its tail the traces of its passage in order to deceive its hunters, simply because he *must* possess this property to function as the image of Christ deleting the traces of human sin by His incarnation. (b) Whether because of the growth of an hallucinatory imagination or because of a symbolic temptation challenging the rights of the allegorical coding, the properties of these creatures are frequently contradictory, so that every item of the medieval encyclopedia can acquire alternative meanings: the lion is at the same time the figure of Christ and the figure of the Devil because of its hideous jaws. How can an interpreter be sure that in a given context the lion stands for Christ and not for the Devil? The allegorical code is open, so as to become a symbolic matrix where the meanings are, if not nebulous, at least manifold. The medieval solution is that a preceding *auctoritas* should have already established the ''good'' contextual selections: once again the vicious hermeneutic circle. The medieval interpreter looks continually for good authorities, knowing at the same time that any authority has a wax nose that can be moulded as the interpreter wants. With humble and hypocritical flexibility, the medieval interpreter knows that he is a dwarf with respect to the *auctoritates*, but a dwarf mounted upon the shoulders of giants, and therefore he is able to look a little further ahead: perhaps he does not see new things (*nova*), but he sees them in a new way (*nove*).

In this way the allegorical mode is inextricably and ambiguously intertwined with the symbolic one: the medieval mind is a divided one, rent by the conflict between confidence in an indisputable truth (repeated by every word and every fact), and the feeling that words and facts must be continually reinterpreted in order to go further and further, beyond their acknowledged sense, since the whole universe is *quasi liber scriptus digito Dei* [like a book written by God's finger], but in this book *aliud dicitur, aliud demonstratur* [what is said is different from what is shown].

Once again, as in the case of mysticism, the gathering of the community around the ever-speaking voices of the Scriptures and of the world has the function of social control. It does not matter what both the Book and the world say; it matters that they *speak* and that there is a centre of elaboration of their speech. When people gather around a flag, it does not matter what exactly the flag symbolically means, since it can have multiple senses: what matters is that the flag undoubtedly *means something to them*. The power consists in possessing the key for the right interpretation, or (what is the same) in being acknowledged by the community as the one who possesses the key. Not only in the Middle Ages does every community (be it a church, a country, a political regime, a scientific school) in which the symbolic mode holds need an *auctoritas* (the Pope, the Big Brother, the Master). The *auctoritas* is indispensable when there is not a code; where there is a code—as a system of pre-established rules—there is no need for a central *auctoritas*, and the power is distributed through the nodes of organized competence. Either power eliminates the other one. Civilizations and cultural groups have to make a choice.

The medieval symbolic mode collapses when, with Aquinas' theology, *a* code wins (the *Summae* are a sort of institutional code: they do not allow for a vague interpretation of reality and the Scriptures). Aquinas definitely destroys with cogent argumentations the medieval tendency toward the allegorical and symbolic reading of reality and reserves a strictly coded allegorical reading only for the facts narrated by the Old Testament.

The language of the Scriptures is purely literal: the Old Testament tells us about facts that, in so far as they have been pre-disposed by God in order to teach us, are to be interpreted allegorically. But these facts are only the facts narrated by the Old Testament. After the Incarnation the possibility of looking at facts as meaning something else no longer exists.

As far as language (be it poetic or scriptural) is concerned, every rhetorical strategy represents an instance of *modus parabolicus* [parabolic mode], but this *non supergreditur modum litterale* [does not exceed the literal mode] (Aquinas 1256: q. 6.

a. 3. ad 2²). This means that since there are rhetorical rules, tropes and allegories can be interpreted univocally as if they were literal expressions. Rhetoric is a natural language.

If the symbolic mode collapses, for a while, in Western thought, it survives, however, and grows in different directions in other forms of mysticism. A paramount example of a different symbolic mode is the Jewish mysticism of the Kabbala, where the Book that the Christian tradition tried desperately to anchor in a fixed allegorical reading blows up, so to speak, in a really unlimited semiosis, even losing the linear consistency of its material expressive level.

4.4. *The Kabbalistic Drift.* Scholem (1960) says that Jewish mystics have always tried to project their own thought into the biblical texts; as a matter of fact, every inexpressible reading of a symbolic machinery depends on such a projective attitude. In the reading of the holy text according to the symbolic mode (ibid.: 36), "letters and names are not conventional means of communication. They are far more. Each one of them represents a concentration of energy and expresses a wealth of meaning which cannot be translated, or not fully at least, into human language". For the Kabbalist the fact that God expresses Himself, even though His utterances are beyond any human insight, is more important than any specific and coded meaning His words can convey.

The *Zohar* says (III, 202a) that "in any word shine a thousand lights". The unlimited quality of the sense of a text is due to the free combinations of its signifiers which, in that text, are linked together as they are only accidentally, but which could be combined differently. In a manuscript of Rabbi Eli-yaku Kohen Ittamari of Smyrna we read why the scrolls of the Torah, according to the Rabbinical law, must be written without vowels and punctuation (Scholem 1960: 74-75):

> This is a reference to the state of the Torah as it existed in the sight of God before it was transmitted to the lower spheres. For He had before Him numerous letters that were not printed into words as is the case today, because the actual arrangement of the words would depend on the way in which this lower world conducted itself . . . . The divine purpose will be revealed in the Torah at the coming of the Messiah, who will engulf death forever . . . . For the God will annul the present combination of letters that form the words of our present Torah and will compose the letters into other words, which will form new sentences, speaking of other things.

Thus, when a man utters the words of the Torah, he never ceases to create spiritual potencies and new lights (ibid.: 76): "If therefore he spends the whole day reading just this one verse, he attains eternal beatitude, for at all times, indeed, in every moment, the composition [of the inner linguistic elements] changes in accordance with the name that flares up within him at this moment".

Such a disposition to interrogate a text according to a symbolic mode still rules many contemporary hermeneutic practices. They can take two alternative (though profoundly connected at their source) routes. Language can be the place where things authentically begin: in Heidegger's hermeneutics the word is not "sign" (*Zeichen*) but "to show" (*Zeigen*), and what is shown is the true voice of Being. In such a line of thought, texts can be indefinitely questioned, but they do not only speak of themselves; they reveal something else and something more.

On the other hand, there is a radically secularized hermeneutics where the text is no longer transparent and symptomatic, since it only speaks of its possibility of eliciting a semiosic "drift". More than "auscultating", the text must (in a more radically Kabbalistic option) be *deconstructed*, until it fractures its own expressive texture. Thus the text does not speak any longer of its own "outside". It does not even speak of itself; it speaks of our own experience in (deconstructively) reading it. There is no longer a dialectics of *here* and *there*, of *signans* and *signatum*. Everything happens *here*—and the dialectics takes place, at most, as a *further-and-further* movement, from *signans* to *signans*.

Only in this way, even in epistemological frameworks devoid of a traditional notion of truth, is it possible that the very act of reading provide a certain approach to what a text truly (even though never definitely) says. From this point of view it is interesting to re-read the fascinating discussion that took place between John Searle (unwillingly playing the role of the "literal" man, who believed that the word *copyright* conventionally means that the excerpt from a given paper cannot be reproduced without permission) and Jacques Derrida, who, in a true Kabbalistic mode, from the unstable combination *copy-right* draws infinite inferences on the instability and fragility of Searle's language, and on the deconstructibility of every linguistic utterance. Focused upon as a new and unfaithful Torah, the text of Searle allows Derrida to read in it something else, something other than what his adversary believed it to mean, something by and through which he, in fact, has been meant (Derrida 1977: 203-204):

> The questioning initiated by the logic and the graphics of *Sec* does not stop at the security of the code, nor at its concept. I cannot pursue this problem too far, since that would only add new complications to a discussion that is already too slow, overdetermined, and overcoded in all respects. I shall simply observe that this line of questioning is opened in the first of *Sec's* three parts, and to be exact by the following phrase: "The perhaps paradoxical consequence of my here having recourse to iteration and to code: the disruption, in the last analysis, of the authority of the code as a finite system of rules, at the same time, the radical destruction of any context as the protocol of code" (p. 180). The same direction, that of an iterability that can only be what it is in the *impurity* of its self-identity (repetition altering and alteration identifying), is charted by the following propositions: "As far as the internal semiotic context is concerned, the force of the rupture is no less important: by virtue of its essential iterability, a written syntagm can always be detached from the chain in which it is inserted or given without causing it to lose all possibility of functioning, if not all possibility of 'communicating', precisely. One can perhaps come to recognize other possibilities in it by inscribing it or *grafting* it onto other chains. No context can entirely enclose it. Nor any code, the code here being both the possibility and impossibility of writing, of its essential iterability (repetition/alterity)" (p. 182). And: ". . . in so doing [i.e., by the iterability *or* the citationality that it permits] it [the sign] can break with every given context, engendering an infinity of new contexts in a manner which is absolutely illimitable. This does not imply that the mark is valid outside of a context, but on the contrary that there are only contexts without any center or absolute anchoring [*ancrage*]" (pp. 185-6).

In this ultimate epiphany of the symbolic mode, the text as symbol is no longer read in order to find in it a truth that lies *outside*: the only truth (that is, the old Kabbalistic God) is the very play of deconstruction. The ultimate truth is that the text is a mere play of differences and displacements. Rabbi Levi Isaac said that "also the white, the spaces in the scroll of the Torah, consist of letters, only that we are not able to read them as we read black letters. But, in the Messianic Age, God will also reveal to us the white of the Torah, whose letters have become invisible to us, and that is what is meant by the statement about the 'new Torah' " (Scholem 1960: 82). The Lacanian acknowledgement of the autonomy of the symbolic as the chain of the signifiers, by inspiring the new deconstructionist practices, has now allowed the new and atheistic mystics of the godless drift to rewrite indefinitely, at every new reading, the new Torah.

5. *Semiotics of the Symbolic Mode*

Our quest for the specific symbolic mode is seriously challenged by the deconstructive practice. If in a text everything can be read beyond its conventional (and delusory) meaning, then *every* text is a reserve of symbols. Once again, the symbolic mode is equated with the semiotic one: each human discourse always speaks indirectly. A fascinating but unsatisfactory conclusion. Symbols looked so mysterious; they promised such a privileged way of knowing. And now we are left with two equally irritating alternatives: either every utterance provides for this privileged knowledge (but where everything is privileged, there is no longer a privilege), or language is always symbolic but only a happy few can deal with it as such. It will be then unclear what the others really understand; they probably misunderstand, but why despise them, since misunderstanding is the only way of interpreting? Or is there a difference between "correct" and "incorrect" misunderstanding?

There is, however, a fully secularized way of conceiving of the symbolic mode, as limited to specific forms of communication, and it is the one proposed by many modern aesthetic theories springing from the experience of French Symbolism. Even though the cultural roots of artists such as Baudelaire go back to many currents of mystical thought, in the modern aesthetic perspective the artist is a free detonator of a vision that he himself produces: an expression purposefully endowed with vague meanings, one which cannot be anchored in a pre-established code (there is no fixed elaboration). The poetic work remains *open*. It is still the Romantic ideal, but definitely dominated by the ideal of poetic ambiguity. It is true that when Baudelaire (in "Correspondances") speaks of Nature as a temple whose living pillars whisper a cryptic speech, so that man wanders among them as in a wood of symbols where colors, perfumes and sounds echo each other, this picture reminds us of the medieval world as a book written by the hand of God. But Baudelairean symbols (be they albatrosses, cats, or serpents) are *private*; they do not need a *Physiologus* to explain their possible meanings. They acquire their full significance only within their poetic context. It is true that Mallarmé's idea of a context made up by empty and white spaces can recall the rabbinical idea of a scroll where even the white spaces are to be read as letters, but this time there is no God to warrant (and to be named by) the combinatory game: the Book is not conceived by God to speak of Himself. On the contrary, it is the whole world which exists in order to give birth to the Book (*Le Livre*), and the Book only speaks of its infinite combinatorial possibilities.

More radically, the symbolic mode is poetically secularized in Joyce's theory of epiphanies and in Eliot's notion of objective correlative. Here events, gestures, suddenly appear as strange, inexplicable, intrusive evidence within a context which is too weak to justify their presence. So they reveal that they are there to reveal something else: it is up to the reader to decide what else.

In this line of thought *not everything can be a symbol*. A symbol has to be textually produced; it requires a specific semiotic strategy. It is exactly such a strategy that should now be in some way outlined—at least under the form of an abstract model. A symbolic strategy can produce aesthetic enjoyment, but it is first of all semiotic machinery.

Let us start from the normal conversational implicatures as described by Grice (1975). They are instances of indirect signification, as described in 2.2., but not necessarily of the symbolic mode: the additional meaning transmitted by an implicature is not a vague one, at least not as far as the intentions of the speaker are concerned (it can become vague only because of a lack of cooperation by the hearer).

In a text, the device of flouting the conversational maxims can be used rhetorically. Metaphors, irony, hyperboles all violate the maxim of quality, since they do not tell (literally) the truth. If I say that a hero is a lion, literally speaking I lie: my addressee, by recognizing such a blatant case of lying, must infer that I probably intend to say something else. But since the correct interpretation of the metaphor is that this hero is a courageous or ferocious man, the metaphorical expression does not necessarily convey a content nebula (even though it could). Many metaphors (and all catachreses) can be disambiguated without vagueness.

More interesting are the violations of the maxims of quantity, relation, and manner. Not every rhetorical violation of these maxims produces the symbolic mode: figures such as periphrasis or laconism violate the maxim of quantity without conveying vague meanings, and certain synecdoches and metonymies violate the maxim of manner without referring to nebulous contents.

Nevertheless, we can say that even though not all the violations of these maxims result in producing the symbolic mode, the symbolic mode springs from certain violations of them and represents a case of *textual implicature*.

Naturally a text can *narrate* a case of conversational implicature, thus encouraging the interpreter to implement the appropriate inferences. If a narrative text reports a conversation in which the first speaker asks the second one about his love affairs, and the second speaker answers by some meteorological remarks, the reader has to infer that the second speaker was making a conversational implicature, meaning "I am not supposed to tell about my private life", and, by means of other co-textual inferences, some additional information about his character can be extrapolated. But all these inferences follow rhetorical or psychological laws, more or less coded, and rely on pre-established frames. This will not be considered an instance of textual implicature but, rather, a case of mere reported conversational implicature.

On the contrary, when in a Zen story the Master, asked about the meaning of life, answers by raising his stick, the interpreter smells an abnormal implicature, whose interpretant keys lie outside pre-existing frames. This gesture means not only that the Master refuses to answer, but also that his (gestural) answer has a still uncoded meaning, and maybe more than one. The textual implicature signaling the appearance of the symbolic mode depends on the presentation of a sentence, of a word, of an object, of an action that, according to the precoded narrative or discursive frames, the acknowledged rhetorical rules, or the most common linguistic usages, *should not* have the relevance it acquires within that context.

The standard reaction to the instantiation of the symbolic mode should be a sort of uneasiness felt by the interpreter when witnessing an inexplicable move on the part of the text, the feeling that a certain word, sentence, fact, or object should not have been introduced in the discourse or at least not have acquired such an importance. The interpreter feels a *surplus* of signification since he guesses that the maxims of relevance, manner, or quantity have not been violated by chance or by mistake. On the contrary, they are not only flouted, but—so to speak—flouted dramatically.

"By an epiphany [Stephen] meant a sudden spiritual manifestation, whether in the vulgarity of speech or of gesture or in a memorable phase of the mind itself. He believed that it was for the man of letters to record these epiphanies with extreme care, seeing that they themselves are the most *delicate* and *evanescent* of moments", wrote Joyce in *Stephen Hero* (i.1904-1906). In producing most of his epiphanies, Joyce puts them within a co-text that explicitly introduces and stresses their strangeness and their revealing intrusiveness. Other authors (see, for example, the objective correlatives in Eliot) present the irrelevant apparitions without justifying their presence. What signals their role is the fact that they *should not be there*. Incidentally, the feeling that something should not be there is the one that accompanies, in the early theory of textual symbolism, the interpretation of an event, of an object, of a precept in the Holy Scriptures. See how Augustine, in the *De Doctrina Christiana* (c.397-426: III. 14. p. 87), explains when an expression of the Bible has to be taken figuratively and not literally (naturally, as we have seen in 4.3., the problem of Augustine and of the Middle Ages will be to reduce the symbolic power of the expression by interpreting it allegorically):

> To this warning that we must beware not to take figurative or transferred expressions as though they were literal, a further warning must be added lest we wish to take literal expressions as though they were figurative. Therefore a method of determining whether a locution is literal or figurative must be established. And generally this method consists in this: that whatever appears in the divine Word that does not literally pertain to virtuous behavior or to the truth of faith you must take to be figurative.

The symbolic mode, as theorized by both decadent and contemporary aesthetics, has also been, and can also be, implemented in different cultural frameworks. In Gérard de Nerval's *Sylvie* (1853) the narrator, in the first chapter, lives a conflict between his actual love for an actress (seen as an unattainable ideal woman) and crude everyday reality. A piece of news read by chance plunges him (at the beginning of the second chapter) into a state of half-sleep in which he recollects the events of an imprecise past—presumably his childhood—in the village of Loisy. The temporal contours of this reverie are blurred and misty: he remembers the apparition of a mysterious and ethereal beauty, Adrienne, destined for the convent.

In the third chapter, when awakening from his state of half-sleep, the narrator compares the image of Adrienne with the actress and is struck by the suspicion that they are the same person, an unreasonable hypothesis, indeed; but he still suspects himself of having superimposed the two images, loving the disappeared girl of his childhood in the shape of the actress of his adulthood. Suddenly he

decides to set foot into reality again. Incidentally, at this point the narration abruptly shifts to the present tense; previously it had been carried on in the imperfect
(a tense that in French stresses a temporal vagueness much more than the supposedly equivalent English tenses can do). Returning to reality, the narrator
decides to go back to Loisy, not to see the girl of his dreams, but to see Sylvie,
who in the second chapter appeared as the representative of humble reality, as
opposed to the enchanted Adrienne. He wonders what time it can be, realizing
that he has no watch. He steps back to ask the doorman, and with this concrete
information he takes a cab to go back physically in space, and ideally in time.

However, between the first question about the right time and his visit to the
concierge, the narrative sequence is interrupted by the following description (Nerval 1853: 80-81):

> Among all the bric-à-brac splendours which it was customary to collect
> at that period to give local colour to an old apartment, shone the restored
> brilliance of one of those Renaissance clocks, whose gilded dome sur-
> mounted by the figure of Time is supported by cariatides in the Medici
> style, resting in their turn on semi-plunging horses. The historical Diana,
> with her arm round her stag, is in low relief on the face, where the
> enamelled numbers of the hours are marked on an inlaid background. The
> works, excellent no doubt, had not been wound up for two centuries. I
> had not bought that clock in Touraine to learn the time from it.

What is the narrative function of this description? None. The reader already knows
that the narrator has no reliable watch. At the discursive level this long digres-
sion does not add much to the knowledge of the habits of the character. The
presence of that clock sounds strange and strangely delays the action. Thus the
clock must be there to mean something else.

What it could mean will be inferred throughout the further course of the story.
In the fourth chapter, Nerval does not narrate the present trip to Loisy. Just at
the end of the third chapter, the author abandons the narrator sitting in the cab
and follows his new memories. The narrator muses on another time, different
from the one of the second chapter. It is some temporal state between remote
childhood and the time of the narration, an imprecise moment of the narrator's
adolescence, and this state lasts from chapter four to chapter six. At the beginning of the seventh chapter, there is a very short return to the present (time and
tense); then the narrator starts a new reverie about a bewitched voyage to the
Abbey of Chaalis—where he *believes* he saw Adrienne for a second time. The temporal contours of this experience are absolutely unclear: was he there before or
after the experiences remembered in the previous three chapters? Moreover, did
he really meet Adrienne, or was it an hallucination? This chapter is a revealing
clue that impels the reader to consider the following, as well as the preceding,
chapters in the light of an unsuccessful quest for the things of the past. Nerval
is not Proust; he does not come to terms with his past. Sylvie is the story of the
failure of memory as well as of the failure of identity: the narrator is unable to
distinguish not only the present from bygone times, but also the imaginary from
the real. Sylvie, Adrienne and the actress are three "actorial" embodiments of
the same *actant*—each woman becoming in her turn the instance of a forgotten
and lost ideal, as opposed to the crude presence (or absence and death) of the

others. The narrator fails to understand which one he really loves and which one he really loved. At this point the reader catches the *possible* symbolic meanings of the Renaissance clock. It is a symbol standing for a nebula of alternative but nevertheless complementary contents: namely, the vagueness of remembrance, the incumbency of the past, the transience of time, the longing for the remnants of an idealized heroic era—perhaps the clock is even the symbol for *Sylvie* as a whole, a story within a story—and so on *ad infinitum*. The novel encourages as many interpretations as there are readings. This symbol is *open*; it is, however, *overdetermined* by the co-text. It is *undoubtedly* a symbol, since its interpretation is *doubtful*, and there were only *doubtful* reasons for its textual appearance.

The episode is interpreted as symbolic exactly in so far as it cannot be definitely interpreted. The content of the symbol is a *nebula* of possible interpretations; open to a semiosic displacement from interpretant to interpretant, the symbol has no authorized interpretant. The symbol says that there is something which it could say, but this something cannot be definitely spelled out once and for all, otherwise the symbol would stop saying it. The symbol says clearly only that it is a semiotic machine devised to function according to the symbolic mode.

In this sense a symbol is different from a metaphor. When facing a metaphor, the interpreter, in discovering that the metaphoric expression does not tell the truth, is obliged to interpret it metaphorically. In the same way, when facing the flouting of a conversational maxim, one is obliged to assume that the expression should express something else.

On the contrary, when confronted with an allegory, the interpreter could also decide to interpret it in its literal sense. The fact that at the beginning of the *Divine Comedy* Dante is in a gloomy wood can be taken as a report of a literal event, disregarding the possibility of seeing it as the adventure of a human soul lost in the wood of sin.

Both symbol and allegory are signaled, at least, by a feeling of literal waste, by the suspicion that spending such a textual energy for saying *only this* is pragmatically "uneconomical".

The further difference between symbol and allegory stands in this: that the allegory is more insisted upon than the symbol and, furthermore, that the allegory is a piece of extended narrativity, whereas usually a symbol is the sudden apparition of something that disturbs the course of a previous narration. Moreover, an allegory should immediately suggest its own key; it should point towards a portion of encyclopedia which already hosts the right frames for interpreting it (it represents an explicitly intertextual reminder), whereas a symbol leaves the interpreter face to face with the uncoded. Thus a symbol cannot send back to a previously coded cultural competence; it is idiolectal because it holds only for the textual environment where it appears (otherwise it is only the "quotation" of a previously catachresized symbol). In this sense aesthetic symbols are removed from every "political" control; they *detonate* but they cannot be *elaborated* from the outside. The aesthetic experience cannot be a mystical one, because it cannot be interpreted and tamed by an external authority. No critical achievement has the force to establish an interpretive tradition; when this happens, the aesthetic symbol has provisionally (perhaps definitively) lost its appeal—it has become something that can be quoted as "shibboleth" by the members of a critical clique, the "gesture" of a frozen ritual, the mere mention of a previous symbolic experience. The living symbol is then replaced by a kitsch label.

6. Conclusions

If one then makes an abstraction from any possible underlying metaphysics or mystical assumption, the symbol is not a particular sort of sign, endowed with mysterious qualities, nor is it a particular modality of sign production. It is a *textual modality*, a way of producing and interpreting the aspects of a text. According to a typology of sign production (Eco 1976: 217-261), there is an actualization of the symbolic mode when, through a process of *invention*, a textual element is produced which could be interpreted as a mere *imprint*, or a *replica*, or a *stylization*. But it can also be identified, by a sudden process of recognition, as the *projection*, by *ratio difficilis*, of a content nebula.

Take the wheel of a carriage at the door of a country house. It can be the sign for the workshop of a carriage maker (and in this sense it is an *example* of the whole class of object there produced); it can be the sign of a restaurant (thus being a *sample, pars pro toto*, of that rural world to which it announces and promises culinary delights); it can be the *stylization* of the sign for the local seat of the Rotary Club. One can *also* decide to recognize it as a manifestation of the symbolic mode: one can focus upon its circularity as suggesting the ability of proceeding *ad infinitum*, or upon the equal distance of the hub from every point of the circle, the radiant symmetry that links the hub to the rim through its spokes. One can disregard as symbolically irrelevant other properties (namely, its wooden material, its artificial origin, its metonymic link to oxen and horses . . .). Starting from the selected properties, one can discover, in one's encyclopedic competence, that these pertinent properties map the properties of something else, even though this something else is a nebula of many things: let us say, time with its forward progress, the perfect symmetry of God, the creative energy that produces, from a unique centre, the circular perfection of every being, the progression of the divine light beams throughout the fall of Neoplatonic emanations . . . that wheel can send us back to all these properties of all these entities, and in its content nebula it conveys all of them, and all of them can coexist at the same time, irrespective of their mutual contradictoriness. The symbolic mode neither cancels the wheel as a physical presence (all the suggested content seems to live *within the wheel* and *because of the wheel*), nor cancels the *token* wheel as a vehicle of a ''literal'' conventionalized meaning. For the profane it could still remain the sign for the carriage maker's workshop. In the same way, the profane only see a cobbler at work where the Kabbalist recognizes in his operation the symbolic action of the one who ''at every stitch of his awl . . . not only joined the upper leather with the sole, but all the upper things with all lower things'', drawing at every step ''the steam of emanation down from the upper to the lower (so transforming profane action into ritual action), until he himself was transfigured from the earthly Enoch into the transcendent Metatron, who had been the object of his meditation'' (Scholem 1960: 132).

The symbolic mode is thus not only a mode of producing a text, but also a mode for interpreting every text—through a pragmatic decision: ''I want to interpret this text symbolically''. It is a modality of textual *use*.

This pragmatic decision produces at the semantic level a new sign-function, by associating new content—as far as possible, undetermined and vague—with expression already correlated to a coded content. The main characteristic of the symbolic mode is that the text, when this mode is not realized interpretively, remains endowed with sense—at its literal or figurative level.

In the mystical experience, the symbolic contents are in some way suggested by a preceding tradition, and the interpreter is convinced (he must be convinced) that they are not cultural units but *referents*, aspects of an extrasubjective and extracultural reality.

In the modern aesthetic experience, the possible contents are suggested by the co-text and by the intertextual tradition: the interpreter knows that he is not discovering an external truth but that, rather, he makes the encyclopedia work at its best. Modern poetic symbolism is a secularized symbolism where languages speak about their possibilities. In any case, behind every strategy of the symbolic mode, be it religious or aesthetic, there is a legitimating theology, even though it is the atheistic theology of unlimited semiosis or of hermeneutics as deconstruction. A positive way to approach every instance of the symbolic mode would be to ask: which theology legitimates it?

15

IRENE PORTIS WINNER

Semiotics of Culture

Semiotics of culture, a very broad domain within semiotics, requires a system of signification (the construction of *sign-vehicles* that, being based on codes, refer back to all possible worlds) and the transmittal of this information so that the system of signification can be perpetuated. Whether the sign itself is a text or a part of text clearly depends upon the context, as Lotman has shown. Methods used to analyze and conceptualize the characteristics of the semiotic object differ, but in this view the meaningful object (the sign or the text) itself must not be dichotomized by such oppositions as abstract/concrete, verbal/nonverbal, synchronic/diachronic, or code/message, but must subsume all of these spheres. Thus semiotics of culture would need to focus on all objects that in some cultural semiotic system and for some person refer back to something that they are not.

1) If we outline the parameters of a semiotics of culture, it appears that this domain is both narrower and broader than a general semiotics conceived in terms of conventional sign encoding. The specifics of a semiotics of culture may be briefly summarized. First of all semiotics of culture draws upon aspects of all studies of particular sign systems that either underlie or are directly a part of culture, in order to investigate the function or correlation of different sign systems in culture, where a culture is seen as a changing hierarchy of semiotic systems which is never isolated from the systems of other cultures. Culture is understood as pursuing a heterogeneity of languages or sign systems that participate in the typical syncretic culture text. Not only are the intersections and homologies and transformations of sign systems within texts to be investigated, but also the higher semiotic system of the text which these relations create. Thus a complex text becomes, in a sense, in its own right a kind of supersign. Furthermore, since the text is not closed, the relation of the text to its context must be considered. Finally, following upon the assumption that in the last analysis all culture texts of a certain culture share some invariants, it is assumed that underlying cultural models may eventually be determined by the study of culture texts.

In order to exemplify more concretely the approach of semiotics of culture to the analysis of a culture text, we may consider a mythological tale. It would not be sufficient to analyze only the universal invariants that structure such texts such as its universal symbols, which would appear in the same form cross-culturally, without attending to their various cultural transformations. Nor would it be sufficient to attend only to the organization of its verbal artistic structure and the internal meanings of its figures of speech as though the text were a closed system. Rather it would be necessary to place the text in the context of the entire culture in time and space and to analyze the role of basic cultural perceptions, beliefs, and values as they underlie participating cultural codes, rules and norms, and all the mechanisms of transformation of these deeper levels to more specific levels. In addition it would be necessary to consider the structural relation of this text to other similar texts, as well as to texts of other types, such as songs, poetry, rituals, etc. Furthermore, the intentions of the senders as they become a part of the text, and the point of view of the receivers who decode and thus also alter the text, would need to be accounted for. Then, within this broad context one would consider all the interrelations, intersections and transformations of the various internal sign systems (Kristeva's intertextuality) including that of natural language, the language of the mythological artistic text, the system of visual images invoked, the purely auditory or musical codes or rhythm, intonation, etc., and the accompanying gestures or actions of the teller of tales. Finally, the text would need to be understood on its own semiotic level. Does it attain some kind of supersign status where it is, in a sense, a system of systems? Of particular relevance in such a complex encoding and decoding is the role of aesthetic function, which, by virtue of its ability to relate heterogeneous units from all levels, discovers new similarities, expositions and equivalences making possible the combination of the uncombinable, and thus giving rise to new meanings. For example, by juxtaposing objects of all kinds, aesthetic images create metonymic metaphors or montages, making it possible for nonverbal objects to render abstract meanings and verbal objects to become more visual and palpable. Thus a pervasive assumption is that sign systems, because of their interrelatedness in culture, are not homogeneous but partake in various ways of the diverse characteristics of other sign systems.

While semiotics of culture is concerned with the most abstract and metatextual levels, such as invariant cultural models, its particular and great strength remains its lack of reduction and its rejection of closed systems. The concrete, rich and specific level of the culture text is never abandoned and is of fundamental interest. Thus a text is understood as polysemantic, polyfunctional, changeable, and preeminently context-sensitive.

2) In certain senses semiotics of culture is narrower than a general semiotics conceived on the basis of a linguistic paradigm, since such a semiotics in general attends to the entire universally based communicating mechanisms of systems of signification of living organisms, and if we include Eco's pseudo-communication we may encompass nonintentional messages on the biological and even inanimate levels. Insofar as general semiotics concerns itself with humans, it attends to panhuman physiologically and psychologically based structures and their philosophical interpretations, all those structures which make the particular type of communication known as human, its types of sign systems and texts, possible and universally present.

Areas in general semiotics which occupy the borders between psycho-biological universals and human variable cultures include the semiotic dimensions of the physiology of medicine (symptomatology); the genetic code understood as a form of communication that has parallels to the structure of language (Roman Jakobson); the functions of the brain as they determine the universal bases for binary oppositions in perception and different levels of semiotic activities such as verbal and nonverbal, abstract and concrete, symbolic and iconic; and the semiotics of the internal communication of psychiatric and diseased minds evidenced by studies of aphasia, of autistic or psychotic individuals (Lacan, Jakobson, Ivanov and others); universal apects of language and of thought that constrain semiotic expression; universal symbols and their universal meanings if they exist, all of which are discussed by linguists, philosophers and psychologists (for example Peirce, Chomsky, Jakobson, Freud, Devereux, Saussure, Hjelmslev, etc.).

Insofar as universal aspects of physical and natural environment and society (Marx, Durkheim and modern ecologists, etc.) are looked upon as universal and invariant structures that precondition general forms and meanings of signs, such concepts are a part of general semiotics.

Semiotics of culture cannot ignore broad findings that define universal structures underlining semiotics of culture, but it cannot achieve this particular type of breadth. The conclusions of the findings in general semiotics are, however, highly relevant to semiotics of culture and may form primitive assumptions or premises in regard to semiotics of culture. This does not mean that such positions are uncritically accepted. Paradigms of science change, and some premises turn out to be negative or debilitating rather than heuristic. Furthermore, the factor of feedback from culture to society and nature is equally important. Semiotics of culture departs from the primary polar relations of nature and culture and the mediating role of society, and thus universals based on nature and society that constrain and underlie culture, and are as well affected by the semiotic structure of culture, provide the foundation for research in semiotics of culture. Society, then, like the empirical ego, is both a creator and a product of culture.

3) Semiotics of culture may also be viewed as more encompassing than a general semiotics glottocentrically conceived, since, while it attends to aspects of all sign systems in culture as they interrelate and does not overlook the more abstract level of underlying invariants and codes, it concentrates upon the infinitely variable and endlessly transformable concrete text in culture in relation to its highly variable context, human and nonhuman. The effect of these factors has been to free semiotics of culture from certain limitations historically dominating the broad field of semiotics, namely the emphasis on *langue* or code to the detriment of *parole*, and the dominance of the linguistic model in the analysis of all sign systems whether verbal or not.

The move in semiotics of culture from emphasis on universal rules and the linguistic model to context, the specific and the concrete, has led to a renewed interest in semantics and pragmatics as affected by varied cultural contexts and to a reassessment of the iconic qualities of the signifier level of the sign itself, no longer seen as simply arbitrarily connected to a symbolic meaning. The fundamental assumption that verbal systems are not the only primary ones does not deny that verbal systems compose privileged systems characterized by double articulation when the minimal unit is apparently devoid of inherent meaning. Nor does it deny that all nonverbal sign systems are more or less translatable into or describable by languages whereas the reverse does not appear to be true. Nevertheless nonverbal sign systems have their own importance and specifics. Thus the various secondary or syncretic sign systems from verbal and nonverbal arts, gestures, and all kinds of ritual activities, from table manners, to cooking, to economic exchange, to wearing of special kinds of clothes, etc., all appear to synthesize and transform, in various degrees, attributes of both verbal and nonverbal primary systems.

Since natural language is no longer viewed as the only primary system, the nonarbitrary nature of other sign systems in culture becomes the more relevant, and since all sign systems interpenetrate in culture, it is not necessary to assume that the linguistic sign is unaffected and remains purely arbitrary. Furthermore, if signs are always a part of systems, and if the system is present in the text level, then no sign, not even the verbal sign, is purely arbitrary from the inner point of view. When cultural signs and texts are not understood as entirely arbitrary or fortuitous, or purely relative, and when they do not represent autonomous units or closed systems, their various types of relations to other systems and their various types of internal logic and dynamics (transformations, oppositions, reversals, evolutionary changes, etc.) are all open to fruitful investigation, bearing upon the elucidation of the principles of communication in culture.

Thus it is clear that investigations of underlying codes and dynamics ordering of texts cannot be limited to those purely reflecting the linguistic model. This is true whether we proceed from Lévi-Strauss' basic oppositions and transformations and type of cultures (cold/hot, concrete/abstract, *bricoleur*/engineer, etc.), Goody's (1977) and Derrida's (1978) *parole* or speech as opposed to *écriture* or writing and associated modes of thought, or Lotman's (1978) typologies of culture or modes of thought based on numerous interpenetrating criteria (discrete/nondiscrete, change by transformation/change by addition of new elements, orientation towards content/orientation toward expression, focus on beginnings/focus on ends) or Kuhn's (1970) shifting paradigms, or Foucault's (1973) archaeology of contemporary modes of thought. Furthermore, insofar as we go beyond the analyses of underlying and interpenetrating verbal and nonverbal cultural codes and the basic cultural meanings they signify, we focus on the richness of culturally textured *parole* of the culture text, although it cannot be separated from *langue*.

Thus semiotics of culture addresses the specificity of human experience, and yet refuses to remain purely descriptive, unsystematic or hermeneutic, static or limited to closed systems. The problems of so broad an approach are large, and particularly challenging is the question of boundary. For example, it is less difficult to see how semiotics of culture could concern itself with those traditionally well-defined texts that humans create, such as formalized texts, a musical piece, a dance, a dramatic performance, a work of visual art, a ritual, ceremony or institution, a game, a joke, an artifact from a simple tool to an artistically rendered piece of pottery, an archaeological structure from a simple house to a cathedral, even a city or an irrigation system or a village unit. But what of the many apparently unbounded units of behaviour that pervade all human life? Here we refer to the many segments of behaviour that lack easily discernible structures or formal easily visible boundaries such as frames, a stage, bindings of various types, or ritualistic beginnings and ends. Here semiotics of culture has a particularly strong contribution to make, for all patterned activities in culture, from segments of conversation to informal visits, to economic exchanges, to routine subsistence activities, to ways of movement, to ways of handling space, to styles of clothes, to gestures, expressions and posture, etc., are culturally coded, and thus they convey many levels of meaning from the most obvious to the most metaphorical and from the iconic to the most conventional. Indeed, following Peirce, "the human sign" demands analysis itself.

16

MICHAEL HERZFELD

Disemia[1]

The central argument of this paper is that the linguistic formulation of "diglossia", whereby a single language may have both literary ("H") and vernacular ("L") "registers", is part of a larger semiotic phenomenon in which individuals are able to negotiate social, national, ethnic, or political boundaries through a potentially inexhaustible range of co-domains. Language, though important, is not necessarily primary in this wider phenomenon, which I propose to call *disemia*. Disemia is thus a higher-order concept, not only than diglossia, but also than all such models as political polarization, class-based differentiation of behavior (including kinesics and proxemics), "folk" versus "urban" culture, and the like. In Ardener's sense (1971), it is a paradigmatic structure, a category of formal social principle rather than of behavior type.[2]

Defining the Issue

Ferguson's seminal presentation of the original diglossia model (1959) treats it as an ideal-type construct, or set of "continuous variables" (Johnson 1975: 39). Intermediate or "mixed" forms represent emic categories which permit a considerable range of variation in actual speaking practice. Like the "register" categories, the isolation of language as a discrete domain seems justified as a reflection of indigenous perceptions, at least as far as Greek ("the language question") and Arabic are concerned, and the crucial role of literacy in determining the choice and range of any one speaker's utterances reinforces that impression (Ferguson 1959; Fishman 1967; Shouby 1957). Yet this perspective shares the *a priori* logocentrism of many sociolinguistic categories (cf. Webber 1973; Crick 1976: 63-68), and demonstrates that a commitment to the reporting of emic *categories* does not adequately guarentee the representation of conceptual *structure*. If emic analysis stops at language, it is in fact rarely emic at all; it becomes instead a passive commitment to the etic view that a spoken language is capable of expressing the entire range of what its speakers are able to mean. It is a rejection of the very possibility of a "symbolic syntax" (Ardener 1970; Crick 1976: 111), or semiotic system, in which linguistic signs have a co-operative rather than a dominant function.

Thus, the alternative model of disemia poses a heuristic challenge. If the social "conditions of use" of diglossic variants in language can be identified, and if these conditions are not merely dependent functions of linguistic discourse, then they must represent principles which can be sought in non-linguistic behaviors also. If language exhibits diglossia, why not seek disemia in gesture, in architectonics, in music (surely a fertile field), in food habits?

The conditions of use for disemic variants generally are likely to be of two kinds. Conditions of the first group are historical or ideological; they consist of those preconditions which have been determined by the culture's prior ideological experience, and which in turn determine the appropriateness of a register-marked usage. Those of the second group are immediate or communicative; as in Fillmore's formulation (1971: 278), they are determined by the utterer's intentions and communicative competence, and constrain the situational appropriateness of a particular *parole*. The two sets thus correspond to the two fundamental kinds of diachrony, that of linguistic (or cultural) evolution and that of particular utterances respectively, and are necessarily linked in an analogous and unceasing dialectic. In other words, the cultural presuppositions which govern an individual's selection of register both influence, and are cumulatively influenced by, the particular choices that are actually made.

I shall attempt to demonstrate the model ethnographically, using the paradigm case of modern Greece. This does not mean, of course, that Greek disemia is necessarily motivated by the same antecedent principles as comparable phenomena elsewhere, but only that the generalization of a linguistic to a semiotic model offers more generous possibilities of explanation. Presumably, the potential of this revised model would then have to be worked out for other cultures on an empirical basis. It is a heuristic rather than an elaborately taxonomic device; otherwise, it could only entangle us in a thankless choice between reification and runaway typologizing—which is where, to some extent, the uncritically exploited diglossia model has already led. One cannot emphasize too strongly that a deterministic model, rather than one which is sensitive to the semiotics of social interaction, will lack heuristic efficacy, by focusing on disemia as rigid sets of rules rather than as a model for folk rhetorics that can be manipulated to achieve ("constitute") all sorts of special effects—irony, contrast, humor, and much else (see Bouissac 1977, Kendall 1981, Schwimmer 1979).

The Greek Paradigm: First Approximations

Greek H (*katharevousa*)[3] is not so much "purely Classical" as definitively European. While Turkish- and Arabic-derived forms were supplanted during the eighteenth- and early nineteenth-century emergence of Greek nationalism by Classical lexemes and syntactic markers, some syntactic elements (notably the genitive relative *tou opiou*) appeared to calque German or French prototypes. It is not clear how far such calquing represents conscious design, but—to anticipate the argument—it is at least consistent with the more general practice in nineteenth-century Greece of adopting Western European cultural *realia*[4] on the grounds that they were "really" (i.e., derivatively) Hellenic. The self-view of the (modern) Greeks as "Hellenes" was directed to external consumption, and was a major ideological component in the articulation of Greek nationalism with Western European political and moral support (Herzfeld 1982). As a recent paper by Sotiropoulos (1977) demonstrates, the development of H-Greek served the economic, political, and ideological subordination of the emergent nation-state to the European Powers, by concentrating communicative control in the hands of an outward-directed, Western-educated elite. Although there may have been deliberate intention in this, given the peculiarly reflexive or metalinguistic properties of language, there is no reason to assume that something analogous was not taking place with regard to other, perhaps less obtrusive co-domains.

L-Greek, on the other hand, came to be associated with a more introverted ideology, one that was concerned with the Byzantine and Turkish roots of the modern culture, and with peasant society, rather than with the Periclean glories. In its extreme development, as *dhimotikia*,[5] it became the clearest index of a speaker's Marxist orientation—a "foreign dogma", in the pronouncements of the H-using political Establishment, and certainly opposed to the "Hellenist" perspectives of the latter.

The principal axis along which these two ideologies were opposed was that of introversion/extroversion (or inclusion/exclusion). They thereby not only reproduce the definitive contours of a "culture text" (cf. Winner & Winner 1976: 106-107), but constitute the basis of a dialectical relationship between two explicitly recognized indigenous models.[6] Moreover, the disemic registers encapsulate "constructions" (Goldstein 1976) of history, so that each social interaction reproduces the tension between extremes, and each utterance has the effect of creating anew ("performing") the lines of social interaction between actors as a microcosm of the wider ideological issue.

Let me clarify, first of all, with a linguistic example. When a rural Greek wishes to explain something to a co-villager, he will normally use the term *yati* for "because". When he wishes to imply some external authority for his opinion, he will use the Neo-Classical (H) form *dhioti*. Note that he never uses *dhiati*, "why", for the L-form *yati* ("why" here); either the questioner assumes the superordinate position in the exchange (cf. Goody 1978: 17-23; Labov 1969: 57; Herzfeld 1980), or else a semiotic claim to the authority of external validation would violate "felicity conditions". When the villager wishes to explain something to an outsider, such as the foreign ethnographer, he is more likely to use *dhioti* than *yati* for "because" as an index of his *interlocutor's* external status and of his own desire to show familiarity with educated usage.

This is more than simply "code-switching". The possibility of such connotative manipulation is part of the code itself. If connotation is not so much a "vaguer" kind of meaning than denotation, than it is a superimposed level of sign-production (Eco 1976: 54-57), the notion of rigidly differentiated codes simply reifies the taxonomy of subcodes and ignores the rich semiotic implications of so-called "mixed forms"—of ordinary discourse, in fact. It is not *the lexical item* that indicates *which code* is being used; rather, it is the *use* of a given lexical item which indicates (a) the burden of historical and ideological implication, and (b) the degree of social closeness between speaker and addressee. Thus, a "use theory" not only serves semantic analysis well in regard to encyclopedic knowledge (Eco 1976: 98-100, 1984: 46ff.), but also provides a more flexible (and less aprioristic) approach to the semiotics of diglossia. Phonologically identical units may and do appear in dictionaries of both registers with identical semantic descriptions. What distinguishes them is the way in which they are used, and this is knowledge of an encyclopedic kind.

Outside language, the same observations hold good. A Neo-Classical house-ornament which originally bespoke an H-orientation, rescued from the demolition of its original home and incorporated into the design of a small Piraeus house surrounded by skyscrapers would now usually convey, not the Hellenic pretensions of its new owner, but his extreme *demoticism* in the threatening face of "Western culture". It is not the sign, but the way the sign is used, that tells us about its motivating ideology. When the once-despised underworld *rebetika* songs began to acquire popularity with the intelligentsia and then gradually with the Establishment generally, good Classical roots were suddenly "discovered" (or "constructed") for them (Veinoglou 1976). Sung by a drunkard in a Piraeus dive, of course, they still connote "low" culture. Sung in an Athenian *saloni*, other cues will enable those who know about such things to determine whether they are "meant" ironically or pretentiously. These are indeed "illocutionary or perlocutionary acts that are unaccompanied by locutionary ones" (Cohen 1975: 8). They achieve their effects in part, at least, by alluding to the presupposition of shared historical knowledge.

An Architectonic Example

Certainly, when one has examined diglossia/disemia as a semiotic rather than as a purely linguistic problem, there is no reason to confine the construct to language at all. This is particularly the case when we consider that the informing ideology is largely the same for language as for the other co-domains. True, language is indigenously treated as a special and discrete problem (*to ghlossiko zitima*). It is also true that non-linguistic artifacts mostly seem to convey their messages as simultaneities rather than as sequential utterances. Such objections are nevertheless hardly radical. We are not necessarily denying the *distinctiveness* of language by refusing to treat it as fully *autonomous*. On the contrary, the shift from diglossia to disemia gives us a context in which the linguistic phenomenon can be treated as a paradigm case rather than as a unique isolate. What makes what we should then call *linguistic disemia* different is what in general makes language different from other cultural artifacts, no more and no less, and it would be merely tautologous to insist on representing it as a special case—what paradigm is not?—of the wider phenomenon.

An architectonic example shows how disemic "marking" can function as an index of ideological orientation and of immediate social relationships simultaneously, in a manner analogous but not identical to that found in language. In an account of the Neo-Classical architecture of Athens and Piraeus, we are told, "It was natural for the newly constituted "good" society—made up of the merchants, the leading local headmen of Turkish times, the klefts and the educated people from the West and from Constantinople—to concede the lead to the Bavarians[7] in determining the measure of social standards. . . . Dances, dress, manners followed Bavarian dictates. The same was true of houses. . . . Thus, the Neo-Classical house came to be adopted. In addition, it had certain advantages of convenience. It created a false impression of Greekness[8] on the exterior. It emphasized the owner's economic pretensions, flattered his newly acquired urban outlook, and, at the same time, protected his private life" (Iakovidhis 1975).

Here, microcosmically, we find the extroversion of the "Hellenist" model and the introversion of the self-critical "Romeic" model combined in a single "utterance". This is a doubling of the indexical function; the protection of the householder's private life was not merely a mechanical function, it was a means of signifying his privacy to the rest of the world. To explain in more detail: the "Hellenistic" exterior was an ideological statement of cultural identity, while the interior harmonized well with the introversion of the "Romeic" ideology in that it was immune to inspection by outsiders. The ideological choice a Greek makes between the two national ideologies may be rhetorically stated in absolute terms. In everyday life, however, the signs of both ideologies are manipulated situationally, whether in language, architecture, *mores*, or any other medium.

Moral disemia is particularly interesting. A villager can praise the aggressive self-regard known as *eghoismos* to his fellow-villagers, then condemn someone as having exhibited precisely that moral quality when describing the latter to an official or a foreigner. Such behavioral disemia can be identified in other cultures hitherto restrictively classified as "diglossic", notably those of the Caribbean. Thus, the evidence adduced by Abrahams and Bauman (1971) and Reisman (1970) shows how an ostensibly negative evaluative term is used of L-behavior that is, in the appropriate social contexts, regarded as positively indicative of "insider" status. Again, while it would be insulting to *label* a Greek villager as a "thief" or a "liar", both terms can convey praise in contexts where the reference is to *particular acts* performed in symbolic defense of the in-group (e.g., sheep-stealing from other villages in the West Cretan highlands, lying to conceal a household's inner workings) (see also Friedl 1962: 80; du Boulay 1974: 77-78). The sense of the "lie" in the latter instance is directly analogous to a style of architecture which protects each household from the prying eyes of the next.

Thus, the disemia model allows us to treat various distinctive codes or co-domains in directly analogous terms. This is infinitely preferable to treating each as so completely *sui generis* that it has to generate a sub-discipline of its own— "sociolinguistics", "the anthropology of aesthetic form", and so forth. Above all, it broadens our understanding of the potential significance of "conditions of use" for a general semiotic theory, and for the penetration of interpretative systems other than our own.

Heuristic Possibilities

Disemia has heuristic potential in two respects. First, it invites a more critical investigation of cultures where H- and L-styles are indigenously recognized, whether or not they include a linguistic component. Stirling, for example (1965: 283-289), evocatively describes such a pairing (urban-rural) in Turkish attitudes; we may now be led to inquire whether, as the Caribbean materials cited above might suggest, there are any situations in which the L-style is evaluated positively, or whether the classification is as static and socially context-free as the ethnograghic description implies.

The second heuristic potentiality of the disemia model is that it points up the marking of social boundaries (insiders vs. outsiders) in such a way as to lessen our dependence on linguistic indices. Pocius' analysis of Newfoundland hooked rugs (1979) demonstrates this well, in the indexical correlation of iconicity (designs) with degrees of socially hierarchical differentiation appropriate to the rooms in which the rugs are situated. Here, the *internal* H/L distinction does not appear to be replicated in language, despite some evidence (Faris 1968) of semantic discrepancies between Newfoundland usage and "standard" English. Pocius' description of the phenomenon does not suffer noticeably through the absence of supporting evidence of a linguistic nature.

One test of the model's flexibility lies in its ability to accommodate some of the effects of tourism on so-called "traditional" cultures. Tourism effectively calls on local people to provide foreigners with an idealized view of their culture, while at the same time encouraging the incorporation of these idealized (or attenuated) cultural forms into the local aesthetic (see, e.g., Hirschfeld 1977 and Sherzer and Sherzer 1976 on San Blas *molas*; cf. also Cretan *touristika*, woven articles partly used domestically). The significance of cultural elements is thus contextually negotiated (cf. also Schwimmer 1979: 272-273). The metasemiotic rhetoric may change too. Especially in and around the coastal town of Rethimno, Crete, the practice has sprung up of scratching designs in cement house-fronts before the latter have dried. The local people claim that this is done ''for beauty'', whereas the wealthier and worldlier Irakliots—who use ''Western'' tiles and facings to a large extent—distain such decoration, and say that they abandoned it many years ago (Herzfeld 1971)! Beauty is in the eye of the impecunious Rethimniot householder who mainly has to demonstrate domestic pride to his local neighbors, whereas the Irakliot is additionally concerned with the impression his town will make on the tourist hordes.

To summarize, the disemia model suggests a broadly holistic use of speech act theory without demanding the presence of (verbal) speech. By incorporating the ideological implications of insider/outsider distinctions, it abstracts the H/L opposition from the restrictive model of diglossia and applies it to the whole range of everyday *realia*. It thereby suggests a new and specifically semiotic perspective on the social basis of aesthetic concerns.

17

ROBERTA KEVELSON

Prolegomena to a Comparative Legal Semiotics

Philip Shuchman (1979: 3-4) recently stressed, in discussing the problem of knowledge in legal scholarship and in analysis of legal discourse and practice, that legal theorists must begin to seriously ask two major questions: 1) how is the authoritative legal actor's knowledge of a reality external to the case at hand brought to bear on the legal judgment or decision, and 2) what are the leading philosophical assumptions about epistemology which underlie explicit legal premises and which influence the actions of legal theorists and their practicing counterparts, legal actors? The answers to these questions, I want to suggest, can fruitfully be sought by applying to legal matters the theory and method of semiotics which derives from Charles S. Peirce. Here, I want only to introduce a perspective on the relation between law and society which may serve to stimulate further inquiry along semiotic lines.

The Background of Legal Semiotics

We know that Peirce's theory of signs as integral with a semiotic epistemology or theory of knowledge has influenced juridical thought directly and indirectly since the close of the nineteenth century. A revolutionary illustration of his impact on jurisprudence is Gény's classic study on legal method (1889; discussion in Kevelson 1981a). We find repeated reference to Peirce in the writings of such distinguished legal historians as Huntington Cairns (1962), and notes of indebtedness to Peirce for the notion of "legal realism" by such controversial legal theorists as Jerome Frank (1930). That Peirce's philosophy was a direct influence on Oliver Wendell Holmes and on Francis Lieber is a reasonable assumption. Certainly the exchange of ideas between Peirce and his colleagues in law, especially during his residence in Cambridge, Massachusetts, appears to have resulted in the formulation of important, innovative legal theory in late nineteenth-century and early twentieth-century legal philosophy (cf. Fisch 1964, 1942; Kevelson 1984, 1985).

What I want to show here are some contributions to be made from the study of law in relation to that of signs. Charles Hartshorne remarked in recent conversation that as long as we continue to become aware of logical possibilities not yet realized, and begin to examine such possibilities, we are faced with the inescapable fact of a growing universe in which we ourselves are interactive partners. The development of legal semiotics is a logical possibility within the doctrine of signs which warrants close attention.

It is a fact that some key terms in modern semiotic research, such as Code, Interpretation, Speech Acts, Interrogation, Definition, and Discovery Procedures, had their origin in law. So it should perhaps not be surprising that a new branch of the study of signs has recently emerged that can be broadly designated Legal Semiotics. Within this area of semiotic inquiry we find the following subdivisions: 1) relations between Law and Legal Systems, 2) relations between Legal Discourse and Legal Practice, 3) exchange of signs between official Legal Actors and non-official members of the General Public, 4) sign structures of inquests and trials, 5) intersystemic communication between Codes of Legality and Codes of Legitimacy, 6) relations between the laws of Logic and the logic of Laws, and 7) a comparative semiotic perspective on Legal Cultures.

Each of these areas of inquiry within Legal Semiotics can be approached in terms of one or a combination of three major considerations: 1) the logical structures of legal reasoning; 2) legal hermeneutics as paradigmatic for the interpretation of signs in general in social systems; 3) isomorphism between legal systems and contextual, coeval social institutions.

In this essay I will be concerned with the seventh subdivision of legal semiotics (a comparative perspective on legal cultures), and I will deal with it in terms of the third approach or emphasis (isomorphism between legal systems and their contextualizing social institutions). Informing my observations, but not directly discussed, will be Peirce's semiotic methodology.

How Are Legal System and Social System Related?

Legal anthropologists and sociologists of law in general use the term "legal culture". This term carries the rhetorical suggestion that law and social custom are two sides of the whole of any given society, a property it has acquired through its use by scholars attempting to understand, on the one hand, the interaction between customs and moral values of a society, and, on the other hand, the order of authority which specifically constitutes the legal institutions of a society.

Oliver Wendell Holmes remarked that the growth of legal systems and codes is logical in form, but in substance these codes follow popular feelings and patterns of behavior deriving from basic emotions concerning loss, namely, revenge: desire for retribution and demand for compensation. He remarks that a legal system is never consistent or complete, but forever attempting to achieve a balance between values emerging from present experience and values carried over by customs rooted in a common-law past. Holmes stresses that the reciprocal relation between law and custom exemplifies an exchange of meaningful signs. In a wide range of legal theory, Holmes's viewpoint is designated as an assumption of "interactional law".

A concept similiar to that of Holmes is expressed by his contemporary, Fritz Berolzheimer, who maintained that society always appears as a whole, a symbolic type of sign, and that there is a necessary relation between every existing society and its laws. He says (1904-1907: xiv-xxxiv): ". . . a legal process is not limited to the formulations of laws, but embraces the economic and social institutions and movements which vitalize them . . .".

Edwin Schur remarks (1968: 73) that ". . . the question of distinguishing law from other social norms . . . has plagued and continues to plague numerous anthropologists and sociologists". Schur refers to Malinowski's conclusion from his work on the Trobrianders, that the stuff we recognize as legal phenomena are consequences of a "configuration of obligations" which cannot be ignored without penalty. The person who breaks the law is testing the strength and power of the Legal Actors who, in their turn, are obliged to make appropriate legal judgment.

It must be noted that some legal systems include rules for the various ways laws may be justifiably broken, while others do not allow for any violation of laws in the name of some presumed and "higher" legitimacy or social sense of justice. In legal systems of the latter type, positive law is absolutely free to oppose social values, and seeks to establish itself as the sole authoritative system. In legal systems of the former type, legality and legitimacy are adjuncts in an ideal according to which positive law and social claims for justice engage in continuous dialogue, which dialogue constitutes the conceived unity of a Legal System as a whole.

Representing the view that legal codes and cultural values are involved in a creative tension is Pekelis (1950: 42), who refutes the theory that "rules . . . are a simple restatement of an existing custom", and reminds us that "rules which are enacted with the very purpose of reversing existing custom . . . should be read as we read the negative of a snapshot: white for black and black for white".

Thus a code of law may be regarded as a system of signs of a predominantly symbolic function which represents abstract, ideal values or leading goals of a society, and as such prescribes and sets forth paradigms of how people ought to behave; or it may be regarded as a description of how people actually behave, inasmuch as a community by definition is a social contract whose rules are agreed upon through the voluntary processes by which individuals transfer their freedoms to one another and become socialized. That is Locke's thesis, which in this important respect affirms the Hobbesian notion of the motivation for social contract.

It has long been believed by legal theorists of many camps that a legal code is a mirror of society. Dietze observes (1964: 74) that "if law, as is usually believed, is a mirror of society, then different mores, circumstances, and times may rationally require different codification . . . ." He goes on to remark (ibid.) that, "characteristically, old German codes were explicitly called 'mirrors' (Spiegel), the most famous of them being the Sachenspiegel".

The problem of recodifying the laws of a society requires that we consider the concepts of "open" and "closed" in at least two different senses. The first involves the study of Legal Hermeneutics referred to above; the second requires that we clearly distinguish between open legal systems and closed legal systems as respectively representative of closed and open societies, and it is some features of this latter relationship that must be discussed here.

To begin with, it is useful to accept Friedman's point (1975) that there is not in actual practice a single Legal System. Rather, as he goes on to show, there are in all societies networks of legal subsystems. These legal subsystems continually conflict and compete with one another for position, influence, and dominant power. As a rule, a closed type of legal system will predominate in a society which derives its working values from an underlying belief in fate, in predetermination, in a universe created once and for all by a divine force. In such societies, the legal code is presumed to extend a divine mandate through its privileged, authoritative legal actors.

An open society, by contrast, is one which has explicitly distinguished between civil and sacred law. Open societies are often but not always characterized by a prevailing belief that the world has not been created once and for all, is not a Being so much as a Becoming. I would mention here that it is this process of Becoming which gives Peirce's philosophy of signs—and especially that part of his Expanded Logic which he calls, synonymously, Methodology, Methodeutic, and Speculative Rhetoric—such critical prominence in our approach toward understanding the "open" aspect of legal systems (Kevelson 1984).

Through the interpretation of signs, new signs for reality emerge. Peirce was very much concerned, in his later writings especially, with methods of discovery for explaining open systems. Traditional logical methods of justification are, as we know, inadequate when it comes to the discovery of new ideas (Russell 1984). Correlatively, as social changes come to be regarded in legal theory as a source of new law, we find rules for discovery procedures in law made increasingly more explicit (Beal 1896; Ross 1912). It is no mere coincidence that Peirce's interest in the logic of discovery developed at the same time that legal theorists were writing texts on procedures for legal discovery. Both in law and in semiotic philosophy the fact of changing societies is a primary fact of experience to be accounted for.

The difference between open and closed societies with their corresponding legal systems may be summarized as follows. In closed society, the dominant, prevailing legal code has become *as though* canonized. It is represented by the guardians of the legal order as embodying fixed and eternal values, somewhat like the holy texts which religious leaders of communities safeguard. In an open society it is assumed that codes of law are man-made, and that new laws must be enacted to fit changes in the times.

These remarks serve to foreground some main assumptions at work in the area of Legal Semiotics.

1) There is no ideal Legal System in any society; there are only relations between legal subsystems which conflict for the position of ascendancy.

2) Verbal Legal Acts are of three kinds: decisions, commands and requests, and rules. There are both verbal and nonverbal Legal Acts, but all legal acts are presumed to derive from a verbal infrastructure, and thus must be examined and accounted for in the context of natural language by appropriate modes of analysis, such as, particularly, Peirce's Methodology, or Speculative Rhetoric.

3) Assumptions of authority, often implied but deleted in explicit Legal Acts, characterize traditional presumptions of trust and legitimacy. Such presumptions are not adequate by themselves in transitional, open societies. The approach of Legal Semiotics to a comparative view of legal cultures has especial need for Peirce's *method of methods* in order to account for different patterns of legal discourse and practice.

4) Coexisting legal subsystems sometimes reinforce one another, at other times they conflict with each other. In order to understand the shifting dialogue between opposing and/or complementary subsystems, we need intersystemic bridge laws. Such bridge laws permit us to describe the kinds of legal dialogue which take place as an exchange of value signs between the predominant and authorized legal actors and the spokesmen for values newly emerging in the general public. In this way, we may begin to explain the age-old symbiosis between legitimacy and the rules of law, or legality.

5) The system of logic which predominates in any given society is a referent model, or sign, for contextual social structures and cultural institutions. We assume

that these derived systems are Interpretants which interpret their object-sign, the legal system. Following Peirce's concept of the three categories or stages in the process of coming to a conclusion about an object, the Interpretant Sign is Firstness, the Immediate Interpretant is Secondness, and the Dynamic Interpretant is Thirdness. These three stages correspond with the functions of the iconic, the indexical, and the symbolic which are simultaneous and coordinate functions in response to context (Kevelson 1981, 1981b, 1984, 1985).

Social Signs and Their Legal Interpretants

A monolithic cornerstone was laid for legal semiotics by Wigmore (1928), when he invited us to think of all institutions of a given society, including artifacts, modes of personal interaction, the design or physical layouts of communities, as well as predominating patterns of thought and value, as extensions or modalities of empowered and effectual legal systems.

Since Wigmore's study of legal systems there has been interest, particularly among sociologists, in the relationships between societies and legal systems. A number of seminal studies in social science pre-date Wigmore by more than a decade; but it is particularly in Wigmore's unique approach that we can begin to examine the topics of edifices, men of law, and legal records, as logical types in a logic of law regarded as a system of signs.

These topics are extensions of two prototypical terms of legal understanding: Justice and The Laws. From the time of ancient Greece these terms have been interconnected in the development of Western legal science. At times, these terms have been regarded as synonymous, at other times they have been taken to be in opposition. When they have been taken as equivalent, this was done on the basis of a well-known strategy of rhetoric, the argument by convergence. The opposite interpretation was brought about rhetorically through an argument by dissociation (Kevelson 1977).

We especially want to distinguish the meaning of the term 'pragmatics' in Peirce's philosophy from the way we use the concept of pragmatics in our ordinary conversation to refer to the direct, practical aspects of certain thoughts, procedures, and action in the world. For Peirce pragmatics is an integral aspect of a Methodology which is not directly applicable to practical affairs, but seeks rather to account for the actual processes by which ideas develop and grow through discourse in the course of practical life. The Speculative Rhetoric or Methodology which intends to describe how new thought-as-sign interprets known thought-as-sign is modelled upon the rhetorical tactics of persuasive discourse. Semiotic methodology is a theoretical representation of experiential arguments in law and in ordinary communication (Kevelson 1984, 1985). Indeed, Toulmin (1958) has called the legal argument the prototype of all other argument in natural language.

Let us try to provide an overview of some of the main features of a number of legal systems which date from antiquity, and which can be conveniently regarded in a global way. I am not suggesting anything approaching an exhaustive description of these selected systems; my intention is merely to compare and contrast certain features of each which may be considered characteristic and significant.

The Egyptian legal system, which endured from about 3200 B.C. until around 800 B.C., underwent great modification, reflecting a changing culture and, particularly, internal political revolutions which took place during that period. These

changes in the society from war, commerce, modifications of the signs of deity—
all contributed to undermine the structure of an indigenous legal system in Egypt.
In response to these pressures, the native court of law held proceedings under
the aegis of the god Osiris. This court evolved to a highly complex system resistant to the influences resulting from foreign conquests; but in the eighth century
B.C. the system was badly weakened by internal civil war, by the conquering
Assyrians, Persians, and Greeks, and finally by the Roman Caesars who imposed
upon Egypt their own legal system, thereby destroying once and for all the native
Egyptian system (Wigmore 1928: 49).

Unlike the Egyptian system of law, the Mesopotamian legal system, which
dates from around 2500 B.C., changed hardly at all during its effective existence.
The earliest people of that area were the Sumerians, a non-Semitic people.
Fragments of their codes, the earliest code-texts to be discovered which are still
intact in modern times, anticipate the "pillar-code" of Hammurabi which dates
from around 2100 B.C. Hammurabi's code governs all of cultural life: crime,
family, property, commerce. It is noteworthy that this is the only legal system
which was organized from a central power source that did not provide for the
special training of legal professionals. The Egyptian laws, which were more regional
than central in their source of issue, and were not encoded as a binding system
as Hammurabi's code was, share with the Mesopotamian laws the absence of training schools for professional lawyers.

A legal system as such was not established within Jewish civilization until 500
A.D.—some 2500 years after the Mosaic Code had become the law of the Hebrews.
A system of law requires that official legal actors enforce the law, interpret the
law, and legislate it; the system must therefore provide the resources needed to
decide cases.

When the Mishnah or book of learning was brought together with the Gemor-
rah or Talmudic commentaries by the priests into an encyclopedia of law which
defined, in a legal framework, major topics of Judaic culture, the legality-legitimacy
dialectic was brought into a marriage under God. Among the major topics discussed were history, mathematics, medicine, theory of metaphysics, and sundry
specific problems in civil law. Neither statutes nor rules are recorded in this text;
it is a documentation of discourse constructed dialogically of questions and answers.

We find in the long history of Hebrew law that the sign-referent of the Highest
Legal Actor changes. The sign, or term of Highest Legal Actor, evolves from
Kings to Prophets to the Judges of the Mosaic Period (1200 B.C. to 400 B.C.)
to the classic period of Hebrew law in which the chief Actor is the Rabbi (300
B.C. to 200 A.D.). Thus the term "god" extends to the term "Rabbi". In the
course of this development, the primary legal texts shift from the canonized Pen-
tateuch of the first period to the reports of cases and Talmudic commentary of
the second or classic period. In the Talmudic Period which follows, the Legal
Digests become the primary sources of legal precedent, and in this period Hebrew
law struggles for survival under imposed Roman law; the culture at this time is
characterized under dual and competing legal systems.

In the history of the Jewish people, what Wigmore calls the Medieval Period
begins around 700 A.D. This corresponds with the Jewish restructuring of the
people as an alien group in a host culture. During this period we find Private
Codes and Talmudic Commentary, until around 1500 A.D., at which time the

cultural development is characterized by emphasis on local custom, on ceremonial and moral rules, and increasingly on borrowed, culturally transforming patterns of living. At this time, legal texts begin to include translated assimilations of ancient texts, and they begin to be printed rather than hand-written. The concept of legal authority has radically altered under the influence of successive Persian, Greek, and Roman conquests, and passed from the Kings to the Sanhedrin or senate, and from the Senate to the community, which may consist of as few as ten men.

The last distinctive legal system I want to include in this brief survey is the Islamic system. It should be stressed that, from its inception, the Islamic legal system was a complex, comprehensive sign of interrelationships between all areas of cultural life: all aspects of one's life were prescribed through a revealed, divine command. It is presumed that everything a member of the Islamic culture should know, believe, and do is written in the summaries attributed to Mohammed and also those written down after his death as gleanings from his thought. These didactic summaries encompass all aspects of religion, ethics, law, politics, and industry. They are in great part easily practiced dicta.

The Islamic legal system reached the peak of its development during precisely those four centuries which are referred to as the Dark Ages in Europe, 800 to 1200 A.D. The world's oldest law school was the Mosque El Azhar in Cairo, founded in 970 A.D.. This was not a seat of the ancient Egyptian law, but an Islamic law school. Wigmore remarks that "in the sciences and arts, the Saracens were the preeminent people" who brought intellectual and cultural activity and progress to all of Europe.

As in the Rome of the emperors, the Islamic legal system, two hundred years after the death of Mohammed, was divided into judicial and juristic functions, both set apart from executive functions. At this time a system of professional legal specialists was developed. By 900 A.D. this institution was so well organized that the writings of these jurists formed the third major source of Islamic law. The first source remained the Koran itself; now, to the second source (the commentary on Mohammed's sayings and writings), a third source was added, the professional legal commentary.

Wigmore suggests (1928: 775) that the Islamic legal system has endured as a native legal system because it realizes the formula for a legal system which reaches into and affects virtually every corner of every life in every aspect of a total cultural system, to wit, it performs the following functions: "Judiciary organization, careful documentation, role of counsellors, use of authority and precedent in argument and in decisions, theoretically religious background of its legal principles". Yet it must be said that the Islamic system of law is not one which exemplifies semiosis as open dialogue (notwithstanding Rescher's analysis [1966] of interrogative patterns in Arabic legal discourse). It is a highly complex structure of signs and sign-relationships, but it is designed to be as resistant as possible to evolutionary processes of exchange and growth, particularly where it is a question of stimuli from beyond the horizons of Islamic authority.

In all, the above examples suggest that certain cultures, perhaps all cultures, exemplify, as signs-in-themselves, the semiotic process of transacting and exchanging meaningful signs between participants in the rounds of daily life. Within these societies as units of culture, sometimes in spite of their explicit structures, each temporal realization of authority adds to a cumulative message of discourse—

tradition—that constantly adapts and modifies through interpretative translation and response to the Other. I have attempted here to correlate patterns of rule with patterns and images of authority which act, in different ways, for different societies, as representations of the society's highest values. Eventually, we will need to attempt a systematic (and not just a selective) presentation of logical pictures of each distinctive type of legal system that can be discerned in human history, replete with its major quests and inquiries, using Peirce's Methodology.

Concluding Remarks

The experimental phenomena of legal systems are systems of behavior, and as such are processes and events in which meaningful signs are exchanged in actual, practical life. The theory of Legal Semiotics does not immediately engage in these transactions, but rather, at a second remove from the exchange of meanings, it seeks to explain how this discourse proceeds and develops.

Because rhetoric plays a central role in the emergence of sign relations within legal cultures, it warrants particular attention within legal semiotics. A semiotic methodology for the study of law, once developed, can contribute to our understanding of practical and nontraditional uses of rhetoric in legal action and legal reaction. It can also point the way toward describing both societies' modes of responding to legal authorities and the internal dialogue between the judge as highest legal actor and as member of society. In addition, legal semiotics casts new light upon the fact that no individual person is a passive object of a legal system, that one can bribe, cajole, outwit, outtalk, and in countless ways use rhetorical strategies to mold a rule or shape its application. As Friedman points out (1975: 105ff.), the use of rhetoric is the act of a person engaging in a communicative event, using signs in persuasive ways in order to shape the understanding of the law.

Legal "commands" do not strike a person directly from the outside, but they are filtered through a semiotic web composed of cultural and personal scales and measures of straights and crookeds. Not the least of the problems confronting a semiotics of law and legal systems is that of understanding the process of how equivalent meanings and values are arrived at and agreed to within these networks of semiosis. This issue dovetails with the object of inquiry within Speculative Rhetoric, which is constituted by "the devices which have to be employed to bring new relations to light" (Peirce c.1903: 4.370). The task of legal semiotics is to bring to light just this open foundation of systems of law as such, and to set them in relation to societies and cultures as a whole.

18

RICHARD L. LANIGAN

Semiotics, Communicology, and Plato's Sophist[1]

The dialogue *Sophist* is often regarded as the most difficult of Plato's writings. In part, it is ambitious in taking up the problem of the Being of Not-Being. Also, it attempts an explanation of the One and the Many that is an enduring philosophical and empirical paradox. Last, the dialogue is an oral illustration of Platonic method (maieutic) as purported in the Seventh Letter. The presence of these varying threads in the one dialogue suggests a major shift from the conversational tone of inquiry present in the early dialogues to the argumentative mode of analysis in Plato's late thinking. The chief result is the creation of an object of consciousness within interpersonal experience that is open to analytic justification as an empirical experience.

My essay attempts to explicate the main features of the Platonic argument in order to establish that the *model* of discourse analysis is semiotic in nature and phenomenological in function. I am using the term *model* in its technical theory construction sense as an "exemplar" (combined "paradigm" and "prototype") in a theory.[2] Thus in a Heideggerian view (1968: 51), "What a model as such is and how its function for thinking is to be understood can only be thought from an essential interpretation of language." The dialogue *Sophist* relies on a binary code that is cast within a rhetorical situation grounded in an analogue logic. The binary coding is made clear with the illustrative use of a modified version of Barthes' model of discourse. The Barthes model is grounded in Hjelmslev's theory (1943, 1943a, 1948; Garvin 1954) in which he describes the structure of language and similar systems with the following theorems:

> 1. A language consists of a content and an expression. 2. A language consists of a succession, or a text, and a system. 3. Content and expression are bound up with each other through commutation. 4. There are certain definite relations within the succession and within the system. 5. There is not a one-to-one correspondence between content and expression, but the signs are decomposable in minor components. Such sign components are, e.g., the so-called phonemes, which I should prefer to call taxemes of expression, and which in themselves have no content, but which can build up units provided with a content, e.g., words (1948: 35).

The Barthian model of Hjelmslevian theory allows a direct comparison between the stages of Platonic method and Barthes' concepts of connotation, denotation, and reality as set in a signifier or rhetoric system and signified or ideology system

(Lyons 1963). The analogue logic is equally applicable in the respective correlation to Merleau-Ponty's (1945) phenomenological model of description, reduction, and interpretation. In short, the logic for a *semiotic phenomenology* is provided
in the dialogue *Sophist* and it points the way for viewing the speaking subject as
an *agent provocateur* in the sociocultural context where empirical reference must
give way to the production of analytic signification. As Heidegger (1968: 51)
specifies: "speaking about ontic models presupposes that language in principle
has an ontic character, so that thinking finds itself in the situation of having to
use ontic models for what it wishes to say ontologically, since it can only make
something evident through words."

My essay does not represent an effort to claim that Plato is either a semiologist
or a phenomenologist. Rather, I argue that the dialogue *Sophist* offers a long
neglected textual model of binary analogue thinking that is foundational to many
of the issues current in the study of the philosophy of communication where
semiology and phenomenology intersect in the problematic of analysis. Indeed,
many of the basic elements in the Platonic investigation are being unnecessarily
reinvented by contemporary theorists. By addressing the fundamental problem
of the Being of Not-Being, Plato provides a semiotic phenomenology of discourse
in which he demonstrates the acceptability of analytic proofs as the concrete analysis
of empirical communication acts. Thus, the dialogue *Sophist* represents a critical,
but often ignored, theoretical foundation for an empirical examination of the sign
relationship between the ontology of the speaking subject and the epistemology
of the discourse system.

As a dialectic examination, my analysis has four steps. First, I review the
exemplar of maieutic that Plato provides in Letter VII. Then I indicate the parallel
between the Platonic model and the one that Barthes (1964) offers. The point
of this comparison is to demonstrate that Barthes adopts a view of "rhetoric"
and "ideology" (and the subsequent view of "text") that is dysfunctional if we
concede the force of Plato's analysis. Third, I examine the Platonic model as it
is applied in substance to the productive art of discourse in the dialogue *Sophist*.
Last, I suggest the way in which Merleau-Ponty's existential phenomenology
(1945) offers a praxis model of philosophic discourse that meets the Platonic standard for theory construction and grounds rhetoric in a dialectic logic consistent
with modern Hjelmslevian notions (1943) in communication theory. That is, I
am concerned to argue that Plato gives us a coherent logic of discourse as a grounding that we readily perceive as information theory. Barthes utilizes this theory
and is trapped by its structure, namely, that context always provides for choice,
but concrete choice is systematically ambiguous. By comparison, Plato helps us
discover that the inclusion of the human agent in the use of information theory
sets the criteria for communication theory, in which a person makes a choice that
systemically constitutes a context. But in specifying the problem in order to locate
the solution, Plato stops short of disclosing the condition for choice in context.
For such an illustration of completed theory, I turn to Merleau-Ponty's philosophy
of communication (1945) and my own extensions of his basic model (Lanigan
1970, 1972, 1979, 1979a). One other feature of these various comparisons needs
to be mentioned before proceeding. In Plato, Barthes, and Merleau-Ponty the
basic philosophic pair of concepts at issue is "rhetoric" and "ideology". In this
regard, it is important to recognize the signification that attaches to these con-

cepts as they are used in dialectic analysis. In brief, "ideology" should be viewed as a condition of discourse that constitutes the *context of choice*, viz., "information". By comparison, "rhetoric" is the practice of discourse that constitutes a *choice in context*, viz., "communication". Indeed, it is the very irony of the dialogue *Sophist* that in seeking out the axiological characteristics of sophistry, we apparently locate the philosopher's condition and thereby discover the logic of human discourse with its full ontological import (Kerferd 1954, 1981).

The Seventh Letter

Plato addresses his letter to the companions and friends of Dion. The letter is occasioned by Plato's attempt to maintain his neutrality in the struggle for power at Syracuse between the exiled Dion and the ruling Dionysius I. We need not encumber ourselves with the history of Syracuse, but it is of consequence to recall that in the dialogue *Sophist* the discussion begins epistemologically with the problem of distinguishing among the sophist, the statesman, and the philosopher. Plato's intellectual problem in the dialogue has its vivid practical illustration in Letter VII, which recalls the threat to his personal existence during the boat trips between the Greek mainland and Sicily. To be sure, the existential flavor of Plato's thinking is all too clear in his rather constant mention of his recurrent, urgent need to get a boat out of town! With less facetiousness, I also need to remind you that Socrates is pursuing the question "What is knowledge?" in the dialogue *Theaetetus*, which ends with a promise to complete the discussion the following day (Klein 1977). Yet, the next day Socrates is arrested and brought to trial. The consequence is that the discussion of knowledge resumes while Socrates is in prison awaiting execution. The resumed dialogue is the *Sophist* (Sallis 1975: 457).

In the key passage of Letter VII, Plato announces the exemplar that informs the Socratic method of maieutic.[3] "For everything that exists there are three classes of objects through which knowledge about it must come; the knowledge itself is a fourth, and we must put as a fifth entity the actual object of knowledge which is the true reality. We have then, first, a name, second, a description, third an image, and fourth, a knowledge of the object" (p.353BC: 342b-343c). And later he adds, "Furthermore these four [names, descriptions, bodily forms, concepts] do as much to illustrate the particular quality of any object as they do to illustrate its essential reality because of the inadequacy of language. Hence no intelligent man will ever be so bold as to put into language those things which his reason has contemplated, especially not into a form that is unalterable—which must be the case with what is expressed in written symbols." The fact that this model is communicated in a written letter points to a momentary paradox. Yet, we recall the dialogue *Sophist* where the contemplated model is in fact articulated according to Plato's criteria for production (Isenberg 1951).

Plato offers us an illustration to demonstrate the model's utility. The example is the concept "circle". First, the articulate use of "circle" is a word that names. Second, we use nouns and verbal expression to describe the circle and thereby suggest its *logos*: "The thing that has everywhere equal distances between its extremes and its center." Third, we discover a class of objects, e.g., the graphic object that we can draw and erase or the wooden object we can turn on a lathe and then destroy. Fourth, we come upon another thing that is not found in sounds or in the shape of bodies, but in the mind. This concept has a degree ranging from knowledge to understanding to current opinion, each displaying a "particular quality". Fifth, there is the real circle, what Plato in his Idealism calls the "essential reality". We immediately perceive that the clear, but epigrammatic presentation of the exemplar in Letter VII is an assertion in want of proof. The desired demonstration of the model occurs in the dialogue *Sophist*, where Plato addresses the question of knowledge and its method, i.e., the *logos* of *logos* (Sallis 1975: 456; Kerferd 1954). But before examining this detailed argument, I would like to compare the Platonic model to that of Barthes (1964).

Barthes' model of discourse

Barthes' 1964 model actually consists of a developmental approach to the question of knowledge that is in spirit like the Platonic quest. In particular, both Plato and Barthes are concerned to formulate a method for discovering and utilizing knowledge that is produced and comes to us in the form of discourse. Also, both theorists provide for a modification in their method when discourse proves to be an inadequate guide. This modification is, of course, the use of myth. As I subsequently suggest, it is Barthes' (1957) model for myth analysis that points to a serious defect in the structuralist theory of *rhetoric* in general and of *text* in particular. It is a defect that is exposed initially by using the Platonic model for epistemology.

In chapter IV of Barthes' *Elements of Semiology* (1964) we have the now classic presentation of the semiotic model of discourse. The model is constructed to account for the production of signification. By comparison, Eco (1976: 54-56, 268-269) presents a less flawed process model of the Hjelmslevian theory and subsequent diagrammatic presentation. Following Hjelmslev, Barthes calls the first element in the system the "plane of expression". The second element is the "plane of content" and the connection between the two planes is simply the "relation". He proceeds to argue that the *Expression/Relation/Content* or ERC condition exists on the two levels of "connotation" and "denotation", this latter being a metalanguage function. Barthes offers two illustrative expressions of this model: one is a symbolic calculus and the other is a pictorial diagram. Last, there is a third diagrammatic illustration of the model that shows the combined models of connotation and denotation as based in the real system. It will be useful to compare the symbolic and diagrammatic versions [*mutatis mutandis* existential graphs] of the models to indicate the logical limitations built into Barthes' approach.

The symbolic version of the model in a propositional calculus is quite simple and straightforward (Figure 1)[4]:

Figure 1. *Barthes' 'connotation' expressed in his propositional calculus*

The first system [noted in "1" in Figure 1] *ERC* becomes the plane of expression of the second system [noted as "2" in Figure 1], so the formulation now reads *(ERC)RC*. In this case we have the connotation, since the plane of expression in the first system *(ERC)* becomes the signifier [Sr] of the second system, i.e., *(ERC)* substitutes for *E* in the second *ERC*. This structure is reversed in the case of denotation, thereby becoming a metalinguistic physical function. Here (Figure 2) we have the plane of expression in the first system by commutation for the plane of

Figure 2. *Barthes' 'denotation/metalanguage' expressed in his propositional calculus*

content in the second system. That is, the formulation reads *ER(ERC)*, in which
the signified *(ERC)* replaces the *C* in the first system of *ERC*. Both connotation
as a signifier and denotation as a signified are apparent in the existentialist graphs
(Figures 3 and 4).

Figure 3. *Barthes' 'connotation' graphically produced*

Figure 4. *Barthes' 'denotation/metalanguage' graphically produced*

At this point a problematic issue arises. If we take Barthes' (1968) symbolic
presentation of connotation *(ERC)RC* and denotation *ER(ERC)* as combinatory,
it should be possible to express the formulation as *(ERC)R(ERC)*. Why is this
formulation not presented by Barthes? If we graphically present the combinatory
formula (Figure 5), it becomes quite apparent. Barthes gives us only one com-

Connotation   2   E   R   C

                   1   2   E   R   C

Denotation   1   E   R   C

Figure 5. *Combinatory overlay of Barthes' propositional calculus for 'connotation' and
'denotation' where the metalanguage function is produced: Rhetoric*

mutation set (Figure 5), while there is at least one other necessary set (Figure
6), and multiple sufficient sets (Figures 7 and 8). In fact, Barthes suggests the

Connotation   2   E   R   C

                   1   2   E   R   C

Denotation   1   E   R   C

Figure 6. *Combinatory overlay of Barthes' propositional calculus for 'connotation' and
'denotation' where the metalanguage function is produced: Ideology*

possibility of an answer when he distinguishes "Rhetoric" (Figure 5) from
"Ideology" (Figure 6). Yet there is not discussion of the production of Ideology;
it is simply asserted. The best explanation for the use of the linear ratio of

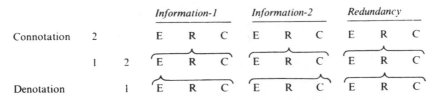

Figure 7. *Examples of combinatory sufficient condition sets that can be demonstrated in communication theory*

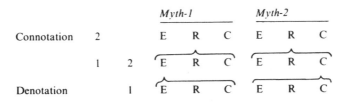

Figure 8. *Examples of combinatory sufficient condition sets that can be interpolated in communication theory*

(ERC)RC:ER(ERC) (see Figure 9) rather than my entailment model *(ERC)R(ERC)*

3	Connotation	Sr: rhetoric		Sd: ideology
2	Denotation: Metalanguage	Sr	Sd	
1	Real system		Sr Sd	

Figure 9. *Barthes' complete model in* Elements of Semiology *(1968: 93)*

(or more elegantly *(ERC)²*) is that such an entailment (see Figure 10) discloses

3	Connotation	Sr: Rhetoric		Sd: Ideology	
2	Denotation: Metalanguage	Sr	Sd	Sr	Sd
1	Real system		Sr Sd		Sr Sd

Figure 10. *Lanigan extrapolation of Barthes' model*

that discourse is dialectic (ontologically reversible) and should be grounded in a theory of the speaking subject (Kristeva 1975: 5, Merleau-Ponty 1945: 174; Eco 1976; Hikins 1977). In contrast, Barthes solves the problem of the ontological status of discourse by making *language (langue)* the ground for Being. For Plato, language is the ground for Not-Being. As one might guess, the Barthian view is that of the classical sophist to which Plato points his many objections. As a limited demonstration of my argument, I suggest a comparison between Barthes' use (1957: 115; 1977) of his model for myth analysis (Figure 11) and one of the

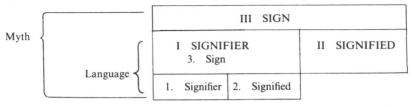

Figure 11. *Barthes' interpolation model in* Mythologies *(1972: 115; graph inverted)*

sufficient variations of my entailment model [see Figure 8: Myth-1], which reveals
an identity of formulation. I am confident about the accuracy of my interpretation since Barthes (1957: 109) specifically argues that "myth is a type of speech",
to which he adds the operational definition: "Innumerable other meanings of the
word 'myth' can be cited against this. But I have tried to define things, not words."
If we follow Barthes' intent in providing this definition of 'myth' and "speech"
as deriving from a "thing", we instead should expect the formulation presented
in Figure 8, Myth-2, which indicates such content signification. The fact that
Myth-2 is asserted, i.e., "to define things, not words", when Myth-1 is used
(Figures 9 and 11) merely confirms the error by omission found in the original
model in the *Elements of Semiology* (see the "Ideology" system in Figure 10).
However, for immediate purposes of comparison with Plato's analysis, I use the
complete model (Figure 9) that Barthes presents in the *Elements of Semiology* (1964).
I think the Platonic argument is clearest if simply formulated according to Barthes'
construction principles, since the comparison thus illustrates the concrete differences involved between the two theorists.

For Plato, the "plane of expression" consists of what I shall call the "verbal
form" (Sr) in relation to what Plato calls the object or "bodily form" (Sd). We
have now the simple *ERC* formulation. For Platonic connotation, the "name"
stands in relation to "description" and this pair becomes the significr in place
of the "verbal form" (Figure 12 ; cf. Figures 3 and 1) or *(ERC)RC*. For denotation

Sr		Sd
Verbal Form (particular quality)		Bodily Form
Sr Name	Sd Description	

Figure 12. *Platonic categories formulated according to Barthes' model of connotation*

Sr Name		Sd
	Description	
	Sr Knowledge	Sd Essential Reality

Figure 13. *Platonic categories formulated according to Barthes' model of denotation*

and the metalanguage function we have the signifier/signified relation of "name" and "description" where "description" is produced by the relation of "knowledge" and "essential reality" (Figure 13; cf. Figures 4 and 2) or the formulation *ER(ERC)*. At this point, we can compare the two possible sets represented by the formula *(ERC)R(ERC)* or *(ERC)²*. The commutation set hypostatized by Barthes (1964) as "rhetoric" is apparent in Figure 14. The key factor to be

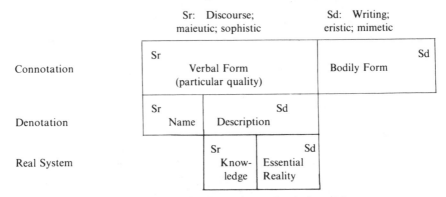

Figure 14.   *Platonic categories formulated according to Barthes' model*

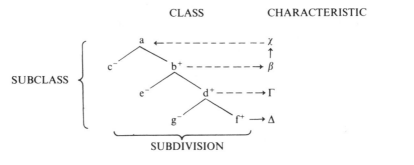

Figure 15. *Plato's method of definition by genus (CLASS) and differentia (CHARACTERISTIC)*

recognized, as Plato argues, is the signifier function, the *verbal form* that is always a "particular quality". Before proceeding, it is helpful to look at my construction of the set that Barthes (1964) suggests is "ideology" (Figure 16). Or, it may be useful to visualize the arrangement of sets as specified by my formula *(ERC)²* in Figures 10 above and 17 below. I believe that it is apparent that the diacritical sign production process of this formulation is consistent with the logical and phenomenological principles of paradigmatic/synchronic and syntagmatic/diachronic production established by Saussure and elaborated by Jakobson in the context of communication theory (Lanigan 1979, Holenstein 1976, Alperson 1975).

Plato's model for knowledge, used as a test of Barthes' model, therefore, allows us to recognize with Plato that an ambiguity exists when dealing with words, actions, or thoughts. This is the Platonic problem of distinguishing sophists,

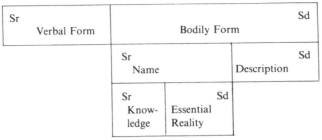

Figure 16.   *Lanigan extrapolation of Barthes' model applied to the Platonic categories*

statesmen, or philosophers. Or more to the point, we have the problematic ambiguity of speaking, writing, and thinking as the labor of sign production (Eco 1976). Here is the philosophic issue. Barthes (1964) resolves the ambiguity by choosing *writing* as a *context* that punctuates both speaking and writing as choice procedures (Lemert 1979). Plato, on the other hand, suggests, as a communication theorist might, that we probably should choose thinking to contextualize speaking and writing (the philosopher's method of maieutic). Or perhaps a second Platonic choice would be to select speaking as a context for writing and thinking (the sophist's method in rhetoric). Let me digress slightly to indicate that in the dialogue *Sophist* Plato suggests that speaking can produce many different qualities, so that just as we might perceive that the speech of philosophers is like the speech of the gods (which for Plato is a correct assessment), we may mistake the pedagogical speech of sophists for those speakers (ideologues) who engage in eristic. As distinguished from philosophers and sophists, Plato has no label to mark the eristic practitioners (see Figure 16 above), who are mere bodily forms for whom there is no verbal form, i.e., they have no *name* because the description of their acts is not produced by any knowledge of essential reality. These "ideologues", as I call them, are embodiments of eristic. They are speakers (particular quality) who are marked by their skill at deception (a denial of essential reality). Yet, philosophers, sophists, and statesmen (Kerferd 1981) are speakers (essential reality) who are to a degree skilled at knowing (particular quality). Barthes' notion of "myth" seems to be an exemplar of Plato's notion of eristic where "III SIGN" (Figure 11) is identical to "Bodily Form" (Figure 16). In the present context, however, to make the extension that the concept of "text" becomes the "Verbal Form" attached to the "Bodily Form" is an error (Figure 17). It is to confuse the very production of ideology with rhetoric (Sallis 1975: 110-117). We might speculate that we now also have an explanation for why Barthes' (1953) "Writing Degree Zero" is so difficult to detect as an explicit object of production (an "essential reality"); or, why Lévi-Strauss avoids contemporary social analysis (Charbonnier 1961; Lévi-Strauss 1960: 49). With this comparison between Barthes and Plato and with my assertion that Plato's dialectic should be the received logical interpretation, I now turn to the argument that Plato offers for the justification of maieutic.

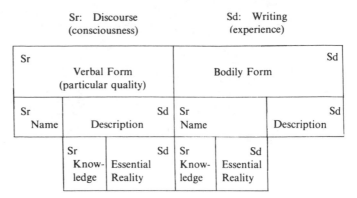

Figure 17. *Lanigan model for Platonic categories*

The dialogue Sophist

The dialogue *Sophist* (i.367-361BC) stands as a ready illustration of Burnyeat's comment (1979: 56) that "Plato's dialogues are a miraculous blend of philosophical imagination and logic". On the one hand, the dialogue *Sophist* entices us to contemplate how we know things by looking to our experience with those persons who articulately profess imagination, i.e., the sophist, statesman, and philosopher. There is a hint of argument by degree in this approach whereby Plato uses the personae of the dialogue to display a scale (of distinctions) of knowable experience. The dialogue opens with Theodorus, a mathematician, introducing the Eleatic Stranger (a philosopher who knows the sophistic method) to Socrates, who spontaneously mistakes the Stranger for a god in playful recognition of the demeanor that a philosopher should have. Art in its fundamental sense is the practice of knowledge that begins with the gods and has its first reflection in number, the art of mathematics. So philosophers, who are like gods in the practice of knowing, must be skilled in the *logos* of *logos*, i.e., the understanding of *collection* and *division*. Hence from the perspective of the dialogue personae, we know that the analysis of knowledge will proceed by the philosopher's ability (the art of distinction) to combine and divide the characteristics of the sophist (representing the acquisitive arts) from those of the statesman (representing the productive arts). In short, the personae represent an analogue logic of degree in which the choice of the philosopher prescribes a context belonging differentially to the sophist or the statesman. This binary analogue model of choice/context construction is, strictly speaking, our contemporary understanding of communication theory (Runciman 1973: 200-201; Lanigan 1979; Marcus 1974).

On the other hand, the dialogue *Sophist* is a concern with logic as separate from philosophical imagination. In Plato's phrase (i.367-361BC: 226c), there is "the art of discerning or discriminating". It is clear that Plato assigns the *art of controversy* to the sophist (ibid.: 232b) and the *art of imitation* to the philosopher (ibid.: 235b). The logical approach indicates one kind of knowledge that can be distinguished from another, so the kind of dialectic used by the sophist can be contrasted with that used by the philosopher. Within the context of dialectic possibilities (Sallis 1975: 478), speakers make choices in discourse that display "controversy" (that which is over against, in opposition to, *logos*) or "imitation" (that which is identical). As opposed to "controversy", which is digital (Prior 1979), "imitation" is binary by degree, in either "likeness" (Plato i.367-361BC: 235d) or "semblance" (ibid.: 236b). In contemporary terminology, Plato is asserting the conditions required by information theory, in which digital choices ascribe a context of choice. That is, the formulation reads: *Either* x *or* y *is true in context* z. One makes a particular choice in a pre-established context; a context of choice predicates a choice in context (Lanigan 1979). Thus, Plato's notion of "controversial" choice is parallel to the technical concept of information "bit", whereas the idea of "imitation" is akin to "redundancy" (see Figure 7).

Plato undertakes to explore the differences between Being and Not-Being, philosopher and sophist, by exploring the binary oppositions that are discovered in the image (Bodily Form) the sophist projects through *discourse* (see Figure 14 above). Plato's goal is to demonstrate that the "Being" (Bodily Form) of the sophist can be discovered in his discourse (Verbal Form), which is produced by the "name" and "description" that can be the "knowledge" we have of the "essential reality" in question. This procedure (Hunt 1921) is the famous Academic method (derived from Plato's use of Socratic maieutic in the Academy) of definition by genus and difference (see Figure 15). Taylor (1956: 377) provides a concise summary of the method:

> In principle the procedure is this. If we wish to define a species *x*, we begin by taking some wider and familiar class *a* of which *x* is clearly one subdivision. We then devise a division of the whole class *a* into two mutually exclusive sub-classes *b* and *c*, distinguished by the fact that *b* possesses, while *c* lacks, some characteristic β which we know to be found in *x*. We call *b* the right-hand, *c* the left-hand, division of *a*. We now leave the left-hand division *c* out of consideration, and proceed to subdivide the right-hand division *b* on the same principle as before, and this process is repeated until we come to a right-hand "division" which we see on inspection to coincide with *x*. If we now assign the original wider class *a* and emumerate in order the successive characters by which each of the successive right-hand divisions has been marked off, we have a complete characterization of *x*; *x* has been defined.

Plato begins his maieutic analysis by saying of the sophist (i.367-361BC), "He is clearly a man of art". The investigation is rather long and involved and I shall not trace it out, since Sallis (1975) provides an excellent schematic illustration (Figure 18), and since this analysis by division is abandoned as merely a discovery of *logos* instead of the sought definition of knowledge, i.e., a *logos* of *logos*. But, it is important to list the defining characteristics of the sophist that Plato discovers. First, the sophist uses flattery. Second, he is a merchant of knowledge regarding virtue. Third, he uses the knowledge of others as a merchant. Fourth, he makes use of one's own knowledge of virtue. Fifth, the sophist makes money by teaching argumentation. And sixth, he is skilled in the educational practice of cross-questioning. Unfortunately, as I indicated, this analysis proves inadequate. It is apparent that Plato, in the person of the Eleatic Stranger who conducts us through this long division, is thinking as an information theorist. His digital choices of names and descriptions turn out to be only a *context of choice*, rather than choice per se. Thus, it is painfully obvious to Plato that the six characteristics belong to the philosopher as well as the sophist. There is not difference in contextual

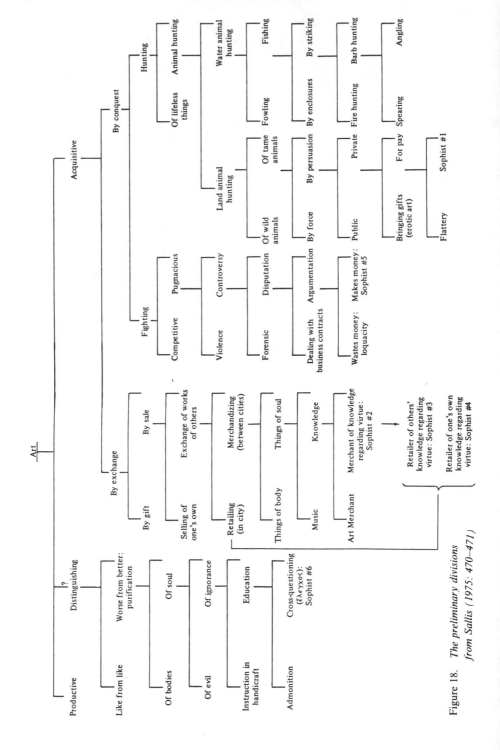

Figure 18. *The preliminary divisions*
from Sallis (1975: 470–471)

kind between the philosopher and the sophist. As Plato argues, there is only a difference of degree—for instance, let us take the fifth characteristic whereby the sophist makes money by argumentation and the philosopher is seen to lose money in the same way!

Plato's judgment is that the analysis has gone astray because it started with the division of characteristics from the perspective of "controversy", i.e., a digital division. Instead, we should start again with the perspective of "imitation" as the basis for a new series of divisions that in fact are "collections". In short, Plato shifts the dialectic into a binary analogue form of combinatory logic in which a choice *of context* is made, i.e., the communication theory perspective: *Both* x *and* y are true *of context* z. This is to say, a choice of context gives context in choice (Lanigan 1979). Thus, certain pairs of defining characteristics will be *both* present (a collection) *and* separate from each other (a division). For example, Plato suggests the typical dilemma of the information theorist: things must be said to be *either* hot *or* cold. This is not a paradox for the communication theorist, who realizes that the Being of things can possess *both* hot *and* cold in any given situation (i.367-361BC: 243b). It is clear to Plato that one should not mistake a difference of kind for a distinction by degree. This is to say, a collection is a difference by contiguity (a distinction and combination) that entails a difference by division (a distinction by disjunction and separation) because the reverse implication disallows a process presence, i.e., a separation cannot lead to a concrete combination. "In this sense, the diagnosis does not establish the fact of our identity by the play of distinctions. It establishes that we are difference, that our reason is the difference of discourses, our history the difference of times, ourselves the difference of masks. That difference, far from being the forgotten and recovered origin, is this dispersion that we are and make" (Foucault 1969: 131; see 1963: 35-36). The same point is made by Peirce (Savan 1976: 16), who says, "a sign is something by knowing which we know something more."[5]

Plato confirms the basis for his new choice of division grounded in collection by taking up the problem of distinguishing among "Being", "One", and "Whole" (i.367-361BC: 244d). He discovers that the collection "Being-One-Whole" is found in the division of both "Being-Whole" and "One", where the collection "Being-Whole" is a division of both "Being and "Whole". Plato is quite explicit (ibid.: 253-258) in suggesting that the binary analogue logic of communication theory is the dialectic discourse that identifies both the sophist and the philosopher as opposed to those who practice eristic, i.e., "ideologues" who rely on the use of information theory to invent their knowledge (Kerferd 1981: 59ff.). Plato proceeds to an elaborate proof of his thinking by showing how the conditions of "Being", "Movement", "Rest", "Same", and "Other" combine and divide. In brief, he argues that Being and Not-Being become mutual proofs of each other by their status as binary boundaries that punctuate knowledge (Figure 19). The proof recognizes two oppositional pairs: *Movement* and *Rest*; and *Same* and *Other*. Either one or the other in each pair is recognized as the Being against which the Not-Being is contrasted when one member of the pair is initially selected as a defining characteristic. For example, in the pair Movement/Rest we could select Movement as characteristic of Being. In turn, Rest is thereby equally characteristic of Not-Being (i.e., not being in motion). Thus, we discover that the Being and Not-Being of Movement is the *Same* and that the Being and Not-Being of Rest is *Other* than Movement (Sallis 1975: 514ff.).

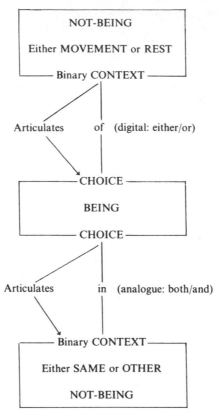

Figure 19. *Plato's entailment of communication theory and information theory in the categories of Being/Not-Being, Movement/Rest, and Same/Other*

Plato's basic illustration for his argument is *language*, where he reviews many of these logical features in terms of language at both the phonological and syntactical levels. And, he offers a review of language in terms of paradigmatic and syntagmatic shifts, i.e., the analogue function of the *one* and the *many* (Plato i.367-361BC: 253d-e). It is plain that the competence of the philosopher matches the performance of the sophist (ibid.: 253b). The speaking subject is the source of Being (ibid.: 263a-e). As proof, Plato offers a comparison between the following sentences:

(1) "Theaetetus sits." (2) "Theaetetus, whom I am talking to at this moment, flies."

Plato tells us that several judgments are possible. First, as Theaetetus remarks about both utterances: "they are about me and belong to me." Hence, (1) is true and (2) is false. And we know that the second utterance is one of the shortest that conforms to the definition of a sentence. The first contains both *name* and *description* in Being. Whereas, the second prescribes Being in the *person* of Theaetetus (". . . whom I am talking to at this moment . . .") and Not-Being in his *name*

"Theaetetus" which is true and Not-Being in his *description* (". . . flies") which is false.

It may be helpful to review this example with the aid of Figure 17. The first sentence *divides* discourse (Sr: Verbal Form) and the person of Theaetetus (Sd: Bodily Form); Not-Being (Sr) is combined with Being (Sd). By contrast, the second sentence *combines* discourse and the person (Sr: Verbal Form and Bodily Form); Being (Sr) is distinguished from Not-Being (Sd: "flies"). The word "flies" becomes the Bodily Form of Not-Being. Recall Barthes' comment about myth as things that are speech! Thus, Plato establishes the dialectic of collection and division as conditions of Being and Not-Being that are mediated by the speaking subject, not language. Mediation by language is myth. As Taylor (1956: 377) remarks, "the satisfaction of these conditions depends on our native acumen and our acquaintance with the subject-matter, and no rules can be given for it, precisely as no rules can be given for the discovery of a promising explanatory hypothesis. The method, like all scientific methods, will not work *in vacuo*". Thus does Plato remark (i.367-361BC: 260a) that ". . . to rob us of discourse would be to rob us of philosophy."

There is more to note here. We have an illusion of how the philosopher and the sophist use thinking to produce discourse. The reverse, using discourse for thinking, is eristic, i.e., bad philosophy and bad sophistry. Indeed, eristic is the crime for which Socrates stands falsely condemned. The dialogue *Sophist* explains the philosopher's method and hence the innocence of Socrates. In accord with the quest for a *logos* of *logos*, the explanation comes through the last minute speaking of a sophistic philosopher, the Eleatic Stranger!

Thus far in my analysis I compared Plato's model of discourse analysis to that of Barthes (1964). Second, I indicated certain errors in structuralist thinking *à la* Barthes by reexamining the detailed argument that Plato gives in the dialogue *Sophist* with respect to the method of discursive analysis. I would now like to briefly suggest the way in which Merleau-Ponty (1945) builds on the Platonic argument by utilizing the speaking subject as the source of sign production to combine the methods of semiology and phenomenology.

Merleau-Ponty and semiotic phenomonology

Discourse according to Barthes (1964), as we recall, exists on the levels of connotation, denotation (metalanguage), and the real system. The object of his structural analysis is *language* (*langue*) or its artifacts: text and myth. By comparison, Merleau-Ponty's (1945) phenomenological analysis takes the consciousness of the person as the object of analysis. The result is the development of a model of analysis consisting of (1) description, (2) reduction, and (3) interpretation (Lanigan 1972). Utilizing this method, I now want to construct a model of discourse that is a semiotic phenomenology. By describing the key features that Plato offers to us and reducing them to essential characteristics in the comparison between Barthes and Plato, I generate a hermeneutic of discourse for the speaking subject. In this model (Figure 20), there are two reversible commutation systems: (1) the *Reflective System* of the signifier (Sr) and (2) the *Prereflective System* of the signified (Sd). Each system consists of three levels (boundaries): the punctuation of *Expression* (comparable to Barthes' "connotation"), the punctuation of *Perception* (comparable to "denotation") and the punctuation of *meaning* (comparable to "real system"). These three paradigmatic levels exist in both the Sr and Sd systems.

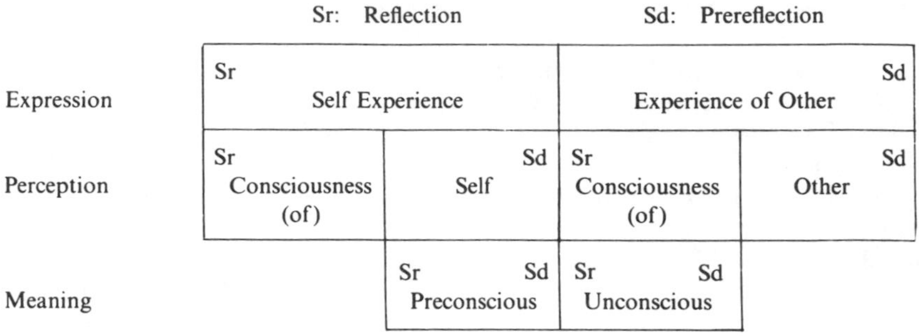

	Sr: Reflection		Sd: Prereflection	
Expression	Sr Self Experience		Experience of Other Sd	
Perception	Sr Consciousness (of)	Self Sd	Sr Consciousness (of)	Other Sd
Meaning		Sr Preconscious Sd	Sr Unconscious Sd	

Figure 20. *Semiotic phenomenology of human communication. Vertical relationships display communication theory: analogue choice, binary coding, metaphor, symbol, and paradigmatic/ synchronic condition. Horizontal relationships display information theory: digital choice, binary coding, metonymy, sign, and syntagmatic/diachronic condition*

The signifier system of *Reflection* illustrates the phenomenological perspective that discourse is a production of the *speaking* subject. In this system, *Expression* is the *Self Experience* that is constituted by *Consciousness of Self* or, in Platonic terms, Expression is the "particular quality" of Verbal Form that is *named* in the *description* of self (cf. Figures 17 and 20). Thus, Expression is constituted by Perception. In turn, *Perception* derives from a *Meaning* infrastructure that is the *Preconscious*. Again in Platonic terms, the Preconscious is equivalent to the knowledge I have of an essential reality. We can see that the phenomenological method of Merleau-Ponty (1945) has the same logical structure as the Platonic dialectic. That is, the methodological *description* of self experience is *reduced* to consciousness of self, which allows the *interpretation* of what has meaning in the preconscious. Recall Plato's method of analysis for sentences (1) and (2) above.

Where Plato and Merleau-Ponty differ is over the ontological status of the maieutic. For Merleau-Ponty (1945) discourse is a proof of the person, the speaking subject, as the incarnation of consciousness. For Plato the analysis shows that the person is an Image [Bodily Form] of an ideal Form ["essential reality"] that is true.[6] For Plato this Image can be known through discourse that is oral (knowledge), i.e., an oral report of what was said (understanding), or written (opinion). But writing converts the "essential reality" into a "particular quality", i.e., writing as an instrument replaces the "person as instrument" just as mimicry of another uses the voice as an instrument to replace my discourse (Plato i.367-361BC: 266d-267e). Opinion is mistaken for knowledge in Writing. Eco (1976: 171) illustrates the semantic sense in which propositional meaning requires a *perceptum* from the communicative point of view of an addressee, which is precisely the point of Plato's view that writing requires (erroneously) the reader to invent, rather than discover, a *perceptum*. Sebeok and Rosenthal (1981) ingeniously point to this same principle (historically found in magic acts of the theatre) as the "Clever Hans" fallacy in scientific research procedures. Thus while Plato and Merleau-Ponty differ on the ontological status of persons and discourse, they are agreed that discourse is a dialectic knowledge of the person, not language.

The signified system of *Prereflection* illustrates the phenomenological view that subjectivity in discourse must be viewed as intersubjectivity. That is, in the Sr

system, Expression comes from the *speaking* subject (experience of self), which entails that Expression in the Sd system is the speaking *subject* (experience of other).
For Plato this is simply another way of suggesting that Being is founded in Not-
Being. Or from the linguistic point of view, it is Saussure's distinction between
parole (*speaking* subject) and *langue* (speaking *subject*). The Sd system of *Prereflection*
is thereby the experience of the *Other*, which is constituted by the *Consciousness*
I have of the *Other*. Or in Platonic terms (Figure 17), experience of an Other (Bodily
Form) is *named* by my conscious *description* of the Other. Expression of the Other
is constituted by my Perception. In turn, Consciousness derives from the grounding of the *Unconscious*. In Platonic terms (i.367-361BC: 265b-266d) the unconscious
is equivalent to the knowledge we have of an object's absence in essential reality.
Or more precisely, we have the Not-Being of Being as Same or Other (Figure
19). In a phenomenological perspective the Unconscious is the Not-Being of my
consciousness or Being. In turn, this knowledge of my Being at the Meaning level
of the Sd system allows me to constitute the perception level in which my consciousness (Being) constitutes the Other (Not-Being [of me]).

Foucault (1961: 191) provides a concrete illustration of the present analysis
in his discussion of the therapeutic force of imitation in "theatrical representations".

> The fulfillment of delirium's non-being in being is able to suppress it as
> non-being itself; and this by the pure mechanism of its internal
> contradiction—a mechanism that is both a play on words and a play of
> illusion, games of language and of the image; the delirium, in effect, is
> suppressed as non-being since it becomes perceived as a form of being;
> but since the being of delirium is entirely in its non-being, it is suppressed
> as delirium. And its confirmation in theatrical fantasy restores it to a truth
> which, by holding it captive in reality, derives it out of reality itself, and
> makes it disappear in the non-delirious discourse of reason.

Foucault's analysis, interestingly enough, draws on a previous exploration by
Merleau-Ponty (1962: 291, 334) of the place of the rationality of the speaking
subject in the problematic of hallucination and delirium (Levin 1945; Lanigan
1979b).

I trust that it is apparent at this point that Merleau-Ponty adopts Saussure's
concept of, and Jakobson's elaboration of (Holenstein 1976), paradigmatic/syn-
chronic and syntagmatic/diachronic shifts to illustrate the reversibility of analysis
that occurs at each level of the system. That is, Expression, Perception, and Meaning in the Sr or Sd system are paradigmatic/synchronic shifts, while there is a
simultaneous syntagmatic/diachronic shift between Sr and Sd Expression, Sr and
Sd Perception, and Sr and Sd Meaning. I illustrate this process in Figure 21 by
citing Merleau-Ponty's categories as they constitute a semiotic phenomenology
of discourse. I have detailed previously Merleau-Ponty's philosophy of communication that informs the content of the schematic in Figure 21 (Lanigan 1970, 1972,
1977, 1979a).

In brief summary, let me say that Plato's dialogue the *Sophist* (i.367-361BC)
provides a maieutic analysis of philosophical imagination that in large part we
methodologically recognize as the contemporary school of *existential phenomenology*.
At the same time, however, the dialogue also gives us a discussion of the logic

Sr: Consciousness   Sd: Experience

Sr		Sd	
Parole (speaking)		Langue (social language)	

DESCRIPTION
[Expression]

Sr	Sd	Sn	Sd
Parole (speech)	Parlante (speaking)	Parole (speech)	Parlée (spoken)

REDUCTION
[Perception]

	Sr Sd	Sr Sd	
	Corps Propre (person: lived- body)	Geste (gesture: body- lived)	

INTERPRETATION
[Meaning]

Figure 21. *Merleau-Ponty's model of human discourse. All relationships are combinatory; this is critical to recall with reference to 'parole parlante' and 'parole parlée'.*

in human conscious experience that we may readily call *semiology*. Indeed, the very argument that I am making for the existence of a *semiotic phenomenology of discourse in the speaking subject* (*corps propre*) comes from the mouth of the Eleatic Stranger, who tells us (257d): ''Knowledge is also surely one, but each part of it that commands a certain field is marked off and given a special name proper to itself. Hence language [discourse] recognizes many arts and forms of knowledge.''

19

BROOKE WILLIAMS

History in Relation to Semiotic

The time has come for history to be classified within semiotics according to its proper characteristics both as a discipline in its own right and in terms of its transdisciplinary place in the development of a doctrine of signs. Sebeok's comment (1979: 67) on the potential of semiotic to integrate the disciplines hits the heart of the matter as regards current controversy over the question of history:

> Precisely how semiotics can function as "an organon" of all the sciences, and the wide humanistic implications of the assumption that semiotics "provides a base for understanding the main forms of human activity and their interrelationship", since all such activities and relations are mediated exclusively by signs, pose a host of further questions that need to be widely as well as urgently debated, since, among other consequences, their satisfactory reformulation might lead to badly needed improvement of the curricula which still inform students of the human sciences worldwide.

The very right to existence of the discipline of history is often called into question passionately these days precisely because the as yet underdeveloped logic of history is neither purely scientific nor purely literary. It seems to have no place in a contemporary curriculum. It is a semiotic anomaly, seemingly grounded in neither fact nor fiction. It raises problems concerning the existence of "reality", and therewith blood-pressures.

If the logic of history resists, on the one hand, a superimposed semiotic analysis (e.g., of Haidu 1982), so has it also resisted attempts to develop a formal logic of history (starting with Hempel 1942). The reasons for the misfit of history are in both cases the same. It is not, as is sometimes argued, that historians are "abnormally stupid", but that the discipline of history is necessarily rooted in temporal human experience that can best be expressed in natural languages. Historians, therefore, find the very material itself that they work with resistant to "any tightly defined system whatever", precisely because such a definition presupposes too much: it "leaves out the heart of the matter" (Tillinghast 1972: 13). It is this "heart of the matter" that needs to be classified logically, and it is this, I claim, that semiotic enables us to do for the first time.

The social scientists agree with the philosophers that it is analysis and classification, rather than the underdeveloped logic of history, that are at the heart of the matter academically, even in the purely humanistic studies. Given our philosophical tradition, in favor of knowledge admitting of universal statements, and of statements set out in the systematic form appropriate to theoretical knowledge— given, in other words, the mind-set that presupposes that the more abstract and general concepts of the physical sciences are closer to "reality" (see Conkin 1971: 155) than are concepts of any other sort—it follows that our modern logicians find it "virtually impossible to describe well the most basic things historians do" (Gallie 1964: 19).

Historians tend to see history as a mediating discipline that "occupies the treacherous middle ground between concrete particulars and abstract relations" (Conkin 1971: 143; see also Marwick 1970: 18). Whereas history once linked philosophy with poetry, today it links social science with literature. The question arises as to whether there really is an epistemological middle ground between art and science, a question that historians have always guessed to be answerable in the affirmative because the nature of historical material itself suggests such an hypothesis. The question is, then, whether the "problem" of history simply reduces to a problem with the humanistic presuppositions of the discipline, as analytic philosophers have unsatisfactorily tried to show, or whether it can be satisfactorily shown to reduce to literature, as some structuralists intimate. For instance, Hayden White (1978: 62, emphasis supplied) writes:

> In my view history is in bad shape today because it has lost sight of its origin in the *literary imagination*. In the interest of appearing scientific and objective it has repressed and denied to itself its own greatest source of strength and renewal. By drawing historiography back once more to an intimate connection with its literary basis . . . we will be arriving at that *"theory" of history* without which *it cannot pass for a "discipline" at all*.

It appears that what we are dealing with is not a "mediating" discipline so much as an anomaly. Although this discipline is very old, what has come to be known as "the crisis of history" (Marrou 1959: 12) still persists—mayhap because the status of history as a discipline is still unresolved. One historian (Conkin 1971: 135) seems—unknowingly—to detect the right answer only after having given up on the wrong tracks: "most disquieting of all, so long as competing views of history retain their ties to mechanistic, mentalist, or vitalistic ontologies, they involve unbridgeable gulfs open to no intellectual reconciliation."

It is at this point of no return that a doctrine of signs can step in and bridge the gulf, pave the way for an intellectual reconciliation. In so doing, semiotic can at last clarify what it is that historians do.

History need no longer serve as a presemiotic "mediator" between science and art, nor need history be caught in between these disciplines and squeezed out of existence by them. What is the source of this "problem"—seen in semiotic perspective—is that history is intrinsically interdisciplinary because of the nature of the material which informs the historian's method. Because the physical, mind-independent being of historical material stands for *mind-dependent human experience*, this material elicits from the historian a human response at the poetic source of creativity that overflows into the historian's work as a form of art. But because historical material consists of *mind-independent* or physical material that is publicly verifiable as to its existence, history also elicits from the historian an ordering of this material that is not only coherent for art's sake, but is perhaps above all coherent (in a publicly verifiable way) for truth's sake, in the same sense that the scientist seeks truth.

Now the "problem" of history, from a semiotic point of view, is not its relation to other disciplines, but that the logic of history has never been properly defined. Some regard it as anomalous to try to combine the imprecision of something relying primarily on natural language with the scientific notion of an objective coherence *verifiable* in relation to things existing that function as signs of a "history" independent of the historian's mind. In the perspective of semiotic, history is revealed to be a discipline that resists all attempts to classify it as characteristic of the modes of reasoning of either science *per se* or art *per se*, precisely because history addresses the interaction and interdependence of nature and mind that seems to constitute human experience through semiosis. Whatever the public or private mind-set of the historian, we find we need no longer couch the problem of the "objective" world of nature and the "subjective" world of mind as if the relation were not correspective, or had to be construed hermeneutically so as to preclude precisely the relation *between* mind-dependent and mind-independent being.

History as a discipline is thus between science and art precisely in the sense that it addresses the interaction of nature and mind through the semiosis that transmits human culture, whether the subject of historical inquiry be, for example, the transmission of science or of art. The seeming anomaly of history appears only when this discipline is forced into prevailing classifications as science ("theoretical") or art ("practical") or both as a hybrid or mediating discipline. The anomaly disappears when the "problem" of history is situated in the context of semiotic.

To classify history in this way requires first of all that the logic of history be seen according to its own characteristics, and, second, that history be seen in relation to science and art neither as opposed to them, nor as mediating between them, nor as cut off from them by its proper autonomy (still less as having no longer a reason to exist), but rather as the *relation* between mind-independent and mind-dependent being that underlies the possibility of "history" as a discipline which is distinct from, but not separated from, science and art—not only because of an overlap and sharing of techniques, but also because it is as historical creations that science and art flourish within culture. In other words, history in its proper being is not first of all a discipline, but is precisely the anthroposemiotic transmission and generation of culture wherein nature and mind mutually influence each other in the shaping and constitution of "reality".

To begin with, history has its own proper mode of reasoning that is distinct, but not separate, from the modes of scientific reasoning. The logic of history characteristically involves, without being circumscribed by, the logic of question and answer typical of detection (for fuller discussion, see Williams 1985: 285-287; see also: Russell 1984; Collingwood 1936-1940: 266-282, 1939: 29-43; and Marrou 1959: 89, 140). This is the logic of abduction as distinct from deductive and inductive modes of inference (in the precise sense explained in Deely 1982: 68-75, after Peirce; see also Sebeok and Umiker-Sebeok 1979, Eco and Sebeok 1983).

The logic of question and answer characteristic of history is underdeveloped, and its potential unexploited, because the possibility of such a logic was itself a non-question in a philosophical tradition wherein realists belittled the reality of becoming, with the result that they reduced becoming propositions into being propositions (see Collingwood 1939: 28-29; Russell 1981: 179-189; also Merrell 1975: 76). The very arising of the question of the logic of history is itself but a part of the whole semiotic web in which the question of historical change arose, at which point the problem of history got structured in terms of the modern realist-idealist debate. That is, it is only in relation to the time dimension of the semiotic web that historical becoming and the logic of history are revealed in the first place precisely as a question.

Because of an awareness of the time dimension of the semiotic web in which even the development of logic itself takes place, it can now be seen that the distinct modes of thinking of history and science need no longer be separated in an artificial way that cuts them off from human thought in its integral wholeness, wherein abstract and concrete, speculative and practical thinking, find a common ground in anthroposemiosis. Far from denying the proper logic of each, a semiotic perspective admits the richness of human experience and consciousness which integrates both modes of thought through semiosis.

In contrast to a lifeless propositional logic, what is characteristic of the logic of history is that it detects, rather than dismisses, the rich web of sign relations in human culture wherein the part can be understood only in relation to some whole, and a whole only in relation to the part. This interconnectedness cannot be observed from without as if the whole and the part were independent entities whose sign relations to each other were only external, that is, mind-independent simply. The historian uses the logic proper to history to penetrate to internal—or mind-dependent—relations that involve purpose and goals underlying external forces, a knowledge that differs radically from, for instance, the knowledge of a planetary system. Moreover, human products, such as a Gothic cathedral, form a semiotic web of temporal and dynamic relationships wherein the later parts of the whole are not only brought into existence by the earlier parts, but the earlier parts are themselves affected by the anticipatory internal relations they entertain to the later parts (see Collingwood 1936-1940: 210-217; Marrou 1959: 58-59; Tholfsen 1967: 243-244). The historian's logic must therefore not only apprehend concrete signs, but also universal sign systems as these develop over time.

Thus being and becoming are two aspects of an indivisible single reality (see Tholfsen 1967: 107), wherein physical, or mind-independent being, and the physically unreal objects or aspects of objects of thought, or mind-dependent being, become interdependent insofar as it is cognition that gives them signification— that is, the use of signs explicitly as signs—in precisely the way in which relations between natural events, which are only extrinsic, cannot do, even if these relations also be classified sometimes as "semiotic" (Deely 1978; 1982: 93-123).

What the historian does is to make explicit the structuring process of signification, not by means of the dichotomous logic of a "before-after" relationship, but by means of the logic of history which deals with signification precisely as changing throughout the interval between given slices across, given cross-sections of, time. Whether a particular historian be oriented toward history as event or as structure, what cannot be escaped is "the heart of the historian's problem", which is "the transition between coherences, the explanation of radical discontinuity" (Struever 1974: 404). The historian's problem must be approached from the anthroposemiotic standpoint that recognizes the "shifting line" between being and non-being, or mind-independent and mind-dependent elements wherein these distinct—but not separated—orders of existence exchange places over time as their interrelationships change according to human design and accident, as, for example, in the case of "heroes" who "shape the development of a given culture through myth and folklore in ways that cannot be reduced to causal lines stemming from actual achievements in the order of physical events, just as stories false in their origin can become true shapers of a course of social events, thus acquiring a reality which must be dealt with in its own right'' (Deely 1982: 64-65).

Thus non-being, or ''unreal'' relations (in the sense of having no being apart from cognition), are notions that are founded on ''real'' relations (in the mind-independent sense in which things are observed to affect one another in their physical existence: cf. Poinsot 1632a: Second Preamble, esp. 83/9-16, 95/18-96/36), and, in turn, by influencing human conduct, these very ''unrealities'' can ultimately acquire sometimes the status of ''reality'' through such consequent incorporation into the network of real relations (Langan 1983: ix-x; Powell 1983) comprising the world of social interaction or of culture. Hence the inevitability of the human condition as *historical*, in the very precise sense of *historicity* as ''the domination of man's existence by a total view of reality (culture, *Weltanschauung*, etc.) not known to reduce to fact'' (Deely 1971: 2).

In the perspective of semiotic, therefore, the old question of whether history be an art or a science or a mediating discipline between the two need no longer be approached by attempts to graft history onto the prevailing interdisciplinary mind-set that combines disciplines without developing the inner logic characteristic of each. Even the best attempts among historians to classify history according to its own proper logic succumb to a kind of double vision of history as a split-level discipline, half art and half science, or some proportion thereof. The noted historian Crane Brinton (1936) once called history an imaginative reconstruction of the past, which, while scientific in its methods and findings, is artistic in its presentation. The question has also been turned inside out: ''All sciences are devoted to the quest for truth; truth can neither be apprehended nor communicated without art. History therefore is an art, like all other sciences'' (Wedgwood 1956: 96).

These approaches to the anomaly of history fall short of resolving the problem. History deals not simply with external relations, but with internal relations as well—that is, not simply with some (now mind-independent) *fact* of the past, but with the *feel* of it as well (see Nye 1966: 140). As Johan Huizinga observed in his 1924 classic, *The Waning of the Middle Ages* (pp. 14-15):

> A scientific historian of the Middle Ages, relying first and foremost on official documents, which rarely refer to the passions, except violence and cupidity, occasionally runs the risk of neglecting difference of tone between the life of the expiring Middle Ages and that of our own days. Such documents would make us forget the vehement pathos of medieval life, of which the chroniclers, however defective as to material facts, always keep us in mind.

The historian Lynn White (1956: 74) makes much the same point: ''Much of life escaped the documents . . . . The historian must create his patterns of probable truth less in terms of specific records and more in terms of relationships intuitively evident to him as he deals with the records.''

What needs to be developed in the perspective of semiotic is the logical connection between fact and fiction. Historians have pointed out to one another for some time that they sometimes ''behave more like writers of fiction than they either admit or know'' (Wedgwood 1956: 95). Illustrative of such an historiographical problem is the question of what took place in the ministries and palaces of Europe during the days following the assassination of Archduke Franz Ferdinand which precipitated World War I. As Remak points out (1967: 117), any narrative of these days must of necessity be partially fictive, or constructed, in view of the difference between life itself and the logic of the historian:

> For what in print is likely to look neat and logical, in truth, more often than not, was chaotic or at best improvised. Decisions were made with no time for proper reflection, messages crossed each other, and some of the most fateful errors were committed from motives no more profound or sinister than lack of information or sleep.

The logical connection between fact and fiction that still needs to be developed is the relation between words and ideas that semiotic can clarify (see Deely 1982: 131-142; also Merrell 1975: 101). While the naming process is a creative act of making something intelligible from the very beginning of historical inquiry, it is pushing an insight too far to say that the word therefore "creates" the object, as Kinser asserts (1981: 65): "The verbal formulas used to describe an object also create it." The question then arises: What was there in the first place to describe? A tennis umpire, for example, may call a serve a fault or an ace, but all the umpire does is create the call, not the serve itself. If a given umpire, moreover, makes too many "wrong calls" according to public perception, this umpire will be removed as "umpire".

To argue that the past does not exist until the historian makes the shots by calling them, that is, to argue that the historian creates the past simply by his or her construction of it, sinks history into a kind of linguistic quicksand which loses all ground upon which to base a semiotically objective inquiry. On the other hand, to fail to recognize the power of the word, or power of naming, in the shaping of thought about an object—in establishing the object's signification—is to fail to recognize the presuppositions built into the naming process itself, and thus to fail to recognize any difference between "what really happened" and what we call "history".

What we call "history" is therefore, to borrow a distinction that Wilden makes (1981: 2-3) about language, "both a representation of reality and a part of reality, part of the human context":

> It is the very task of language to bring its structure to the representation of reality, for where there is no structure, there is no sense. Structure structures content. And any language can be restructured in both form and content so as to deal with changing ecological and historical realities.

Thus history as transmitted through language is something flexible: semiosically, it structures the human *Umwelt*, but by reordering it continually. While the contemporary historian thus shares with the scientist a semiotically objective method of inquiry, the historian also possesses, because history is structured through natural language, a kind of poetic license in the crafting of historical reality.

Semiotic *in principle* thus distinguishes in order to unite the artistic and scientific, practical and speculative knowledge, as these are integrated in the method of history as historians practice it. The developing logic of semiotic and the heretofore underdeveloped logic of history are seen thus to converge toward a doctrine of signs that resolves of itself the anomaly presented by history in the presemiotic context of modern philosophy and science.

This "doctrine of signs", of which history forms part, is precisely the "semiotic" that Locke called for in ending his *Essay Concerning Human Understanding* as a foundational doctrine of the structure of experience and consciousness. It is this new logic, "different", as Locke put it, and more encompassing, as Poinsot remarked, than the "logic and critic we have been acquainted with heretofore", that provides the perspective required to account for history.

Locke the physician—to draw an imaginary analogy—did not sever the connection between the two hemispheres of the brain; on the contrary, he shows how the two communicate. Semiotic thus integrates logically what is already integrated in the historian's awareness. In so doing, semiotic, in contrast to traditional philosophy (Deely 1982: 64) opens the door to studying the orders of external and internal relations, mind-independent and mind-dependent relations, being and non-being (the "real" and "unreal"), not as if their boundaries were staked out in advance, but as constantly shifting because of the interaction between these two orders as the mind participates in what it observes—through the function of signs. Semiosis thereby structures experience *flexibly*. It is just this flexibility— publicly verifiable in part but suffused throughout with poetry (the free initiatives of human creativity)—which is the object of historical inquiry, and which the method of history is required to accommodate *before all else*—as, so to speak, its point of rest.

20

LUIGI ROMEO

Heraclitus and the Foundations of Semiotics

If semiotics is accepted as the study, the doctrine, or the science of signs, the history of semiotics must perforce include investigations into the nature of the sign as well as into its evolution at various stages of the historiography of science. While all aspects of history may be relevant to semiotic studies, considerations on the development of the sign according to records are more reliable than speculations on the initial awareness of the sign. That is because such considerations encompass only a relatively short segment of thinkers' efforts throughout the ages, i.e., barely twenty-five centuries or so, if we limit our research to the West. Genesis of the sign, or the initial grasp of consciousness by *Homo semeioticus* through speculations reaching back some 50,000 years, however, will doubtless excite inquiries which, no matter how scientific in nature, will always be tainted with conjecture by anthropologists, biologists, archeologists, and semioticists. In this essay I shall limit myself to historiographic aspects of recorded "history"— not necessarily true history—stressing "original" sources collected and analyzed during approximately the last hundred years.

General Observations

For the sake of its history, constraints are imposed upon its researchers insofar as the foundations of semiotics are concerned, constraints arising not only from traditional boundaries of culture, but also from the paucity of systematic inquiries regarding virtually uncoverable and unrecoverable stages of development. In certain cases it is not possible to delve deeply into observable foundations, owing to the interpretation of basic concepts that have been commonly accepted without the ἀρχή of meaning having been probed. In other words, key terms are often employed anachronistically and out of context. It becomes necessary, therefore, for scholars to return repeatedly to original sources in the history of science in order that those meanings be reinterpreted in the light of contemporary findings and tools of work.

In regard to the history of the sign, traditional scholarship (by that I mean scholarship *en vogue*) seems to be entangled in a maze of obscure (or at least colorless) interpretations involving the diverse acceptations in ancient history given to anything deriving from σημ-, such as σημεῖον, σημαίνω, etc. Similar problems stem from anything related to λέγ- and λόγ-. As a matter of fact, it is difficult to separate σημ- from λέγ-/λόγ- in the process of understanding *Homo semeioticus*. It is, to say the least, bewildering and depressing to read endlessly how, for generations, standard meanings have been accepted as dogma *in toto* without anyone asking what "logic" supports them in particular contexts. This phenomenon is not new. In the case of Heraclitus, it began with Plato. And that is why stress has always been comfortably laid upon post-Socratic doxography for the interpretation of basic terms when the semantic value was already altered in accordance with the development of new concepts (mostly for applied purposes) in logic, medicine, *ars grammatica*, and so forth. It is true that terms are sometimes appropriated to suit a particular intellectual climate and to satisfy a polysemous exigency. With regard to semiotics, this has also been the case. Such an intricate state of affairs was further complicated, even in Aristotelian times, by philological and exegetic difficulties.

A typical example related to Heraclitus' work is Aristotle's difficulty in relating "ἀεì" to the rest of the sentence at the very beginning of what is now Fragment 1 in Diels' editions. Punctuations before or after ἀεì can matter a great deal (changing the accent accordingly) in whether Heraclitus' λóγος is eternal or whether men will ever understand it. Of course, a third possibility, if intentionally hinted at by Heraclitus in a semiotic key, would validate the oracular character of his maxims, leaving the reader to interpret it "correctly" after understanding the meaning of λóγος.

All that we have gleaned to date from the probings of Steinthal 1863, for λóγος in general, to the painstaking research of Weltring 1910 for σημεῖον in its budding stage (but after Socrates), deserves—and always will—periodical reanalysis due to current interest, if not for the sake of questioning repetitive taken-for-granted interpretations.

As for the history of semiotics (still to be written in a comprehensive way), its problems are so ancient that it seems almost vulgar to ask why we should return to them after twenty-five centuries, starting, at least, with Heraclitus. One logical answer may lie in that, after all, the pre-Socratic fragments have been analyzed systematically by only a few generations of scholars periodically disturbed, as they were, or interrupted by evils concocted by *Homo* allegedly *sapiens*—proving, incidentally, Heraclitus' views contained in Diels Fragment 80, or even 53. Moreover, each "modern" discipline tends to dissect fragments which emphasize certain fields or points immediately related. Only recently has semiotics begun to exploit the fruitful labors of countless philologists and philosophers who, mostly over the last century, have analyzed Western thought exegetically and at the international level. It will be a long time before semiotics, as a discipline, can succeed in freeing itself from the complexity (and the "complex") of its intellectual longevity and from a currently factional tendency to stress local and fashionable "politics" *où tout se tient*—e.g., some literary critics in particular, having drained their methodological resources and historic validations, attempt to use semiotics by forgetting or ignoring its philosophical foundations (cf. the Fall 1974 issue of *Diacritics*, A Review of Contemporary Criticism, devoted to "Semiotics").

With a reanalysis of semiotic scholarship, two things become apparent. First, there appears a tendency, if not a need, to either assign a paternity to someone (almost to validate contemporary theories) or to seek reassurance in the *auctoritas* of past scholars who occupied a central position in the most favorable climate of opinion. For example, Kleinpaul 1888: 103 was probably satisfied with labeling Hippocrates as "der Vater und Meister aller Semiotik", suggesting perhaps a father for the Western community of thought. (Cf. Sebeok 1971; but also Coseriu 1969: 108, in which Augustinus "enthält die ausführlichste Semiotik der Antike". Of course, it is already too late in history for Augustinus, and Hippocrates was an applied semioticist only.) In parochial schools such as ours in the West, the title of "Vater", or its kindred variants in Germanic "Vaterland" tradition, might be subject to contention between, say, Europeans for Locke and Americans for Peirce. No matter what the genealogical tree, whether for the sake of either pedagogical or aphorismic purposes, the tendencies are understandable; and, while intrinsically irrelevant, they nevertheless serve to indicate clearly the state of the art in time and place.

Second, the history of the fragments themselves, i.e., the "fortune" of the pre-Socratic fragments and how they have been utilized to trigger, consciously or not, a novel interpretation—not necessarily a sounder one—on the basis of a different focus [becomes apparent as a semiotic phenomenon].[1]

Fragment 93 and a Seed for Semiotics

The tendency of claiming the beginning of semiotic studies each time any term connected with σημ- appears is dangerous, but one cannot afford to disregard a reanalysis of the term and its congeners whenever they surface in earliest historical times. In our case, long before Protagoras for the sake of philosophy, and long before Hippocrates for the sake of medicine, the term involving a semanteme (or free morpheme in American terminology) that contains σημ- is attested in Heraclitus.[2] Of course σημ- is not merely a term, but a seminal concept represented by it which, if validated, would make its impact felt upon a whole kinship of concepts and their ἀρχή.

Now, a basic problem deriving from reanalysis of Heraclitus' fragments is encountered in Diels 93 (Bywater 11, and Pasquinelli 83). Because of Diels' availability to most scholars in the West over the last two generations, and the continuous re-edition under Kranz, Diels will remain for the time being as the most reliable corpus in Greek from a philological standpoint. Nevertheless, in the West we are in the Diels "paradigm", and so be it pending acceptance of a new one, although I am qualmish about humans engaging in a completely new edition of the fragments. Frankly, I believe it would be easier to put a man on Mars.

Fragment 93 is also, from a history of science standpoint, the most ancient document containing a semanteme within a cadre of semiotic theory. (For a derivation of the term *semeiotica* before *semiotics*, see Romeo 1977, and cf. Sebeok 1971.) All other semantemes (or allomorphs) are latecomers and found with increasing frequency in post-Aristotelian records. Heraclitus' Delphic aphorism, the most baffling at first to the neophyte, is recorded as follows: ὁ ἄναξ, οὗ τὸ μαντεῖόν ἐστι τὸ ἐν Δελφοῖς, οὔτε λέγει οὔτε κρύπτει ἀλλὰ σημαίνει.

First of all, the Heraclitean meaning might seem difficult of immediate abstraction for various reasons, most of them simply "historical". But the primary and most "logical" is that, if after twenty-five centuries we still labor on it, the palm of success should undoubtedly go to Heraclitus for keeping himself alive among us at the purely exegetical level. Another reason arises from the fact that the three verbs in 93 seem to be uttered by the Sibyl in 92, without any trimmings. In other words, those verbs are intentionally chosen by Heraclitus for proper stylistic and oracular purposes. Also, it is commonly agreed that in antiquity no one would "explain" an oracle through audio-visual aids to morons—else it would not have been an oracle to start with—and that has not changed in the last twenty-five centuries. Moreover, it was the tradition of Greek philosophers of the time to be stenoglottic, incisive, compact, if not lapidary *in posse* and *in esse*. The contents of the fragments, and particularly in the maxims, was intended not for consumption by olive pickers and wine makers, but for an elite who would transmit culture to another generation.

The other difficulty arises from the danger of taking Diels 93 in isolation and thus interpreting it in any "literal" manner leading to a flat rendering of incoherent or contradictory meaning. However, when it is related to the entire corpus of fragments (especially to those belonging to the same "category") additional light is shed not only on the single fragment but on the work as a whole. Heraclitus is, first of all, a master of interrelationships, of correlations, of interdependencies: nothing is in isolation (and there is no need for "structuralism" to verify this). Indeed, it is not by pure chance that 93 follows 92 in Diels, that they are 11 and 12 in Bywater, and 85 and 86 in Pasquinelli. Besides, any interpretation must be accepted by taking into consideration not only those fragments immediately related to each other (as are 93 to 92) but all fragments and anything else surrounding the work, whether in the area of drama, religion, medicine, cookery, or even erotica, and whether from doxographic sources or pseudo-works.

The Tradition of Translation

Starting with Diels, how does he render the fragment into German? In a literal way:

Der Herr, dem das Orakel in Delphi gehört,
sagt nichts und birgt nichts, sondern er bedeutet.

Here Diels was over-hasty, and a few generations of "translators" from German erred with him. Let us analyze the fragment. In both Greek and German the syntax is plain enough to be used for homework after a couple of weeks' elementary Greek or German. There are no structural complexities or punctuative disfunction leading to Aristotelian or sophomoric variants. The problem is merely semantic in terms of correlations among the verbs λέγει, κρύπτει, and σημαίνει.

According to Diels' literal interpretation as if made in Aristotelian times, the contents are somewhat obscure, which is why, after twenty-three centuries, Heraclitus continued to be labeled "dunkel" (the term originally used by Aristotle in his *De Mundo* might have been understandable twenty-three centuries ago, but it is preposterous to employ it still, when there is actually nothing "obscure" in Heraclitus). The verb λεγέι rendered by "sagt" is parochial, and σημαίνει by "bedeutet" extremely ungrammatical for semantic and syntactic reasons. In fact, Diels translates roughly:

The Lord, . . . says nothing and hides
nothing, but means.

Naturally I am aware that, although in German it might be more wholesome, no matter how allotropic (even admitting "signifies" instead of "means"), the sense one derives from Diels is zero, since the logic behind that interpretation is tenuous. First, is the oracle to be understood as a function of magic or of religion? In magic, people *demand* an answer which must be clear especially in terms of positive/negative results. In religion, however, as in the case of the oracle in those times, people *asked for*, not demanded, an answer. An answer was always given, but how to interpret it was the mystery of the oracle's intercourse with humans. (Even later in the Roman tradition, the answer to *Ibis redibis non morieris in bello* depended on how the intonation or pause was imagined. The oracle did not use "commas", a latter-day luxury.) Too, an oracle *must* always say something, if not very much; but at the same time it must not hide *everything* in order to mean *something*. Otherwise, as in Diels' interpretation, how could it *bedeuten*? One should also ask: What does it *bedeuten*? Undoubtedly, the equation σημαίνει = *bedeutet* is the literal admission of a generally accepted dictionary listing, without probing into the whole corpus but remaining within proper chronological parameters. Nor did Diels correlate the archaic meaning of λέγεται with that of σημαίνει.

As for ourselves we should also bear in mind the maxim Φύσις δὲ καθ' Ἡράκλειτον κρύπτεσθαι φιλεῖ (Diels 123), that nature loves to hide, yes, but not to remain eternally concealed from the inquirer. In other words, does intimate nature love to hide in order to trigger a seeking action in the human who must find an answer in himself (Diels 101: ἐδιζησάμην ἐμεωντόν)? By going into the realm of "English" interpretation, things become necessarily more Delphic. Take, for example, one of the most popular English translations with which a whole generation of young minds have struggled (Freeman 1948: 31; but cf. also Freeman 1946):

> The lord whose oracle is at Delphi neither
> speaks nor conceals, but indicates.

In essence, Freeman's version is a translation from Diels' German interpretation, and thus in it one still faces identical problems that are compounded by "indicates" which, according to normal syntax, calls for a direct (and potentially for an indirect) object. In other words, what does it indicate, and to whom?

It is obvious that the meaning of σημαίνω suffers from hyperdefinition, since in similar cases its interpretation does not vary. Hyland, one of the latest interpretations in a century-old tradition, falls into a similar trap (1973: 151), although methodologically he was quite close to grasping a less pallid meaning. Indeed Hyland, along the line of Pasquinelli's innovations, had grouped at least four fragments and tried to obtain the Heraclitean *signifié* of λόγος through Fragments 18, 54, 123, and 93, quoted as follows (italics added):

> Unless you expect the unexpected, you will never
> find it. For it is hard to discover and difficult.
> A hidden harmony is better than an apparent one.
> Nature loves to hide.
> The lord whose oracle is at Delphi neither speaks
> nor conceals, but *gives a sign*.

Here "gives a sign" is more etymological though more fallacious than in previous cases, because semantically the entire sentence lacks color. It is the result of Hyland extracting *medical* (or clinical) semantic values of later times, as in Galenus, or even earlier in Hippocrates. Surely one can supply a genitive of some kind to the last verb, as Sanctius might have done later; but is the whole maxim, then, satisfactory in terms of "logic"?

There are fortunately less literal interpretations. In French, the one more consonant with Heraclitus' archaic meaning is from Burnet 1919:

. . . l'oracle de Delphe qui n'exprime ni ne cache
sa pensée, [il veut] la faire voir par signe (Rey 1933: 313).

The "French" tradition continues until the most recent rendition by Ramnoux (1968: 302):

Le Mâitre a qui appartient l'oracle, celui de Delphe:
il ne parle pas, il ne cache pas, il fait des signes.

The only improvement here is that in Burnet the oracle makes *one* sign; in Ramnoux's time, he makes several.

Another example expressive of a more "logical" force of thought and meaning, almost with semiotic overtones, is Pasquinelli (1958: 189):

Il signore che ha l'oracolo in Delfi
non dice e non nasconde, ma accenna.

This "Italian" tradition continues with few stylistic variants, as in Salucci and Gilardoni (1968: 38):

. . . né dice, né nasconde . . .

So the difference between a French and an Italian Apollo is that in French he does not *speak*, and in Italian he does not *say* (anything). Nevertheless, like everyone else, Pasquinelli is still bound to the most used *later* meaning of λέγω "I say", but he *almost* hits the nail on the head with "accenna" ("he hints", "he alludes", or "he intimates").

At this juncture it would serve no purpose to devise a typological inventory of Western language translations. I have read two dozens in West European cultures, and all of them follow the German interpretation given by Diels. How, then, can one place the oracle's answer into a "logical" and semiotic framework? By considering several frames of reference before validating the final answer. It is, thus, important to reflect upon the following points of reference in mutual correlations:

(1) The archaic meaning of λέγω related to an oracle.
(2) The semantic charge of κρύπτω as antithetical to (1) within Heraclitean thought.
(3) The interpretation of σημαίνω outside vocal language.
(4) The assumption that *intimate* nature loves to hide.
(5) The solution suggested by Heraclitus—to seek within oneself—anticipating the concept of *Homo mensura* much before Protagoras' μέτρον.
(6) The implied answer that man himself is an oracle when he searches within himself.

Before reflecting on the points listed above, however, it is necessary to take into consideration certain oracular traditions.

The Oracular Tradition in Greece

In order to correlate the meaning of the three verbs among themselves and the "whole" work, it is important to remember the function as well as the types of the oracles in Greece. At the same time, one should recollect the power that divination exercised not only on the individual but also on society at all levels. Divination through the oracle was, then, the strongest psychological tool in the hands of any individual or group. It was actually ''institutionalized psychiatry''. But in my particular assumption of the ''intuitive'' aspect of the oracular function, it is known that in Greece the divination through the oracle could be accomplished in two ways. One was based on *external* (visible, acoustic, sensible) ''signs''. This was actually ''inductive'', and indeed the Greeks called it τεχνική since it implied the technical knowledge of practical devices in order to interpret the will of the gods and thus know the future.

The other way was performed by the god's direct inspiration to either the local psychiatrist (i.e., the priestess) in charge of the oracle or to the individual seeking an answer derived from the meaning of *internal* ''symptoms'', without external tools of interpretation (ἄτεχνος). In our specific case, although it is on record that all oracles could function through either inductive or intuitive means, Delphi's oracle was not only the most prestigious one in Greece but operated exclusively in an ''intuitive'' manner. In other words, Delphi's oracle was ''endosemiotic'' and thus more human in resources. It was also the most sophisticated, aristocratic, and learned. It is no wonder that Heraclitus, himself an aristocrat, chose Delphi from among a hundred oracles in Greece alone. (See Bouché-Leclerq 1879-1882 in connection with the religious role of the oracles, and Ferri 1916 for their classification.) For Delphi was, indeed, since Homeric times, the seat of Apollo, a god who knew everything in the past, present, and future (cf. Homer c.700-600BC: III, 277), as any standard classical mythology manual will amply illustrate.

Toward a Semiotic Solution of Diels 93

Consideration is now directed to the six points listed above, in an attempt to solve the Heraclitean ''riddle''.

(1) The sixth century meaning of λέγειν can be analyzed, in Diels 93, either independently or in connection with ''λόγος. Since λόγος will be discussed at length in another paper, I choose to dissect Heraclitus' ''λέγει'' independently from his obsession with λόγος. Moreover, I believe Diels 93 contains all data necessary for a solution. Although already in the sixth century λέγειν had also, if not primarily, the meaning of ''to say'', ''to speak'', and related synonyms, there were other coexisting meanings including, naturally, the archaic ones and the newer ones, derivatives of ''to say''. Before scanning basic literature of Heraclitus' time, a brief etymological review would refresh our memory regarding λέγειν, and not λόγος, as a basic semanteme—for the verb is the fundamental form since Homeric times. Etymologically, and thus historically, λέγω meant simply ''I put things together'', ''I select'', ''I gather'', ''I separate (one from a group)'', ''I enumerate'', and so forth. When viewed within Indo-European, it corresponds to Latin *lego* having similar meanings, in addition to that of ''I read'' which was *not* so in Homeric Greek (cf. Latin *legiō, -onis*, and Oscan *leginum* corresponding to Latin *legionem*). (See, among many, Boisacq 1916: 563, for a comprehensive presentation of the I.-E. situation.)

The archaic meaning of λέγω, especially when analyzed in relation to derivatives and compound forms, leaves no doubt as to the original acceptation devoid of "to say" (even Scapula 1637: 934-950 [see gloss in References on Scapula 1579-1580] lists hundreds of attestations, starting with the *Iliad* [Homer c.700-600BC]). An entire book could be written on the subject; hence I find it irrelevant to transcribe here what one can see for oneself consulting "original" sources for pre-Heraclitean times.

At this stage, therefore, since the key to the oracle lies in the archaic meaning of three verbs (and Heraclitus would employ nothing but the most archaic semantic charge), let us assume as a frame of reference Diels' interpretation which lingers in each and every "translation":

The lord, who . . . , neither λέγει nor κρύπτει but σημαίνει.

It is now only a matter of "substituting" English for the Greek, and, although this replacement can be done singly at any of the three positions, I prefer to follow the "linear" progression, not only because it must have been the manner Diels chose by generating "sagt", but because λέγει seems to have troubled everybody since Diels' interpretation. Thus,

(2) Once any of the archaic semantic values for λέγει have been accepted, it should not be an arduous task to find the oracular meaning of κρύπτει because, by "logical" tenets, it must be the opposite of λέγει and because it is dictated by a reading of the whole corpus of Heraclitus' fragments. Moreover, if we remember Heraclitus' philosophical views on opposites, and apply basic rules of logical syntax, the second step should be as follows:

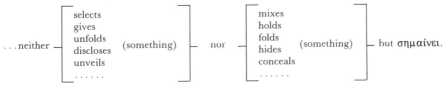

(3) At this point the selection of a semantic force for σημαίνει is pleasant not only because of its own characteristics that can be uncovered independently of the preceding two verbs, but also because of the base for its archaic meaning *per se*. This is especially so for the reason that, in the oracle, vocal language is excluded, and hence meaning must be conveyed by non-verbal expressions. Again, even in Homeric times, σημαίνω might have meant an infinitude of things—from "I mark with a sign" to "I reveal" or "manifest something through signs", in addition to "I make a sign", "I indicate through signs", etc. Note that "sign" or "signs" can be physical, natural, sensible, conceptual, internal, external, imaginary, real, etc. Once more, it would be redundant to quote from standard literature the archaic value of σημαίνω.

Later meanings were derived and applied for various purposes—in medicine, philosophy, economics, military science, astrology, meteorology, and so forth. It was a matter of "applied" semiotics in its infant stage. Thus, it is dangerous to construct, according to popular tendency nowadays, a whole semiotic theory based on, say, the literature of medicine.

Even the term "semeiotics" itself (via Latin *ars semeiotica* from τέχνη σημειοτική) is a late result of "applied" science. But to make this paper short, let us consider the last stage, where I assume once more:

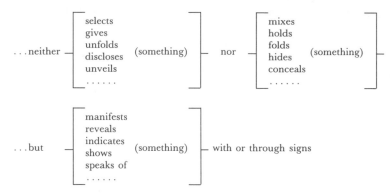

The selection can now be made by knowing that the direct object contained in any verb must be the lord's thought on the matter solicited by the inquirer (thought being in keeping with the pair λέγ-/λόγ-):

> The lord, who has the oracle in Delphi, neither discloses nor hides his thought, but indicates it through signs.

The problem now is what we should understand by "signs", obviously not external ones such as smoke or noises. Thus, if the interpretation above is valid, a whole semiotic theory can be formulated—especially if σημαίνει is understood as "the oracle *speaks* through signs", a verb that could not fit any traditional interpretation where οὔτε λέγει is rendered "neither speaks". The oracle does indeed speak, and says a lot to one who knows how to listen. That is what an oracle is for.

(4) The considerations made for (1)-(3) above, leading to the suggested solution, when correlated with Heraclitean conceptions on human nature, are corroborated by the view that such characteristics do not yield anything (or any answer) so easily. But, before continuing, one should first understand what human "nature" means. It is assumed that Heraclitus' fragments are those remaining from his work entitled *On Nature*; therefore the "behavior" of one's nature must be of prime consideration. This quality is uniquely characteristic of humans, not of rocks, and not of beasts. Therefore, it is the nature of *Homo sapiens, oeconomicus, intuens*, in short, *Homo semeioticus*, and as such may be subject to self-analysis. Thus, "hides" is not to be construed as an innate permanent feature of human nature. That is to say, nature loves to hide (but notice the verbal aspect of κρύπτεσθαι φιλεῖ indicating the desultory and periodical "present" tense); however, again, to linger in the depth is part of its natural "behavior". One has to seek within himself in order to elicit something that was already latent in *Homo intuens* (Diels 101: ἐδιζησάμην ἐμεωυτόν "I searched within myself"). The reason for searching

arises from the condition of something being hidden. Finally, this deep seeking is correlated with Diels 99: εἰ μὴ ἥλιος ἦν, ἕνεκα τῶν ἄλλων ἄστρων εὐφρόνη ἂν ἦν—"If there were no sun there would be no night".

Heraclitus, thus, appears clear to anyone who knows that he must rely upon his own intrinsic resources. This is not to suggest that Heraclitus enjoys shifting all the responsibility onto his own or man's intuition. He does not even trust himself since, rather than painstakingly researching within his mind, he would prefer to trust his five senses, as evident in Diels 46, 101a, 107, and 63, whenever coping with "reality".

(5) The implications from Diels 101 are fundamental for the problems of cognition. It is evident that, the intimate nature of things being hidden in all of us, each person must analyze himself on the basis of internal signs (as well as external ones that might act only as catalysts), i.e., in relation to the reasoning powers which distinguish *Homo semeioticus* from *non-Homo*. There is another implication, however, that required a longer time to be formally declared by another aphorism. This implication was caught later by Protagoras, who did not hesitate to declare that πάντων χρημάτων μέτρον ἐστίν ἄωθρωποσ, but the concept of *Homo mensura* is already in Heraclitus. Indeed, in semiotic matters Protagoras was to Heraclitus what in logic Aristotle was to Plato. If man is the measure of everything, then all his answers are to be found inside himself merely by seeking the meaning of his own signs, i.e., by intuitions.

(6) If all of the above is valid, each human being has his own built-in oracle as part of his mind. Heraclitus indeed speaks of "ψυχες". This is consistently and erroneously interpreted, since Diels' translation of Fragment 115 as "soul" ("Seele"): "ψυχες ἐστι λόγος ἑαυτὸν αὔξων", which I interpret simply "The mind has its own nature to expand itself". The problem is that since Heraclitean times man still has not fully exploited the potential of his mental capacity.

To those who put forward *non-Homo* speculations Heraclitus replies very clearly indeed (Diels 82): πιθὴκων ὁ κάλλιστος αἰσχρὸς ἀνθρώπων γένει συμβάλλειν "The most beautiful ape is horrible when compared with humans". Heraclitus did not have to read Darwin to single out the uniqueness of *Homo semeioticus*, for only in *Homo* (Diels 113): ξυνόν ἐστι πᾶσι τὸ φρονέειν "The faculty of reasoning is common to all". At last the anticipation of Protagoras' μέτρον attests the primacy of *Homo semeioticus* through Diels 116: ἀνθρώποισι πᾶσι μέτεστι γινώσκειν ἑωυντοὺς καὶ σωφρονεῖν "Every human being has the faculty not only of knowing himself but also of reasoning rightly", and reinforces Fragment 113. Both fragments 113 and 116, among many, lie at the foundations of theoretical semiotics.

Conclusions

In the realm of semiotics there actually cannot be any conclusions, especially if an attempt is made to base them upon the thought of pioneers whose work, already twenty-five centuries old, remains still at an infant stage. However, if in the history of semiotics there may be an ἀρχή *in nuce*, it must be found in Heraclitus and in his Delphic oracle, properly correlated with virtually his entire corpus. There is no doubt that the three Delphic verbs constitute the semiotic synthesis of a thesis-antithesis statement leading to the formulation of signs inside and outside of *Homo semeioticus*. We are at the ἀρχή of semiotics, and in it Heraclitus is one of the thinkers climbing a lonely path, fencing only with Parmenides in an infinite world replete with interior and exterior signs. There is so much to be done for the study of these semioticists that the task may well intimidate anyone attempting to dissect in a semiotic framework the period encompassing the sixth and the fifth centuries. But in spite of the long road ahead, if there is at this stage any *Vater*, he is Heraclitus—not Hippocrates, a rather tardy heir to theoretical tenets on which applied aspects of semiotics were later based. And I should not be surprised if, someday, the label of *Vater* were to be lifted from Heraclitus and laid upon another. For, in the history of semiotics (also a history of mankind), every *Vater* must have a previous Father, and the ultimate will inevitably be *Homo semeioticus*.

V

The Name and Its Direction

21

JOSEPH RANSDELL

Semiotic Objectivity

The central purpose of this paper is to explain a conception of objectivity which may be taken as a liberalized conception of what it means to be scientific, and to argue that what I call "conventionalist semiotics" cannot lay claim to objectivity, in the sense explained. The conception of objectivity is not itself argued for here, though I hope it has enough *prima facie* plausibility to generate some reflective response. Since successful sciences usually generate technologies as a matter of course, the conceptions of the scientific and the technological are often confused. For that reason I spend some time making clear that it is not a technological semiotics that I am attempting to promote, though such a thing is by no means impossible. In fact, it already exists. Some of my remarks in this connection are motivated by a belief that there is a very real possibility that the present semiotics movement will mistakenly come to conceive itself as a movement toward a technological semiotics, particularly when it becomes clear that conventionalist semiotics (which has dominated in contemporary semiotic theorizing) is an essentially empty enterprise—a realization which will occur quite apart from anything I have to say.

I

The popular conception of science as a form of magical power, the unrestrained exploitation of the technologies which successful sciences normally generate, and the highly successful attempt of positivistic philosophy of science to establish the belief that the value of science can only be technological or instrumental, have combined to give to the term *science* conceptual and emotional associations which make me hesitant even to suggest that semiotics should be scientific to academicians largely humanistic in orientation. For, as I understand it, semiotics is a movement toward a comprehensive theory of communication, construed in terms of interpretational response to meaning-properties, and it seems likely to me that, if the present movement is intellectually successful, it will generate technologies of human control fully comparable in power to the technologies the "hard" sciences generate. The question is whether semiotic technology will, and must be, yet one more deadly weapon in the hands of fools, or whether it can instead be a path leading us out of our foolishness. It is only because I think it can be the latter that I find it possible to encourage the development of semiotics along scientific lines.

But as I construe the term *science*, following the conception of the scientific which Charles Peirce developed, it really means much the same as could otherwise be expressed by talking of *objectivity*, as that term is applied to an inquiry or cognitive quest. By *objective inquiry* I mean inquiry which incorporates in the form of its practices, procedures, or methods, the idea of arriving at publicly stated conclusions based on publicly observable data, such conclusions being put forth *as* conclusions with which any other competent and devoted inquirers into the same subject matter, with the same explanatory aim, will or would agree in due time. This involves the idea that every scientific *assertion* implicitly involves a meta-statement of the inquirer to other inquirers into the same matter, attesting that the conclusion drawn is a result of observation mediated by inference, with an indication of what was observed and what was observed about it, and with further indication of the inferential mediation which led to the conclusion, both sorts of indications being articulated sufficiently as to allow the other inquirers to attempt to "replicate" the observation/inference/conclusion sequence. By *observation* I do not mean sensory perception. I mean rather an active acquaintance with something which results in a belief that it had certain properties. *Observation* thus primarily means the activity of observing, or becoming acquainted with, something insofar as this activity eventuates in a belief about it. This may be a highly inferential process itself, and perhaps always involves some inference, but the scientific function of observation is to provide *starting points* for inferential development.

As regards the meaning of "being acquainted with", I will explain by indicating my usage of it, which I think you will find similar to your own. Thus I consider myself to be very well-acquainted with some things, fairly well-acquainted with others, not well-acquainted at all with still others, and to have no acquaintance with a good many things. And I suppose you would say the same about yourself. I couldn't tell you what this last class of things consists of (the things I have no acquaintance with), because whatever I told you about them would imply an acquaintance with them, in the sense of "acquaintance" I have in mind. It may even be an impossible class. If so then I would say that my acquaintance with things ranges from extensive to practically nil, and I suppose you would say the same for yourself. The things in question may be individual objects, laws, rules, fictional beings, real beings, illusions, ideals, abstractions, emotions, thoughts—you name it, or otherwise identify it, and you *are* acquainted with it *ipso facto*. (This raises the question of what it is to identify something, a question I will discretely evade here.) Now, *observation* is getting acquainted with something, or perhaps I should say *getting better acquainted with* something, insofar as this takes on the form of an intentional activity. *An observational datum* is something believed to be true of that thing as the result of observation of it, functioning logically in the form of a premise for a conclusion asserted as such in a scientific claim.

An observational datum is a starting point, but its status as a datum is purely contextual: it is a datum for *this* inference; but it may itself be a conclusion from observational data, and, so regarded, it is no longer a datum. There are no absolute observational data, no ultimate first premises from which we all must begin: one person's datum is another's conclusion, and vice versa. So in putting something forth as an observational datum functioning as a (partial) basis for a conclusion, one is assuming that others either have found or will in due time find it equally acceptable as a starting point—perhaps because their observations yield (have yielded, will yield) the same result, or perhaps because they are willing to accept it on trust, at least provisionally, because they respect one's ability and scrupulosity as an observer (a far more important factor in the establishment of a data base than is usually acknowledged). In any case, though, a scientific assertion will be a waste of words if it does not rest upon observational data acceptable to others, for whatever reason or cause.

I believe you will see that this conception implies nothing about the kind of subject matter involved or the logical use to which the conclusions may be put. It does not imply that the subject matter is physical or sensory, for example, nor does it imply that the conclusion is descriptive or predictive in function, as opposed to critical or evaluative. It consigns no intellectual interest to the domain of the unscientific. For it is not *what something is about* which makes it scientific or unscientific, but rather *how one goes about it*. One of its root ideas is that an objective inquiry is one which exhibits in its procedure the assumption that whatever the inquirer claims about or attributes to the subject matter is to be regarded as being true of it, or false of it, as the case may be, independently of the claim itself, and indeed independently of what any individual or finite set of individuals claims or thinks it to be. For it only involves a belief that others will agree about the matter if they start from a certain point and move in a certain way towards a conclusion. Whether they will indeed be willing to start from that point, or infer in that way, is of course another matter. Even if they do, however, there is no implied guarantee that the resulting agreement will be the truth; so the truth about the matter is never constituted by any such actual agreement. On the other hand, what is agreed to be the truth about the matter may well be the truth. So the truth claims are not in vain. They serve the function of achieving further agreement (sometimes) on what is true, among those willing to work from the same starting points, and such agreements may well capture the truth.

Nothing is assumed about the kind or kinds of inference involved: deductive, inductive, hypothetical, or any other varieties there may be. An experimental report from a physics lab will explain the role of the physical activities and the instrumentation involved in the inferential process in one way, and a literary critic will explain his inferential moves in quite another. Poor inferential moves may be made. No matter, so long as they are made public for the possible criticism of the other inquirers. Objectivity is not a matter of results or even of types of inferential procedure, but rather a matter of the recognition *in* one's communication with other inquirers that where one started from, and how one got to the conclusion (or how one thinks one can get to that conclusion), may be capable of being corrected by them, and hence are to be shared so that they can be subjected to the real possibility of such a correction. The metaphor behind it is that of the *communal hunt*: "Hey, everybody! I think it went that way! Look; here are the signs. Now I interpret them to mean that . . . ." But it really is no metaphor. Human beings were hunters before they were warriors or growers even, and we will always be on the hunt for something. Objectivity is the form of the communal hunt for the truth, and it seems to me that this is what *scientific* should be construed to mean as well.

I should emphasize that, although this conception of objective inquiry may be regarded as an analysis of what is implicit in making a responsible truth claim in a scientific context, it does not constitute a *criterion* for distinguishing a truth from a falsehood. That is, the fact that an objective method of inquiry is followed does not imply that any particular conclusion drawn in accordance with it is thereby a truth, or even that the conclusion can be assigned any determinate likelihood of being true. Objectivity is not an algorithmic decision procedure. (I might add that nearly every discussion of Peirce's analysis of truth errs in supposing that his shift to a methodic conception is an attempt to provide a criterion for truth in the form of a method, whereas the essence of Peirce's approach lies in the abandonment of the idea that there is any such thing as a criterion of truth. It is remarkable that the quest for a criterion still absorbs the energies of epistemologists when reflection upon the actual practice of inquiry in any area will show clearly that no such thing is either used or missed.) The analysis is based rather on the idea that a scientific truth *claim* amounts to saying something like this:

> I have done my best to come to the same conclusion anyone else would come to about this matter, were they to enquire into it with the same explanatory aim as I. Here is my conclusion, of which I am sufficiently convinced to be willing to take the responsibility of putting it forth publicly, well aware of the fact that anything publicly asserted may be taken as a basis of thought and action by others, thereby helping or harming them in their own pursuits. My belief is that this conclusion can only be helpful in increasing our common understanding of the matter in question. And here is an indication of the way I arrived at this conclusion: see if you find yourself similarly compelled to draw this same conclusion, provided you think my starting points, and my way of moving toward a conclusion, are acceptable as such. If you do not find yourself in agreement with me, please state publicly your reasons for this so that I and others can reconsider the matter and see if we can come to an agreement with you.

Perhaps my formulation is not exact, but it can be regarded as an attempt to capture the logical force of a claim made in the context of a scientific or scholarly journal, or other such context. In an era when "publish or perish" is the working ethic of academia, it is based on the opposing ethic that one should perish before publishing anything—which is to say, before *asserting* anything formally and publicly to one's intellectual colleagues—which could be misleading, without having done one's best to make sure it will not have that deleterious effect, taking due account of the practical constraints and limitations upon all of us in our pursuit of a reliable and fruitful understanding of what mutually concerns us.

As a final remark, let me urge that semioticians should, above all others, be sensitive to the multiple techniques of communication that are available for conveying starting points, inferential processes, and conclusions. I am not thinking here primarily of non-verbal media—though they are pertinent, too—but rather of the various possible uses of language in cooperative inquiry. Some things are best conveyed in one way, some in another. Research reports are best for some things; poetry best for others. "What? Scientific claims made in the form of poetry?" I don't see why not. But of course the poet has to bear in mind the poetic interpretational capacities of his or her fellow inquirers, in deciding whether it is best put in that form. Such interpretational skill is not very widespread at present, for example. Philosophy—much of which is semiotics—has been done in a variety of idioms: poetry, drama, letters, notebooks, confessions, meditations, formal proofs, even intentional non-sense, as well as the forms favored in the professional journals. Plato wrote philosophy in the form of plays, for example, and, to a large extent, at least, I think I understand what he is talking about, what he takes as his observational data, how he draws his conclusions, and what his conclusions are. That is, I began to understand these things when I began to respond to his works *as* plays. And I find these things far clearer in him than in much material I read in professional journals, which often exhibit a pseudo-objectivity because their authors do not grasp that they have to situate themselves in a real communal hunt in order to make clear where they are really starting from and what they are talking about.

There is much else that could be said about this conception of objectivity; but perhaps this is sufficient for present purposes, and will indicate that this conception of the scientific is one according to which science is primarily a *code of conduct*—something rather more like a code of honor than like a linguistic code—which is constitutive of an ideal and shared form of life, that ethic being derived logically from an analysis of how we must relate to one another communicationally if we are to achieve our common goal of a shared understanding of our subject matter. It is, if you will, a semiotic conception of objectivity and science. I cannot defend this conception here, and can only commend it for consideration on the basis of its *prima facie* plausibility, but it is not one which is being put forth in a divisory or exclusionary spirit. If it seems to be remote from science, as you understand it, perhaps it is because you are accustomed to thinking of the scientific in terms of its subject matter (e.g., something quantifiable) or its results (e.g., instrumentalities of practical use) or its subject-specific methods (e.g., the use of special physical instruments, mathematical calculi and conceptions, etc.), rather than in terms of its being a shared form of thinking and communication: in short, an ethics of the intellect.

The conception is Peirce's, as I understand him; and I think it is worth remarking in this connection that Peirce was himself an adept in nearly every science of his time, working in the forefront of several of them, and doing so always with a sustained focus on the question: "What does it *mean* to be a scientist? What does it mean to devote one's life to the service of the discovery of truth?" When the truth about Peirce's life and accomplishments becomes generally known, it will be perceived that he was not only the most omnicompetent scientific mind of his time, perhaps never subsequently to be equalled, but also a moral hero of the intellect, of the stature of Socrates: a veritable icon or paradigm of *philosophia*—which really means devotion to the search for truth, not *philosophy*, as that is currently conceived in academic orthodoxy. In any case, Peirce's conception of the scientific is not that of a dilettante, but that of a person whose qualifications for advancing such a conception are far higher than those of the amateurs who have dominated philosophy of science during this century. This does not imply that his conception is thereby the superior one, but it does mean that one is well-justified in taking what he says seriously, regardless of how it may appear *prima facie*, for he certainly did not arrive at his conception on the basis of a naive understanding.

II

In working toward an effective semiotic theory we are working toward the creation of a human enterprise the value of which could be so deleterious as to insure definitely the destruction or permanent degradation of human life. I think such a Doomsday semiotics is possible, even likely, if no attention is paid to the *alternatives*, and their practical implications, at this early stage in the present movement. For although a semiotics that works in the service of human interests is also possible, there is more than a little danger that it will never be actualized. It may seem odd to talk about alternatives, as if one could choose between competing theories *a priori*, and on a moral basis at that. If it were a question of a physical theory I would make no such suggestion, but the fact is that we do have a latitude of choice about how we are to conceive human life which is not available to us in respect to our conception of the physical order. This is not a "conventionalist" thesis: I am *not* saying that we can conceive things any way we decide to conceive them (assuming we wish to arrive at a valid understanding) by simply defining them according to our whims. My point is rather this: human life is not fixed in its overall form, due to the fact that reflection upon it can enter into the determination of its form, such that the conclusions drawn in such reflection have (at least to some extent) the power of self-actualization and, thereby, self-validation. For example, a person who conceives of himself as a helpless pawn in the games of others will tend to be such a pawn in the games of others; a person who conceives of himself as unattractive to others will tend to be unattractive to others; a person who feels himself to be a loser will tend to be a loser. That is, there are tendencies for self-perceptions to validate themselves, though of course I don't mean that there are no exceptions, or that "the power of positive thinking"—the popular phrase for this idea—is anything miraculous. The basic idea is simply that, by and large, we will live within the range of what we *conceive* to be possible—or necessary—regardless of what the actual possibilities and necessities are.

This is why ideologues of every stripe are so bent on convincing us that such-and-such is inevitable, and in fact characteristically speak so much of what is desirable as of what must happen, anyway. We will accept nearly anything, regardless of how unattractive to us at the beginning, once we become convinced that we have no real alternative. I recall watching an interview with a certain physicist some years ago concerning weapons-policy, a matter on which he had (at that time at least) extraordinarily rigid views. It became clear in due time that the man was literally incapable of entertaining alternatives about what *will* happen: the future was as fixed and determinate for him as the past, and his beliefs about it simply unquestionable, at least insofar as it bore on the point at issue. Thus the interviewer several times said: "Yes, but what if . . . ?", whereupon he would simply say, in effect, there are no "ifs" about the matter. I had not until then realized that fanaticism is not an extreme case of moral commitment, but rather an abandonment of the moral perspective altogether (through the abandonment of alternatives), and that it is in this abandonment that the power of the ideologue lies; moreover, that in a very real sense this stance toward human reality has some genuine *logical* force, because the very fanaticism or dogmatism supporting the belief actually increases its likelihood of turning out to be true, at least under some conditions. (This is what William James was trying—confusedly—to express in his paper on "the will to believe", which, like nearly all of James' philosophical ideas, is a bowdlerization of something he learned from Peirce).

A case more directly pertinent to our purposes here is that of B. F. Skinner, whose psychology can be interpreted as a form of semiotics, and who has been attempting to convince us that he has discovered the only possible way in which human life can be understood, and therefore the only way in which it can be lived. From this supposed necessity he infers that he—that is, some likeness of himself—should be put in charge of us as our keeper. Now it would surely be a mistake to think that a life "beyond freedom and dignity" is not possible for human beings, or to think that Skinner does not know what such a life would be like. Moreover, when he says that this is what all human life really is, he comes far closer to the truth than those who oppose him are usually willing to recognize. The fact is that the modern world *is* much as he says it is, and the modern consciousness *is* largely constrained within the purview of the possibilities he recognizes. Take what he says not as a metaphysical/political doctrine, but as a description of the dominating tendencies in our life and thought, and Skinner's confused and amateurish philosophizing reveals a valuable insight about our current situation.

A conception of what human life (intellectual or practical) can *only* be has a tendency to validate itself by driving out other possibilities from our awareness, so that, in due time, it is the only model available and, consequently, the only kind of life there actually is. Might really does make right, in this sense. Though he undoubtedly never thinks about it this way, Skinner wants to rule the world because that is a part of his method of verification: he will *make* his theory true, if he can, simply by persuading us that we have no option. But when I refer to Skinner here I really mean Skinner the sign, not Skinner the person: Skinner as index of the present state of our intellectual culture, and Skinner as icon of a form of life "within which we live, move, and have our being" (Bishop Berkeley's definition of God). For Skinner's theory of human nature is nothing new. On the common sense level, his psychology is just what we all began to learn in the cradle as we learned about the effects of reward and punishment in the control of others. All his theory does is to sophisticate that common sense idea.

In western philosophy he was first clearly identified by Plato, who called him "Gorgias" and pointed out that his follower was Callicles, a demagogic politician who is the Thrasymachus of the *Republic* under another name. Plato knew that Skinner was not just wrong: people *are* pigeons (a con man's name for a sucker, by the way) and those who know the secrets of the carrot and the whip *can reduce* people to mere button-peckers, whether from desire for the carrot or from fear of the whip. The key to their success is that we keep believing them when they tell us:

> Get wise! You're nothing but a pigeon, but some pigeons are more equal than others, namely, those pigeons who learn the science of pigeon-training. You'll be amazed to learn how much more positive reinforcement you can get once you are in charge of the pellet-dispenser. Now if you show a lot of aptitude for pecking, we'll let you control the dispenser every now and then. And who knows but what we might reassign you permanently to this exalted position? Why, all of us trainers were once mere button-peckers ourselves!

We forgot the reports of those who have told us that there is a world outside of the laboratory where pigeons can actually fly. A flying pigeon is still a pigeon, to be sure, but there may be more to being a pigeon than is dreamt of in the philosophy of button-peckers and pellet-dispensers.

The relevance of this to semiotics? Skinner's theory *is* a kind of semiotics, or can be so construed, and I am thinking of it from that point of view here. In Peirce's terms, it is a semiotics in which only the indexical meaning of things is recognized, and the other basic semiotic functions—the symbolic and the iconic—are reduced to special cases of the indexical, which is to say that they are eliminated as theoretically distinct functions. Now, an actual reduction in our abilities to respond to the various meaning-potentials of things can be effected to a greater extent than is usually recognized—not completely, to be sure, but sufficiently to seem to validate the thesis that there is but one type of meaning. Our capacity for iconic interpretation is already badly atrophied: we hardly even try to see the meanings *in* things: we only focus on them long enough to identify their indicative properties, their indexical meaning, which points us away from the things themselves to other things, which in turn point us to other things, which . . . "Say, conductor, where and when does this train stop?" "Sir, this train *never* stops; you are on The Indexical Express. But isn't it great to travel and see all the sights? Look quickly, now, and you'll catch a glimpse of the famous Leaning Tower of Pisa between those two buildings. Isn't it—whoops, there it went!— wasn't it exciting?"

What is meant by *iconic interpretation*, by seeing the meaning *in* things? Well, what is the meaning in the following anecdote?

> I went to the World's Fair in New York, back sometime in the early 60's. Michelangelo's *Pieta* was on exhibit there, and let me tell you of the wonderful efficiency with which the authorities handled the problem of the vast crowd that flocked to see this Great Work of Art (rumored to be just as great as the Mona Lisa, that is, worth just as much money.) The way they handled it was to put the spectators on a conveyor belt which conveyed us right by it, not so slowly that we had time to get bored, but not so quickly as to blur the vision.

There is a meaning in this anecdote which is much the same as the meaning in the story of The Indexical Express, and in both there is something about the atrophy of our capacity to interpret things iconically, according to what they can intrinsically reveal.

Indexical meaning is at the foundation of our understanding of the causal order of the world, and therefore at the foundation of our ability to control portions of it. Technology is indexical sophistication, and the technological society—of which the United States is the most extreme case—is one of which human life is controlled much as the physical order is controlled. In such a society it becomes increasingly difficult to imagine how human life might be otherwise controlled, although control by the manipulation of indexical meaning is not in fact the only option. For example, control by tradition is an alternative, and such control is based primarily on iconic rather than on indexical meaning: myths, rituals, models, heroes, folk art, and so on, are primarily iconic control techniques, the basic principle being that of *mimesis* or imitation. People model themselves on more or less unchanging forms, and act primarily with an eye to achieving a formal correctness and identity through the roles they play. *Getting things done* is not so important as *being* this or that sort of person. The reason why the technological or indexical mode of control has triumphed so totally in the United States is obvious enough, I think: as a nation of immigrants of diverse origins we not only have no traditions universally shared, except at the most superficial level, but naturally tend to look upon anything traditional with great suspicion, seeing in any given tradition the potential for divisiveness. *E pluribus unum*—but one *what*? Hence the technological or indexical type of control meets little opposition and seems, in fact, to be the only method really viable for us. I am not urging tradition against technology, but only attempting to convey that the Skinnerian view of life—the technological view, indexical semiotics—is not the only possibility, while at the same time pointing out that it can become—and indeed largely has become—the only possibility we ever see actualized. From a semiotic point of view, this can be expressed by saying that although our capacity to respond to several different types of meaning can never really be eliminated, the fact is that it is possible for one of these—in this case the indexical interpretational capacity—to so totally dominate in practice that the others become atrophied to the point where we cannot achieve a clear vision of what these others actually are. On the theoretical level, the result is that we try to reduce these other capacities to being special cases of the dominating one (which is precisely what Skinner's *Verbal Behavior* is all about, for example).

Just as the intrinsic meanings of things (their iconic potential) can be nearly obliterated by the cultivation of habits of thought which simply ignore that semiotic dimension, except on the most superficial level, so also with the symbolic meanings of words, that is, that dimension of the meaning of words which makes them distinctively linguistic. Now words do not have *only* symbolic meaning, and advertisers, politicians, public relations experts, and other demagogues and tricksters specialize in the destruction of the symbolic by exploiting the indexical meanings which words bear, while at the same time so conjoining them that no coherent overall interpretation of their symbolic dimension is possible. What is *said* may add up to nothing, but at the same time the words keep *pointing* us, involuntarily, to this or that other thing (feeling, image, whatever) which it is advantageous for the manipulators to keep pushing our thoughts towards. This is a radical oversimplification of the techniques of trickery involved in the sophist's art; but the essence of sophistry lies in inducing confusion on the symbolic level while at the same time stimulating involuntary indexical interpretation advantageous to the sophist or his client. The result is that what seem to be words are not really words at all. One gets the impression that words have been said, when nothing in fact was said, though something was certainly being *done* with these word-imitations. The capacity to interpret symbolically, in a sophisticated way, is an *art* which requires continual cultivation, and our self-control is a function of this development. Sophism is the attempt to destroy this art, and it is no accident that there is no conception of self-control in Skinnerian psychology, and that from the time of John Watson to the present the psychologists of this school have frequently moved into the world of advertising and other forms of professional sophism.

In sum, my point is that there is a special logical feature of semiotic inquiry which arises from the fact that human self-perception has a *causally* determining efficacy in respect to its subject matter: as we conceive ourselves, so shall we be, to some extent at least. Now there is certainly a logical fallacy involved in a claim, such as Skinner's, that human life can *only* be as he describes it. No empirical hypothesis can claim itself to be the only alternative; for this is a meta-judgment about the hypothesis which can draw upon no empirical evidence in its support, inasmuch as all such evidence is already logically appropriated to the hypothesis itself. Minimally, such a claim is just empty, and any attempt to justify it *a priori* would produce a self-contradiction since it would involve a simultaneous claim that the hypothesis is and is not an empirical one. However, there is a certain peculiar logical force to such a claim in the sense that, by *causally* determining how its subject matter actually is, it tends to validate itself. I am unable to determine whether or not my definition of objectivity in Part I of this paper rules out the exploitation of this peculiarity; as it stands, I believe it does not, but it may be that a more sophisticated formulation of the same idea would do so.

But however that may be, the fact is that we, as theoreticians, are engaged not merely in trying to understand human life (among other things) but also in *making* it something thereby. Our power in this respect is certainly limited, but it is sufficient to make it obligatory upon us that we consider the *effects* of the conceptions we develop and not delude ourselves that we are only finding out the facts, as if those facts are altogether causally independent of our ideas of them. If we conceive semiosis in such a way as to preclude anything but a Skinnerian vision of life then we are simply helping to insure that such a vision *will* be the true one. Indeed, it already is largely true and, in my opinion, the reigning tendencies of our time—tendencies that have been continually on the increase since the Renaissance—are such that its truth is on the increase, in the sense that his type of theory actually does account for more and more human behavior as time goes on, and is true of more and more people, as the technological or manipulative mentality it expresses spreads to every culture on the globe.

In the rest of this paper I will be concerned with another type of semiotics, which I will call a "conventionalist" semiotics, and I will be arguing that it clearly does violate the principle of objectivity, as I have formulated it. This second type of semiotics often sees itself in opposition to the Skinnerian type—as is well-illustrated in Chomsky's justly famed review of Skinner's *Verbal Behavior*, for example—but I contend that there is an unrecognized alliance in practice between a manipulative semiotics of the Skinnerian type and a conventionalist semiotics of the type I will be discussing next, this alliance arising from the fact that the implicit authoritarianism in the latter is itself technologically sterile; so that it will always in practice draw upon the semiotics of manipulation to put its visions into effect.

III

I think it will generally be agreed that, in semiotics, we must work minimally with a distinction between an entity which bears some meaning or significance of some sort (a *sign*) and a possible response relative to that entity as bearer of that property (an *interpretant*). Some semioticians are primarily oriented toward the relationships which signs do or can stand in to one another, others more toward interpretational considerations; but a distinctively semiotic approach is, I take it, one in which both sorts of factors are ultimately to be regarded from a unitary theoretical point of view. Let us restrict our attention here to sign-interpretation processes, which I will call *semiosis* processes. An analysis of meaning properties and relationships may have no overt reference to any interpretational process, but there would be no point in referring to it as a distinctively semiotic analysis unless it was thought of as being concerned with entities implicitly relative, one way or another, to such a process.

Semiotic theorizing and analysis is itself a form of semiosis. Semiosis processes such as human beings engage in have the capacity to become reflexive or self-reflective: semiosis takes the form of semiotics and thereby takes itself as part of its subject matter. It was this which was at the base of the considerations discussed in Part II of this paper; and just as it gives rise to a certain logical peculiarity pointed out there (self-validating theorizing), it also puts limits upon how semiosis is to be conceived if we are to allow for the possibility of semiotic inquiry having the property of objectivity. For the basic conception of semiosis put forth in a semiotic theory must either allow for the possibility of semiosis taking on the form of objectivity or else it disqualifies itself from entering into an objective inquiry process as a guiding theory. A theorist cannot (validly) deny the possibility of objectivity (implicitly or explicitly) if that very denial is put forth *as* being made within the context of objectivity. To put it another way, that which is asserted cannot (validly) contradict what is implicit in the very act of asserting. The kind of contradiction involved here is, to be sure, one which involves a relationship between two "logical levels", and I cannot adequately explicate it here; but I think it is clear that there is a logical impossibility involved. Note, though, that this does not prove that there *is* any such thing as objective semiosis, or that semiotic conceptions which do not allow for such a possibility are false. It only proves that any semiotics which wishes to be objective must abandon any conception of semiosis which does not allow for that possibility. My thesis is that a type a semiotic theory which I call *conventionalism*, and which is quite widely held at present, is in this sense incompatible with the achievement of objectivity in semiotics. The scientific pretensions of such theories are therefore quite bogus.

Does the semiotic value of the sign, that which constitutes it *as* a sign, that is, its meaningfulness or significance, accrue to it because of any particular act in which it is interpreted, or is it a property possessed by the sign independent of *any* given interpretation? Any theory according to which any sign acquires its meaning through any given interpretant of it (regardless of the number of persons participating in it) is, insofar, a conventionalist thesis, as I conceive it here. This formulation is unusual, but I think you will see the point to it if I explain it in terms of linguistic signs, in particular, which are commonly regarded as being conventional signs.

Take any word: the English word *table*, let us say. The meaning of this perceptual configuration is no doubt *arbitrary* in the sense that it has the meaning it has only because it just happened to have entered into an activity or practice of some people (just as, say, *mesa* or *Tisch* happened to have entered into similar activities or practices of other peoples). Perhaps *accidental* would be a more exact word for arbitrariness, in this sense. In any case, though, there is nothing about the configuration itself which makes it mean what it means linguistically. Only considerations of history and convenience, of no logical import, seem to account for its having this property. But note that the arbitrariness here is not a property of the configuration but rather of the *fact* of its having acquired that linguistic meaning rather than some other, or none at all, and of that meaning having been given to it rather than to some other configuration. Since such meaning-properties come and go across time, it seems, therefore, that there must have been a point in time prior to which this configuration had no such meaning, and subsequent to which it did, which suggests that there must have been at that point in time an *act* of meaning-bestowment, or something *logically equivalent* to an act. For even if the meaning-relation is thought of in terms of an *habitude* or rule, there must have been a moment at which such an entity (the rule or habitude) came into existence, and it is difficult to see how that is to be construed except in terms of an *act* of *relating* that configuration to whatever it means, though of course the act may have been unreflective and the exact moment at which it occurred undiscoverable, practically speaking. Thus the arbitrariness is ultimately to be predicated of the *act* of meaning-bestowment, which is "unmotivated" in the sense that no property of the physical configuration as such necessitated that it, rather than some other configuration, be the recipient of that meaning. In glyphic writing, for example, the likeness of a sign to something is often a valuable clue to its linguistic meaning for the archaeologist, and the providing of such clues was undoubtedly an aid to the remembrance of the meaning of such signs for the persons who originally wrote and read the glyphs; but that likeness is not constitutive of their meaning (except for their iconic meaning), and thus has a purely auxiliary function, relative to linguistic decipherment. That is, such configurations are motivated psychologically, but not logically.

This seems to me to be a fairly precise statement of what is meant in saying that linguistic signs are conventional. The use of the term *convention*—which is perhaps more widespread in philosophy than in linguistics—originates in the idea of a convening of persons for the purpose of an explicit act of meaning-bestowment, a laying down of the law, as it were; and it is fundamentally the same idea as that of the social contract theory of the state. (Thomas Hobbes' theory of meaning and his social theory are almost exact isomorphs of one another, for example.) Of course, hardly anyone—perhaps no one—holds to a literal social contract theory of meaning, according to which linguistic signs get their present meaning by an actual historical convening of linguistic legislators who unanimously decided to give words the meaning they have, any more than political versions of the contract theory are couched in historical terms nowadays. However, logically equivalent views are very widespread, at present, I believe, in both domains. For any view is logically equivalent to this which holds that (a) the meaning of linguistic signs is a function of codes or rules, and that (b) these rules or codes *exist at a given moment*, such that (c) acts of interpretation or use *at that moment* are correct or incorrect depending upon whether they do or do not conform to those co-existing rules. More simply, any view according to which an act of linguistic interpretation or use is correct or incorrect in virtue of agreement or disagreement with a co-existing rule is equivalent to a social contract or conventionalist theory of meaning.

Why? Because a rule or a code is essentially a *trans-temporal* entity, that is, it essentially extends across time; hence, if it is supposed that it exists at a moment of time it must be supposed to exist in the form of an *act*, since there is no other way in which a rule can be conceived to exist at a moment. In the case of this particular sort of rule, moreover, it must be conceived as an interpretational act *constituting the meaning* of the sign, relative to which any other non-constituting interpretation of the same sign (*qua* configuration) is right or wrong, depending upon its agreement with the constituting act. That is, the meaning-constituting interpretational act which *is* the rule at a given moment must be supposed to be somehow *authoritative* relative to the non-constituting interpretations, the agent or circumstance somehow having the power to make the sign meaningful in this way. But this is the social contract theory, assuming a plurality of agents.

Let me state this in a slightly different way. I pointed out that the point in time at which a linguistic *habitude* or rule came into existence must, it seems, be thought of as the time of an initial act of relat*ing*, subsequent to which, and in virtue of which, the relat*ion* exists. Suppose, then, that for a certain word the date of that supposed occurrence can be roughly fixed at one hundred years ago. If that word has that meaning now, it is clearly quite irrelevant to its having that present meaning that originally received it one hundred years ago: all that counts now is that it is now so related. Its *possession* of that meaning now is logically equivalent to its *initially receiving* that meaning now, for it means what it means now regardless of how long it has had that meaning. Its relat*ion* is logically equivalent to a present relat*ing*; the presently existing *habitude* or rule is logically equivalent to a present act of *habitude*—or rule—adoption: the logical upshot is the same in either case, as regards its present meaning. It is as if the fictional convening of the legislators is actually an act repeated at every successive moment, so long as the word has that meaning. Indeed, it is difficult to understand how an original act of relating can establish a temporally enduring relation, anyway, unless we think of the latter as equivalent to a series of trans-temporal acts of relating. (Descartes' idea that God is continually re-creating the world, at each successive moment in time, this being the only way it can be *sustained* in existence, is a theological analogue to this, by the way.) We can say, at a given time, "Let the meaning of this configuration henceforth be _____"; but what logical force can such a fiat have? The Doomsday Machine might go off in the next moment, or we might suffer a lapse of memory, or we might change our minds immediately, and so on. So how can the relating bring about the enduring relation, in a logical sense? The relation must, then, be regarded as if it were an ongoing series of acts of relating, each prior act devoid of present logical force precisely because it is prior. In other words, the historical factor is really quite irrelevant, except of course when we are concerned with what something used to mean, as distinct from what it means now.

Conventionalism originated as a thesis about linguistic signs in particular, and some conventionalists either explicitly restrict the thesis to linguistic signs or are concerned only with signs of this type, anyway. However, the dominant tendency of the past few decades has been to attempt to extend the thesis to all signification or meaningfulness whatever, so that both "natural signs" (indexical signs) and signs by likeness (iconic signs) are also regarded as conventional. The basic rationale for extension— sometimes called "linguistic imperialism"—lies in the tenuousness of the distinction between "truths of meaning" and "truths of fact" (sometimes also called the distinction between "analytic truths" and "synthetic truths"). A truth of meaning would be one whose truth is ascertainable by reference to a linguistic meaning-rule (meaning-convention): for example, *All swans are birds* is supposedly true because there is a rule to the effect that whatever *swan* applies to *bird* applies to also. (There are a variety of ways in which the rule could be stated.) A truth of fact is one which is not so ascertainable—for example, if *All swans are white* is true, it is so on some basis other than a rule of meaning (the other basis usually being thought of vaguely in terms of conformity to the facts, or something like that). In semiotic terminology, this distinction would correlate with a distinction between linguistic and "natural" signs: *swan* is a linguistic sign meaning *bird* (in part), but being a swan, though perhaps a "natural" sign of whiteness (an indicator or index of it) is not such because of any rule of meaning, but because of a regular factual correlation.

However, a variety of considerations can be adduced which suggest that there either is no such distinction, or else that the distinction is itself a conventional one in its application. For example, it may be pointed out that the ability to interpret natural signs is culturally learned, just as is the ability to interpret linguistic signs; or it may be claimed that even in the highly controlled context of scientific inquiry definitional statements are often indistinguishable from supposedly empirical hypotheses and that the distinction between theoretical and empirical propositions is impossible to draw in principle; or that there really is no such thing, in scientific practice, as absolutely "hard" empirical fact which can refute a contradicting theory, it always being a matter of decision as to whether to treat an apparent diversification as a real one; and so on. (I cannot here do justice to the sophisticated arguments in question but only hint at them.) In general the idea is that what is treated as conventional is itself a matter of convention; hence even a "truth of fact" is such only by a conventional agreement to regard it as such, which, in effect, makes the "truth of fact" into a special case of a "truth of meaning". Thus, to treat *All swans are white* as factual in import is to permit *This is a black swan* to be an acceptable locution; but whether such a decision is actually made depends upon what is contextually at stake at the time of the appearance of an apparently black swan; hence a "truth of fact" is really only a combination of words for which no corresponding rule of meaning has yet been established. It thus functions *as* a truth only on the basis of a tentative acceptance of it; but this is tantamount to saying that its truth is a matter of convention. (Perhaps the point would be clearer if I were to say that the idea is that there really is no distinction between "truths of meaning" and "truths of fact"; the apparent distinction is really due to the fact that the theory in question is not fully determinate relative to rules of meaning at a given time: the "truths of fact" are the presently indeterminate parts of it.)

In any case, the result is the same: a conventionalist model, originally set up only with linguistic meaning in mind, is extended to cover all sign phenomena whatever. Everything semiotical in character is to be understood in terms of rules and codes, everything is an expression of a language or something logically equivalent to a language, and the meaning of everything is arbitrary, in the sense in which language is arbitrary. The continental semiotic called "semiology" illustrates this very well in its movement from Saussurian linguistics to structuralist analyses of literature, fashion, music, myth, and so on. In this country, the movement has been retarded owing to the relatively late appearance of Chomskyan linguistics (I'm thinking here of Chomsky's "rationalism", not his innovations in the representation of rules), which is its natural base in Anglo-American linguistics. Also, Chomsky's own reticence about hyper-enthusiastic extensions of his approach, in addition to the existence of a powerful empiricist opposition here in the social and psychological sciences, has kept the *Schwärmerei* under some control. But the theoretical groundwork has long been laid in philosophy of science for the absorption of *all* of science within the sphere of linguistics, as it has become nearly an article of faith among the *avant garde* that a scientific theory is a language, and that everything in a language is conventional in one way or another—which means there is no reason in principle why the Universal Grammarians aren't already giving kindly advice to physicists on how to construct their theories. Interestingly enough, as this "linguistic imperialism" advances it keeps locating the ultimate conventions at ever deeper levels of the psyche, and the conventions begin to appear as the whims of a God-like universal *esprit* rather than as the results of human choice (as in Lévi-Strauss's anthropology), so that a doctrine whose original appeal was surely due in part to a vague idea that it recognized human freedom, now begins to appear in the form of a determinism beyond anybody's power to alter. I think myself that Chomsky's "innate ideas" doctrine is cut from the same cloth as Lévi-Strauss's doctrine of the determining *esprit*, but Chomsky would deny that this doctrine is itself conventional, and I cannot try to show the contrary here.

IV

My argument to the effect that conventionalism is incompatible with objectivity in semiotic inquiry is based on the impossibility of *asserting* a convention to be a fact. Since a conventionalist semiotician must make such assertions if any substantive statements are to be made about the subject matter, it follows that no conventionalist semiotics is possible that is also objective, in the sense of the term I have explained here. It is not denied that a conventionalist may say something about conventions, but whatever the force of such sayings may be, they do not have the force of a claim functioning in a context of objective inquiry.

Perhaps the most effective way to show this will be to work with the idea that a sign system can be given a "synchronic" description, an idea generally taken for granted among linguists and widely believed to represent a Great Leap Forward in linguistic theory. The idea is intrinsic to conventionalism in one form or another, I believe, since the basic idea of conventionalism is that a sign has the meaning it has at a given time by virtue of a co-existing rule of meaning or interpretation, and it should therefore be possible to describe these rules, some way or another, as existing at the moment when the signs in question exist *as* signs (as meaningful configurations). I will discuss this only in terms of linguistic meaning, but the same considerations apply regardless of the type of signs involved, assuming that their meaning is supposed to be conventional.

A sign system is supposed to be a set or code of rules, present in behavior as temporally (though temporarily) enduring *habitudes* of a sign-using community, and a synchronic description is one which would "slice across" the language at a moment in time, revealing, as if in a cross-section, the structure of the rules (*habitudes*) constituting the language at the moment of the "slice". This is often spoken of as yielding a "state-description" of the language (*langue*) at a moment in time. It is supposedly on the basis of two or more such state-descriptions of the *langue* at different times that the "diachronic" or historical study of a language is possible. There is a massive confusion here. A state-description of the world, or any part of it, at a moment in time, would contain no descriptions of rules as such; for such a description could only contain singular propositions, whereas any statement of a rule will be universal in logical form. All that could appear in such a description would be *parole* instances: a *langue* cannot be synchronically described. The usual answer to this is that the "synchronic slice" can be regarded as extending across a small amount of time (rather more like a cucumber slice, it would seem, than a cross-sectional cut). But this won't do either. For the only evidence that a rule holds across any finite period of time would be constituted by singular occurrences of its actualization during that time period (whatever form that actualization might take); but since the time period is finite so also will be the number of its actualizations, which means that the rule inferred can only be construed to be logically equivalent to the sum total of its actualizations, and the description of it is therefore logically redundant and eliminable: the rule *is* its actualizations, and nothing more than that, during that period, no matter how thick the slice. So, again, there is nothing to be revealed by a "synchronic slice" (even one having thickness) except *parole* occurrences.

What the linguists apparently have in mind is not really a "state-description" but rather a list of rules, all of which are supposed to *hold* or *be in effect* at a certain time. But what does this mean? Such rules supposedly function to *constitute* the linguistic (or, more generally, the semiotic) *identity* of the signs, that is, give them their distinct meaningfulness or significance or sign status. Since the rules change across time, the fact that a given rule holds at a moment *t*, thereby giving semiotic identity of some sort to an occurrence at *t*, implies nothing about any prior or subsequent moment; hence, the only thing that could be meant by saying that such a rule holds at *t* is that, at *t*, a meaning-constitutive interpretation occurs (or it is as if it occurs), in virtue of which any similar configuration at *t* is a sign (a *meaningful* configuration), and such that an interpretation of the latter can be assessed as correct or incorrect depending upon its agreement or disagreement with the meaning-constitutive interpretation. Thus a state-description at a time must either be supposed to include a description of a (probably fictitious but possibly actual) meaning-constitutive act of interpretation for every rule that supposedly holds at that time, or else a description of only those corresponding to actual instances of interpretation which occur but are non-meaning-constitutive, and which thereby require the simultaneous occurrence of meaning-constitutive interpretations in order to be genuine instances of interpretations of *signs* (as distinct from meaningless configurations). The first alternative would appear to be pointless: it is stretching things far enough to posit fictional acts when necessary to account for something, and surely going altogether too far to posit them when these ghosts have no logical role to play. The state-description at *t*, then, must be supposed to contain, for every description of a non-meaning-constitutive interpretational occurrence, at least one (possibly fictional) meaning-constitutive interpretation.

Let us suppose that interpretational act A1 at *t* is a meaning-constitutive act, and a second act, A2, is a non-meaning-constitutive interpretation of the same configuration (that is, of something having the same configuration). Now, what is the force of assigning to A1—and denying to A2—the property of being meaning-constitutive? (Bear in mind that this is, according to my argument, the only sense we can give to the claim that a rule of meaning exists or holds at that time.) This would have to be due to some logical *condition* which A1 meets but A2 does not.

What could that be? Would it be something like, say, the condition of being an interpretation made by the Pope *ex cathedra* on a matter of faith or morals, the satisfaction of which condition guarantees its canonical character? Or would it be the condition of being a conjoint interpretation of the entire linguistic community, exclusive of the person who utters A2? Or would it be the condition of being uttered by a "fluent speaker of the language"? Regardless of what it is, the linguist who identifies A1 as having the favored status of being meaning-constitutive must claim that it is meeting that condition that gives it that status. But in that case what he is saying is that it is a rule that if condition C is met, then an act, A, which satisfies it, is a meaning-constitutive act, which means that the linguist is himself affirming a general conditional rule for meaning-bestowment. But the affirmation of such a rule is not the description of a fact, for if it were then the bestowment of meaning would not be conventional or "unmotivated" but rather contingent upon a certain factual condition being met by the interpreting act, which would in turn be a relational property of the interpreted configuration. Hence the affirmation can itself only be a conventional act, a fiat, and it turns out that *the linguist is the legislator*. But, to legislate conventionally is not to assert anything. Hence the linguist can make no assertion about his subject matter, and therefore cannot participate in a process, such as objective inquiry, which is essentially assertive in character.

Let me recapitulate the basic argument more formally. The linguist must be able to make assertions about his subject matter, predicating of individual *parole* instances (utterances) that they have this or that linguistic property. Such an assertion must be capable of being true or false, depending upon whether the linguist ascribes to them properties which they actually have or not. To say that any such instance, P2, has such a property is to say that a linguistic rule applies, somehow, to the case of P2. Since such rules come and go, and historical considerations are essentially irrelevant, a given rule in effect at a given time need neither have been in effect the moment before or the moment after, so the rule being in effect at that time is equivalent to another *parole* instance, P1, occurring at the same time, which has the same configuration as occurs in P2, being *assigned* a property—though not by assertion, as this would imply the possibility of error—thereby being the one relative to which the other is to be assessed for actually having the property *asserted* of it. P1 is indisputably and paradigmatically what P2 may or may not be. To say, therefore, what property P2 has, say F, is to say that it is thereby like P1, *and* that P1 is not simply F, but is in some sense indisputably F (definitionally F, necessarily F, paradigmatically F, whatever). But what is the force of this latter part of the claim? It can only be that P1 meets some condition, C, in virtue of the nature of the interpreting act, A1. (It cannot be in virtue of the configuration because the meaning-property would then be a "motivated" one.) So A1 must meet some condition C. But whatever that condition is, A1's satisfaction of it is also a relational property of P1 (for it is the act of interpreting which meets the condition). But this paradigmatic *parole* instance is not "unmotivated" or arbitrary or conventional if the condition, C, is a factual one. Hence, in saying that the paradigmatic instance meets the condition, the linguist cannot be asserting a fact. He can only himself be issuing a fiat (with what right I do not know). In that case, though, the claim that A2 has F is based on an unasserted premise. But no conclusion can be drawn from a premise which is unasserted. The conclusion (that A2 has F) therefore cannot be asserted. Hence the linguist can assert nothing about his subject matter, and therefore cannot engage in an objective inquiry.

Without elaborating further on it here, let me simply say that this argument is not intended to show or suggest that linguistic meaning is not a function of rules, but only that it not a function of conventional rules, as that concept has been defined here.

V

I remarked, in Part I, that my definition of objectivity is not being put forth in a divisory or exclusionary spirit, but my criticisms of technological and conventionalist semiotics may seem to contradict that. They do not, however. My objection to technological semiotics (as exemplified by Skinner's type of psychology) is directed only at its misguided pretensions to being an adequate conception *by itself*: a claim which cannot possibly be justified empirically, which is deeply alien to the scientific spirit (which attempts to *find out* rather than to *rule out*), and which is made in the service of a conception that is disastrously inadequate to the human need for self-understanding and self-control. I have not attempted to justify this last point here, however, and I put it forth chiefly in order to obviate any possible confusion between my conceptions of the scientific and the technological.

As regards conventionalist semiotics, I have concentrated on its incompatibility with objectivity, because I think its pretensions to being scientific have perhaps constituted its chief appeal. I believe it is also a product of the technological mentality, as is suggested by the ubiquity of the machine analogy in the writings of its theorists, the machine-image in this case being a computer model: conventionalism is the expression of the "soft-ware" technologist, whereas indexical semiotics is the expression of the "hard-ware" technologist. But the former is utterly empty apart from its ultimate connections with the latter. To paraphrase Kant: Chomsky without Skinner is empty; Skinner without Chomsky is blind. Together they mutually compensate. The conventionalist legislates under the guise of description, but his legislations are idle without the engineer to pump substance into him. For those who don't see immediately why I associate them as I do, I suggest a careful reading of Thomas Hobbes' *Leviathan*, and pondering the force of his comment that "convenants without the sword are but words, and of no strength to secure a man at all."

But I'm concerned with deflating groundless and irresponsible theories and meta-theories, not with the substantive progress that has been achieved by those who have worked within their distorting and misleading perspectives. For the fact is that all of the first-order thinkers in these traditions—such as de Saussure, Lévi-Strauss, Chomsky, Skinner—have produced valuable work that will survive their methodological and meta-theoretical nonsense, as have numerous others who have worked under their aegis. Just as Kepler's informing vision of the divinity of the sun motivated him to achievements that nobody now regards as having theological reference, or denigrates on that account, so also these mistaken images of man of the technologist will in due time be largely forgotten, while the substantive achievements of their proponents will survive, thereby demonstrating again what has been demonstrated often in the history of human thought: that a bold error is often more valuable than a pedestrian truth. I recall in this connection a story (the source for which I cannot now locate) about a Taoist sage who said that wise persons never feel resentment or disappointment because someone has not told them the truth; for to one who knows how to read signs, *all* signs reveal only the truth. But this depends upon not taking signs as having only the value which the sign-producer puts on them.

What, then, can a genuinely fruitful, comprehensive, and objectively informed semiotics be? Well, I believe it can be the realization of the Delphic Oracle's "Know thyself": but in order to realize this possibility the other inscription at Delphi, "Nothing in excess", must be heeded. These tendencies to monomaniacal exaggeration of what are really only one or another aspect or kind of meaning, to the exclusion of the rest, are the chief hindrances at the present time, which is a time of fanaticism, *Schwärmerei*, "tunnel vision", *hybris*. Skinner seizes upon indexical meaning, and everything is to be reduced to that. The conventionalists seize upon symbolic (distinctively linguistic) meaning, and everything is to be reduced to that. The third type of meaning, the iconic, has had no similar fanatical development thus far in our century; but it, too, is susceptible of being the bearer of this disease of lack of moderation, and the sign of its emergence as *idée fixe* will be the exaggeration of the role of the mythical, the mystical, the poetic, and the religious as the be-all and end-all of human life.

The history of humanity could be read, I believe, in terms of the radical and ever-shifting imbalance in the relations of these three types of meaning to one another: *Eidos, ergon, logos*; form, act, word; icon, index, symbol. How can they be brought together in a triadic coordination? That is, I suggest the fundamental task for semiotics, both practically and theorectically. It is necessary for this, however, to get control of ourselves by recognizing our limitations, both as individuals and as a species. We are not gods and these blasphemous dreams of omnipotence—in whatever guise they take—must be forsworn. This brings us to a third dictum of the Delphic Oracle: that Socrates was the only truly wise person in Athens because he was the only one aware of his own essential fallibility and limitations as a human being (for that is what Socratic wisdom actually is). Semiotically interpreted: no sign is ever given its meaning by anyone's interpreting act, no matter who it is or how many collaborate in that act. That is, in addition to the sign and the interpretant, a third term of the relation must be recognized: the *object*. Signs make objects available to us by providing a basis for interpretation. If we interpret aright, then the object *is* revealed to us in our interpretation. But we can never be certain, beyond any possibility of doubt, that any given interpretant rightly reads the meaning of the sign. This is no cause for skepticism: about many things there is no actual doubt and no reason why any should be raised. But that third term must be borne in mind. It signifies our fallibility, which is the human condition, the recognition of which constitutes the *daimon* of *philosophia*, the guiding spirit of the communal hunt for truth. My definition of objectivity here is merely an attempt to state certain implications of the theoretical adoption of that triadic relation as basic in semiotics, which is, of course, Charles Peirce's conception of the fundamental form of semiosis. The line of thought in this paper can thus be regarded as an argument for its adoption in lieu of the essentially dyadic conceptions of semiosis held in common by the types of theories I have criticized here.

22

THOMAS A. SEBEOK

"Semiotics" and Its Congeners

> . . . a long-standing result of linguistic study, of whatever period
> or school, is the denial of the existence of perfect
> synonyms. . . . Synonyms are the most probable substitutes, in
> any given situation—but in one situation only, which is
> an important limitation.
>
> —Hill 1958: 412—

A theory of signs was variously developed on the part of the Epicureans, and especially the Stoics, as a way of proceeding by inference from what is immediately given to the unperceived, and was thus analogous to a doctrine of evidence, particularly medical. Bodily motions were interpreted as a sign of the soul, blushing as a sign of shame, and fever as a sign, viz., symptom—later considered as an "unintended index"—of a disease. Since none of the many works of the Stoic logicians and semanticists, those of Chrysippos (c. 280-206BC) included, nor a full account of their Epicurean critics [cf. also Philodemus c.54 BC], is extant—their ideas are known to us largely through such surviving sources as Sextus Empiricus and Diogenes Laërtius, that postdate by nearly half a millennium their greatest period of efflorescence—the detailed nature of their philosophy of language remains "the most tantalizing problem in the history of semantics" (Kretzmann, 1967: 363; the fullest relevant exposition is Weltring's 1910 dissertation). In any event, the Greek doctrine of signification, with strong medical overtones (in special reference to Galen), acquired the designation *semeiotiké, from sēma* "sign", *sēmeiōtikos* "observant of signs".

At the end of the 17th century, the Greek word *semeiotiké* was injected into the mainstream of English philosophical discourse by John Locke (1632-1704). Locke declared the "doctrine of signs" to be that branch of his tripartite division of all sciences—namely, logic, physics, and ethics—"the business whereof is to consider the nature of signs, the mind makes use of for the understanding of things, or conveying its knowledge to others" (1690: Bk. IV, Ch. XXI, 4). Specialists like Aaron (1937: 309) find Locke's use of *semeiotiké* for that part of philosophy which is logic rather perplexing, because the Gassendists seemingly made no use of the term, and because there is no evidence, either, that Locke, who was a physician by profession, came across the word in his medical studies and converted it to his own uses (he certainly does not explicitly connect it with symptomatology). L. J. Russell (1939), however, has convincingly argued that Locke adapted *semeiotiké* from neither logical nor medical writings, but from writings on Greek music. His immediate source was probably John Wallis' 1682 edition of Ptolemy's *Harmonics* (although Russell does not mention this, the fact that the word does not occur in Locke's first draft of the *Essay*, in 1671, strengthens his argument). Wallis, Locke's friend and former mathematics professor in Oxford, appears, in turn, to attribute the term *semeiotiké*, as the art of musical notation, to Marcus Meibomius, with two references to the latter's *Antiquae musicae auctores septem* (1652).[1]

The English word, and some of its congeners, first apppear, nearly two centuries later, in the works of C. S. Peirce (1839-1914), as *semeiotic* (c.1896: 1.444), rarely *semeotic* (1908: 8.377), but most commonly as *semiotic* (never, however, as far as I have been able to determine, as *semiotics*). Moreover, he also uses *semeiosy*, "or action of a sign" (c.1906: 5.473), and, of course, *semiosis*, pluralized as *semioses* (ibid.: 5.490) (he claims that its variant, *semeiosis*, "in Greek of the Roman period, as early as Cicero's time, if I remember rightly, meant the action of almost any kind of sign" [ibid.: 5.484]). Peirce undoubtedly took the term "*semiotic (semeiotiké)*" over, with attendant definition as the "quasi-necessary, or formal, doctrine of signs" (c.1897: 2.227), directly from the usage of Locke, of whose work he had written elsewhere: "The celebrated *Essay Concerning Humane Understanding* contains many passages which . . . make the first steps in profound analyses which are not further developed" (1878: 2.649). In a famous remark, Peirce viewed himself as "a pioneer, or rather a backwoodsman, in the work of clearing and opening up what I call *semiotic*, that is, the doctrine of the essential nature and fundamental varieties of possible semiosis . . ." (c.1906: 5.488).

Although Peirce makes repeated references (e.g., c.1903: 4.353) to J. H. Lambert (1728-1777), he seems, puzzlingly enough, not to have explicitly mentioned the latter's ten masterful chapters on "Semiotik oder Lehre von der Bezeichnung der Gedanken und Dinge" [*"Semiotic, or the Doctrine of the Signification of Thoughts and Things"*] (Lambert 1764: 5-214), where the cardinal principles of communication and signification are well grasped and lucidly set forth in a consistently semiotic frame (cf. Söder, 1964), prefiguring his own opus in several important respects, including his very use of the term *semiotic*.[2] In fact, as was pointed out by Resnikow (1968: 189), despite Lambert's interesting contributions, "beeninflussten seine Arbeiten die Entwicklung der logisch-semiotischen Problem kaum" [*"his work hardly influenced the development of logical-semiotic problems"*]. In common German usage, until lately, *Semiotik* continued to mean symptomatology. To cite only one example, Rudolf Kleinpaul, the author of one of the first and most comprehensive books on nonverbal communication, employed the term with its conventional meaning: "Die Mediziner haben eine Wissenschaft, die sie *Semiotik* nennen, die Lehre von den *Kennzeichen* der Krankheiten oder, wie wir gewöhnlich sagen, der Symptomen . . ." [*"Physicians have a science they call* semiotic, *the theory of the characteristic signs of illness or, as we usually say, of* symptoms . . ."] (Kleinpaul 1888: 103), although, he quickly added, "Es wäre nun wohl schön, wenn . . . auch die Gesundheit ihre *Semiotik* hätte" [*"It would indeed be a fine thing if there were also a semiotic of health"*] (106). Husserl, on the other hand, equated *Semiotik* with "Logik der Zeichen" [*"The Logic of Signs"*], as spelled out in his important essay on the subject written in 1890. The usage of Hermes (1938), who meant by *Semiotik* pure general syntax, in contradistinction to descriptive syntax, seems highly idiosyncratic. Nowadays, the impact of American Pragmatism, especially of Peirce, and of quasi-behavoristic social science, namely, semiotic, particularly as represented by Morris, is such in Germany that *Semiotik* has come to be equated overwhelmingly and, it would seem, conclusively, with the "Allgemeine Theorie der Zeichen" ["*General Theory of Signs*"] (cf., e.g., Bense 1967).

Meanwhile, back in America, *semiotic* became commonplace in philosophical usage, and beyond, through the incentive and persuasive stimulation provided by Charles Morris in a series of publications dealing with various aspects of the general theory of signs, particularly his now classic 1938 monograph, *Foundations of the Theory of Signs*, and his more elaborate 1946 book, *Signs, Language and Behavior* (both included, among others, in Morris 1971). According to Read (1948: 85), neither *semiotic* nor *semeiotic* had appeared in print during Peirce's lifetime, but, of course, he did use variants of the term, ca. 1908, in his correspondence with Lady Victoria Welby (a part of which was first published in Ogden and Richards 1923: 281f.; cf. Peirce 1908: 8.342). Read cites a Polish mathematician, Leon Chwistek, as having actually used *semeiotics*, rendering in English his German *Semantik*, in 1924; but *semiotic* was not truly launched in printed English until its appearance in the work of Morris.

Morris (1971: 106) told his readers that " 'Semantics' is perhaps the most widely accepted name for the discipline which studies signs. 'Semiotic', the term here chosen, was used by the Stoics, John Locke, and Charles Peirce. Linguists and logicians restrict 'semantics' to a part of the whole field, namely, the part which deals with the significata of signs. Hence we use 'semiotic' as a general term; 'semantics' will be employed for that part of semiotic which deals with significata." Morris' terminology was immediately and prestigiously propagated by Carnap (1942: 9), who assigned "The whole science of language", consisting of syntax, semantics, and pragmatics, a tripartite distinction previously introduced by Morris, to *semiotic*.

Leaving aside here a detailed treatment of the entangled historical interplay of *sem(e)iotic* with *semantics*, and most of their multifarious rivals—some of the lexicographical aspects are expertly discussed by Read (1948)—it does seem worthwhile to enumerate, in this connection, at least those that can be traced back to Greek *sēmeîon: sem(e)iology*, the only terms in the set I return to below; Reisig's *Semasiologie* (1839-), in English, *semasiology* (1877-); Benjamin H. Smart's *sematology* (1831-), and the perhaps independent coinage of Bühler, *Sematologie* (1934: 34f.), which, employed by the latter with a meaning very close to that of *semiotic*, have both more or less disappeared now; and Noreen's *semology* (cf. Lotz 1954: 58, 61f.), currently popular in certain American linguistic circles (e.g., Joos 1958 or Lamb 1966: 31f.). One should also mention, in passing, Lady Welby's *sensifics* (1896), and her much better known *significs*, that, in 1917, became the rallying cry of a group of Dutch scientists calling themselves the *significi* (Mannoury 1969).

Then there is the curious case of *semiotics*, which belongs to the form class of "*-ics* words" that once preoccupied Hill, who demurred that "at least a part of the confusion which learners experience in handling the *-ics* words . . . is caused by the fact that no dictionary makes clear that the final *-s* in these words, no matter what its origin, is not identical with the familiar plural morpheme of nouns which happens to be homonymous with it" (1948: 11). As I have already observed, Peirce never used *semiotics* at all, and neither does Morris, who, in fact, requested the editor of the *Approaches to Semiotics* series, in which his collected writings were recently republished, to add a special "Terminological note" to his book to account for the divergence between his usage and that of the series (Morris 1971: 9-10).

Almost every true *semiotician*—another Morris coinage (1971: 81), to label a prac-
titioner of the art—working in the Peirce tradition, notably, the philosophers
clustering around the Charles S. Peirce Society (see the eleven volumes of their
Transactions 1965-), as well as such prominent linguist partisans and promoters
of Peirce as Roman Jakobson (1971 *passim*), assiduously shun *semiotics*, which
they tend to regard as a barbarism. Nevertheless, the term has cropped up in
print all along, including in some peculiar ghostly manifestations: thus, in the
Index of Subjects to the 5th volume of the Peirce papers (p. 425), there is an entry
"Semiotics", but in the paragraph referred to (488) this form does not occur;
perhaps the same gremlin is responsible for the identical entry in the Index of
Subjects to Bochenski's monograph (1954: 134), but the sole variant that I have
been able to locate in his text is *semiotic* (30ff.). Each of the sporadic occurrences of *semiotics*, since the 1940s, must be presumed to have been impelled by
an identical mechanism of analogical recreation on the model of what Hill has
called the *-ics* words of English, most probably *semantics* (Michel Bréal's late
19th century coinage of which was itself anticipated, in 17th century English, by
semantick). Its eventual diffusion and, since the mid-1960s, its increasing acceptance, or as Hermann Paul might have put it, the summation of repetitive shifts
in idiolects culminating in a novel Language Custom, must surely be ascribed
to the forceful intervention of one individual, Margaret Mead, who, on May 19,
1962, in the final moments of the first American conference ever held on aspects
of the emerging field, announced: "It would be very nice if we could go away
from here with at least a preliminary agreement on the use of some phrase that
we could apply to this whole field. . . . If we had a word for patterned communications in all modalities, it would be useful. I am not enough of a specialist
in this field to know what words to use, but many people here, who have looked
as if they were on opposite sides of the fence, have used the word 'semiotics'.
It seems to me the one word, in some form or another, that has been used by
people who are arguing from quite different positions" (Sebeok, Hayes, and
Bateson 1964: 275). I then wrote in the editorial Preface: "Implying the identification of a single body of subject matter, this summative word was incorporated, overburdened as it is, and not without remonstrations from several
quarters, into the main title of our work", that is, *Approaches to Semiotics* (Sebeok,
Hayes, and Bateson 1964: 5). This same phrase was later selected to serve as the
over-all title of a series designed to accommodate book-length contributions to
the theory of signs (Sebeok 1969). On the other hand, at the formative meeting, on January 21, 1969, of what was to become the International Association
for Semiotic Studies (IASS), the issue what to call the Association's journal
was hotly debated, in part because of its intended bilingual character, but in
part also because the by then very real rivalry of the synonyms *semiotic/semiotics*
had become acute. The matter was ingeniously resolved by naming our fledgling
journal *Semiotica*. My impression of the present state of affairs is that *semiotics*
has made irreversible inroads over its competitor, and is likely to entirely replace *semiotic* within a decade or so, in spite of a residue of strong, variously
rationalized, scholarly predilections in this regard. Furthermore, a minute holdout
dismisses both, in favor of *semeiotics*, on the argument that "the spelling is better
etymology than semiotics, and it avoids the ambiguity of semi-. Semi-otics would
be nonsense" (Count 1969: 76n.).

   In broad strokes, then, it can be recorded that the family of labels that has become attached to the theory of signs is *sem(e)iotic(s)*. In the Soviet Union, where the discipline flourishes with unmatched concentration and distinction (Meletinsky and Segal 1971), and where the first colloquium devoted to its foundations was held in 1962—almost coincidentally with our own intiatory efforts— the favored terms are likewise *semiotic(s)*. It is interesting to note, however, that the famed center of semiotic studies, established about 1964 at the University of Tartu, where lectures and summer courses on the structural study of secondary systems giving rise to models are offered at regular intervals, publishes its Proceedings under the revivalistic banner *Semeiotiké* (subsequently echoed in the title of Kristeva, 1967), subtitled, in Russian, "Works on Systems of Signs", which is then explicitly rendered, both in English and Estonian, on the verso of the half-title page, as "Works on Semiotics—Tööd semiootika alalt" (Lotman 1964). In Poland, a country which has contributed heavily to the advancement of the theory of signs, and where the impetus for the IASS actually germinated, a clear preference is shown for *semiotics*; cf. the name of the International Conference on Semiotics (convened in Poland, in September 1966), and M. R. Mayenowa's report about "Semiotics Today" (reprinted in Kristeva *et al.* 1971: 57-62), or the usage of Polish logicians, as reflected, e.g., in the studies of Pelc (1971, *passim*) and his associates. The situation is much the same throughout the rest of the Slavic world; and the word used in Hungarian is likewise *szemiotika*) (cf. Voigt 1969a: 337f.).

   In contrast to what might be called the "Locke-Peirce-Morris pattern", outlined so far, that prevails generally in America, as it does, too, in both Northern and Eastern Europe, there exists quite another tradition, widespread throughout the Romance areas, but not confined to them, since reflexes of it occur in English, particularly British. This tradition, that I shall refer to as the "Saussure pattern", actually has two different sources: originally, Greek medicine; then, superimposed much later, the direct heritage of Ferdinand de Saussure (1857-1913). Synchronically, we are dealing here with the simultaneous multilingual interplay of polynymy (involving several similar forms) and polysemy (involving several connected meanings). Let French serve as the Romance prototype (data from Robert 1967: 1633): there are two forms, a. *sémiologie* and b. *séméiologie*, both with two definitions, 1. "Partie de la médecine qui étudie les signes des maladies" [*"The part of medicine which studies the signs of illnesses"*], and 2. "Science qui étudie la vie des signes au sein de la vie sociale" [*"The science which studies the life of signs at the heart of social life"*], or "Science étudiant les systèmes de signes (langues, codes, signalisations, etc.)" [*"The science studying systems of signs (languages, codes, ways of signaling, etc."*], in brief, 1., meaning symptomatology, dated 1752 (*Dictionnaire de Trévoux*), and 2., meaning the general theory of signs, illustrated by a quotation from Saussure, dated about 1910. This information can be displayed as a simple matrix:

Forms	a.	b.
Meanings	1.	2.

There are also two additional forms, dated 1555, c. *sémiotique* (Ambroise Paré, livre XX bis, 23),[3] and d. *sémeiotique*, both with essentially the same two definitions, 1. "Sémiologie" ["*Semiology*"], and 2. "Théorie générale des signes" ["*General Theory of Signs*"], or reconverted into an expanded matrix:

Forms	a.	b.	c.	d.
Meanings	1.		2.	

The situation is, *mutatis mutandis*, the same in the other Romance languages: in Italian, however, forms c. and d. are polarized in respect to meanings 1. and 2., that is, *semiotica* has come to refer to the theory of signs, whereas *semeiotica* continues to be confined to the medical context; in Romanian, on the other hand, *semiologie* means only "parte a medicinii care se ocupă cu diagnosticarea bolilor după simptomele lor" ["*a branch of medicine that deals with the diagnosis of illnesses from symptoms*"], whereas a Romanian form c. is used for a meaning 2. (e.g., Golopentia-Eretescu 1971; on increasing activity in this field in Romania, cf. also Pop 1972); in Brazilian Portuguese, the preferred term is *semiótica*, with an awareness that "Na Europa, a Semiótica é chamada de Semiologia . . ." ["*In Europe, semiotics is called semiology . . .*"] (Pignatari 1971: 27).

Meaning 1. need not detain us (cf. Barthes 1972); our prime concern is with *sémiologie* in the secondary sense, which, as every linguist knows, was launched by Saussure. In one variant, the key citation read (Saussure i.1906-1911: 46-49 [Baskin trans. p. 16]):

> La langue est un système de signes exprimant des idées, et par là, comparable à l'écriture, à l'alphabet des sourds-muets, aux rites symboliques, aux formes de politesse, aux signaux militaires, etc., etc. Elle est simplement le plus important de ces systèmes.
>
> On peut donc concevoir *une science qui étudie la vie des signes au sein de la vie sociale*: elle formerait une partie de la psychologie générale: nous la nommerons *sémiologie* (du grec *sēmeîon* "signe"). Elle nous apprendrait en quoi consistent les signes, quelles lois les régissent. Puisqu'elle n'existe pas encore, on ne peut dire ce qu'elle sera: mais elle a droit à l'existence, sa place est déterminée d'avance. La linguistique n'est qu'une partie de cette science générale, les lois que découvrira la sémiologie seront applicables à la linguistique, et celle-ci se trouvera ainsi rattachée a un domaine bien défini dans l'ensemble des faits humains.
>
> [*Language is a system of signs that express ideas, and is therefore comparable to a system of writing, the alphabet of deaf-mutes, symbolic rites, polite formulas, military signals, etc. But it is the most important of all these systems.*
>
> *A science that studies the life of signs within society is conceivable: it would be a part of social psychology and consequently of general psychology. I shall call it semiology (from the Greek sēmeîon "sign"). Semiology would show what constitutes signs, what laws govern them. Since the science does not yet exist, no one can say what it would be; but it has a right to existence, a place staked out in advance.*

Linguistics is only a part of the general science of semiology; the laws discovered by semiology will be applicable to linguistics, and the latter will circumscribe a well-defined area within the mass of anthropological facts.]

After the word *sémiologie*, the *Cours* has a footnote reference to a book by Naville (1901: 104), who recorded this early version of his Geneva colleague's views on the subject: Saussure insists on the importance "d'une science très génerale, qu'il appelle *sémiologie*, et dont l'objet serait les lois de la creation et de la transformation des signes et de leur sens. La sémiologie est une partie essentielle de la sociologie. Comme le plus important des systèmes de signes c'est le langage conventionnel des hommes, la science sémiologique la plus avancée c'est la *linguistique* ou science des lois de la vie du langage" [*"of a very general science which he calls* semiology, *and which would have for its object the laws governing the creation and transformation of signs and their sense. Semiology is an essential part of sociology. Since the most important of the systems of signs is the conventional language of men, the most advanced semiological science is* linguistics *or the science of the life of language"*] (cf. Godel 1957: 181). The notion, and its designation as *sémiologie*, appear to have been first recorded in a note of Saussure's, dated November, 1894 (Godel 1957: 275). Beginning 1916, and especially after the monographic treatment of the subject by Buyssens (1943), the word spread throughout French scientific, viz., linguistic discourse, and is now featured in such standard texts as those by Barthes (1964), Mounin (1970), and Guiraud (1971). However, this seemingly straightforward story has recently become considerably muddled by a double crossover: while *sémiologie* has come across the English Channel, in the guise of *semiology*, meaning "semiotic", *semiotic* has travelled in the opposite direction, returning across the Atlantic, by a zigzag track, to revitalize *sémiotique*, meaning "sémiologie". Thus Barthes' influential essay, *Éléments de sémiologie*, was published in England (1967) (and subsequently distributed in America [1968] as well) under the title, *Elements of Semiology*, and this is the term that, reinforced by the prestige of Parisian intellectual life, now turns up regularly in British newspapers and magazines, such as *The Times Literary Supplement*, and in an outpouring of volumes on the most diverse verbal and nonverbal arts, ranging from architecture ("Semiology of Architecture", Part 1 of Jencks and Baird 1969; in a comparable context, see Spanish *semiología*, in Gandelsonas, et al., 1970) to cinematography; a nice illustration of the latter emerges from the contrast of an English chapter, on "The Semiology of the Cinema" (Wollen 1969: 116-62), with an American essay, published simultaneously, on "The Development of a Semiotic of Film" (Worth 1969). At the same time, *sémiotique* occurs with such frequency in French (e.g., cf. Kristeva et al. 1971), that one scholar has even issued a prescriptive caution: for *semiotics*, "La meilleure traduction française reste: sémiologie. Le terme *sémiotique* a pénétré en français . . . pour désigner la sémiologie en général—usage à déconseiller . . ." [*"The best French translation is: semiology. The term* semiotic *has made its way into French . . . as a designation for semiology in general—an ill-advised usage . . ."*] (Mounin, 1970: 57n.)! Summarizing once more: in British English, the form *semiology* seems to be firmly established, whereas its success in American English, in competition with *semiotic(s)*, appears negligible; in French, *sémiologie* now has a rival in *sémiotique*, with the eventual outcome of the competition still in doubt.

Even in the narrow sense, excluding, that is, their medical uses, *semiotic*, *semiotics, semiology*, to mention only the three most common English congeners, are by no means wholly interchangeable. While every contributor to *Semiotica*— to stick with a parochial illustration—may indulge his personal taste when attaching a label to the theory of signs, his terminology within the same piece of discourse will not oscillate *ad libitum*, for his initial selection will have signaled to his sophisticated readership whether he has chosen to align himself with the Locke-Peirce-Morris tradition, the Mead variation, or the Saussurean pattern of thought and action. And while these words may—though they need not, of course—all share the same denotatum, the intellectual ambiance evoked by each is so different that Hill's dictum about synonymy, featured in the epigraph to this article, is reconfirmed once again.

A few scholars have deliberately kept the denotatum of *semiotic* distinguished from that of *semiology*. Such was the eventual English practice, notably, of Hjelmslev (1943: 85, 87), who provided these formal definitions: for *semiotic* (Danish *semiotik*)—"hierarchy, any of whose segments admits of a further division into classes defined by mutual relation, so that any of these classes admits of a division into derivatives defined by mutual mutation"; and for *semiology* (Danish *semiologi*)—"metasemiotic whose object semiotic is a non-scientific semiotic". Hjelmslev, moreover, used *semiotics* as well, although casually and informally (ibid: 69), and was responsible for the introduction, with formalization, of *metasemiotic* (vs. *object semiotic*) and *metasemiology*. His select followers seek to perpetuate the cleavage: "The independent science that is sought turns out to be rather an immanent semiology—the science that studies semiotics [*sic*], or sign systems in general" (Francis Whitfield, in Hill 1969: 258); and, sporadically, others: "It may be useful", a social anthropologist pleads, "to retain *semiology* to describe the study of *semiotics*, used as the plural [!] of *semiotic*. In its turn, a *semiotic* is a sign system" (Ardener, 1971: lxxxvi, n. 16). In French, denotata of *sémiotique* and *sémiologie* are variously distinguished from one another, for instance, by Kristeva (1967, 1970), and by Mounin, who, as already mentioned, objects to the designation of "la sémiologie en général" [*"semiology in general"*] by the term *sémiotique* [semiotic], although he would appear to be content if the employment of it were restricted "pour désigner un système de communication non linguistique particulier: le code de la route est une sémiotique, la peinture en est peut-être une autre, etc." [*"to the designation of a specific non-linguistic communication system: the code of traffic signals is a semiotic, the code of painting is perhaps another, etc."*] (Mounin 1970: 57n.). In Italian, the meaning of *semiologia* on the one hand is sharply differentiated from that of *semiotiche* on the other, by the author of the most interesting textbook on the subject so far, not at all on the basis of existing usage, but, so to say, *ex cathedra*, in order to establish a convention—how viable this will be remains to be seen—intended to clarify ensuing discussion (Eco 1968: 384).

In conclusion, I should like to adjoin, very briefly, two sets of observations:

1. In 1963, I set afloat a new compound, *zoosemiotics*. Since its first appearance in *Language*, I tried to keep track of its passage from a linguistic context to all sorts of other scientific texts and, eventually, to fiction and comic strip, as well as of its transmutation from English into other Indo-European and Finno-Ugric languages, and Japanese. My accounts of these events (Sebeok 1968, 1970) can be regarded as companion pieces to this article.

2. A comment on another related term, *asemasia*: Jackson, in his paper on affections of speech, expressed reservations about the term aphasia, on the cogent grounds that "there is, at least in many cases, more than loss of *speech*; pantomime is impaired; there is often a loss or defect in symbolising relations of things in any way", and went on to say that "Dr. Hamilton proposes the term Asemasia, which seems a good one" (Jackson 1932: 159). His somewhat recondite reference is to Allan McLane Hamilton, a prominent neurologist who practiced in New York City, and who had written a book on nervous diseases, wherein he remarked: "It has occurred to me that the word 'aphasia' as at present used, has too restricted a meaning to express the various forms of trouble of this nature, which not only consist of speech defects, but loss of gesticulating power, singing, reading, writing, and other functions by which the individual is enabled to put himself in communication with his fellows. I would, therefore, suggest 'asemasia' as a substitute for 'aphasia'" (Hamilton 1878: 161n.). It is possible, as Jakobson claims (1971: 289), that Hamilton not only proposed but actually coined this term as a cover for the general deficit of semiotic activities beyond the merely verbal, but, if so, he was anticipated by Steinthal, who had recognized, at least by 1871, that "die Aphasie . . . erweitert sich . . . zur allgemeinen Mangel an Erkenntniss von Zeichen, Asemie" [*"aphasia can be expanded to a general theory of the understanding of signs: asemia"*] (Steinthal 1871: 458).

23

JOHN DEELY

Semiotic as Framework and Direction

It is a cliché of current intellectual culture that we have entered upon a "post-modern" phase of society and culture. I say this is a cliché because, everywhere repeated, the phrase is nowhere defined. Nonetheless, it says something true, something widely felt toward the exact expression of which we are still groping.

One of the characteristic features of self-consciously "post-modern discourse" is a rejection, usually ill-defined and often virtually incoherent, of the "subject-object" dichotomy. What is sound about this rejection is the notion of dichotomy as applied simply to the relation between what is being cognized and what organism is doing the cognizing. What is also sound about the rejection is the implicit understanding of objectivity that has become common today, as meaning either "detachment" on the side of some "observer", or, at the other extreme, a supposedly independently existing domain of physical being.

What I want to suggest here is that semiotics constitutes the transdisciplinary framework which makes the idea of a "post-modern" development intelligible, in just the way that modern thought provided the framework which made the idea of a "post-medieval" and "post-renaissance" development intelligible; and that, in addition, the development within semiotics of the foundational doctrine of signs—semiotic, in precisely the sense outlined by Poinsot (1632a) but named by Locke (1690) and undertaken full-scale only by Peirce (1867 and after) in our own day—already points out the direction in which this post-modern development is bound to reach its mature and fully recognizable form by way of contrast to the idealism of typically modern thought or the realism of typically pre-modern thought.

It has been a mistake of the self-proclaimed post-modern (but pre-semiotic) prophets to think that they could somehow do away with the notion of objectivity altogether. In fact, what is needed rather is a *new understanding* of objectivity as it is properly an irreducible feature of any communicational relationship. The object/thing distinction, never properly developed in modern thought, as Cahalan has shown in a somewhat devastating manner (1985 throughout), becomes almost impossible to mistake at the heart of semiotic development. I will develop this below.

But alongside this new notion of objectivity—semiotic objectivity, in Ransdell's phrase (1979)—and, indeed, of a piece with it, a new appreciation and notion of *history itself* is called for, not the common notion of history as calendar of events, or the typically modern notion in philosophy of history as list of errors, but rather

a full-scale development of the notion of history as laboratory of thought first suggested by Gilson (1937) and brought into mainstream semiotic development with
the fine descriptive expression of Umberto Eco, who showed (after Zumthor and
Vance 1977) how the "archeology of concepts" is at the heart of any perspective
or method fully semiotic (Eco 1980 lecture series; comments in Deely 1982: 1-3).

Dr. Leach (lecture of 9 October 1984) has already taken the position that in
fact none of us—with the possible exception of Dr. Sebeok—are semioticians, on
the ground that each of us has a specialized training in the traditional disciplines.
Semiotics, he has said, is something peripheral, that yet somehow helps the
specialties and is common to all of them.

These remarks require considerable qualification to be acceptable—and yet
they are not so far wrong. His exasperation at the effort to define semiotics as
a distinct domain of inquiry is understandable, but it is perhaps the impatience
of the man too long used to the compartmentalization and specialization that have
become the hallmark of intellectual life in the age of science, that is to say, since
the great revolutions so intimately associated with the 17th century. The habits
of thought engendered by this perspective over some three centuries now run deep,
and yet, in spite of them, Dr. Leach also advises us that there is something common to all our pursuits, something that is in need of being given a common
language.

My remarks are made from the perspective of a philosopher, familiar equally
with the traditions of his discipline both before and after the magic 17th century—
equally, that is, at least in what concerns the Latin tradition and the national
language traditions which supplanted it in the later modern times. From this
perspective, it seems to me that what is "new" about semiotics is really new,
both in its foundations and as a superstructure or explicit notion and theme
developing in the academies that have generally become unable to envision the
possibility of unity to intellectual life, or to recognize the importance of tradition—
history—at the very center of intellectual life even in its most purely "scientific"
and perhaps mathematical constructions. What is new is the frame of reference,
or perspective, if you like, in which the sign is seen to mediate knowledge over
time (*eo ipso* historically) regardless of the logical methods characteristically employed by the given discipline, be it humanistic or scientific; and the realization
that semiosis is a correspective process, a process structured by and structuring
of "reality".

The dialectic between humanistic and scientific modes of inquiry to which
Dr. Sebeok has recently directed attention in his Indiana University seminar (Fall
of 1984) is at the heart of the matter. For one thing that did not change in the
17th century as scientific understanding came to displace philosophy from the
central role in the academies and culture of Western civilization was an uncom-
promising sense of "reality" as a natural world prejacent to and independent of
the human mind, a world governed in its interactions by laws which form the
proper object of human understanding, laws and interactions which formed the
object and goal of understanding of the natural philosophers from the remotest
times in their pursuit of a science called by the Stoics and Aristotelians alike
"Physics", i.e., *scientia seu philosophia naturalis*.

What changed in the 17th century was not at all this notion of reality as the
mind-independently real, or "given". What changed was only the methodological

conviction about how this world of nature could best be penetrated by human understanding. In the ancient physics, Stoic or Aristotelian, the emphasis was on an intelligible content superior to what the senses could attain even in the most refined achievements of perception, imagination, and estimation of material possibilities, a content given the general designation of "being" (ὄν), and refined discursively (λόγος) in the science of metaphysics or ontology. The modern physics abandoned not the goal of knowing reality (the "mind-independently 'given'"), but only the emphasis on being as distinct from the observable and the methods of dialectic and deductive logic as the way to bring out for the understanding the proper content of the real. In place of dialectic they recommended observation, and in place of deduction ("syllogismus") mathematical inferences which would make possible precise calculations of consequences and expectations in the realm of what can be observed.

"Reality", however, remained the unquestioned final goal of the inquiry. Only the means had changed. This simplifies the picture somewhat, but is true in its essential lines. It was no accident that Newton labelled his watershed work (1686) *Principia Mathematica Philosophiae Naturalis*—"philosophia naturalis" being the favorite Latin expression for the "physica" of Aristotle. Of course, the controlling principles in a science mathematical in form and experimental in its matter are of a radically different character from whatever knowledge of nature may be possible in the guise of intelligible being unfolded by the understanding according to the form of logical principles resident in the structures of natural language, as Jacques Maritain in our own time has best explained (1941a; 1959[1]). But my point is that, despite this misunderstanding which for a long time masked the differences between the ancient and the modern physics under the label of "natural philosophy", the guiding idea of reality as the prejacently and mind-independently given provided the common fixation of the two ages.

If we turn to the side of philosophy, we find that the break from classical and Latin traditions takes the form of a substitution of discourse for being at the center of philosophers' preoccupations, *a shift from ontology to epistemology*, as it appears in hindsight. Originally, this shift took the form of a search for new methods, an obsession of sixteenth and seventeenth century philosophers dissatisfied by scholasticism and made forever memorable by the title of one of Descartes' most enduring works, the *Discours de la méthode* of 1637. In its original context, however, this work was but a preface to his works of "natural philosophy", which were of a scientific character so primitive that they have long been forgotten. But the shift soon came to focus on the presuppositions of the new types of inquiry into nature, with the curious result that, without exception, the modern philosophers both in England and on the Continent found themselves absolutely baffled when it came to explaining how the realist pretensions of the new sciences might be justified at the level of the theory of knowledge. Thus rose with Berkeley idealism in the distinctively modern sense of that term, and with Hume skepticism also in the modern sense. Kant, the master of all the moderns in philosophy and the systematizer of an idealism so ruthless as to strangle even the hope of a knowledge of whatever of nature be in any sense prejacent to and independent of human thinking, nonetheless took it for a scandal in philosophy that no proof of the existence of a mind-independent natural world had so far been given. He set his considerable genius and energy of mind to remedy this situation, aiming to overcome idealism in modern thought, with what success the subsequent history of philosophy plainly tells—in a word, none.

André Lalande, meeting with the group concerned to produce the marvellous *Vocabulaire technique et critique de la philosophie* just after the turn of the century (from 1902-1923), arrived at perfectly clear definitions of "realism" and "idealism" in philosophy, but considered that realism in whatever form was definitively surpassed by the typically modern development of philosophy, which has been, to be sure, idealist to the core and for the most part solipsistic.

To all this semiotic provides a welcome and long-overdue alternative, an idea whose time has come. I cannot emphasize this point too strongly. The rise of semiotic consciousness today seems to me to be absolutely revolutionary respecting the past of philosophy and science alike. It is at once an antidote for the unbridled and atomizing specialism of academic pursuits that science has brought in its wake, and a restoration of historical thought to its properly central place in humanistic inquiry.

The reasons for this claim stem directly from the peculiar character of the process in nature which is at least as old as life and doubtless in some sense as old as the universe itself, the process labelled by Peirce "semiosis", which process semiotic inquiry studies in its multifarious manifestations (see my *Introducing Semiotic*, p. 65—the diagram illustrating the contrast between semiosis as process and semiotic as study thereof). The results of such study lead inexorably far beyond the confines of human language and consciousness, into the depths of nature itself, which reveals itself more and more intimately, and throughout, as a network or web of sign-relations, to borrow the felicitous analogy of Thomas Sebeok.

Semiosis, in the simplest terms, and at least in the sphere of living things, is the process whereby experience is developed and structured by means of sign relations. It is this building process that provides with its products in various ways the common object of semiotic inquiries, and it is something remarkable in nature. Glimpses of this process occur scattered throughout the medical, philosophical, and theological literature of ancient times, glimpses we seek to recapture and systematize, for example, in our "Neglected Figures in the History of Semiotic Inquiry" Sessions which have become a regular part of the Annual Meeting of the Semiotic Society of America, to the astonishment (and in fact consternation) of those who fail to appreciate the antiquity of these questions, and their complexity.[2] For to tell the truth, there is almost no figure who cannot be considered "neglected" from a thoroughly semiotic point of view.[3]

What is remarkable about semiosis as a process in nature is twofold. In the first place, it involves but does not consist in exchanges of physical interaction. That is to say, it lies outside the order of efficient or "productive" causality—in Peircean terms, it belongs to the order of thirdness. Second, and as a consequence of this, it proceeds with a certain indifference to physical reality in the classical sense characterized above.

To explain and to foreground these characteristics of semiosis in the living world, Dr. Sebeok has taken over from Jakob von Uexküll the concept of *Umwelt* and its correspective *Innenwelt*. Deeply rooted in classical German philosophy— that is to say, Kant—von Uexküll had a lively sense of the role of mental construction in our experience of any "reality". But, unlike Kant and fortunately for us, von Uexküll was a remarkably attentive observer of the world of plants and other than human animals. Out of these two preoccupations von Uexküll forged some of the most remarkable and semiotically fruitful notions available to us for understanding the phenomenon of semiosis.

Umwelt, by all accounts, is difficult to translate. What this means, however, is that there is no equivalent vocabulary standard in French or in English, etc., to facilitate the rendering of von Uexküll's text. Of course, this should not obscure the fact that his *Umwelt* is an original term in the use he makes of it in German to begin with. So the problem is not so much a problem of translation as it is a problem of understanding. It is not that the term is lucid in German but that the other national languages are deficient. Already in von Uexküll's German, a new understanding of the animal world is at stake and being forged, and it is this that is semiotically important and interesting for the present context.

The easiest way in my opinion to explain what is central to the notion of *Umwelt* is to revive a term of Renaissance scholasticism that fell into desuetude around the time of Descartes, namely, the term *objective being*. Pay attention to what I say here, for the notion of "objectivity" I wish to bring to your notice is a purely semiotic one. Christine Hasenmueller (presentation of 10/9/84) insisted on the "textuality" of art as against its "objectivity". The "objectivity" of which I am about to speak, however, is precisely what she calls textuality, but so conceived as to be free of the glottocentric analogy at the base of "textual" notions. For the Latins, an *objective being* is something that exists only in awareness. It is something existing precisely *as and insofar as and only insofar as it is known*. The sun or the sea, for the Latins, as parts of our experience of nature, are *objective beings*; they are *also* physical beings, but *it is not as physical that they are said to be objective beings*. Objective beings, as such, are something known: they need have no other status. The celestial spheres of Plato (c.427-347BC), Eudoxus (c.400-347BC), Ptolemy (fl.127-145), John of Sacrobosco (d.1256), these were objective beings thought—wrongly—to be physical beings as well. Ether and phlogiston, constructs of the scientific understanding seeking to explain nature at an earlier time, turned out to be pure fictions of a would-be understanding which nonetheless served to support and promote inquiry into nature along definite "scientific" and cultural lines. Like true unicorns and centaurs, they are *purely* objective beings, but were once believed in and exercised a control over behavior within the human Umwelt.

Within experience, all beings, therefore, by definition, are objective beings. Not all, however, are physical beings. Experience consists of an irreducible admixture of the two. I say that this admixture is irreducible: it is not that we cannot sometimes tell the difference between the purely objective and the objective that is also physical or that also has a physical embodiment or dimension; we can—sometimes. The point is rather that experience depends, root and branch, upon signs, and signs by their nature make things objectively present even when and in ways that are wanting physical counterparts. Signs, that is, establish networks able to sustain in experience what does not exist with as much facility as what does—where "existence" carries the meaning of physical existence or, classically, existence independent of human thought and interest.

Thus, something can exist—physically—and yet not exist at all—objectively— for some particular organism or observer. Again, something may not exist at all— physically—and yet exist as a matter of central importance and interest—objectively—for some observer or group.

If these points are well understood, we are in a fair position to see that "reality", so far as experience is concerned, is not first of all something given prejacently to human understanding. On the contrary, reality, as experienced, consists precisely in an admixture of objective elements and factors, some of which come from the physical environment in its proper being—nature, if you will—and others of which come from the beliefs and customs of the community assimilated through the normal processes of socialization—nurture, if you will (and provided you understand, contrary to the impoverished anthropology brought to the colonies by Radcliffe-Brown, the irreducibility of enculturation to socialization, the latter of which is independent of language whereas the former is not).

If we now translate *Umwelt* as *objective world*, we are also in a fair position to see the significance of this notion for the understanding of semiosis as a unique process in nature. An *Umwelt*, von Uexküll tells us, is the physical environment as filtered or transformed by the given organism according to what is important or "significant" to it. Elements of the physical environment are networked objectively, i.e., so as to establish the sphere of experience as something superordinate to and strictly transcending, all the while containing partially and resting upon aspects of, the physical environment in its "natural" or "mind-independent" being. Umwelts thus are species-specific: No two types of organisms live in the same objective worlds, even though they share the same physical environment. What the bat seeks (nourishment) the moth avoids (providing nourishment for bats), and conversely. "The differences of things as things are quite other than the differences of things as objects and in the being of object", was the statement of a so-far neglected figure in the history of semiotic inquiry, the 16th century Thomas Gaeta. It is this insight that Poinsot saw as foundational to the doctrine of signs, and that von Uexküll recaptures and extends to the understanding of zoosemiotic phenomena with the notion of *Umwelt*, at the same time expanding it to show that objective structures are total networks or webs of relationships redistributing the physical environment so as to make it habitable and improve its habitability for the species.

The differences between the human *Umwelt* or *Lebenswelt* consequent upon the "tinker-toy" structure of true language in its primary modeling role (as opposed to its exaptation [cf. Gould and Vrba 1982] in speech for communicative purposes, which is strictly derivative and secondary) and the *Umwelt* of animals which communicate but without the sort of critical control of objectivity required for language in the human sense, lie beyond our point here. Suffice it to say that the *Umwelt* as such is objectively structured cathectically according to positive and negative affect into the desirable and to be sought, the undesirable and to be avoided, and the indifferent. The human *Umwelt*, or *Lebenswelt*, as I prefer to call it, adds over and above this basic trichotomic differentiation all the further differentiations—infinite, practically speaking—made possible by the recognition of differences in objects obtaining as a result of what they may be or are independently of their relation to us and our desires.

Our point here is to realize that reality, *so far as it is a matter of direct public experience and not just of hypothesis or inference*, is an objective affair superordinate and strictly irreducible to what exists independently of human thoughts and actions. The physics unable to account for the role of the observer is a pre-semiotic science, hardly paradigmatic for human understanding, as positivist and most analytic philosophers of science continue to believe. Human understanding must account first of all and in the final analysis for the objectively real, not just for the physically real, and not just for what the prejudices of a given time label as "real". "Reality" is not the physically given, it is the semiosic total of which physical being forms a part. The Mississippi River physically is not the boundary between Iowa and Illinois, but it is so objectively. Ronald Reagan physically is not President of the United States, but he is so objectively. More to the point, Thomas Sebeok is not physically a semiotician, but only objectively; in fact, he is a kind of legend or myth, much more interesting than a mere physical organism, and pretty much independent of one too as far as the future of semiotics goes.

There is a real problem here, as Williams details in her Prefatory Essay (1985a) to the new edition of Sebeok's *Contributions to the Doctrine of Signs*, and as Herzfeld put it in his remarks opening the "State-of-the-Art" conference (10/8/84), of making semiotics serve positivistic goals by the manipulation of antipositivistic rhetoric. Should we seek to develop a *science* of signs or, as Locke and Sebeok suggest, a *doctrine* of signs? A would-be science of signs, in the modern sense of science, buys in to the now sterile and stale debate in philosophy between "realisms" and "idealisms". What Locke calls for, however, and what we find in Poinsot, Peirce, and the best of Sebeok, is the unfolding of an objective discipline, not a discipline having at its primary focus the physical environment as such. This discipline belongs to a higher order of human understanding, of which scientific understanding forms only a substructure. The dialectic of scientific and humanistic modes of understanding is the dialectic of an understanding ordered to the grasp of physical reality in its proper being and an understanding which also seeks to account for the objective elements of experience irreducible to physical being. It is, in a word, a semiotic enterprise, beyond realism and idealism.

What then are we left with—field or discipline? In its foundations, by explicating the nature of the sign as making present in experience what the sign itself is not, semiotics is a kind of discipline, but a discipline which uncovers the structure of experience in all its parts, not just in those which have a conveniently physical identification. Umberto Eco maintained (1980) at the first Toronto ISISSS that semiotics is therefore a philosophical discipline, and I would agree with this, except to wonder whether there is point in assimilating semiotics to a discipline which has abandoned its heritage and become as sterile as philosophy today has become. Perhaps this future thought, as Heidegger suggested (1947), should no longer be called philosophy.

More important is its function in identifying and exploring a process that cuts across all the possible lines and fortifications of the "specialists": the inherently transdisciplinary nature of semiosis inevitably imposes itself upon those who come to study it, that is to say, semioticians. We have reached, in the MacCannells' fine expression (1982), "the time of the sign".

It is no accident that semiotics has moved so far from its early glottocentric biases, at a rate roughly proportional to the increasing number of inquirers. Nor is it by chance and fashion alone that Peirce has increasingly been recognized as the true modern pioneer of semiotics, far greater in general importance for semiotics than the linguist Saussure. In fact Peirce is not a "modern" philosopher. He is the beginning in philosophy of something new, as I have tried to indicate (1985: 492-498), something radically philosophical and transdisciplinary, but better than philosophy in any form it has taken so far, namely, semiotics.

The semiotics movement is a movement toward establishing new foundations for and a redistribution of the traditional areas of academic specialization. Semiotic consciousness is rooted in the realization that the ideas by which any debate is joined are already signs, not paths to what is independent of observation so much as perspectives making observation possible in the first place and elevating the physical to the level of experience which redistributes the physical to make the world habitable as well as "given", and to further within nature the highest possibilities, not the least common denominator, of physical existence and life.

It is in such a direction that the development of semiotics points, and it is such a framework that semiotics can become, if we continue to bring out the requirements of its object, the semiosic aspects and processes present and at work throughout the natural world, as including our species.

Notes

(to page ix, 18)

Notes

Notes for Editors' Preface:
"Pars Pro Toto"

[1] Much of what follows in this Section I of the Preface is abstracted from a longer treatment by John Deely, "A Context for Narrative Universals or: Semiology as a *Pars Semeiotica*", presented first as an ISISSS 84 Evening Lecture (Toronto, June 21) and scheduled for publication in *The American Journal of Semiotics* 4.2.

[2] What we here call "the Poinsot-Locke-Peirce tradition" is substantially identical with what Sebeok, looking more at the contemporary inspiration than at the foundational development historically conceived as such, earlier called "the Locke-Peirce-Morris tradition", in contrast to "the Saussurean pattern of thought and action" (p. 256 above). See the updated discussion in "Challenging Signs at the Crossroads", Williams' Preface (1985a) to the reprint of Sebeok 1976; see also Sebeok 1982. Doctrinal links between Peirce and Poinsot, as they appear in Locke's doctrinal perspective, are spelled out in Deely 1985: 491-498.

Notes for Reading 2:
John Deely, "The Coalescence of Semiotic Consciousness"

[1] Let us ask whether ideas as semiotically conceived, that is, as (formal) signs, might not be simply states of our nervous system. The answer is that ideas and neural conditions cannot be so identified, for the reason that brain states are in principle (under appropriate instrumentation) directly sense perceptible, while, by contrast, ideas in principle—that is, in order to be ideas and to function according to the rationale of their admission as real— are not sense perceptible, but are rather that on which every sense perceptible object as actually perceived here and now depends. Let us call them "mental events" in contrast to "physical events", that is, in contrast to items of possible sense apprehension. Thus, in a semiotic perspective, the same reasoning that leads us to affirm the reality of ideas as mental in contradistinction to brain states as physical, also requires us to preclude the reduction of the mental to the physical, and to preclude as well identification of the mental with that of which we are directly aware in cognition. The reduction and identification are alike incompatible with the semiotic (sign) structure of apprehension itself as underlying all observation and constituting its ground.

Moreover, this analysis removes the principal ground on which behaviorists and analytic philosophers have repudiated the existence of ideas, namely, the ground that we have no direct awareness of them in our experience as something distinct or separable from the objective "physical" being of the marks seen and expressions heard. Indeed, the thrust of this argument is heuristically just what the semiotic analysis of ideas would lead us to expect. In short, the line of argument from which contemporary Anglo-American analysis of language rejects the existence of ideas in the modern sense, supports the acceptance of the existence of ideas in the semiotic sense, i.e., as making present in our consciousness objects which they themselves are not. The recent attempts of mainstream philosophers to explain away the mental somehow in terms of the physical is shown by semiotic analysis to be misguided. That same line of analysis demonstrates the wrongheadedness of the more enduring modern tendency to close thought within its own constructions, with the result of making experience of communication unintelligible or merely apparent at best. What the analysis of cognition from a semiotic point of view quickly reveals is that the solipsistic and reductionistic tendencies of mainstream modern and contemporary philosophy and psychology have as their common root an inadequate understanding of the phenomenon of signifying which is at the heart of cognitive life.

The counter to both these tendencies, accordingly, and the opening of a new era of understanding, can be found in a careful establishment of the foundations of the doctrine of signs (semiotic in the strict sense) and in the extension of such an analysis to all the phenomena of which signs make up part (the interdisciplinary field of semiotics). The possibilities of such a work and perspective seem to have been first secured systematically as early as 1632a in the *Treatise on Signs* of John Poinsot, while the actual project has begun to go forward only in most recent times, especially under the influence of Charles S. Peirce. Thus the dominant interest of Poinsot's *Treatise* is the prospective significance of a seminal treatment, illuminating possibilities of a future age. "Poinsot's thought", commented Sebeok (1982: x), belongs to the mainstream of semiotic discourse "as the 'missing link' between the ancients and the moderns in the history of semiotic, a pivot as well as a divide between two huge intellective landscapes the ecology of neither of which could be fully appreciated" prior to the publication of his *Treatise* in a modern edition.

2 "It should now be apparent how great is the too frequently committed blunder of representing the opposition of the syllogism and induction as the simple opposition of two movements proceeding in contrary directions on the same road. Such a representation betrays a complete misunderstanding of the true nature of this opposition and even risks confusing the syllogism with *descensus*. The opposition between the syllogism and induction is much deeper: it is a fundamental opposition. The very paths which they pursue are different. One moves entirely upon the intelligible plane; the other leads from the plane of sense experience to the intelligible plane, from the plane of the particular or the singular to the plane of the universal (or inversely). The syllogism is based entirely upon the connection of two terms with a same third term (the middle term). Induction replaces the middle term by an enumeration of parts and is entirely based upon the connection of individuals or of parts with the universal whole" (Maritain 1923: 267).

3 If this is understood, it will also be seen that, far from providing a tool for adjudicating philosophical disputes, as has been commonly supposed, philosophical dispute precisely is tacitly set aside and taken as settled whenever and as long as one has recourse to logistic methods, notably propositional functions and quantifiers. This point is beginning to be recognized among contemporaries, so that one may hope its importance will eventually sink in. (For extended discussions from very different standpoints, see Strawson 1952: esp. 193-194; Deely 1975a: esp. 266-267, 1985a; Küng 1967: 8-9.)

Notes for Reading 3:
Thomas A. Sebeok, "The Doctrine of Signs"

1 The reasons therefor were forcefully argued by Karl R. Popper in his 1977 book on *The Self and the Brain*, with John C. Eccles.

2 This man-sign analogy, and implications of the semiotics of identity more generally, constitute the central themes of *Man's Glassy Essence*, an important new book by the distinguished Chicago anthropologist, Milton Singer.

Notes for Reading 6:
Umberto Eco, Roberto Lambertini, Costantino Marmo, and Andrea Tabarroni,
"Latratus Canis, or: The Dog's Barking"

1 Aquinas introduces under ''non significativa'' a twofold distinction—*litterata/non litterata* and *articulata/non articulata*—which poses some difficulties. Aquinas seems to have gotten

the distinction from Ammonius' *Commentary on the Perihermenias* (c.400), translated by Moerbeke in 1268; for it is the position of Ammonius, according to which these two distinctions are handled as basically synonymous, which Aquinas follows—but choosing his own words and examples—in his own uncompleted *Commentarium super libros Perihermenias* (c.1269-1274), lectio iv.

This point is important in the history of semiotics, because there is a rather different use made of these same expressions among the Latin grammarians, from Priscian (c.526) to the modistae, and these materially overlapping but formally divergent uses serve to identify semiotically two cultural heredities among the Latins, one of a logico-linguistic character in which the bark of the dog has a fixed place of marginality, another of a naturalistic character in which the bark proves to occupy a position which is neither fixed nor strictly marginal.

None of the Latin predecessors of Priscian present a scheme according to the oppositions *articulata/inarticulata litterata/illiterata.* For them, *vox* is simply divided into *articulata* on the one hand and *confusa* (*seu inarticulata*) on the other. If one turns to the Greek tradition, however, at least three passages are known which present a clear parallelism with Priscian's treatment "De voce" in his *Institutions*, the earliest in Apollonius Dyscolus (i.100-200), and two later ones in Ammonius (loc. cit.) and John Damascene (i.742-749). Moreover, Ammonius, probably writing against Apollonius Dyscolus, expresses, in his commentary on the *De Interpretatione*, an irritation with the incongruity of the classification of the grammarians ("...risibile utique erit") which arises from their way of drawing the twofold distinction in question, which may be summarized in the following table, and is precisely the classification introduced into Latin grammatical tradition by Priscian:

	articulata	inarticulata
litterata	quae possunt scribi et intelligi ut "homo"	coax (the bellowing of an ox) cra (the cawing of a cow)
illitterata	sibilus hominis gemitus	mugitus (mooing of a cow) crepitus (croaking of a frog)

In this way of drawing the twofold distinction, the *articulatio* of the *vox* is identified with its *significatio*, a point on which Priscian is followed, as we have said, by all the medieval grammarians. In a more complete discussion of this research (Eco, Lambertini, Marmo, and Tabarroni 1984: 9-12), a possible reason for this identification is conjectured, and problems about the internal coherence of this way of drawing the matrix are raised. Here, it is enough to note that, if we view Aquinas from the standpoint of Priscian, we cannot understand why the *voces articulatae* don't coincide with the *voces significativae*, whereas to speak of non-signifying and articulated sounds is a contradiction in terms. (And, in general, this classification in the hands of the philosophers has in common with that of the grammarians only some homonymies, such as to create an impression of overlap and generate unbearable confusion when an effort is made to place them in a common scheme. For Aquinas the feature "litterata" is a grammatological or graphematic one, whereas the feature "articulata" is a phonological one in the linguistic sense of 'second articulation'. For the grammarians, on the contrary, the feature "litterata" concerns the phonological second articulation, while "articulata" meant "endowed or correlated with a meaning", and was a semantic feature.) Thus we find ourselves on the road toward identifying two differing semiotic traditions, each of which assigns to the bark of the dog a different status.

In the logico-philosophical tradition, directly dependent on the lessons of Ammonius and remaining foreign to the lessons of the grammarians, the *articulatio* continues to be identified with the *litteratio* and therefore with the possibility of a written translation of sound. How this affects the bark of the dog we will see on resuming our main discussion. In the logico-linguistic tradition of the grammarians, along the line of Priscian, the bark of the dog has from this point only a most sad destiny—that is, one devoid of further interest.

It is perhaps natural for a grammarian that the only interesting things are the sounds articulated by a man, according of course to a grammar, in order to express meanings. The
sounds of animals, therefore, have no interest whatsoever. And so it is that in the texts
of the grammarians one sees that the bark of the dog goes to occupy positions always more
marginal.

At this point the tradition of the grammarians no longer interests us. It is obvious that
the grammarians are concerned exclusively with the grammar of human languages, and
not with general semiotics, not to mention zoosemiotics. What interests us instead is the
tradition of the philosophers who continue to grant to the dog a certain honorable and
labile position in the classification of signs; the philosophers also interest us because, beyond
the classifications they stretch out from the reserves of the Aristotelian *De Interpretatione*,
they are continually inclined to make supplementary observations, such as those of Aquinas
to which we now return.

2 It is not immediately clear why Bacon distinguishes the signs of type 1.1. from those
of the type 1.3. It would seem that while in the type 1.3. there is a clear relation of cause
and effect, in those of the type 1.1. there is only a relation of concomitance between events,
certain where the concomitance is a necessary concomitance, uncertain where the concomitance is merely likely or probable. Yet it remains obscure why the wet earth, as a
probable sign of rain in the past, is not classified among the *vestigia*. Even more curious
is the locating of pictures and images, intentional products of man, among the natural
signs. Bacon reasons that what is intentionally made is the object (statue or portrait), but
the resemblance between the real person and the representation is owing to a kind of
homology between the form of the *signans* and the form of the *signatum*; Augustine had
been much more subtle in his *De doctrina christiana* (II.35.38-39) with his perception of the
widely conventional nature of images and mimetic representations.

3 *Intentio* is assumed by Bacon in its epistemological sense developed by the Scholastics,
as a turning of the soul toward a cognitive object, as distinct from any act of will (cf. Vescovini
1965: 64-69). It is thus clear how there can be *intentio* even in cases absent reason and will;
for it is enough that there be an immediate impulse of the sensitive soul "quasi subito
per privationem temporis sensibilis". Thus those signs ordered by the soul without any
deliberation of reason or choice by the will—type 2.2—are said to function "naturaliter",
but they have no connection with the natural signs of type 1. These natural signs—type
1.—are called "natural" with reference to nature as substance, while the naturally functioning signs of 2.2. are called "natural" because they are born from an impulse of the
soul in the order of operative quality. In any event, the distinction is clear: the *signa naturalia*
of type 1. perform their function without regard to any intention, while the *signa naturaliter
ordinata* of type 2.2.—the wail of the infirm and the bark of the dog, etc.—are considered
precisely as springing from an intention, an impulse of the sensitive soul tending to express that which the animal, human or not, feels. So it is that in this classification the bark,
without finding itself next to Holy Scripture and separated from the wail, as in the provocation of Augustine, yet comes to stand more or less on the same side with the other
signs (type 2.1.) emitted by and with deliberate intention of reason and will.

4 For the wrong attribution to Marsilius see A. Maieru 1972.

Note for Reading 9:
Martin Krampen, "Phytosemiotics"

1 Editors' note: In the original publication of Krampen's essay, this section was preceded
by a technical section titled *Measurements of oxygen and carbon dioxide*. The omitted section
contains a technical discussion summarized in a series of tables, and aims "to demonstrate
the meaning of plants to human life and to point out the necessity for further investigation
in phytosemiotics". Considerations of space required the omission of this quantitative discussion in reprinting the essay for general readership in the present volume. Readers interested

in the technical details are referred to Krampen 1981: 197-203. The opening sentence of the present section has been edited to smooth the transition.

Notes for Reading 10:
John Deely, "On the Notion of Phytosemiotics"

1 "Il me semble, quand je suis a Fontainebleu, que je sympathise de toutes mes forces avec la vitalité puissante des arbres qui m'entourent. Quant à réproduire jusqu'a leur forme, je suis sans doute trop encroûté dans la mienne pour cela; mais, en y réfléchissant bien, il ne me paraît pas deraisonnable de supposer que toutes les formes de l'existence dorment plus ou moins profondément ensevelies au fond de chaque être; car sous les traits bien arrêtés de la forme humaine dont je suis revêtu. Un oeil un peu percant doit reconnaître sans peine le contour plus vague de *l'animalité*, qui voile à son tour la forme encore plus flottante et plus indécise de la simple *organisation*: or l'une des déterminations possibles de l'organisation est *l'arboréité*, qui engendre à son tour la *chênéité*. Donc la *chênéité* est cachée quelque part dans mon fond, et peut être quelquefois tentée d'en sortir et de paraître à son tour *dias in luminis oras*, bien que l'humanité, qui a pris les devants sur elle, le lui défende, et lui barre le chemin."

2 Liber II, lect. 9, n. 347: "Definit ipsam primam animam, quae dicitur anima vegetabilis; quae quidem in plantis est anima, in animalibus pars animae. . . . Ad cuius definitionis intellectum, sciendum est, quod inter tres operationes animae vegetabilis, est quidam ordo. Nam prima eius operatio est nutritio, per quam salvatur aliquid ut est. Secunda autem perfectior est augmentum, quo aliquid proficit in maiorem perfectionem, et secundum quantitatem et secundum virtutem. Tertia autem perfectissima et finalis est generatio per quam aliquid iam quasi in seipso perfectum existens, alteri esse et perfectionem tradit. Tunc enim unumquodque maxime perfectum est, ut in *quarto Meteororum* dicitur (8), cum potest facere alterum tale, quale ipsum est. Quia igitur iustum est, ut omnia definiantur et denominentur a fine, finis autem operum animae vegetabilis est generare alterum tale quale ipsum est, sequitur quod ipsa sit conveniens definitio primae animae, scilicet vegetabilis, *ut sit generativa alterius similis secundum speciem.*"

3 Sebeok 1974a: 108-109: "le fond du problème de l'analogie entre code génétique et code linguistique est en réalité très different quand on le prend d'un point de vue linguistique. Le langage est un mécanisme très particulier, organisé de manière hiérarchique. Cette organisation hiérarchique est généralement désignée sous le nom de dualité, mais en réalité ce terme prête à confusion car il signifie essentiellement que l'on a un ensemble de sous-systèmes, et que le sous-système de base comporte un répertoire universel de traits binaires. C'est ce que les linguistes appelent des traits distinctifs (*distinctive features*), traits qui sont en eux-mêmes dépourvus de signification, mais à l'aide desquels on peut fabriquer un nombre infini de phrases, lesquelles forment un autre sous-système. Pour ce qui est de l'ensemble des systèmes de communication des organismes, ceci constitue un phénomène unique, car nulle, part ailleurs dans le monde animal on ne trouve traçe d'une telle organisation hiérarchique. Le code génétique, si je le comprends bien, fonctionne de manière analogue. On a quatre unités de base qui sont en elles-mêmes dépourvues de signification, mais qui se combinent en des unités plus grandes, lesquelles se combinent en unités encore plus grandes qui, finalement, donnent lieu à un nombre infini de suites. C'est là le coeur de l'analogie, mais Jakobson est allé encore plus loin et a trouvé des analogies beaucoup plus fines, et je suis un peu gêné de devoir ajouter qu'il se réfère la explicitement à Monod."

Notes for Reading 11:
T. L. Short, "Life Among the Legisigns"

1 For example, in writings of as late as c.1907 (MS 318) Peirce identified the emotional/energetic/logical trichotomy with the immediate/dynamic/final trichotomy of interpretants, despite the fact that he based these trichotomies on different principles which,

if consistently followed, lead us to the view that the two trichotomies are not identical but intersect, yielding nine types of sign in all. Similarly, Peirce explicitly identified the final and ultimate interpretants even in the same paragraph, where he defined them quite differently (1905: MS 298). I believe that keeping these distinctions distinct gives us the best systematic reconstruction of Peirce's most mature thought. It seems to me, especially, that Peirce's late (1908) division of signs by 10 trichotomies into 66 classes depends upon there being emotional, energetic, and logical examples of *each* of the immediate, dynamic, and final types of interpretant. And it seems to me that Peirce's view that pragmatism is a theory of meaning and not of truth requires him to admit that final logical interpretants may occur in verbal as well as in ultimate form and that some ultimate interpretations may be less than final. For details, see Short (1981).

2 The late Douglas Greenlee suggested (1973: 48) that because a qualisign, in itself, is only a possibility, it is not a sign but "only an aspect or factor of any sign". Peirce of course admitted that a qualisign "cannot actually act as a sign until it is embodied . . ." (1903: 2.244). But he goes on to say that "the embodiment has nothing to do with its being a sign". The point is that even if it cannot function as a sign until it is embodied, the quality is *itself* significant. Hence, the quality is an *embodied sign* and not just *an aspect of an embodying* sign. (It will of course be the latter also; for the fact of embodiment is significant, too. But that constitutes another sign—a sinsign—with another significance.) Despite their being significant in themselves, Greenlee was right when he said that qualisigns are aspects of all other signs; for no sinsign can be such without qualities, and every legisign is a type of sinsign.

3 The ground of a sign is not to be confused with the significance which it grounds: these are two distinct relations of sign to object. Even in the case of symbols there is a distinction between the rule that specifies its interpretation and the interpretation thus specified. It follows that while significance is irreducibly triadic, the ground, in itself, need not be. When the ground is itself triadic and semeiotical, Peirce described the sign as "genuine" and all other signs as "degenerate". Symbols alone are genuine signs (1885: 3.359-363). Several commentators have thought for this or for other reasons that Peirce either held or should have held that symbols are the only real signs. But Peirce always included degenerate signs among his classes of signs. For more details, and for references, see Short 1981: 221 n. 5.

4 The principles referred to in this paragraph have been discussed in print by Weiss and Burks (1945: 383-388), and by Lieb (1953: Appendix B). Where Lieb differs from Weiss and Burks, I find that I agree with Lieb.

5 Greenlee (1973, 88) claims that "Since the sign cannot represent its object solely by virtue of dyadic action, we must look elsewhere for the ground of the sign-object relation. And again, as in the case of the icon, we shall find this ground in a symbolic connection." But mere symbols, which are always general, could never serve by themselves to pick out an individual thing. Therefore, indexical significance is irreducible to symbolic significance, and our application of symbols to individual things can only occur by means of indices. Greenlee bases the claim quoted on an example of pointing to an object; but as I explain in the text, such pointing requires a cooperation of pointing as an index of direction with other sorts of signs, and hence, does not prove or illustrate a reduction of indexical to symbolic significance. Another argument Greenlee makes for his claim is that indices signify dyadically if at all, while significance is triadic. But this confuses the ground of significance with significance itself. The ground can be dyadic, but the possibility of forming an interpretant on such a ground brings in a third factor.

6 Peirce indicates otherwise in 1904: 8.335, where he says that a symptom of disease in general is a legisign. But this would make the general type of *any* sign a legisign; so I think we must conclude that Peirce slipped here.

7 "Meaning" is not a technical term of Peirce's semeiotic, and those commentators who ask, with respect to Peirce's semeiotic rather than with respect to his pragmatism, "What

is Peirce's theory of meaning?'' are not asking a very helpful question. The same can be said of the question, ''What is Peirce's theory of reference?'' This is not to say that Peirce did not use the words ''meaning'' and ''reference'' in presenting his theory of signs; but he used them informally, sometimes to refer to one thing, sometimes as meaning another. Still, if we insist on finding a theory of reference, it would be in Peirce's account of the relation of a sign to its dynamic object: for that is what answers to what most philosophers have in mind when they speak of reference. And in the case of meaning, Peirce did come, eventually, to give ''meaning'' a technical definition as being the interpretant of a sign (c.1907: MS 318, 00238). The occasion for this seems to have been his semeiotic reformulation of the pragmatic theory of meaning, beginning in about 1903. However, Peirce sometimes spoke of the immediate interpretant and other times of the final interpretant as being the meaning of a sign, and sometimes of all three types of interpretant as three different types of meaning (c.1907: MS 318). On Peirce's view, then, ''meaning'' is best defined as referring to an *effect* which the sign is fit to produce or does produce or would eventually produce. Meaning is thus entirely different from reference.

8 I have been privileged to read in typescript portions of Professor Jarrett Brock's extensive and careful work on Peirce's theory of what Searle and others call ''speech acts''. For the tip of this particular iceberg, see Brock 1981.

9 A rigid designator will continue to refer to the same thing under any counter-factual condition under which it refers to anything at all. Thus, ''Ronald Reagan'' is a rigid designator whereas ''the President of the United States in 1981'' is not; for the former would still refer to the same person under the supposition that Jimmy Carter was re-elected, whereas the latter would not. Rigid designators cannot be symbolic or iconic; for then they would refer to whatever satisfied the general type they either describe or exemplify. Hence, they must be indexical legisigns. They continue to refer to the same things under counter-factual conditions because their significance has been established by existential connections in the actual world. It is the actual person actually named ''Ronald'' to whom we refer even under the supposition of various counter-factual conditions, such as that he lost the election or such as that he is really named ''Sylvester''. I do not mean to suggest that Peirce anticipated the important implications which Kripke has drawn from his account of rigid designation. See Kripke (1980, *passim*).

10 Peirce's commentators have been none too clear about legisigns and symbols For example, Greenlee argues (1973: 85) that all legisigns are symbolic; in particular, while Peirce classified demonstrative pronouns as indexical legisigns, Greenlee argues that they are symbolic because ''. . . it is by virtue of a convention that a demonstrative pronoun is used demonstratively; dynamical connection appears to be an unnecessary condition . . .'' But this overlooks the distinction between a convention which tells us to attend to a dynamic connection and a convention which establishes significance without further ado. One cannot know to what a pronoun refers only by hearing that pronoun and knowing the convention that governs its use. One has also to notice with what this individual instance of the pronoun is connected.

11 See my discussion (Short 1981) of ''existing for a purpose'' and ''acting for a purpose''.

12 Thus, discourse itself appears to commit us to certain aims. For a related view of the ethical import of semeiotic, see Krois 1981.

13 While I would not dare to ascribe any of the views I express here to Professor I. C. Lieb, such little sensitivity as I have to the present topic (of arguments, propositions, etc.) is due to courses I have been privileged to take from him.

14 In this way, Peirce's semeiotic leads to a unified theory of rationality in thought, *and* conduct, without reducing either form of rationality to the other. But this theory remains to be developed. See also the penultimate paragraph of the present paper.

[15] J. L. Austin once wrote (1961: 87 n.1), "With all his 66 divisions of signs, Peirce does not, I believe, distinguish between a sentence and a statement." But Peirce's analysis of assertion as a particular way of replicating certain legisigns does make that distinction, in effect. For the legisigns assertions replicate are, typically, declarative sentences, and assertive replications of these are statements. Ironically, Peirce's analysis of assertion, as making oneself liable to penalty if proven wrong, is echoed nearly to the word by Austin's own, later analysis of what is done in saying, "I know . . ." (ibid.: 66-71).

[16] All the parts of Peirce's confusion about propositions can be seen in MS 517, which has recently been dated 1904 (Fisch, Ketner, and Kloesel 1979: 17). This manuscript, which is peculiar in representing *all* signs as having replicas and, therefore, as being legisigns, has been published by Carolyn Eisele (Peirce 1904a).

Notes for Reading 12:
Floyd Merrell, "Structuralism and Beyond: A Critique of Presuppositions"

[1] The basic premises of structural linguistics were first articulated, albeit rather sketchily, by Ferdinand de Saussure (i.1906-1911). This formulation may be understood primarily as a reaction against nineteenth century historical studies of language. Consequently, Saussure's concerns lie chiefly in the realm of synchronic aspects of linguistic phenomena. During the 1930's N. S. Trubetskoy (1939) and Roman Jakobson (1931) of the Prague school of linguistics attempted to account for historical change in language without discarding the fundamental tenets of Saussurean linguistics. More recently, the Danish linguist Louis Hjelmslev (1943) set the foundation for future linguistic studies by reformulating the "structuralist" conception of language in an elaborate methodological scheme.

[2] For a perceptive critique of the particular methodologies of Lacan, Lévi-Strauss, and Piaget, see Wilden 1972.

[3] I do not include in my generalizations the "genetic structuralisms" of Piaget and Lucian Goldmann, since their methodology constitutes a departure from the "static" variety of structuralism which I scrutinize. Nevertheless, on another level, "genetic structuralism" can be subjected to a similar line of inquiry.

[4] However, see Émile Benveniste's influential critique (1966) of Saussure's concept of arbitrariness.

[5] This intransigent synchrony-diachrony opposition is part of the Saussurean conception of language. On the other hand, Jakobson was one of the first to suggest (1931) that this opposition is to a large degree illusory, that it is a convenient device for analysis rather than a particular mode of being.

[6] This presupposition leads directly to the "principle of immanence" which limits structural analysis to that which occurs in the mind, a tentative basis for the accusation that structuralism in general, and Lévi-Strauss' structuralist methodology in particular, adheres to a Kantian approach to man and his cultural products (Dubois 1969: 46-60). It is significant, therefore, that Paul Ricoeur (1963: 596-652) refers to Lévi-Strauss' structuralist method as Kantism "without a transcendental subject".

[7] Lévi-Strauss proposes (1964: 13) that it is "immaterial whether . . . the thought processes of the South American Indians take shape through the medium of my thought, or whether mine takes shape through the medium of theirs. What matters is that the human mind, regardless of the identity of those who happen to be giving it expression, should display an increasingly intelligible structure as a result of the doubly reflective forward movement of the two thought processes acting one upon the other, either of which can in turn provide the spark or tinder whose conjunction will shed light on both."

[8] Similarly, Wylie Sypher, in his study of modern art and literature, maintains (1968: 78-79) that an overemphasis on the visually perceptible qualities of art tends to "spatialize

time". Henri Lefebvre (1966: 121-76) alludes to this "spatialization" in Lévi-Strauss' variety of structuralism as a "new Eleatism". It can be provisionally concluded, then, that this static quality of orthodox structuralist methodology, as well as any other analogous view of reality, is the result of an implicit "spatialization".

[9] See also, for instance, Greimas, who maintains (1970: 13-27) that the scientific conception of the universe is that of a great "semiotic hierarchy".

[10] There has, however, been controversy concerning the respective positions of each system in the total hierarchy. For instance, Saussure originally forwarded the notion that the linguistic system is subordinate to general semiological systems. Barthes inverts this formulation suggesting the primacy of the linguistic system over all aspects of human activity. These two central propositions are antithetical, but tenable on their own grounds, as are the Kantian antinomies of thought. The argument could go on forever.

[11] Capek (1961: 299) attempts to demonstrate how this tendency of human thought to follow the "pathways of least resistance" is a psychological phenomenon and that psychology for this reason cannot be divorced from epistemology. He believes that epistemological conventions can become ingrained in the "subconscious" such that it is well nigh impossible to go beyond these conventions to view reality in a different light. The Newtonian paradigm has over the centuries become ingrained so as to "condition our minds" and prevent us from eliminating it overnight. Newtonian subconsciousness is incompatible with the conscious convictions of those modern physicists who outwardly profess allegiance to the relativity theory. These subconscious barriers must fall. Hence, the epistemology of modern physics "would profit enormously from a sort of 'psychoanalysis of knowledge' in Gaston Bachelard's sense which would unmask the inhibiting influence of our Euclidean and Newtonian subconscious in the minds of those physicists who sincerely believe themselves to be entirely free from them." In conjunction with this view of the cultural "embedding" of ideas, see Bateson 1972.

[12] This line of reasoning follows Bertrand Russell's theory of logical types. To paraphrase and simplify (I hope without doing violence to a sophisticated and quite complex theory), all entities referred to in a *corpus* submitted for analysis may be thought of as a macrosystem which includes systems of systems, all arranged in a hierarchy of classes, or types. An individual of a particular class cannot be considered as the class itself, and conversely, a class cannot be a member of itself. To do so introduces paradox. The paradox of Epimenides the Cretan who said that all Cretans were liars effectively illustrates Russell's point. In this statement a member of a particular class is considered on the same level as the class itself and the sentence is for this reason rendered nonsensical. In the context of the present commentary, to treat, as does structuralism, myths, the mind, dress codes, narrative texts, etc., *as if* they were language is to establish language as a model. However, whereas the explanatory model for structural linguistics is binarism, structuralism generally adopts binarism as a sort of "second order" model, language being the primary model. Therefore, the binary principle is for linguistics the model while for structuralism it is a metamodel, the model of a model. It is the use of this model of a model that constitutes a violation of the boundaries separating logical types and brings about a fundamental methodological problem.

[13] This is an apparent contradiction of Lévi-Strauss' notion that anthropology studies structures through space while history constitutes a "functional" study through time. The fact does remain that "primitive" societies in twentieth century Brazil exist simultaneously with comparable societies ten or more centuries past. On the other hand, Edmund Leach maintains (1970: 15-52) that Lévi-Strauss' culinary triangle and other similar devices do not depend on the temporal status of societies but apply equally well to the so-called "hot" (industrialized) and "cold" (preindustrial) societies. Similarly, Jakobson's phonemic triangle supposedly applies equally well to both "primitive" and modern languages.

[14] This is Wittgenstein's early thesis in *Tractatus Logico-Philosophicus* (1919). We may "intuit" a particular reality but on attempting to describe that reality we are lost, for its essence is, *ipso facto*, unutterable. The unutterability will be reflected in what is said but cannot be explicitly stated. Hence poetic discourse displays, but cannot tell in an objective fashion, and the reader must "intuit" that linguistic display just as the writer intuited the reality he displayed through language.

[15] Nevertheless, it was only on the basis of this Linnaean classificatory system that a viable model of evolution could be constructed (Wiener 1967: 93).

[16] Similarly, even though structuralism purports to be a holistic way of looking at man and at the world, in certain respects it is, as Capek says of the more "conservative" interpretation of relativity physics, still tied to the world view it attempts to supersede.

[17] Georg Lukacs' critique (1968: 6) of Western empirical science is analogous to my own critique, even though from a distinct vantage point. Lukacs maintains that the traditional empirical method wrenches "facts" from their living content, isolates them, and fits them into an abstract theory. Phenomena, by means of this method, are reduced "to their purely quantitative essence, to their expression in numbers and numerical relations". A method of analysis based on immediately perceivable facts fails in so far as it cannot, as does dialectical materialism, take account of the historical character of the facts and glimpse their underlying reality. Both "bourgeois science" and "vulgar Marxism" abstract the parts and prevent them "from finding their definition within the whole and, instead, the whole was dismissed as unscientific or else it degenerated into the mere 'idea' or 'sum' of the parts. With the totality out of the way, the fetishistic relations of the isolated parts appeared as a timeless law valid for every human society" (ibid.: 9). These "timeless laws" have become an ideological weapon. For the bourgeoisie, "it is a matter of life and death to understand its own system of production in terms of eternally valid categories: it must think of capitalism as being predestined to eternal survival by the eternal laws of nature and reason. Conversely, contradictions that cannot be ignored must be shown to be purely surface phenomena, unrelated to this mode of production" (ibid.: 10-11). Although Lukacs is referring to empirical "facts" in contrast to my criticism of "isolated structures", the timeless character ultimately implied in both methodologies is analogous. Julia Kristeva's contention (1967: 27-42) that one must consciously rise above the ideologies that are implicit in traditional Western World heuristic models is also comparable. Furthermore, Capek's "ingrained Newtonian mentality" prevents integration of the concrete and the abstract just as does Lukacs' ideologically motivated bourgeois science.

[18] And in Goldmann's case, structure is conceived within a deterministic Marxist framework which becomes, in the long run, a "static" explication of the "static" relationships between instantaneous structures of a given point in history.

[19] According to Lévi-Strauss (1964: 12), "Mythological analysis has not, and cannot have, as its aim to show how men think. In the particular example we are dealing with here, it is doubtful, to say the least, whether the natives of central Brazil, over and above the fact that they are fascinated by mythological stories, have any understanding of the systems of interrelations to which we reduce them . . . I, therefore, claim to show, not how men think in myths, but how myths operate in men's minds without their being aware of the fact."

[20] Newton compared the function of space to the function of the Supreme Being (see Capek 1961: 7-10, 12-15).

[21] I have taken the liberty of constructing a "structural scheme" of the relations between the Newtonian, existentialist, and structuralist world views, aware of the fact that it might appear that I am employing the very analytical method I criticize. I do, however, believe that structural schemes are economical and potentially illustrate relations between structures and between elements in a structure more effectively than the conventional expository

method. My criticism in this article is not directed toward the use of such schemes but toward the purpose for which they are used.

22 While Frederick Suppe (1974: 3-232) in a penetrating essay comments on various *Weltanschauungen* analyses of science, I will summarize what I consider the two approaches most applicable to the present study.

23 It is worthy of note that Michel Foucault develops a "structuralist" method of historical analysis which bears resemblance to that of Kuhn. Language, according to Foucault (1966), constrains and limits human mental capacities, and only within this limiting horizon can human thought processes be properly understood. These constraints reduce the parameters of mental activity to invariant "epistemes", which are used much as Kuhn's "paradigms" to portray particular *Weltanschauungen*. Compare also this line of inquiry to Althusser's "epistemological breaks", a concept introduced by Gaston Bachelard in his *La formation de l'esprit scientifique* (1938: 249) which describes "the leap from the pre-scientific world of ideas to the scientific world; this leap involves a radical break with the whole pattern and frame of reference of the pre-scientific (ideological) notions, and the construction of a new pattern".

24 Einstein once said, "If you want to find out anything from the theoretical physicists about the methods they use, I advise you to stick closely to one principle: don't listen to their words, fix your attention on their deeds" (quoted in Toulmin 1953: 16). In many cases that same advice may apply to leading structuralists, for the language they themselves use in building their models is perhaps not entirely conscious.

25 It is conceded that structuralism generally assumes a subject who is incapable of taking an "objective" stance *vis-à-vis* the object under study. He is himself an "activity" rather than an entity, when observing the object, and as such rests on a level coequal with the object. Hence subject and object apparently become mutually inclusive and complementary, and neither has any being apart from the reciprocal activity between both. Nevertheless, the picture becomes confused, for it becomes difficult to "classify" without maintaining a distance from the *corpus*. Lévi-Strauss himself states (1962b: 40-45) that structures can appear only as the result of observation from outside.

26 It has been as much as demonstrated that language is not the determinant of thought (or, by extension, world view) but that language is grounded in thought. See the studies of Piaget (1972), Vygotsky (1962), and Schaff (1964).

27 This concept relates indirectly to one aspect of the Sapir-Whorf hypothesis. Contrary to the thesis forwarded in this paper, Whorf believes that language governs an individual's perception of the universe to provide him with a particular world view. However, bracketing out this aspect of the Whorfian hypothesis, it might be stated that a language, given its syntactic structure, the breadth of its lexical repertoire, and its semantic scheme, is limited in its capacity to describe the universe from divergent and contradictory perspectives, a concept which is in line with Eddington, Bridgman, Capek, Toulmin, et al. The Hopi language, for example, contains a particular "metaphysics", just as our language reveals the "naive" Newtonian view of space and time all Western languages are specifically designed to describe. On the other hand, the Hopi language describes a particular structure of the universe which cannot be perfectly duplicated in Western languages. In the Hopi view, "time disappears and space is altered, so that it is no longer the homogeneous and instantaneous timeless space of our supposed intuition or of classical Newtonian mechanics." To extrapolate, Western languages, fettered as they are by Newtonian categories, are incapable of effectively describing the Einsteinian universe of space-time continuity, and they inexorably manifest what Capek calls "semantic inertia" (see Whorf 1956: 57-64).

Notes for Reading 14:
Umberto Eco, "On Symbols"

1 Correcting Eco's reference to *In Gen.* 9.1, i.e., Jerome c.389-392.
2 Correcting Eco's reference to *Quodlibetales* 8.6.16. *ob* 1, *ad* 1.

Notes for Reading 16:
Michael Herzfeld, ''Disemia''

[1] Editors' note: This reading is an inversion vis-à-vis the other readings in this part. Herzfeld does not so much come to a traditional sphere of culture from a semiotic perspective as take over an existing linguistic model of cultural anthropology—diglossia, as established by Ferguson—with its ideological implications of insider/outsider, in order to show that the model's own possibilities are constricted in ways that of themselves expand holistically to the postlinguistic aspects of cultural life (along with the diglossic, but paralinguistic to and beyond it and, so to speak, as *presupposed*) as soon as the model is reconceptualized semiotically, i.e., so as to focus on the signifying patterns as such (*pro toto domus et civi*) rather than (*pro parte nominali*) linguistically signifying. Herzfeld shows that the ideological implications and assumptions built into this model and ''all such models as political polarization, class-based differentiation of behavior (including kinesics and proxemics), 'folk' versus 'urban' culture and the like'', are part of a larger phenomenon which must be viewed semiotically in order to be analyzed according to its proper unity, and which he proposes to call ''Disemia''.

[2] In Ardener's formulation, the paradigmatic/syntagmatic opposition produces such pairings as opposition/conflict, exchange/transaction.

[3] H (''High'') and L (''low''), though judgmental, partially reproduce indigenous attitudes, as, e.g., the view of *katharevousa* as ''good Greek'' which then leads to the classification as *katharevousa* of urban speech forms that are not technically of that register.

[4] Cf. Ardener's (1970) *Realien*.

[5] This term is marked by one of its own most characteristic syntactic markers (fem. sing. ending in *-i'a* rather than *-i* or *-'ia*.

[6] I.e., *Ellinismos* (Neo-Classical model, extroverted and ''Europeanizing'') vs. *Romiossini* (Christian-Byzantine, introverted acknowledging Turkish and other non-European influences) (cf. Herzfeld 1981). Note that it is not only *symbols* that are dialectical (as, e.g., El Guindi and Selby 1976); shifters (cf. Silverstein 1976) indicating the lines of inclusion and exclusion may provide a means for reproducing the extroverted/introverted dialectic in immediate social interaction. When one is classified as a *ksenos* (''outsider to reference-group'') in Greek, one is shown an essentially *Ellinismos-related view of the speaker; not so, when one is treated as his dhikos* (''co-insider''), a situation which may occur within the same conversation.

[7] I.e., because the first king of the new Greek state was a Bavarian (Otho I), as were many of his advisers.

[8] *Éllinikotita*, i.e., ''Hellenic-ness''.

Notes for Reading 18:
Richard Lanigan, ''Semiotics, Communicology, and Plato's Sophist''

[1] Editors' note: ''Communicology'' is Professor Lanigan's preferred term for communication theory and the communication sciences generally.

[2] Heidegger 1968: 51: ''A thinking which thinks in models must not immediately be characterized as technological thinking, because the word 'model' is not to be understood in the technological sense as the repetition or project of something in smaller proportions. Rather, a model is that from which thinking must necessarily take off in such a way that that from which it takes off is what gives it impetus. The necessity for thinking to use thinking is related to language. The language of thinking can only start from common speech. And speech is fundamentally historico-metaphysical. An interpretation is already built into it. Viewed from this perspective, thinking has only the possibility of searching for models in order to dispense with them eventually, thus making the transition to the speculative.''

[3] While I follow the standard codex practice of using Stephanus numbers for textual citation, the edition of translations I am using is that of Hamilton and Cairns 1961. It should be further noted that I am using Letter VII for convenience of explanation; I realize that the authenticity of authorship for this letter is in dispute. It simply offers a concise statement of issues with which to begin my analysis of the dialogue *Sophist*, which is the text of concern.

[4] Editors' note: The numerous diagrams accompanying the text are here presented, in accordance with the author's original design, on the first occasion of their mention, with the exception of Figure 15, which is presented together with Figure 14 (p. 200 above) for the reason that its textual mention (p. 203 above) occurs only after the later introduction of Figure 17.

[5] I am indebted to Professor Luis Perez, University of Saskatchewan, for bringing this point to my attention.

[6] Edmund Husserl's phenomenology, with its emphasis on the transcendental Ego, would be compatible with the Platonic ontology in a way that Merleau-Ponty's existential phenomenology clearly is not. It is also important to recall that the Greeks did not have our ontological tendency to separate signifiers and signifieds: "Even a non-human object can, in the archaic period, take on a life of its own—as when an inscription on a pot reads 'I greet you'" (Havelock 1978: 99).

Note for Reading 20:
Luigi Romeo, "Heraclitus and the Foundations of Semiotics"

[1] Editors' note: A section from this article entitled *Sources for Research on Heraclitus' Semiotic Views* (Romeo 1976: 75-79) is omitted here. The omitted section contains a mainly philological discussion of more technical than general interest, but provides an overview of the history of Heraclitean scholarship during the last hundred years, in particular the establishment of editions of Heraclitus' fragments from Bywater 1877 through Diels 1903 to Pasquinelli 1958. Readers are referred to the original publication for the details of the discussion.

Notes for Reading 22:
Thomas A. Sebeok, "'Semiotics' and Its Congeners"

[1] Editors' note: Luigi Romeo, in a subsequent "re-evaluation of the derivation for the term in question" (1977), glosses this passage as follows (pp. 40-41): "as illustrated in the quotation above, the whole probing was confined to logical, medical, and even musical writings; no attempt was made to analyze the philological and lexicographic aspects of the problem, for both concordances and dictionaries reflect not only the cultural currency of the times but also the intellectual atmosphere. After all, how could one quote Galenus' 'semeiotice' without realizing that the Latin version was published much before later speculations from logic to music? Indeed, the oldest *Latin* edition is Galenus 1490." In a later note (ibid.: 47 n. 18) Romeo adds: "Russell 1939 is unaware (and Sebeok 1976: 48 [= Sebeok 1971 in References to the present collection]: along with him) that σημειωτική could not have come 'from writings on Greek music' since the chronology of the documentation in print indicates that the term existed before Meibom's and Wallis' but did not appear in Alypius. In addition, Russell himself declares he does not know whether the term was introduced by Meibom [1652]. It is, thus, obvious that Meibom, who must have read the term in either the *Thesaurus* or Scapula printed at least a century earlier, either reconstructed the Greek term by transliterating it from still earlier 'semeiotice', or borrowed it from Stephanus 1572-1573 (or Scapula 1579, 1605, 1637, 1652 [see editorial gloss on Scapula entry in References]). Moreover, the reference adduced by Russell 1939: 406, saying that 'The medical term given in Liddell and Scott is τό σημειωτικόν', constitutes an explanation that needs no elaboration, for Russell apparently never heard of philological tools such as the *Thesaurus* and its tradition".

Romeo's main abductions may be summarized by the following citation (Romeo 1977: 43): "Actually, Locke had [in his library] two editions [of the pirated abridgment of the original 1572-1573 *Thesaurus Graecae linguae* of Henricus Stephanus], Scapula 1605 and 1663. I have Scapula 1637. So, after going in circles for so long, I had no alternative than that of assuming a very simple thing: Locke, the physician, must have read Hippocrates in his younger days; but Locke, the philosopher, must have consulted Scapula in his later days. Apparently, Locke did not have Galenus' edition of 1490, or any later one edited with a Latin translation containing *semeiotice* (as well as *semioticam* and *semiotice* [Romeo 1977: 47 n. 13, adds here: "'Semiotice', with the monophthongized *ei*, would naturally be closer to Locke's 'σημιοτική as a transliteration of Latin into Greek!"]) for σημειωτική. Thus, one can presume that when Locke the philosopher was confronted with employing a term in philosophy, the medical concept of which he had acquired in his younger years, he doubtless borrowed the idea from Hippocrates' σημεῖον. But on consulting Scapula he found, among the several variants, 'σημειωτική'. And, since Scapula refers to Hippocrates, as well as because Locke must have remembered all the various allotropes involving σημ-, he must have taken Scapula's term and reference (actually the *Thesaurus*' initial reference) for granted, without rechecking the original source. On the other hand, although Locke did not have Galenus in his library, it is also possible (but not probable) that Locke read Galenus' work containing the terms *semeiotice, semioticam,* and *semiotice.*

"At my present stage of research, I personally prefer to believe that either Scapula overcame Locke (there was no *Thesaurus* in Locke's library, although this does not mean that he might not have had access to it), or Locke transliterated Galenus' 'semiotice' into Greek. No other solution now seems feasible until we locate further records evidencing that others may have used σημειωτική before the *Thesaurus Graecae linguae.* In other words, *the first time in history* that 'σημειωτική' appears as such is in the *Thesaurus* [of Stephanus, 1572-1573], then in Scapula [1605], for lexicographic purposes, and in Locke [1690] for philosophical reasons as 'σημιωτική' which suggests an influence from 'semiotice' without the Greek diphthong. If it did appear anywhere for musical or medical reasons, so far we only have evidence for Latin *semeiotice* through Galenus 1490 and later editions, but the Greek term never appeared in print *before* the *Thesaurus.* It is, indeed, significant that neither Meibom (1652) nor Wallis (1682 edition of Ptolemy c.150) was in Locke's library according to Harrison and Laslett (1965)."

Romeo concludes: "Until new documentation is brought to light (be it in future excavations at Herculaneum or in Peirce's oenological notes), the only fact we have, based on historical records, is that 'σημειωτική' never existed before it was printed in the *Thesaurus Graecae linguae.* Scapula (or Galenus) might have given the source to Locke. And Locke, via Peirce, found his way across the Atlantic into *The Century Dictionary* before returning eastward into the pages of the *Oxford English Dictionary.* If there is any instance of σημειωτική in any manuscripts still to be edited and published, let us hope that it will be made known to the scholarly world. Meanwhile, we only know that the ancients used either 'σημειω-τικος' for the *ars* and 'σημείωσις' for the action (or process) of σημεῖα in all their morphological variants. Thus, the term 'σημειωτική' and Locke's 'σημιωτική' have been borrowed from classical philology, not from medical or musical sources in post-Renaissance times. Any other account for the introduction of 'semiotics' into the discipline must remain, at present, a matter of conjecture."

These remarks, of course, concern the matter of looking at the name "semiotic" from Locke backwards, and are included here for the reader's interest and as a stimulant to further researches; but the principal interest of Sebeok's own essay for the present volume is rather its look at the name in the present context and as it indicates the main lines of development and the taking shape of semiotics today—its prospective rather than its retrospective significance.

2 Peirce (in 1903b: 5.178, but unindexed) does refer to Lambert's "large book in two volumes" on logic ("and a pretty superficial affair it is"), clearly meaning the *Neues Organon,* in whose second volume the *Semiotik* appeared; Peirce's set is still at The Johns Hopkins, although there are no annotations in it (Max H. Fisch, personal communication).

3 Besides its medical use, French *sémiotique* was also used, towards the middle of the 19th century, in a military context: "Art de faire manoeuvrer les troupes en leur indiquant les mouvements par signes . . ." (Alain Rey, personal communication), a sense for which sometimes *sémantique* was also used (Rey 1969: 6).

Notes for Reading 23:
John Deely, "Semiotic as Framework and Direction"

1 Maritain (1959: 39) summarizes his researches in the following table:

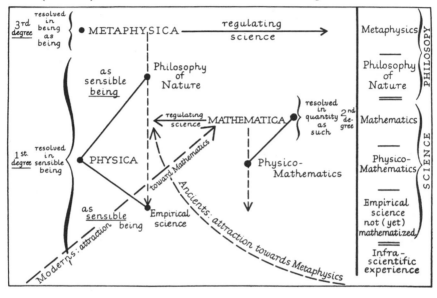

2 Derisive and divisive reference to "ancestor worship" among semioticians is sometimes used as a tactic to belittle or ostracize so far as possible semiotic developments along traditionally humanistic, literary, and philosophical lines. Indeed there is such a thing as ancestor worship, but its polemic invocation in this context is an inappropriate tactic in a misguided strategy. Present-mindedness, with its blindness to the historicity of human thought and its ideological adhesion to scientism (and covert worship of the ghosts of positivism to boot!) is a far greater threat to the healthy development and possible realization of the perspective of the doctrine of signs. Modern scholarship, with its inclination to follow into postmodern times the positivistic biases modern culture imbibed with the powerful belief that the scientific modes of understanding alone have validity (despite their reduction of experience to its merely physical and environmental components, and despite their notorious difficulty as classically conceived to account for the role of the observer, so nicely explored at the 1982 seventh Annual Meeting of the Semiotic Society of America), hardly needs these exhortations, which tend in fact to promote ignorance of the past and rediscoveries of not only the wheel but even the club. (Edmund Leach's counsel to semioticians, in his "Concluding Remarks" to the October 8-10, 1984, State-of-the-Art Research Conference organized by Professor Herzfeld, that "Peirce has been dead over sixty years; let him rot in peace"—is surely a high-water mark of modern culture in the distinctly ideological line of scientism. What are we to do with those Neill describes [1958] as "makers of the modern mind", all but one of them "rotters" dead well more than sixty years?)

We have had enough of the rhetoric of two cultures. We do not need to further this modern division within semiotics; we need to transcend it. Exhortations against "ancestor worship" as incantations to close down avenues of properly humanistic inquiry, or to replace them entirely with scientific inquiry, are radically out of place in semiotics.

What is called for is a profound understanding of both humanistic and scientific modes of investigation, in order to transform them, to render both modalities as "traditionally" (i.e., currently) understood *aufgehoben* in the higher synthesis semiotic consciousness makes possible but cannot guarantee. What is needed are new foundations. In this perspective, the attempt to polarize debate in terms of the established genres of "the commentaries of traditional scholarship" on the one hand and "the scientific constructs compatible with the tenets of logical empiricism" on the other hand (Gardin, Bouissac, and Foote 1984) already appears as a missing of the point and a regression to the confines of classical modern philosophy—that is to say, to a point before which semiosis doubtless occurs, but semiotic has yet to reach the *prise de conscience* wherein it discovers what is proper to it.

[3] A case in point is John Locke. It would be possible to include Locke in the Semiotic Society of America's Annual Meeting as a Neglected Figure in the History of Semiotic Inquiry. This statement may seem at first ludicrous, since it is well known that Locke invented the term "semiotic" as far as concerns the English speaking world, and it has long been customary to make honorific mention of his *Essay concerning Human Understanding* in this regard. How then can he be considered neglected?

Easily. For how many realize the synecdochal function played by Locke's key terms in the crucial and rich—but almost entirely unexplicated—passage in which he seemingly casually introduces the term "semiotic" into the universe of signs as the conclusion of his essay on human understanding? This is a matter on which the famous "scientific" modes of understanding, not even the most advanced neurophysiological manifestations thereof, can shed so much as a wave or a particle of light. And yet it is a matter which goes to the heart of semiotic consciousness. In fact, the re-definition of reality and the *Innenwelt-Umwelt* correspectiveness discussed in the present essay are already present in the suggestion of Locke that if "words and ideas as the great instruments of knowledge were duly weighed and distinctly considered, they would perhaps provide us with a different sort of Logic and Critic than we have hitherto been acquainted with." But to see this, just as, for example, to "see" Professor Bouissac as the founder and moving spirit of the remarkable ISISSS Institutes, it is necessary to already know something, and to think a while besides.

In the case of Locke's text, for example, it is necessary to know Aristotle's original distinction between speculative and practical knowledge, and in particular to know how this version of the distinction differs from the very version Peirce employs. It is necessary to know that "physics" was an ancient name common to all the major Greek and Latin schools as the designation for the study of nature in very specific ways distinguished from mathematics and metaphysics, a name which Locke takes over and expands synecdochically to cover the realm of speculative knowledge *tout court*, just as he takes over the term "ethics" and makes it apply by a synecdochical expansion to the entire realm of practical knowledge in the ancient sense, that is, not only to moral and ethnic questions but also to all questions of artistic and technical production as well.

Just so, "words and ideas" function in Locke's key passage in the literal or "obvious" sense of human linguistic expressions and intellectual conceptions, and also synecdochically to cover the entire range of outward expressions of inward conditions, factors, and states whereby organisms orient themselves and thrive in their environment. Already implied here is the discovery that the "observed world" is not just physical, but also objective in the special sense introduced and explained above—that is to say, it is more than can be accounted for by reduction to fact in the physical sense. "Reality", in short, is not just physical, but semiosic.

With this discovery, we are beyond the classical realism and idealism debates, and on the path of semiotic consciousness. How well and how broadly Locke sketched the foundations for this possible development will require a good deal more than passing honorific mention of his invention of a term. Until the synecdoches in Locke's seminal text—physics, ethics, logic, words, ideas—have been fully explored, he will remain in a curious way neglected.

References

Explanation of Reference Style

The present volume is intended to exhibit the synthetic and synoptic perspective, at once synchronic and diachronic, proper to the treatment of semiosis. The volume itself as a physical artifact, not just in its conceptual content, but also in its editorial design and reference style, is intended to be part of the exhibition; and, for this, it was necessary to find ways to amalgamate the economy of presentation required by scientific style with the depth of sensitivity to temporal context of sources ideally required by humanistic understanding.

The main instrument for accomplishing the synthesis aimed at is the device of "historical layering" systematized in *Semiotics 1984*: 715-739 (q.v.) as the "Style Sheet for Semiotic Society of America Proceedings", and illustrated earlier in Powell 1983 and Deely 1982. The essays for the volume, accordingly, have been edited in conformity with the plan of this Style Sheet, and the master list of references which follows is formed according to the same plan, particularly the governing principle of historical layering.

This system of layering every source historically manifests to the reader, conveniently and directly, the period of origin of each contribution to the dialogue underway, by exacting that primary reference dates throughout be taken from within the lifetime of the author of each given text or attributed insight. The system may be reduced to three essentials (*Semiotics 1984*: 716): 1. only references explicitly made in the text or notes of a presentation are included in the master reference list; 2. the reference date for every author must fall within a determinate individual lifespan—be it individual or collective (*Semiotics 1984*: 734ff.); and, 3. when a modern or secondary edition of any source—*any edition other than an original edition (including unaltered reprints) or manuscript text*—is presented or used, then the editor and/or translator or whatever 'interpreter' of the source drawn upon, *as well as* the publisher and copyright year of the edition used, must be included as part of the complete reference list, together with whatever glosses thereon might be deemed necessary or useful in the circumstances.

When this manner of reference style is properly used, two advantages accrue: the references so compiled are easily translated—by deletion of included material—into every other major style sheet (including notably the MLA and University of Chicago *Manual of Style*), whereas translations from other style sheets into the framework of historical layering can be made normally only via a library visit; and the relationship of inner discourse to experience—discourse with the world invading the self willy-nilly—as well as the experimental continuities underlying and giving comprehension to material differences of language and expression ("parole", in a word) are brought to the fore in ways likely to develop sensitivities to the historicity, the irreducibility to "physical fact", of the human condition when it comes to understanding.

Specific abbreviations employed throughout the references are properly explained here. Before a date, the prefix c. means *circa* or "approximately"; a. means *ante* or "before"; p. means *post* or "after"; i. means *inter* or "between" ("in the interval"); fl. anywhere means *floruit* or "the time of blossoming"; while q.v. means *quod vide*—the command for "take a look at" (*lit.* "which see")—or, in our case, "complete information under the author and year referred to".

Annotations are made throughout the references as seems useful.

Beyond these points, the references follow the standard techniques of existing style sheets, notably that of being arranged alphabetically by author.

AARON, Richard I.
  1937. *John Locke* (London: Oxford University Press).
ABELARD, Peter.
  i.1118-1137. *Dialectica*, first complete edition of the Parisian manuscript, ed. L. M. De Rijk (2nd,
      revised ed.; Assen: Van Gorcum, 1970).
  a.1120. *Summa Ingredientibus* or *Logica Ingredientibus*, in *Peter Abelards Philosophische Schriften*, ed. B.
      Geyer (Münster: Aschendorff, 1927).
ABRAHAMS, R. D., and R. BAUMAN.
  1971. "Sense and Nonsense in St. Vincent", *American Anthropologist* 73, 762-772.
ADLER, Mortimer J.
  1967. *The Difference of Man and the Difference It Makes* (New York: Holt, Rinehart, & Winston),
      esp. p. 320 n. 8, p. 327 n. 10, p. 331 n. 11. In this work, Adler uses "the ideas without
      the terminology" of Poinsot, or so he would have it.
  1968. "Sense Cognition: Aristotle vs. Aquinas", *The New Scholasticism* XLII (Autumn), 578-91.
d'AILLY, Pierre.
  c.1372. *Concepts and Insolubles*, an annotated translation by Paul Vincent Spade (Dordrecht, Holland:
      D. Reidel Publishing Company, 1980).
  a.1396. *Destructiones Modorum Significandi (secundum viam nominalium)*, nach Inkunabelausgaben in
      einer vorläufigen Fassung neu zusammengestellt und mit Anmerkungen versehen von
      Ludger Kaczmarek (Münster: Münsteraner Arbeitskreis für Semiotik, 1980).
ALBERTUS MAGNUS. Chronology for this reference is based on Weisheipl 1980, 1980a.
  c.1250-1252. *Ethica libri X per modum commenti*, in the Cologne edition of the *Opera Omnia*, Vol. 16,
      Part 1 (Münster: Aschendorff, 1968-1972).
  c.1250-1264. *Liber Primus et Liber Secundus Priorum Analyticorum*, in the *Opera Omnia Alberti Magni*, ed.
      Auguste Borgnet, vol. 2 (Paris: Vivès, 1890), 459-809.
  i.1254-1257. *De Anima*, Vol. VII, pt. 1 of *Opera Omnia*, ed. Clemens Stroick (Münster: Aschendorff,
      1968).
  c.1264-1270. *Libri Topicorum*, in the *Opera Omnia*, ed. Auguste Borgnet, Vol. 2 (Paris: Vivès, 1890),
      233-524.
ALPERSON, Burton L.
  1975. "In search of Buber's ghost: A calculus for interpersonal phenomenology". *Behavioral Science*
      20, 179-190.
ALTHUSSER, Louis.
  1966. *Pour Marx* (Paris: F. Maspero). The English trans. by Ben Brewster, *For Marx* (New York:
      Random House, 1970), was used.
AMMONIUS HERMEIOU.
  c.400. *Ammonius in Aristotelis de Interpretatione commentarius*, Vol. V of *Commentaria in Aristotelem graeca*,
      ed. Adolfus Busse (Berlin: G. Reimer, 1897).
ANDERSON, Myrdene, John DEELY, Martin KRAMPEN, Joseph RANSDELL, Thomas A.
      SEBEOK, and Thure von UEXKÜLL.
  1984. "A Semiotic Perspective on the Sciences: Steps toward a New Paradigm", *Semiotica* 52.1/2,
      7-47.
APOLLONIUS DYSCOLUS.
  i.100-200. *Apollonii Dyscoli quae supersunt*, II, in *Grammatici Graeci*, vol. II, iii, rec. Richard Schneider
      and Gustav Uhlig (Leipzig: Teubner, 1910).
AQUINAS, Thomas.
  1256. *Quodlibetum VII*. *Quaesitum est de quibusdam pertinentibus ad substantias spirituales, ad sacramen-*
      tum altaris, ad corpora damnatorum, in *Quaestiones Quodlibetales*, cura et studio Raymundi Spiazzi
      (9th ed.; Turin: Marietti, 1956), 132-156. (Chronology based on Weisheipl 1974: 367).
  c.1266. *Summa theologiae prima pars*, ed. P. Carmello cum textu ex recensione leonina (Turin: Marietti,
      1952).
  c.1266-1272. *In Aristotelis Librum de Anima Commentarium*, ed. A. M. Pirotta (3rd ed.; Turin: Mariet-
      ti, 1948).
  c.1269. *In decem libros ethicorum Aristotelis ad Nicomachum expositio*, cura et studio Raymundi Spiazzi
      (Turin: Marietti, 1950).
  c.1269-1272. *In libros Politicorum Aristotelis expositio*, cura et studio Raymundi P. Spiazzi (Turin: Mariet-
      ti, 1951).
  c.1269-1272a. *In libros posteriorum analyticorum expositio*. Cum textu ex recensione leonina cura et studio
      R. M. Spiazzi (Turin: Marietti, 1955).
  c.1269-1274. Uncompleted commentary (after Book II, lectio 14: see Deely 1982: 188ff. n. 16 and
      entry for Cajetan 1496) *In Aristotelis libros perihermenias expositio*, pp. 5-144 of the Spiazzi

edition based on the leonine text (1882) of this commentary together with that of St. Thomas on the *Posterior Analytics* (Turin: Marietti, 1955). English trans. in Oesterle 1962: 17-137.

1272-1273. *Summa theologiae tertia pars et supplementum*, De Rubeis, Billuart, P. Faucher et aliorum notis selectis ornata cum textu ex recensione leonina (Turin: Marietti, 1948).

ARDENER, E., ed.

1971. *Social Anthropology and Language* (London: Tavistock).

ARDENER, E. W.

1970. "Witchcraft, Economics, and the Continuity of Belief," in *Witchcraft Confessions and Accusations*, ed. M. Douglas (ASA 9; London: Tavistock).

1971. "The New Anthropology and Its Critics", *Man* n.s. 6, 449-467.

ARISTOTLE. Chronologizing based on Gauthier 1970.

c.353BC. *Refuting Sophisms* (*De Sophisticis Elenchis*), trans. W. A. Pickard-Cambridge, in McKeon, ed. 1941: 207-212 (incomplete).

c.335-334BC. *Rhetorica*, trans. W. Rhys Roberts, in Vol. XI of *The Works of Aristotle*, ed. W. D. Ross (Oxford: Clarendon Press, 1924).

c.335-334BCa. *Meteorologica*, trans. E. W. Webster, in Vol. 3 of *The Works of Aristotle*, ed. W. D. Ross (Oxford: Clarendon Press, 1931).

c.335-334BCb. *Nicomachean Ethics*, trans. W. D. Ross, in McKeon ed. 1941: 927-1112.

c.330BC. *De Interpretatione*, trans. Boethii, in *Aristoteles Latinus*, Vol. II, parts 1-2, ed. L. Minio-Paluello (Bruges and Paris: Desclée de Brouwer, 1965). English trans. by E. M. Edghill, *On Interpretation*, in McKeon, ed. 1941: 38-61.

c.330BCa. *On the Soul*, trans. J. A. Smith, in McKeon, ed. 1941: 533-603.

c.330BCb. *De Memoria et Reminicentia*, trans. J. L. Beare, in McKeon, ed. 1941: 607-617.

ARNAULD, Antoine, and Pierre NICOLE.

1662. *La Logique, ou l'Art de Penser* (Paris).

ASHBY, Hal, director.

1979. *Being There*, produced by Andrew Braunsberg (film; New York: United Artists). Film based on Kosinski 1970, q.v.

ASHLEY, Benedict.

1973. "Change and Process", in *The Problem of Evolution*, ed. John N. Deely and Raymond J. Nogar (Indianapolis: Hackett), 265-294.

AUGUSTINE of Hippo.

c.397-426. *De doctrina christiana libri quattuor*, in *Patrologiae Cursus Completus*, ed. J. P. Migne, *Series Latina* (P.L.), Vol. 34, cols. 15-122. The *édition Bénédictine* of 1949 (Paris: Desclée), in *Oeuvres de Saint Augustin*, Vol. ll, was also consulted, as was the edition recensuit et praefatus est Guilelmus M. Green, Vol. LXXX of *Corpus scriptorum ecclesiasticorum latinorum*, editum consilio et impensis Academiae Scientiarum Austriacae (Vienna: Hoelder-Pichler-Tempsky, 1963). Page references in Eco are to the English trans. by D. W. Robertson, *On Christian Doctrine* (Indianapolis: Bobbs-Merrill, 1977).

AUSTIN, J. L.

1961. *Philosophical Papers* (Oxford: Oxford University Press).

1962. *How to Do Things With Words* (Oxford: Oxford University Press).

BACHELARD, Gaston.

1938. *La formation de l'esprit scientifique: contribution à une psychanalyse de la connaissance objective* (Paris: J. Vrin).

BACHI, Riccardo.

1936. "Semiologia", entry in Vol. 31 of *Enciclopedia Italiana di Scienze, Lettere ed Arti* (Rome: Istituto della Enciclopedia Italiana), 348-349.

BACON, Francis.

1620. *Novum Organum*, ed. Thomas Fowler (Oxford, 1889); English trans. ed. by Fulton H. Anderson, *The New Organon* (Indianapolis: Bobbs-Merrill, 1960).

1623. *De Dignitate et Augmentis Scientiarum*, the first part of a planned work of which the above 1620 work formed the second part.

BACON, Roger.

c.1250. *Sumule Dialectices*, in *Opera hactenus R. Baconi*, fasc. XV, ed. R. Steele (Oxford: Clarendon Press, 1937), 191-371.

1267. *De Signis*, in K. M. Fredborg, L. Nielsen, and Jan Pinborg, "An Unedited Part of Roger Bacon's 'Opus Maius': 'De signis'", *Traditio* 34 (1978), 75-136.

BAER, Eugen.

1985. "The Unconscious Icon: Topology and Tropology", in *Iconicity: Essays on the Nature of Culture* (Festschrift for Thomas A. Sebeok), ed. Paul Bouissac, Michael Herzfeld, and Roland Posner (Tübingen: Stauffenburg, in press).

1983. *Medical Semiotics: The State of the Art* (forthcoming). This remarkable manuscript has recently been contracted as a volume in the University Press of America Sources in Semiotics series, to appear updated and revised according to the SSA Proceedings "Style Sheet" in late 1986.

BALLARD, Carroll, director.
1979. *The Black Stallion*, produced by Fred Roos and Tom Sternberg (film; New York: United Artists).

BAMBROUGH, Renford.
1961. "Universals and Family Resemblances", *Proceedings of the Aristotelian Society* 61, 207-222.

BARTHES, Roland.
1953. *Le degré zéro de l'écriture* (Paris: Éditions du Seuil). English trans. by Annette Lavers and Colin Smith, *Writing Degree Zero* (New York: Hill and Wang, 1968).
1957. *Mythologies* (Paris: Éditions du Seuil). Incomplete English trans. by Annette Lavers, *Mythologies* (New York: Hill and Wang, 1972).
1964. *Eléments de sémiologie*, in *Communications*, no. 4 (Paris: Seuil), 91-135, trans. by Annette Lavers and Colin Smith as *Elements of Semiology* (London: Jonathan Cape, 1967; American edition with pagination unchanged, New York: Hill and Wang, 1968). References in Sebeok are to the French ed.; references in Merrell and Lanigan are to the English trans.
1966. "Introduction à l'analyse structurale des écrits", *Communications* 8 (1966), 1-27.
1972. "Sémiologie et médecine", in *Les sciences de la folie*, ed. Roger Bastide (Paris: Mouton), 37-46.
1977. *Leçon* (Paris: Editions du Seuil). Trans. as "Lecture in inauguration of the chair of literary semiology, Collège de France", *October* 8 (1979), 3-16. Also trans. as "Inaugural Lecture, Collège de France", in *A Barthes Reader*, ed. Susan Sontag (New York: Hill and Wang, 1982), 457-458.

BATESON, Gregory.
1972. "Style, Grace, and Information in Primitive Art", in *Steps to an Ecology of Mind* (New York: Ballantine Books), 128-152.

BEAL, Edward.
1896. *Cardinal Rules of Legal Interpretation* (London: Stevens and Songs).

BENSE, Max.
1967. *Semiotik: Allgemeine Theorie der Zeichen* (Baden-Baden: Agis).

BENVENISTE, Emile.
1952. "Animal Communication and Human Language: The Language of the Bees", *Diogenes* 1, 1-7.
1966. "La nature du signe linguistique", in *Problèmes de linguistique générale* (Paris: Gallimard), 49-55.
1969. "Semiologie de la langue", *Semiotica* 1, 1-12; 127-135.

BERGER, Arthur Asa.
1982. *Media Analysis Techniques* (Beverly Hills/London/New Delhi: Sage Publications), particularly Part I.1., "Semiological Analysis", 14-43.

BERGSON, Henri.
1932. *Les Deux Sources de la Morale et de la Religion*, 7th ed. (Paris: Alcan). English trans. by R. A. Audra and C. Brereton, *The Two Sources of Morality and Religion* (New York: Henry Holt, 1935).

BERKELEY, George.
1710. *A Treatise Concerning the Principles of Human Knowledge*, complete and unabridged text in *The English Philosophers from Bacon to Mill*, ed. E. A. Burtt (New York: The Modern Library, 1939), 509-579.
1732. *Alciphron, or the Minute Philosopher*, Volume III of *The Works of George Berkeley, Bishop of Cloyne*, ed. T. E. Jessop (London: Thomas Nelson and Sons, 1950).

BEROLZHEIMER, Fritz.
1904-1907. *System der Rechts-und Wirtschaftsphilosophie* (Munich: Beck). The English translation by R. S. Jastrow, *The World's Legal Philosophies* (Boston: The Boston Book Company, 1912), was used.

BERTALANFFY, Ludwig von.
1967. *Robots, Men and Minds* (New York: George Braziller).

BLOOMFIELD, Leonard.
1939. *Linguistic Aspects of Speech* (Chicago: University of Chicago Press).

BOCHENSKI, I. M.
1954. *Die Zeitgenössischen Denkmethoden* (Bern, Switzerland: Francke Verlag), trans. by Peter Caws as *The Methods of Contemporary Thought* (Dordrecht, Holland: D. Reidel Publishing Co., 1965; reprinted New York: Harper Torchbook, 1968). Page references are to the Harper reprint.

1970. *A History of Formal Logic*, translated and edited "with the author's full concurrence" by
       Ivo Thomas from *Formale Logik* (Freiburg: Verlag Karl Alber, 1956) (2nd ed., with cor-
       rections; New York: Chelsea Publishing Company).
BOEHNER, Philotheus.
1957. "Introduction" to *Ockham. Philosophical Writings*, edited and presented in bilingual format
       (London: Thomas Nelson and Sons, Ltd.), ix-lix.
BOHR, Niels.
1958. *Atomfysik og menneskelig erkendelse* (Copenhagen: Schultz). The English translation, *Atomic
       Physics and Human Science* (New York: John Wiley, 1958), was used.
BOISACQ, Emile.
1916. *Dictionnaire éthymologique de la Langue grecque étudiée dans ses rapports avec les autres langues indo-
       européennes* (Heidelberg: Universitätbuchhandlung).
BOOLE, George.
1847. *The Mathematical analysis of Logic, being an essay toward a calculus of deductive reasoning* (Lon-
       don: Cambridge).
BOS, Egbert P.
1983. "Introduction" to Marsilius of Inghen, *Treatises on the Properties of Terms* (Dordrecht: D.
       Reidel), 3-48.
BOSSEREL, J. B.
1615. *Synopses in quibus doctrina dialectica R. [i] P. [i] Petri Fonseca ad Ordinem Aristotelicum revocatur, Anno
       Domini 1615* (University of Graz MS 133; reprinted in Ferreira Gomes 1964, II, 779-861).
BOUCHÉ-LECLERQ, Auguste.
1879-1882. *Histoire de la divination dans l'antiquité*, in 4 vols. (Paris: Leroux).
BOUISSAC, Paul.
1977. "Semiotics and Spectacles", in *A Perfusion of Signs*, ed. T. A. Sebeok (Bloomington: In-
       diana University Press).
BRÉAL, Michael.
1900. *Semantics. Studies in the Science of Meaning* (New York: Holt).
BRIDGMAN, Percy W.
1950. *Reflections of a Physicist* (New York: Philosophical Library).
1959. *The Way Things Are* (Cambridge: Harvard University Press).
BRINTON, Crane.
1936. "The New History: Twenty-Five Years After", *Journal of Social Philosophy* I (January),
       134-137.
BROCK, Jarrett.
1981. "An Introduction to Peirce's Theory of Speech Acts," *Transactions of the Charles S. Peirce
       Society*, 17.4 (Fall), 319-326.
BROGLIE, Louis de.
1937. *La physique nouvelle et les quanta* (Paris: Flammarion). The English trans. by Ralph W.
       Niemeyer, *The Revolution in Physics: A Non-mathematical Survey of Quanta* (New York: The
       Noonday Press, 1953) was used.
BRONOWSKI, Jacob.
1955. *The Common Sense of Science* (Cambridge: Harvard University Press).
BROUWER, L. E. J.
1913. "Intuitionism and Formalism", *American Mathematical Society Bulletin* 20, 81-96.
1927. *Consciousness, Philosophy, and Mathematics*. Unpublished MS.
BROWN, Clarence, director.
1944. *National Velvet*, produced by Pandro S. Berman (film; Metro-Goldwyn-Mayer).
BÜHLER, Karl.
1934. *Sprachtheorie: Die Darstellungsfunktion der Sprache* (Reprint ed.; Stuttgart: Gustav Fisher, 1965).
BURNET, John.
1908. *Early Greek Philosophy* (2nd ed.; London: A. & C. Black). The French trans. by A. Rey-
       mond, *L'aurore de la philosophie grecque* (Paris: Payot, 1919), was also used.
BURNYEAT, M. F.
1979. "The Virtues of Plato", *New York Review of Books*, September 27, 56-60.
BUYSSENS, Eric.
1943. *Les langages et le discours: Essai de linguistique fonctionnelle dans le cadre de la sémiologie* (Brussels:
       J. Lebègue). A revised version is incorporated in Buyssens, *La communication et l'articula-
       tion linguistique* (Brussels: Presses Universitaires, 1967).
BYWATER, Ingram, ed.
1877. *Heracliti Ephesii reliquae* (Oxford: E Typographo Clarendoniano).

CAHALAN, John C.
1985. *Causal Realism. An essay on philosophical method and the foundations of knowledge* (= Sources in Semiotics, Volume II; Lanham, MD: University Press of America).
CAIRNS, Huntington.
1962. *Law and Its Premises* (New York: Association of the Bar of the City of New York).
CAJETAN, Thomas de Vio ("Thomas Gaeta").
1496. *Commentaria in reliquum libri secundi peri hermenias*, in *Sancti Thomae Aquinatis Opera Omnia*, Leonine ed., Tomus Primus (Rome: 1882, ed. Zigliara), pp. 87-128. English translation in Oesterle 1962: 139-255.
1507. *Commentaria in Summam Theologicam. Prima Pars* (Rome). Reprinted in the Leonine ed. of the *Sancti Thomae Aquinatis Doctoris Angelici Opera Omnia*, vols. 4 and 5 (Rome, 1888-1889).
CAPEK, Milic.
1961. *The Philosophical Impact of Contemporary Physics* (New York: American Book Company).
CARNAP, Rudolf.
1934. *Logische Syntax der Sprache* (Vienna), published in English trans. by Amethe Smeaton, with additions, as *The Logical Syntax of Language* (London: Routledge & Kegan Paul, 1937).
1942. *Introduction to Semantics* (Cambridge, MA: Harvard University Press).
CARROLL, Ronald C., and Carol A. HOFFMAN.
1980. "Chemical feeding deterrent mobilized in response to insect herbivory and counteradaptation by *Epilachna tredecimnotata*", *Science* 209 (July 18), 414-416.
CASSIRER, Ernst.
1923-1929. *Philosophie der symbolischen Formen*, in 3 vols. (Berlin: Bruno Cassirer). English trans. in 3 vols. by Ralph Mannheim, *The Philosophy of Symbolic Forms* (New Haven: Yale University Press, 1955-57). Page refs. are to Eng. Vol I.
CATAUDELLA, Quintino, ed.
1958. *I frammenti dei Presocratici tradotti* (Padua: Cedam).
CAWS, Peter.
1970. "What Is Structuralism?", in Hayes and Hayes 1970 [q.v.]: 197-215.
CHARBONNIER, Georges.
1961. *Entretiens avec Claude Lévi-Strauss* (Paris: Plon, Julliard). English trans. by John Weightman and Doreen Weightman, *Conversations with Claude Lévi-Strauss* (London: Jonathan Cape, 1969).
COHEN, Jonathan.
1975. *Spoken and Unspoken Meanings* (Lisse, Netherlands: Peter de Ridder Press).
COHEN, Morris R., and NAGEL, Ernest.
1934. *An Introduction to Logic and Scientific Method* (New York: Harcourt, Brace & World).
COLLINGWOOD, R. G.
1936-1940. *The Idea of History*, posthumous publication (Oxford: Oxford University Press, 1946).
1939. *An Autobiography* (Oxford: Oxford University Press).
COMAS DEL BRUGAR, Miguel ("Michael Comas").
1661. *Quaestiones minoris dialecticae* (Barcelona: Antonius Lacavalleria). Available in Lilly Library, Indiana University, Bloomington; on microfilm at Loras College Library, Dubuque, IA.
COMPAGNON, André.
1979. *La Seconde Main* (Paris: Seuil).
CONIMBRICENSES.
1607. "De Signis", being Chap. 1 of their commentary on Aristotle's *De Interpretatione*, in *Commentarii Collegii Conimbricensis et Societatis Jesu. In Universam Dialecticam Aristotelis Stagiritae. Secunda Pars* (Lyons: Sumptibus Horatii Cardon), 4-67.
CONKIN, Paul K., and Roland N. STROMBERG.
1971. *The Heritage and Challenge of History* (New York: Dodd, Mead & Co).
COPI, Irving M.
1982. *Introduction to Logic* (6th ed.; New York: Macmillan).
COSERIU, Eugenio.
1969. *Die Geschichte der Sprachphilosophie von der Antike bis zur Gegenwart. Eine Übersicht (Teil I: Von der Antike bis Leibniz)*, autorisierte Nachschrift besorgt von Gunter Narr und Rudolf Windisch (Stuttgart: Polyfoto).
COUNT, Earl W.
1969. "Animal Communication in Man-Science", in *Approaches to Animal Communication*, ed. Thomas A. Sebeok and Alexandra Ramsay (The Hague: Mouton), 71-130.
CREUZER, G. F.
1810-1812. *Symbolik und Mythologie der alten Völker* (Leipzig and Darmstadt: Leske).

CRICK, M.
1976.   *Explorations in Language and Meaning* (New York: John Wiley).
CSIKSZENTMIHALYI, Mihaly, and Eugene ROCHBERG-HALTON.
1978.   "Reflections on materialism: People and Things", *University of Chicago Magazine* 70.3, 7-15.
CULLER, Jonathan.
1973.   "The Linguistic Base of Structuralism", in *Structuralism: An Introduction*, ed. David Robey
          (Oxford: Clarendon Press), 20-36.
1976.   *Structuralist Poetics: Structuralism, Linguistics and the Study of Literature* (Ithaca, NY: Cornell
          University Press).
DALBIEZ, Roland.
1936.   *La méthode psychoanalytique et la doctrine freudienne* (Paris: Desclée de Brouwer). English trans.
          by T. F. Lindsay, *Psychoanalytical Method and the Doctrine of Freud*, in 2 vols. (London:
          Longmans, Green and Co., 1941).
DALGARNO, George.
1661.   *Ars signorum, vulgo character universalis et lingua philosophica, etc.* (London: Excudebat J. Hayes,
          sumptibus Authoris).
DANTE ALIGHIERI.
i.1312-1317. *Epistula XIII*, Latin with Italian trans. in *Opere minori*, ed. Alberto del Monte (2nd ed.;
          Milan: Rizzoli Editore, 1966), 793-816.
DARWIN, Charles.
1872.   *The Expression of the Emotions in Man and Animals* (London: John Murray).
DE LUBAC, Henri.
1959.   *Exégèse Médiévale, Les Quatre Sens de l'Ecriture*, Part 1 (Paris: Aubier).
1962.   *Exégèse Médiévale, Les Quatre Sens de l'Ecriture*, Part 2 (Paris: Aubier).
DE MORGAN, Augustus.
1847.   *Formal Logic, or the calculus of inference, necessary and probable* (London).
DE RUGGIERO, Guido.
1967.   *La filosofia greca*, Vol. I of *Storia della filosofia* (Bari: Laterza).
DEELY, John N.
1971.   *The Tradition Via Heidegger* (The Hague: Martinus Nijhoff).
1971a.   "The Myth as Integral Objectivity", ACPA *Proceedings* XLV, 67-76.
1972.   "The Ontological Status of Intentionality", *The New Scholasticism* XLVI, 220-233.
1972a.   "How Language Refers", *Studi Internazionali di Filosofia* 4, 41-50.
1974.   "The Two Approaches to Language. Philosophical and Historical Reflections on the Point
          of Departure of Jean Poinsot's Semiotic", *The Thomist* XXXVII.4 (October), 856-907.
1975.   "Modern Logic, Animal Psychology, and Human Discourse", *Revue de l'Université d'Ot-
          tawa* 45.1 (janvier-mars), 80-100.
1975a.   "Reference to the Non-Existent", *The Thomist* XXXIX.2 (April), 253-308.
1976.   "The Doctrine of Signs: Taking Form at Last", *Semiotica* 18.2, 171-193. (Essay review
          of Eco 1976.)
1977.   " 'Semiotic' as the Doctrine of Signs", *Ars Semeiotica* 1.3, 41-68.
1978.   "What's in a Name?", *Semiotica* 22.1-2, 151-181 (essay review of Sebeok 1976).
1978a.   "Toward the Origin of Semiotic", in *Sight, Sound, and Sense*, ed. Thomas A. Sebeok (Bloom-
          ington: Indiana University Press), 1-30. This work erroneously conjectured (p. 7) that
          "the explicit thematization and appellation of the division of signs into formal and in-
          strumental may well have been original with Poinsot." Romeo (1979), working from Her-
          culano de Carvalho 1970 (q.v.), shows that while Poinsot's thematization in Book II,
          Question 2, of the *Treatise* was indeed original, the appellation of this contrast was already
          in use with Petrus Fonsecus' *Institutionum dialecticarum libri octo* (1564), a work with which
          Poinsot was certainly familiar. See Romeo 1979: 194-195, for a translation of Fonseca's
          summary remarks "about formal and instrumental signs". Further in Doyle 1984.
1978b.   "Semiotic and the Controversy over Mental Events", ACPA *Proceedings* LII, 16-27.
1980.   "The Nonverbal Inlay in Linguistic Communication", in *The Signifying Animal*, ed.
          Irmengard Rauch and Gerald F. Carr (Bloomington: Indiana University Press), 201-217.
1980a.   "Antecedents to Peirce's Notion of Iconic Signs", in *Semiotics 1980* (Proceedings of the
          Semiotic Society of America), ed. Margot Lenhart and Michael Herzfeld (New York:
          Plenum), 109-120.
1981.   "Cognition from a Semiotic Point of View", in *Semiotics 1981*, ed. John N. Deely and
          Margot D. Lenhart (New York: Plenum, 1983), 21-28.
1982.   *Introducing Semiotic. Its History and Doctrine* (Bloomington: Indiana University Press).
1983.   "Neglected Figures in the History of Semiotic Inquiry: John Poinsot", in Eschbach and
          Trabant 1983: 115-126.

1985. "Editorial Afterword" (EA, 391-415), Semiotic Markers, notes, and indices to Poinsot 1632a (q.v.), including an exhaustive discussion of the "nationality" and proper name of this author.

1985a. *Logic as a Liberal Art* (Queen's University: Toronto Semiotic Circle Monograph, Volume 2, 1985). Extensive discussion of Umwelt, Innenwelt, and related notions.

1985b. "Semiotic and the Liberal Arts", *The New Scholasticism* LIX.3 (Summer), 296-322.

DELBRÜCK, Max, J. DEGENKOLBE, and K. H. LESTER.

1977. "Discussion to IV. light and dark adaptation of the photoreceptor cell", *Biophysics of Structure and Mechanism* 3:181-182.

DELBRÜCK, Max. A. KATZIR, and David PRESTI.

1976. "Responses of Phycomyces indicating optical excitation of the lowest triplet state of riboflavin", *Proceedings of the National Academy of Science* (Washington), 78 (1969-1973).

DERRIDA, Jacques.

1967. *De la grammatologie* (Paris: Éditions de Minuit). References in Romeo are to this edition; references in Baer are to the English translation by Gayatri Chakravorty Spivak, *Of Grammatology* (Baltimore: Johns Hopkins University Press, 1976).

1967a. *L'Ecriture et la Différance* (Paris: Editions du Seuil). Page references are to the English trans. by Alan Bass, *Writing and Difference* (Chicago: University of Chicago Press, 1978).

1970. "La Structure, le signe et le jeu dans le discours des sciences humaines", ms. trans. as "Structure, Sign, and Play in the Discourse of the Human Sciences", in *The Languages of Criticism and the Sciences of Man*, ed. Richard Macksey and Eugenio Donato (Baltimore: Johns Hopkins Press), 247-265.

1977. "Limited Inc abc . . .", trans. Samuel Weber, *Glyph* 2 (Johns Hopkins Textual Studies), 162-254.

DESCARTES, René.

1637. "Discourse on the Method of Rightly Conducting the Reason and Seeking for Truth in the Sciences", trans. Elizabeth S. Haldane and G. R. T. Gross, in *The Philosophical Works of Descartes* (corrected reprint edition; New York: Dover, 1955), I, 79-130.

1641. *Meditations on First Philosophy*, trans. Elizabeth S. Haldane and G. R. T. Gross, in *The Philosophical Works of Descartes* (corrected reprint edition; New York: Dover, 1955), I, 131-199.

1648. Letter to Picot in *Oeuvres de Descartes*, ed. Charles Adam and Paul Tannery (Paris: 1897-1910), Vol. IX, 1-20.

DIELS, Hermann, ed.

1903. *Die Fragmente der Vorsokratiker*. The 1975 ed. of this work by Walther Kranz (Zürich: Weidmann) was used.

DIETZE, Gottfried.

1964. "The Limited Rationality of Law", in *Rational Decision*, ed. W. Friedrich (New York: Atherton Press), 63-88.

DOBZHANSKY, Theodosius.

1962. *Mankind Evolving* (New Haven: Yale University Press).

DODDS, John H., and Michael A. HALL.

1980. "Plant hormone receptors", *Scientific Progress, Oxford* 66, 513-535.

DOYLE, Arthur Conan.

1892. "The Adventure of Silver Blaze", *The Strand Magazine*, 4 (December), 645-660.

DOYLE, John P.

1983. "Suarez on Truth and Mind-Dependent Beings: Implication for a Unified Semiotic", in *Semiotics 1983* (Proceedings of the Eighth Annual Meeting of the Semiotic Society of America), ed. John N. Deely and Jonathan Evans, with assistance from Margot D. Lenhart (in preparation).

1984. "The *Conimbricenses* on the Relations Involved in Signs", in *Semiotics 1984*, ed. John N. Deely (Washington: University Press of America), 567-576. Breakthrough presentation of research into Poinsot's immediate semiotic predecessors.

DRYSCH, K.

1980. "Tagesverlauf der Kohlendioxidkonzentration im Experimentalgewächshaus" (LOGID/ Schempp). Working paper (mimeographed), Institut für Arbeits- und Sozialmedizin, Universität Tübingen.

DU BOULAY, J.

1974. *Portrait of a Greek Mountain Village* (Oxford).

DUBOIS, Jean.

1969. "Estructuralismo y lingüística", trans. Antonio G. Valiente, in *Estructuralismo y marxismo* (Barcelona: Ediciones Martínez Roca), 46-60.

DUMITRIU, Anton.
    1977.   *A History of Logic*, being a revised, updated and enlarged 4-vol. ed. of the 1-vol. Rouman-
             ian work *Istoria Logica* (Bucharest: Editura Didactica, 1975), trans. Duiliu Zamfirescu,
             Dinu Giurcaneanu, and Doina Doneaud (Turnbridge Wells, Kent, England: Abacus Press):
             Vol. I.   Logic in Non-European Cultures. Logic in Ancient Greece. Rhetors and Com-
                        mentators.
             Vol. II.   Scholastic Logic. Renaissance Logic.
             Vol. III. Methodological Logic. Development of Modern Logic.
             Vol. IV.   Mathematical Logic.
DUMMETT, Michael.
    1967.   "Frege, Gottlob", in *The Encyclopedia of Philosophy*, ed. Paul Edwards (New York: The
             Free Press), Vol. 3, 225-237.
ECO, Umberto.
    1968.   *La struttura assente: Introduzione alla ricerca semiologica* (Milan: Bompiani). German version,
             Einführung in die Semiotik (Munich: Fink, 1972). Cf. Paolo Valesio's 1971 review article,
             "Toward a Study of the Nature of Signs", *Semiotica* 3, 155-85.
    1975.   *Trattato di semiotica generale* (2nd ed.; Milan: Bompiani).
    1976.   *A Theory of Semiotics* (Bloomington: Indiana University Press). Reviewed in Deely 1976.
    1979.   *The Role of the Reader* (Bloomington: Indiana University Press).
    1980.   "Current Issues in Semiotic Theory", lecture course given at the first International Summer
             Institute for Semiotic and Structural Studies (ISISSS '80; Toronto, June 2-27).
    1980a.   *Il nome della rosa* (Milan: Bompiani). Page references are to the English trans. by William
             Weaver, *The Name of the Rose* (New York: Harcourt Brace Jovanovich, 1983).
    1984.   *Semiotics and the Philosophy of Language* (Bloomington: Indiana University Press).
    1985.   "Latratus Canis", *Tijdschrift voor Filosofie* 47.1 (March), 3-14.
ECO, Umberto, Roberto LAMBERTINI, Costantino MARMO, and Andrea TABARRONI.
    1984.   "On Animal Language in the Medieval Classification of Signs", *Versus* 38/39 (maggio-
             dicembre), 3-38.
ECO, Umberto, and Thomas A. SEBEOK, eds.
    1983.   *The Sign of Three. Dupin, Holmes, Peirce* (Bloomington: Indiana University Press).
EDDINGTON, Arthur.
    1958.   *The Philosophy of Physical Science* (Ann Arbor: The University of Michigan Press).
EHRENZWEIG, Anton.
    1967.   *The Hidden Order of Art* (Berkeley: University of California Press).
EL GUINDI, F., and H. A. SELBY.
    1976.   "Dialectics in Zapotec Thinking", in *Meaning in Anthropology*, ed. K. Basso and H. Selby
             (Albuquerque, NM: University of New Mexico Press).
ESCHBACH, Achim.
    1978.   "Einleitung" to his trans. of Smart 1831, 1837, 1839 as one (see Deely 1982: 215, 230).
ESCHBACH, Achim, and Jürgen TRABANT, eds.
    1983.   *History of Semiotics* (= Foundations of Semiotics, Vol. 7) (Amsterdam: John Benjamins).
FARIS, J. C.
    1968.   "Validation in Ethnographical Description", *Man* n.s. 3. 112-124.
FERGUSON, C. A.
    1959.   "Diglossia", *Word* 15, 325-340.
FERREIRA GOMES, Joaquim.
    1964.   Introdução, Estabelecimento do Texto, Tradução e Notas for Fonseca 1564, q.v.
FERRI, S.
    1916.   "Saggio di classificazione degli oracoli", *Athaeneum* IV, 396-415.
FILLMORE, C. J.
    1971.   "Verbs of Judging", in *Studies in Linguistic Semantics*, ed. C. J. Fillmore and D. T. Langen-
             doen (New York: Holt, Rinehart & Winston).
FIRTH, Raymond.
    1973.   *Symbols Public and Private* (London: Allen & Unwin).
FISCH, Max H.
    1942.   "Justice Holmes, the Prediction Theory of Law, and Pragmatism", *Journal of Philosophy*
             39.12, 85-97.
    1964.   "Was There a Metaphysical Club in Cambridge?", in *Studies in the Philosophy of Charles
             S. Peirce. Second Series*, ed. Edward C. Moore and Richard S. Robin (Amherst: Univer-
             sity of Massachusetts Press), 3-32.
    1980.   "Foreword" to *"You Know My Method": A Juxtaposition of Charles S. Peirce and Sherlock Holmes*,
             by Thomas A. Sebeok and Jean Umiker-Sebeok (Bloomington: Gaslight Publications), 7-13.

FISCH, Max H., Kenneth Laine KETNER, and Christian J. W. KLOESEL.
    1979. "The New Tools of Peirce Scholarship, With Particular Reference to Semiotic", *Peirce Studies* 1 (Lubbock: Institute for Studies in Pragmaticism), 1-17.

FISHMAN, Joshua A.
    1967. "Bilingualism with and without Diglossia; Diglossia with and without Bilingualism", *Journal of Social Issues* 23, 29-38.

FONSECA, Petrus ("Pedro da").
    1564. *Institutionum dialecticarum libri octo* (Coimbra: Apud haeredes Joannis Blauij). The most important edition of this work thus far is the bilingual presentation comparable to Poinsot 1632 (q.v.) of Joaquim Ferreira Gomes, *Instituições Dialecticas (Institutionum dialecticarum libri octo)*, 2 vols. (Instituto de Estudos Filosoficos da Universidad de Coimbra, 1964). Discussion in Romeo 1979.

FOUCAULT, Michel.
    1961. *Histoire de la folie à l'âge classique* (Paris: Plon). The English trans. by Richard Howard, *Madness and Civilization* (London: Lowe and Brydone Printers, Ltd., 1965), was used.
    1963. "Préface à la transgression", *Critique*, 19.195-196, 751-769. The English trans. by Donald F. Bouchard and Sherry Simon, "A Preface to Transgression", in Michel Foucault, *Language, Counter-Memory, Practice: Selected Essays and Interviews*, ed. Donald F. Bouchard (Ithaca: Cornell University Press, 1977), 29-52, was used.
    1966. *Les Mots et les choses: une archéologie des sciences humaines* (Paris: Gallimard). The English translation, *The Order of Things: An Archaeology of the Human Sciences* (New York: Pantheon, 1970), was used.
    1969. *L'Archéologie du savoir* (Paris: Gallimard). The English trans. by A. M. Sheridan-Smith, *The Archaeology of Knowledge* (New York: Pantheon/Random House, 1972), was used.
    1971. *L'Ordre du discours* (Paris: Gallimard). English translation by Rupert Swyer, "The Discourse on Language", *Social Science Information*, April 1971, 7-30. Page references are to the reprint of this translation in Michel Foucault, *The Archaeology of Knowledge* (New York: Pantheon/Random House, 1972), 215-237.

FRANK, Jerome.
    1930. *Law and the Modern Mind* (New York: Doubleday).

FRASER, Alexander Campbell.
    1894. "Prolegomena", Notes, and Critical Apparatus to new edition of John Locke, *An Essay concerning Human Understanding* (Oxford).

FREEMAN, Kathleen.
    1946. *The Pre-Socratics: A Companion to Diels, Fragmente der Vorsokratiker* (Oxford: Blackwell).
    1948. *Ancilla to the Pre-Socratic Philosophers* (Oxford: Blackwell).

FREGE, Gottlob.
    1879. *Begriffsschrift, eine der arithmetischen nachgebildete Formelsprache des reinen Denkens* (Halle).

FREUD, Sigmund.
    1900. *Die Traumdeutung* (Leipzig and Vienna: Franz Deuticke). The English translation under the general editorship of James Strachey, *The Interpretation of Dreams*, in Vols. 4-5 of *The Standard Edition of the Complete Psychological Works of Sigmund Freud* (London: Hogarth Press, 1953), Vol. 4, 1-338; Vol. 5, 339-627, was used.
    1905. *Der Witz und seine Beziehung zum Unbewussten* (Leipzig and Wien: Deuticke). The English trans. under the general editorship of James Strachey, *Jokes and their Relation to the Unconscious*, Vol. 8 of *The Standard Edition of the Complete Psychological Works of Sigmund Freud* (London: Hogarth Press, 1960), was used.
    1920. *Jenseits des Lust-Prinzips* (Leipzig: Internationaler Psychoanalytischer Verlag). The English translation under the general editorship of James Strachey, *Beyond the Pleasure Principle*, in Volume 18 of *The Standard Edition of the Complete Psychological Works of Sigmund Freud* (London: Hogarth Press, 1955), 7-134, was used.
    1937. "Die endliche und die unendliche Analyse", *Internationale Zeitschrift für Psychoanalyse* 23.2, 209-40. The English translation under the general editorship of James Strachey, "Analyses Terminable and Interminable", in Volume 23 of *The Standard Edition of the Complete Psychological Works of Sigmund Freud* (London: Hogarth Press, 1953-74), 216-253, was used.

FRIEDL, E.
    1962. *Vasilika: A Village in Modern Greece* (New York: Holt, Rinehart & Winston).

FRIEDMAN, Lawrence.
    1975. *The Legal System* (New York: Russell Sage).

FRISCH, Karl von.
    1950. *Bees, Their Vision, Chemical Senses, and Language* (Ithaca: Cornell University Press).

FUTUYMA, D. J.
   1979.   *Evolutionary Biology* (Sunderland, MA: Sinauer Association).
GALENUS, Claudius.
   c.150-200.   *Claudii Galeni Opera omnia*, in 22 vols., ed. Carolus Gottlob Kuhn (Leipzig: Cnobloch,
            1821-1833). Semiotics is discussed, in this standard edition, in Vol. XIV: 689ff., 693,
            and in Vol. XVIII [B]: 633. Though not complete, this edition is bilingual (Greek and
            Latin), and is available in a recent reprint (Hildesheim: Olms, 1965). The Venice edition
            (Per Philipum de Caneto Impressa, 1490) is referred to by Romeo. For bibliographical
            details concerning Galen's writings, see Sarton 1954: Ch. IV.
GALLIE, W. B.
   1964.   *Philosophy and the Historical Understanding* (New York: Schocken Books).
GANDELSONAS, Mario, *et al.*
   1970.   "Semiología arquitectonica", *Summa* 32, 69-82.
GARDIN, Jean-Claude, Paul BOUISSAC, and Kenneth E. FOOTE.
   1984,   June 15, October 10. "A Program for Semiotics", position paper circulated among the
            participants of the fifth International Semiotic Summer Institute for Semiotic and Structural Studies
            (ISISSS 84) for signatures (none were obtained), and re-presented polemically by Paul
            Bouissac at an afternoon session of the Research Conference "Semiotics: Field or
            Discipline?" held at the Bloomington campus of Indiana University, October 8-10.
GARVIN, Paul.
   1954.   Review of Louis Hjelmslev, *Prolegomena to a Theory of Language, Language* 30, 69-96.
GAUTHIER, René Antoine.
   1970.   "Introduction" to *L'Ethique à Nicomaque, traduction et commentaire*, par R. A. Gauthier et
            Jean Yves Jolif (12th ed., avec une introduction nouvelle; Paris: Beatrice-Nauwelaerts),
            Tome I, première partie.
GEACH, Peter.
   1968.   *Reference and Generality. An Examination of Some Medieval and Modern Theories* (emended edi-
            tion; Ithaca: Cornell University Press).
   1972.   "History of the corruptions of logic", in *Logic Matters* (Berkeley: University of California
            Press), 44-61.
GÉNY, François.
   1889.   *Méthode d'interprétation et sources en droit privé positif* (Paris: A. Chevalier-Marescq).
GILBERT OF STANFORD.
   a.1153. *In Canticum Canticorum*. Source: *Studia Anselmiana*, Fasciculus XX, edited by Jean Leclerq,
            O.S.B., entitled *Analecta Monastica, Première Serie* VIII (1948), 240 pp. Leclerq subsequent-
            ly published eight volumes of *Analecta Monastica* for *Studia Anselmiana* (Rome: Pontificium
            Institutum S. Anselmi).
                This Fascicle XX contains ten selections of which the *In Canticum Canticorum* attributed
            to Gilbert of Stanford is contained in Chapter 10. Leclerq quotes only a text from the
            Preface, pp. 225-229, and a text from Book V, pp. 229-230. Eco quotes from p. 225. Leclerq
            gives his own interpretation of these selections at the beginning of Chapter 10, pp. 205-224,
            suggesting that Gilbert of Stanford never existed, that the text is by an anonymous author—
            "c'est le fruit d'un milieu autant que le travail d'un homme" (Leclerq 1948: 209):
            "Retenons donc le nom de Gilbert de Stanford, mais continuons à le considérer comme
            anonyme, puisque, nous ne savons pas quel personnage recouvre cette désignation" (ibid.:
            212).
                De Lubac 1962: 48 says that Gilbert of Stanford quotes some sentences of St. Bernard
            as "sicut ait quidam sapiens". St. Bernard died in 1153. Hence our dating of the text
            as "ante 1153". De Lubac treats Gilbert of Stanford prior to treating "l'Age Scholas-
            tique" in Chapter IX, pp. 263-344. Now the Scholastic theology is thought to begin with
            Anselm of Canterbury (d. 1109). Hence we could place "Gilbert of Stanford's" text in
            the very early scholastic age, but still during the life of St. Bernard.
GILSON, Etienne.
   1937.   *The Unity of Philosophical Experience* (New York: Scribner's).
   1952.   *La Philosophie au Moyen Age. Des Origines Patristiques à la Fin du XIVe Siècle* (2nd ed., rev.
            et aug.; Paris: Payot).
   1955.   *History of Christian Philosophy in the Middle Ages* (New York: Random House).
GODEL, Robert.
   1957.   *Les sources manuscripts du* Cours de linguistique générale *de F. de Saussure* (Geneva: Droz).
GOETHE, Johann Wolfgang von.
   1797.   "Über die Gegenstände der bildenden Kunst", in Vol. 31 of *Sämtliche Werke* (Stuttgart
            and Berlin: Cotta, 1902-12).

1809-1832. "Maximen und Reflexionen", in Vol. 12 of *Goethes Werke* (Hamburg: Christian Wegner, 1953), 365-547.

GOLDSTEIN, Leon J.
1976. *Historical Knowing* (Austin, TX: University of Texas Press).

GOLOPENTIA-ERETESCU, Sanda.
1971. "Explorari semiotice", *Studii çsi cercětari linguistice* 22, 283-91.
1977. "Contribution à la Doctrine des Sémiotiques", *Revue Roumaine de Linguistique* XXII, *Cahiers de Linguistique Théorique et Appliquée* XIV.2 (juillet-décembre 1977), 117-130.

GOODY, E. N.
1978. *Questions and Politeness* (Cambridge).

GOODY, Jack.
1977. *The Domestication of the Savage Mind* (Cambridge: Cambridge University Press).

GOULD, Stephen J., and Elisabeth S. VRBA.
1982. "Exaptation—A missing term in the science of form", *Paleobiology* 8.1 (Winter), 4-15.

GOUX, Jacques.
1973. *Freud, Marx: Economie et symbolique* (Paris: Seuil).

GREENLEE, Douglas.
1973. *Peirce's Concept of Sign* (The Hague: Mouton).

GREIMAS. A. J.
1970. "Sémantique, sémiotique et sémiologies", in *Sign, Language, Culture*, ed. C. H. van Schooneveld (The Hague: Mouton), 13-27.

GRICE, H. P.
1957. "Meaning", *Philosophical Review* 66, 377-88. References in Eco are to this version; references in Short are to the reprint in *Philosophical Logic*, ed. P. F. Strawson (Oxford: Oxford University Press, 1967), 39-48.
1968. "Utterer's Meaning, Sentence-Meaning, and Word-Meaning,' *Foundations of Language* 4, 1-18. References in Eco are to this version; references in Short are to the reprint in *The Philosophy of Language*, ed. John Searle (Oxford: Oxford University Press, 1971), 54-70.
1975. "Logic and Conversation", in *Speech Acts*, Vol. 3 of *Syntax and Semantics*, ed. Peter Cole and Jerry L. Morgan (New York: Academic Press), 41-58.

GUIRAUD, Pierre.
1971. *La sémiologie* (Paris: Presses Universitaires de France). [English version—*Semiology* (London and Boston: Routledge & Kegan Paul, 1975).]

GUTHRIE, W. K. C.
1971. 'Rhetoric and Philosophy", in *The Sophists* (Cambridge: Cambridge University Press), 176-225.

HABERLAND, G.
1902. "Culturversuche mit isolierten Pflanzenzellen", *Sitzungsberichte der Akademie der Wissenschaften*, (Wien): *Math. Nat. Classe* 111, 69-92.

HAIDU, Peter.
1982. "Semiotics and History", *Semiotica* 40.3-4, 187-228.

HALVERSON, William H.
1976. *A Concise Introduction to Philosophy* (3rd ed.; New York: Random House).

HAMILTON, A. Mc.
1878. *Nervous Diseases: Their Description and Treatment* (Philadelphia: Henry C. Lee).

HAMILTON, Edith, and Huntington CAIRNS, eds.
1961. *The Collected Dialogues of Plato, Including the Letters* (New York: Pantheon).

HARDWICK, Charles S., ed.
1977. *Semiotic and Significs: The Correspondence between Charles S. Peirce and Victoria Lady Welby* (Bloomington: Indiana University Press).

HARRISON, John, and Peter LASLETT.
1965. *The Library of John Locke* (London: Oxford University Press).

HASENMUELLER, Christine.
1984, October 9. "A Picture is Worth a Thousand Words: How We Talk About Iconic Signs", presentation in the Research Conference "Semiotics: Field or Discipline?" at the Bloomington campus of Indiana University, October 8-10.

HAVELOCK, Christine.
1978. "Art as Communication in Ancient Greece", in *Communication Arts in the Ancient World*, ed. Eric Havelock and Jackson Hershbell (New York: Hastings House), 95-118.

HAWKES, Terence.
1977. *Structuralism and Semiotics* (Berkeley, CA: University of California Press).

HAYES, E. Nelson, and Tanya HAYES, eds.
  1970.   *Claude Lévi-Strauss: The Anthropologist as Hero* (Cambridge, MA: The M.I.T. Press).
HEGEL, G. W. F.
  1817-1829. *Ästhetik* (Berlin: Aufbau, 1955). Page references are to the English trans. by F. P. B.
            Osmaston, *The Philosophy of Fine Arts* (London: Bell, 1920).
HEIDEGGER, Martin.
  1927.   *Sein und Zeit*, originally published in the *Jahrbuch für Phänomenologie und phänomenologische
            Forschung*, ed. Edmund Husserl. Page references are to the 10th edition (Tübingen:
            Niemeyer, 1963).
  1929.   *Vom Wesen des Grundes* (Frankfurt: Klostermann).
  1947.   *Platons Lehre von der Wahrheit, mit einem Brief über den Humanismus* (Bern: Francke).
  1957.   *Identität und Differenz* (Pfullingen: Neske).
  1968.   *Zur Sache des Denkens*, in *L'Endurance de la pensée* (Paris: Plon). The English translation by
            Joan Stambaugh, *On Time and Being* (New York: Harper & Row, 1972), was used.
HEISENBERG, Werner.
  1959.   *Physics and Philosophy: The Revolution in Modern Science* (London: George Allen & Unwin).
  1967.   *Das Naturgesetz und die Struktur der Materie* (Stuttgart: Belser). References are to the English
            trans. by Werner Heisenberg, *Natural Law and the Structure of Matter* (London: Rebel Press,
            1970).
HEMPEL, Carl.
  1942.   "One Function of General Laws in History", *Journal of Philosophy* 39 (January), 35-47
            (reprinted in Patrick Gardiner, ed., *Theories of History* [Glencoe, IL: The Free Press, 1959],
            344-356).
HENDERSON, Lawrence J.
  1913.   *The Fitness of the Environment* (Boston: Beacon Press).
HERACLITUS.
  c.500BC. *Fragments*, in Vol. I of Diels 1903 (q.v.).
HERCULANO DE CARVALHO, José G.
  1969.   "Segno e significazione in João de São Tomás", in *Estudos Linguísticos*, Vol. 2
            (Coimbra: Atlântida Editora). Pp. 129-153 are exposition; 154-168 reproduce selected
            passages of Latin text. This careful essay, a most important piece of work on Poinsot's
            semiotic, stands along with the essay of Maritain (1938, 1941) as a firsthand presentation
            of Poinsot's views on the subject of signs. It is excerpted from Herculano de Carvalho
            1970, q.v.
  1970.   *Teoria da linguagem. Natureza do fenómeno linguístico e a análise das línguas* (reprint with addi-
            tions of 1967 work of same title, and now as "Tomo I" with a second volume of the same
            name published in 1973; Coimbra: Atlântida).
HERMES, Hans.
  1938.   *Semiotik: eine Theorie der Zeichengestalten als Grundlage für Untersuchungen von formalisierten Sprache.*
            Forschungen zur Logik und zur Grundlegung der Exakten Wissenschaften 5 (Leipzig: Hirzel).
HERSCHEL, Sir John.
  1831.   *A Preliminary Discourse on the Study of Natural Philosophy* (London: Longman, Rees, Orme,
            Brown and Green).
HERZFELD, Michael.
  1971.   "Cost and Culture", *Kritika Khronika* 23, 189-198.
  1980.   "The Dowry in Greece", *Ethnohistory* 27, 225-241.
  1982.   *Ours Once More: Folklore, Ideology, and the Making of Modern Greece* (Austin, TX: University
            of Texas Press).
  1984, October 8. "Semiotics: Saying 'No' to Narcissus", Introductory address to the Research
            Conference "Semiotics: Field or Discipline?" (Bloomington: Indiana University, October
            8-10).
HIKINS, James.
  1977.   "Discourse, Dialectic and Intrapersonal Rhetoric: A Reinterpretation of Plato's Rhetorical
            Theory", paper presented at the Speech Communication Association Conference,
            Washington, D.C., December 4.
HILBERT, D.
  1905.   "Über die Grundlagen der Logik und der Arithmetik", *Verh. d. 3. Int. Mathem.-Kongr.*
            (Leipzig), 174-185.
HILL, Archibald A.
  1958.   *Introduction to Linguistic Structures: From Sound to Sentence in English* (New York: Harcourt Brace).
HILL, Archibald A., ed.
  1969.   *Linguistics Today* (New York: Basic Books).

HILLGARTH, Jocelyn Nigel.
   1971. *Ramon Lull and Lullism in Fourteenth Century France* (Oxford: Clarendon Press).
HIPPOCRATES.
   c.460-350BC. *Hippocrates*, with an English trans. by W. H. S. Jones (The Loeb Classical Library), in
      4 vols. (Cambridge: Harvard University Press, 1923-1931).
HIRSCHFELD, L. A.
   1977. "Art in Cunaland", *Man* n.s. 12, 104-123.
HJELMSLEV, Louis.
   1943. *Omkring sprogteoriens grundloeggelse* (Copenhagen: Ejnar Munksgaard). References in Sebeok
      are to the English trans. by Francis J. Whitfield, *Prolegomena to a Theory of Language* (Baltimore:
      Waverly, 1953). References in Eco, Lanigan, and Merrell are to the revised trans. by
      Francis J. Whitfield under the same title (Madison: University of Wisconsin Press, 1961).
   1943a. "Langue et parole," in *Cahiers F. de Saussure* 2, 29-44. Page references are to the reprint
      in Hjelmslev 1970: 69-81.
   1948. "Structural Analysis of Language", *Studia linguistica* I, 69-78. Page references are to the
      reprint in Hjelmslev 1970: 27-35.
   1970. *Essais linguistiques* (= Travaux de cercle linguistique de Copenhague XII) (2nd ed.;
      Copenhagen: Nordish Sprogog Kulturforlag).
HOFFMANN, E.
   1925. *Die Sprache und die archaische Logik* (Tübingen: Niemeyer).
HOLENSTEIN, Elmar.
   1976. *Roman Jakobson's Approach to Language: Phenomenological Structuralism* (Bloomington: Indiana
      University Press).
HOMER.
   c.700-600BC. "Ιλιας, trans. by Robert Fitzgerald as *The Iliad* (Garden City, New York: Double-
      day, 1975).
HUIZINGA, Johan.
   1924. *The Waning of the Middle Ages* (New York: Doubleday & Co.).
HUME, David.
   1748. *An Enquiry concerning Human Understanding*, complete and unabridged text in *The English Philos-
      ophers from Bacon to Mill*, ed. E. A. Burtt (New York: The Modern Library, 1939), 585-689.
HUNT, Everett L.
   1921. "Dialectic—A Neglected Method of Argument", *Quarterly Journal of Speech* 7, 221-232.
HUSSERL, Edmund.
   1890. "Zur Logic der Zeichen (Semiotik)", in *Philosophie der Arithmetik*, ed. Lothar Eley, Vol.
      12 of *Gesammelte Werke*, ed. H. L. Van Breda (The Hague: Martinus Nijhoff), 340-72.
IIYLAND, Drew A.
   1973. *The Origins of Philosophy, Its Rise in Myth and the Pre-Socratics* (New York: Putnam's).
IAKOVIDHIS, Khristos.
   1975. "Introductory Note" in Greek to *Neoklassika Spitia Tis Athinas (Neoclassical Houses of Athens
      and Piraeus)* (Athens: Dhodhoni).
INNIS, Robert E.
   1982. *Karl Bühler. Semiotic Foundations of Language Theory* (New York: Plenum).
   1985. *Semiotics: An Introductory Anthology*, with Introductions to each reading by the editor (Bloom-
      ington: Indiana University Press).
ISENBERG, M. W.
   1951. "Plato's *Sophist* and the five stages of knowing", *Classical Philology* 46, 201-211.
JACKSON, J. H.
   1932. "On Affections of Speech from Disease of the Brain", in *Selected Writings of John Hughlings
      Jackson* (London: Allen Lane).
JAKOBSON, Roman.
   1931. "Prinzipien der historischen Phonologie", *Travaux du Cercle Linguistique de Prague* 4, 247-267.
      References are to the French trans. by J. Cantineau, "Principes de phonologie histori-
      que", Appendix I to the French ed. of Trubetskoy 1939 [q.v.], 315-36.
   1936. "Sur la théorie des affinités phonologiques entre les langues", rapport au Quatriéme
      Congrés International de Linguistes (Copenhague: août 1936), in *Phonological Studies*, Vol.
      I of *Selected Writings* (The Hague: Mouton, 1962), 234-246.
   1962. "Concluding Remarks", in *Proceedings of the Fourth International Congress of Phonetic Sciences*,
      ed. A. Sovijärvi and A. Aalto (The Hague).
   1963. "Parts and Wholes in Language", in *Parts and Wholes*, ed. Daniel Lerner (New York:
      The Free Press), 157-62.
   1971. *Word and Language*, Volume 2 of *Selected Writings* (The Hague: Mouton).

JAKOBSON, Roman, and Linda WAUGH.
  1979. *The Sound Shape of Language* (Bloomington: Indiana University Press).
JAMESON, Fredric.
  1972. *The Prison House of Language* (Princeton: Princeton University Press).
JAZAYERY, Mohammed Ali, Edgar C. POLOMÉ, and Werner WINTER, eds.
  1976. *Linguistic and Literary Studies in Honor of Archibald A. Hill, I: General and Theoretical Linguistics* (Lisse: The Peter de Ridder Press).
JEANS, James.
  1958. *The Mysterious Universe* (New York: Dutton).
  1959. *The New Background of Science* (Ann Arbor: The University of Michigan Press).
JENCKS, C., and G. BAIRD.
  1969. *Meaning in Architecture* (London: Barrie & Jenkins).
St. JEROME ("S. Eusebius Hieronymus").
  c.389-392. *Liber Hebraicarum Quaestionem in Genesim*, in *Patrologiae Cursus Completus*, ed. J.-P. Migne, Series Latina (P.L.), Vol. XXIII (Paris: Garnier, 1883), cols. 985-1062.
  c.397. *Epistola LXIV* (Ad Fabiolam), in Pars I of *Sancti Eusebii Hieronymi Epistuli*, rec. Isidorus Hilberg, in *Corpus scriptorum ecclesiasticorum latinorum*, editum consilio et impensis Academiae Litterarum Caesareae Vindobensis (Vienna: F. Tempsky, and Leipzig: G. Freytag, 1910), vol. LIV, 586-615; also in *Patrologia Cursus Completus*, ed. J.-P. Migne, *Series Latina* (P.L.), Vol. XXII (Paris: Garnier, 1877), cols. 607-622.
  c.411. *Commentariorum in Ezechielem: Praefatio in librum XIV*, in J. P. Migne, ed., *Patrologia Latina*, vol. XXV (Paris, 1845), col. 448.
JEVONS, W. S.
  1864. *Pure Logic, or the Logic of Quality apart from Quantity* (London).
JOHN DAMASCENE.
  i.742-749. *Dialectica*, in Vol. I of *Die Schriften der Johannes von Damaskos*, ed. B. K. Kotter (Berlin: de Gruyter, 1969), 27-147.
JOHN OF SACROBOSCO.
  a.1230. *Tractatus de sphaera*, trans. Lynn Thorndike in *The Sphere of Sacrobosco and Its Commentators* (Chicago: University of Chicago Press, 1949), 76-142. Edition includes Sacrobosco's Latin original with English translation, the commentaries by Robertus Angelicus, that ascribed to Michael Scot, that of Cecco D'Ascoli, four anonymous commentaries, and the *Sphere* of John Peckham. It needs to be understood that Sacrobosco's work, though derivative and secondary by comparison with that of Ptolemaeus, was yet the primary source for most students (as well as many professors) of the arcane knowledge of the spheres and stars in the mediaeval university world.
JOHNSON, B. C.
  1975. "More on Diglossia", *Language Sciences* 37, 37-38.
JOOS, Martin.
  1958. "Semology: A Linguistic Theory of Meaning", *Studies in Linguistics* 13, 53-70.
JOSEPH, H. W. B.
  1916. *An Introduction to Logic* (2nd ed., rev.; Oxford: Clarendon Press).
JOYCE, James.
  i.1904-1906. *Stephen Hero. A Part of the First Draft of A Portrait of the Artist as a Young Man*, ed. from the ms. in the Harvard College Library by Theodore Spencer (New York: New Directions, 1944).
JUNG, Carl Gustav.
  1954. "Über die Archetypen des kollektiven Unbewussten", in *Von den Wurzeln des Bewusstseins. Studien über den Archetypus* (Zürich: Rascher, 1954), 3-56. English trans. by R. F. C. Hull, "Archetypes of the Collective Unconscious", in *The Archetypes of the Collective Unconscious*, Vol. 9, Pt. 2 of *The Collected Works of C. G. Jung* (2nd ed.; New York: Bollingen, 1968), 3-41.
KACZMAREK, Ludger.
  1980. Introduction, critical apparatus, and notes to d'Ailly a.1396, q.v.
  1981. "Modi Significandi and Their Destructions: A 14th Century Controversy about Methodological Issues in the Science and Theory of Language", paper read at the Seconde Conférence Internationale d'Histoire des Sciences du Langage (ICHOLS II), Lille, September 2-5, 1981.
  1983. "Significatio in der Zeichen- und Sprachtheorie Ockhams", in Eschbach and Trabant 1983 [q.v.]: 87-104.
KANT, Immanuel.
  1781, 1787. *Kritik der reinen Vernunft* (Riga). References are to the English trans. by Norman Kemp Smith, *Kant's Critique of Pure Reason* (New York: St. Martin's Press, 1963), and to *Kant's*

Gesammelte Schriften, issued by the Königlich Preussischen Akademie der Wissenschaften, Band III, *Kritik der reinen Vernunft*, 2nd ed. (1787) (Berlin: Druck und Verlag von Georg Reimer, 1911).

KENDALL, M. B.
    1981.   "Towards a Semantic Approach to Terms of Address", *Journal of Language and Communication* 1, 237-254.

KERFERD, George B.
    1954.   "Plato's Noble Art of Sophistry", *Classical Quarterly* 48, 84-90.
    1981.   *The Sophistic Movement* (New York: Cambridge University Press).

KETNER, Kenneth Laine, and James Edward COOK, eds.
    1975.   *Charles Sanders Peirce: Contributions to The Nation*, Vol. I (Lubbock: Texas Tech Press).

KEVELSON, Roberta.
    1977.   *Inlaws/Outlaws: A Semiotics of Legal Systems* (= Studies in Semiotics 7) (Lisse: Peter de Ridder Press).
    1981.   "Semiotics and the Art of Conversation", *Semiotica* 32.1/2, 53-80.
    1981a. "Semiotics and Structures of Law", *Semiotica* 35.1/2, 183-192.
    1981b. "Semiotics and Law", in *Encyclopedic Dictionary of Semiotics*, ed. Thomas A. Sebeok et al. (New York: Plenum, forthcoming).
    1981c. "Francis Lieber and the Semiotics of Law and Politics", in *Semiotics 1981*, ed. J. N. Deely and M. D. Lenhart (New York: Plenum, 1983), 167-177.
    1984.   "Charles Sanders Peirce's Speculative Rhetoric: Method and Discovery", *Philosophy and Rhetoric* 17.1.
    1985.   *Charles S. Peirce's Method of Methods* (Amsterdam: John Benjamins).

KEYSER, Cassius J.
    1956.   "The Group Concept", in Vol. III of *The World of Mathematics*, ed. James R. Newman (New York: Simon and Schuster), 1538-1557.

KINSER, Samuel.
    1981.   "Annalistic Paradigm? The Geohistorical Structure of Fernand Braudel", *American Historical Review* 86.1 (February), 63-105.

KLEIN, Jacob.
    1977.   *Plato's Trilogy: Theaetetus, the Sophist, and the Statesman* (Chicago: University of Chicago Press).

KLEINMAN, Arthur.
    1980.   *Patients and Healers in the Context of Culture* (Berkeley: University of California Press).

KLEINPAUL, Rudolph.
    1888.   *Spache ohne Worte: Idee einer allgemeinen Wissenschaft der Sprache* (Leipzig: Friedrich). Reprinted as Vol. 19 of *Approaches to Semiotics* (The Hague: Mouton, 1972).

KNEALE, William, and Martha KNEALE.
    1962.   *The Development of Logic* (London: Oxford).

KOEHLER, O.
    1956.   "Thinking Without Words", *XIV International Congress of Zoology* (Copenhagen), 75-88.

KOSINSKI, Jerzy.
    1970.   *Being There* (New York: Harcourt Brace Jovanovich).

KRADER, Lawrence.
    1974.   "Beyond Structuralism: The Dialectics of the Diachronic and Synchronic Methods in the Human Sciences", in *The Unconscious in Culture: The Structuralism of Claude Lévi-Strauss in Perspective*, ed. Ino Rossi (New York: E. P. Dutton), 336-61.

KRANZ, Walter.
    1939.   *Vorsokratische Denker* (Berlin: Weidmann).

KRAMPEN, Martin.
    1981.   "Phytosemiotics", *Semiotica* 36.3-4, 187-209.

KREMPEL, A.
    1952.   *La doctrine de la relation chez St. Thomas* (Paris: Vrin).

KRETZMANN, Norman.
    1967.   "Semantics, History of", entry in Vol. 7 of *The Encyclopedia of Philosophy*, ed. Paul Edwards (New York: Macmillan), 358-406.

KRIPKE, Saul.
    1980.   *Naming and Necessity* (Harvard: Harvard University Press).

KRISTELLER, Paul Oskar.
    1961.   "The Aristotelian Tradition", in his *Renaissance Thought* (New York: Harper), 24-47.
    1961a. "Humanism and Scholasticism in the Italian Renaissance", in op. cit., 92-119.

KRISTEVA, Julia.
    1967.   *Semeiotikè: Recherches pour une sémananalyse* (Paris: Seuil).
    1970.   "La mutation sémiotique", *Annales économies, sociétés, civilisations* 25, 1497-1522.
    1975.   *The System and the Speaking Subject* (Lisse: The Peter de Ridder Press). Page references are
             to this monograph version. Concurrently published in *The Tell-Tale Sign: A Survey of Semiotics*,
             ed. Thomas A. Sebeok (Lisse: The Peter de Ridder Press, 1975), 47-55.
KRISTEVA, Julia, Josette REY-DEBOVE, and Donna Jean UMIKER, eds.
    1971.   *Essays in Semiotics/Essais de sémiotique* (= *Approaches to Semiotics* 4) (The Hague: Mouton).
KROIS, John Michael.
    1981.   "Peirce's Speculative Rhetoric and the Problem of Natural Law", *Philosophy and Rhetoric*,
             14.1 (Winter), 16-30.
KUHN, Thomas S.
    1962.   *The Structure of Scientific Revolutions* (= Foundations of the Unity of Science, No. 2) (2nd
             ed., enlarged; Chicago: The University of Chicago Press, 1970).
KÜNG, Guido.
    1967.   *Ontology and the Logistic Analysis of Language* (rev. ed.; Dordrecht, Holland: Reidel). A
             remarkable and extremely valuable book which shows perhaps more of the limits of logistic
             philosophizing than any other single study—or than its author hoped.
LABOV, W.
    1965.   *The Study of Nonstandard English* (rev. ed.; Chicago: NCTE; Washington: Center for Ap-
             plied Lingusitics).
LACAN, Jacques.
    1953-1954. *Les Écrits Techniques de Freud*, Livre I de *Le Séminaire*, texte établi par Jacques-Alain
             Miller (Paris: Seuil, 1975).
    1956.   "Fonction et champ de la parole et du langage en psychanalyse", *La Psychanalyse* I, 81-166.
             References are to the English translation with notes and commentary by Anthony Wilden,
             The Language of the Self: The Function of Language in Psychoanalysis (Baltimore: Johns Hopkins
             Press, 1968).
    1966.   "L'instance de la lettre dans l'inconscient", in Jacques Lacan, *Ecrits I* (Paris: Éditions
             du Seuil), 249-289. English trans. of this article by Jan Miel in *Structuralism*, ed. Jacques
             Ehrmann (Garden City, N.Y.: Anchor, 1970), 101-137.
LACHELIER, Jules
    1933.   *Oeuvres de Jules Lachelier*, Tome I (Paris: Alcan).
LALANDE, André.
    1902-1923. *Vocabulaire Technique et Critique de la Philosophie*, édition originale en fascicules, dans le
             Bulletin de la Société française de Philosophie. References in Deely are to this edition; references
             in Eco are to the 1926 ed. (Paris: Presses Universitaires de France).
LAMB, Sydney M.
    1966.   *Outline of Stratificational Grammar* (Washington, D.C.: Georgetown University Press).
LAMBERT, J. H.
    1764.   *Neues Organon oder Gedanken über die Erforschung und Bezeichnung des Wahren und dessen
             Unterscheidung vom Irrthum und Schein*, 2. Band (Leipig: Wendler).
LANGAN, Thomas.
    1983.   "Foreword" to Powell 1983 (q.v.): ix-xi.
LANIGAN, Richard L.
    1970.   "Semiotic Expression and Perception: Merleau-Ponty's Phenomenology of Communica-
             tion", *Philosophy Today* 14, 78-88.
    1972.   *Speaking and Semiology* (The Hague: Mouton).
    1977.   *Speech Act Phenomenology* (The Hague: Martinus Nijhoff).
    1979.   "A Semiotic Metatheory of Human Communication", *Semiotica* 27, 293-305.
    1979a.   "The Phenomenology of Human Communication", *Philosophy Today* 23, 3-15.
    1979b.   "The Objectivist Illusion in Therapeutic Philosophy", paper presented at the Merleau-
             Ponty Circle, State University of New York at Stony Brook, October 12.
LASSALLE, Ferdinand.
    1858.   *Die Philosophia Herakleitos des Dunkeln von Ephesos* (Berlin: Duncker).
LEACH, Edmund R.
    1970.   *Claude Lévi-Strauss* (New York: Viking Press).
    1984, October 9. "Semiotics, Ethology, and the Limits of Human Understanding", Patten Lecture
             delivered at Indiana University, Bloomington, adjunct to Leach's participation in the Oc-
             tober 8-10 "Semiotics: Field or Discipline" State-of-the-Art Research Conference.
    1984, October 10. "Concluding Remarks" to the "Semiotics: Field or Discipline" State-of-the-
             Art Research Conference held at Indiana University, Bloomington, October 8-10.

LECLERQ, Jean.
  1948.   "Gilbert of Stanford, Le commentaire de Gilbert de Stanford sur le cantique des cantiques",
          Studia Anselmiana XX, 205-230.
LEFEBVRE, Henri.
  1966.   "Claude Lévi-Strauss et le nouveau éléatisme", in *L'Homme et la société*, Vol. 7, No. 1,
          21-33, No. 2, 81-104 (Paris: Editions Anthropos). Page references are to the Spanish trans.
          by Alejandro Ferrieros, "Claude Lévi-Strauss y el nuevo eleatismo", in *Estructuralismo
          y filosofía*, ed. José Sazbón (Buenos Aires: Ediciones Nueva Visión, 1971), 121-176.
LEIBNIZ, G. W. F.
  1704.   *Nouveaux Essais sur l'entendement humain* (first published posthumously in Amsterdam, 1765),
          English trans. by A. G. Langley as *New Essays Concerning Human Understanding* (Chicago,
          1916).
LEMERT, Charles C.
  1979.   *Sociology and the Twilight of Man: Homocentrism and Discourse in Sociological Theory* (Carbon-
          dale: Southern Illinois University Press).
LEVIN, David.
  1979.   "Sanity and Myth: Merleau-Ponty's Understanding of Human Space", paper presented
          at the Merleau-Ponty Circle, State University of New York at Stony Brook, October 12.
LÉVI-STRAUSS, Claude.
  1945.   "L'Analyse structurale en linguistique et anthropologie", *Word* 1.1 (April), 33-53.
  1947.   *Les Structures élémentaires de la parenté* (Paris: Presses Universitaires de France).
  1950.   "Introduction à l'oeuvre de Marcel Mauss", in Marcel Mauss, *Sociologie et anthropologie*
          (Paris: Presses Universitaires de France), ix-lii.
  1955.   *Tristes Tropiques* (Paris: Plon). References are to the English translation by John Russell
          under the same title (New York: Atheneum, 1961).
  1958.   *Anthropologie structurale* (Paris: Plon). References are to the English translation by Claire
          Jacobson and Brooke Grundfest, *Structural Anthropology* (New York: Doubleday, 1964).
  1960.   "Leçon inaugurale", lecture delivered on 5 May at the Collège de France. References
          are to the English trans. by Sherry Ortner Paul and Robert A. Paul, *The Scope of Anthropology*
          (London: Jonathan Cape, 1967).
  1962.   *La pensée sauvage* (Paris: Plon). References are to the English translation, *The Savage Mind*
          (Chicago: University of Chicago Press, 1966).
  1962a. "Histoire et dialectique", Ch. IX of Lévi-Strauss 1962: 324-357. Page references are to
          the English translation, "History and Dialectic", Ch. IX of the English version of Lévi-
          Strauss 1962 [q.v.]: 245-269.
  1962b. "Les limites de la notion de structure en ethnologie", in *Sens et usages du terme structure*,
          ed. R. Bastide (The Hague: Mouton), 40-45.
  1964.   *Le cru et le cuit* (Paris: Plon). References are to the English trans. by John and Doreen
          Weightman, *The Raw and the Cooked* (New York: Harper & Row, 1969).
LÉVY-BRUHL, Lucien.
  1899.   "Essay on Descartes", added "as it appeared in the author's *History of Modern Philosophy
          in France* (Chicago: Open Court, 1899) by way of a general introduction" to *The Medita-
          tions and Selections from the Principles of René Descartes*, trans. by John Veitch and published
          by Open Court of Chicago in 1905 under the editorship of T. J. McCormack, vii-xxx.
  1938.   Letter to Jacques Maritain dated 8 May. Published in *Revue Thomiste* 44 (July 1938), 482-483.
LIEB, Irwin C.
  1953.   Appendix B to Charles S. Peirce, *Charles S. Peirce's Letters to Lady Welby*, ed. Irwin C. Lieb
          (New Haven: Whitlock's). Reprinted in *Semiotic and Significs: The Correspondence Between
          Charles S. Peirce and Victoria Lady Welby*, ed. Charles S. Hardwick (Bloomington: Indiana
          University Press, 1977), 160-166.
LOCKE, John.
  1690.   *An Essay Concerning Humane Understanding* (London: Printed by Elizabeth Holt for Thomas
          Basset). The copy from this original edition located at the Lilly Library on the Bloom-
          ington campus of Indiana University was consulted in preparing this book. Also consulted
          were the Alexander Campbell Fraser edition (Oxford, 1894; reprinted New York: Dover
          Publications, 1959) and the Peter H. Nidditch edition (Oxford, 1975; 1979 corrected paper-
          back edition).
LOGID.
  1981.   *Grüne Archen* (Frankfurt a. M.: Fricke Verlag).
LOMBARD, Peter.
  c.1150. *Libri Quattuor Sententiarum* ("The Four Books of the Sentences"), in *Patrologiae Cursus Com-
          pletus*, ed. J.-P. Migne, *Series Latina* (P.L.), Vol. 192 (Paris: Garnier, 1880), cols. 522-963.

(One of the very earliest printed editions of this formerly ubiquitous work appeared in Venice: Vandelin Spire, 1477.)

LOTMAN, Jurij M.
1969. "O metajazyke tipologičeskix opisanij kul'tury", in *Trudy po znakovym sistemam* [Works on Semiotics] IV, 460-477. Page references in Winner are to the English trans., "On the Metalanguage of a Typological Description of Culture", *Semiotica* 14.2 (1975), 97-123.

LOTMAN, Jurij M., ed.
1964-. *Semeiotiké: Trudy po znakovym systemam* [Works on Semiotics] (Tartu: Acta et Commentationes Universitatis Tartuensis). Lotman's *Lekcii po struktural'noj poetike* was published as Trudy 1 (1964).

LOTZ, John.
1954. "Plan and Publication of Noreen's Vårt Språk", in *Portraits of Linguists* 2, ed. Thomas A. Sebeok (Bloomington: Indiana University Press), 56-65.

LOTZE, Hermann.
1843. *Logik* (Leipzig; English trans. Oxford 1884).

LUKACS, Georg.
1968. *Geschichte und Klassenbewusstsein* (Neuwied a.Rh.: Luchterhand). References are to the English trans. by Rodney Livingstone, *History and Class Consciousness: Studies in Marxist Dialectics* (Cambridge, MA: The M.I.T. Press, 1971).

LULL, Ramon.
1274. Composition of the first version of the *Ars Magna*, the *Ars compendiosa inveniendi veritatem*, which "has only once been published, by Salzinger" as the opening work in the 8-volume *Beati Raymundi Lulli Opera*, ed. Ivo Salzinger (Mainz, 1721-1742). "The Catalan original (*Ars abreujada d'atrobar veritat*) is lost but it certainly existed; it is referred to by Lull, *Ars demonstrativa*, c.1275." (Hillgarth 1971: 8 n. 32.)

LYONS, John.
1963. *Structural Semantics. An Analysis of Part of the Vocabulary of Plato* (Publications of the Philological Society XX) (Oxford: Basil Blackwell).

MacCANNELL, Dean, and Juliet Flower MacCANNELL.
1982. *The Time of the Sign* (Bloomington: Indiana University Press).

MADAY, Stefan von.
1912. *Psychologie des Pferdes und der Dressur* (Berlin: P. Parey).

MAIERÙ, A.
1967. "'Signum' dans la culture mediévale", in *Sprache und Erkenntnis im Mittelalter*, Vol. 13, No. 1 of *Miscellanea Mediaevalia* (Berlin and New York: Walter de Gruyter, 1981), 51-72.
1972. *Terminologia logica della tarda scholastica* (Rome: Edizioni dell' Ateneo).

MAKOWSKI, Simon Stanislaus.
1679. *Cursus Philosophicus* (Cracow: University of Cracow Press). At Lilly Library.

MANNOURY, G.
1969. "A Concise History of Significs", *Methodology and Science* 2, 171-80.

MARCUS, Solomon.
1974. "Fifty-Two Oppositions between Scientific and Poetic Communication", in *Pragmatics of Human Communication*, ed. Colin Cherry (Dordrecht, Holland: D. Reidel), 83-96.

MARITAIN, Jacques.
1923. *Eléments de Philosophie. II. L'Ordre des Concepts. I. Petite Logique (Logique formelle)* (Paris: Tequi). Citations and page references are from the English trans. by Imelda Choquette, *Formal Logic* (New York: Sheed and Ward, 1937).
1924. *Réflexions sur l'intelligence et sur sa vie propre* (Paris: Nouvelle Librairie Nationale).
1937-1938. "Sign and Symbol", trans. Mary Morris in *Journal of the Warburg Institute* I, 1-11.
1938. "Signe et symbole", *Revue Thomiste* XLIV (avril), 299-330.
1941. "Sign and Symbol", English trans. of 1938 entry above (q.v.) by H. L. Binsse in *Ransoming the Time* (New York: Charles Scribner's Sons), text pp. 217-254, Latin notes from Poinsot 1632a and 1644e pp. 305-315. See gloss on 1943 entry following.
1941a. "The Conflict of Methods at the End of the Middle Ages" (in effect a précis of Maritain 1959), *The Thomist* III (October), 527-538.
1943. "Sign and Symbol", English trans. of 1938 entry above (q.v.) by H. L. Binsse in *Redeeming the Time* (London: Geoffrey Bles), text pp. 191-224, Latin notes pp. 268-276. Except for pagination, this text is identical to that of 1941 above. We have referred to the pagination of the 1943 text because that was the edition available to us.

1956. "Le Langage et la théorie du signe", Annexe au Chapitre II (= Maritain 1938) de *Quatre Essais sur l'esprit dans sa condition charnelle* (revised and augmented ed.; Paris: Alsatia), 113-124. This Annexe is substantially identical with Maritain 1957, q.v.
1957. 'Language and the Theory of Sign", in *Language: An Enquiry into Its Meaning and Function*, ed. Ruth Nanda Anshen (New York: Harper & Row), 86-101.
1959. *Distinguish to Unite, or The Degrees of Knowledge*, trans. under the supervision of Gerald B. Phelan of the 4th French edition of *Distinguer pour unir: ou les Degrés du Savoir* (orig. ed. Paris: Desclée, 1932).
1966. *God and the Permission of Evil*, trans. Joseph Evans (Milwaukee: The Bruce Publishing Co.). (Original French publication, *Dieu et la Permission du Mal* [Paris: Desclée de Brouwer, 1963]).

MARROU, Henri-Irénée.
1959. *De la connaissance historique* (4th ed., rev.; Paris: Seuil). Page references are to the English trans. by Robert J. Olsen, *The Meaning of History* (Montreal: Palm Publishers, 1966).

MARSHACK, A.
1976. "Some Implications of the Palaeolithic Symbolic Evidence for the Origin of Language", in *Origins & Evolution of Language and Speech*, ed. S. R. Harnad, H. D. Steldis and J. Lancaster (New York: New York Academy of Sciences), 289-311.

MARWICK, Arthur.
1970. *The Nature of History* (London: Macmillan).

MARX, Karl.
1857. *Einleitung zur Kritik der politischen Ökonomie*, reprinted in Marx/Engels, *Werke*, vol. 13 (Berlin [East]: Dietz Verlag, 1961). Page references are to this 1961 reprint.

MATSON, Floyd W.
1966. *The Broken Image: Man, Science and Society* (Garden City, N.Y.: Doubleday and Company).

MAYENOWA, Maria R.
1967. "Semiotics Today: Reflections on the Second International Conference in Semiotics", *Social Science Information* 6, 59-64. Page references are to the reprint in Kristeva et al. 1971 [q.v.]: 57-62.

MAZZANTINI, Carlo.
1945. *Eraclito* (Turin: Chiantore).

McKEON, Richard.
1940. "Plato and Aristotle as Historians: A Study of Method in the History of Ideas", *Ethics* 51, 66-101.

McKEON, Richard, ed.
1941. *The Basic Works of Aristotle* (New York: Random House).

McKECHNIE, George E.
1977. "The Environmental Response Inventory in Application", *Environment and Behavior* 9.2, 255-276.

MEIBOMIUS ('Meibom'), Marcus.
1652. *Antiquae musicae auctores septem Graece et Latine*. M. Meibomius restituit ac notis explicavit. 2 vols. (Amsterdam: Apud Ludovicum Elzevirium). Refs. in Romeo cited in Reading 22 n. 1 (p. 285) are to the microprint copy of the original in the Sibley Music Library, Eastman School of Music (Rochester, N.Y.: University of Rochester Press, 1954).

MELETINSKY, Eleazar, and Dmitri SEGAL.
1971. "Structuralism and Semiotics in the USSR", *Diogenes* 73, 88-155.

MENNE, Albert.
1962. "Preface of the Editor" to *Logico-Philosophical Studies* (Dordrecht, Holland: D. Reidel), vii-ix.

MERLEAU-PONTY, Maurice.
1945. *Phénoménologie de la perception* (Paris: Gallimard). References are to the English trans. by Colin Smith, with revisions by Forrest Williams, *Phenomenology of Perception* (London: Routledge & Kegan Paul, 1962).

MERRELL, Floyd.
1975. "Structuralism and Beyond: A Critique of Presuppositions", *Diogenes* 92, 67-103.
1982. *Semiotic Foundations. Steps toward an Epistemology of Written Texts* (Bloomington: Indiana University Press).
1985. *Deconstruction Reframed* (West Lafayette, IN: Purdue University Press).
1985a. *A Semiotic Theory of Texts* (The Hague: Mouton).

MILL, John Stuart.
1843. *System of Logic* (London).

MISNER, C. W., K. S. THORNE, and J. A. WHEELER.
1973. *Gravitation* (San Francisco: W. H. Freeman).

MONOD, Jacques.
    1970.   *Le Hasard et la nécessité: essai sur la philosophie naturelle de la biologie moderne* (Paris: Seuil).
            References are to the English translation by Austryn Wainhouse, *Chance and Necessity: An
            Essay on the Natural Philosophy of Modern Biology* (New York: Knopf, 1971).
MORRIS, Charles W.
    1938.   *Foundations of the Theory of Signs* (= *International Encyclopedia of Unified Science* 1.2) (Chicago:
            University of Chicago Press).
    1946.   *Signs, Language and Behavior* (New York: Prentice-Hall).
MOUNIN, Georges.
    1970.   *Introduction à la sémiologie* (Paris: Minuit).
NAVILLE, Adrien.
    1901.   *Nouvelle classification des sciences* (Paris: Alcan).
NEILL, Thomas P.
    1958.   *The Makers of the Modern Mind* (2nd, enlarged ed.; Milwaukee: Bruce Publishing Co.).
NERVAL, Gérard de.
    1853.   *Sylvie*, in Vol. I of *Oeuvres* (Paris: Editions Garnier Frères, 1958), 589-620. Page references
            are to the English trans. by R. Aldington under the same title, in *Aurelia* (London: Chatto
            and Windus, 1932), 73-111.
NEWMAN, Mildred.
    1979.   Mimeographed working paper (SUNY Buffalo: Center for Study of Cultural Transmission).
NEWTON, Isaac.
    1686.   *Philosophiae Naturalis Principia Mathematica* (London: Jussu Societatis Regiae ac Typis Josephi
            Streater), translated into English by Andrew Motte in 1729, revised and supplied with
            an historical and explanatory appendix by Florian Cajori under the title *Sir Isaac Newton's
            Mathematical Principles of Natural Philosophy and his System of the World* (Berkeley: University
            of California Press, 1946).
NICOLAS DE LYRA.
    c.1330. *Commentarium in Epistolam ad Galathas*, caput IV, col. 4, in *Biblia cum postillis Nicolai de Lyra*
            (Nuremberg: Arthur Koberger, incunabula 1485), vol. 4, no pagination. The cited text
            is at the bottom of the fourth column.
NIDDITCH, Peter H.
    1975 (hardcover), 1979 (corrected paperback). Foreword, Notes, and Critical Apparatus to new
            Oxford edition of Locke 1690.
NIETZSCHE, Friedrich.
    1883-1888. *Der Wille zur Macht*, in Vols. XV and XVI of *Nietzsche's Werke* (Leipzig: Alfred Kröner,
            1911), Vol. XV: 129-489; Vol. XVI: 1-521. References are to the English trans. by An-
            thony M. Ludovice, *The Will to Power*, Vol. XV of *The Complete Works of Friedrich Nietzsche*
            (London: T. N. Foulis, 1930).
NOVALIS (Friedrich, Freiherr von Hardenburg).
    a.1801. *Sämtliche Werke*, Ergänzungsband (Leipzig: Eugen Diederichs, 1901).
NUTINI, Hugo.
    1970.   "Some Considerations on the Notion of Social Structure and Model Building", in Hayes
            and Hayes 1970 [q.v.]: 70-107.
NYE, Russel B.
    1966.   "History and Literature: Branches of the Same Tree", in *Essays on History and Literature*,
            ed. Robert H. Bremner (Columbus: Ohio State University Press), 123-159.
OESTERLE, Jean.
    1962.   Translation with Introduction (pp. 1-15), *Aristotle: On Interpretation. Commentary by St. Thomas
            and Cajetan* (Milwaukee: Marquette University Press).
OESTERLE, John A.
    1944.   "Another Approach to the Problem of Meaning", *The Thomist* VII, 233-263. A valuable
            analysis of key distinctions in Poinsot, which does not however penetrate to the level of
            his semiotic proper, concluding with a point-by-point comparison between Poinsot and
            Ogden and Richards 1923.
OGDEN, Charles K., and Ivor A. RICHARDS.
    1923.   *The Meaning of Meaning: A Study of the Influence of Language upon Thought and of the Science
            of Symbolism* (New York: Harcourt, Brace). Page references are to the 1938 reprint edition.
ORIGEN.
    c.232-250. *Origenis in Ezechielem*, in *Patrologiae Cursus Completus*, ed. J.-P. Migne, Series Graeca (P.G.),
            Vol. XIII (Paris: Migne, 1857), cols. 665-787.

c.232-250a. *Origenis in Genesim Homiliae*, translated by Rufino, in *Patrologiae Cursus Completus*, edited by J.-P. Migne, Series Graeca (P.G.), Vol. XII (Paris: Migne, 1857), columns. 146-262.

OXFORD ENGLISH DICTIONARY.
1933. Original edition by Oxford University Press in 13 volumnes; reprinted by micrographic means in 2 volumes by the same press, 1971.

PANTALEONI, M.
1892. "Osservazioni sulla semiologia economica", *Revue d'économie politique* (octobre).

PARKER, F. H., and Henry VEATCH.
1959. *Logic as a Human Instrument* (New York: Harper).

PARMENIDES of Elea.
i.500-400BC. Fragments, in Vol. I. of *Die Fragmente der Vorsokratiker*, ed. Hermann Diels (Berlin: Weidmann, 1934), 217-246.

PARRETT, Herman.
1984. "Peirce and Hjelmslev: The Two Semiotics", *Language Sciences* 6.2, 217-227.

PASQUINELLI, Angelo, ed.
1958. *I presocratici. Frammenti e testimonianze*, Vol. I (Turin: Einaudi).

PEANO, G.
1889. *Arithmetices principia, novo methodo exposita* (Turin: Augustae Taurinormu).

PEIRCE, Charles S. CP references in this entry are to *The Collected Papers of Charles Sanders Peirce*, Vols. I-VI ed. Charles Hartshorne and Paul Weiss (Cambridge, MA: Harvard University Press, 1931-35), Vols. VII-VIII ed. Arthur W. Burks (same publisher, 1958), and are here abbreviated as CP followed by volume and paragraph numbers (separated by a point or 'period' according to the custom that has been established in this matter among users of the Collection). Chronology for CP references is based on the Burks bibliography in Volume VIII of the *Collected Papers*, pp. 249-330.

　　Numbers and dates of unpublished manuscripts are as listed in Richard S. Robin, *Annotated Catalogue of the Papers of Charles S. Peirce* (Worcester, MA: The University of Massachusetts Press, 1967).

　　References to Peirce's *The New Elements of Mathematics*, in 4 vols., ed. Carolyn Eisele (The Hague: Mouton, 1976), are abbreviated NEM. Chronology is based on the Robin catalogue.

1865-1909. "Logic", notebook listed as MS 339 in the Robin catalogue.
1867. "On a New List of Categories", in Vol. 2 of *Writings of Charles S. Peirce: A Chronological Edition*, ed. Edward C. Moore et al. (Bloomington: Indiana University Press, 1984), 49-59. Also in CP 1.545-567. (Burks p. 261.)
1868. "Grounds of Validity in the Laws of Logic. Further Consequences of Four Incapacities", CP 5.318-357. Originally in *The Journal of Speculative Philosophy* 2, 193-208. (Burks p. 262.)
1871. Review of Fraser's Edition of the Works of George Berkeley, CP 8.7-38. Originally in *The North American Review* 113 (October), 449-472. (Burks p. 262.)
1878. "The Doctrine of Chances", CP 2.645-660. Originally in *Popular Science Monthly* 12 (March), 604-615. (Burks p. 265.)
1885. "On the Algebra of Logic: A Contribution to the Philosophy of Notation", CP 3.359-403. From an article of the same title originally published in *The American Journal of Mathematics* 7.2, 180-202. (Burks p. 273.)
1889. Letters to the editor of *The Nation* dated 13 June, 20 June, and 27 June, in Ketner and Cook, eds. 1975 [q.v.]: 75-78.
c.1893. Segments from "The Short Logic", CP 2.282, 286-291, 295-296. (Burks p. 280.)
c.1895. Segment from "That Categorical and Hypothetical Propositions are one in essence, with some connected matters", CP 2.332-356. (Burks p. 286.)
c.1896. "The Logic of Mathematics; An Attempt to Develop My Categories from Within", CP 1.417-519. (Burks p. 287.)
c.1897. "Ground, Object and Interpretant", CP 2.227-229. (Burks p. 287.)
1898. "The Logic of Events", CP 6.1-5, 6.214-221. (Burks p. 288.)
1898a. "The Logic of Continuity", CP 6.185-213 (with deletions). (Burks p. 288.)
1898b. "Detached Thoughts Continued and the Dispute between Nominalists and Realists", Robin MS 439, 30-31.
1902. "Symbol", CP 2.307. Originally an entry in Volume II of the *Dictionary of Philosophy and Psychology*, edited by James Mark Baldwin (New York: Macmillan), 640. (Burks p. 292.)

c.1902.   Segments from "Syllabus", CP 2.274-277, 283-284, 292-294, 309-331. (Burks p. 296.)
c.1902a. "A Detailed Classification of the Sciences", CP 1.203-283. Originally Section 1, ch. 2
          of the *Minute Logic* (Peirce c.1902b, q.v.). (Burks p. 294.)
c.1902b. *Minute Logic*, draft for a book complete consecutively only to Ch. 4. Published in the *Col-
          lected Papers* in extracts scattered over six of the eight volumes; details in Burks, pp. 293-294.
1903.   "Nomenclature and Divisions of Triadic Relations, as far as they are determined", CP
          2.233-272. (Burks p. 296.)
1903a.   "The Categories Continued", Lecture III of the Lectures on Pragmatism, CP 5.66-92.
          (Burks p. 294.)
1903b.   "Three Types of Reasoning", Lecture VI of the Lectures on Pragmatism, CP 5.151-179.
          (Burks p. 294.)
c.1903.   "Of Euler's Diagrams", CP 4.350-371. (Burks p. 296.)
p.1903?   (undated ms.) From "Lady Welby, *What Is Meaning?*", CP 8.177-185. (Burks p. 301.)
1904.   "On Signs and the Categories", CP 8.327-341. (Burks p. 321.)
1904a.   Καινὰ στοιχεῖα, MS 517 in the Robin catalogue. Published in NEM 4: 235-263.
1904b.   Letter to Lady Welby dated 12 October, in Hardwick, ed. 1977 [q.v.]: 22-36.
1905.   "Phaneroscopy", MS 298 in the Robin catalogue.
1906.   "Prolegomena to an Apology for Pragmaticism", CP 4.530-572. Originally in *The Monist*
          16, 492-546. (Burks p. 297.)
1906a.   "Basis of Pragmaticism" portions, CP 1.573-574, 5.549-554 (continuing 1.574), 5.448
          n. 1 (following somewhat after 5.554). (Burks p. 298.)
c.1906.   "A Survey of Pragmaticism", CP 5.464-496. (Burks p. 299.)
c.1907.   "Pragmatism", MS 318 in the Robin catalogue. (A small segment of this MS is pub-
          lished under the title of "From Pragmatism" in NEM III.1: 489-494.)
1908.   "On the Classification of Signs", from a partial draft of a letter to Lady Welby dated
          24, 25, and 28 December, CP 8.342-379. (Burks p. 321.)
c.1910.   "Additaments", comments on "A Neglected Argument for the Reality of God", CP
          6.486-490. (Burks p. 301.)
PEKELIS, Alexander.
1950.   "Legal Techniques and Political Ideologies", in *Law and Social Action*, ed. M. R. Konvitz
          (Ithaca: Cornell University Press), 42-74.
PELC, Jerzy.
1971.   *Studies in Functional Logical Semiotics of Natural Languages* (The Hague: Mouton).
PERRON, Paul.
1983.   "Preface" to *Paris School Semiotics: Texts and Documents. I. Theory* (Victoria University: Toronto
          Semiotic Circle Monograph, Number 3).
PHILODEMUS.
c.54BC.   Περὶ Σημειώσεων, trans. Philip Howard De Lacy and Estelle De Lacy with Greek text
          facing as *Philodemus: On Methods of Inference. A Study in Ancient Empiricism* (Philadelphia:
          American Philological Association, 1941). This edition contains considerable critical ap-
          paratus; text of Philodemus' work on pp. 22-120.
PIAGET, Jean.
1968.   *Le Structuralisme* (Paris: Presses Universitaires de France). References are to the English
          trans. by Chaninah Maschler, *Structuralism* (New York: Harper & Row, 1970).
1972.   *Problèmes de psychologie génétique* (Paris: Denoël/Gothier). References are to the English trans.
          by Arnold Rosen, *The Child and Reality: Problems of Genetic Psychology* (New York: Grossman,
          1973).
PIGNATARI, Decio.
1971.   *Informação* (São Paulo: Perspectiva).
PLATO. All textual references are by Stephanus numbers.
i.367-361BC. *Sophist*, trans. F. M. Cornford, in Hamilton and Cairns, eds. 1961: 957-1017.
          (Stephanus numbers 216a1-268d5.)
i.367-361BCa. *Theaetetus*, trans. F. M. Cornford, in Hamilton and Cairns, eds. 1961: 845-919.
          (Stephanus numbers 142a1-210d4.)
p.353BC. *Letter VII*, trans. L. A. Post, in Hamilton and Cairns, eds. 1961: 1574-1598. (Stephanus
          numbers 323e1-352a5.)
PLOCHMANN, George K.
1954.   "Socrates, the Stranger from Elea, and Some Others", *Classical Philology* 49, 223-231.
POCIUS, G. L.
1979.   "Hooked Rugs in Newfoundland", *Journal of American Folklore* 92, 273-284.
POINSOT, John.
1631.   *Artis Logicae Prima Pars* (Alcalá, Spain). The opening pages 1-11a14 of this work and the

"Quaestio Disputanda I. De Termino. Art. 6. Utrum Voces Significant per prius Conceptus an Res" pages 104b31-108a33, relevant to the discussion of signs in the *Secunda Pars* of 1632 (entry following), have been incorporated in the 1632a entry (second entry following, q.v., pp. 4-30 and 342-351 "Appendix A. On the Signification of Language", respectively) for the independent edition of that discussion published by the University of California Press. The Reiser edition of Poinsot's work (Vol. I; Turin: Marietti, 1930: pp. 1-247, arranged by columns—a, b—and line numbers within each column) was used as source for the Latin text.

1632.   *Artis Logicae Secunda Pars* (Alcalá, Spain). The Reiser edition of this work (also arranged as described in preceding 1631 entry; Vol. I; Turin: Marietti, 1930: pp. 249-839) was used as source for the Latin text.

1632a.   *Tractatus de Signis*, subtitled *The Semiotic of John Poinsot*, extracted from the *Artis Logicae Prima et Secunda Pars* of 1631-1632 (above two entries) and arranged in bilingual format by John Deely in consultation with Ralph A. Powell (First Edition; Berkeley: University of California Press, 1985), as explained in Deely 1985, q.v. Pages in this volume are set up in matching columns of English and Latin, with intercolumnar numbers every fifth line. (Thus, references to the volume are by page number, followed by a slash and the appropriate line number of the specific section of text referred to—e.g., 287/3-26.)

POLANYI, Michael.
1969.   *Knowing and Being: Essays by Michael Polanyi*, ed. Marjorie Grene (Chicago: The University of Chicago Press).

POP, Mihai.
1972.   "Le laboratoire de sémiotique de l'Université de Bucarest, Roumanie", *Semiotica* 5, 301-302.

POPPER, Karl R., and John C. ECCLES.
1977.   *The Self and the Brain* (New York: Springer International).

POWELL, Ralph Austin.
1977, July 30. "Memorandum on the Translation of 'Ratio' in Poinsot", published in substantially complete form in Deely 1985: 468-471.
1983.   *Freely Chosen Reality* (Washington, D.C.: University Press of America).

PRESTI, David, Wan-Jean HSU, and Max DELBRÜCK.
1977.   "Phototropism in Phycomyces mutands lacking β-Carotene" *Photochemistry and Photobiology* 26, 403-405.

PREZIOSI, Donald.
1979.   *The Semiotics of the Built Environment* (Bloomington: Indiana University Press).

PRIOR, William.
1979.   "Plato's Account of Being and Non-Being in the *Sophist*", paper presented at the American Philosophical Association Western Division Conference, Denver, Colorado, April 19.

PRISCIAN of Lydia.
c.526.   "De Voce", chapter of *Institutiones Grammaticae*, ed. M. Hertz, in Vol. II of *Grammatici Latini* (Leipzig, 1855; rpt. Hildesheim, 1961).

PSEUDO-MARSILIUS of INGHEN (Anonymous).
1495.   *Commentum emendatum et correctum in primum et quartum tractatus Petri Hyspani et super tractatibus Marsilii de Suppositionibus, ampliationibus, appelationibus et consequentiis* (Hagenau). Reprinted as Marsilius von Inghen, *Commentum in primum et quartum tractatum Petri Hispani* (Frankfurt: Minerva, 1967). For discussions of the mistaken attribution of this work to the fourteenth-century philosopher Marsilius of Inghen by the Frankfurt editors, see Maierù 1972: 234 n. 57 and Bos 1983: 32.

PTOLEMY ("Claudius Prolemaeus").
c.150.   Κλαυδιου Πτολεηαιου άρηονικων βιβλια γ́ *Claudii Ptolomaei Harmonicorum libri tres*, J. Wallis . . . edidit, versione et notis illustravit, et auctarium adjecit (Oxford: E Theatro Sheldoniano, 1682).
p.150.   *Almagest*, trans. annotated by G. J. Toomer (London: Duckworth, 1984).

RADCLIFFE-BROWN, A. R.
1941.   "The Study of Kinship Systems", *Journal of the Royal Anthropological Institute of Great Britain and Ireland* 71.1, 1-18: seminal source of the reductive influence of Radcliffe-Brown discussed in Deely 1980: esp. 215 n. 7, and Deely 1982: 122. Gathered with other influential essays in 1952 following.
1952.   *Structure and Function in Primitive Society* (Glencoe, IL: The Free Press).

RAMNOUX, Clémence.
1968.   *Heraclite ou l'homme entre les choses et les mots* (2nd ed.; Paris: Les Belles Letters).

RANDALL, Jr., John Herman.
1961.   *The School of Padua and the Emergence of Modern Science* (Padua: Editrice Antenore).

1962.   *The Career of Philosophy*, Volume I, *From the Middle Ages to the Enlightenment* (New York: Columbia).
RANSDELL, Joseph.
1966.   *Charles Peirce: The Idea of Representation* (New York: Columbia University, unpublished doctoral dissertation).
1979.   "Semiotic Objectivity", *Semiotica* 26.3/4, 261-288.
1980.   "Semiotic and Linguistics", in *The Signifying Animal*, ed. Irmengard Rauch and Gerald F. Carr (Bloomington: Indiana University Press), 135-185.
READ, Allen Walker.
1948.   "An Account of the Word Semantics", *Word* 4, 78-97.
REISIG, Karl.
1839.   *Professor K. Reisig's Vorlesungen über lateinische Sprachwissenschaft*, hrsg. mit Anmerkungen von Dr. Friedrich Haase (Leipzig: Lehnhold).
1872.   This work, presumably the English of Reisig 1839, is referred to by Sebeok 1976: 50 (p. 257 above). We were unable to track down the specific reference, and rely for our date on a letter from Professor Sebeok dated 8/16/85.
REISMAN, K.
1970.   "Cultural and Linguistic Ambiguity in a West Indian Village", in *Afro-American Anthropology*, ed. N. E. Whitten and J. Szwed (New York: Free Press), 129-144.
REMAK, Joachim.
1967.   *The Origins of World War I* (Hinsdale, IL: The Dryden Press).
RESCHER, Nicholas.
1966.   *The Logic of Commands* (New York: Dover).
RESNIKOW, Lasar Ossipowitsch.
1968.   *Erkenntnistheoretische Fragen der Semiotik* (Berlin: VEB Deutscher Verlag der Wissenschaften). [Enlarged edition from the original Russian, 1964; in 1967 an Italian translation was published under the title, *Semiotica e Marxismo: I problemi gnoseologici della semiotica* (Milan: Bompiani).]
REY, Abel.
1933.   *La jeunesse de la science grecque* (Paris: La Renaissance du Livre).
REY, Alain.
1969.   'Remarques sémantiques", *Langue Française* 4: 5-29.
1973.   *Théories du Signe et du Sens, I* (Paris: Klincksieck).
RICOEUR, Paul.
1962.   "Herméneutique et réflection", in *Demmitazione e immagine*, ed. E. Castelli (Padua: Cedam).
1963.   "Structure et herméneutiques", *Esprit* 31, 596-652.
1968.   "Structure, Word, Event", *Philosophy Today* 12, 114-129.
1975.   *La Métaphore vive* (Paris: Seuil). English trans. by Robert Czerny, *The Rule of Metaphor* (Toronto: University of Toronto Press).
ROBERT, Paul.
1967.   *Dictionnaire alphabétique & analogique de la langue française* (Paris: Société du Nouveau Littré, Le Robert).
ROCHBERG-HALTON, Eugene.
1979.   "Cultural signs and urban adaptation: The meaning of cherished household possessions", dissertation summary (mimeographed), Behavioral Sciences, University of Chicago.
ROLLAND, Romain.
1952.   *Le Cloître de la rue d'Ulm* (Paris: Albin Michel).
ROLLIN, Bernard E.
1976.   *Natural and Conventional Meaning: An Examination of the Distinction* (The Hague: Mouton).
ROMEO, Luigi.
1976.   "Heraclitus and the Foundations of Semiotics", *Versus* 15.5 (dicembre), 73-90.
1977.   "The Derivation of 'Semiotics' through the History of the Discipline", in *Semiosis* 6.2, 37-49.
1977a.   "The Semiotic Foundation of Linguistics", *Semiotic Scene* I.2, 31-38.
1979.   "Pedro da Fonseca in Renaissance Semiotics: A Segmental History of Footnotes", *Ars Semeiotica* II.2, 187-204.
ROSS, Robert E.
1912.   *The Law of Discovery* (London: Butterworth & Co.).
ROSSI-LANDI, Ferrucio.
1974.   "Linguistics and Economics", in Vol. 12 of *Current Trends in Linguistics*, ed. Thomas A. Sebeok (The Hague: Mouton).
1975.   "Signs about a Master of Signs", *Semiotica* 13, 155-197. Review article of Morris 1971.
RUNCIMAN, W. G.
1973.   "What Is Structuralism?", in *The Philosophy of Social Explanation*, ed. Alan Ryan (London: Oxford University Press), 189-202.

RUSSELL, Anthony F.
  1981.   "The Logic of History as a Semiotic Process of Question and Answer in the Thought
          of R. G. Collingwood", in *Semiotics 1981* (Proceedings of the Semiotic Society of America),
          ed. John N. Deely and Margot D. Lenhart (New York: Plenum Press, 1982), 179-189.
  1984.   *Logic, Philosophy, and History* (Washington, D.C.: University Press of America).
RUSSELL, Bertrand.
  1905.   "On Denoting", *Mind* XIV, 479-493. See gloss on entry for Russell 1919.
  1910.   "Incomplete Symbols", third introductory chapter to Whitehead and Russell 1910-1913
          (q.v.): 66-84. See gloss on entry for Russell 1919.
  1919.   *Introduction to Mathematical Philosophy* (London: George Allen and Unwin Ltd.). Russell's
          so-called "Theory of Descriptions" first appeared in 1905 (q.v.). The most technical and
          "logically simple" exposition of the theory is perhaps the version incorporated into the
          third introductory chapter of the *Principia Mathematica* under the title "Incomplete Sym-
          bols". See entry for 1910. But insofar as philosophy is more concerned with underlying
          assumptions and principles than with the resolution of problems into definite conclusions,
          the most philosophically important exposition of the theory is perhaps the one set out in
          Chapters 15-17 of this 1919 book. Discussion in Deely 1975a: 262ff.
RUSSELL, L. J.
  1939.   "Note on the Term ΣΗΜΕΙΩΤΙΚΗ [sic] in Locke", *Mind* 48, 405-06.
RUSSMAN, Thomas A.
  1981.   "Two Paradigms of Reality and Objectivity", *The New Scholasticism* LV (Winter), 1-15.
SALLIS, John.
  1975.   *Being and Logos: The Way of Platonic Dialogue* (Pittsburgh: Duquesne University Press).
SALUCCI, Brunero, and Giovanni GILARDONI, eds.
  1968.   *Eraclito. Tutti i frammenti* (Florence: Le Monnier).
SARTON. George.
  1954.   *Galen of Pergamon* (Lawrence: University of Kansas Press).
SARTRE, Jean-Paul.
  1943.   *L'Être et le néant, essai d'ontologie phénoménologique* (Paris: Gallimard). References are to the
          English trans. by Hazel E. Barnes, *Being and Nothingness: A Phenomenological Essay on Ontology*
          (New York: Philosophical Library, 1956).
SAUSSURE, Ferdinand de.
  i.1906-1911. Lectures delivered at the University of Geneva and published from auditors' notes by
          Charles Bally and Albert Sechehaye under the title *Cours de linguistique générale* (Paris: Payot,
          1915). Page references in Sebeok are to the ed. of R. Engler (Wiesbaden: Otto Harrassowitz,
          1916); see also the critical ed. of Tullio de Mauro (Paris: Payot, 1972). Page references
          in Merrell are to the English trans. by Wade Baskin, *Course in General Linguistics* (New
          York: McGraw-Hill, 1966).
SAVAN, David.
  1976.   *An Introduction to C. S. Peirce's Semiotics: Part I* (Toronto: Toronto Semiotic Circle Mono-
          graphs).
  1983.   "Toward a Refutation of Semiotic Idealism", *Recherches Sémiotiques/Semiotic Inquiry* 3.1, 1-8.
SCAPULA, Joannes.
  1579-1580. *Lexicon Graeco-Latinum* (Basel: Ex officina Hervagiana). This work went through several
          editions: *Lexicon Graeco-Latinum novum* (Basel: Per Sebastianum Henricpetri, 1605); *Lex-
          icon Graecorum novum* (London: Impensis Ioscosae Norton, 1637); *Lexicon Graeco-Latinum*
          (Lyons: Typis B. & A. Elzeviriorum & F. Hackii, 1652). Romeo (1977: 46 n. 5) explains
          this series of editions as follows: "Henricus Stephanus' *Thesaurus Graecae linguae* was first
          published in 1572. Joannes Scapula's pirated abridgement of the *Thesaurus* started in 1579
          and generated several editions until the nineteenth century". It must be noted that Romeo
          (1977: 43) mentions a 1663 edition of Scapula as in Locke's possession along with the
          1605 edition, but Romeo gives no bibliographical information whatever concerning this
          1663 edition.
SCHAFF, Adam.
  1964.   *Jçezyk a poznanie* (Warsaw: Państwowe Wydawnictwo Naukowe). References are to the
          English trans. by Olgierd Wojtasiewicz, *Language and Cognition* (New York: McGraw-Hill,
          1973).
SCHLEIERMACHER, Friedrich D. E.
  1807.   "Herakleitos der Dunkel, von Ephesos", *Museum der Alterthums-Wissenschaft* I, 313-533.
SCHOKNECHT, W., E. KARRER, and K. DRYSCH.
  1980.   "Sauerstoffmessungen in pflanzenreichen Räumen". Working paper (mimeographed),
          Institut für Arbeits- und Sozialmedizin, Universität Tübingen.

SCHOLEM, Gerhardt.
  1960. *Zur Kabbala und ihrer Symbolik* (Zürich: Rhein). Page references are to the English trans.
      by Ralph Mannheim, *On the Kabbalah and Its Symbolism* (New York: Schocken, 1965).
SCHOLES, Robert.
  1974. *Structuralism in Literature* (New Haven: Yale University Press).
SCHRÖDER, E.
  1877. *Der Operationskreis des Logikkalkuls* (Leipzig).
  1890-1905. *Vorlesungen über die Algebra der Logik* (Leipzig: I, 1890; II.1, 1891; III, 1895; II.2, 1905).
SCHRÖDINGER, Erwin.
  1945. *What Is Life?* (New York: Macmillan).
SCHUCHMAN, Philip.
  1979. *Problems of Knowledge in Legal Scholarship* (Storrs, Conn.: University of Connecticut Law
      School Press).
SCHUR, Edwin M.
  1968. *Law and Society* (New York: Random House).
SCHUSTER, Paul Robert.
  1872. *Heraklit von Ephesus. Ein Versuch, dessen Fragmente in ihrer ursprünglichen Ordnung wiederherzustellen*
      (Leipzig: Teubner).
SCHWIMMER, Eric.
  1979. "Reciprocity and Structure", *Man* n.s. 14, 271-285.
SCRUTON, Roger.
  1980. "Possible Worlds and Premature Sciences", in *The London Review of Books*, 7 February
      1980, reviewing Preziosi 1979 and Eco 1976, without much good to report, but without
      much depth, either.
SEARLE, John R.
  1965. "What Is a Speech Act?", in *Philosophy in America*, ed. Max Black (London: George Allen
      and Unwin), 221-39. Page references are to the reprint in *The Philosophy of Language*, ed.
      John Searle (Oxford: Oxford University Press, 1971), 39-53.
SEBEOK, Thomas A.
  1963. "Communication among social bees; porpoises and sonar; man and dolphin", *Language*
      39, 448-466.
  1968. "Zoosemiotics", *American Speech* 43, 142-44.
  1968a. "Is a Comparative Semiotics Possible?", in *Échanges et communications: Mélanges offerts à
      Claude Lévi-Strauss à l'occasion de son 60ème anniversaire*, ed. Jean Pouillon et Pierre Maranda
      (The Hague: Mouton), 614-627, reprinted in Sebeok 1976: 59-69.
  1970. "The Word 'Zoosemiotics'", *Language Sciences* 10, 36-37.
  1971 (original composition), " 'Semiotics' and Its Congeners", first published in Jazayery, Polomé,
      and Winter 1976: 283-295, and reprinted in Sebeok 1976: 47-58 [q.v.]. Page references
      are to Sebeok 1976.
  1972. *Perspectives in Zoosemiotics* (The Hague: Mouton).
  1974. "Semiotics: A Survey of the State of the Art", in *Linguistics and Adjacent Arts and Sciences*,
      Vol. 12 of the *Current Trends in Linguistics* series, ed. by Sebeok (The Hague: Mouton),
      211-264. Page references are to the reprint in Sebeok 1976 (q.v.): 1-45.
  1974a. "La dynamique des signes", in *L'Unité de l'homme: Invariants biologiques et universaux culturels*,
      ed. Edgar Morin and Massimo Piattelli-Palmarini (Paris: Seuil), 61-77, reprinted in Sebeok
      1976: 95-110.
  1975. "The Semiotic Web: A Chronicle of Prejudices", *Bulletin of Literary Semiotics* 2, 1-63, as
      reprinted with essential corrections and additions in Sebeok 1976 (q.v.): 149-188.
  1975a. "Zoosemiotics: At the Intersection of Nature and Culture", in *The Tell-Tale Sign*, ed.
      Thomas A. Sebeok (Lisse, The Netherlands: Peter de Ridder Press), 85-95.
  1976. *Contributions to the Doctrine of Signs* (Lisse: Peter de Ridder Press; reprinted with a new Preface
      by Brooke Williams and with arabic pagination unchanged as Volume IV of the Sources
      in Semiotics Series of the University Press of America, 1985).
  1976a. "Final Report: Narrative" for the National Endowment for the Humanities on the Pilot
      Program in Semiotics in the Humanities at Indiana University's Bloomington campus,
      1 August 1975-31 July 1976; report dated 1 June 1976, distributed by the Research Center
      for Language and Semiotic Studies, 14 pages; subsequently published as "Appendix III.
      Teaching Semiotics: Report on a Pilot Program", in Sebeok 1979: 272-279. Page references
      are to this published copy.
  1977. "Ecumenicalism in Semiotics", in *A Perfusion of Signs*, ed. Thomas A. Sebeok (Bloom-
      ington and London: Indiana University Press), 180-206.
  1977a. "The French Swiss Connection", *Semiotic Scene* I, 27-32.

1978. "Looking in the Destination for What Should Have Been Sought in the Source", *Diogenes* 104, 112-138.
1979. *The Sign & Its Masters* (Austin: University of Texas Press).
1979a. "Prefigurements of Art", *Semiotica* 27, 3-73.
1980. *Statement* distributed to participants in the colloquium "The Role of the Observer" held as a Plenary session of the seventh Annual Meeting of the Semiotic Society of America, Buffalo, New York, October 1982.
1981. *The Play of Musement* (Bloomington: Indiana University Press).
1982. "Foreword" to *Introducing Semiotic. Its History and Doctrine* (Bloomington: Indiana University Press), ix-xi.
1984. "S601. Introduction to Semiotic Studies", graduate seminar taught in the Fall at Indiana University, Bloomington.
1984a. "Signs of Life", *International Semiotic Spectrum* 2 (June 1984), 1-2.
1984b. October 12. "Vital Signs" (Presidential Address to the Ninth Annual Meeting of the Semiotic Society of America), *The American Journal of Semiotics* 3.3 (1985), 1-27.
SEBEOK, Thomas A., ed.
1969. *Approaches to Semiotics* 1- (The Hague: Mouton).
SEBEOK, Thomas A., Alfred S. HAYES, and Mary Catherine BATESON, eds.
1964. *Approaches to Semiotics: Cultural Anthropology, Education, Linguistics, Psychiatry, Psychology* (The Hague: Mouton).
SEBEOK, Thomas A., and Robert ROSENTHAL, eds.
1981. *The Clever Hans Phenomenon: Communication with Horses, Whales, Apes, and People* (New York: The New York Academy of Sciences).
SEBEOK, Thomas A., and Jean UMIKER-SEBEOK.
1979. " 'You Know My Method': A Juxtaposition of Charles S. Peirce and Sherlock Holmes", *Semiotica* 26: 203-250. Subsequently reprinted in an enhanced monograph form under the same title (Bloomington: Gaslight Publications, 1980).
SEBEOK, Thomas A., and Jean UMIKER-SEBEOK, eds. (Further under UMIKER-SEBEOK).
1976. *Speech Surrogates: Drum and Whistle Systems*, in 2 vols. (The Hague: Mouton).
1980. *Speaking of Apes. A Critical Anthology of Two-Way Communication with Man* (New York: Plenum). This anthology is a landmark in the study of man-animal communication, bringing to bear, as it does, a state of the art critical consciousness that has so far been conspicuously lacking in this area of research. Further under Umiker-Sebeok.
SEMIOTICS 1984 (10th Annual Proceedings of the Semiotic Society of America).
1984. "Style Sheet for Semiotic Society of America Proceedings", in *loc. cit.*, ed. J. N. Deely (Lanham, MD: University Press of America, 1985), 715-739.
SEVE, Lucien.
1969. "Método estructural y método dialéctico", trans. Antonio G. Valiente, in *Estructuralismo y marxismo* (Barcelona: Ediciones Martínez Roca), 108-150.
SEXTUS EMPIRICUS.
c.200. *Outlines of Pyrrhonism*, bilingual Greek/English text with an English trans. by R. G. Bury (The Loeb Classical Library), Vol. I of *Sextus Empiricus* (London: Heinemann, 1933).
SHAFFER, Peter.
1974. *Equus*, in *Equus and Shrivings: Two Plays* (New York: Atheneum), 1-106.
SHERZER, D., and J. SHERZER.
1976. "Mormaknamaloe", in *Ritual and Symbol in Native Central America*, ed. P. Young and J. Howe (University of Oregon Anthropology Papers, Number 9).
SHORT, T. L.
1981. "Semeiosis and Intentionality", *Transactions of the Charles S. Peirce Society*, XVII.3 (Summer), 197-223.
1981a. "Peirce's Concept of Final Causation", *Transactions of the Charles S. Peirce Society*, XVII.4 (Fall), 369-382.
1983. "Teleology in Nature", *American Philosophical Quarterly* 20.4 (October), 311-320.
SHOUBY, E.
1951. "The Influence of the Arabic Language on the Psychology of the Arabs", *The Middle East Journal* 5, 284-302.
SILVERSTEIN, Michael.
1976. "Shifters, Linguistic Categories, and Cultural Description", in *Meaning in Anthropology*, ed. K. Basso and H. Selby (Albuquerque, NM: University of New Mexico Press), 11-55.
SIMON, Yves R.
1955. "Foreword" to *The Material Logic of John of St. Thomas*, selections made and trans. from the Latin of Poinsot 1632 by Yves R. Simon, John J. Glanville, and G. Donald Hollenhorst

(Chicago: The University of Chicago Press), pp. ix-xxiii. This work is unusable as a guide to Poinsot's semiotic—details in Deely 1985: 406 n. 15, here quoted in part: "Nonetheless, in view of the scarcity of works in this area and the difficulty of the problems involved in their mastery, this pioneering effort of Simon and his collaborators is an indispensable mine of scholastic lore in Simon's 'Notes' and 'Foreword' to the text. Simon's vignettes of reflection on the distinction between formal and material logic in the scholastic context (pp. ix-xviii) bear particular mention in this regard."

1961.   "To Be and To Know", *Chicago Review* 15.4 (Spring), 83-100.
SIMPSON, George Gaylord.
1963.   "Biology and the Nature of Science", *Science* 139, 81-88.
SINGER, Milton.
1984.   *Man's Glassy Essence: Explorations in Semiotic Anthropology* (Bloomington: Indiana University Press).
SLUGA, Hans.
1980.   *Gottlob Frege* (Boston: Routledge & Kegan Paul).
SMART, Benjamin Humphrey.
1831.   *An Outline of Sematology: or an Essay Towards Establishing a New Theory of Grammar, Logic, and Rhetoric*, in Smart 1839.
1837.   *Sequel to Sematology. An Attempt to Clear the Way for the Regeneration of Metaphysics*, in Smart 1839.
1839.   *Beginnings of a New School of Metaphysics: Three Essays*, with an Appendix (London: J. Richardson).
SÖDER, Karl.
1964.   "Beiträge J. H. Lamberts zur formalen Logik und Semiotik". Dissertation, Greifwald.
SONTAG, S.
1978.   *Illness as Metaphor* (New York: Vintage Books).
SOTIROPOULOS, Dimitri.
1977.   "Diglossia and the National Language Question in Modern Greece", *Linguistics* 197, 5-31.
SPADE, Paul Vincent.
1980.   Critical apparatus and notes to d'Ailly c.1372, q.v.
STAIANO, Kathryn Vance.
1979.   "A semiotic definition of illness", *Semiotica* 28: 107-25.
STEINTHAL, Heyman.
1863.   *Geschichte der Sprachwissenschaft bei den Griechen und Römern mit besonderer Rücksicht auf die Logik*, in 2 vols. (Berlin: Dümmler).
1871.   *Einleitung in die Psychologie und Sprachwissenschaft* (Berlin: Dümmlers).
STEPHANUS, Henricus.
1572-1573. *Thesaurus Graecae linguae*, in 6 vols. (Geneva: Excudebat H. Stephanus). Two subsequent editions are important for the present context. [1] *Thesaurus Graecae linguae, editio nova auctior et emendatior*, in 8 vols. (London, 1815-1828). Of this edition Romeo remarks (1977 original publication: 46 n. 5): "all lexica to date are still based on the original *Thesaurus* which, itself, had several editions. However, Locke could only have been exposed to the original edition, for only in the nineteenth century was a major change made through the *Editio nova auctior et emendatior*, London: 1815-1828 (8 volumes)." Unfortunately, Romeo gives no indication as to those responsible for the alleged "increased authority and corrections" of this posthumous edition, as neither for the publisher. (Compare discussion of the 1663 Lyons edition of Poinsot's work in Deely 1985: 396, 397, 402 n. 7, 403 n. 8, 442, 459 n. 95.) [2] *Thesaurus Graecae linguae ab Henrico Stephanus constructus. Post editionem Anglicam novis additamentis auctum ordineque alphabetico tertio ediderunt*, ed. C. B. Hase et al. (Paris: 1831-1865; reprint Graz: Akademische Druck- u. Verlagsanstalt, 1954-1955). Romeo continues (ibid.): "I was able to consult only the Paris edition of 1831-1865 (*Thesaurus Graecae linguae ab Henrico Stephano constructus. Post editionem Anglicam novis additamentis auctum ordineque alphabetico tertio ediderunt*, C. B. Hase [et alii]), reprinted in Graz by Akademische Druck- u. Verlagsanstalt, 1954-1955".
STIRLING, Paul.
1965.   *Turkish Village* (London: Weidenfeld & Nicholson).
STRAWSON, P. F.
1952.   *Introduction to Logical Theory* (London: Methuen).
STRUEVER, Nancy S.
1974.   "The Study of Language and the Study of History", *Journal of Interdisciplinary History* 4, 401-415.
SUAREZ, Francis.
1605.   *De Sacramentis* (Venice: Apud Societatem Minimam). Vol. XX of the *Opera omnia editio nova*, a Carolo Berton (Paris: Vivès, 1860) was used in preparing the present work.

SUPPE, Frederick.
    1974. "The Search for Philosophical Understanding of Scientific Theories", in *The Structure of Scientific Theories*, ed. Frederick Suppe (Urbana: University of Illinois Press), 1-241.
SWIFT, Jonathan.
    1726. *Gulliver's Travels*, critical edition by Robert A. Greenberg (2nd redaction; New York: W. W. Norton, 1970).
SYPHER, Wylie.
    1968. *Literature and Technology* (New York: Random House).
TATE, Allen.
    1952. "The Angelic Imagination and the Power of Words", *Kenyon Review*, 14.3 (Summer), 455-475.
TAYLOR, A. E.
    1956. *Plato: The Man and His Work* (New York: World Publishing Co.).
THOLFSEN, Trygve R.
    1967. *Historical Thinking: An Introduction* (New York: Harper & Row).
THOM, René.
    1972. *Stabilité structurelle et morphogénèse: essai d'une théorie générale des modèles* (Reading, MA: W. A. Benjamin). References to this work are to the version updated by the author and translated into English by D. H. Fowler, *Structural Stability and Morphogenesis: An Outline of a General Theory of Models* (same publisher, 1975).
    1973. "De l'icone au symbole: Esquisse d'une théorie du symbolisme", *Cahiers Internationaux du Symbolisme* 22/23, 85-106; English version entitled "From the Icon to the Symbol" is reproduced in Innis ed. 1985: 275-291, q.v.
TILLINGHAST, Pardon E.
    1972. *The Specious Past* (Menlo Park, CA: Addison-Wesley Publishing Company).
TODOROV, Tzvetan.
    1977. *Théories du symbole* (Paris: Seuil).
    1978. *Symbolisme et interprétation* (Paris: Seuil).
TOPOROV, N.
    1972. "K proiskhozhdeniiu nekotorykh poeticheskikh simvolov (Paleoliticheskaia epokha)", in *Rannie formy iskusstva* [Early Forms of Art] (Moscow). Page references are to the English translation, "Toward the Origin of Certain Poetic Symbols: the Palaeolithic Period", in *Semiotics and Structuralism: Readings from the Soviet Union*, ed. Heinrich Baran (White Plains, New York: International Arts and Sciences Press), 184-225.
TOULMIN, Stephen.
    1953. *The Philosophy of Science* (London: Hutchinson's University Library).
    1958. *The Uses of Argument* (Cambridge: Cambridge University Press).
    1961. *Foresight and Understanding* (New York: Harper and Row).
TRUBETSKOY, N. S.
    1939. *Grundzüge der Phonologie, Travaux du Cercle Linguistique de Prague* 7. References are to the French trans. by J. Cantineau, *Principes de Phonologie* (Paris: Klincksieck, 1964).
UEXKÜLL, Jakob von.
    1899-1940. *Kompositionslehre der Natur. Biologie als undogmatische Naturwissenschaft*, selected writings ed. and with an introduction by Thure von Uexküll (Frankfurt a. M.: Ullstein).
    1920. *Theoretische Biologie* (Berlin). The English trans. by D. L. MacKinnon, *Theoretical Biology* (New York: Harcourt, Brace & Co., 1926) was consulted.
    1922. "Wie sehen wir die Natur und wie sieht sie sich selber?" *Die Naturwissenschaft* 14, 316-322.
    1934. *Streifzüge durch die Umwelten von Tieren und Menschen*, with illustrations by Georg Kriszat (Berlin). The English trans. by Claire H. Schiller "A Stroll through the Worlds of Animals and Men", in *Instinctive Behavior: The Development of a Modern Concept*, ed. Claire H. Schiller (New York: International Universities Press, Inc., 1957), 5-80, was used.
    1935. "Die Bedeutung der Umweltforschung für die Erkenntnis des Lebens", *Zeitschrift für die gesamte Naturwissenschaft* 7, 257-272.
    1940. "Bedeutungslehre", *Bios*, vol. 10 (Leipzig). Reprinted in *Streifzüge durch die Umwelten von Tieren und Menschen/Bedeutungslehre*, by Jakob von Uexküll and Georg Kriszat (Frankfurt a. M.: S. Fischer Verlag, 1970). Page references are to the 1970 reprint. English trans. by Barry Stone and Herbert Weiner as "The Theory of Meaning", *Semiotica* 42.1 (1982), Special Issue guest edited by Thure von Uexküll, 25-82. See commentary on the translation of "Umwelt" in this Special Issue in Deely 1985a References.
UEXKÜLL, Thure von.
    1980. "Vorwort des Herausgebers" (pp. 7-15), "Einleitung: Plädoyer für eine sinndeutende Biologie" (pp. 17-85), and "Vorbemerkungen des Herausgebers" (passim) to Jakob von Uexküll 1899-1940, q.v.

UEXKÜLL, Thure von, ed.
   1979.   *Lehrbuch der psychosomatischen Medizin* (München: Urgan & Schwarzenberg).
ULLMANN, Stephen.
   1951.   *The Principles of Semantics* (Glasgow: Jackson, Son & Co.).
UMIKER-SEBEOK, Jean, and Thomas A. SEBEOK.
           (The five articles comprising this entry constitute a single, jointly produced, ongoing critique,
           substantially expanded and—between 1979-1981—continually updated in each stage or
           version, that probably marks a turning point in the discussion of animal "language".
           The order of the names in this particular case does not uniformly represent priority of
           authorship for the component entries, as this seems to have shifted, e.g., between the 1980
           and 1981a versions.)
   1979.   "Performing Animals: Secrets of the Trade", *Psychology Today* 13.6, 78-91.
   1980.   "Questioning Apes", in Sebeok and Umiker-Sebeok eds. 1980: 1-59.
   1981.   "Clever Hans and Smart Simians: The Self-Fulfilling Prophecy and Kindred Methodo-
           logical Pitfalls", *Anthropos* 76.1-2, 89-165.
   1981a. "Smart Simians: The Self-Fulfilling Prophecy and Kindred Methodological Pitfalls", in
           Sebeok 1981: Chapter 8, 134-209.
   1982.   "Rejoinder to the Rumbaughs", *Anthropos* "Reports and Comments" 77, 574-578.
VALÉRY, Paul.
   a.1945. *Oeuvres*, Vol. I (Paris: Gallimard, 1957).
VEATCH, Henry B.
   1952.   *Intentional Logic* (New Haven: Yale University Press).
VEINOGLOU, Tzon ("John").
   1976.   "Ελλινικοτατεσ ι ριζεσ τοθ ρεβετικοθ" ("The roots of the *rebetika* are very Hellenic"),
           Ta Nea, in Greek, May 10, 11, 12.
VESCOVINI, G. Federici.
   1965.   *Studi sulla prospettiva medievale* (Turin: Giappichelli).
VOIGT, Vilmos.
   1969.   "Modellálás a folklorisztikában", *Studia Ethnographica* 5, 347-430.
VYGOTSKY, Lev Semenovich.
   1962.   *Myshlenie i rech'*, trans. by Eugenia Hanfmann and Gertrude Vakar as *Thought and Language*
           (Cambridge, MA: The M.I.T. Press, 1962).
WALLACE, William A.
   1980.   "Albertus Magnus on Suppositional Necessity in the Natural Sciences", in Weisheipl,
           ed. 1980 [q.v.]: 103-128. Wallace documents a remarkable discussion in Albert's *De
           Praedicabilibus*, tract. 7, ch. 2, and tract. 8, ch. 10 (in Vol. I of the *Opera Omnia*, Borgnet
           ed. pp. 122a-b and 140a, respectively) of the conditions of egg-formation under which
           a crow that was not black would be produced.
WALLIS, J., ed.
   1682.   Latin trans. of Ptolemy c.150, q.v.
WALZER, Richard R.
   1939.   *Eraclito* (Florence: Pubblicazione della Reale Scuola Normale di Pisa; reprinted Hildesheim:
           Georg Olms, 1964).
WEBBER, J.
   1973.   Review article, *Journal of the Anthropological Society of Oxford* 4, 32-41.
WEDGWOOD, C. V.
   1956.   *Literature and the Historian*, Presidential Address to the English Association (London: Ox-
           ford University Press). Page references are to the reprint in *Truth and Opinion* (New York:
           Macmillan, 1960), 62-81. *Truth and Opinion* was reissued in 1967 under the title of *The
           Sense of the Past. Thirteen Studies in the Theory and Practice of History* (New York: Collier Books),
           with pagination identical to the 1960 edition.
WEISHEIPL, James A.
   1974.   *Friar Thomas d'Aquino. His Life, Thought, and Works* (New York: Doubleday).
   1980.   "Life and Works of Albert the Great", in Weisheipl, ed. 1980 [q.v.]: 13-51.
   1980a. "Appendix I. Albert's Work on Natural Science (*libri naturales*) in Probable Chronological
           Order", in Weisheipl, ed. 1980 [q.v.]: 565-577.
WEISHEIPL, James A., ed.
   1980.   *Albertus Magnus and the Sciences. Commemorative Essays 1980* (Toronto: Pontifical Institute
           of Mediaeval Studies).
WEISS, Paul, and Arthur W. BURKS.
   1945.   "Peirce's Sixty-six Signs", *The Journal of Philosophy* 42.13 (June 21), 383-388.

WEIZENBAUM, Joseph.
    1977. "Computers as 'Therapists' ", *Science* 198, 354.
WELBY, Victoria Lady.
    1896. "Sense, Meaning, and Interpretation", *Mind* V.17-18, 24-37 (Vol. 17), 186-202 (Vol. 18).
WELTRING, Georg.
    1910. *Das* Semeion *in der aristotelischen, stoischen, epikureischen und skeptischen Philosophie. Ein Beitrag zur Geschichte der Antiken Methodenlehre* (Bonn: Hauptmann'sche Buchdruckerei).
WEYL, Hermann.
    1932. *The Open World* (New Haven: Yale University Press).
WHEELER, John Archibald.
    1981, July. Lecture presented at "Scientific Concepts of Time in Humanistic and Social Perspective" Conference, held at the Rockefeller Foundation's Study and Conference Center in Bellagio, Italy, 6-10 July 1981.
WHEWELL, William.
    1837. *History of the Inductive Sciences, From the Earliest to the Present Time* (London), in 3 volumes.
    1840. *Philosophy of the Inductive Sciences* (London).
WINNER, Irene P. and Thomas G.
    1976. "The Semiotics of Cultural Texts", *Semiotica* 18, 101-156.
WHITE, Hayden.
    1978. *Tropics of Discourse. Essays in Cultural Criticism* (Baltimore: The Johns Hopkins University Press).
WHITE, Jr., Lynn.
    1956. "The Changing Past", in *Frontiers of Knowledge in the Study of Man*, ed. Lynn White, Jr. (New York: Harper & Brothers), 68-78.
WHITEHEAD, Alfred North.
    1948. *Science and the Modern World* (New York: Macmillan). References in Baer are to the 1967 reprint (New York: The Free Press).
WHITEHEAD, Alfred North, and Bertrand RUSSELL.
    1910-1913. *Principia Mathematica* (Cambridge), 3 vols.
WHITNEY, William Dwight, ed.
    1897. *The Century Dictionary and Cyclopedia*, in 10 vols. (New York: The Century Co.).
WHORF, Benjamin Lee.
    1956. "An American Indian Model of the Universe", in *Language, Thought, and Reality*, ed. John B. Carroll (Cambridge: The M.I.T. Press), 57-64.
WHYTE, Lancelot Law.
    1944. *The Next Development in Man* (London: Cresset Press). Page references in this volume are to the New American Library edition, New York, 1950.
WIENER, Norbert.
    1967. *The Human Use of Human Beings* (New York: Avon).
WIGMORE, John H.
    1928. *A Panorama of the World's Legal Systems*, in 3 vols. (St. Paul: West Publishers).
WILAMOWITZ-MOELLENDORFF, Ulrich von.
    1922. "Gedächtnisrede des Hrn. v. Wilamowitz-Moellendorff auf Herman Diels", in *Sitzungsberichte der Preussischen Akademie der Wissenschaften* (Berlin: Verlag der Akademie der Wissenschaften), 104-107.
WILD, John.
    1947. "An Introduction to the Phenomenology of Signs", *Philosophy and Phenomenological Research* VIII (December), 217-244.
    1956. Review of *The Material Logic of John of St. Thomas* (see entry for Simon 1955, above), in *Philosophy and Phenomenological Research* XVII (June), 556-559.
WILDEN, Anthony.
    1968. "Lacan and the Discourse of the Other", in Wilden's English trans. of Lacan 1956 [q.v.], 159-311.
    1972. *System and Structure* (London: Tavistock Publications).
    1981. "Semiotics as Praxis: Strategy and Tactics", *Recherches Sémiotiques/Semiotic Inquiry* 1.1, 1-34.
WILLIAMS, Brooke.
    1981. "The Feminist Revolution in 'Ultramodern' Perspective", *Cross Currents* XXXI.3 (Fall), 307-319.
    1985. "What Has History To Do with Semiotic?", *Semiotica* 54.3/4, 267-333; preprinted in revised monograph form with index and historically layered bibliography under the title *History and Semiotic* (Victoria College of the University of Toronto: Toronto Semiotic Circle Number 4, Summer).

1985a. "Challenging Signs at the Crossroads", prefatory essay to Thomas A. Sebeok, *Contribu-
        tions to the Doctrine of Signs* (= Sources in Semiotics IV; uncorrected reprint edition of 1976
        original; Lanham, MD: University Press of America), xv-xlii.
WINANCE, Eleuthère.
1983.   "Review" of *Introducing Semiotic* (Deely 1982), *Revue Thomiste* LXXX (juillet-aôut), 514-516.
1986.   "Echo de la querelle du psychologisme et de l'antipsychologisme dans l'Ars Logica de
        Jean Poinsot", *Semiotica* 55.3/4, 225-259.
WITTGENSTEIN, Ludwig.
1919.   *Tractatus Logico-Philosophicus*, German with English trans. by D. F. Pears and B. F. McGuin-
        ness (London: Routledge and Kegan Paul, 1961).
WOLLEN, Peter.
1969.   *Signs and Meaning in the Cinema* (Bloomington: Indiana University Press).
WOOD, W. B.
1961.   *From Miasmas to Molecules* (New York: Columbia University Press).
WORTH, Sol.
1969.   "The Development of a Semiotic of Film", *Semiotica* 1, 282-321.
XENOPHON.
c.365BC. περὶ ἱππικῆς, *On the Art of Horsemanship*, Greek with facing English trans. by E. C. Mar-
        chant, in Vol. VII of *Xenophon* (Loeb Classical Library ed.; Cambridge, MA: Harvard
        University Press, 1925), 296-363.
ZUMTHOR, Paul, and Eugene VANCE, organizers.
1977, August 2-12: Colloquium "L'Archéologie du Signe", held at Centre Culturel International
        de Cérisy, Cérisy-la-Salle (Normandy), France.

Index

Aalto, A.: 303
Aaron, Richard I.: 255, 291
Abelard, Peter: 70, 72, 291
Abraham: 170
Abrahams, R. D.: 189, 291
Academicians: 64
Adam, Charles: 297
Adler, Mortimer J.: 15, 291
Aegidius Romanus: 9, 10
Ailly, Pierre d': 9, 10, 291, 304
Albert the Great ("Albertus Magnus"): 9, 10, 11, 26, 64, 291, 320
Alcmaeon: 39
Aldington, R.: 310
Alice in Wonderland: 57
Alperson, Burton L.: 206, 291
Althusser, Louis: 125, 283, 291
Ammonius Hermeiou: 64, 66, 275, 291
Anderson, Fulton F.: 292
Anderson, Myrdene: xviii, xix, 291
Angelicus, Robertus: 304
Anselm of Canterbury: 300
Anshen, Ruth Nanda: 309
Apel, Karl-Otto: 7
Apollonius Dyscolus: 275, 291
Aquinas, Thomas: xvi, 7, 9, 14, 20, 58, 63, 68, 69, 99, 171, 274, 275, 277, 283, 291, 320
Archduke Franz Ferdinand: 222
Ardener, E. W.: 185, 262, 284, 292
Aristotle: xiv, 7, 8, 9, 13, 14, 19, 23, 25, 26, 58, 64-67, 99, 102, 149, 225, 227, 233, 291, 292, 295, 309
Arnauld, Antoine: 292
Ashby, Hal: 39, 292
Ashley, Benedict: 19, 292
Audra, A.: 293

Augustine, Saint ("Augustinus"): 5, 10, 12, 14, 65, 66, 70, 72, 170, 176, 226, 292
Austin, J. L.: 111, 280, 292
Bacchus: 11
Bachelard, Gaston: 281, 283, 292
Bachi, Riccardo: 292
Bacon, Francis: 26, 292
Bacon, Roger: 69, 71, 72, 276, 292
Baer, Eugen: xx, 292, 297
Baird, George: 261, 304
Baldwin, James Mark: 311
Bally, Charles: 315
Bambrough, Renford: 154
Baran, Heinrich: 319
Barnes, Hazel E.: 315
Barthes, Roland: 120, 121, 125, 126, 199, 200, 202, 204-207, 213, 260, 261, 281, 293
Baskin, Wade: 315
Bass, Alan: 297
Basso, K.: 298, 317
Bastide, Roger: 293, 307
Bateson, Gregory: 258, 281, 293
Bateson, Mary Catherine: 317
Baudelaire, Charles Pierre: 174
Baumann, Richard: 189, 291
Beal, Edward: 194, 293
Beare, J. L.: 292
Bense, Max: 257, 293
Benveniste, Emil: xii, 55, 280, 293
Berger, Arthur Asa: viii, 293
Bergson, Henri: 57, 58, 135, 293
Berkeley, Bishop George: 17, 35, 242, 266, 293, 311
Bernard of Clairvaux: 300
Berolzheimer, Fritz: 192, 293
Bertalanffy, Ludwig von: 134, 135, 293
Billuart: 292

Binsse, H. L.: 308
Black, Max: 316
Blonsky, Marshall: viii
Bloomfield, Leonard: 74, 293
Bochenski, I. M.: 25, 31-33, 258, 293
Boehner, Philotheus: 8, 294
Boethius: 15, 66-68, 292
Bohr, Niels: 36, 125, 138, 294
Boisacq, Emile: 230, 294
Boole, George: 30, 294
Borgnet, Auguste: 292, 320
Bos, Egbert P.: 294
Bosserel, J. B.: 11, 294
Bouchard, Donald F.: 299
Bouche-Leclerq, Auguste: 230, 294
Bouissac, Paul: 186, 288, 292, 294, 300
Braudel, Fernand: 305
Braunsberg, Andrew: 292
Breal, Michel: 258, 294
Bremner, Robert H.: 310
Bremond: 126
Brereton, C.: 293
Brewster, Ben: 291
Bridgman, Percy: 132, 133, 283, 294
Brinton, Crane: 221, 294
Brock, Jarrett: 279, 294
Broglie, Louis de: 124, 294
Bronowski, Jacob: 125, 294
Brother Klaus von der Flue: 165
Brouwer, L. E. J.: 141, 142, 294
Brown, Clarence: 41, 294
Brunschvicq, Leon: 153
Buber, Martin: 291
Bucephalus: 41
Buhler, Karl: xii, 257, 294, 303
Burks, Arthur W.: 278, 311, 312, 320
Burnet, John: 229, 294
Burnyeat, M. F.: 208, 294
Burtt, E. A.: 293, 303
Bury, R. G.: 317

323

Designer:	Chet Grycz and John Deely
Compositor:	Bud MacFarlane of Composition Specialists
Text:	Baskerville, Text 10/11, Description of Contributions
	and Notes 9/10, References 8/8.5, Index 8/8
Display:	Names 12/36, Titles 24/26
Printer and Binder:	Bookcrafters, Inc., Chelsea, Michigan